FASCISM'S EUROPEAN EMPIRE

This is a controversial reappraisal of the Italian occupation of the Mediterranean during the Second World War, which Davide Rodogno examines for the first time within the framework of Fascist imperial ambitions. He focuses on the European territories annexed and occupied by Italy between 1940 and 1943: metropolitan France, Corsica, Slovenia, Croatia, Dalmatia, Montenegro, Albania, Kosovo, western Macedonia and mainland and insular Greece. He explores Italy's plans for Mediterranean expansion, its relationship with Germany, economic exploitation, the forced 'Italianization' of the annexed territories, collaboration, repression and Italian policies towards refugees and Jews. He also compares Fascist Italy and Nazi Germany through their dreams of imperial conquest, the role of racism and anti-Semitism, and the 'Fascistization' of the Italian army. Based largely on unpublished sources, this is a ground-breaking contribution to genocide, resistance, war crimes and occupation studies as well as to the history of the Second World War more generally.

DAVIDE RODOGNO is Academic Fellow in the School of Modern History at the University of St Andrews.

ADRIAN BELTON is a freelance translator specializing in the humanities and the social sciences.

NEW STUDIES IN EUROPEAN HISTORY

The aim of this series in early modern and modern European history is to publish outstanding works of research, addressed to important themes across a wide geographical range, from southern and central Europe, to Scandinavia and Russia, and from the time of the Renaissance to the Second World War. As it develops the series will comprise focused works of wide contextual range and intellectual ambition.

For a full list of titles published in the series, please see the end of the book.

FASCISM'S EUROPEAN EMPIRE

Italian Occupation During the Second World War

DAVIDE RODOGNO
University of St Andrews

Translated by Adrian Belton

CAMBRIDGE
UNIVERSITY PRESS

CAMBRIDGE UNIVERSITY PRESS
Cambridge, New York, Melbourne, Madrid, Cape Town, Singapore, São Paulo

Cambridge University Press
The Edinburgh Building, Cambridge CB2 2RU, UK

Published in the United States of America by Cambridge University Press, New York

www.cambridge.org
Information on this title: www.cambridge.org/9780521845151

Originally published in Italian as *Il nuovo ordine mediterraneo: Le politiche di occupazione dell'Italia fascista in Europa (1940–1943)* by Bollati Boringhieri editore 2003, and

First published in English by Cambridge University Press 2006 as *Fascism's European Empire: Italian Occupation During the Second World War.*

Printed in the United Kingdom at the University Press, Cambridge

A catalogue record for this publication is available from the British Library

ISBN-13 978-0-521-84515-1 hardback
ISBN-10 0-521-84515-7 hardback

The translation of this work has been funded by SEPS
SEGRETARIATO EUROPEO PER LE PUBBLICAZIONI SCIENTIFICHE

SEPS
SEGRETARIATO EUROPEO PER LE PUBBLICAZIONI SCIENTIFICHE

Via Val d'Aposa 7-40123 Bologna–Italy
seps@alma.unibo.it-www.seps.it

Contents

Illustrations

Maps

Foreword

Amid an abundance of studies on the first half of the twentieth century, Davide Rodogno's book stands out for two reasons: first its intrinsic quality, and second its interest, for it jointly addresses two topics of prime historical interest: the history of Fascism and Italy's military occupations.

Fascism continues to be much studied, especially in regard to Italy, and for indubitably good reasons: the Italians were both the protagonists and the victims of its history. Yet the international dimension of Fascism has been somewhat neglected, with the exception of some studies on foreign policy and the colonial empire.

The first merit of Rodogno's book is that it furnishes us with a more complete understanding of Fascism as regards both its ambitions and the realities of one of its essential dimensions, that of territorial expansion.

First, the ambitions. Numerous projects for the 'new order' were put forward by the Italian press and by the regime's propaganda in 1941, the year when hopes were highest that Italy's 'historic mission' was soon to be accomplished. These projects – whose content, it must be said, was vague – referred to the empire then being built, an empire which once again centred on Rome because it added Mediterranean territories in Europe itself to the already-existing possessions in North and East Africa. By examining the European order of the new 'Roman' empire, Rodogno's book conducts a comprehensive survey of the territories occupied by Fascist Italy in Greece, Yugoslavia, France and Albania, a protectorate since 1939.

Second, the realities. That the new order was not accomplished was due to the prolongation of the war and the obstacles raised by relations with Nazi Germany. The Fascist regime had to combine – unsuccessfully, as we know – its endeavour to achieve its imperial aims with defence of its interests against its principal ally. Rodogno's examination of Fascist imperial expansion provides a fascinating account of the differentiated administration of the occupied territories, and in particular of Mussolini's pivotal 'Napoleonic' role, as well as those of military leaders and diplomats.

The second merit of the book lies in its contribution to the history of military occupations. This is a relatively neglected area; and especially so in Italy, given that its historical experience in such matters is not comparable to that of France or Germany. Yet this is an extremely interesting topic because a military occupation involves not only the superimposition of one administrative apparatus upon another within the same territory (provided the victor allows the defeated country's administration to continue), but also face-to-face confrontation between two societies.

In this regard, Rodogno cleverly marshals the scant documentation available to furnish original insights into the relationships between the occupiers and the occupied. One reads with profit everything that he writes about the lives of soldiers – almost none of whom had ever been away from home – as they struggled to cope with alien climates, lands and societies. The relationships he describes range among love affairs, dealings on the black market, the 'd system' (from the French *système débrouille*, 'being resourceful') and vicious reprisals. The harshness of the Italian army's repressive measures in the occupied territories has often been minimized. While we await entirely free access to the archives to be granted to scholars, the account in this book is sufficient to provide a more realistic idea of what those measures actually were.

Of equal interest is Rodogno's treatment of another topic (better known but usually treated in isolation): Fascist policy towards Jewish refugees in the territories controlled by the Italian army. It seems that this policy was determined less by the alleged 'humanitarianism' of the Italians – although this nevertheless existed – than by a set of important factors, principal among which was the conflictual and competitive relationship with the Nazi senior partner. Rodogno's analysis is a fine example of how broader contextualization yields further understanding of a phenomenon thought to be already thoroughly known.

Finally, considering that Rodogno's study is based on painstaking archival research and mastery of a large body of secondary sources, it is bound to 'make history', so to speak. I greet its publication with pleasure.

Philippe Burrin

Acknowledgements

This book sets out the results of research for my doctoral thesis in international relations submitted in 2001 to the Institut Universitaire de Hautes Études Internationales of Geneva. I wish to express my profound gratitude to Philippe Burrin for his unstinting support and inspiration during these years. He has stimulated my interest in the subject and encouraged me to explore new avenues, constantly furnishing new interpretations and insights. I am also indebted to Bruno Arcidiacono for his guidance both personal and scientific as I wrote this book. I also thank Pierre Milza for his acute observations on my work; the Fonds National de la Recherche Scientifique Suisse, without whose assistance I could not have conducted my research; and the Istituto di Studi Politici of the Università 'La Sapienza' of Rome. I am especially grateful to Emilio Gentile, Mario Toscano and Giuseppe Conti for constantly treating me with such cordiality, for making their vast knowledge available to me, and also for their valuable advice. Crucial for the writing of this book have been my correspondence and interviews with Matthew Leitner, Gerold Krozewski, Stevan Pavlowitch and Giorgio Rochat, and my conversations with Michele Sarfatti, Spartaco Capogreco, Piero Crociani and Raffaele Rodogno. No less valuable has been the assistance of Adrian Belton, with his acute comments and careful reading of my research, and Adolfo Mignemi, who prepared the section of photographs. As regards the CUP edition in particular, I am immensely grateful to LSE London professors MacGregor Knox and David Stevenson, and I am indebted to Anita Prazmowska, who encouraged me to send a synopsis of the book to the editor, and to my friends Jasna Dragovic Soso, Dejan Djokic and Ilaria Favretto. I owe a particular debt of gratitude to Ms Lina Panetta of the London Italian Cultural Institute. The Cambridge edition has been published with the financial assistance of the Italian Ministry of Foreign Affairs through the Istituto Italiano di Cultura, London, and the Segretariato Europeo per le Pubblicazioni Scientifiche.

Obviously, the usual disclaimer applies: responsibility for the contents of this book is mine alone.

I thank the curators and staff at all the archives and institutes at which I carried out my research, in particular Marisa Giannetto of the ACS, Stefania Ruggeri of the ASMAE, General Nicola Della Volpe, Alessandro Gionfrida and Maresciallo Antonio Sangiovanni of the USSME, Annarita Rigano and Angelo Battilocchi of the ASBI, Fabrizio Bensi of the ACICR, Marshal Gerardo Severino at the Customs and Finance Police Archives, Fotini Tomai-Konstantopoulou at the Diplomatic Archives of the Greek Ministry of Foreign Affairs, and Mr Depastas at the Archives of the Greek Ministry of Defence. I am also grateful for their help to the librarians at the CDEC of Milan, of the CBUCEI of Rome and, especially, to the staff of the Institut Universitaire de Hautes Études Internationales of Geneva. Among those many people who have assisted me I would make especial mention of Salvatore Blanco, Umberto Cuzzola, Alexandros Dimitrakopoulos, Francesco Maugeri and my wife Giovanna . . . and finally, more than all others, Anna and Daniele, who believed in me and gave me constant support.

Note on the translation

Italian and French place names are generally translated into English. Greek, Yugoslav, Albanian, Macedonian and Bulgarian place names lack uniformity. As far as an English translation was found they have been translated; otherwise I have chosen to maintain the place names as they appear in the Italian documents. Therefore some errors may remain.

Most data points in the tables taken directly from the archives are given in this book as they appeared in the original, including some obvious mistakes.

Abbreviations

'A'	Assistenza (Welfare)
AA.CC.	Affari Commerciali (Commercial Affairs)
AA.CIV.	Affari Civili (Civil Affairs)
AA.FF.	Affari Finanziari (Financial Affairs)
AA.GG.	Affari Generali (General Affairs)
AA.GG.RR.	Affari Generali e Riservati (General and Confidential Affairs)
AA.PP.	Affari Politici (Political Affairs)
AA.RR.	Affari Riservati (Confidential Affairs)
AC	Alto Commissario / Alto Commissariato (High Commissioner / High Commission)
ACICR	Archives du Comité International de la Croix-Rouge (Archives of the International Committee of the Red Cross)
ACJ	Anonima Commercio Jonico (Ionian Commercial Joint-Stock Company)
ACP	Affari Collettivi Prefetture (General Prefecture Affairs)
ACS	Archivio Centrale dello Stato, Rome (Central State Archive)
AGIP	Azienda Generale Italiana Petroli
ALI	Azienda Ligniti Italiane (Italian Lignite Corporation)
AMMI	Azienda Minerali Metallici Italiani (Italian Metallic Minerals Corporation)
AOI	Africa Orientale Italiana (Italian East Africa)
ARMIR	Armata Italiana in Russia (Italian Army in Russia)
ASBI	Archivio Storico della Banca d'Italia (Historical Archive of the Bank of Italy)
ASMAE	Archivio Storico del Ministero degli Affari Esteri (Historical Archive of the Ministry of Foreign Affairs)
b.	*busta* (envelope)

BAC	Banda Anticommunista (Anti-Communist Band)
BCI	Banca Commerciale Italiana (also COMIT)
BDI	Banca d'Italia (Bank of Italy)
BK	Balli Kombëtar (National Union)
BNL	Banca Nazionale del Lavoro
CBUCEI	Centro Bibliografico dell'Unione delle Comunità Ebraiche Italiane (Documentation Centre of the Union of Italian Jewish Communities)
CC.NN.	Camicie Nere (Blackshirts)
CC.RR.	Carabinieri Reali (Royal Military Police)
CdA	Corpo d'Armata (Army Corps)
CDEC	Centro di Documentazione Ebraica Contemporanea (Centre for Contemporary Jewish Documentation)
CEPIC	Commissione Economica Permanente Italo-Croata (Permanent Italo-Croat Economic Commission)
CIAF	Commissione Italiana d'Armistizio con la Francia (Italian Armistice Commission with France)
CIB	Controllo Industrie Belliche, Sottocommissione CIAF (CIAF War Industry Control Subcommission)
CIOM	Compagnia Italiana Oriente Mediterraneo
COM. SUP.	Comando Superiore (High Command)
COMIT	Banca Commerciale Italiana (also BCI)
CONI	Comitato Olimpico Nazionale Italiano (Italian National Olympic Committee)
CONSUVI	Consorzio per le Sovvenzioni su Valori Industriali (Industrial Subsidies Consortium)
Cp	*compagnia* (company)
CRI	Croce Rossa Italiana (Italian Red Cross)
CS	Comando Supremo (Supreme Command)
CSI	Comando Supremo Interforze (Supreme Inter-Force Command)
CSIR	Corpo di Spedizione Italiano in Russia (Italian Expeditionary Force in Russia)
CSM	Capo di Stato Maggiore (Army Chief of Staff)
CSMG	Capo di Stato Maggiore Generale (Army General Chief of Staff)
CTA	Commissione Tedesca d'Armistizio con la Francia (German Commission on Armistice with France)
DDI	*Documenti diplomatici italiani* (Italian diplomatic documents)

DEGRIGES	DeutscheGriechische-Warenausgleichgesellschaft (German–Greek Trade Balancing Association)
DGAC	Direzione Generale Affari Commerciali, Ministero degli Esteri (Department of General Commercial Affairs, Ministry of Foreign Affairs)
DGDR	Direzione Generale Demografia e Razza, Ministero dell'Interno (Department for Demography and Race, Ministry of the Interior)
DGFP	Documents on German Foreign Policy
DGPS	Direzione Generale Pubblica Sicurezza, Ministero dell'Interno (Public Security Department, Ministry of the Interior)
DPF	Département Politique Fédérale, Bern
DRA	Delegazione Rimpatrio e Assistenza (Delegation for Repatriation and Assistance)
EAM	Ethniko Apelefterotiko Metopo (Greek National Liberation Front)
EIAA	Ente Industrie e Attività Agrarie (Agricultural Industry and Assets Board)
EIAR	Ente Italiano Audizioni Radiofoniche (Italian Radio Broadcasting Corporation)
EFTF	Emanuele Filiberto Testa di Ferro (Army Division)
ESCATA	Ente per gli Scambi Commerciali e gli Approvvigionamenti nei Territori Annessi (Authority for Trade and Supplies in the Annexed Territories)
fasc.	*fascicolo*
FF.AA.	Forze Armate (Armed Forces)
FIAT	Fabbrica Italiana Automobili Torino
GABAP	Gabinetto Armistizio–Pace (Armistice–Peace Cabinet)
GaF	Guardia alla Frontiera (Border Guards)
GAN	Gruppi d'Azione Nizzarda (Nice Action Groups)
GdF	Guardia di Finanza (Financial Police)
GIL	Gioventù Italiana del Littorio (Fascist Youth Organization)
GILE	Gioventù Italiana del Littorio all'Estero (Fascist Youth Organization Abroad)
GILL	Gioventù Italiana del Littorio di Lubiana (Ljubljana Fascist Youth Organization)
'I'	Informazioni (Intelligence)

ICRC	International Committee of the Red Cross
IFI	Istituto Finanziario Italiano (Italian Financial Institute)
INA	Istituto Nazionale delle Assicurazioni (National Insurance Institute)
IRI	Istituto per la Ricostruzione Industriale (Industrial Reconstruction Institute)
ISPI	Istituto per gli Studi di Politica Internazionale (Institute for International Political Studies)
ISR	Istituto Pavese per la Storia della Resistenza e dell'Età Contemporanea
ISTAT	Istituto Centrale di Statistica (Central Statistical Institute)
KKE	Komunistikon Komma Ellados (Greek Communist Party)
MAE	Minisetro degli Affari Esteri (Ministry of Foreign Affairs)
MI	Ministero dell'Interno (Ministry of the Interior)
MINCULPOP	Ministero di Cultura Popolare (Ministry of Popular Culture)
MVAC	Milizie Volontarie Anticomuniste (Anti-Communist Voluntary Militias)
MVSN	Milizia Volontaria Sicurezza Nazionale (Voluntary Fascist Militia)
NDH	Nezavisna Drzava Hrvatska (Independent State of Croatia)
OF	Osvobodilna Fronta (Liberation Front)
OKW	Ober Kommando Wehrmacht (Armed Forces High Command)
OND	Opera Nazionale Dopolavoro (National Working-Men's Guild)
OUL	Organizzazione Universitaria di Lubiana (Ljubljana University Organization)
OVRA	Opera vigilanza Repressione Antifascista (Anti-Fascism Intelligence Agency)
'P'	Propaganda
PCM	Presidenza del Consiglio dei Ministri (Cabinet Office)
PFA	Partito Fascista Albanese (Albanian Fascist Party)
PNF	Partito Nazionale Fascista (National Fascist Party)
POW	prisoner of war
PS	Pubblica Sicurezza (police)

QG	*Quartier Général* (headquarters)
RDL	*Regio decreto legge* (royal decree)
RGF	Regia Guardia di Finanza (Royal Customs and Finance Police)
Rgt	regiment
RKKS	Reichskreditkassenscheine (Reich credit cashier bills)
RM	Reichsmark
SACA	Società Anonima Commercio Adriatico (Adriatic Trade Corporation)
SACIG	Società Anonima Commercio Italo-Greco (Italo-Greek Trade Corporation)
SAMIA	Società Anonima Mineraria Italo-Albanese (Italo-Albanian Minerals Corporation)
SAPIC	Società Anonima per i Lavori Pubblici in Croazia (Croatian Public Works Corporation)
SCAEF	Sottocommissione Affari Economici e Finanziari della CIAF (CIAF Economic and Financial Affairs Subcommission)
ser.	*serie*
SIE	Servizio Informazioni dell'Esercito (Army Intelligence Service)
SIM	Servizio Informazioni Militare (Military Intelligence Service)
SM	Stato Maggiore (General Staff)
SMG	Stato Maggiore Generale (Joint General Staff)
SMRE	Stato Maggiore del Regio Esercito (General Staff of the Royal Army)
sottofasc.	*sottofascicolo*
SPD	Segreteria del Duce (Duce's Secretariat)
SPE	Servizio Permanente Effettivo (Permanent Staff)
UAC	Ufficio Affari Civili (Civil Affairs Office)
UCEI	Unione delle Comunità Ebraiche Italiane (Union of Italian Jewish Communities)
UIC	Ufficio Italiano Cambio (Italian Exchange Office)
USC	Ufficio Speciale Coordinamento (Special Co-ordination Office)
USSME	Ufficio Storico dello Stato Maggiore dell'Esercito (Historical Office of the Army General Staff)
WiRüAmt	Wirtschaftsrüstungsamt des Oberkommandos der Wehrmacht (Economic and Armaments Office of the German High Command)

Introduction

Between 1940 and 1943, with the decisive military assistance of its German ally, Fascist Italy conquered a number of territories in the Mediterranean area of Europe: a part of metropolitan France, Corsica, southern Slovenia, south-western Croatia, the Dalmatian coast, Montenegro, most of Kosovo, western Macedonia and a large part of Greece and its islands. The expression 'conquered territories' denotes those that were annexed to the Kingdom of Italy and those occupied following an armistice or administered by military governors, as well as territories of allied states in which Italian troops were stationed. It is important to specify from the outset that the case of Albania – a territory occupied before the outbreak of the Second World War, and in circumstances radically different from those of subsequent conquests – will be given due consideration in this book, but the short-lived occupation of Tunisia will not be treated.

On examining the historiography on Fascist occupations in Mediterranean Europe, one notes the presence of striking lacunae but also of a number of pioneering studies: the three volumes by Oddone Talpo on Dalmatia, the works by Tone Ferenc and Marco Cuzzi on Slovenia, by Jean-Louis Panicacci on Menton, by Romain Rainero on the relationships between Italy and Vichy France, by Mark Mazower on Greece and especially the numerous studies by Enzo Collotti and Teodoro Sala on Yugoslavia.[1] The works of Daniel Carpi, Léon Poliakov and Jacques Sabille, Michele Sarfatti, Jonathan Steinberg, Klaus Voigt and Susan Zuccotti have concentrated on matters concerning the Jews, with the occupation acting as a backdrop to their researches.[2] Yet no comprehensive analysis of Italy's

[1] Talpo, *Dalmazia*; Ferenc, *La provincia 'italiana' di Lubiana*; Cuzzi, *L'occupazione italiana della Slovenia*; Panicacci, *Les Alpes Maritimes*; Rainero, *Mussolini e Pétain*; Mazower, *Inside Hitler's Greece*; Collotti, *L'amministrazione tedesca dell'Italia occupata*; Collotti and Sala, *Le potenze dell'Asse e la Jugoslavia*; Sala, 'Programmi di snazionalizzazione del "fascismo di frontiera"'.

[2] Carpi, 'Rescue of Jews in the Italian Zone of Occupied Croatia'; Carpi, 'Notes of the History of the Jews in Greece'; Carpi, *Between Mussolini and Hitler*; Panicacci, 'Les juifs et la question juive dans

occupation policies has been attempted. This, therefore, is the purpose of this book; an endeavour prompted by the following remarks by Collotti and Renzo De Felice:

> [While] it is important to acknowledge that Fascism failed to achieve its objectives, it is of equal importance to identify Fascism's components and its projects . . . understanding their history in relation to the regime's aspirations and achievements.[3]
>
> Still lacking is any study on Italy's reasons for going to war or, more generally, on how it conceived the post-war 'new order' and the place and role within it of Fascist Italy, and on how [Mussolini] contrived to curb National Socialist ambitions and assert his vision or, at least, carve out a role for himself amid those ambitions.[4]

The documentation on which this book is based is conserved in the archives of the Italian Army General Staff, the historical and diplomatic archives of the Ministry of Foreign Affairs, the Central State Archives, the historical archive of the Bank of Italy, the archives of the Union of Italian Jewish Communities, the archive of the International Committee of the Red Cross, and Greek archives. Much of the material has never previously been published. However, it should be borne in mind that the documentation available is not exhaustive: a large quantity of archival material has been lost (for example, the documents of the War Commissariat for the occupying armies and those of the Fabbriguerra[5]) because numerous local authorities burned registers, reports, correspondence, ledgers and lists, as well as numerous other documents as soon as the armistice was signed. Research is also hampered by Italian law, which does not permit consultation of documents on, for example, war crimes. I would finally stress that, even after decades of collation and organization, numerous other Italian archives are still closed to researchers. Those of greatest importance for the present study are the diplomatic archives on Albania, those on the

les Alpes Maritimes'; Picciotto Fargion, 'Italian Citizens in Nazi-Occupied Europe'; Poliakov and Sabille, *Jews Under the Italian Occupation*; Sarfatti, 'Fascist Italy and German Jews in South-Eastern France'; Shelah, *Un debito di gratitudine*; Steinberg, *All or Nothing*; Voigt, *Il rifugio precario*; Zuccotti, *The Italians and the Holocaust*; Zuccotti, *The Holocaust, the French, the Jews*.

[3] Collotti, *Fascismo, fascismi*, pp. 165 and 17. Gerhard Schreiber has written (here translated into English from the German): 'Ideas have to be taken seriously, no matter how abstruse and remote from all possible realization they may be. This applies not only to Hitler, and it means not only a rejection of the kind of downplaying of Hitler's programme which has often been, and still is, attempted on the grounds of its remoteness from reality . . . As for historical relevance, this stems from the fact that even the most unrealistic planning is, in itself, also real, and that ideas, if given half a chance of realization, seldom remain mere ideas. In other words, they reveal the dimension of volition, i.e. what moves history forward, and usually influence it more powerfully than that which has manifestly taken place' (Schreiber, 'Political and Military Developments in the Mediterranean Area', p. 301).

[4] De Felice, *Mussolini l'alleato*, p. 133.

[5] Fabbriguerra (short for Commissariato Generale per la Fabbricazione di Guerra) procured raw materials and allocated them among factories requisitioned for the war effort.

war tribunals, the censored letters of soldiers, the files of the various Fascist economic ministries and the archives of the Foreign Ministry's general directorate for trade.

As regards secondary sources, the literature on the French, Greek and Yugoslavian resistance movements does not concern itself with the role of the Italians in the occupied territories. It sometimes omits them entirely from events and often caricatures Italian occupation policy. It depicts the Italian occupiers as amiable and indifferent to a war which they did not feel to be their own, and as fraternizing closely with the occupied populations, forming sentimental attachments and friendships. It thus seems that comparison with the brutal and ruthless Germans is impossible, or else that the Italian occupations were nothing but occupations on Germany's behalf. But is this really the case?

The book divides into two parts. The first examines Fascist Italy's relationships with Germany, its plans for expansion in the Mediterranean area, actual occupation, the co-ordination of policies, and the 'conquerors'. The second part explores the various aspects of occupation policy, relations with the governments of the occupied countries, economic penetration, the forced Italianization of the zones annexed, collaboration, repression, the internment of civilians, the 'refugee question' and the so-called Jewish Question. The treatment is organized thematically, and each chapter proceeds by examining in parallel, and sometimes comparing, events in the various territories conquered. The reader is advised that aspects of this historical period pertaining to the occupied territories which have already been examined by historians will only be outlined here. I refer to the conquest – the western Alps (June 1940) and the Balkans, the wars against Greece (26 October 1940–23 April 1941) and against Yugoslavia (6–12 April 1941) – and to the period following the armistice of 8 September 1943.

The first chapter reviews the main phases of development in relations between Italy and Germany, and demonstrates that the Fascist regime had failed to achieve its objectives even before the conquest of its European territories. The chapter examines the relationship between the two Axis powers and argues that Italy's diplomatic, military and economic subordination to its ally substantially altered Fascism's plans for Mediterranean domination. It describes the principal features of the Italians' reaction to Nazi encroachment on 'their' living space and reconstructs the perceptions entertained by Italian diplomats, Fascist Party hierarchs and senior German army officers.

The second chapter addresses the following questions: what were the ideological, political and economic motives for the conquest and domination of the Mediterranean? What geopolitical configuration of the

Mediterranean would have come about after the war, which the regime believed it would win? How would territories falling, in one way or the other, within the Fascist sphere of influence have been governed? The chapter furnishes definitions of the expressions *nuova civiltà*, *nuovo ordine* and *comunità imperiale*, or the geo-political space in which the satellites of the Fascist empire would orbit under the motive principle of the nation's ethnic unity (one people for one nation).

The third chapter examines the discrepancies between intentions and outcomes in the territories ruled from Rome, and it classifies the territories conquered into annexed provinces and militarily occupied territories. It shows that Italy's expansionary plans clashed with complex local realities, and also that the geographical extent of the territories which the Italians were able to occupy depended on the benevolence of the Germans. The new frontiers were ill-considered boundaries which severed social, political and economic ties among the occupied zones. They posed both strategic and administrative problems because of territorial discontinuity and because different regimes obtained in contiguous zones of occupation.

The fourth chapter describes how the conquered territories were administered. It examines the roles of Mussolini, the organs of the state, and the Partito Nazionale Fascista (PNF, National Fascist Party) in co-ordinating policies in Rome, and also the role of 'the men on the spot' (to borrow an expression from historians of the British Empire). It then dwells on the administrative tasks of the Regio Esercito (Royal Army) and examines conflicts of jurisdiction. Although the subject of the book is military occupations, its concern is not with the preparedness of the Regio Esercito; and it does not assess the military and strategic capabilities of its commanders, the technological level of its armaments or the strategies adopted for the campaigns of conquest. On these matters the reader is referred to the studies by Lucio Ceva, MacGregor Knox, Fortunato Minniti, Leopoldo Nuti and Giorgio Rochat.[6]

The final chapter – entitled 'The conquerors' – in this first part of the book examines the experiences of more than half a million Italians in the occupied territories between 1940 and 1943. For more than fifty years, historians have concentrated on the occupied populations as the victims of aggression by the Axis powers. Numerous studies have been published on national liberation movements: some have exalted the romance of national

[6] Ceva, *Le forze armate*; *Ceva*, 'Vertici politici e militari'; Knox, *Mussolini Unleashed*; Knox, *Hitler's Italian Allies*; Knox, *Common Destiny*; Minniti, 'Profili dell'iniziativa strategica italiana'; Nuti, 'I problemi storiografici connessi con l'intervento italiano'; Rochat, 'Mussolini chef de guerre'; Rochat, 'Appunti sulla direzione politico-militare della guerra fascista'; Rochat, 'Lo sforzo bellico'; Rochat, *L'esercito italiano*.

histories; others have elaborated on epics of resistance; yet others, more recently, have examined the vicissitudes of civil societies under the Nazis. But none of them has analysed the experiences of hundreds of thousands of Italian soldiers in the occupied countries, where they remained for more than two years confined in military enclaves, subject to military rule and discipline, and far from their homes, their families and their jobs. Little study has been made of the impact of everyday reality on the occupiers, on their morale, sanitary conditions and relations with the occupied populations, or of their racism, or above all of the role of Fascist ideology in the Italians' treatment of the populations under their control.

The second part of the book examines the policies pursued in the occupied territories. The sixth chapter analyses the exercise of authority and relationships between the occupying power and the executive and administrative branches in a first subset of territories: those occupied militarily and which possessed a government. The economic exploitation of the countries occupied – the topic of the seventh chapter – is undoubtedly a new departure in the literature on Fascism. Setting aside the thorny question of the consequences of this exploitation,[7] the chapter describes the 'projects' (i.e., the regime's long-term objectives) and their 'realization' (i.e., the short-term exploitation) of the occupied territories. It takes due account of the role of the Germans in the Fascist economic space and examines the expenses arising from occupation and the obstacles encountered by the conquerors as they set about exploiting the dominated territories industrially, commercially and financially.

The eighth chapter concentrates on the forced Italianization of the annexed territories, singling out four distinct yet interconnected dimensions: the ethnic and racial mapping of the territories; the erasure of national identity and the internment, transfer and expulsion of native-born residents; the 'Fascistization' of the latter (especially those of younger age) through education and the 'totalitarian' action of all the organs of the state and the Fascist party; and the colonizing of further provinces.

The ninth chapter addresses the theme of collaboration. It is founded on the conviction that the division of the occupied societies between those that collaborated and those that resisted is simplistic and obsolete. Studies such as Philippe Burrin's *La France à l'heure allemande* (1995) or Claudio Pavone's *Una guerra civile. Saggio storico sulla moralità nella Resistenza* (1991) have shown that there was a grey zone of accommodations and compromises that encompassed the actions of the majority of the occupied populations. The

[7] On this, see the brilliant study by Etmektsoglou-Koehn, 'Axis Exploitation of Wartime Greece', which examines the heavy responsibility of the Axis for famine in Greece.

upheavals brought by defeat induced not only individuals but also entire strata of societies to seek a *modus vivendi* with the occupiers, and they did so for the most diverse of reasons. There were in fact various degrees of compromise, so that lumping the few collaborationists, Yugoslav Četniks, Greek gendarmes and French prefects into a single category would be inappropriate. Distinctions must be drawn between those who fought side by side with the occupiers for ideological reasons and those who collaborated to secure the means for their survival, between those who provided military assistance and those who enlisted with the voluntary anti-communist militia.

The penultimate chapter compares the provisions and application of the rules on public order issued by the authorities in the occupied territories and the criteria used when they conducted round-ups and took reprisals. It analyses differences among the methods used to put down rebellions, compares the treatment of rebels in the various zones of occupation and conducts a geographical survey of the concentration camps for civilian internees.

The final chapter interweaves the 'refugee question' with the 'Jewish question'. It argues that, for a certain period of time, Jewish refugees who fled into the Italian-occupied zones to escape persecution or deportation were treated in entirely the same manner as all other refugees. They were refused entry or escorted back to the border and consigned to their persecutors. With reference to Italian policies towards Jews, Poliakov has written:

> 'The action of the Rome government displayed a plurality of motives – what is known as the permanent national interest, some remote calculation, a vague quest for reassurance and even a latent Germanophobia – all certainly played a part. The fact still remains, however, that it was the attitude of the Italian people as a whole that determined the position adopted by the government. It was responsible for the mindset of those charged with deciding what action to take, who forced . . . Mussolini himself to oppose German demands . . . [There was] a profound incompatibility between the two Axis partners.'[8]

Poliakov's thesis could have been the point of departure for new research on the topic as early as the 1960s, given that the bulk of the documentation had already been microfilmed and was available to scholars at that time. Analysis of the 'plurality of motives' would probably have led to abandonment of a genocide-centred view of events and to the recontextualization of the history of the Greek, Yugoslav and French Jewish refugees within the Fascist occupation. It would also have prompted examination of Italian policy within the framework of relations with the Germans and with the

[8] Poliakov and Sabille, *Jews Under the Italian Occupation*, p. 44.

other occupied countries, in the light of the particular circumstances of a territorial expansion *sub condicione* and amid the contingencies of war. In this sense, the chapter is revisionist because, as Pierre Milza puts it, historical analysis applied to the contemporary age should conceive itself as a sequence of established 'truths' to be subsequently re-examined in the light of new sources, new questions and new revelations.[9]

The documentation in my possession belies the claim that 'Mussolini's government did not release a single Jew to the Nazis for deportation.'[10] And it prompts investigation of the circumstances in which Jews were consigned to the Germans or to collaborationist governments, or expelled. Was there really a concerted effort to rescue the Jews, planned from upon high, co-ordinated by the various branches of the Italian administration and pursued on the basis of a humanitarian imperative? Can we describe Italian policy as 'rescue of the Jews during the Holocaust',[11] as 'humanitarian deliverance' or even as establishing a 'debt of gratitude' towards the occupiers by the 'saved'?

Although military occupations are ancient phenomena, they have only recently been subject to study. They can be distinguished into two main types: classic military occupations and those that can be described as 'Napoleonic'. Both ensue from a military victory. The former serve to weaken the adversary and their purpose is neither the physical incorporation of the occupied territory into the occupying nation nor the cultural assimilation of its identity. They are temporary arrangements, and it is assumed that they will conclude with a peace treaty or with cessation of conflict. In the latter case, the occupier imposes its political, social, cultural and economic system on the occupied territory and society. Napoleonic occupations had this feature, and in certain respects so did those by Japan and the Soviet Union. Distinctive of occupations of this kind is the eschatological missionarism of the occupiers. Driven by the conviction that they alone possess the truth, they impose not only their hegemony but also their value systems and beliefs, the purpose being to 'save' the occupied population, which has no other option but submit to their 'liberators'.

The occupations by the Third Reich do not match this definition. The main purpose of the Nazi conquests was to acquire territories whose inhabitants were then to be removed, except for those who could be Germanized and some others for use as slaves. The expulsion of the peoples inhabiting

[9] Milza, *Mussolini*, p. vii. [10] Zuccotti, *The Italians and the Holocaust*, p. 54.
[11] The subtitle to Herzer, *The Italian Refuge*.

the *Lebensraum*, the settlement therein of only populations with German blood, and the genocide of the Jews were essential components of the project to accomplish the 'racial catharsis' of Nazi Europe.

And the Fascist occupations? They shared certain features with classic occupations and also with Napoleonic ones; but ideologically they were akin to the Nazi occupations, although they were much less radical in intent (during the implementation phase). Of course, if we consider only the outcomes, it is difficult to decide what was distinctively Fascist about the occupations of Mediterranean Europe. Violence and brutality were not unique to them. Suffice it to consider – in more recent times – what the United States did in Vietnam or the Soviet Union in Afghanistan: two superpowers whose armies failed to defeat the guerrilla movements ranged against them despite the advanced technological means at their disposal.

Consequently, if we are to adumbrate the distinctive features of the Fascist occupations, we must go further than mere acknowledgement that Fascism failed to achieve its objectives. We must also identify the components, aspirations and 'projects' of the Fascist domination of a part of Mediterranean Europe, however short-lived it may have been.

Emilio Gentile has written that Italian Fascism was a political and cultural revolution. It sought to destroy the liberal regime and to construct a new state in the unprecedented form of totalitarian organization of civil society and the political system.[12] The totalitarianism of the Fascist regime – which was less radicalized than that of the Third Reich – would conquer a living space in which the *uomo nuovo*, the conqueror born of the revolution, would prosper. Though the circumstances of this conquest and Italy's peculiar status in the Axis profoundly conditioned the extent and nature of its *dominio*, we should not forget that the regime did indeed partly achieve its 'historic objective' of territorial expansion. The Fascist project for the territorial conquest and occupation of Mediterranean Europe cannot be ignored, therefore. Instead, it must be examined with care and framed within the history of the Fascist regime, of Italy and of the Second World War.

[12] Gentile, *Le origini dell'ideologia fascista*, p. 13.

PART I

The time of idiocy

There are exceptional moments in the life of an individual in which the inhibitory centres seem to relax their control over the irrational and unreflecting impulses of the spirit and mankind lapses into error. Similar circumstances arise in the lives of nations. While in normal times a wise man errs seven times a day, in emergencies he does so seven times seven. The unwise now come to the forefront and their stupidity, no longer restrained by fear of the judgement of others, reaches the heights of absurdity. In times of war, as in periods of revolution, there is no possibility of choice and in the general turmoil the scum rises to the surface. This is the case of the excesses committed in revolutionary uprisings and it also explains why error is the norm in warfare, so that the side which commits fewer errors is victorious; or, better, the side more able to exploit the errors of its adversary. It is inevitable that in a country so unprepared for war as Italy a staggering array of follies will be committed.

Luca Pietromarchi, unpublished diary, 14 March 1942

Prologue
The conquered territories

On 10 June 1940 Italy entered the war on Germany's side. Between the end of that month and November 1942 the Italians occupied or annexed various territories in Mediterranean Europe, but they were able to do so always and only by virtue of Germany's decisive military intervention on their behalf.

After the armistice of 24 June 1940, the Italians occupied a number of French *communes* along Italy's western frontier, among them Menton. In April 1941, the defeat of Yugoslavia led to its territorial partition among Germany, Italy, Bulgaria, Hungary and Albania, and to the creation of the two independent states of Croatia and Montenegro (although the independence of the latter was short-lived), while Serbia was occupied by the German army.

Between May and June 1941, the Italians annexed the cities of Kotor and Split, while a number of towns in the interior were incorporated into the province of Zara (Zadar), which had been Italian since the First World War. These three cities – Kotor, Split and Zadar – formed the Governorate of Dalmatia. Ljubljana and its province constituted what was called the Italian Province of Ljubljana, while territories in the Kupano, a strip of land between Slovenia and Croatia comprising the small town of Suak, were merged with Italy's province of Fiume.

Again with regard to the Yugoslavian territories, it was decided at the Vienna conference (21–24 April 1941) that Montenegro should become a protectorate of Rome. The same fate was decreed for Croatia, although there was no protocol or treaty to sanction that decision. Albania acquired a large part of Kosovo and the western area of Yugoslavian Macedonia (the rest went to Bulgaria), while it extended its frontiers northwards into the Montenegrin region of Metohija. Although Germany imposed no restrictions on Italian ambitions officially, it made sure that zones of key importance to the Reich's interests did not end up in the possession of Italy or its satellites. It was for this reason that it backed Sofia's claims in western Macedonia (the zone of Ohrid and Skopje) and directly occupied zones with mineral or other natural resources (northern and eastern Kosovo, for example). In the summer of 1941, the western and central part of Croatia, including broad swathes of Bosnia and the whole of Herzegovina, as well as Montenegro and the western Sanjak, were militarily occupied by the troops of the Italian Regio Esercito.

Greece was occupied by the Axis powers after it had been defeated militarily as a consequence of German intervention in April 1941. The troops of the Regio Esercito, which between 20 October 1940 and 23 April 1941 had sought in vain to defeat and invade Greece, occupied almost all Hellenic continental territory except for the wealthy province of Greek Macedonia, which had been taken over by the Germans, and Thrace, which had been annexed by Bulgaria. The Italians occupied numerous Greek islands as well: the Ionian islands – administered by civil commissioners who prepared the way for annexation – the Cyclades and the (southern) Sporades.

Finally, from 12 November 1942 onwards, the Regio Esercito occupied Corsica and eight French *départements* lying to the east of the Rhône; it also occupied the principality of Monaco. The Italian occupation of all these territories officially came to an end with the armistice of 8 September 1943; but the Italians withdrew voluntarily from some of them between the spring and summer of 1943 following accords with the Germans.

Many of the militarily occupied areas were part of Fascism's imperial 'project'. They pertained to its ambition for *spazio vitale*, or 'living space',

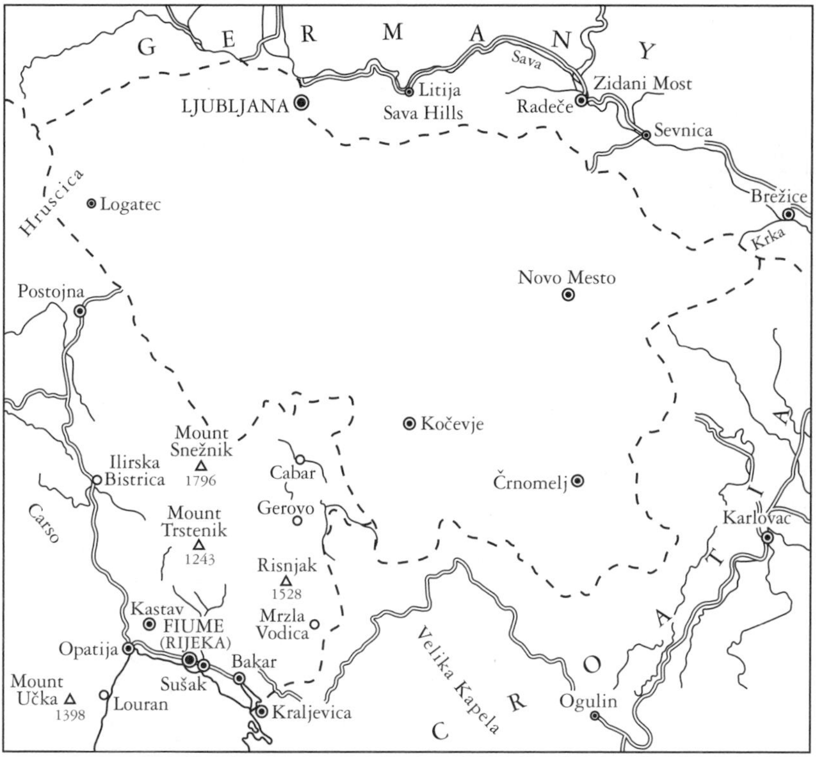

Map 1. The situation in Slovenia in spring 1942 (from Cuzzi, *L'occupazione italiana della Slovenia*, p. 361)

and they were to be controlled or directly administered according to the 'race' or level of development of the population concerned. Military occupation was to be a transitional phase that theoretically would last only until Italy's victory. Other territories, however, were earmarked for annexation. Yet the actual circumstances of their occupation upset the Fascist regime's plans, for it was the 'senior partner' in the Axis that decided which territories Italy might take over. The Fascist regime managed to gain a grip over a large part of the European territories belonging to its envisaged *spazio vitale*, although Rome never enjoyed full freedom of political and military action in any of the territories occupied after 1940. The expression 'gain a grip' is apt because – as we shall see – the occupied territories were economically exploited and politically controlled almost entirely by the Third Reich.

Map 2. The Governorate of Dalmatia, 1941–3 (from Mori, *La Dalmazia*, 1942)

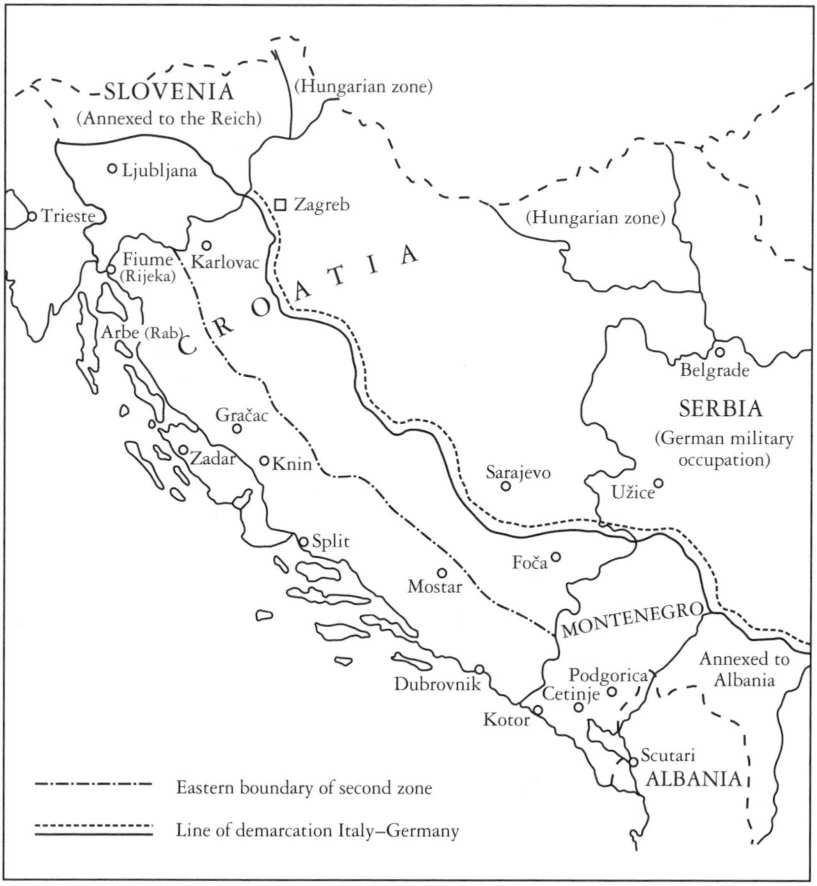

Map 3. Occupied Yugoslavia, 1941–3

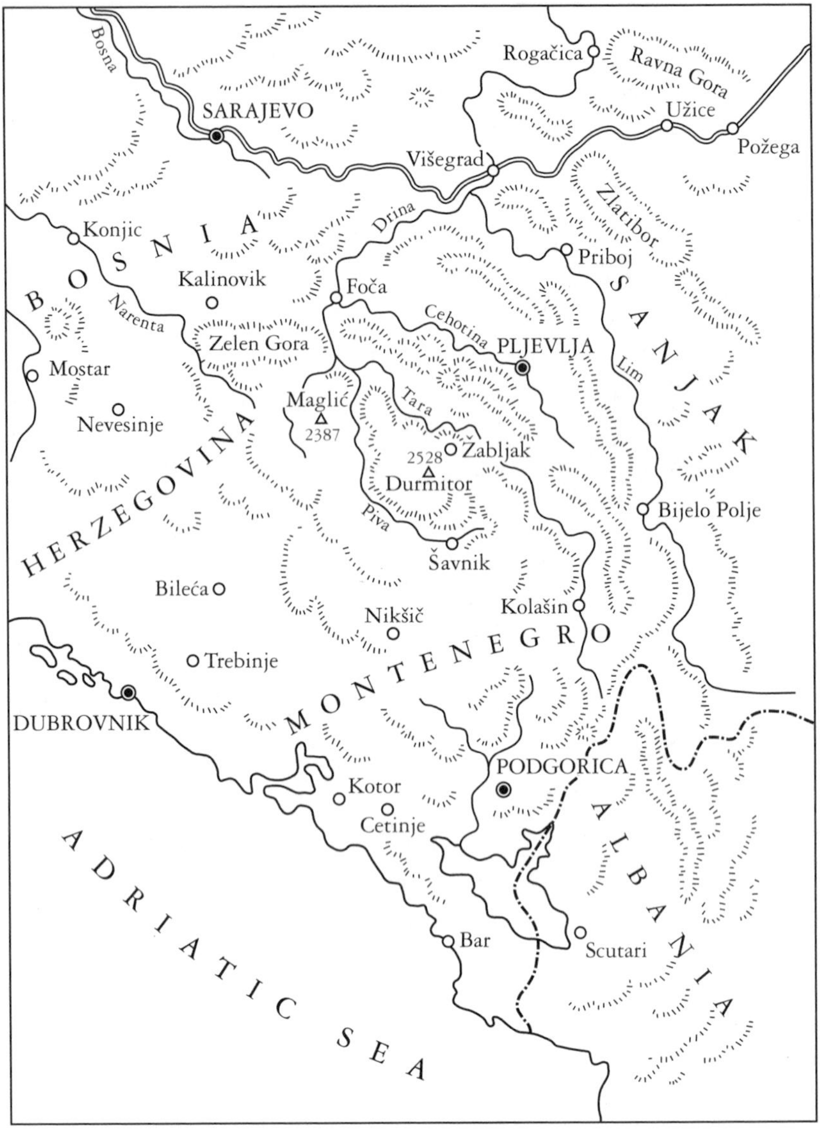

Map 4. Geographical features of Montenegro (from Scotti and Viazzi, *Le aquile delle montagne nere*, p. 18)

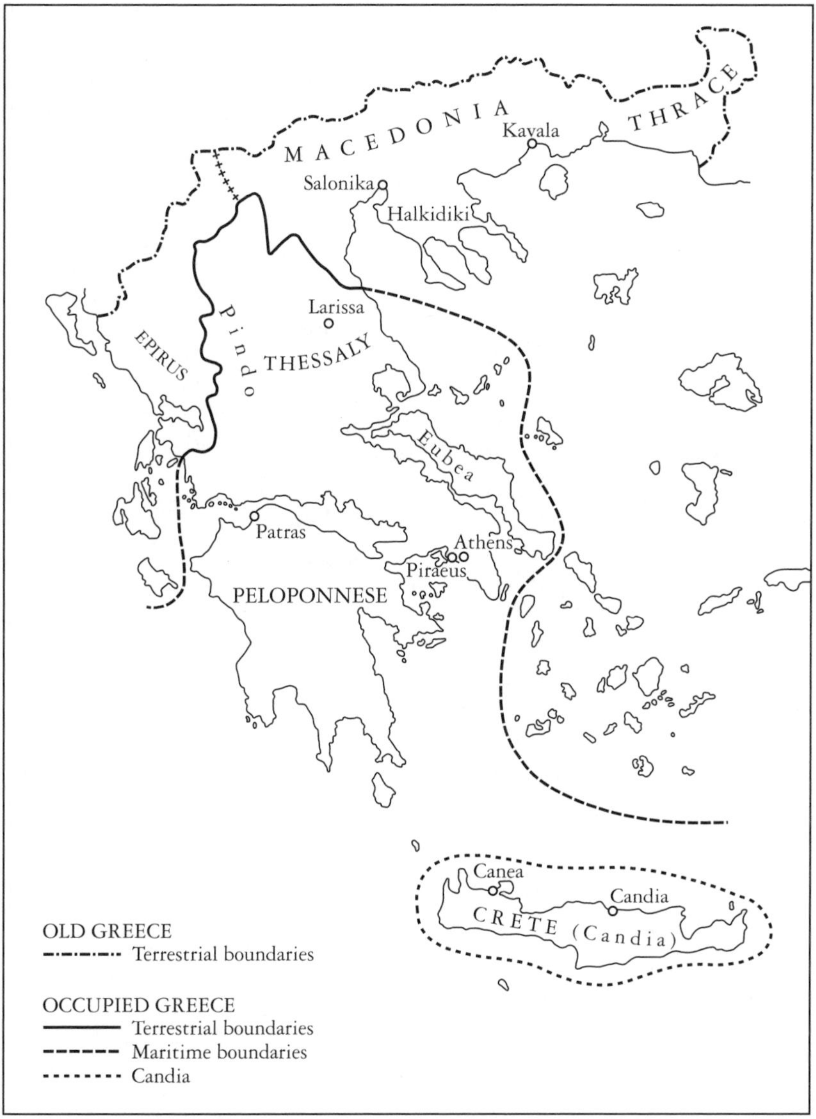

Map 5. Occupied Greece, 1941–3

Map 6. Occupied France, 1942–3

CHAPTER I

Italo-German relations in Mediterranean Europe

The chapter surveys the main phases in the relationship between Italy and Germany. It pays particular attention to the Mediterranean, as the theatre of various conquests and occupations. The rationale of the chapter is that a thorough understanding of Italy's occupation policy during the Second World War can be gained only by examining the degree of Italy's diplomatic, economic and military dependence on the 'senior partner' in the Axis.[1]

FROM THE AXIS TO THE ALLIANCE WITH GERMANY

Until 1935, Fascist expansionism looked in two directions: southward to Africa and the Mediterranean, and eastward to the Danube–Balkan basin. Mussolini was aware that Italy could not pursue these two objectives simultaneously – or, at least, not in the short or medium term. Expansion eastward would have made any rapprochement with Hitler's Germany impossible (especially in view of the Austrian question). But then, during the war against Ethiopia, Hitler discreetly assisted Italy by not complying with the international sanctions ordered against Rome; and in return he obtained Mussolini's tacit endorsement of Germany's re-occupation of the Rhineland. After the Fascist regime's proclamation of its 'empire', Italy concentrated more closely on expansion in the Mediterranean – as evinced by its massive intervention in the Spanish Civil War (around 4,000 dead and 11,000 wounded among the 35,000 Italian soldiers sent to fight in Spain, and more than six billion lire spent on war matériel).

Germany's recognition of Italy's annexation of Ethiopia and the joint German–Italian support for Franco during the Spanish Civil War drew

[1] In writing this chapter I have drawn on the following: André, 'L'Italia nella seconda guerra mondiale'; Collotti, 'L'Italia dall'intervento alla guerra parallela'; Collotti, 'L'alleanza italo-tedesca'; De Felice, *Mussolini il duce*; De Felice, *Mussolini l'alleato*; Mallett, 'The Anglo-Italian War Trade Negotiations'; Milza, *Mussolini*, pp. 658–825; Pastorelli, 'La politica estera fascista'; Militärgeschichtliches Forschungsamt, *The Mediterranean, South-East Europe, and North Africa, 1939–1941: From Italy's Declaration of Non-Belligerence to the Entry of the United States into the War.*

Rome and Berlin closer together. A visit to Rome in 1936 by the Nazi minister Hans Frank gave Germany an early opportunity to ascertain how Mussolini would react to a proposal of alliance. Frank intimated to the Duce that Hitler would consider the Mediterranean Italy's if Rome refrained from intervening should Germany launch an *Anschluss* against Austria. Then, on 1 November 1936, in the Piazza Duomo of Milan, Mussolini delivered the speech in which he pronounced the fateful words 'the Berlin–Rome Axis'. Yet the birth of the Axis was not the result of perfect ideological intercourse between the two regimes. Rome continued to deal with the British, and in January 1937 concluded 'a gentlemen's agreement' with them on free movement in the Mediterranean and mutual respect for each country's interests, followed by a joint undertaking to maintain the territorial *status quo*. The year 1937 was a transitional one in which Italian foreign policy oscillated between two fronts: on the one hand, Britain, Austria, Hungary and Yugoslavia (the bilateral agreements with Belgrade were made public in March 1937); on the other, Germany (visits were made to Rome by Hermann Göring, Konstantin Alexander von Neurath and Werner Eduard von Blomberg). But Italy's signing up to the Anti-Comintern Pact (on 6 November) and its withdrawal from the League of Nations (on 11 December) cannot be taken as unequivocal signals that it had now decided whose side it was on. The road to alliance with Germany was still a long and tortuous one, and far from ineluctable.

On 11 March 1938, the Germans notified Rome that their advance on Vienna had begun. The announcement was greeted with surprise and concern by Mussolini and Galeazzo Ciano, despite Hitler's reassurances that the Brenner frontier would remain inviolate. Although the Germans' belated announcement was an affront to Rome, Mussolini, to the astonishment of some Fascist hierarchs and of numerous diplomats, accepted what was to be the first of a long series of *faits accomplis* which in substance spelled the end of fifteen years of Danubian and Balkan policy. The German annexation of Austria signified – and of this both Mussolini and Palazzo Chigi (the Foreign Ministry) were well aware – that Berlin had taken possession of the Danubian basin, with its communication routes, Romanian oil, Hungarian cereals and Yugoslavian and Bulgarian minerals and timber. The states of the Danubian–Balkan area would now look to Berlin rather than to Rome for fulfilment of their revisionist claims.

The *Anschluss* further accelerated the *Drang nach Südosten*[2] already begun by Germany before 1938 with a policy of economic penetration and

[2] Mitrović, *Ergänzungswirtschaft*; Breccia, 'Le potenze dell'Asse e la neutralità della Jugoslavia'.

propaganda whose ultimate purpose was incorporation of south-eastern Europe into the *Grosswirtschaftsraum* (great economic space). To this end the Nazis had elaborated the notion of *Ergänzungswirtschaft* (a complementary economy founded on the exchange of local natural resources for capital and German finished products). Pseudo-scientific publications 'proved' that south-eastern Europe was inseparable from Germany and 'explained' that the Western powers were *raumfremden Mächte* – powers extraneous to a region Germanic by allegedly natural and 'organic' affiliation.

Mussolini and his ministers were kept constantly informed on how Germany was strengthening its commercial and financial positions in the Danubian–Balkan area, and on the Nazis' methods of economic penetration: these being, for instance, the purchase of French or American mining companies or plants, or location in the area by firms with the economic power of IG Farben and Krupp. They were aware that, thanks to the clearing system, the Reichsmark's bloc was now an economic reality: indeed, by 1938 Germany monopolized 50 per cent of Balkan trade. The Italian ambassador in Berlin wrote to Ciano that the Germans had excluded any Italian presence in the Balkans. The extent of the area allocated to Rome in the great European-African-Middle Eastern economic space, the ambassador explained, would be 'only' the Mediterranean basin, with its geographical centre in Egypt and Asia Minor.[3]

The impossibility of competing with Germany in the Balkans stiffened Italy's resolve to expand in the Mediterranean, even though this would have sooner or later led to a showdown with London and Paris. The logical consequence of this political calculation should have been an endeavour to acquire the support of the Reich, which was indispensable. Yet both Mussolini and his hierarchs knew perfectly well that alignment with Berlin would be fraught with risk. For example, alliance with Germany very likely meant that it would be impossible to achieve a satisfactory territorial share-out with diplomatic threats alone, and without armed intervention – which was a scenario attractive to a militarily weak power unprepared for war, such as Fascist Italy.

Until the end of 1938, the idea that Italy's role was to be that of the 'decisive weight' (*peso determinante*) in the international balance – a notion devised in the early 1930s by Foreign Minister Dino Grandi – continued to be the guiding principle of Rome's foreign policy. Hence, in April 1938, Italy made various overtures to the Western democracies. The Easter Agreements were concluded with Britain to settle Italo-British rivalry in the

[3] DDI, ser. IX (?), 1939–43, vol. 5, doc. 321, 'Dino Alfieri a Ciano', 1 August 1940.

Mediterranean, East Africa and the Near East, while talks began with the French *chargé d'affaires* in Rome, Jules-François Blondel. Mussolini hinted at the possibility of a war in which, should Hitler not respect the inviolability of the Brenner frontier, he himself would lead a Europe-wide coalition against Germany. Hitler, for his part, talked to the Duce about a possible alliance during an official visit to Italy, but received only evasive responses in return.

Then, when the Sudetenland crisis erupted, it was Mussolini's hope that Germany would prevail, for this would upset the territorial *status quo* established at Versailles, give greater fluidity to the European situation and open the way for Italian expansion. Mussolini saw Hitler's Sudetenland campaign as instrumental to the revisionist policy that he had pursued since taking power. He wanted Hitler to succeed; but he wanted him to do so without resorting to force, because Italy, still trapped in the morass of the Spanish Civil War, was weak and unprepared. Consequently, at the Munich conference convened on 29 September 1938 to resolve the Sudetenland crisis, Mussolini assumed the 'role of the arbiter of Europe', 'the saviour of peace', but also the role of Germany's *de facto* ally.

In 1938, amid the waverings of Italian foreign policy, a short-lived attempt at rapprochement with France led to resumption of normal diplomatic relations and the arrival in Rome of the French ambassador André François-Poncet. However, the initiative foundered on 29 November. On a visit to the Camera dei Fasci e delle Corporazioni (the erstwhile Chamber of Deputies), the French diplomat was greeted with raucous cries of 'Savoy', 'Nice', 'Corsica' and 'Djibouti'. The immediate effect of the anti-French barracking – orchestrated by the Fascist Party secretary Achille Starace – was outright rejection by Paris of any Italian request whatever, but most notably for Italo-French condominium in Djibouti and Tunisia, and a discounted tariff for Italian ships through the Suez Canal. Relations with Paris deteriorated further when Mussolini delivered speeches proclaiming that his regime's short-term expansionist objectives concerned, besides Albania, also France's metropolitan and colonial territories.

On 15 March 1939, the Italian government took concrete action. First, Mussolini issued an ultimatum to King Zog of Albania; then, on a specious pretext, Italian troops occupied Albania, which on 8 April became an Italian protectorate. On 16 April the Albanian crown was offered to Victor Emmanuel III. The manoeuvre served two purposes: it demonstrated to the Western powers that Rome took its decisions regardless of Germany's wishes; and it warned Berlin that Fascist Italy had not renounced its expansionist ambitions in the Balkans.

Italy had two options for strategic alignment at the time of the Albanian occupation. Alliance with Berlin offered good prospects for Mediterranean expansion, but it also carried the risk of Italy's involvement in a war for which it was entirely unprepared. Mussolini knew that sections of the population, as well as the ruling class, the industrialists and even the party hierarchs, were resistant to the idea of an alliance. On the other hand, bridges had not yet been burned with either London (visits were made to Rome in January 1939 by Neville Chamberlain and Lord Halifax) or Paris (in February Edouard Daladier sent an emissary to Rome – Paul Baudouin – with orders to ascertain the extent of Italy's claims). Then Germany's aggression against Czechoslovakia, and its annexation of Bohemia, prompted Ciano – a fervent supporter of alliance in 1936 – to write in his diary that he would strive to persuade the Duce to reach agreement with the Western powers. Mussolini nonetheless preferred the hazardous option of alliance with Germany. He did so for reasons to do with his self-perceived role as the charismatic leader of the nation and because he was convinced that the alliance would enable his regime to bring its revolution to completion and carve out Italy's *spazio vitale*. Moreover, he was reluctant to set himself against Hitler and feared Italy's diplomatic and military isolation. Although there was nothing to prevent Mussolini from changing his mind, it was probably too late for a humiliating climbdown – especially after Daladier's public proclamation that France would not yield an inch of its metropolitan and colonial possessions, and above all after Mussolini's pronouncement in Berlin (on 26 September 1937) that Fascism would march beside its ally *sino in fondo* or until the bitter end.

Ciano and Joachim von Ribbentrop conducted the negotiations on the alliance. The Italian minister made it plain that Italy would not be ready to enter the war until 1943; but at a meeting in Milan on 6 May 1939 he received only vague reassurances from Ribbentrop in that regard. Then, following French press reports of anti-German demonstrations in Italy, Mussolini ordered Ciano to announce the imminent signing of an Italo-German pact. Ciano foolishly left the task of drawing up the treaty to the Germans, who contrived for its article 3 to place Italy at the mercy of Germany's decision when war would be declared. The Pact of Steel was signed in Berlin on 22 May 1939.

FROM THE PACT OF STEEL TO THE END OF THE PARALLEL WAR

No article, nor indeed any clause, of any document concerning the Pact of Steel stipulated that Germany must not declare war before 1943. The objectives of the alliance were not stated, nor was any formal recognition made of Italy's and Germany's respective spheres of influence. There was no protocol that defined frontiers apart from the declared inviolability of the Brenner, and no jointly defined military strategy. In August 1939, Italy had no military plans in the event of a war against France or Great Britain. Its response against any Anglo-French attack would be the defence of its frontiers combined with an offensive against Greece, and a probable second offensive against Yugoslavia 'after fomenting internal uprisings'. Thus, any aggression against Italy was to be countered by an offensive against third countries, not against the aggressors themselves: a strategy with a political significance at odds with the regime's foreign policy and which suggests that Italy's interests were compatible with those of its probable enemies.

On 17 June 1939, Joseph Goebbels delivered a violent speech in Gdańsk against the Polish government, which he accused of violating the rights of the German-speaking minority. The Italian ambassador in Berlin, Bernardo Attolico, realized that a German invasion of Poland was imminent and notified Ciano and Mussolini to that effect. His warnings were largely ignored, however. In August, at a meeting held in Salzburg, Ribbentrop and Hitler explained to their Italian counterparts that the international situation had changed: the assault on Poland would now begin before 1942. They also opined that the Western democracies would not have the courage to declare war against Germany. Ciano left the meeting convinced that there was nothing more to be done: Hitler had decided to strike and nothing and nobody could dissuade him. On his arrival in Italy, Ciano tried to persuade Mussolini to abandon the Pact of Steel and not bring Italy into the war as Germany's satellite, adding that if he did so, the Third Reich would acquire power which one day it would turn against Italy.

On 23 August 1939, the announcement of the German–Soviet pact changed the situation once again. Ciano now believed that circumstances in Europe had altered so radically that Italy should ready itself to grab some of the spoils in Dalmatia and Croatia. On 25 August 1939, Hitler wrote a long letter to Mussolini in which he apologized for not keeping him abreast of the negotiations with the Soviet Union and for not informing him that the attack against Poland was imminent. Mussolini replied that, if the conflict remained localized, Italy would give Germany the political and economic support that it requested; but if the conflict spread Italy could not take any military initiative unless Germany delivered the military supplies and raw materials that Italy required to resist attack by the French and the British. The Fabbriguerra estimated that such resistance would require 17,000 trainloads of materials and supplies: a deliberately exaggerated request which

Berlin could only refuse. Hitler was forced to relent, but he asked Mussolini not to inform the Western powers of his decisions, to support Germany with a propaganda campaign and to send Italian workers to the Reich. Already humiliated at being obliged to acknowledge Italy's unpreparedness for war, the Duce now failed in his attempt to organize a second Munich conference. Thus, on 1 September, he informed the Italians of their country's 'non-belligerence'. Some days later a ministerial reshuffle eliminated the pro-German ministers, including Starace, and replaced them with men close to Ciano: Grandi, Alessandro Pavolini and Raffaello Riccardi.

At the beginning of 1940, the minister of foreign affairs successfully concluded an economic agreement with the British (coal in exchange for aeroplanes and war matériel). Trade with France continued unabated. In May, Daladier announced his willingness to grant important concessions to Rome in eastern and northern Africa. On 10 March, Ribbentrop travelled to Rome intent on persuading Mussolini to abandon his non-belligerence. He was informed by the Duce that Italy intended to wage a 'parallel war' in the Mediterranean, but it would do so only after Germany's western offensive had begun. During a meeting held at the Brenner Pass on 18 March, Mussolini reiterated his position to Hitler and announced that he alone would decide the date of Italy's entry into the war. Whether or not Italy would go to war alongside Germany now depended on only two residual conditions: firstly that Italy could delay its entry to the extent that honour and dignity allowed; secondly that the war must be short.[4]

A secret memorandum circulated by Mussolini on 31 March 1940 confirmed that his policy was unyielding defence on land (except in Ethiopia and, as regards only air bases, against France in Corsica). The memorandum also outlined his plans for an offensive in the Balkans, as well as an general maritime offensive, which was wholly incongruous given the lack of terrestrial strategic objectives. This was an indirect strategy by which the threat of war served the purpose of political and diplomatic, more than military, coercion.

The German occupation of Denmark, the defeat of Norway, the offensive against the Netherlands and Belgium and above all the collapse of France persuaded Mussolini that the time had come for Italy to enter the war. The decision was probably taken on 31 March. Then, on the following day, Mussolini reiterated to his army commanders the political-military directives set out in his memorandum of 31 March: the military engagement was to be coercive, dissuasive, but above all rapid in its consummation. But

[4] Ceva, 'Vertici politici e militari', p. 692.

these were objectives that increased Italy's military dependence on Germany, for the timing of intervention would be determined by the success of the German offensive – with the added danger (which, in fact, transpired) that Italy's contribution would not be of sufficient magnitude to justify its claims to territory. According to the historian Fortunato Minniti, Mussolini did indeed have a strategic vision; but its purpose was to achieve absolute freedom of action, with the consequence that political considerations took priority over operational ones.[5] Although the army commanders were aware of this priority, and of its attendant problems, they raised no objections, confident that Italy's entry in the war alongside the Germans would come about only in the distant future. Consequently, in the belief that the war was a political contrivance, and reassured by the king's acquiescence, they did as the Duce wanted.

The doctrine of Italy's absolute freedom of action from Germany bred the notion of the 'parallel war': independent and brief military action which Italy would wage rapidly and ruthlessly before sitting down at the peace table. It was to be a war, Mussolini told Giuseppe Bottai, 'which does not overlap or mesh with the greater and more general conflict: rather, it is a war with its own and specifically Italian objectives, and it has nothing to do with the present adversaries'. It was to be fought 'not for Germany, nor with Germany, but alongside Germany'.[6] The notion was prompted by these considerations: that Italy's armed forces were still far from war-ready, that the economy was unprepared for long-drawn-out conflict and that Hitler's real intentions were unknown.[7] It was predicated on certainty that Germany would achieve rapid victory – this being a concrete possibility after the defeat of France – and on fear that, if Germany triumphed without adequate Italian support, Rome would be reduced to a second-rate power. Thus confirmed was the gulf between Italy's ambitions for autonomy and expansion on the one hand, and the instruments available for their accomplishment on the other. Italy rejected any form of strategic collaboration with Berlin, so that the Fascists might demonstrate their military prowess to the German ally, to the nation and to the world. Should this strategy prove successful, Italy could cash it in at the peace table for territorial gains.

On 10 June 1940, Italy declared war against France and Great Britain. After the defeat of France, and in view of Britain's difficulties, the Italians believed that their ambitions in the Mediterranean and Africa could be easily realized. Nevertheless, if a 'parallel' victory were to be achieved, new

[5] Minniti, 'Profili dell'iniziativa strategica italiana'. [6] De Felice, *Mussolini il duce*, p. 685.
[7] De Felice, *Mussolini l'alleato*, p. 101.

theatres of war would have to be found. This was an exigency which redirected attention to the arena for Fascist expansionism that the regime had never abandoned: the Balkans.

On 17 June, Hitler announced to Mussolini that France had sued for armistice. But if armistice were granted, Italy could not sit at the peace table as one of the victors, and its role in the war would consequently be only that of a supernumerary. The Duce reacted by ordering his army chief of staff, General Pietro Badoglio, to attack France within three days. Whereupon he left for Munich to discuss the conditions of the armistice with the Führer.

The French armistice represented 'an acid test . . . for determining whether and to what extent Germany intended to support Italy's claims'.[8] It was in its aftermath, in fact, that realization dawned on the Italians that German policy and the German war were damaging Fascism's vital interests and betraying the promises made before the conflict. Between 17 and 24 June 1940, Rome wavered between two opposing strategies. It could either anticipate German encroachments on the *spazio vitale* by immediate annexation and consolidation of acquired positions by means of border treaties; or it could avoid definitive territorial demarcations and rely instead on rapid victory by the Axis and a further and more advantageous redrawing of the map of Europe. The same dilemma would arise when the armistices were signed with Yugoslavia and Greece.

On 18 June 1940, on the train bound for Munich, Ciano, Assistant Army Chief of Staff Mario Roatta, director general of European and Mediterranean Affairs at the Foreign Ministry Gino Buti, Rear Admiral Raffaele De Courten and General Egisto Perino drew up a plan that reflected the former of the above policies. Italy, they decided, would press the following demands upon the Germans: demobilization of the French army until the peace settlement; French disarmament; Italian occupation of French territory as far as the Rhône; Italian occupation of Corsica, Tunisia and French Somalia; Italian occupation of strategic areas, factories and military bases in France and its empire; the immediate consignment of French naval vessels, aircraft and railway rolling stock in the territory occupied; an obligation on France not to destroy fixed plant or supplies of any kind; and a denunciation of the French alliance with Great Britain.[9] Hitler raised no objections,

8 Collotti, 'L'Italia dall'intervento alla guerra parallela', p. 36.

9 DDI, ser. IX, 1939–43, vol. 5, doc. 45, 'ministro degli Esteri Ciano al capo del governo Mussolini'; doc. 65, Ciano's diary, 19 June 1940, 'colloquio Mussolini–Ciano'; doc. 75, 'capo di gabinetto Filippo Anfuso al ministro degli Esteri Ciano', Rome, 21 June 1940; doc. 83, 'capo del governo Mussolini all'ambasciatore a Berlino Alfieri'.

except in regard to the French fleet, which he feared might pass to the British. He then presented the final draft of the German armistice. But it imposed conditions much less stringent than expected by Mussolini, who returned to Rome dismayed at the Germans' moderation, which he believed presaged their imminent reconciliation with the French. He also disapproved of the conclusion of two separate armistices, and he was annoyed by the scant consideration shown him by Hitler. Immediately on his arrival in the capital, he ordered Badoglio to begin the offensive against France. The campaign effectively started on 20 June and lasted for four days; the French defended themselves exceptionally well against a surprise attack which left more than 600 dead and more than 2,000 wounded on the Italian side. The most 'brilliant' achievement by the Fascist troops was the occupation of the town of Menton and of some small *communes* in the French Alps.

On 24 June, almost none of the items on the ambitious list initially drawn up by Ciano and colleagues remained in the armistice signed at Villa Incisa. The French plenipotentiaries discovered that Italy's only demands were the creation of a fifty-kilometre demilitarized zone to the west of Italy's western frontier and the occupation of the *communes* conquered during the campaign. The Italians also wanted demilitarization of the strongholds and naval bases of Toulon, Bizerte, Ajaccio and Mers-el-Kebir.[10] Gianluca André describes the Italian change of mind as a 'sincere attempt at reconciliation with France' prompted by fear that Germany was about to become the absolute master of Europe: it was an attempt, that is to say, made in the hope of counterbalancing German hegemony.[11] According to Renzo De Felice, what changed the Italian delegation's mind was the Germans' unexpected opposition to a punitive armistice.[12] Convinced that peace was at hand, Mussolini realized that the conditions of 18 June would have compromised future relations with France. Adjustment of the Italian demands to the contents of the Franco-German armistice was necessary to avert possible reconciliation between France and Germany – an outcome that would have severely damaged Italy's interests. The most recent and accurate reconstruction of these events has been made by Romain Rainero, who maintains that Mussolini and Hitler sought during their meeting of 18 June to forestall the flight from metropolitan France of a *de facto*

[10] DDI, ser. IX, 1939–43, vol. 5, doc. 95, 'Convenzione di armistizio tra il CSMG Badoglio e il capo della delegazione francese per l'armistizio Charles-Léon-Clément Huntzinger'.

[11] André, 'La guerra in Europa'; Borgogni, *Mussolini e la Francia di Vichy*; Borgogni, *Italia e Francia durante la crisi militare dell'Asse*.

[12] De Felice, *Mussolini l'alleato*, p. 135.

government which in the future might prove a valuable interlocutor while the Axis powers waited for victory to clarify France's future in the new European order. This preoccupation, however, induced neither Italy nor Germany to relinquish its ambitions.

Proof of this is that, when the Italian delegation returned to Rome, it used the decisions taken at Munich (and therefore the Fascist demands embodied in them) as the basis for a draft armistice with France whose entry into force would have conditioned the entry into force of the Franco-German armistice. Italy's 'Protocol on the Conditions for Armistice Between Italy and France' consisted of fully six sections of clauses: political-military, military-terrestrial, military-naval, aeronautic, financial, and general.[13] Though the text diluted Italy's territorial claims, it was not a sincere revision of the regime's overall project. Rather, it was a stopgap expedient which the Axis powers believed they could revise at the forthcoming peace talks with London and Paris. Yet, as Enzo Collotti has remarked, the decisions of 24 June closely and permanently conditioned relations between Italy and France, for 'Germany was in no hurry to reach peace with France, because the uncertainty of the armistice made it easier to control . . .: Italy was in a hurry to reach a conclusion because the passage of time heightened the uncertainty and frailty of its hopes of realizing its [ambitions]'.[14]

The campaign in the Alps was by no means the success that Italy needed if it was to sit at the peace table as an outright victor. Rome consequently decided to seek its fortune elsewhere: in northern Africa and the Balkans, areas which held out attractive prospects of easy military victories. Fascist objectives ranged across broad swathes of territory from French metropolitan territories to Tunisia; from Algeria to French and British Somalia; from Aden and Perim to Socotra; from Malta to Greece; from eastern Switzerland to Yugoslavia; from Egypt to British Egyptian Sudan.[15] The death of the governor and commander-in-chief of the troops in Libya, Italo Balbo, on 28 June 1940 – the same day on which Badoglio launched the offensive

[13] Rainero, *Mussolini e Pétain*, vol. I, pp. 42–51; vol. II, pp. 15–27, doc. 1, with the text of the 21 June plan.

[14] Collotti, 'L'Italia dall'intervento alla guerra parallela', p. 37.

[15] DDI, ser. IX, 1939–43, vol. 5, docs. 114 and 677; doc. 65, Ciano's diary, 4 October 1940, 'Colloquio al Brennero fra Mussolini e Hitler': 'As far as Italy is concerned [Mussolini] confirms our well-known demands, namely: Nice, Corsica, Tunisia and Djibouti. Of these, only Nice and Corsica are part of metropolitan territory. This is a matter of only eight thousand square kilometres and the Duce is willing to concede to the inhabitants of those zones the right to opt for French nationality. The Führer says that he is perfectly in agreement with the Italian requests and repeats that he will never make peace with France unless Italy is satisfied.' These requests were reiterated in a GABAP note written on or around 26 October 1940 in preparation for the Florence meeting between Mussolini and Hitler: DDI, ser. IX, 1939–43, vol. 5, doc. 793.

against the Suez Canal – delayed the start of operations in northern Africa by almost three months. Only on 13 September did General Rodolfo Graziani, who had been sent in the meantime to replace Balbo, attack the British positions and manage to occupy Sidi el-Barrani. But after this first advance – hailed as a triumph by the regime's propaganda machine and by the general himself – the Italians failed to proceed any further. If they had accepted the two armoured divisions offered by Hitler, events would have turned out otherwise. But Mussolini brusquely rejected Hitler's offer: he wanted an entirely Italian victory, and he refused to countenance any deviation from the fundamental principle of the 'parallel war'. By February 1941, which was when the five divisions of the German Afrikakorps arrived in northern Africa under the command of General Erwin Rommel, the Italian troops had lost the whole of Cyrenaica, and the British had captured more than 130,000 soldiers and disabled all the Italians' tanks and 1,000 of their aircraft. In East Africa, on 5 May 1941, the British triumphantly escorted the Negus into Addis Ababa; and on 21 May the Duke of Aosta was forced to capitulate.

As regards the other theatre of war – the Danube–Balkan basin – Mussolini informed Hitler that Italy was ready to launch an attack against Greece, whereupon the Führer enjoined his ally not to undertake any military operations at all in south-eastern Europe. As absolute master of the economies of the Balkan countries, the Reich was concerned to keep the region out of the war, and it had no need – unlike Italy – to assert its hegemony in the concrete form of direct military occupation. As Collotti has shown, a policy of collaboration without occupation enabled Germany to save on the Wehrmacht's forces and on military expenditure. But above all it conveyed the image of unprecedented cohesion within the Axis – with the prospect of swelling the crusade against Bolshevism with Slav populations always responsive to the pan-Slav ideal embodied by Russia (and therefore the USSR). Italian expansionism in the Balkans was instead the expression of a weak capitalism, which in order to obtain outlet markets for its industry, and especially to source raw materials directly, was forced to rely more on military conquest than on economic power. The German veto on military operations in south-eastern Europe frustrated Italian aspirations and intensified competition between the two allies in the Danube–Balkan basin, which was the only directly accessible source of raw materials for Italy.[16]

[16] DDI, ser. IX, 1939–43, vol. 4, doc. 210, 'incaricato d'affari a Berlino Guelfo Zamboni al ministro degli Esteri Ciano', Berlin, 26 April 1940; doc. 270, 'ministro a Belgrado Francesco Mameli al ministro degli Esteri Ciano', Belgrade, 2 May 1940; vol. 5, doc. 161, 'ambasciatore a Berlino Alfieri al ministro degli Esteri Ciano', 1 July 1940. See also vol. 5, doc. 65, Ciano's diary, 7 July 1940.

Increasingly dependent on Germany, Rome did not have the wherewithal to oppose its ally's will. After entering the war, it received no guarantees from Berlin that it would have access to the supplies – steel, oil and coal – essential for its prosecution of the war. Indeed, 'Germany strove to give orders to Italian industry so that production plant would be diverted away from the war effort, and it endeavoured to prevent Italy from acquiring the raw materials that it needed from countries dominated by the Axis.'[17]

In September 1940, the failure of operations against Britain, postponed *sine die*, and the German occupation of Romania (on 12 October, and which the Italians had known about several weeks beforehand) increased Italian fears that the war was about to conclude with a negotiated peace between London and Berlin from which Rome would be excluded. For this reason, heedless of Hitler's veto of July, Mussolini chanced his hand on achieving rapid victory in Greece.

The Italian political and military leaders were perfectly aware of Greece's administrative organization, its domestic and international political situation, its geography, industry, foreign trade, the minorities in the country, its border disputes and its military strength.[18] Reports by the War Ministry depicted the country as anything but poorly armed and nowhere near internal collapse. Nevertheless, at a meeting held on 15 October 1940, Mussolini and his closest advisers agreed that the occupation of Greece would be entirely straightforward. The military objective was possession of Greece's western coast, Zante, Cephalonia, Corfu and Salonika, followed by 'complete occupation of Greece, the purpose being to disable it militarily and ensure that it [will remain] within Italy's political-economic space'.[19] Responsibility for the decision cannot be placed on Mussolini alone. The generals dared not explain to him that Greece was impossible to defeat with the meagre military means allocated to the campaign (an expeditionary force of 60,000 men) or that the proposed demobilization of 300,000 soldiers (between the end of 1940 and the beginning of 1941) would render any rapid reinforcement of the front in Greece practically impossible. The politicians, too, bore heavy responsibility for the

[17] Collotti, 'L'alleanza italo-tedesca', p. 477. See DDI, ser. IX, 1939–43, vol. 6, docs. 308, 323, 327, 343, 347.

[18] USSME, N I–II, 'Diari storici', b. 2245, XI Armata, 'Relazione Pirtille'; H 3, b. 46, Ministero della Guerra, SIM, pubblicaz. 566s, *Grecia*, October 1940, copy 280.

[19] USSME, N I–II, *Diari storici*, b. 2245, 15 October 1940, 'Verbale della riunione tenuta alle ore 11 nella sala di lavoro del duce a palazzo Venezia (resoconto stenografico), presenti: il Duce, Ciano, Badoglio, Ubaldo Soddu, Francesco Jacomoni, Roatta, Sebastiano Visconti Prasca'; DDI, ser. IX, 1939–43, vol. 5, doc. 728, 15 October 1940, 'Riunione presso il capo del governo del ministro degli Esteri e del CSMG'.

miscalculation, Ciano most of all: for in the hope of increasing his prestige and power, and considering Albania some sort of personal fief, he claimed that Italy had the Albanians' support, that the Greeks had little stomach for a fight and that a pro-Italian faction in Athens was ready to oust Ioannis Metaxas. There was not a grain of truth to any of Ciano's assertions, but they prompted Mussolini to launch an attack against Greece, but with only five divisions, without the support of the Bulgarians and without the advantage of surprise. The Greek campaign was an utter disaster. An advance from the Albanian frontier to Epirus while fighting an enemy defending its homeland and during an early and particularly harsh winter was always bound to fail. Little by little the expeditionary force disintegrated into a rabble: of its fully 500,000 soldiers, 32,000 were killed and more than 100,000 wounded. Moreover, the British disabled part of the Italian fleet in the Bay of Taranto (12 November 1940) and thus regained control over the seaways of the southern Mediterranean.[20]

Mussolini thus had to resign himself to accepting Germany military assistance. Berlin could now have obliged Rome to place the Regio Esercito under the command of the Germans, as numerous Nazi generals and diplomats recommended, Ribbentrop most vociferously among them. Hitler resisted, however, although he did not do so out of sympathy with Italy, nor for any confidence that he might have had in the Italian army, but because of his friendship with and admiration for the Duce, and perhaps also because he feared the decision would have undesirable political repercussions. Germany attacked Yugoslavia and Greece:[21] between 6 and 23 April, both countries were defeated and armistices were signed, and on 24 April, in Vienna, Yugoslavia was erased from the map of Europe. When Ciano left Rome for the former Austrian capital, Mussolini spelled out Italy's demands for him: the incorporation of Slovenia into the Kingdom of Italy, the redrawing of the province of Fiume's terrestrial and insular boundaries; the annexation to the kingdom of all the territory from Segna to Kotor; the merging of Montenegro with Albania, although it would retain its autonomous status; and the annexation to Albania of Kosovo and of the Yugoslav regions populated by Albanians (between 700,000 and 1,000,000 persons).[22]

As we shall see in more detail in chapter 3, the Germans agreed at Vienna to almost all of Italy's demands, as well as to those of Bulgaria and Hungary. Serbia was to be reduced 'to the minimum necessary to prevent it from

[20] Sadkovich, 'The Italo-Greek War in Context', p. 453.
[21] DDI, ser. IX, 1939–43, vol. 6, doc. 766, 23 March 1941.
[22] DDI, ser. IX, 1939–43, vol. 6, docs. 923, 924 and 931.

[becoming once again] a hotbed of plotting and intrigue',[23] while Croatia obtained its independence. When Ciano pointed out to Ribbentrop that the zone of Slovenia allocated to the Reich was overextended to the south, Ribbentrop replied that the frontier could not be changed because it had been 'irrevocably' fixed thus by Hitler. Then, when discussion turned to Croatia, Ribbentrop gave permission for Italo-Croatian border negotiations to begin. Although Germany could have installed the pro-German Marshal Slavko Kvartenik as head of the Croatian state, it nevertheless accepted Rome's man: Ante Pavelić. The Germans 'only' secured their right to exploit Croatia's resources and economy while guaranteeing the superior status of the *Volksdeutschen*.[24] As the senior partner in the alliance, Germany could offer this purely formal sop to Rome because Italy was by now no more than a satellite of the Reich. In an article published in 1941, Ulrich von Hassel calculated the disparity between the two competitors in the Yugoslav market as being 10 to 1 in favour of the Reich, while he emphasized Germany's 'crushing' supremacy in industrial shareholding.[25] When the Italians suggested to the Germans that their respective spheres of influence might be established according to a rigid division of geographical zones (Yugoslavia and Greece to Italy, all the rest to the Germany), the Germans rejected the proposal and obliged its 'junior partner' to accept the principle of 'prevalence'[26] in a particular zone for each of the two powers, so that Germany could maintain a presence in those controlled by Italy. The upshot was therefore that, however much Fascist propaganda might proclaim the priority of Italy's interests in the Balkans, there was no doubt that the Reich had absolute superiority.[27]

By now certain of its hegemony in the Danubian–Balkan area, Berlin permitted Italy to occupy areas of territory (even large ones) and to settle the political question and the boundary dispute with the Croats as it wished.[28] From a political point of view, playing the role of the 'honest broker' enabled Germany to consolidate its position and prestige even further, and the Croatian government now acceded to every German demand without demur. Italy's negligible economic significance, but extensive military

[23] DGFP, ser. D, vol. 12, docs. 291, 379, 394, 398, 534, unsigned; DDI, ser. IX, 1939–43, vol. 6, docs. 956, 962 and 967.

[24] Miletić, *The Volksdeutschen of Bosnia, Slavonia and Srem Regions*; Krnic, 'The German Volksgruppe in the Independent State of Croatia'; Trifković, 'Rivalry Between Germany and Italy in Croatia', p. 892.

[25] Hassel, 'Die Neuordnung im Südostraum', 1941.

[26] In Nazi parlance, 'prevalence' meant that there would be German troops and emissaries in Italian zones; and vice versa, Italian troops and emissaries in German ones.

[27] Collotti, 'L'alleanza italo-tedesca', p. 480.

[28] DGFP, ser. D, vol. 12, docs. 391 and 394.

occupation, gave Nazi propagandists an opportunity to rebut accusations of German hegemony and sell the idea that the Axis allies were co-participants in the 'new order'. Under Hitler's oft-repeated distinction between political and economic influence, Italy obtained political, and therefore only formal, recognition of the Fascist *spazio vitale*. Rome's restricted room for manoeuvre became plain when the armistice was signed with Greece. At the negotiating table in Salonika, the Italian Foreign Ministry's delegate, Filippo Anfuso, sought to have a territorial clause included in the text of the armistice. His counterpart, Felix Benzler, objected on the ground that the sole purpose of the negotiations was to form a government that would serve the interests of the Axis for the period of the war. There was, consequently, Benzler said, no need to alarm the Greeks.[29] Italy found itself in a situation similar to that of 18–24 June 1940 and the negotiations with France. But whereas at Villa Incisa Rome had decided on its own to relent and conclude a 'moderate' armistice, at Salonika it was the German veto that prevented the Italians from demanding an armistice imposing drastic territorial conditions. Berlin had not the slightest intention of taking decisions that might subsequently prove disadvantageous, whilst, compared to the year before, Rome was in a situation of greater diplomatic, economic and military subordination.

The 'desire not to rule out any possibility, to take every possible initiative', had vanished entirely by the end of the Balkan campaigns.[30] The armistice with Greece marked the end of the parallel war, with no mingling of forces and in an entirely Italian war theatre. Between May 1941 and July 1943, Italy was forced to accept Germany's supremacy and the role benevolently granted by the ally. There thus came about what diplomats had predicted at the beginning of 1941: the Balkans, politically and territorially, were entirely under the hegemony of the swastika, and the Fascist *spazio vitale* had been much reduced.[31] Italy had lost the 'parallel war', and it was now fighting what was – to use Giorgio Rochat's apt expression – a 'subordinate war' as regards its interests. With only a narrow margin for initiative, but paradoxically thanks to the magnanimity of the Germans, Italy had gained a foothold in the Balkans.

In order that Italy might share in the Axis's eventual victory, and true to his promise to march with Hitler 'until the end', in the years that followed Mussolini sent an Italian expeditionary force (the CSIR, later ARMIR) to

[29] Mazower, *Inside Hitler's Greece*, p. 18; DDI, ser. IX, 1939–43, vol. 7, doc. 17.

[30] De Felice, *Mussolini l'alleato*, p. 278.

[31] DDI, ser. IX, 1939–43, vol. 6, doc. 405, 'l'ambasciatore a Berlino Alfieri al ministro degli Esteri Ciano', Berlin, 5 January 1941.

the Soviet Union. In 1942 and 1943, around half of the 200,000 Italian soldiers fighting at the Soviet front died in battle and many others were lost or taken prisoner. The military situation improved slightly for the Axis between the end of 1941 and the autumn of 1942 but then rapidly deteriorated. In northern Africa, the defeat at El Alamein in early November was only a prelude to large-scale operations by the Allies, whose landings in Morocco and Algeria led to the loss of Libya and to headlong retreat by the Axis troops in Tunisia. At the end of 1942, the Axis war effort in the Mediterranean was in disarray, while the capitulation of the German Sixth Army at Stalingrad on 31 January 1942 marked a turning point in continental Europe as well. The question was no longer whether the Axis would lose the war but when.

It was the Allied landings in Africa – these being taken to be a crucial change of circumstances with respect to the armistice of 1940 – that induced Germany to occupy the whole of France and invite Italy to join the operations mounted on 11 and 12 November 1942. Once again, as previously in Yugoslavia and Greece, it was action by the Germans, not Italy's own military initiative, that enabled it to occupy almost all the territory as far as the Rhône originally intended for annexation. The circumstances of the occupation explain why the annexation so strongly desired by Rome did not take place. At 5.30 p.m. on 11 November 1942, the German consul Krug von Nidda handed to Charles Rochat, general secretary of the French Foreign Ministry, a letter prepared by Hitler for Philippe Pétain that announced the occupation of the whole of France and of Corsica according to a plan drawn up in full accord with Italy. Pétain and Pierre Laval protested to the Germans, demanding that the naval base of Toulon remain in French hands and that Nice not be occupied by the Italians. The Italian troops advanced very slowly, with few motorized vehicles and a large number of soldiers, convinced that the French would raise fierce resistance, although this did not actually happen. Rome wanted to avoid another display of military incompetence and was worried about the political repercussions on relations with France of a further military failure. It feared that, once the Germans had moved into territories which did fall within their occupation zone, they would renege on agreements with Rome and not withdraw to make way for the Italian troops. Indeed, important cities like Avignon, Lyons, Marseilles and Toulon were occupied by the Germans. The Italian troops, tasked with defence and with maintaining the order established by the Germans, deployed themselves along the line of the Rhône, occupying all the *départements* to the east of the river (Alpes-Maritimes, Var, Hautes-Alpes, Alpes de Haute-Provence, Isère, Savoie, Haute-Savoie and the eastern part of Drôme, Ain, Vaucluse and Bouches-du-Rhône) as well as Corsica. The Rhône line began at the frontier with Geneva, passed through the valley of the Durance, Peyrolles-en-Provence, Trets, Saint-Zacharie, Cuges-les-Pins and La Ciotat, and ended at Marseille.

The military subordination of the Italian occupation forces in Mediterranean Europe increased *pari passu* with the defeats suffered by the Axis. Until the end of 1942, the Germans left the Italians a semblance of command and a limited margin of autonomy in military decisions concerning the occupied territories. However, this largely sympathetic treatment by the Germans was deemed unacceptable by the generals of the Regio Esercito resentful of what they regarded as a humiliation. The German commanders had serious doubts that the Italian occupying forces could resist and defend the territories under their control. And so, at the beginning of 1943, the question once again arose of who should command the Italian army, after the matter had already been raised when the Wehrmacht intervened in the Mediterranean. Whereas on that first occasion Hitler had refrained from emphasizing Mussolini's subordinate role in the Axis, the defeats in Africa, the Allied landings in Morocco and the war of resistance in the Balkans now changed his mind.

The Führer's Instruction no. 47 of 28 December 1942 put an end to the Italians' scant freedom of manoeuvre in the occupied territories. In the Balkan area, the Regio Esercito was wholly subordinate to the Wehrmacht. General Alexander Löhr, commander-in-chief south-east (Oberbefehlshaber Südost), and under Hitler's direct orders, had territorial command over Serbia, Salonika-Aegean and southern Greece. The Italian Supreme Command gave Löhr the task of co-ordinating the Axis armed forces, but it did not specify whether or not he exercised tactical command over the Italian troops – although these had in effect become the executors of orders from the German high command. In Greece, Löhr interpreted 'co-ordination' as meaning 'command' and attended so meticulously to every military detail that it was no longer clear who had operational command.[32] In early 1943, Löhr announced to the commander of the Italian Eleventh Army, General Carlo Geloso, the arrival of a German division to reinforce the defence of the Peloponnese, which had not been placed under Italian command although it was in the Italian zone. The Italian general proposed that the whole of the zone be taken over by the Germans, in order to avoid interferences and complications but also the humiliation of his soldiers. In

[32] USSME, L 13, b. 105, *Con l'XI Armata nella guerra contro la Grecia*, typescript by General Geloso, pp. 215–21.

spring 1943, a further two German divisions were deployed to the rear of the Italian troops in Attica and the area of Thebes. The Eleventh Army was thus kept under German supervision.

In Yugoslavia, on 17 March 1943, the Italian ambassador in Zagreb, Raffaele Casertano, informed Rome that the Germans were deliberately pushing the largest possible number of partisan bands towards the coast, their purpose being to increase the Italian occupiers' difficulties even further.[33] Two months later the Wehrmacht and the SS moved into the towns garrisoned by the Regio Esercito. Ignoring the Italian authorities, they attacked the anti-communist militias armed by the Italians and seized telephone and telegraph installations and railway lines.[34] According to the general of the Carabinieri Reali (Royal Military Police), Giuseppe Pièche, the Germans' aim was to sap the Italians' military capabilities until they were definitively forced out the war.[35] The army chief of command in Yugoslavia, General Mario Robotti, and the consul in Sarajevo, Paolo Alberto Rossi, confirmed Pièche's suspicions by reporting that the Germans intended to take possession of the Sanjak, Bosnia and Herzegovina.[36] German officers, they reported, already commanded 40,000 Croat legionaries and *domobrans* (regular soldiers of the Croatian army), Croats returned from the Soviet front, Muslim troops from Bosnia-Herzegovina, groups of refugee White Russians in Yugoslavia and bands of gypsies, and they were demanding the disarming and arrest of the local militias recruited or regimented by the Italians.

The upshot of this brief excursus is that Italo-German relations were marked by mutual suspicion throughout the war: 'The two partners in the coalition were weighed down by a psychological handicap, for distrust constantly characterized their relations.'[37] The Germans were sure that the Italians were militarily incapable of defending the occupied territories against enemy attacks; the Italians suspected, and later became certain, that the

[33] ASMAE, GABAP, b. 32, 'Casertano a Pietromarchi', 17 March 1943.

[34] ASMAE, GABAP, b. 38, 'Ufficio di collegamento del Ministero degli Esteri con il Comando della II Armata', 17 May 1943, 'Appunto per il sottosegretario agli Esteri, firmato Vittorio Castellani'.

[35] USSME, M 3, b. 19, fasc. 8, 'General Pièche al GABAP, 19 maggio 1943, Notizie dalla Croazia'.

[36] USSME, M 3, b. 19, MAE, 29 May 1943, 'Promemoria per il generale Vittorio Ambrosio'; b. 71, 'Comando v CdA al Comando della II Armata', Ufficio "I", 26 June 1943, 'Agenti tedeschi sul litorale croato'; b. 78, 'console Rossi, legazione a Sarajevo, al Comando della II Armata, 3 marzo 1943, Situazione politico-militare – Pressione croato-tedesca sull'Erzegovina'; b. 78, 'Comando II Armata, 21 maggio 1943, Sintesi del colloquio Casertano-Pavelic dopo l'incontro di questi col Führer'; ASMAE, GABAP, b. 31, 11 May 1943, 'Appunto del GABAP, Ufficio Croazia, per il sottosegretario di stato'; b. 27, 'legazione di Belgrado al MAE, 1 giugno 1943, Aspetti dell'attuale situazione in Serbia'; b. 37, 'console generale a Sarajevo Rossi, 15 febbraio 1943, Situazione politica – Ampliamento dell'influenza tedesca – Tentativi di accaparramento dei musulmani'.

[37] Schreiber, 'Les structures stratégiques de la conduite de la guerre', p. 32.

Germans had hegemonic designs on 'their' *spazio vitale*. As a consequence the two sides never co-ordinated their political and military choices and decisions. The 'dysfunctionality' of the alliance was most evident in the occupied territories, where an ill-concealed conflict of interest ruled out any possibility of collaboration. In 1941, no Fascist soldier or hierarch was willing to comply passively with the dictates of the senior partner. The psychological impact of Italy's downgrading from equal to junior partner in the Axis, and the memory of having once been the leader of Fascism in Europe, provoked resentful defiance of German supremacy. As manifested by numerous Italian political leaders, this attitude was irrational because Italy was by now a *de facto* satellite of the Reich. Until the end of 1942, the upper echelons of the Italian state and armed forces sought to prevent the war from being fought under the orders and command of the Germans, and for the Germans' purposes. Only after the Allied landings in North Africa and the retreat from Stalingrad, and with the certainty of defeat, did the Italians gradually come to accept their country's rank of satellite and resignedly, sometimes disdainfully, submit to Germany.

After 1941, had it so wished, Berlin could have left no territory at all for the Italians. But it wanted to shore up Fascist morale and was loath to treat Rome on a par with the other European satellites – for military reasons (hundreds of thousands of Italian soldiers had something to contribute, after all), for reasons of propaganda (if the Reich's satellites believed that the Axis was united, they could more convincingly contribute to the crusade against Bolshevism) and for political and economic ones (to disguise the Nazis' project for sole European dominion). Rather than be left with nothing, the Fascist regime accepted whatever Germany might concede. Italy's was an example of dependent imperialism, similar to Portugal's with respect to Great Britain, or, if one wishes, a case of opportunistic bandwagoning – added to which was the Italians' belief that they could beguile the senior partner and become masters of their *spazio vitale*. Certainly influenced, perhaps befuddled, by Fascist ideology, Mussolini and his executive refused to accept subordination to Germany. They repressed the idea that Italy was effectively Germany's servant and satellite, and they forgot that Italy was no longer a great power, especially in relation to occupation policies. They reacted with determination against all German interventions in 'Italian zones', considering them unjustified intrusions into what was exclusively the Fascists' sphere. The civil and military authorities in the occupied territories deluded themselves into believing that they effectively controlled Fascist living space, and they acted accordingly.

THE FEAR OF GERMANY: THE FASCISTS' PERCEPTION OF THE NAZIS

Italy waged what it termed a 'parallel war' in the occupied territories. The Germans, however, took the Italians' state of mind for what it really was: *Minderwertigkeitsgefühl*, or an inferiority complex. On their side, the Italians fashioned an image of the Germans as greedy and dangerous bullies.

Suspicion, fear of the real aims of German expansionism and anxiety over the place reserved for Italy in the new European order characterized relationships between Rome and Berlin from the Pact of Steel onwards. For Rome, Hitler's and Ribbentrop's declarations on the Mediterranean theatre were solemn and sacrosanct pledges: indeed, numerous such declarations circulated among Italian diplomats, the following being an example:

> Be informed of the Führer's decision that, in all questions concerning the Mediterranean, Axis policy shall be determined by Italy, and that Germany will therefore never pursue a policy which is independent of Italy's in the Mediterranean countries. This decision by the Führer is to be an immutable law of German foreign policy. As the Duce has taken no interest in Czechoslovakia, so Germany has no interest in the Croatian question, and in any event shall act in that regard only in close accordance with Italian desires.[38]

Every breach of these pledges was treated as a betrayal, as detrimental to Italian authority and prestige, as proof of German hegemonic designs on Italy's *spazio vitale*. For Berlin, by contrast, after the German intervention in the Balkans, such pledges no longer had any substance to them. In January 1941, General Efisio Marras, military attaché at German army headquarters, reported that the Reich intended to achieve hegemony over the whole of south-eastern Europe.[39] The manner in which Marras described the Germans is particularly interesting because it illustrates clearly how the Fascists perceived their ally. In 1940, he wrote, Germany declared the entire Mediterranean basin to be Italy's zone of influence. It then maintained that the Balkan peninsula would be a zone of influence in which Berlin had economic interests. At the Vienna conference of 21–24 April 1941, the Nazis significantly reduced Italy's Balkan zone of influence. Subsequent military operations and intense political activity revealed Berlin's hegemonic intentions and its determination to demote the Italian armed forces to executors of merely secondary tasks, thereby emphasizing to world opinion Germany's predominance in the Axis, regardless of what the Italo-German power

[38] ASMAE, GABAP, b. 29; b. 33, 12 December 1941, 'Colloqui Ambrosio–Pietromarchi'.
[39] Pelagalli, 'Le relazioni militari italo-germaniche', p. 6.

relationship might actually be. According to Marras, therefore, by deliberately restricting Italy's influence, Germany had revealed its hegemonic intent. He failed, however, to mention the circumstances in which Italy had been able to establish its foothold in the Balkans, concentrating instead on analysis of the German character: 'ready to profit from any opportunity to penetrate, widening the breach to accomplish its purposes' and 'prone to abusing its strength as soon as it [perceives] an absence of reaction'.[40] This perception of the Germans grew stronger in the course of the war. Fear of the ally and suspicion of Germany's real purposes were also manifested by Mussolini, who, in 1941, confessed that an Axis victory would give Hitler political and economic supremacy and relegate Italy to the role of a German province.[41] In a paper entitled *Vincere la Guerra*, written before the conclusion of the Italo-Greek conflict, General Bongiovanni declared thus:

> To us there will remain above all the merit of having, with great sacrifice and little glory, kept a conspicuous part of the enemy forces engaged; but with the war finished and won, this merit will be afforded scant recognition by foreigners and by the Germans themselves. The *brillant Sekundat*, as the Germans, at their most generous, describe their allies, whoever they may be, will diminish in the common perception to that of the meek collaborator, if not the lucky profiteer.[42]

General Arturo Vacca Maggiolini, head of the Commissione Italiana d'Armistizio con la Francia (CIAF, Italian Armistice Commission with France) accused the German authorities in France of deliberately seeking to damage Italy.[43] The Italian civil and military authorities in France were convinced that the Germans had no intention of granting the Italians' territorial demands and were 'plotting behind their backs'.[44] General Geloso declared that the Germans' sole aim was to 'harm Italian prestige and status'.[45] But it was not only the military commanders who described the Germans thus: the chief of Ciano's cabinet, Blasco Lanza d'Ajeta, alleged the existence of a Nazi plan whereby, on conclusion of the war, 'Great Germany' would reunite all the territories that had belonged to Austria-Hungary before the First World War, including Fiume, Gorizia and Istria. The Reich, he claimed, was ready to conquer these territories and others besides.[46] Amedeo Mammalella, consul in Dubrovnik (Ragusa), declared

[40] Quoted ibid., pp. 28–30.
[41] Schreiber, 'Les structures stratégiques de la conduite de la guerre', p. 9.
[42] USSME, M 3, b. 4, 'Relazione del generale Bongiovanni', pp. 2–3.
[43] ASMAE, GABAP, b. 1, 'presidenza della CIAF al CS', 26 May 1942.
[44] ASMAE, GABAP, b. 1, 'Michele Scammacca al GABAP', 26 April 1942.
[45] USSME, L 13, b. 105.
[46] DDI, ser. IX, 1939–43, vol. 8, doc. 461, 'capo di gabinetto Lanza d'Ajeta al console generale a Vienna Romano', Rome, 17 April 1942.

that the 'blatant German raid on the Adriatic' was intended to 'create a new Austria-Hungary'.[47] The general of the Carabinieri, Pièche, on a mission in the Balkans, was so riddled with resentment and fear of the Germans that he wrote as if the recipients of his reports were perfectly aware of the Nazis' intentions. He invariably recommended that a reactive strategy be adopted in Italo-German relations in all the occupied territories. For example, he suggested that German brutality should be exploited to stoke resentment in the Balkans and thereby hamper the ally's incursions.[48] On 31 July 1941 the head of the Gabinetto Armistizio–Pace (GABAP, Armistice–Peace Cabinet), Luca Pietromarchi, noted in his diary as follows:

> The state of public opinion in Italy is not good: the future, whatever fate it may hold in store, is regarded with the greatest anxiety. In the event of victory, Europe will remain under German hegemony for some centuries; in the event of defeat, the entire African empire will be lost. Perhaps national unity itself will be mutilated and independence reduced to servitude. In the event of equilibrium between the two opposing forces, the war will last for years.[49]

Dino Alfieri, Rome's ambassador in Berlin, wrote of the Germans thus: 'good soldiers, and strong men, given more to action than to thought. Nazism has laid bare the quintessence of their race, brutally bellicose, whilst their reasoning is convoluted, subordinate and sluggish.'[50] The ambassador in Zagreb, Raffaele Casertano, for his part, viewed disloyalty as the salient trait of the German character, this being amply borne out, he affirmed, by Berlin's policy of the *fait accompli* and deliberate disinformation.[51]

During the first six months of 1943, the war in the Mediterranean grew more uncertain as the days passed, and the domestic front began to disintegrate. Mussolini was increasingly absent from Rome, doing nothing to extricate himself from an alliance which was destroying his regime. Political and military circles began to voice doubts that the alliance served any practical purpose. The civil and military authorities stationed in the occupied territories differed in their reactions to Germany's interference. Some resigned themselves and complied with the decisions of the senior partner; others reacted angrily, and with a disdain for the Germans that induced them to stress their differences from them, especially in occupation policies; others advocated a separate peace; and yet others refused to relinquish their ideological vision of *spazio vitale* and the *guerra parallela*.

47 ASMAE, GABAP, b. 31, 'consolato di Ragusa alla legazione di Zagabria', 4 June 1943.
48 USSME, M 3, b. 6, fasc. 1, 'generale Pièche al GABAP', 12 August 1942, 'Rapporto sulla Serbia'.
49 Pietromarchi, unpublished diary, 31 July 1941 (Fondazione Luigi Einaudi, Turin).
50 DDI, ser. IX, 1939–43, vol. 8, doc. 507, 3 May 1942.
51 USSME, M 3, b. 51, fasc. 2, 'legazione di Zagabria al MAE', 15 August 1942, pp. 2–3.

At the beginning of 1943, doubts about the alliance were for the first time being openly expressed by the men closest to the Duce. On 21 January 1943, Alfieri, whose pro-German sentiments were well known, explained to the foreign minister that Germany regarded the occupied territories as merely storehouses of materials to be exploited for the war. Every resource was to be placed at the immediate and discretionary disposal of the occupier, without regard to the needs of the local population and the organization of the country concerned. The harsh treatment of certain ethnic groups, excessive exploitation and uncertainty about the future were raising doubts among some of the allies and considerable fears as to their prospects in the event of a German victory. This policy, Alfieri argued, was the typical expression of the mentality of the men who directed it and of the doctrines that inspired them. The German politicians, he wrote, had risen to power without taking active part in the political life of the state. They had been schooled on rigidly dogmatic principles, and imbued with the belief that the German race possessed inherent supremacy over other Europeans. This supremacy was to be imposed by force, with no possibility of compromise or peaceful coexistence. For these men only total victory or total defeat was possible; any concession, any negotiation or any victory achieved by means other than military force was inconceivable to them. The German ruling class saw the conflict as a war destined to realize the Nazi hegemonic doctrine, and this world-vision had been exasperated by the difficulties of the war. The only hope for Italy, given its utter dependence on Germany, was the 'clarity and sincerity' of the German leaders, for on its own Italy was unable to feed itself or to produce sufficient arms with which to fight the enemy. The ambassador concluded his letter with the Duce's 'historic' dictum to the effect that 'marching together until the bitter end does not mean following'.[52] Italy, though, had followed until the point of no return.

The *Carta d'Europa* produced in the spring of 1943 was closely bound up with the situation of those months, and it matched Alfieri's reflections. The Germans were informed of the project at the Klessheim discussions (7–10 April 1943), when Mussolini presented them with the text of a joint declaration enumerating four points: respect for the principle of nationality and the right of states to establish themselves on the basis of ethnic homogeneity; respect for the full sovereignty and the unconditioned internal order of the European states; the principle of collaboration founded on the moral unity of Europe and on the full and free development of

[52] DDI, ser. IX, 1939–43, vol. 10, docs. 61, 188, 196, 198.

national individuality; a pledge that the Axis powers would lead Europe to international peace, to be achieved by the fair distribution of the world's resources, in partnership with labour, and with trade among all nations.[53] The Germans brusquely rejected the proposal and forbade Rome to make any further unilateral declarations on such matters.

There is no doubt that the 'New Europe Project' set out in the *Carta d'Europa* was a mere propaganda device, an expedient for Italy to find a way out of its disastrous situation. However, it prompts considerations on the extent to which the vision of the new order in 1943 differed from the projects of 1940–1. After two years of experience as Germany's ally, and in a situation close to catastrophe, the Italians berated the Nazis for their lack of a 'communitarian' vision and admonished them that organizing Europe hierarchically was not enough. They argued that political and economic co-operation must be grounded on the 'vital energies of peoples', and thus without brutally exploiting the occupied territories, but rather involving and enhancing forces which later would be crucial in the struggle against the great non-European powers. They were much preoccupied by the thought that the Italians would be considered accomplices in the Nazi terror, and they were aware that hatred of the Nazis had grown enormously in Italy since the catastrophe of the 1942–3 winter, when the remnants of the Italian army in the USSR had returned home, and thousands of survivors had described their vicious treatment at the hands of German soldiers.[54] But was there really such a marked ideological and political difference between the Fascist and Nazi visions of the new European order?

[53] The *Carta d'Europa* was drawn up by Foreign Under-Secretary Bastianini and senior officials at the Foreign Ministry, among them Leonardo Vitetti, Francesco Babuscio Rizzo and the head of the GABAP, Pietromarchi. See Bastianini, *Uomini, cose e fatti*, 1967, pp. 91–2.

[54] Petersen, 'Italia e Germania'.

CHAPTER 2

The New Mediterranean Order

Between 1939 and 1942 the Fascist regime envisioned a world organized according to the dictates of the 'new European order' and springing from conquest of the *spazio vitale* and accomplishment of the Fascist revolution. De Felice called this projection the 'logic of afterwards', by which he meant the vision of the Fascist Italy that would ensue from a victorious war – a feasible world towards which, the regime decreed, all Italians must strive. This chapter describes how the leader-nation of the *spazio vitale* intended to organize the lands conquered, and how it would have managed relations with the Mediterranean basin countries brought within an ideal sphere of exclusive interest. After describing the ideal type of the Fascist living space, the chapter examines aspects of the organization of that space and shows how Italy's colonial experience in Libya, *Africa Orientale Italiana* (AOI, Italian East Africa), Albania and its Aegean possessions (the Dodecanese) determined the constitutional framework of the territories conquered after 1940 and influenced the organization of their governments and administrations.

In 1997, a book entitled *Les empires occidentaux de Rome à Berlin* was published as part of an interesting series of studies on the history of political systems. In the introduction, the editor explains why the book examines the Roman, Byzantine, Russian and Carolingian empires, the Holy Roman Empire, the Austrian empire and the Napoleonic empire, and the First and the Third Reich, but not the colonial empires. He justifies the exclusion of the Fascist empire thus: 'Fascism may have been inspired by ancient Rome in its attempt at colonial expansion. But Mussolini was not an emperor at all; he was merely a dictator. Hitler was contemptuous of Mussolini's presumptions: "Germany took thirty years to rise again", he said, "Rome has never again regained its supremacy".'[1] If we look at the achievements of the Fascist regime we may agree with Tulard; but if we analyse the Fascist

[1] Tulard, *Les empires occidentaux*, p. 15.

imperial project according to its definition as proposed by this book, we may conclude that the Fascist empire had features which place it squarely among the Western empires.

The first condition for an empire to qualify as such is geographical extension. Space is the distinctive feature of an empire. A kingdom coincides with a country; an empire consists of a set of countries. The notion of spatial extension is specified by the notion of *limes*[2] and by the desire for conquest. An empire seeks to protect itself (consider Hadrian's Wall or the Great Wall of China) while at the same time endeavouring to extend its boundaries further: from Genghis Khan to Napoleon, from Hitler to Stalin, emperors have been conquerors. The second defining feature of an empire is its organization of space. An empire is usually centralized and cannot conceive of itself without an emperor at its head – whether or not he actually bears that title. Obviously, depending on the extent of the territories under his rule, an emperor delegates his powers to governors, satraps or prefects who administer the provinces or *départements* in his name. He is the centre and the pivot of the empire. Roads (as communication routes) are vital for the exercise of imperial authority: indeed, no empire from Rome to Napoleon ever ignored this rule. Also distinctive of empires is the intent to meld their subject populations into a unified whole wherein law overrides language and religion, wherein political and fiscal institutions are essential and wherein the material and symbolic hegemony of imperial power must cow the subject populations into submission. An empire is also founded on the civilizing process. Whether Chinese or Roman, an empire aspires to universality and uniqueness. Beyond its boundaries lies a realm of barbarians who, according to circumstances, must be ignored, exterminated or civilized. An empire is destined eventually to die, however. Its death is ineluctable: it may be lingering as its authority gradually wanes; or it may be swiftly and brutally brought about by external enemies, by rivals or by the barbarians.

The purpose of this chapter is to show that the Fascist regime nourished imperial ambitions. Its intent, that is to say, was to expand geographically, to conquer and dominate territories and to have an emperor. Mussolini's project for himself was to organize the space conquered and

[2] Martin, 'L'empire': un espace conguis, p. 60. The word *limes* denoted the boundaries of the Roman Empire. Its literal meaning of 'strip of land marking the boundary between two territories' shifted to that of 'axis of communications', in that it referred to a frontier zone comprising one or more roads used for troop movements. The term finally came to comprise all the semantic elements relative to the presence of troops: camps, fortifications, etc. Control was maintained from the *limes* over entries, infiltrations and the comings and goings of tradesmen.

to impose Fascist law and civilization on subject peoples of which he did not hesitate to term himself the 'liberator'. Historians have either ignored the Fascist imperial project or treated it in reductive terms. I contend instead that it should be given due consideration, both in itself and because analysis shows that it closely influenced Fascist occupation policies. We shall then see how these policies went awry from the original imperial purpose.

THE RIGHT TO FOUND AN EMPIRE: THE NEW CIVILIZATION AND FASCISM'S CIVILIZING MISSION

There is a distinctive feature shared by the Fascist and Nazi regimes which evinces the close kinship (but not the identity) between the two ideologies and the two regimes. I refer to the conquest of a living space – of an empire – as an essential component of a totalitarian project to transform society. The revolution of 1922 should have founded a 'new civilization' – that of Fascism. Mussolini accelerated the process after the conquest of Ethiopia (1935–6). The war in Africa was to provide a new context for Fascism's schemes of social engineering. It would drive the renewal of Italian society; it would represent the apogee of the Fascist myth of national regeneration; and it would be the crucible for a new civilization which would give Italy leadership of Europe.[3] The colonial war would generate 'a new kind of humanity' bred for conquest and dominion.

What the Italian historian Emilio Gentile termed the *svolta totalitaria* – the shift from authoritarianism to totalitarianism – sprang from the Duce's conviction that relationships among nations were about to change radically, and that his regime could finally renege on its compromise with the conservative forces in the country and accomplish its revolutionary endeavour to create the *uomo nuovo*. Mussolini – Gentile has written – was certain that he could 'divine the nature of his century'. He was convinced that he was living through one of the watersheds of history when destiny afforded the Italian people an occasion to demonstrate their 'virtue'. After centuries of decadent obscurity, the Italians could now create a new civilization. But they could do so only if they had faith in the new Fascist religion, and if they submitted to the Duce as he fashioned them into a race of dominators and conquerors.[4]

[3] Ben-Ghiat, *La cultura fascista*, p. 207; Knox, *Common Destiny*, p. 62.
[4] Gentile, *Il culto del littorio*, pp. 153–4 and 180–95.

For Fascism, the Italian revolution would reconsecrate worship of the nation. It would regenerate the population into a 'community' endowed with the unity and strength necessary to confront the challenges of the modern world, to regain supremacy and to undertake a civilizing mission that would resurrect the spirit and grandeur of ancient Rome in the modern age.[5] The regime's appeal to the myth of Rome served various purposes: to give the Italians the pride necessary to overcome their inferiority complex with respect to the other European great powers; to highlight the differences between Italy and the other 'pettily nationalistic civilizations' (Germany among them); to depict Italy as a nation on the ascendant; and, finally, to imbue the masses with a national-fascist consciousness. Racial policy, in its colonial, metropolitan and anti-Semitic variants, was part of a broader endeavour to create a racial consciousness in the Italians which would prevent 'cross-breeding and mongrelization' as the empire spread through the world. Racism, observes Ruth Ben-Ghiat, was the most radical part of the Fascist project to transform Italians and to regenerate the nation.[6] Fascism would prepare the 'Italian race' for 'its appointment with history': strong in numbers and bold in spirit, Fascism would reverse power relations with the other European nations, and with the United States – that 'country of negroes and Jews, the disruptive element of civilization'. Accomplishment of the revolution would require war and territorial expansion.[7]

The conquest was to be politically, philosophically and morally grounded on a Spenglerian and Darwinist vision of international relations, and on a distorted interpretation of Gioberti's notion of Italy's 'primacy' and of Mazzini's conception of Italy's civilizing mission. Territorial expansion was to be the logical outcome of the Italian race's spiritual and demographic supremacy in the Mediterranean. Fascist doctrine affirmed that people were subject to the 'laws of nature' – and especially to the primordial law that all must constantly struggle against each other and against the elements for survival, growth and development.[8] Destiny was a concept central to Fascist ideology; so too was determinism and the idea that 'history orders human societies into great collectivities living geopolitically in great spaces'.[9] Amid

[5] Ibid., p. 44. [6] Ben-Ghiat, *La cultura fascista*, pp. 245–6.

[7] Bottai, 'Contributi dell'Italia al nuovo ordine', 1941, p. 1. Bottai explained that revolution and war were inextricably bound up with each other. He wrote that he dreamed of an Italian people who, on winning the war and its revolution, would propagate their revolutionary principles by means of another war.

[8] Gray, *Dopo vent'anni*, 1943, p. 21.

[9] Selvi, 'Le basi dell'ordine nuovo', 1942; Selvi, *Nuova civiltà per la nuova Europa*, 1942.

the apparently chaotic movement of populations, amid great changes and conflicts, the Fascist theoreticians believed they could discern a slow but steady evolutionary process by which ethnic groups superior to others by race and civilization constantly expanded.[10]

The right to conquer *spazio vitale* was granted to only a few select nations. It was the direct consequence of their demographic vitality, their particular geophysical conditions and their specific ethnic, historical and cultural values.[11] The 'great nations' would be the spiritual, moral, racial, political and economic leaders of the world community, and they would shape the political, social and economic life of a 'great space'. Fascist Rome would organize a complex of nations which gravitated around Italy but kept their languages and cultures. It would have absolute supremacy over its dependent states but would also be duty-bound to ensure their security and development. For Fascist ideology, the purpose of expansionism was to civilize the peoples subjugated and export the revolution to their countries, to impose moral and racial values, the law and then *virtus*, *vis* and *libertas*. These values sublimated in the Italians would be transmitted to the dominated territories by the new man, the 'custodian and bearer of a superior civilization' who carried 'in his blood that rare privilege of being able to grasp, effortlessly and naturally, a universal conception of life inspired by the principles of justice and equity'. Like the ancient Romans, wrote Giuseppe Bottai in his 'Contributi dell'Italia al nuovo ordine', 'the new Italians will illuminate the world with their art, educate it with their knowledge, and give robust structure to the new territories with their administrative technique and ability, with their enterprise and organization of trade'.[12]

This vision of the Italian race's mission in the territories of the imperial community was not mere propaganda. The purpose of Fascist expansion was not to annihilate the subject population. It was instead to affirm a 'natural right to expansion' while also obeying a moral obligation to 'civilize' the territory conquered.

[10] Piccoli, 'La nazione e l'ordine nuovo', 1942. Gianturco wrote, in *Lineamenti della nuova Europa*, 1941, p. 97, citing H. Hunke (in 'Die deutsche Volkswirtschaft', 16, 1940): 'Life is motion . . . hence one deduces that the lives of peoples . . . obey the natural necessity for growth to which life is subject as it seeks to propagate itself and to expand.' The history of nature is an uninterrupted sequence of the increasingly elaborate and cohesive organization of the elements of which it is made up. This explains why states tend to join together into great supranational complexes. Hierarchy, which is 'inherent to the historical development of humanity', is not a 'form of disguised international enslavement . . . but is founded on labour and has the existence of living space as its natural corollary'.

[11] Bottai, 'Contributi dell' Italia al nuovo ordine', 1941.

[12] Soprano, *Spazio vitale*, 1941, p. 8.

ORGANIZATION OF THE *SPAZIO VITALE*: THE NEW ORDER

What exactly was meant by the term *spazio vitale*? The definition ran as follows: 'that part of the globe over which extends either the vital requirements or the expansionary impetus of a state with strong unitary organization which seeks to satisfy its needs by expanding beyond its national boundaries'.[13] What was to be the geographical extent of the *spazio vitale*? Though Fascism did not draw its *limes* with precision, for political reasons the compass of the *spazio vitale* was clear from the outset: it was to be the Mediterranean. Mussolini said that if Italy had been governed well, if it had been 'directed towards its glorious destiny', with 'the Italians projected as a single force towards world duties', and if the Mediterranean had become an 'Italian lake', as early as 1922 'a grandiose period of Italian history would have begun'.[14] Twelve years later, in a speech delivered to the regime's third quinquennial assembly on 19 March 1934, Mussolini described the form that Italy's expansion would take: 'We may confidently speak of a plan extending until the next millennium, until 2000 . . . Italy's historic objectives have two names: Asia and Africa, South and East . . . this is not territorial conquest . . . but territorial expansion.'[15] He then announced that the revolution would culminate with conquest and expansion: 'a march to the Atlantic Ocean' through French North Africa, and 'a march to the Indian Ocean' through Sudan which would 'weld' Libya to Ethiopia. Conquest of the *spazio vitale* would divide into three phases: short-, medium- and long-term. Mussolini then enumerated the objectives to be achieved after 1942 in speeches to the Grand Council on 30 November 1938 and 5 February 1939: Tunisia, Corsica, 'everything this side of the Alps' and Albania. A second set of (medium-term) objectives was to be Malta and Cyprus; then, in the very long term, Suez and Gibraltar, the 'keys to the Mediterranean'. Moreover, Yugoslavia, Greece, Turkey and Egypt, 'states ready to link up with Great Britain and complete the political and military encirclement of Italy . . . [were to be] considered virtual enemies of Italy and its expansion'. The schedule was accelerated by the war – though this the Duce and part of the population did not see as a danger to the regime, but rather as an opportunity to realize Fascism's totalitarian project.[16]

[13] Messineo, 'Spazio vitale e grande spazio', 1942, p. 66; Titta, 'Concetto di spazio vitale', 1941.

[14] Mussolini, 'Discorso della Sciesa di Milano', 4 October 1922, in Orano, *Le direttive del duce*, 1937, p. 37.

[15] Ibid., p. 151.

[16] DDI, ser. IX, 1939–43, vol. 5, doc. 65, Ciano's diary, 19 June 1940, 'Colloquio Mussolini–Ciano'.

Until the defeat of France, the 'Italian comrades' failed to realize that Nazi expansionism was driven by a desire for an unlimited and exclusive dominance which would relegate Italy to what at best would be a subordinate role to the Reich. Until realization dawned on the Italians, they deluded themselves that the Euro-African space would be divided thus: Central Europe to the Nazis; the Mediterranean, Africa and the Near East to the Fascists.[17] Evidently, the propaganda machine explained, the 're-organizers of Europe', Mussolini and Hitler, would set about redrawing the map of Europe only on conclusion of the war. They would take account of ethnic and religious situations, the contributions of the various nations to the war, the attitudes of the defeated populations and the various necessities of the immediate post-war period. The fact that the Italians envisaged two spheres of influence points up a difference with respect to the Germans, whose plans for dominance showed not the slightest regard for Italy's interests. Although Rome had its own imperial project in mind, it had to take account of the awkward presence of the ally even in its most secret and ambitious plans.

The *spazio vitale* comprised a *piccolo spazio* which would be inhabited only by the Italian 'race', and a *grande spazio* inhabited by other populations under Italy's dominion: the *spazio vitale* was the sum of that small and that large space.[18] No other great power would be allowed to encroach upon it. At its core lay 'the ancient and renewed values' of Italian culture, the intrinsic civilizing capacity of which provided the rationale for Rome's mission in the Mediterranean. Within that space Rome would impose the *nuovo ordine* (or *ordine nuovo*: the two expressions were interchangeable) and organize a community 'both for the peoples of which it was made up and for those other peoples which, though less civilized, would nevertheless grow and develop, like those which had belonged to the Roman Empire and had come into contact with its superior civilization'.[19]

The new European order would be founded 'on the superiority of the political sphere over the economy; on the subordination of individual interests to collective ones; on the state's right to assume economic management of the multiple entities making up the *spazio vitale*; on the recognition of private firms and their elevation to public utilities; on the collaboration of

[17] Mainardi, *Nazionalità e spazi vitali*, 1941, pp. 172–82.

[18] Sertoli Salis, *Imperi e colonizzazioni*, 1941, pp. 23–5; Tamagnini, 'Lo "spazio vitale" nell'organizzazione del nuovo ordine', 1942.

[19] De Felice, *Mussolini il duce*, p. 300.

all classes in the achievement of social order and well-being and a higher level of output'.[20]

The new order would guarantee what Wilsonian self-determination had failed to deliver: peace in Europe, as well as the co-ordination of economic activity and a fair division of labour among great state bodies. This would give rise to enduring peace. The subjects of international law would be the new geographical agglomerates – these being empires and no longer individual states. The disappearance of small states after their incorporation into new empires would substantially reduce the number of armed independent organizations, curb economic and demographic growth and foster economic development and prosperity.[21] The principles of the self-determination of peoples and national sovereignty would be abolished under the new order, their place being taken by the supranational principle of international relations – an arena which only the protagonist nations would have the right to enter. Individual nationalities would be 'integrated' (in reality, violently crushed) under the 'imperial Roman and Fascist organizing principle, which does not intend to deny, but rather to safeguard, ethnic and cultural individualities, thereby completing the mission begun by Mazzini'.[22] Rome, the propaganda proclaimed, would not act exclusively in its own interests as did the imperialist powers; it would also pursue the interests of the 'associated' (i.e., dominated) states *sub specie universali*, fashioning relations of hierarchical subordination into a system of joint and several responsibility.[23] Within the *spazio vitale*, universality was conceived as the relationship between diverse elements and a common and superior element under which the former would be 'spontaneously' subsumed without being suppressed by force. Rome would rule its *imperium* like an enlightened despot, 'with the methods that . . . the degree of civilization of the conquered peoples suggested',[24] keeping firm hold of the reins of supreme power, 'since a consortium without a head is inconceivable'.[25]

The empire would not be a confederation of states, for only Rome would be empowered to regulate the lives of the 'associates'. The process of aggregation would not lead to the creation of a United States of Europe, because Europe was made up of 'too many and diverse races', nor to arrangements like Plato's Republic, Campanella's City of the Sun, the British Empire or

[20] Bottai, 'Contributi dell'Italia al nuovo ordine', 1941, p. 6.
[21] Soprano, *Spazio vitale*, 1941, p. 60; Orestano, 'Nuovo ordine europeo', 1942.
[22] *Critica fascista*, 19, 17, 1 July 1941.
[23] Pellizzi, 'Italia e Germania,' 1941–2; Baratelli, 'Unità romana nel Mediterraneo', 1941; Schmidt, *Rivoluzione nel Mediterraneo*, 1942, p. 117.
[24] Bottai, 'Contributi dell'Italia al nuovo ordine', 1941, p. 11.
[25] Spampanato, *Perché questa guerra*, 1942, p. 199.

a Napoleonic federation under the aegis of France. States shorn of their sovereignty and protectorates would be subject to the leader-nation.

Such were the conceptual foundations, the postulates, of the new order. Prior to and during the war, they bred a proliferation of nebulous projects, labyrinthine theories on the organization of the *spazio vitale*. Mussolini was reluctant to intervene personally in the discussion because he did not wish to commit himself to any particular scheme before conclusion of the war. He repeatedly declared, or had his hierarchs declare, that the new order could not manifest itself in all its components before the end of the conflict. This is not to say, however, that he did not have his own vision of the future: indeed, he was constantly interested in the discussion and, as we shall see, always ready to dictate occupation policies.

Some examples of these projects follow. Giorgio Quartara believed that the Roman Empire's organization of its *provinciae* and *coloniae* and their gradual fusion into a unitary state provided the model for European unification, and that the Austro-Hungarian federal constitution should represent the transitional stage prior to its introduction.[26] Quartara wrote of a *foedus iniquus* (unequal alliance), which entailed the submission of the defeated to Rome, the obligation to assist it with money, arms, soldiers and ships, to renounce war and to accept the imposition of free trade. After the victory, the Axis would impose the *foedus iniquus* on the vanquished, who would never regain their independence. The European territories adjoining Italy would receive the *lex lata* and the status of *provinciae*, while the African colonies would be bound to Rome as *civitates foederatae*. They would enjoy the right to free movement and have a system of free internal trade, with customs posts on the frontiers of the *orbis romanus*. Like ancient Rome, Fascist Rome would introduce a single currency, unify weights and measures and harmonize commercial rules. Italy would take possession of the public and private territory of the defeated peoples, transforming it into *agrum publicum* confiscated from the vanquished and then leased back to them. Omitted from the ancient *foedus iniquus*, however, would be its requirement that all prisoners of war must be enslaved. Croatia, Serbia, Greece, Dalmatia, Albania and some regions of France would constitute a single bloc with Rome, but unification would come about gradually: a sub-bloc would first be created with a federal constitution based on the Austro-Hungarian model.[27]

[26] Quartara, *La futura pace*, 1942.

[27] Ibid., pp. 486–7. On the Roman Empire as a model of post-war peace, see also Gini, 'Autarchia e complessi economici supernazionali', 1942.

While for Quartara the Habsburg solution was transitional, for Mario Gianturco it was permanent. Gianturco wrote – distorting and bending to his purposes the thought of Dante, Gioberti and Mazzini – that the new order would be a confederation of peoples bound together by a single religious, political and moral creed – Fascism – but operating independently of each other in their domestic affairs. 'The Europe of tomorrow', 'born in blood' under the leadership of the two nations that had assumed the task of disseminating 'forceful ideas', would celebrate the triumph of labour, the end of capitalism and the advent of a 'producers' justice' within a totalitarian state.[28] La Torre put forward a vision inspired by the British Empire. Flanking the Italian state, 'which by dignity and power assumes imperial nature', he wrote, there would be a federation of minor states united with Italy in a hierarchical arrangement of relationships of 'spiritual and economic solidarity'. The imperial state would not exercise sovereignty over the lesser members of the imperial association because they would be juridically independent, especially as far as their domestic policies were concerned. But those member-states would have to accept a 'certain subordination' in international affairs, this being 'necessarily imposed by the exigencies of life'. The hierarchy would not impede the creation of 'a relationship of solidarity and assistance' in the international set-up of the *ordine nuovo*. The minor state would be neither overwhelmed nor exploited by the imperial state; rather, it would receive protection from the latter by virtue of the distribution of tasks between them and the complementarity of their economies.[29]

For Bottai, the imperial community represented the future organization of Western civilization. It would be based on flexible forms of government adapted to the levels of civilization achieved by the empire's various peoples. 'The associative forms, the methods of collaboration, the institutions and the laws may vary, but the principle is by now evident':[30] the *spazio vitale* would impose relationships of a constrictiveness that varied according to the minor states' positions *vis-à-vis* the leader. Some states would be associated as equals, with the leader-state representing and directing the consortium; others would stipulate pacts of friendship and form an economic and political association. Yet others would become constitutional 'living parts' of

[28] Gianturco, *Lineamenti della nuova Europa*, 1941, p. 84.

[29] La Torre, 'Ingrandimento dello stato italiano e del suo spazio vitale', 1941 (La Torre was closely influenced by Schmitt, 'Il concetto imperiale di spazio', 1940); Evola, 'Elementi dell'idea europea', 1940; Perticone, 'Il problema dello spazio vitale e del grande spazio', 1940; La Torre, 'Il compito direttivo dell'Italia imperiale', 1940; Barendson, 'L'economia della Grecia', 1941.

[30] Bottai, 'Contributi dell'Italia al nuovo ordine', 1941.

the leader-state's body politic. The empire would also possess colonies in Africa and Asia.[31]

Fascism's ideal imperial community can be depicted as a set of three concentric circles organized hierarchically on racial principles, and each with a different form of government or control. The first circle, or the 'small space', comprised the Italian peninsula and the zones to be annexed to the kingdom: the Ionian islands, the Dalmatian coast, Slovenia, the province of Nice and Corsica (plus perhaps Bosnia-Herzegovina and Savoy). This 'small' space would contain the executive nucleus – the civilizational core of the 'great space' – of the imperial community constituted by diverse political, social and economic structures and organized into a hierarchy based on the level of development and the features and traditions of each 'race'. The second circle would comprise the 'European members' of the imperial community. Included among these would be state entities created by the 'necessary' dismemberment of countries like Yugoslavia and Greece: Croatia, Montenegro, Serbia and a Greater Albania incorporating the Greek territory of northern Epirus and Yugoslav territories such as Macedonia. The 'great space' would also include other states with which Rome had forged political and economic bonds – though always according to the development, civilization and position of the 'race' – Bulgaria, Romania, Hungary, Portugal, Spain and France.

France, with its more advanced level of development, would presumably be one of the associate states with equal status; but Italy, as the leader-state, would represent and direct the consortium. Like Albania, Montenegro would be one of the states constitutionally 'a living part of Rome's body politic'. Other already-existing Mediterranean states – or those which would become such when 'liberated' – would gravitate around Rome, their status oscillating between the second and third circles: these states would be Turkey, Egypt, Palestine, Iraq and Yemen. According to Bottai's definition, they would be 'states limited to living – with their political independence intact – within Rome's sphere of economic gravitation'.[32] The third circle

31 Spampanato, *Perché questa guerra*, 1942, p. 200.

32 Bottai, 'Contributi dell'Italia al nuovo ordine', 1941; De Felice, *Mussolini l'alleato*, pp. 233–42. The political programme for action in Iraq and its economic exploitation drawn up by the Foreign Ministry suggested that the countries of North Africa, the Middle East, Iraq, the Saudi peninsula and Yemen should form a Mediterranean commonwealth founded on 'political and social order, justice, equal rights, the distribution of wealth according to work, with nations joining together in groups operating on the basis of commonality and in harmony'. Italy would 'help' in the reconstruction of identities destroyed by the war and ensure the independence of the Arab states, 'binding and guiding them' with treaties of alliance and co-operation (Magugliani, 'Impostazione geopolitica del bacino mediterraneo', 1942; DDI, ser. IX, 1939–43, vol. 5, docs. 656, 676 and 687, 'progetti per l'occupazione militare dell'Egitto, elaborati nel giugno 1942').

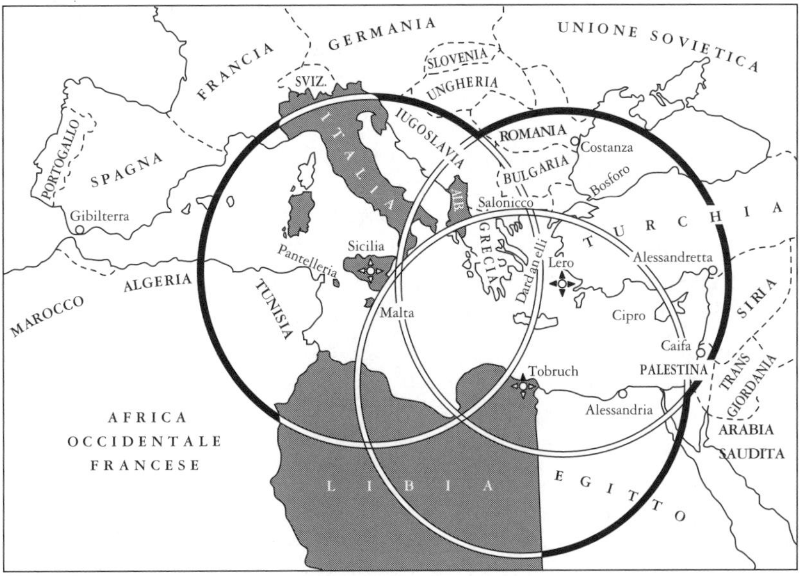

Map 7. The Mediterranean *spazio vitale* (from Schmidt, *Rivoluzione nel Mediterraneo*, 1942)

in the geopolitical community comprised the African colonies (territorially enlarged), whose political status would be inferior to those of all the other members owing to the 'racial inferiority' of their inhabitants.

The racial hierarchy was as follows. The lowest level consisted of the indigenous peoples of Africa (those of the AOI being of inferior status to the North Africans of Libya). The middle level comprised the 'Europoids'. At the apex stood the Italian imperial race. 'The new order would be fascist because in the Mediterranean area only Italy has effectively achieved racial unity and full political consciousness', wrote Renzo Sertoli Salis,[33] in whose view there were three Mediterranean races: Latin, Slav and Hellenic, all of which were inferior to the Italian race, but superior to the Turkish, Semitic and Hamitic ones.

To assist the reader, the above-discussed theories are arranged in a table (see appendix, table 1) in which alongside each 'race' at a given 'stage of development' is the political regime that the authors deemed 'suited' to it. The European territories conquered by Italy after 1940 either fell within the first circle, and therefore among territories which were to become Italian

[33] Sertoli Salis, 'L'elemento antropico e il nuovo ordine politico mediterraneo', 1942; Landra, 'Presente e avvenire del razzismo italiano', 1943.

provinces, or within the second, and therefore among those that would obtain independence or autonomy under the aegis of Rome.

THE NEW ECONOMIC ORDER IN THE EUROPEAN TERRITORIES OF THE IMPERIAL COMMUNITY

The theories of the *novus ordus oeconomicus* propounded between 1939 and 1943 were concerned with a variety of aspects which can only be outlined here. Virginio Gayda wrote that the new international order would not be the promised land: it would not solve all problems, nor would it bring perpetual peace. Rather, it was a means to resolve Europe's economic crisis. It would dampen the harmful effects of European political fragmentation and lead nations towards more genuine solidarity.[34] The Fascist war was propagandized as a war to liberate Europe, a crusade against the monopolies and international cartels of the Western plutocracies, an instrument necessary to achieve 'economic order, justice and peace among nations and solidarist social progress'.[35] The disappearance of the economic system imposed at Versailles, of liberalism and of the corruption intrinsic to capitalism would eliminate the causes of economic disparities among nations. So too would disappear the dichotomy between the rich nations, with their underuse of the land and the natural resources in their possession, and the poor nations forced to send migrants to populate other continents with their labour. The new economic order would introduce a system of 'controlled national economic management' founded on solidarist relations among national economies, with no speculation in money or gold, and organized according to individual capacities to give and to produce. It would establish a 'true democracy' based on the hierarchy of the needs and aptitudes of peoples. The dominion of minorities would be replaced by the dominion of majorities, as expressed by numbers and by productive capacity.

According to the Fascist theoreticians, Europe's economic and political evolution would tend naturally towards the formation of larger and more

[34] Gayda, *Profili della nuova Europa*, 1941, p. 64. Curcio wrote in 'La rivoluzione europea', 1940, pp. 515–18: 'Men – two Men – have been stronger than things. The new civilization . . . springs from the torment of two national revolutions . . . A new European order is installed on the hierarchical basis of intrinsic political values. Great imperial aggregates, spatial, ethnic, economic bodies arise from the chaos . . . In the international order that will ensue . . . [there will be] controlled freedom. The cessation of all conflict, both political and social, political and economic co-operation, an ethic of solidarity which does not alter the national personality . . . What liberalism and socialism have been unable to accomplish the great European and world revolution in progress will construct.'

[35] Gayda, *Profili della nuova Europa*, 1941, p. 21.

organic communities extending beyond, though not eliminating, political boundaries and national identities. The group led by the 'great' nations would generate a sort of European economic regionalism.[36] But which nation would be entitled to operate as the central organizing 'core' of an economic community of this kind, and by virtue of what criteria? The first criterion was demographic growth; the second was an aptitude for economic organization and a capacity to attract economic resources and export financial and knowledge resources to the countries of the 'economic community'. Italy, the Fascist doctrine claimed, had proved that it fulfilled both these requirements in Africa, where it had refrained from the exploitation and pillage typical of the capitalist states.[37] What other European countries were eligible? Undoubtedly Germany, which had created the economic community of continental Europe; perhaps Great Britain; but certainly not France. How would the *limes* of the community be established? A state's membership of one economic community rather than another would be determined by geographical contiguity, by similarity of traditions, by convergence of economic interests, by communications systems, by the complementarity of national economies and by the utility yielded by the association. The economic communities should consist of zones of equivalent size and wealth.

The leader-state of the community would assume executive, organizational and redistributive responsibilities. It would ensure the provision of raw materials and guarantee access to outlet markets. The economic dependence of lesser states on the organizer state would not entail their servitude, however: with 'the myth of the small states' dispelled, they would regain that 'place which nature, geography and history' had allocated to them, although they would have to recognize that their autonomy was 'dependent on the discretion of the machinery of great forces' and that their will was 'subject to the external conditions' created by the great nations.[38] According to this theory, each community would sustain its economy with its own output and intra-community trade, the latter being assisted by the creation of a *Zollverein*, a system of preferential customs tariffs (similar to the German imperial customs union), and by long-term commercial agreements. The leader-state would regulate economic relations among national entities. It would establish a hierarchy in relationships with its associates and then implement a pre-established plan, allocate and co-ordinate tasks and interests, and develop an autarkic manufacturing and commercial economy

[36] Ibid., p. 39. [37] Ibid., p. 67.
[38] J. Mazzei, 'La chiusura economica delle grandi unità statali', 1942.

within its area – but without isolating it from the other European communities.[39] Not permitted, therefore, was the interference, intrusion or indeed the presence of other economic actors in a community's domestic market (in other words, Germany was *persona non grata* in the Mediterranean economic space).

But how could the products and raw materials needed by the community be obtained? A clearing system of balanced exchange rates run by the executive state would solve the problem. Exports and imports among communities would be organized on the basis of internationally balanced exchange rates. This clearing system would regulate commercial relations among communities, and there would be as many clearing systems as there were communities. An international financial organization would act as the clearing house: it would represent communities, not individual states, with a multi-lateral clearing system which efficiently balanced debits and credits. Trades between community countries would pass for settlement through the organizer countries – these being the guarantors of foreign economic and financial transactions. For the system to be practicable, however, a fixed exchange rate for the currencies of the organizer states would have to be established, so that a select group of currencies regulated trade in Europe.

Reciprocal respect for communities' economies would also apply in financial markets, because the Fascist new economic order did not contemplate capital investments or possession of financial or industrial securities by one community in the zone of another. Each member would subordinate its interests to those of the organizer nation, which in exchange would ensure the availability of supplies and prevent speculation, fluctuations in foreign markets, competition and overproduction. The Fascist texts on the matter, however, do not explain how Italian capital would replace British and French capital in the territories of the Fascist economic community; and they simply ignore the problem of how the financial factor might give way to the trio of production, work and trade.[40] As to the 'monetary question', the financial specialists proposed two solutions: monetary union among the members of the community, or the creation of a 'lira zone' which would not eliminate the other national currencies but fix their exchange rates. Only the currency of the leader-state would be used in foreign trade.[41] What,

[39] Gayda, *Profili della nuova Europa*, 1941, p. 46.

[40] See e.g. De Cesare, 'Il riordinamento economico danubio–balcanico', 1941.

[41] This was advocated by Minister of Trade and Exchange Raffaelo Riccardi and by the contributors to the journal of which he was editor, *Economia fascista* (on whose editorial board sat leading representatives of the establishment, industry and the Fascist intelligentsia: Giacomo Acerbo, the

one may ask, would the geo-economic space of Rome's community be? Although its boundaries were not yet definable with precision, geography, traditions and trade routes since the times of the Roman Empire and the Venetians made clear that its compass would be the Mediterranean and the Balkans.

The foregoing description shows that the new economic order would have projected the regime's autarkic principles on a 'community' scale – with co-ordination and management of the economy as the exclusive province of the leader country.[42] Interestingly, the Fascist economists drew a clear distinction between the economic role of the European territories making up the community on the one hand, and the role of the colonies on the other (see chapter 7 for more detailed discussion). The former would be economically integrated into the *spazio vitale*; the latter would belong to the *spazio vitale* to solve demographic problems.

ALBANIA AND THE COLONIAL EXPERIENCE AS BLUEPRINTS FOR CONSTRUCTION OF THE NEW ORDER

The ideal type of the *spazio vitale* has now been described, and the economic principles on which it was supposed to work have been outlined. Now let us turn to how the Fascists drew on past experience when envisioning the political, governmental and administrative system of their imperial community. In this regard, although Albania was not among the territories conquered after 1940, description of its political and administrative status highlights features of the territories that were occupied after 1940.

Albania was the only European conquest that Fascism accomplished without the help of the Germans. Numerous authors of articles and monographs on the *ordine nuovo* and the *spazio vitale*, as well as numerous civil servants and military authorities posted to the territories conquered after 1940, made reference to an 'Albanian model' – although it was never realized in practice. A distinctive feature of the model was its provision for personal union of Italy and Albania under Victor Emmanuel III. This is a choice difficult to understand, for it was made by a regime headed by a dictator minded to do away with the monarchy. Even today one can only speculate as to the reasons for it. Was it the result of a compromise

governor of the Bank of Italy, Vincenzo Azzolini, Paolo Orano and Giuseppe Volpi di Misurata). See Riccardi, 'Collaborazione economica europea', 1942; Riccardi, 'Rapporti economici italo-tedeschi', 1942. See also Gayda, *La politica italiana nei Balcani*, 1938.

42 Volpi di Misurata, 'L'economia di domani', 1940; Fossati, 'Carattere, oggetto e soggetti del commercio in regime di autarchia', 1940.

reached with the Church, monarchy and the traditional élites from which Mussolini was unable to extricate himself? Was it the result of a Machiavellian plan to get rid of the monarchy on conclusion of the war, and also to provoke upheavals in the community's territories, specifically Albania? Was personal union a device for maintaining temporary control over the Italian protectorates until a more original and more markedly Fascist plan was put in place?

It should be pointed out, however, that when territorial plans are implemented, they are often conditioned by concrete circumstances. Napoleon, too, resorted to temporary solutions after 1800 when he replaced the *républiques-soeurs* with monarchical satellite states, his purpose being to have them replicate the 'superior' French model. So the discrepancies between transitional political-institutional solutions and the initial projects cannot be used on their own to appraise the viability of those projects.[43] In Albania, unlike the territories occupied after 1940, Rome decided to create an indigenous Fascist party headed by Mussolini. This decision was important because Tirana thus had the same dualism between state and party that characterized Fascist Italy, and Mussolini could consequently take on the arbiter's role that he performed in Rome, *mutatis mutandis*, in Albania as well (on this, see chapter 4).

It should also be pointed out that, in 1939, Italy decided not to annex Albania and turn the country into a military bridgehead or into a possession to which it could send large contingents of emigrants. It probably decided thus because the illusion of Albania's independence could be used by the regime's propagandists to launch the idea of the imperial community while also peddling Fascism's civilizing and liberating mission.[44] In an article eloquently entitled 'L'Italia e i Balcani nel pensiero di Mazzini', the journal *Geopolitica* sought to demonstrate that Mussolini's hoped-for intimate alliance with the various Balkan countries was conceptually close to the 'external form assumed by the brotherhood between Italy and Albania'.[45] Italy, which had been bred from the principle of nationhood, should talk to the Balkan nations in the same language that it used with the Albanians, distinguishing among the national characteristics of each of those nations but imposing itself as the 'superior' yet 'civil and dispassionate' power. This was the mission that Mazzini had assigned to Italy and that Fascism had taken upon itself to fulfil by occupying the Balkan states.

[43] Tulard, *Napoléon;* Dufraisse and Kerautret , *La France napoléonienne*; Jourdan, *L'empire de Napoléon*.
[44] Morandi, 'La comunità imperiale e l'Albania', 1942.
[45] Scocchi, 'L'Italia e i Balcani nel pensiero di Mazzini', 1940, p. 487.

Fascist doctrine and propaganda strove to distinguish Italy from the capitalist powers and from the Nazis, who pursued a plan centred solely on racial domination. Contrary to the Nazi 'project', the European territories of the imperial community would not be emptied of their populations to make room for Italian colonizers.[46] The occupation of Albania would evince the political doctrine, the social intentions and the economic principles and systems of Rome's empire. For this reason Fascism supported Albanian nationalism and created an Albanian Fascist party. 'It was not possible,' said Ciano to the Senate Foreign Affairs Committee on 30 May 1942, 'to export Fascism to a country and simultaneously deny it the principle of nationhood, which is the essence itself of the [Fascist] doctrine . . . Our action in Albania constitutes concrete proof before the world that in the new order envisaged by Rome nations will not be subjugated but valued.'[47] Yet there was no truth to the claim that Italy would not exploit the occupied territories and let them retain their culture, customs, traditions and legal institutions. Rome was not interested in the principle of nationhood, and it would not have allowed the Albanians to govern themselves: Albanian national interests were to be entirely subservient to imperial ones.

As regards Albania's legal and political status, although its independence was constantly trumpeted, it was obviously neither an independent state nor an autonomous entity. Its status, as the Fascist jurists themselves admitted, was that of a protectorate: 'the kingdom of Albania is not to be considered a state but an entity subordinate to the Italian government'.[48] Indeed, it was not the Partito Fascista Albanese (PFA, Albanian Fascist Party) that wielded executive power but the king's lieutenant governor: he could appoint and dismiss ministers without being obliged to consult the parliament, and he convened and presided over the Council of Ministers. Though officially answerable only to the king, the ministers could take no initiative without the consent of the lieutenant governor.[49] Legislative power was exercised by the king with the collaboration of the Superior Corporative Fascist Council, consisting of representatives from the PFA and members of the Central Council of Corporative Economy. The provisions of the PFA's statute applied to all Albanian citizens, whether or not they were enrolled in the party.[50] In the absence of a Grand Council and a head of government,

[46] Ambrosini, *L'Albania nella comunità imperiale di Roma*, 1940, p. 63.

[47] DDI, ser. IX, 1939–43, vol. 8, doc. 573.

[48] Lucatello, *La natura giuridica dell'unione italo-albanese*, 1943, p. 70.

[49] Cansacchi, 'La luogotenenza generale d'Albania', 1941.

[50] Morandi, 'La comunità imperiale e l'Albania,' 1942; Ambrosini, *L'Albania nella comunità imperiale di Roma*, 1940, p. 59.

the PFA acted on behalf of the Duce and gave him responsibility for the Albanian fascist organization (article 9 of the PFA statute required swearing of the Fascist oath). The secretary of the party was appointed by the lieutenant governor and was instructed by the PNF. To be stressed as well is that, in Albania, the foreign minister had authority over the other organs of the state – this being due to Ciano's solicitude and because the Under-Secretariat of State for Albanian Affairs – later the Ufficio Albania – was installed at that ministry and supervised all relationships between the two countries, taking its instructions from the lieutenant governor (Francesco Jacomoni).

The Albanian solution would probably have been applied to other Balkan countries as well, had not the circumstances of their occupation induced the Fascist regime to take contingent measures at variance with the 'model'. Although the conditions under which the Balkan occupations of 1941 occurred were very different from those of Albania, the latter set the precedent for application of the principle of territorial ethnic uniqueness ('one territory for one race'). In a speech to the Camera dei Fasci on 10 June 1941, Mussolini reiterated that race, nation and state must coincide to ensure the health of peoples.

Finally to be noted is that the idea of a Mediterranean and Balkan Europe constituted by protectorates of Rome was generally endorsed by the Fascist establishment. For example, Raffaele Casertano, Italian ambassador to Zagreb, was a fervent proponent of Croatia's organization on the Albanian 'model'; this, he maintained, would give Rome closer control over domestic policy, the population's living conditions and military policy.[51] Only six months before the fall of the regime he was still advocating personal union between the Independent State of Croatia (NDH) and Italy. The General Staff of the Regio Esercito (SMRE) recommended an Albanian-style solution for the province of Ljubljana, on the ground that it was the arrangement best suited to Italy's interests.[52]

Besides the Albanian model, the Fascist regime could also draw on its previous colonial experiences when organizing the political structures of the conquered countries. Fascist imperialism had indubitable continuities with the 'liberal' period, both in its purposes ('the place in the sun', 'the civilizing mission', 'the settlement colony') and in the men who transferred from one regime to the other, thereby maintaining some sort of bureaucratic

[51] ASMAE, GABAP, b. 36, 'legazione di Zagabria al Ministero degli Esteri, 28 ottobre 1942, firmato Casertano'.

[52] USSME, N 1–11, 'Diari storici', b. 654, 'Comando Divisione Isonzo, Ufficio del capo di Stato maggiore, sezione "I", 28 febbraio 1942, Relazione sulla seconda quindicina di febbraio 1942'.

continuity.[53] But it also had distinctive features: the switch from indirect to direct rule (which massively involved the state and all its apparatuses, including the PNF), the violent repressive methods used in all the territories of the empire, and the principle of demographic colonization. According to the regime's propagandists, Fascist imperialism differed from capitalist imperialism in that the Italian state intervened in the colonies on the basis of the organization of military, political and administrative services. The aim was economic, social and cultural enrichment: this was to be achieved by immigration, the selection of areas to be brought under cultivation, industries to be established and towns to be built – all according to a comprehensive design that took account of differences in civilization and the exigencies 'of integration and differentiation'. In fact, Italian colonial bureaucracy, both in eastern and northern Africa, entirely subjugated the indigenous populations to the occupying authority, and in this it was no different from late nineteenth-century European imperialism.

A decree law of 3 December 1934 unified Tripolitania and Cyrenaica into a single colony which was given the name of Libya. With its own legal personality and ruled by a governor general, Libya was divided among four provincial commissariats (Tripoli, Misurata, Benghazi and Derna), with a military territory in the south (in its turn divided into sub-zones). Then, each provincial commissariat was subdivided into wards (administered by ward commissars), residencies (administered by residents) and districts (administered by district agents). A decree law of 9 January 1939 introduced a partial administrative union, which transformed the commissariats into provinces within the metropolitan territory. The chief towns of the provinces and wards became municipalities governed by a *podestà* assisted by councillors. Instituted within the Libyan government was a General Council presided over by the governor general and consisting of senior colonial officials, representatives of the fascist trade unions, the Colonial Council of the Corporative Economy and representatives of banks. Finally, a Governing Council formed of senior functionaries, including the chief magistrates, and a provincial Administrative Council were established.

Ethiopia – which, according to the colonizers, was populated by a 'race' inferior to the inhabitants of Libya – was administered by a viceroy and a governor general and then, in descending order, by local governors, resident commissioners, vice-resident commissioners and village chiefs, these being the native Ethiopians who ranked highest in the administrative hierarchy.[54] Although the Ministry of the Colonies (which in 1937 became the Ministry

[53] Goglia and Grassi, *Il colonialismo italiano.*

[54] Tritonj, *Politica indigena africana*, 1941, pp. 255–8.

of Italian Africa) should have supplied the administrators, owing to understaffing these were replaced by military personnel: the viceroys Badoglio, Graziani and the Duke of Aosta, the governors Guglielmo Nasi and Pietro Gazzera, and the commissioners and vice-residents, these being respectively majors and lieutenants (so that career soldiers were transformed into governors and administrators, and the civil administration was 'contaminated' by the military).[55]

A different kind of government was imposed on the Aegean, where the regime's objective was to achieve economic development and military consolidation, and to bring the Dodecanese definitively under Rome's sway, with 'the moral transformation of the subject populations'. The regime's intent was to imprint its 'civilization . . . inspired by the political and administrative institutions and the three great principles of authority, order and justice' and to assimilate local entities to Rome. The municipal statutes were revised and the councils were dissolved, their place being taken by *podestà* whose decisions were authorized by the governor. The Gioventù Italiana del Littorio (GIL, Fascist Youth Organization) committees were introduced and the school system was reformed, although the teaching of modern Greek and Turkish, alongside Italian, was still permitted. Judicial reform brought the confessional courts under the jurisdiction of the state. Extended to the islands were the rules on registration that applied in Rome, a provision deemed essential 'for the purposes of public order' and 'racial assessments'. The aim of these jurisdictional reforms was to accomplish a 'totalitarian reform' which abolished minority communities as legal entities and created the new status of Aegean citizen. Also introduced were all the organs of the PNF.[56]

The government of the Aegean enjoyed a certain amount of autonomy from Rome. It issued its own laws and decrees, and the governor exercised full powers. Its relationships with the central government were supervised by the Ministero degli Affari Esteri (MAE, Ministry of Foreign Affairs). It had a bureaucratic structure whereby the governor presided over a civil cabinet as well as a military cabinet which, in 1940, took the name of the Comando delle Forze Armate dell'Egeo, and over the Offices for Civil Affairs and

[55] Del Boca, *Gli italiani in Africa orientale*, vol. I. The governors of Ethiopia included General Geloso and the future governor of Montenegro Pirzio Biroli. No comparative study has yet been produced on the colonial military cadres and those that served in the occupied territories. It would be interesting to know the percentages of the former (career officers) transferred to the territories occupied by the Italians between 1941 and 1943. The military personnel present in the colony in 1930 amounted to 90 per cent of the total in Amhara, 80 per cent in Hara, 90 per cent in Galla and Sidama, 33 per cent in the governorate of Addis Ababa, 70 per cent in Eritrea and 20 per cent in Somalia.

[56] Roletto, *Rodi*, 1939; Fanizza, *De Vecchi – Bastico – Campioni*, 1947.

Personnel, Economic and Financial Affairs, Public Works, the Post Office, Customs, and Education. The governor was flanked by a general secretary who attended mainly to civil matters (in 1940 his post was redesignated 'vice-governor'). Rhodes was governed by a *podestà*, the larger islands by government delegates with a *podestà* for each town, while in the smaller islands the delegate also performed the functions of a *podestà*. As we shall see in chapter 8, the structure of the Governorate of Dalmatia and of the Ionian islands was partly modelled on the government of the Aegean. More generally, Italy's colonial experience provided the template on which the regime based all the state organs when it set about organizing the political, administrative, economic and repressive structures of the territories under Italian domination.

THE INHABITANTS OF THE IMPERIAL COMMUNITY

Ancient Rome had granted individual and collective citizenship in order to augment the number of its citizens, to absorb the local ruling élites and to ensure their loyalty to imperial power. By contrast, from the second half of the 1930s onwards, the essential requirement for the acquisition of citizenship in Fascist Italy was race. In the Italian anti-Jewish legislation, the normative definition of 'person belonging to the Jewish race' – observes Michele Sarfatti – was racist not religious: more precisely, it hinged on biological factors as well as on esoteric-traditionalist criteria (the phobia that even one drop of Jewish blood threatened the health of the individual and of society). Italy, in short, had embarked on construction of a 'racial state', though in confused and haphazard manner due to the difficulties of participation in the Second World War.[57]

Consequently, the regime moved in a direction which was the reverse of that of the Roman Empire. Italian citizenship was to be granted only to the inhabitants of the 'small space'. The inhabitants of the European territories would keep their nationalities, these being anyway inferior to that of the 'civilizers', while the Africans would continue to be mere subjects.[58] Like the Western empires, the Fascist empire would be multi-national and multi-ethnic, but a hierarchy would be established among the subject nationalities and ethnic groups, and an insuperable barrier erected between them and the 'imperial race'. No people, not even the European ones, would be assimilated into the 'civilizing race' with the exception of the Italian minorities

57 Sarfatti, 'Il razzismo fascista'; Sarfatti, *Gli ebrei nell'Italia fascista*.

58 Sertoli Salis, *Imperi e colonizzazioni*, 1941, pp. 330–1; Tritonj, *Politica indigena africana*, 1941, pp. 402–24; Pozzi, 'Il valore razza nel problema coloniale', 1942.

living beyond national borders. Confirmation that the Fascists pursued a racist programme and embraced a racist imperial conception was provided both by the regime's intellectuals and by the organs of the state, notably the General Directorate for Demography and Race, which in a prospectus issued in September 1938 listed the following 'non-Aryan' groups in the Italian peninsula: Africans (Negroes and Arab-Berbers) and Asiatics (Mongols, Armenians, Turks and others – Yemenis, Palestinians, Indians, etc.). A circular of 1939 on the application of the law against mixed marriages specified that Arabs, Chinese, Turks and Libyans were not Aryans. Indians, Iranians and Armenians were to be considered of 'Aryan race', as well as the Albanians, 'Christian or Muslim', while Egyptians were to be defined 'case by case'.[59]

The colonial legislation embodied the principles of preserving the Aryan race and separating the races. For example, it gradually turned the so-called *meticci*, or half-breeds born of a union between a colonizer and a native, into the pariahs of society. The notion of their presumed inferiority had formed before the advent of Fascism, and it had developed before the conquest of Ethiopia. Evidence of this are the studies by the Florentine anthropologist Lidio Cipriani, for whom 'the African mulatto was a degeneration of the white race, a threat, an abnormal biological product that increases racial chaos, as opposed to the unsullied purity of the "superior races"'.[60] A royal decree of 1 June 1936 (no. 1019 – 'Ordinamento e Amministrazione dell'Africa Orientale Italiana') omitted the articles relative to the acquisition of Italian citizenship by *meticci* of unknown parenthood (according to Gianluca Gabrielli, on the legal principle that *ubi lex voluit dixit, ibi noluit tacuit*, we should construe this omission as an abolition[61]). The judge of the colony ascertained fulfilment of the requirements for acquisition of citizenship, the criteria being possession of certain physical characteristics and a wholly Italian upbringing. The acquisition of citizenship therefore depended on an anthropological examination and a test of cultural knowledge. In 1938 the regime drew up a 'Questionario per le Ricerche sull'Incrocio delle Razze Umane in AOI' (Questionnaire on Miscegenation in Italian East Africa) and conducted a census of *meticci* (although the results were never made public). These were measures necessary to proceed with discrimination against persons with one Italian parent, to study their

[59] Sarfatti, 'Il razzismo fascista', pp. 327 and 328. I am grateful to Michele Sarfatti for providing me with copies of the documents referred to: ACS, MI, DGDR, 1938–43, b. 13, fasc. 43, sottofasc. iv/1, '24 settembre 1938, Situazione non ariani presenti in Italia'; b. 3, fasc. 14, sottofasc. 2, 'massimario Matrimoni'.

[60] Gabrielli, 'Un aspetto della politica razzista nell'impero'. [61] Ibid.

'inferiority or dangerousness' and to persecute them. A law enacted on 13 May 1940 – no. 822, 'Norme Relative ai Meticci' – prohibited the adoption or filiation of natives and *meticci* by Italian citizens and required *meticci* to assume the status of the non-Italian parent: they could no longer be recognized by the Italian parent, and they could not be given his or her surname.

The regime's policy on the *meticci* is not the only substantial proof of its racism. Equally eloquent is its legislation on the 'sexual question'. Law no. 1004 of June 1929 criminalized sexual relations between an Italian citizen and a member of an 'inferior race', punishing such behaviour with imprisonment for up to five years (article 10). This law amended royal decree no. 880 of April 1937, which 'only' punished Italians who entered into conjugal relations with subjects of Italian East Africa. Under the law of 1939 any person who engaged in sexual relations with 'natives of Italian Africa' was to be prosecuted: punishable relations included those between Italian citizens and Libyans. Mention should be made of a corollary to these measures: the royal decree of 17 November 1938 prohibited marriage between Italian citizens of Aryan race and persons of another race (Jews and Africans) or of foreign nationality, except in the case of prior consent by the Ministry of the Interior and with the obligation that the Office of Civil Status ascertain the race of the future spouses. The most zealous racists of the regime, writing in journals with such titles as *La difesa della razza*, pressed for a ban on sexual relations between persons of different races in order to prevent both the absorption into the national environment, so contrary to the principle of the integrity of the 'race', and the formation of a differentiated category of 'half-breeds'.

Brief mention should also be made of the norms regulating the acquisition of citizenship in Italian East Africa, where the regime imposed the status of subjecthood on the native inhabitants (a royal decree of 1 June 1936 deemed to be Italian subjects those residents of Italian East Africa born to a subject parent or of unknown parenthood, of a woman married to an Italian subject, of an African who was serving or who had served in the armed forces or the civil service; eligible for Italian citizenship were two-year residents of AOI who applied to the authorities). In Libya, by contrast, considered a 'presumed Libyan citizen' was anyone with residence in the country who was not a metropolitan citizen (royal decree of 3 December 1934, article 34). After the aggregation of the Libyan provinces to the Kingdom of Italy (royal decree no. 70 of 9 January 1939), certain Muslim Libyans were granted a special form of Italian citizenship which did not affect their personal or successional Muslim status. Obtained by order of the governor general, such citizenship was granted only on merit, and it afforded only limited rights and protections: among them were individual freedom, inviolability of domicile, access to a military career in the Libyan divisions and eligibility for senior posts in the Fascist trade unions. This was a propagandist gesture which the governor, Italo Balbo, directed towards the Arab countries but with obviously anti-British intent. Nevertheless, the decree law eliminated the already limited opportunities for Libyan–Italian citizens (Muslims and Jews) to acquire metropolitan Italian citizenship, while also revoking their right to compete for military appointments.

In the Dodecanese, finally, a law enacted on 14 June 1912 had entitled all inhabitants of the islands to claim Italian citizenship, although, after 1938, those of Jewish faith were subject to the legislation that applied to Jews in Italy.[62] Laws prohibiting miscegenation[63] were not promulgated in the Aegean possessions, while royal decree no. 1379 of 19 October 1933 (converted into law no. 31 of 4 January 1934) stated that all residents of the islands could acquire full Italian citizenship either by royal decree or, *ipso jure*, by military service. The question of whether citizenship should be granted to native islanders occasioned debate among the Fascist theoreticians on race. Many odd views were expressed on the matter, but one of especial peculiarity was put forward by a contributor to *La Difesa della razza*, who suggested that the Aegean islanders should be encouraged to emigrate, since this would avert the problem of denationalization of Italian subjects, their assimilation into the 'dominant race' and their indefinite segregation. In effect, the natives of the Aegean, except for Jews, obtained the status of 'semi-citizens' in that they were subject to the Italian flag but, unlike the natives of Italy's African possessions, could become Italian citizens; the *jus connubii*, or right to marry, would not be denied them, only limited in its extent. We shall see in the following chapters whether and how segregation between natives and dominators was achieved in the conquered territories, and to what extent the Dodecanese set a juridical precedent for the territories of the 'small space'.

Colonization, Marc Ferro has written, is the occupation of a foreign land, its cultivation and the settlement of colonies on that land. In the West, it is a phenomenon that, like imperialism, reaches back to ancient Greece. The driving force of colonial expansion has always been the colonizer's determination to make its dominions secure.[64] Fascist Rome, too, set out

[62] Sertoli Salis, *Le isole italiane dell'Egeo*, 1939; Orlandi, *Le isole italiane dell'Egeo*.
[63] Di Caporiacco, 'Cittadini e sudditi nel Dodecanneso', 1943.
[64] Ferro, *Histoire des colonisations*, pp. 13 and 32–4.

to dominate territories and to organize the space that it was able to conquer into a 'new order'. Like the other Western empires, Fascism's empire was to be centralized and it would have an emperor at its head, although he would be Mussolini, not Victor Emmanuel III. In this respect, the Fascist imperial project was neither new nor original. The Fascists copied the Romans' pragmatism in adjusting political structures to local circumstances. The Romans had done so in their eastern provinces by utilizing already-existing powers, and in their western provinces by establishing territorial and legal unity and direct rule. Not only had the Roman Empire exploited its provinces, it had also imposed upon them the 'Roman way of life', with its political and cultural values. This was the system that inspired the Fascist imperial vision; and when it was translated into actual practice it took the form of violent subjugation.

Like the Roman, Napoleonic and British imperialists before them, the Fascists believed that the Italians had reached a more advanced stage of development and civilization than other peoples. They consequently felt they had a moral duty to transmit their values. They would create cities, and develop those already in existence, convinced that this purely material undertaking was essential and should be completed with the passing of laws to improve the quality of urban life. Where the Fascist ideal type differed from the previous Western empires was in its intent to merge the peoples under its control into a unified whole. The Fascist empire would subjugate the peoples that it conquered and establish a hierarchy – a superior/inferior relationship – that would last forever. No people would be allowed to mix with the civilizing race, and the civilizing process would not induce the conquered to identify themselves with the race of the conquerors. In this respect, the new Fascist order closely resembled the Nazi one – testifying to which is the fact that, besides its diplomatic, military and economic dependence on the Third Reich, Italy was (to some extent) an ideological and intellectual tributary to Berlin (remember that the expression *spazio vitale* was the Italian translation of *Lebensraum*).

In regard to the Nazi new order, a brief description of certain of its distinctive features follows, the purpose being to highlight similarities and differences with respect to the Fascist new order. On 10 July 1939, the Nazi regime prohibited use of the expression 'Third Reich' to designate the German empire. The official name was now to be *Grossdeutsches Reich*. The Nazi regime had its conception of empire as defined in *Mein Kampf* and the Führer's speeches and conversations. It consisted of the following: the Reich would exclude or strip of their rights individuals not recognized as ethnically German, and it would include all the Germans of Europe. The

German *Volk* was entitled to its living space and would accomplish absolute hegemony in Europe.[65] The notions of *Volkstum* and *Volksgemeinschaft* were of central importance to Nazi doctrine, with the consequence that from 1933 onward relations were intensified with all groups of the *Volksdeutschen* (communities of Germans living outside the Reich's frontiers).

As soon as he assumed power, Hitler set about conquering land and colonies to feed the Germans and solve the problem of Germany's overpopulation. Like Mussolini, he was convinced that human history was a permanent struggle to conquer living space, and that once this had been acquired it should be safeguarded by the unity of the race. In this regard, aside from differences in emphasis and in the directions that expansion would take, the Nazi and Fascist ideologies were very similar. However, more ambitiously than the Fascists, the Nazis made no secret of their project for world domination, and this they founded, as Norbert Frei put it, on the triad of purification, exploitation and extermination.[66] Three closely interconnected ideological elements drove the project to realize the Nazi empire: expansion to the east, or the conquest of *Lebensraum*; the annihilation of Bolshevism; and the extermination of Judaism, or the triumph of the German race. Expansion, anti-communism and anti-Semitism were components of Fascism as well; but there is a distinction to be made in regard to anti-Semitism, for this, though central to Italian racial discourse and policy, was less essential to them than in Nazi doctrine. Nazi colonization envisaged the acquisition of territories to be exploited for the German race, and it was founded on the necessary expulsion of the peoples inhabiting those territories, and the exclusive settlement thereon of populations with 'German blood'. The Nazi conquest foresaw the absorption of territories, not of their populations.

There is therefore a profound difference between the colonial empires and that envisioned by the Nazis, and it is not just that the latter was to be created in Europe. Hitler admired Britain's ability to dominate the Indian continent with a handful of men; but he was extremely critical of its lax approach and the degree of autonomy that it granted to the natives. He pursued an objective completely different from Britain's: to eradicate the indigenous populations of eastern Europe.[67] The Nazi regime founded its expansion on biological racism: 'genocide and resettlement were inextricably linked, for Hitler's war aimed at the complete racial reconstruction

[65] Dufraisse, 'Le Troisième Reich'; Gross, *Polish Society Under German Occupation*, pp. 29–41; Mulligan, *The Politics of Illusion and Empire*.
[66] Frei, *Lo stato nazista*, p. 172.
[67] Mazower, *Dark Continent*, pp. 141–85; Mazower, 'Hitler's New Order'.

of Europe'.[68] There is no similar project in the history of the Western empires: neither Napoleon nor the Habsburgs aspired to accomplishing such exclusive domination.

The Nazi empire would have comprised one single population: the Germans. Citizenship in the Great Reich would have be reserved solely for persons of German blood, and any other ethnic groups would have been oppressed, and then in the long term forced to emigrate or be eliminated. It was not by chance that the task of Germanizing the *Lebensraum* during the Second World War was given to the SS and personally supervised by Heinrich Himmler, appointed by Hitler Reich commissar for the strengthening of the German race (Reichskommissar für die Feistigung deutschen Volkstum). Nor was it by chance that Himmler established the Central Race and Settlement Office (Rasse- und Siedlungshauptamt) responsible for ensuring the racial purity of the colonies.

The modern notion of Europe as a set of independent states in equilibrium would thus disappear. Extending across the centre of the continent would be the Great Germany inhabited by the *Herrenvolk*, the community of German blood, on whose periphery would lie, as epigones of previous nations, some allied provinces – one of them Fascist Italy – and a federation of subject peoples with no independent armies or political systems or economies. The territories of the *Untermensch* would be plundered, and the sub-humans deported and physically eliminated. Domination of the European continent would enable the Reich to erect an insurmountable barrier against the barbarian hordes in the East, and to destroy the British Empire before embarking on conquest of the world.

Both Hitler and Mussolini shared an ambition to establish and organize an empire in Europe; both talked of a community of European peoples. But the two dictators gave a meaning to the notion of community very different from that usually attributed to it as association, co-operation, recognition of and respect for others, and equality of rights. In the Nazi vision, Europe would not simply be brought under German domination; it would entirely disappear. Projects for the resettlement of populations or mass transfers and expulsions were also part of the Fascist imperial vision (suffice it to consider the scheme conceived by Renzo Sertoli Salis for exclusion of all Jewish communities from the Mediterranean). But, in Europe, Fascism intended to create protectorates and satellites of Rome where the populations or nationalities would not be expelled or exterminated to make way for Italian colonists. Fascism would make sure that each territory of

[68] Mazower, 'Hitler's New Order', pp. 50–5.

the community was inhabited by a single ethnic group; but neither Mussolini nor his hierarchs, nor the intellectuals closest to the regime and with greatest influence over it, ever envisaged the expulsion of the Greeks or the Albanians from their territories so that room could be made for colonists of 'pure Italian race'.

In the Fascist case, the 'small space' – the one reserved exclusively for the civilizing ethnic group – interacted with a great Mediterranean space in which the European populations would have the right to exist. In the Nazi case, a large part of continental Europe would constitute the 'small space' reserved exclusively for the Germans and in which no other population, except for the Germanized Nordic peoples and some enslaved natives, would be permitted to live. In the case of Italian Fascism, the Europeans would receive the same treatment as the Indians under the British; in that of the Nazis they would suffer the same fate as the Native Americans. In this respect the Fascist conception of empire resembled British and French imperialism of the nineteenth century: it also had elements of Napoleonic (and later American and Soviet) imperialism, in the sense that the occupier of the conquered territories transferred its political, social, cultural and economic system to them.[69]

It also shared features with Japanese imperialism. Unfortunately, no comparative studies have been conducted on the Fascist and Nippon ideologies. It should be mentioned here that, at the end of the nineteenth century, a Japanese political theorist, Yamagata Aritomo, argued that colonial expansion was necessary, on the basis of a theory of circles in which each of the territorial spheres around Japan should be strengthened and protected. Subsequently, with the advent of the Meiji period, the need to imitate the European model of development spread to colonial practice as well. Acquiring an empire became a mission which, at least initially, did not serve economic interests. For some, it was a 'divinely ordained' civilizing mission, and the colonies were imagined as territories to be treated paternalistically; for others, the colonies' populations were to be assimilated – Nipponized, that is – which was deemed 'possible' because of the close ethnic similarities among the Asiatic peoples, and deemed 'just' by virtue of the Confucian principle that equality should reign under the same domination – in this case that of the emperor.

Before the Second World War, this conception was supplanted by another: colonial conquests were justified by Japanese superiority. This expansionist project was given the name of the 'Co-Prosperity Sphere'. It

[69] Woolf, *Napoleon's Integration of Europe*; Naimark, *The Russians in Germany*; Soulet, *L'empire stalinien*.

was a racist conception of empire, but the term 'race' was used in the sense of *minzoku*, that is, of the culture embodied by a people – the Japanese – standing at the summit of a ladder of cultures akin to it and destined to lead them as a result of its synthesis of East and West. The 'Project for a Global Policy of Which the Yamato Race is the Nucleus', written by a group of forty researchers at the Ministry of Population and Health, advocated the establishment of colonies grouped around Japanese cities scattered throughout the region. Mixed marriages with natives would be kept to the minimum, 'not because persons of mixed blood are inferior' but because they would destroy the mental solidarity of the Yamato race. Twelve million Japanese would be resettled in Korea, Indochina, the Philippines, Australia and New Zealand. In each of these territories all would be required to 'remain in their place' and the Japanese would occupy the dominant position. The slogan 'eight directions for a single roof' defined the Japanese notion of colonization, where the 'Co-Prosperity Sphere' was identified with a large family led by the eldest brother, namely Japan, given its superiority over the other populations. Japan's racial superiority would make it possible to put an end to Western dominance and erect a barrier against it. To be discerned in the Japanese conception of empire just outlined are the same determination to dominate, the same overweening hegemonic ambitions, the conviction of being the superior civilization and the superior race, and the idea of a civilizing and liberating mission that were distinctive of Fascism.[70]

The *spazio vitale* was only partly conquered; what is more, this was done in particular circumstances. It could be organized according to the tenets of the new order only to a minimal extent. The progress of the war, the direct and indirect influence exerted by Germany (to which Italy was entirely subordinate), weakness and an inability to deal with unexpected situations or to adapt to them thwarted Fascism's project for imperial dominion.

[70] Ferro, *Histoire des colonisations*, pp. 138ff.; Goodman, *Japanese Cultural Policies in Southeast Asia*; Myers and Peattie, *The Japanese Colonial Empire*; Duus, Myers and Peattie, *The Japanese Wartime Empire*; Duus, 'Imperialism Without Colonies'.

CHAPTER 3

The discrepancy between Fascism's plans for domination and actual occupation

The chapter describes the territories conquered by Italy between 1940 and 1943, distinguishing between those that were annexed and those that were militarily occupied. Examined in particular are the purposes and circumstances of the occupations and the role of the Germans, while assessment is made of the discrepancy between the regime's ambitions and its actual accomplishments.

THE TERRITORIES ANNEXED

Apart from the Swiss cantons of Ticino and Grisons – which, along with Malta, were never occupied – the territories of the 'small space' claimed by Italy were Nice, Corsica, Savoy, Dalmatia and the Ionian islands. For each of these territories, putative 'historical' evidence of their *italianità* was adduced, and Italy's equally putative inalienable right to their annexation asserted. The *italianità* of the territory concerned and that of its language, civilization, culture, traditions and race were propounded as the reasons for its necessary return to the 'rightful owner'. For example, the eastern coast of the Adriatic was 'undeniably' Italian because it had once been Venetian, and before that Roman. Corsica was Italian because it had belonged to Genoa, and Savoy because it had been the cradle of the dynasty of the House of Savoy. Indeed, history was distorted to such an extent that the Morlachs of Dalmatia became a 'rural Latin population' directly descended from the Romans, and 'the blood of Dalmatia' became the blood of a mythic Italy.[1] Little matter that for centuries those territories had belonged to other states, or that there were no Italian communities in the Ionian islands, or that there was only a tiny minority of 4,020 Italians in Dalmatia

[1] Some examples: ASMAE, GABAP, b. 25, 'Profili', *Dalmazia*, typescript by Oscar Randi; Franchi, 'La Dalmazia nel pensiero degli artefici del Risorgimento', 1942; Bobich, 'I discendenti degli illiri', 1940; Bernardy, 'La tradizione romana e veneziana della Dalmazia', 1941.

(2,220 of them living in Split, 300 in Šibenik, 500 in Dubrovnik, and 1,000 in Krk (Veglia), besides some 10,000 persons of Italian origin who had acquired Yugoslav citizenship after the First World War).[2] Between 1940 and 1941, the Servizio Informazioni dell'Esercito (SIE, the Army Intelligence Service), the consulates, specialists at various ministries, academics, and experts at the Istituto per gli Studi di Politica Internazionale (ISPI, the Institute for International Political Studies) published numerous studies on the geography, ethnicity, customs, languages, administrations and economies of the territories in the 'small space' and furnished the regime with the purported legal bases and 'scientific' proofs that it needed to justify its annexations.[3]

Dalmatia

A notion recurrent in plans for the conquest of Dalmatia was its 're-Italianization' or the elimination of all incomers to the region since 1919 and the repatriation of all Dalmatians resident on metropolitan territory or in other former Yugoslavian regions.[4] The Fascist regime maintained that it was necessary to 'infuse blood into the small nucleus of Italians', 're-establish the original beneficial flow from shore to shore of the Adriatic' and 'restore pre-eminence to the Italian ruling class'. Erasing all recent Slav accretions would nourish the region's true Italian subsoil, 'which the facts prove to be deeper than at first appears'.[5] A feature shared by many of the plans for Dalmatia was their intent to 'denationalize' the native population through education and the action of the Fascist state: 'those who are not Dalmatian and demonstrate that they cannot become such shall be returned to their countries of origin'.[6] But what was the geographical extent of Dalmatia intended to be, and what territories were actually annexed?

Projects based on the ethnic criterion explained that the annexations should be limited to towns in which there were, or had been, large Italian communities: Split, Šibenik and the islands. The consul of Sušak, Gigli, and the prefect of Fiume, Temistocle Testa, argued

[2] ASMAE, GABAP, b. 25, *Dalmazia*, pp. 6–8. [3] Serra, *L'occupazione bellica germanica*, 1941.

[4] ASMAE, GABAP, b. 25, 1 May 1941, 'relazione 6', E. Coselschi, *Ragusa nel quadro della Dalmazia occupata*; Cocchiara, 'Le tradizioni della Dalmazia', 1941.

[5] ASMAE, GABAP, b. 25, 3 May 1941, 'relazione 6, Dati statistici sulla popolazione di Spalato': 'The current situation [is] the result of a violence and a contrivance: . . . the forced Croatization imposed by the Habsburg government and . . . by the iniquitous government of Belgrade with the brutal persecution of the already preponderant Italian community, with the closure of all its schools and the total elimination of the Italian language.'

[6] Mori, *La Dalmazia*, 1942.

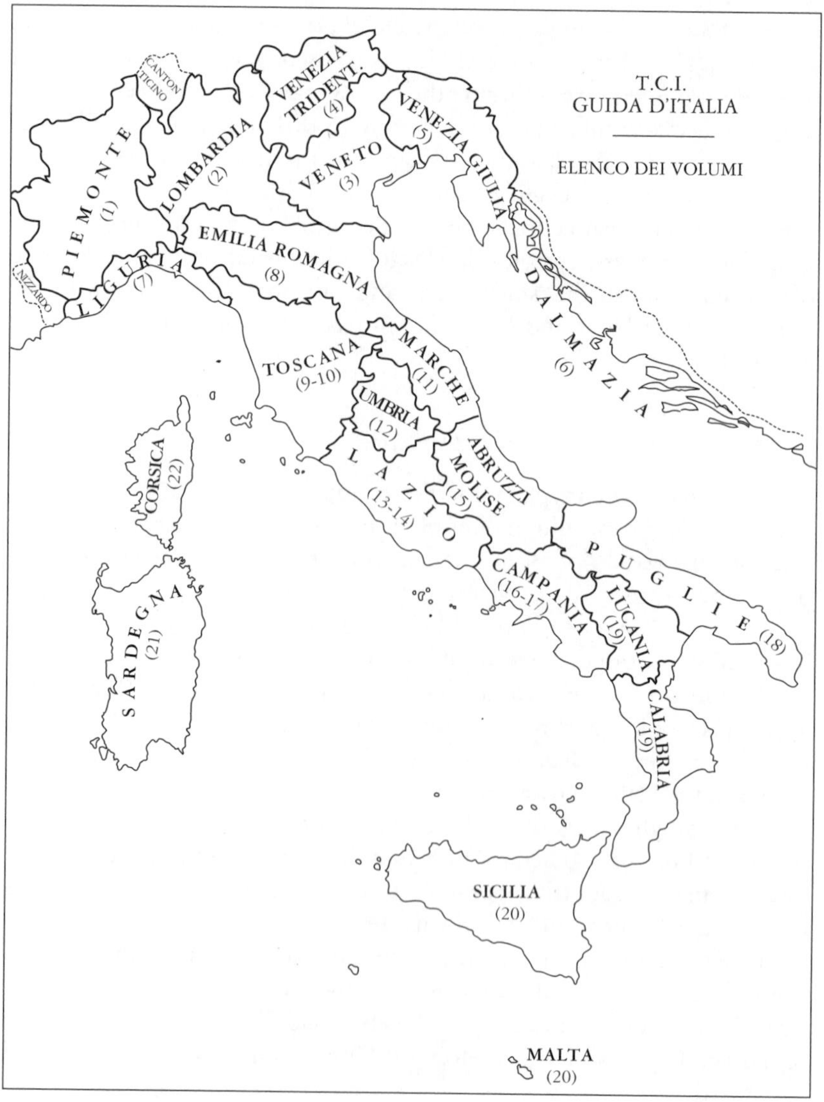

Map 8. Map with Malta, Canton Ticino, the province of Nice and Corsica included among the Italian regions (from Touring Club Italiano, *Guida d'Italia*, 1942)

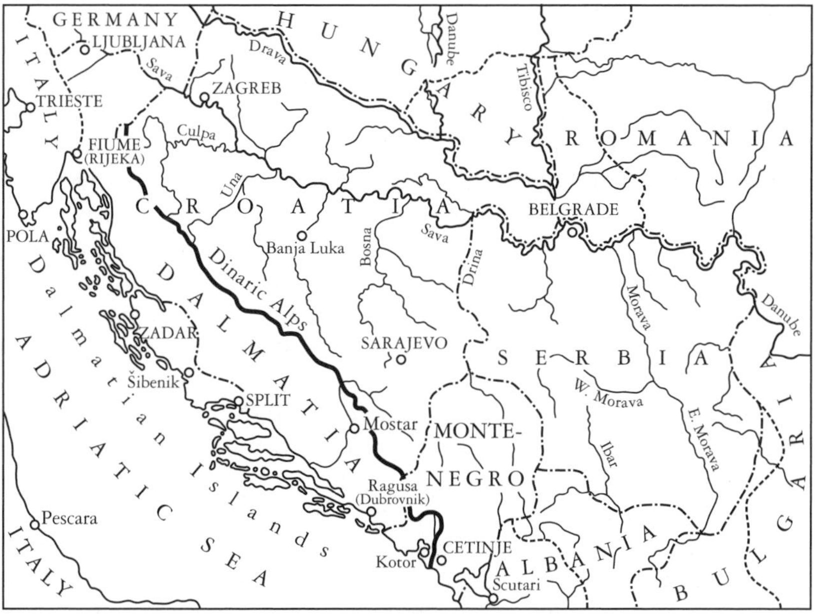

Map 9. Dalmatia, annexation plan (from Missoni, *Luci ed ombre sulle Dinariche*, 1942)

that 'it would be damaging' to occupy extensive territories because the inclusion of a large number of Slavs would change the character of Italy. Instead, by restricting the acquisitions to those absolutely necessary, it would be easy to Italianize the lands *redente* (redeemed) by gradually expelling populations not possible to assimilate and replacing them with 'native Italian elements'.[7] The consul in Dubrovnik (Ragusa), Giorgio Tiberi, argued that, as well as taking over the islands, Italy should expand the Zaratine area, annex Split, Šibenik and Kotor, and then push inland as far as the Dinaric Alps, thus giving the Yugoslavian hinterland access to commercial outlets.[8]

Plans centring on economic exploitation proposed two opposing strategies: annexation of very broad areas (from the coast as far as Bosnia) or annexation of a smaller zone which would give the region political equilibrium and foster trade, with deeper Italian industrial and financial

[7] ASMAE, GABAP, b. 28, 'consolato di Sussak al MAE', *Il pensiero locale su quella che potrà essere la sistemazione dei confini fra l'Italia e la Croazia*; b. 29, 'Testa a Guido Buffarini Guidi, 19 aprile 1941'; Missoni, *Luci ed ombre sulle Dinariche*, 1942.

[8] ASMAE, AA.PP. – Jugoslavia, b. 105, 'console di Ragusa alla Direzione generale del MAE, 12 aprile 1941'.

penetration into the former Yugoslavian interior. A number of studies argued that the former strategy should be adopted because the main industries on the coast (such as the cement works of Split) depended on the interior regions for their raw materials and energy supplies and therefore formed an indivisible economic system with them.[9] Other projects cited geo-political reasons for extending the territories to be annexed. The PNF national counsellor, Giovanni Maracchi, wrote to Mussolini advising him that Dalmatia, Herzegovina (to be renamed 'Val Narenta', Narenta being the Italian for Neretva) and the entire littoral from Zadar to Albania and from the Adriatic to the watershed of the Danube basin should be made part of metropolitan territory, and that 'Italy should also become a Slav state so that it may have decisive influence in the Danube–Balkan basin.'[10]

Immediately before and after the annexations, Mussolini – convinced more than ever that the territorial arrangement was provisional – repeatedly announced that further (and more favourable) territorial changes would be made on conclusion of the war. He wavered between annexation of the entire Dalmatian coast and respect for the Croatian protectorate, since this could be propagandized as manifesting the regime's respect for nationalities 'integrated' into the imperial community. But he would not contemplate forgoing annexation in order to curry favour with the Croat nationalists: Italy had historical claims to Dalmatia and, besides, the region was also a war objective, given that not only the Duce but also soldiers, diplomats and politicians were convinced that the Adriatic must be defended from its eastern shore.[11] Rome consequently settled for a compromise that would later prove disastrous.

In April 1941, for reasons connected with the partition of Yugoslavia, the strategy of 'limited' annexations prevailed. Rome 'generously' decided to 'impose self-restraint' and forgo part of the Adriatic seaboard (the area of Dubrovnik, nostalgically called 'Ragusa'[12]). This decision was far from congenial to the Croatian nationalists, however, and they only formally

[9] Calestani, 'Dalmazia e Italia', 1943. The bauxite deposits of Drniš supplied the aluminium works in Šibenik and the Mount Promina coal works, while Split obtained its electricity from power stations located in the interior.

[10] ASMAE, GABAP, b. 46, 'Relazione dell'11 aprile 1941'.

[11] ASMAE, AA.PP. – Jugoslavia, b. 106, 'Appunto del Ministero degli Esteri'; ASMAE, GABAP, b. 29, 'Supermarina, 8 maggio 1941, Nota sull'isola di Curzola'.

[12] The Italian literature and documents of the time referred to Dubrovnik as 'Ragusa'. Established in the thirteenth century, the Republic of Ragusa enjoyed independence until the Napoleonic army entered the city on 27 December 1807, with the consent of the city government. The use of the term 'Ragusa', rather than 'Dubrovnik', signified that the Fascist regime did not consider the city to be Croatian.

accepted the new territorial arrangement established by the Rome agreement of 18 May.

Given that much of the diplomatic documentation for the period has been lost, a useful source of information is the diary kept by Luca Pietromarchi, head of the Gabinetto Armistizio–Pace (the GABAP, the Armistice–Peace Cabinet), which gives a detailed account of events during the days that led up to and followed the Vienna meetings at which the Axis partners divided up their Balkan spoils. Pietromarchi's diary furnishes a clear description of the vacillations of Italian policy and its subordination to the Third Reich. It also raises the same questions that subsequently dogged the two years of Italian occupation in the Balkans.[13] On 15 April 1941, Pietromarchi wrote that the problems of Dalmatia, Montenegro and Albania's claims were closely interconnected, and that finding a solution for them was impossible without knowing what was going to happen to the countries of the interior. The MAE exercised itself with the question of how far southwards the new Albanian frontier should be pushed. According to Zenone Benini, under-secretary of state for Albanian affairs, the border should start at the Bay of Arta and extend as far as the inland watersheds. But in that case, asked Pietromarchi, would not the town of Ohrid be left outside the Albanian state? Was it not desirable for part of Lake Ohrid to be brought under Italian control? Was it necessary to treat the Macedonian minorities so generously? Should a free state be created, or should Macedonia be annexed to Bulgaria? And would Bulgaria remain under German control? For Pietromarchi, Italy's organization of the Balkan territories depended entirely on Germany. If the Third Reich extended its possessions as far as Salonika, what sense was there in the Adriatic arrangement if the formidable might of Germany lay just behind the fragile buffer of Dalmatia and Albania? What sense was there in Benini's plan (which emulated the policy once pursued by the Venetians) to occupy the Adriatic islands, create a neutral zone fifty kilometres in width, and build a road from Arta to Fiume flanked by the fortresses of Kotor and Šibenik, if the Nazi empire loomed over the Italian zone? According to the head of the GABAP, the military policy that pivoted on Albania and Montenegro – the peripheral marches of Italy's Mediterranean empire in the Balkans – was not realistic. And then there were further questions to complicate the situation, most importantly relations with the Croats: in the event of personal union with Italy, asked Pietromarchi, with which territories would they be satisfied?

[13] Pietromarchi, unpublished diary, 15 April–8 May 1941 (Fondazione Luigi Einaudi, Turin).

On 16 April 1941, with public opinion fervently in favour of Dalmatia's annexation, a frenetic round of meetings by senior officials at the Foreign Ministry, Admiral Giuseppe Rainieri Biscia, Colonel Manfredi of the General Staff, Professor Morandini of the National Research Committee, Professor Oscar Randi,[14] and Senator Francesco Salata came up with the idea that Italy should annex 'historic' Dalmatia at least from the Morlach region to the River Neretva, and also Kotor and all the islands. On the same day Filippo Anfuso notified Pietromarchi that Ciano had been invited by Ribbentrop to a meeting in Vienna on 20 April. It was therefore necessary 'that very day' to define Italy's agenda for dismemberment of Yugoslavia, and in particular to give precise formulation to Italian claims in the Adriatic. A telegram arrived from Berlin specifying the territories that the Germans intended to annex in Slovenia (Carniola and Styria). While the Army General Staff drew up a map plotting the boundaries of the territories distributed among the numerous states bordering on Yugoslavia, Pietromarchi and Randi drafted a memorandum on the Dalmatian question for the Duce. Pietromarchi, although he had no idea of Mussolini's actual intentions, decided to take the most aggressive line possible, in the belief that any half-measures would leave Italy empty-handed, and starting from the principle that Italy could not ask for less than it had requested in 1915.

According to Pietromarchi, the crucial issue was the coastal ports. If some of these were allocated to Croatia, those remaining in the Italian zone would no longer serve any purpose, because Croatia would channel traffic away from them to its own harbours: it was therefore necessary to force Croatia to use the Dalmatian ports. Hence Dalmatia should be annexed in its entirety to Italy; otherwise everything would be taken over by the Croats. On the same day Pietromarchi handed the memorandum to Mussolini in the presence of the secretaries general of the armed forces and Gaetano Polverelli from MINCULPOP. Mussolini told Pietromarchi that the memorandum reflected his thoughts exactly, and then commented on each of its points. A prefect would be appointed for Slovenia, he said, although the region would be largely autonomous from Italy. Dalmatia was an indivisible whole and should be annexed to Italy with autonomous

[14] Oscar Randi worked at the Istituto per l'Europa Orientale, for which he published numerous articles in *L'Europa orientale*; he contributed to nationalist journals, most notably *La vita italiana*, *L'idea nazionale*, *Politica* and *Il giornale d'Italia*. A Dalmatian irredentist and, after the First World War, an official in the Press Office of the Ministry for Foreign Affairs and then of the Ministry of Popular Culture (MINCULPOP), Randi was a prolific editorialist of fervent nationalist and anti-Slav convictions.

status, possibly taking the name of the 'Regency of Dalmatia' or the 'Illyrian Kingdom' under the Italian flag. Pietromarchi asked Mussolini for further instructions on the Adriatic littoral and was told that none of it should be left to the Croats, and that the eastern border should run along the crest of the Dinaric Alps. Montenegro would be merged with Albania but given an autonomous government. The Duce declared that he was opposed to the 'formation of small *operetta* states'. As regards Macedonia, he agreed that its border should not be pushed as far as the mouth of the River Vardar, and that the town of Ohrid should be left to the Macedonians even in the event of Macedonia's annexation to Bulgaria.

On 18 April Pietromarchi took the map marking out the new boundaries to Palazzo Venezia. Some changes were made in regard to the Morlachian Channel (Canale della Morlacca) and Pietromarchi was told that that the Lakes of Prespa and Ohrid in Macedonia must be annexed, with the option of creating a Bulgarian enclave around the town of Ohrid (the birthplace of St Clement). Later that day Pietromarchi held a meeting with the ministers Ciano and Giovanni Host Venturi. Then, on the day after, he left for Vienna in the company of Ciano, Leonardo Vitetti and the German ambassador in Rome, Hans von Mackensen. On 21 April the Italian foreign minister held wide-ranging talks with Ribbentrop, who informed him of the dividing line drawn by the Führer for the partitioning of Slovenia: 'The line is definitive and non-negotiable', wrote Pietromarchi. 'It traverses Slovenia from east to west, passes just three kilometres north of Ljubljana, leaving part of the suburbs to the Germans, and finishes with a deviation to the south of our border at Idrija. Thus from Tarvisio to Idrija our border remains unchanged, with the aggravating circumstance that instead of the Yugoslavs on its other side we now have the Germans.' Pietromarchi knew perfectly well that the border had been drawn thus for economic reasons. The whole of the wealthy part of Slovenia had been annexed to Germany, while the poor Italian zone 'would have to be supported economically'. The only positive outcome was that the Germans 'had not got as far as the Adriatic'. Ribbentrop recognized Italy's rights in Dalmatia and Montenegro but refused to pronounce on Croatia, pointing out instead that Italian claims in Albania were contested by the Bulgarians and saying that he was wholly opposed to the allocation of Mitrovica to the Italians, given the presence in that region of important mineral deposits.

What was the upshot of the meeting? Pietromarchi noted that the Germans had moved their border to only seventy kilometres' distance from Trieste. If Switzerland were dismembered ('as seems decided'), Italy and Germany would share a border stretching from Mont Blanc to Ljubljana, and its weakest point would be precisely the Slovenian frontier. Pietromarchi was astounded at the effrontery of the Germans in citing the principle of nationality when objecting to Italy's claims, while Ciano criticized the Germans for 'applying to us the principle of nationality whereas they themselves apply that of *Lebensraum*'. Moreover, the Germans' affectation of sympathy for Greece was the 'usual' tactic employed by a victor to weaken its ally on conclusion of a war. Pietromarchi foresaw 'a period of perilous intrigues' fuelled by the ever-growing problem of Croatia. He declared at a meeting with Ciano that, as far as the Italo-German balance of power was concerned, Italy's situation was similar to Piedmont's relationship with the France of Louis XIV – except that it could not rely on the support of other countries to counter the overbearing power of its neighbour. He reminded Ciano of Ribbentrop's letter written in March 1939 after the invasion of Czechoslovakia (see chapter 1), in which he guaranteed that Italy would be given a free hand in dealing with Croatia.

Hitler decided not to concern himself further with Croatia and advised the Italians to reach agreement with Ante Pavelić as soon as possible: it was now up to Rome to disentangle the situation in Croatia. The MAE at first discarded the idea of personal union and thought that a guarantee (like that stipulated by the Germans in Slovenia) together with monetary and customs union might be the solution. In any alternative scenario Italy would have to relinquish its ambitions for Dalmatia and settle for the creation of a single economic and monetary area: but who would be willing to assume historical responsibility for the decision to forfeit Dalmatia forever? The idea thus gained ground of a compromise solution whereby Italy would advance only minimal claims: negotiations accordingly got under way with Pavelić and lasted until 18 May.

On 7 June 1941, by royal decree, Italy annexed the districts of Kastav, Cabar and Delnice; the reefs of St Mark; the islands of Veglia and Arbe, and the smaller ones as far as Jablanazzo; all the islands of the Zadar archipelago; the territory marked out by a line starting at the promontory of Prevlaka and extending to the Morlachian Channel, moving inland as far as Lake Novgonod, along the northern shore of that lake past Bucovica as far as the River Krka, then following the watercourse to encompass the territory of Šibenik, Traù and the town of Split – including its suburbs but excluding the islands of Brazza and Lesina. Also annexed were the islands of Bua, Zirona, Solta, Lissa, Bisevo and Sv. Andrija, and adjacent minor islands except for Pago; the islets of Curzola and Meleda; the district comprising all the inlets of Kotor (Bocche di Cattaro), including Gruda and the massif of Mount Orjen as far as the border with Montenegro. The zone from Sušak to Kraljevica was incorporated into the province of Fiume (see appendix, tables 2–5, on the inhabitants and towns of the zones annexed).[15]

The way in which Mussolini justified the geography of the annexations *a posteriori* is interesting: he affirmed that, although the borders could have been extended from the Velebit mountains as far as the Albanian Alps, this would have been an error, because hundreds of thousands of Slavs endemically hostile to Italy would have thus been brought within its national borders. The territorial discontinuity of the annexation (the Croatian littoral extended between Split and Kotor) had 'no practical significance', said Mussolini, because no important railways or roads ran along the northern coast, and in any case the strategic areas – Šibenik, Lissa, the inlets of Kotor – were in the hands of the Italians. Furthermore, Mussolini was certain that he could quell the Dalmatian irredentism which the Zagreb government had set about fomenting as soon as the annexation was announced.

Despite the Duce's reassurances, however, veiled criticisms were voiced by economic commentators because the Dalmatia–Croatia treaty of monetary and customs union had not been concluded. Owing to the limited extent of the annexations, Dalmatia was still economically dependent on Croatia, with the aggravating circumstance that at the Vienna conference the Germans had obtained signature of a memorandum which guaranteed the Reich's rights in Croatia and the annexed territories.[16]

The provinces of Split, Kotor and Zadar formed the Governorate of Dalmatia from 18 May 1941 until 19 August 1943, when it was abolished and powers of governorship were transferred to three prefects (Paolo Valerio Zerbino in Split, Francesco Scassellatti Sforzolini in Kotor, and Vezio Orazi in Zadar).[17] Use of a crest with three lion heads on a blue background, flanked by a stylization of the Dalmatian littoral, was granted (royal decree no. 827) by the Italian college of heraldry to the governor of Dalmatia, Giuseppe Bastianini (replaced in February 1943 by Francesco Giunta). The

[15] DDI, ser. IX, 1939–43, vol. 7, doc. 131. The treaty of 18 May did not include a convention (although one was initially foreseen) relative to Split, Castella and Curzola and granting Croatia administration of the municipalities, harbours, the police force, the financial management of municipalities, and the institution of mixed law courts for the Italian minority. Had the convention entered into force in those municipalities, the Italian and Croatian flags would have flown side by side. Pavelić rejected the proposed agreement, hoping that Split would soon revert to Croatia.

[16] Talpo, *Dalmazia*, vol. I, p. 315, refers to DGFP, ser. D, vol. 12, doc. 398, p. 630, 'Sintesi delle decisioni italo-tedesche prese nei colloqui di Vienna da Ciano e da Ribbentrop': 'In view of Germany's special interests in the former state of Yugoslavia . . . it was agreed that German economic interests should receive special consideration in the zones allocated to Italy. Germany was mainly interested in developing bauxite production in Dalmatia . . . satisfaction of German requests shall receive preferential consideration in relation to exports.'

[17] ACS, PCM, 1.1.13.16542.123; *Gazzetta ufficiale*, Regio decreto n. 747, 'Soppressione del governatorato della Dalmazia'.

MAE used Yugoslavian census data of 1931 to project the Dalmatian population in 1940: on the assumption of a 17.8 per cent rate of increase, the total number of inhabitants was estimated at 380,100 (see appendix, table 6).[18]

Slovenia

According to Marco Cuzzi, the principal reason for the annexation of the south-western territories of the former *banat* of Slovenia was that Italy intended to react in kind to the Reich's annexation of Styria and Carniola.[19] Although the territory did not initially figure among Fascist territorial claims, the regime had no difficulty in finding 'valid' reasons for its annexation. Rome hastily assembled purported historical proof of the *italianità* of the region, pointing out that it had once belonged to the county of Gorizia, to the patriarchate of Aquileia, to the duchy of Friuli and to the Illyrian provinces of the Roman Empire. Italy was therefore annexing territory which, although it did not actually belong within Italy's geographical region, nevertheless had close historical ties with it: 'Rome during its penetration of Pannonia established an important hub of road communications at Emona (Ljubljana); and Venice, by means of a slow process of economic penetration, forged close links with Carniola.' Reasons of internal order were also cited in justification of the annexation. The Julian territories (the region of Primorska) annexed to Italy in 1918 were populated by a large Slovenian minority always hostile to the central government, and especially so since the advent of Fascism: in those lands 'Slav' and 'Slovene' were synonymous with 'anti-Fascist', 'Bolshevik' and 'Third Internationalist'. The claim, therefore, was that incorporation of Ljubljana would remove the entire province from communist influence.

The annexations on the Dalmatian littoral were conditioned by the Croatian question; but the frontiers of the province of Ljubljana were decided directly by the Germans. On 17 April 1941, Berlin informed Rome that the upper territories of former Yugoslavia as far as the northern part of the city of Ljubljana had been occupied with a view to their future annexation to the Reich. Hitler's directives of 3 and 12 April had allocated to Italy the southern part of central Slovenia, the Notranjsko region (inner Carniola) and the city of Ljubljana. The Germans annexed the Slovene territories of Carinthia, upper Carniola and Styria from Vrlika, with the border continuing to three kilometres north of Ljubljana, then descending to just north of Mirna and Kostanjevica, thereafter extending as far as Drava and Petranec.

[18] ASMAE, GABAP, b. 25. [19] Cuzzi, *L'occupazione italiana della Slovenia.*

When the Nazis drew the Reich's southern frontier (which became the northern frontier of the province of Ljubljana), they ignored existing provincial boundaries; indeed, the new border cut across the cadastral bounds of the commune, leaving the Germans in possession of the uplands of Dolenjsko from which they could dominate the Italian zone.[20] The future province of Ljubljana bordered to the north on German Slovenia, to the east on Croatia, to the south on Fiume and to the west on Trieste and Gorizia. The Italian authorities posted to the province advised Rome that, 'had a rational demarcation of the border sought to create an economic entity such as to ensure the area's livelihood, it would not have disregarded the boundaries of the former prefecture of Ljubljana'.[21] The new frontiers meant that agricultural production was unable to meet the minimal requirements of the city of Ljubljana. Even the best-quality timber remained in the German zone, with the consequence that fully seventy-nine manufacturing enterprises were deprived of raw materials. Local mines could only just satisfy demand in the province, and its metallurgical industry (forty-six firms) relied on supplies from German-controlled plants in Bosnia and Croatia. The province's forty-one chemical works obtained their raw materials from German Slovenia, and the power stations supplying the province remained in German territory, so that Ljubljana had to purchase 75 per cent of its electricity.[22] Nevertheless, on 3 May 1941 the annexation was ratified (royal decree no. 291; on 27 April 1943 Mussolini and the king signed the act converting the decree into law).

According to Ciano, Ljubljana would become 'an Italian province with broad administrative, cultural and fiscal powers'. He declared that he was working with the Ministry of Interior under-secretary Guido Buffarini Guidi to draw up a constitution founded on extremely liberal principles, the purpose being to attract the sympathies of the Germanized Slovenia that had suffered such harsh repression.[23] Thus, on the one hand, Italy

[20] ASMAE, GABAP, b. 25. Created at the Ministry for Foreign Affairs was a General Commission charged with drawing the new boundaries in collaboration with the general office of the CS represented by O. Toraldo di Francia.

[21] ASMAE, GABAP, b. 28, 'Raffaele Casertano al MAE'; USSME, M 3, b. 5, 'Comando II Armata – UAC al Ministero della Guerra e per conoscenza al CS, 16 maggio 1941, Relazione politico-economica'. General Vittorio Ambrosio wrote on the same day that the Reich authorities had unilaterally established the following demarcation line for the eastern part of Slovenia: Mirna-Sv. Peter-Sp. Iera-Jecmenisce-Stojdraya-Gabrizza-course of the River Bregana.

[22] ASMAE, GABAP, b. 25, 'Aspetti economici della Slovenia e della nuova provincia di Lubiana'.

[23] ACS, A 5 G, b. 63, MI – DGPS – AA.GG.RR., 'alle prefetture di Trieste, Fiume, Pola, e alla Direzione generale Culti, prot. 442/15758, 31 maggio 1941': 'Representation was made of the particular opportuneness, at this time, of benevolent treatment of the Slovenes resident in the kingdom, given the favourable repercussions that this would have in the lands now occupied . . . clemency for persons in confinement or internees not deemed to be dangerous, use of the Slav language . . . the Duce expressed his approval on these matters.'

intended to turn Slovenia into a model province so that it could distinguish itself from Germany in the Danube–Balkan basin; on the other, the Fascists could only devise annexation schemes similar to those that they had used in Dalmatia, and consequently based on forced Italianization and colonization. Autonomy was only a propaganda device, for the annexation was followed, as we shall see in chapter 8, by violent denationalization involving deportations, resettlements and the eradication of the customs, culture, language and indeed the inhabitants of southern Slovenia.

The journal *Critica Fascista* opined that the annexation was decided because the Slovene people had never been a nation. Little matter that the Slovenes did not see themselves as ethnically, politically or morally Italian, or that their mentality was Germanic and their 'spirituality' Slav: 'in one or two generations the problem would be solved'. Political reorganization, the removal of boundaries, with the consequent economic effects, would open the way for 'spiritual, moral, cultural and perhaps ethnic' penetration, and sooner or later the Italian language would 'spontaneously' impose itself.[24] The introduction of all the bodies and institutions of the Fascist state and party, the Federazione dei Fasci di Combattimento, the GIL (which was given the task of teaching physical education in schools and was styled GILL, Gioventù Italiana del Littorio di Lubiana), the Opera nazionale dopolavoro (OND, National Working-Men's Guild), and the Massaie rurali (the Fascist Party organization for peasant women), manifested the occupying power's real intentions towards the native population.

On 31 July 1941 the Italian administration carried out a census of the population, finding that of the province's 339,751 inhabitants, 318,773 were 'of Slovene ethnicity' (93.8%), 13,580 German, 5,053 Croatian, 511 Serbian, 458 Italian and 1,376 of another nationality (among them 45 Jews and 108 refugees). The population of Ljubljana was approximately 100,000 persons, added to which were 20,000 displaced persons, mostly from the German zone (see appendix, table 7).

Annexed against its will, the province of Ljubljana remained Dalmatia's poor relation: a region that, as Cuzzi writes, aroused no irredentist passions and was not even comparable to Montenegro with its ties to the House of Savoy.

Territories annexed de facto*: the Ionian islands, Cyclades and Sporades*

Italy laid claim to the Ionian islands on the grounds that they had once belonged to the Venetian Republic, but it also regarded their possession

[24] Lodoli, 'Realtà e problemi di Lubiana', 1941.

as vital for gaining 'control of the Adriatic' and exerting influence over Greece.[25] After the defeat of Greece, General Carlo Geloso was informed by Mussolini that the Ionian islands (Paxos, Antipaxos, Cephalonia, Santa Maura (Leucadia), Zakynthos, Thiaki and Corfu) and the minor islands of Fanò, Erikoussa, Mathraki and Meganisi would constitute an Italian province without formal annexation. But at the end of May 1941, Rome was forced to acknowledge that the fate of the Ionian islands was still undecided because the Germans were opposed to any territorial reduction of the Hellenic state. The Italian authorities nevertheless continued to prepare the ground for annexation. A memo to the Duce dated 9 March 1942 reads as follows: 'It has been stated by Minister Pietromarchi that the islands must be considered land redeemed to Italy, as announced to the Germans, who have taken note.'[26]

According to the Fascist plans, the Cyclades and Sporades[27] were to be included among Italy's Aegean possessions. At the end of the campaign in Greece, the Italians reacted to the German occupation of the northern Sporades by themselves occupying the Cyclades. The archipelago had 130,000 inhabitants, 28,000 of them resident in the chief town of Sira, 57,000 on the island of Samos, 15,00 on Furni and 11,500 on Nicaria.

France

One of the territories that the regime annexed *de facto* was a small strip of France (the *linea verde*), approximately thirty kilometres wide, abutting Italy's western frontier. Mussolini's *bando* (announcement of orders and directives) of 30 July 1940 on the administrative and legal order to be imposed on the French occupied territories confirmed that *de facto*

[25] DDI, ser. IX, 1939–45, vol. 6, doc. 766, 'Mussolini a Dino Alfieri, 23 marzo 1941'; Cappuccio, 'Epiro, Acarnania ed isole Jonie', 1941; Nocera, '120 anni', 1942; ACS, PCM, G 7/8 20506, 'Attribuzioni del plenipotenziario per la Grecia', GABAP – 'Grecia 5, luglio 1941, firmato Ciano': 'The Duce has instructed that the Italian plenipotentiary for Greece – without prejudice to his ordinary powers with regard to political matters – shall assume control of the civil administration in the occupied territories except for the Ciamuria and the Ionian islands. Instructions for the Cyclades and Sporades islands will follow.'

[26] ASBI, 'Rapporti con l'estero', prat. 485, fasc. 1, bob. 104, 23 June 1941, 'Promemoria riservatissimo sulla riunione di Vittorio Forte con Piero Parini, Benini e Francesco Jacomoni a palazzo Chigi'; ASBI, Ispettorato generale, n. 313.

[27] The main Cyclades islands are: Naxos, Andros, Tenos, Mykonos, Delos, Kea, Kytnos, Gyaros, Syros, Seriphos, Sifnos, Paros, Antiparos, Folegrandos, Sikinos, Ios (Nio), Iraklia, Schinoussa, Keros, Koufonisia, Amorgos, Kinarose and Levita, Melos, Kimolos, Polinos, Santorini, Therasia and Anafé (Stampalia and Sirino were part of the Aegean possessions). The Northern Sporades, islands close to Asia Minor, consist of: Chios, Thasos, Samothrace and Lemnos, Skiathos, Skopelos, Chiliodromia (Alonnisos), Peristera, Pelagos (or Kyra Panagia), Gioura, Psathoura, Skyros. The Southern Sporades are: Samos, Furni, Ikaria, Patmos, Lissos, Leros, Kalymnos, Cos, Nisyros, Piscopi, Chalki, Simi (except for Samos, Furni and Ikaria, the southern Sporades were Aegean possessions).

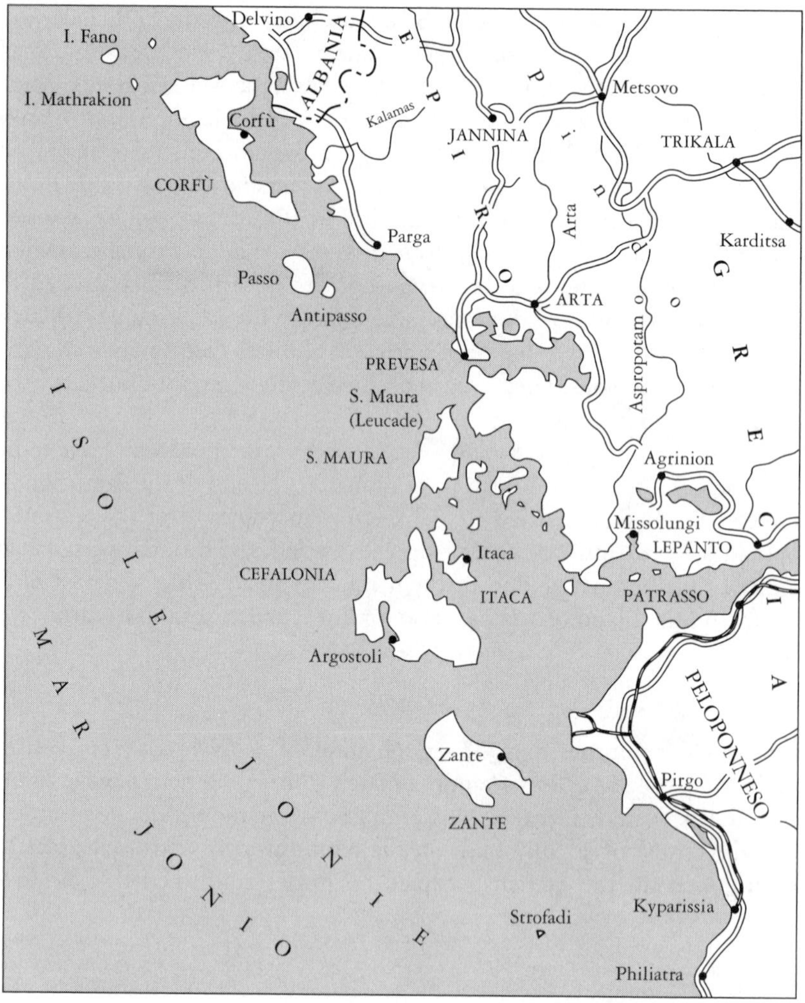

Map 10. Ionian islands (from *Relazioni internazionali*, 1941)

annexation had taken place. The *départements* concerned were Savoie, Hautes-Alpes, Alpes-de-Haute-Provence and Alpes-Maritimes. Occupied in Savoie were the *communes* of Séez, Montvalezan and Sainte-Foy; in the upper Val d'Isère: Bessans, Bramans, Lanslevillard; Lanslebourg, Termignon, Sollières, Sardières, the hamlet of Les Mottet-Versoye in the *commune* of Bourg-Saint-Maurice on the flanks of the Saint Bernard Pass; and the *communes* of Aussois and Avrieux were partially occupied (a total

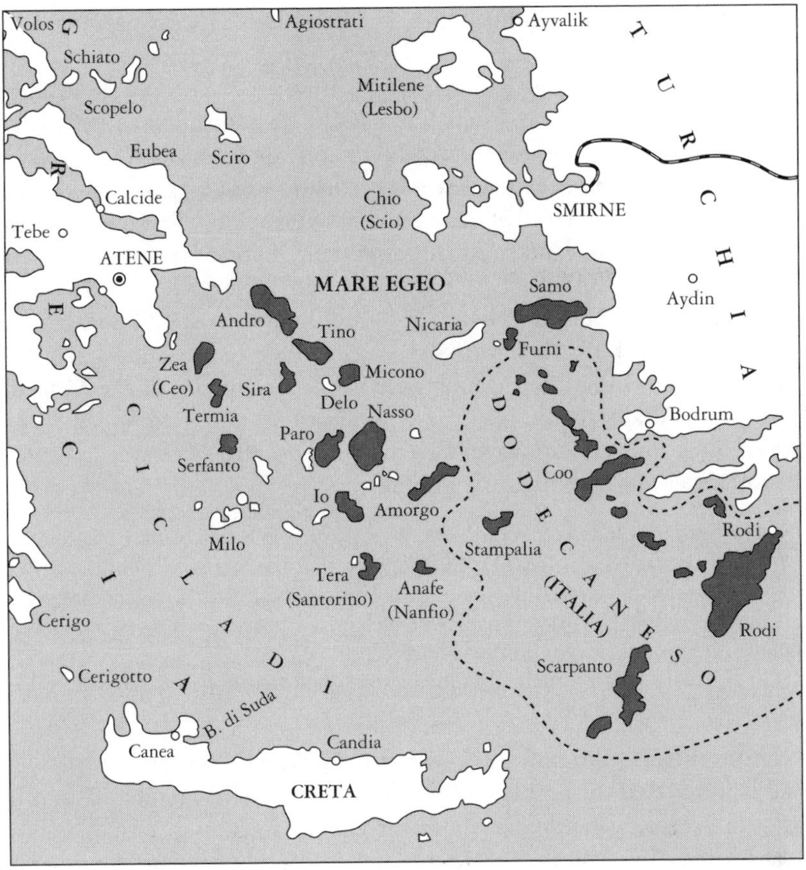

Map 11. The Cyclades and the Sporades (from *Relazioni internazionali*, 1941)

of 5,301 inhabitants). In the *département* of Hautes-Alpes, Italy occupied the *communes* of Mont-Genèvre and Ristolas, the hamlet of Roux in the *commune* of Abriès and part of the *communes* of Névache and Cervières (370 inhabitants). Taken over in the Alpes-de-Haute-Provence were the hamlets of Combremond in the *commune* of Saint-Paul-sur-Ubaye and Roche-Méane in the *commune* of Larche (32 inhabitants). Occupied in the Alpes-Maritimes were the *communes* of Menton, Fontan (Fontano), the hamlets of La Blanche and Doans, both in the *commune* of Saint-Etienne-de-Tinée, and a number of houses in the *commune* of Isola. The *communes* of Castellar, Breil, Saorge, Sospel, Rimplas, Valdeblore,

Saint-Martin-Vésubie, Roquebillière and Belvédère (a total of 22,820 inhabitants, 21,700 of them resident in Menton) were partly occupied.[28]

In the 1920s and 1930s, a large body of literature drew on an array of nationalistic arguments to assert Italy's 'right' to annex French territory.[29] Leafing through the monumental bibliography on Corsica gives an idea of the profusion of these texts: at least 103 articles and monographs published between 1922 and 1943, all of them seeking to prove, in one way or another, the *italianità* of the island.[30] Equally abundant, if not even more so, was the literature on Nice and its district, the Nizzardo. It would be superfluous to dwell on these publications here. Of greater interest is that, if nothing else because of their bulk, these works served to convince the Italians that they had 'rights' and that their claims were valid. The library of the Ministry of Foreign Affairs acquired all these publications, and it compiled a long list of illustrious quotations and events 'proving' that Nice was Italian on historical, ethnic and linguistic grounds:

> 'The border of Italy is the Var; consequently Nice is a part of Italy' (Petrarch);
> 'Denying that Nice is Italian is like denying that the Sun gives light';
> 'Corsica and Nice must not belong to France; there will come the day when an Italy mindful of its true worth will reclaim its provinces now so shamefully languishing under foreign domination';
> 'In February 1861 Emmanuel Filibert established that Italian is the official language of Nice' (Garibaldi).[31]

From August 1940 onwards – writes the historian Romain Rainero – it was believed that the problem of Italy's western frontier could be solved by annexing a tract extending to the River Var and including Antibes, and by moving the Alpine border to Mont Blanc. A second plan – propounded by Senator Francesco Salata, editor of a special ISPI series on Italy's territorial claims – also envisaged direct control over the Principality of Monaco,

[28] ACS, A 5 G, b. 405, 'prefettura di Imperia al Ministero dell'Interno', DGPS, prot. 05807, 18 June 1941, 'Rientro della popolazione a Mentone'; Panicacci, *L'occupazione italiana di Mentone*; Rainero, *Mussolini e Pétain*, vol. I, pp. 117–18, and vol. II, doc. 9 for the full text of Mussolini's order of 30 July 1940.

[29] *Mostra sull'italianità della Corsica*, Venice, November–December 1940: 'Corsica is most intimately connected with Italian geography, and its ethnic, linguistic, cultural, religious and economic features are distinctly Italian. In the strategic picture [it is] vital for security.'

[30] Starace, *Bibliografia della Corsica*, 1943; Savelli, 'Corsica italiana', 1940; Vlora, 'L'italianità della Corsica', 1943; Isnardi, *La Corsica*, 1942.

[31] ASMAE, GABAP, b. 8, 'Ragioni geografiche, storiche, etniche, linguistiche che fanno di Nizza una città italianissima'; AA.PP., 'Francia', b. 70, July 1940, 'Confine italo-francese e Appunto sulle controversie di confine tra l'Italia e la Francia'; Pettinato, *La Francia vinta*, 1941; Gray, *Le terre nostre ritornano*, 1941; Istituto di Studi Liguri, *Nizza nella storia*, 1943; Appiotti, 'Cenni geo-topografici sul Nizzardo', 1942.

while a study by the Foreign Ministry reinstated the former boundary of the Nizzardo. The Air Ministry, however, had little enthusiasm for any annexation plans. Opinions also clashed on the use to be made of Nice and its territory: some functionaries and members of the Fascist establishment maintained that Italian sovereignty should be extended just to Nice; others that Nice should become an autonomous county and be fashioned into a town of superior elegance – a 'salon of Europe' – so that it could overtake its rival Cannes.[32]

In a letter sent to Hitler on 9 October 1940, Mussolini wrote that the time had come to decide the future metropolitan and colonial physiognomy of France, which should be reduced to proportions that would forestall any resumption of its ambitions for expansion and hegemony. The 850,000 Italians that made up the largest foreign community in the country, Mussolini wrote, should be repatriated: at least 500,000 of them in one year. Then Italy's and Germany's territorial acquisitions would remove a further quarter of a million of France's inhabitants; and the peace treaty would reduce its population to 34 to 35 million inhabitants, with further decreases thereafter.[33] As for metropolitan and colonial acquisitions, Mussolini added, 'These shall be restricted to the Nizzardo, Corsica and Tunisia. Somalia does not count because it is only a desert.'[34]

Although Italy's plans for France's territorial reorganization, and for the political role that France and its colonial empire would fulfil in the new order, followed the intricate evolution of relations with the Vichy regime, they nevertheless remained entirely dependent on decisions taken in Berlin. Of the numerous plans mooted for the dismemberment of France, one of the most complete and detailed was drawn up in 1942 by the CIAF. It is of particular interest because it was conceived when the war was well advanced, and by which time Italy was wholly subordinate to Germany.[35] Italy had a Plan A and a Plan B, both of which started from the assumption that military occupation would be only a transitional phase until final victory was achieved.

Plan A, or the 'Maximum Project for Occupation of France as far as the Rhône and Corsica', also entitled 'General Governorate' (see appendix, tables 8–9), envisaged a regime of military occupation in which France would maintain its territorial sovereignty, except for the Nizzardo and

[32] Rainero, *Mussolini e Pétain*, vol. I, pp. 243–7.

[33] DDI, ser. IX, 1939–43, vol. 5, doc. 753, 'capo del governo Mussolini al cancelliere del Reich Hitler', Rocca delle Caminate, 19 October 1940.

[34] 'Direttive ribadite da Mussolini ad Anfuso', in DDI, ser. IX, 1939–43, vol. 7, doc. 79, 9 May 1941.

[35] USSME, M 3, b. 35, 'Progetto d'occupazione della Francia'.

Corsica, which would be directly administered by the Italians. French law would remain in effect, although all provisions contrary to Italian interests would be removed. Extraordinary legislation would take the form of directives issued by a supreme commander or governor, while the French civil authorities would continue to perform their functions unless they were replaced for political or military reasons or for the purposes of public order. The prefects would be dismissed, as well as their chiefs of staff and the vice-prefects, while subordinate functionaries and the administrators of municipalities and *départements* and other minor local authorities would continue in service. The administrative structure would consist of a governor general, a superintendent of civil affairs, eleven provincial governors assisted by civil and extraordinary commissioners and a high commissioner for the Principality of Monaco. The plan set out a detailed description of the allocation of powers, plotted an organization chart and estimated that a total of 594 middle- and senior-level officials would have to be posted to France (see appendix, table 10).[36] The governor general, commander of the occupying armed forces, would be the president of CIAF, flanked by an army chief of staff (the secretary-general of CIAF). These men would head an office which attended to military matters and co-ordinated the activities of the land, sea and air forces and the Carabinieri Reali (CC.RR., Royal Military Police), as well as a civil department presided over by a superintendent of civil affairs and consisting of an Office of Political and Classified Affairs, a Press Office, a Cipher Office, a Public Security Office, a Military Liaison Office, a General Secretariat, and Inspectorates of Judicial, Financial and Economic Control.

Each governorate would be divided into districts administered by civil commissioners or directly by the governor. The civil offices of the governor would be run by a chief of staff responsible for an Office of Political and Classified Affairs, a Prefecture, an Office of Public Security and a Press Office; and by the head of the Civil Office, who performed the functions of a vice-prefect and was in charge of offices responsible for administration, accounts, purchasing and assistance to Italians.

[36] ASMAE, AA.PP. – Francia, b. 65, SCAEF '(presidente Tommaso Lazzari) al presidente della CIAF Arturo Vacca Maggiolini, 17 luglio 1942, Corsica: riflessi economico-finanziari, risorse alimentari, problemi amministrativi (in caso di annessione)'. The CIAF proposed that from a legal point of view the Nizzardo and Corsica should be considered 'Italian lands', so that Italy would not have to assume part of the French national debt. According to the commission, citation could be made of the case-law relative to the Treaty of Versailles, when the French re-annexed Alsace and Lorraine on the grounds that they had never legitimately been part of the German empire; *mutatis mutandis*, the treaties relative to the cession of Nice, Savoy and Corsica would be deemed void.

Plan B, or the 'minimum' project for the 'French Territory in the Alpine Area Subject to National Claims and Corsica', encompassed the Alpes-Maritimes, the Principality of Monaco and a mountainous zone comprising parts of the three *départements* of Alpes-de-Haute-Provence, Hautes-Alpes and Savoie (the heads of the valleys of Isère, Arc, Durance, Ubaye and the districts of Verdon, Albertville, Saint-Jean-de-Maurienne, Gap, Briançon, Barcelonnette and Digne). This would constitute the province of Alpi Occidentali with sixteen communes and 76,000 inhabitants, the provincial capital of which would be Briançon. It was acknowledged, however, that creation of this province would pose serious problems, given the difficulty of communications, diversity of language and of sentiment. If the intention was to annex a zone on the western side of the Alps, in addition to Corsica and the Nizzardo, the report concluded, it should extend further than envisaged so that it encompassed an area that constituted a viable entity. If Plan B was adopted, the superintendents for civil affairs would introduce the Italian legal order and furnish the cadres required for the administration of the new Italian province of Alpi Occidentali: a prefecture, sub-prefectures and provincial offices (Public Works, Finance, Post and Education). In Corsica, a general would immediately replace the French prefects and vice-prefects with civil commissioners installed in Bastia, Corte and Sartène. Other commissioners would be appointed for Grasse, Barcelonnette and the metropolitan districts of Bourg-Saint-Maurice and Modane, thereby ensuring that the local administrations continued to function. Implementing this plan would require only 326 officials.

As for Corsica, mention should be made of a specific plan drawn up in 1941 by the SMRE and Admiral Vannutelli, according to whom no reliance should be placed on the Corsican separatist movement because it was hostile to Italy. 'The following will be granted: the acquired pension rights of Corsican civil servants, the right to choose between French and Italian citizenship, and the right to use Corsican dialect during trial proceedings. As to the form of government, a special regime for an even more prolonged period of transition is suggested, so that Corsica will autonomously flank Italy with ties and guarantees for progressive national fusion.' Corsica would be governed by a viceroy or high commissioner installed in Ajaccio with full executive powers, and by a local administration that left ample space for local traditions to continue. The plan made explicit reference to the autonomous government of Fiume prior to its annexation to the Kingdom of Italy, to the special government of the Dodecanese under the aegis of the Ministry of Foreign Affairs and to the personal union with Albania. It also envisaged a complete customs union, the incorporation of Corsican soldiers serving in the French army into Italy's, the unification of international relations and the commonality of political bodies. The civil administration would be divided into two sub-governorates or provinces corresponding to the island's historical partition between Bastia and Ajaccio.[37]

However, as had happened in Yugoslavia and Greece, it was once again entirely owing to a decision taken by the Germans, and not by virtue of any military initiative on its own account, that Italy was able to occupy the territories as far as the Rhône designated for annexation. When, in November 1942, French metropolitan territory was occupied by the Regio Esercito, Mussolini imposed a regime of military occupation that took no account of the initial plans for conquest and partition.

The Principality of Monaco

The Principality of Monaco was included implicitly or explicitly in all the lists drawn up by Italy of the areas in metropolitan France to be annexed. Relations between the Monégasque and Italian authorities closely followed the ups and (especially) the downs of those between Rome and Vichy – or, better, among Berlin, Vichy and Rome. The Germans, as in all the other occupied territories, interfered in Monégasque affairs and profited from friction between Rome and Monaco to play the role of arbiter and penetrate the principality politically and economically.[38] From the signing of the armistice until the occupation of November, Rome adopted an indecisive policy which neither supported the aspirations of the Fascist groups active in Monaco's Italian community nor openly condemned them. However, important changes occurred towards the end of 1941: closer attention was paid to how the principality's economic and financial resources could be exploited, and a new consul was appointed: Stanislao Lepri, who was much less ardently Fascist than his predecessor Antonio San Felice. It seems that this change was consequent on an instruction from the head of the GABAP, Pietromarchi, who in August 1941 wrote that, if Italy annexed the Alpes-Maritimes, Monaco would remain an enclave within Italian territory. Instead, if Monaco was occupied militarily, it would be brought under the authority of the Regio Esercito. In the latter case, the CIAF delegates would have to be present in the principality, measures would have

[37] USSME, I 10, b. 91 (Admiral Vannutelli would have commanded the Italian landings in Corsica, had they taken place); ACS, PCM, 1940–3, G 23/2 30582, 'Programma per la Corsica del 9 novembre 1941, studio dell'ammiraglio di divisione Vannutelli'.

[38] ASMAE, AA.PP. – Monaco, b. 1, CIAF – 'Sottocommissione AA.GG. al Ministero degli Esteri', 3 April 1942. The Germans repeatedly attempted to open branches of German banks in the principality and conducted surveys on commercial exploitation of its port.

to be taken to defend it, all disloyal Franco-Monégasque elements would have to be replaced and anti-Italian agitators ejected, with Italians replacing the French in all possible areas of official activity. It was necessary to penetrate the Monégasque and to direct propaganda at a hungry population which, 'amounting to just 20,000 inhabitants, certainly did not represent a significant burden for Italy'.[39] Italy maintained this course of action until the occupation. Indeed, in August 1942, when the Monégasque government refused outright to accept the presence of Italian armistice bodies, the CIAF did no more than impede Anglo-American espionage and monitor maritime traffic. On 16 November 1942, Consul Lepre, after Monaco's minister Emile Roblot had rejected a proposal for peaceful and temporary occupation, announced to the local authorities that the principality would be occupied at noon on that same day.[40]

Croatia

During the 1930s Italy had supported and given political asylum to the Ustaše, a group of Croatian separatist terrorists led by Ante Pavelić. When Yugoslavia was partitioned, Rome applied pressure on Berlin for Croatia to obtain independence and for Pavelić to be installed as the head of the new state. The Italians hoped that this move would be enough to ensure their pre-eminence in the region, or at least to counterbalance German hegemony to an adequate extent. The assumption of power by the Ustaše corresponded largely to a plan for insurrection drawn up in January 1940 by Pavelić and Ciano, according to which a member of the House of Savoy would become king of Croatia in exchange for its independence. Theoretically, personal union on the Albanian model would have guaranteed control over Croatia's political and economic system and presented Italy as the 'liberator' of the Balkan peoples. Above all, however, it would have served to block Germany's *Drang nach Südosten*.

The organization of the Ustaša state was inspired by the Fascist model.[41] The Decree on the Composition of the Ustaša Movement (23 June 1941) served as a constitution because the Ustaše did not want to institutionalize their party and had decided to give the state the form of a movement. The decree divided the movement's general activities into three sectors:

[39] ASMAE, GABAP, b. 4, 'Pietromarchi al consolato di Monaco principato', 6 August 1941.

[40] USSME, N I–II, 'Diari storici', b. 1099, 'IV Armata'. On the history of the Principality of Monaco during the Second World War, see Abramovici, *Un rocher bien occupé*.

[41] ASMAE, GABAP, b. 30, document neither signed nor dated but certainly from the second half of 1941.

political-organizational affairs, the militia and the Ustaša political police. The supreme authority was the Ustaša General Command – with a role similar to that of the Grand Council of Fascism – presided over by the *poglavnik*.[42] The second sector, the Ustaša militia, had three main tasks: to secure the acquisitions resulting from the Ustaše's struggle and the revolution of the Croatian people, to defend the state and to train squads physically and militarily.[43] The third sector was 'the Ustaša control service' – a political police force similar to the Opera vigilanza repressione antifascista (OVRA, Anti-Fascism Intelligence Agency) – whose principal task was to supervise the work of the offices and organs of the state, autarkic bodies and the law enforcement agencies.

The Germans' policies were not affected in the slightest by Pavelić's accession to power, nor by the fact that the Croatian state was largely Fascist in its organization. Yugoslavia had been defeated and dismembered by Germany, not by Italy; Croatia had obtained its independence by virtue of Berlin, not of Rome; and now it was Berlin and not Rome that installed Pavelić at the helm of the new Croatian state. As we shall see, Rome rapidly lost its already scant political influence, and at no time did it gain control of Croatia's huge economic resources. As for the Germans, once they had taken over Croatia's manufacturing industry, they left it for Rome to negotiate with Zagreb on the awkward territorial and political issues now being exacerbated further by Dalmatian irredentism.

In 1941 and 1942 Italy and Croatia concluded a series of agreements: Croatia undertook not to create a war navy; permission was granted for Italian armed forces to transit along Croatia's part of the Adriatic coast; Italy agreed to provide military training for the Croatian army; a joint customs and currency regime was installed; privileges were granted to émigré citizens

[42] This consisted of twelve deputy leaders (*doglavniki*) and the assembly of the seven senior counsellors (*glavni pobočniki*), appointed and dismissed by the *poglavnik*. The General Command appointed by decree the fiduciaries and special commissioners, who were allocated among sections and offices. The periphery was organized into *stozeri* (provinces) governed by a *stozernik*, *logori* (districts) governed by a *logornik*, *tábori* (municipalities) governed by a *tabornik*, and *roji* (villages) governed by a *rojnik*. The members of the movement were 'first-category' citizens because, according to article 11 of the decree of 23 June, 'those who have served in the Ustaša militia are given priority in the allocation of state and public posts, and their families shall have precedence in obtaining land'.

[43] ASMAE, GABAP, b. 28, 'II Armata – UAC allo SMRE, 11 giugno 1941, Milizia ustascia'. According to this document the Ustaša militia was organized as follows: legion (*pukovinija*), cohort (*bojnica*), century (*satnija*), maniple (*vod*), squad (*roj*). The battalions were headed by the militia General Staff consisting of the commanders of the regular army units – the *domobrani* – and of special formations. The chief of General Staff was directly subordinate to the *poglavnik*, the supreme commander of all military forces.

of both countries; and cultural relationships were strengthened. But no agreement was reached in resolution of the 'Dalmatian question'.[44]

Now, in an endeavour to make up the ground lost to the Germans in the race for control of Croatia, the Italians attempted to carry through their plan for personal union: Aimone of Savoy (brother to Amedeo), Duke of Spoleto, was to be proclaimed king by the Sabor (assembly) and crowned Tomislav II at Dunansko Polje (Duvno) in Bosnia – as Tomislav I, the first Croatian king, had been in 925 BC. The project soon foundered, however, because of the Dalmatian question, and Aimone-Tomislav passed into history as the 'king that never was'.[45] Devoid of political experience and ignorant of the Italian government's exact intentions, he refused to leave for Croatia, saying so in letters to Victor Emmanuel and Mussolini, in which he told them that the question of Dalmatia, 'a land that could never be Italianized', was an obstacle against any reconciliation with the Croats. Never, he declared, would he agree to be king of a nation amputated from Italy.

After the failure of the plan for personal union, and until the armistice of September 1943, the Italians sought in vain to assert their hegemony in Croatia. The first opportunity arose in the summer of 1941, when the Ustaše, responsible for atrocities against the civilian population, proved unable to maintain law and order despite the barbarism of their repressive methods. To prevent the situation from degenerating, Berlin and Rome decided on complete occupation of Croatia. They established two occupation zones and a demarcation line extending from north to south through Samobor, Sarajevo and Ustipraca. The Italian authorities protested at the term 'demarcation line' because it suggested that Croatia had been divided into 'zones of influence'. They insisted that the expression be used in its merely conventional sense, 'adopted purely and simply for contingent

[44] Reale Accademia d'Italia, *Italia e Croazia*, 1942.

[45] Pavlowitch, 'The King *That* Never Was'; ASMAE, GABAP, b. 35, 'La corona del re Zvonimir, informazioni storiche raccolte dal MAE'. The letters to the king are conserved in GABAP, b. 28. Other documents concerning Aimone have been published in Amoretti, *La vicenda italo-croata*. Pietromarchi refers in his diary entry for 10 May 1941 to a meeting with the 'future king of Croatia'. Duke Aimone of Spoleto informed Pietromarchi that he would accept the crown only in obedience to the king, and then only very reluctantly. The duke was not at all convinced that it was necessary for him to accept the Croatian crown, and he was sceptical about the advantages that Italy would derive from his doing so. Pietromarchi explained the situation to him, saying that the original proposal had been personal union between Croatia and Italy, but because the example of Albania had alarmed the Croats it was now necessary to resort to the solution of a king from the House of Savoy. According to Volpi, if the new king had fully worked in the interests of the Croatian state he would have alienated Italy; if he had worked in the interests of Italy he would have been murdered.

military purposes'; otherwise it would remove 'every foundation from the reality acquired by the agreements with the Reich: Croatia, Italy's *spazio vitale*'.[46] This reality was in fact an illusion because Croatia was already a *Reichsprotektorat.*

On 26 August 1941, the Italians and Croats decided on their relative powers in the zone occupied by the Regio Esercito (see appendix, table 11).[47] The second zone, in which the Italian army wielded extensive powers, was created on 7 September; a third zone followed. The second zone was bounded to the north by the River Kolpa between Osilnica (excluded) and Zdikovo (this place name might be misspelled in the documents); to the west by a line drawn from Osilnica to the Pelješac (Sabbioncello) peninsula, including all the islands; to the south by a boundary extended from Gruda to Triglav; and to the east from Triglav to Zdikovo along the line between Bjolasca (possibly Bjelišca?) and Tounj. The third zone, where civil powers remained in the hands of the Croats, encompassed the territory between the boundaries of the second zone and the Italo-German demarcation line.

Despite the geographical extensiveness of the Italian military occupations in Croatia, the authorities in Rome and those *in loco* soon realized that it was impossible to penetrate Croatia economically and politically. In November, Ciano noted in his diary that there was no longer an Italo-Croatian problem, but rather an Italo-German problem with regard to Croatia. After meetings with Ribbentrop (24–26 November) and Pavelić (15–16 December), the foreign minister wrote: 'It seems that the boat is only just staying afloat . . . Everything depends on the Germans; . . . if . . . they force our hand and push their penetration further, all we can do is roll up our flags and go home.'[48]

At the end of 1941, the German military attaché in Rome, General Enno von Rintelen, proposed to Mussolini the wholesale occupation of Croatia.[49] The Germans' offer was prompted by awareness that their political and economic control over Croatia was now unassailable and that they had to send support to the Wehrmacht in Serbia, reinforcing it with troops presently deployed in the new Croatian state. At a meeting with the Duce on 18 December 1941, Ciano, Raffaele Casertano and Generals Mario Roatta (SMRE), Giovanni Magli (CS) and Vittorio Ambrosio (commander of

[46] DDI, ser. IX, 1939–43, vol. 8, doc. 606, 'ministro a Zagabria Casertano al ministro degli Esteri Ciano, 10 giugno 1942'.

[47] USSME, M 3, b. 45, 'Sintesi degli accordi stabiliti nella conferenza del 26 agosto 1941 a Zagabria'.

[48] The Italo-Croat permanent economic committee met in Abbazia (Opatija) on 15–16 November: 1941: DDI, ser. IX, 1939–43, vol. 8, doc. 26.

[49] DDI, ser. IX, 1939–43, vol. 8, doc. 40, 'comandante della II Armata Ambrosio al CSMG Ugo Cavallero, da palazzo Venezia, 18 dicembre 1941'.

the Second Army, Supersloda) made a realistic assessment of the German proposal. Ambrosio explained that occupation of the third zone was the 'basis for the occupation of the whole of Bosnia', while Italy's positions in the second zone should be consolidated by means of a large-scale campaign of political penetration, given that the zone delimited by the Dinaric Alps was both militarily and economically the natural completion of Italian Dalmatia.[50] He declared that all efforts would be in vain if the German position was not clarified. Two alternative solutions emerged from the discussion:

(1) withdrawal of all Regio Esercito troops into the second zone (Croatian littoral and Herzegovina), with the (secret) intention of its future annexation, leaving administration of the third zone to the Croats, in the hope that the trust placed in them would bring Zagreb within Italy's orbit; or

(2) complete occupation of the third zone, breach of the demarcation line and occupation of eastern Bosnia, with the dispatch of sufficient troops to 'surmount the obstacle of German economic penetration'.[51]

However, the Italian occupation of eastern Bosnia never came about. General Edmund Glaise von Horstenau, plenipotentiary at the German legation in Zagreb, warned the Croats of an 'Italian plan' for complete occupation of Croatia – though he omitted to mention that Rome's proposal was prompted by a request made expressly by the Germans. On 2 January 1942, General Ambrosio proposed the withdrawal of the occupation troops into the second zone and the progressive elimination of all Croatian influence.[52] Pietromarchi agreed that the occupation of the third zone could not be considered an end in itself, because it would require an expenditure of blood, money, energy and prestige absolutely disproportionate to the returns. Mussolini ordered Ambrosio to 'eliminate Croatian influence from the second zone and give the impression that Italy will never again

[50] ASMAE, GABAP, b. 33, 12 December 1941, 'Colloqui Ambrosio–Pietromarchi'; USSME, M 3, b. 45, 28 September 1941, 'Verbale della riunione tenuta a Venezia tra Volpi, Bastianini, Casertano, Pietromarchi e il generale Ambrosio'; ibid., 'Appunto dell'Ufficio Croazia': 'There is no alternative but to occupy only eastern Bosnia. On the day that this happens practically the whole of Croatia will be under our control. We will then be able to give a definitive structure to the country, culminating with the king's accession to the throne'; b. 46, 12 December 1941, 'Colloqui Ambrosio–Pietromarchi'.

[51] USSME, M 3, b. 59, 30 December 1941, 'Processo verbale della riunione di Ambrosio con tutti i capi di CdA di Supersloda'. During the meeting the general declared: 'The Germans must retreat from all the positions that they have acquired. It is not right to risk the lives of our soldiers and then be degraded to garrisoning the new localities while others lord it over the country.'

[52] USSME, N 1–11, 'Diari storici', b. 1361, 'Comando II Armata – Ufficio "I" allo SMRE – Ufficio Operazioni, 2 gennaio 1942, firmato Ambrosio', p. 5. This also contains the secret SMRE memorandum, 'Ufficio Operazioni, gennaio 1942'.

leave, to prevent the Croatian garrisons from receiving reinforcements, and to obtain definitive ejection of the Ustaše'.[53] (We shall see in chapter 6 what happened when, after 24 June 1942, the Italians withdrew into the second zone.)

Having decided not to relinquish their Balkan *spazio vitale*, the Italians considered further strategies with which to counter Nazi hegemony in the former Yugoslavia. After the occupation, and precisely because of the situation that had arisen in Croatia, they weighed up the so-called Bosnian solution. As early as 1940, the Foreign Ministry had drawn up a plan for the partitioning of Yugoslavia and the creation of a state of Bosnia-Herzegovina – 'the second Muslim entity of the imperial community' after Albania – which would enable Italy to exploit the region's abundant resources[54] (see appendix, tables 12–16). A report by the former consul in Sarajevo, Marcello Zuccolin (1923–38), recommended that Bosnia-Herzegovina be annexed to Italy: 'Bosnia', his report affirmed, 'possesses everything that we lack: timber and iron, coal, livestock, minerals . . ., certainly oil.' Zuccolin argued that the Muslims would be loyal Italian citizens provided they were allowed to preserve their traditions and to practise their faith like the Muslims in Albania and the colonies.[55]

General Giuseppe Pièche maintained that Bosnia-Herzegovina should be occupied separately from the rest of Croatia, for Italy could only reap advantages from separating off the richest region in the entire Balkans region. A potential adversary would be weakened by the creation of a counterweight consisting of more than two and a half million inhabitants, the majority of them Serbs and Muslims. The Dalmatian hinterland would be made secure, and 'for the first time in the history of unified Italy' the country would possess a region endowed with the huge natural resources that its industry required. Moreover, all the resources in the region were state-owned, with the consequence that Italy would not have to resort to difficult and costly private expropriations to take possession of them. Pièche declared that the Muslim community, if 'appropriately worked upon', was almost certain to support occupation, because it feared Croat chauvinism and Serb nationalism and manifested a desire for 'the protection of a strong regime' against the abuses and excesses of both.[56]

53 USSME, M 3, b. 59, 28 December 1941, 'Colloquio Ambrosio–Mussolini'.

54 ASMAE, AA.PP. – Jugoslavia, b. 105, 'console di Ragusa Tiberi alla Direzione generale del MAE', 12 April 1941; GABAP, b. 25, fasc. 1, 'Bosnia-Erzegovina'.

55 ASMAE, GABAP, b. 25, 'Abbazia 19 aprile 1941, Appunto per il Gabap dell'ex console Zuccolin'; USSME, M 3, b. 58, 'Comando II Armata, Ufficio "I", aprile 1942, Bosnia'.

56 USSME, M 3, b. 6, 9 September 1942, 'Relazione del generale Pièche al GABAP'.

The SMRE pointed out that no district in Bosnia-Herzegovina had a Croatian majority, and that no zone in the region was attracted to Croatia; moreover, there was 'an extremely strong independence movement' whose leaders would view Italian occupation as 'the best means to achieve their ends'. According to other sources, the region already had 'an autonomous Bosnian-Herzegovinian government' consisting of 'leading Serbian notables and the extremists in the Muslim movement', which had demanded that Pavelić grant it autonomy and whose members had been arrested.[57] In addition to this information, the consulate in Sarajevo provided lists of pro-Italian 'autonomists' and concurred that, if Bosnia-Herzegovina were detached from Croatia, the autonomist project would be viable. There was a faction within the Italian diplomatic corps, however, that was hostile to any such eventuality. It was led by Giuseppe Bastianini and by Pietromarchi, who noted in his diary that he was opposed to the idea of an Italian protectorate over Bosnia-Herzegovina, arguing instead that, whatever Croatia's sentiments towards Italy might be, the true enemies were the Serbs, who made no secret of their desire to regain access to the Adriatic by annexing Bosnia-Herzegovina, Montenegro and Dalmatia. Pietromarchi envisaged a Croatia 'able to curb a resumed offensive by a small Serbia' as the basis for Italian policy. In support of his thesis he cited Count Giuseppe Volpi, for whom Croatia protected Italy's possessions in the eastern Adriatic. Amputating 'Bosnia-Herzegovina as well as its Dalmatian territories from Croatia would create an inveterate enemy and induce it to join forces with Serbia in united assault against us'.[58]

At no stage of the conflict did the Italians 'play the Muslim card' in order to change the political structure of Croatia. The same applied to the Serbian minority in Bosnia, which was either squeezed into the 'small' Serbia or absorbed by the Croatian ethnic majority. During the two years of Italian military occupation, Croatia remained a *Reichsprotektorat* partly occupied by Italian troops with broad administrative powers and charged with the task of maintaining order and putting down the Resistance, but with no political power in Zagreb and, above all, no chance of achieving economic penetration and exploitation of Croatia.

Montenegro

In November 1940, a report by the MAE on the 'future arrangement of the Yugoslavian territory' proposed the creation of a small Montenegrin state

57 USSME, M 3, b. 5, SMRE, 'Ufficio Operazioni "I" – III sezione al CS, 8 dicembre 1941'.
58 Pietromarchi, diary, 27 February 1942.

with a structure that would replicate Albania's.[59] According to the extant documentation (which is extremely fragmentary), the military authorities endorsed the proposal. In 1941, Victor Emmanuel let it be known that he was in favour of restoration of his wife Elena's dynasty, the Petrovićs. But Ciano dissented, aware that restoration of the crown would fuel similar aspirations in Albania, while, for once, Mussolini agreed with Victor Emmanuel. The episode is reminiscent of the Aimone-Tomislav affair in Croatia: the king would have been chosen from among Elena's grandsons – Danilo, Michele or Roman (entirely unknown in Cetinje) – but since none of them accepted the throne, the idea was 'temporarily' shelved.[60]

Also in Montenegro events turned out very differently from what Rome foresaw. And on this occasion it was not solely because of intervention by the Germans, who were entirely uninterested in Montenegro, which lacked any strategic or economic value. The former Yugoslavian *banat* was left 'the fruit of its conquests in the Balkan wars', a small zone extending from Berane southwards to the Sanjak region, including the towns of Prijepolje, Bijelo Polje, Sjenica and a number of villages around Tutin and Rožaj, and with a minority of around 80,000 Muslim Albanians. It instead lost important territories largely inhabited by Montenegrins.[61] Italy assigned to Albania the region of Metohija situated on the southern border of Montenegro and comprising the town of Antivari (Bar), a strip of territory to the north of Lake Scutari, the town of Dulcino (Ulcinj, which had salt pans of importance to Montenegrin sheep-herders), territory to the north-east of Podgorica, a broad swathe of the district of Andrijevica with Plav (the Plav basin) and Gusinje. To the east, the Albanians obtained the whole of western and central Kosovo (including the towns of Prizren, Dragaš and Priština,[62] which Commissioner Serafino Mazzolini called 'living space that guaranteed bread' for Montenegro. Mitrovica and the Ibar Valley (with the important zinc mines of Trepča), Kukavica, Podujevo and Medvedja remained with German-occupied Serbia. The Germans occupied

[59] ASMAE, GABAP, b. 50, 'Relazione sull'opera svolta dall'alto commissario Mazzolini al ministro Ciano, luglio–agosto 1941' (undated); ASMAE, AA.PP. – Jugoslavia, b. 105, 'console di Ragusa Tiberi alla Direzione generale del MAE, 12 aprile 1941'.

[60] ASMAE, GABAP, b. 48, states the reasons for the Petrovićs' refusal of the throne.

[61] ASMAE, GABAP, b. 48, 'Ciano all'Alto commissariato per il Montenegro a Cettigne, 9 luglio 1941'. The boundary between the governorate and Albania was considered 'purely moral and merely administrative in purpose'. Albania and Montenegro belonged to the same customs union, and until conversion of the dinar their currencies were pegged to a fixed exchange rate with the lira.

[62] ASMAE, AA.PP. – Jugoslavia, b. 106, conserves the copy of a note not unlike the one that Ciano took with him to Vienna, followed by a second one with the results of the meeting; DDI, ser. IX, 1939–43, vol. 7, doc. 367, 'ministro degli Esteri Ciano all'alto commissario per il Montenegro Mazzolini, Roma 9 luglio 1941'; see also docs. 369, 372, 384.

the eastern part of the Sanjak, including the strategically important town of Novi Pazar, leaving part of the Sanjak to the Croats on the specious pretext that this would create a buffer between Montenegro and Serbia – thus increasing tension with the Italians, who were reluctant to satisfy Zagreb's demands.[63] Also Foča and Čajnice were assigned to Croatia, while Kotor was annexed to Italy. The Montenegro–Croatia border followed the course of the River Lim in the Drina region as far as Hum, and then continued to Dobričevo and the sea. According to the Duce, this line was 'the fairest from the ethnic point of view' 'because the ethnic criterion should have absolute precedence over the religious criterion if constructive and enduring work is to be done'.[64]

On 18 April 1941, the commander of the 18th Army Corps, General Giuseppe Pafundi, received from the lieutenant general of Albania, Francesco Jacomoni, a letter approving the formation of a committee for the liberation of Montenegro 'spontaneously constituted in Tirana' and whose members would serve as a provisional government under the aegis of Italy.[65] The 'Interim Administration Committee' was installed in Cetinje and was symbolically vested with civil powers after the 'liberation'. Decision-making power remained with the Italian military authorities, which replaced the government of the *banovina*, appointing sub-committees in various municipalities and reactivating the civil services.[66] The committee (rather like a decoy) served solely to attract Montenegrin separatist political groups such as the *zelenasi* (greens), and to avert administrative chaos.

The installation of civil commissioners, similar to those in Dalmatia and Slovenia, did not signify that Rome had opted for annexation of Montenegro to Italy, although some ordinances suggested that the country was on the point of becoming an Italian province. Italian flags were distributed with orders that they be flown immediately, photographs of the Duce and the king were displayed in public offices, and the Roman salute was made compulsory. Measures were taken to establish the Fascist party organizations, and the press was subjected to stringent censorship. The financing of public bodies, insurance institutes and banks was supervised by Italian experts. The

63 ASMAE, GABAP, b. 28, 'Ministero dell'Interno – DGPS al GABAP – Ufficio Croazia, 27 giugno 1941'; b. 48, 10 May 1941, 'Relazione del capitano Ugo Villani'.

64 ASMAE, GABAP, b. 28, 'lettera di Pavelić – vista dal Duce – del 23 giugno 1941 e risposta di Mussolini del 30 cm'. On the question of the boundaries between Montenegro and Croatia, see DDI, ser. IX, 1939–43, vol. 7, docs. 381, 383, 384, 387, 699, 709.

65 Scotti and Viazzi, *Le aquile delle montagne nere*, p. 54; ASMAE, GABAP, b. 52, fasc. a81, 'Aspirazioni montenegrine, con la lista dei membri della consulta amministrativa'.

66 USSME, N 1–11, 'Diari storici', b. 2245, 'maggiore del SIM Alfredo Angeloni, Cettigne, al generale Cavallero, Com. sup. Superalba, Tirana, 26 aprile 1941'; ASMAE, GABAP, b. 51, 'comitato provvisorio al presidente della Corte di cassazione di Podgoritza, Cettigne 20 aprile 1941'.

schools were closed and ordered not to re-open until the end of the year.[67] On 28 April, judicial power was transferred to the civil commissioner of Cetinje, Mazzolini, who was subordinate to the High Command of Armed Forces Albania – styled Superalba.[68] On 22 May, the Interim Administration Committee was dissolved, while the Yugoslavian public functionaries, including sub-prefects, revenue officers and gendarmes, remained in their posts after they had sworn an oath of allegiance to Italy.[69] On 19 June, the Civil Commission became the High Commission (as in Ljubljana) and Mazzolini was appointed high commissioner (like Emilio Grazioli) representing the MAE.[70] In early June, he assembled a collaborationist 'consultative council' (sixty-five deputies in Italy's pay) in Cetinje and convened the Constitutional Assembly to 'declare the restoration of Montenegro'.[71]

On 12 July the declaration was approved by acclamation. Montenegro's servitude to Serbia was abolished, as was the dynasty of the Karageorgevićs, and the constitution of 1931. Montenegro was proclaimed a sovereign and independent state taking the form of a constitutional monarchy which would share its life and its destiny with Italy: it would enter 'Rome's orbit' after the relative accords had been stipulated. The National Assembly, in the absence of a head of state, decided to institute a regency (similar to the Lieutenancy of Albania) and requested the king to nominate a regent of the kingdom of Montenegro who would promulgate the statute. The government would be headed by the sovereign and by the regent acting on his behalf with the power to appoint and dismiss the prime minister, who was answerable only to the king. The ministers would remain in office but would exercise no effective powers.[72] On 13 July 1941, a few hours

[67] Scotti and Viazzi, *Le aquile delle montagne nere*, p. 60.

[68] ASMAE, GABAP, b. 51, 25 April 1941, 'Bando del duce concernente l'amministrazione della giustizia nei territori occupati dalle forze armate italiane'.

[69] ASMAE, GABAP, b. 51, 'Cettigne 26 maggio 1941, Dichiarazione di lealismo'; b. 48, letter of 5 May from Mazzolini to the MAE following the latter's order that all civil servants must swear allegiance to the Italian government.

[70] ASMAE, GABAP, b. 51, 'Bando del duce, disposizioni concernenti i poteri dell'alto commissario per i territori del Montenegro'.

[71] DDI, ser. IX, 1939–43, vol. 7, docs. 375, 379, 382, 389, 391, 398, 419.

[72] Scotti and Viazzi, *Le aquile delle montagne nere*, p. 74; ASMAE, GABAP, b. 48, 'Pietromarchi a Mazzolini, 8 luglio 1941': The head of the GABAP reminded the high commissioner that 'with the annexation of the Sanjak a considerable number of Muslims will become Montenegrin subjects. I believe that their presence in a rather higher percentage than previously in Montenegro should somehow be made evident by a distinctive sign (a half-moon or similar) on emblems and the national flag . . . A solution should be adopted which impresses upon . . . the Muslim community that it is not entirely extraneous to the Montenegro state apparatus.' See also b. 48, 'alto commissario al MAE, Cettigne 9 luglio 1941, Statuto del Montenegro'; the same envelope contains Mazzolini's allocution and the texts of all the speeches made to the National Assembly.

after the declaration of independence, revolt erupted and the Kingdom of Montenegro was already defunct.

On 25 July 1941, General Alessandro Pirzio Biroli – formerly governor of Asmara – was invested by Mussolini with full military and civil powers in Montenegro and authorized to appoint a new civil commissioner if and when he considered it necessary.[73] Pirzio Biroli was appointed governor in October 1941. Repression of the revolt lasted for around a month: pacification was not achieved, but the Italian troops slowly regained control of the territory. In reports sent to Rome on 2 and 12 August, Pirzio Biroli wrote that Montenegro was cramped by borders that deprived it of all autonomy and that had created a 'spiritual situation of discontent, distrust and resentment at the precarious economic and political situation'. The economy could be self-sufficient only if it included Kotor and Dubrovnik, the Herzegovinian belt as far as the Drina region, Novi Pazar and the Sanjak, Metohija and the whole of Kosovo (which was also important for sentimental reasons).[74] Pirzio Biroli proposed two solutions: either formal independence, with narrow boundaries if necessary but including Kotor ('the lung through which Montenegro breathes') or annexation to Italy, with consequent division into three or four provinces (Giacomo Scotti and Luciano Viazzo believe that the general preferred the latter solution).[75] According to Pirzio Biroli's sources, should annexation to Serbia not prove possible, the Montenegrins would prefer annexation to Italy rather than independence. He added that if Montenegro's borders persisted in their present form, creating an independent state would be risky, because the elements essential for its survival would not exist unless Italy provided entirely for the needs of its inhabitants. Independence would only be practicable if the borders were altered so that they were geographically and ethnically 'fair'. Annexation was the fall-back solution if territorial amputation was maintained as it was, because the territory would never be able to support itself. Throughout the period of the Italian occupation Montenegro remained a military governorate.

Greece

In Greece, 'Mussolini's intention was to create an independent state within the Italian zone of influence, but not with all the provinces and islands of

[73] ASMAE, GABAP, b. 50, 'CS al GABAP, Poteri civili e militari nel Montenegro'.
[74] USSME, M 3, b. 4, fasc. 13, 'Com. sup. FF.AA. Albania, Ufficio Operazioni dello SM, al CS, Situazione in Montenegro, firmato Pirzio Biroli'.
[75] Scotti and Viazzi, *Le aquile delle montagne nere*, pp. 249–50.

1940.'[76] With respect to its original project for expansion, Rome was only able to accomplish the *de facto* annexation of the Ionian islands. A German veto precluded the inclusion of a territorial clause in the armistice which would have permitted annexation of the Cyclades and the Sporades, the separation of the Epirus and Akarnania regions from the rest of Hellenic territory, and the annexation to Albania of the territory between the Hellenic north-western frontier and the Florina-Pindus-Arta-Prevesa line.[77]

The Fascist project for domination had never foreseen that a territory of the *spazio vitale* would be occupied in condominium. For Rome this was a major setback: every decision had to be endorsed by the Germans, and Italy was also forced to accept the Bulgarian occupation of Thrace and the eastern part of the Macedonian province, as well as the German occupation of Hellenic Macedonia, including Salonika, and the islands of Lemnos, Mytilene, Chios, Skyros, Melos, Kitira, Anti-Kitira and Crete. There were numerous German enclaves in Italian territory: the coasts of Attica and the Piraeus, the islands of Salamis, Egina and Euboea (though this was transferred to the Italians in October 1941) and the airfields of Larissa, Araxos and Molai. Furthermore, the Wehrmacht's troops remained in Athens and the German navy patrolled the Hellenic coasts of the Aegean. The defence of Crete depended on the German Command, while Italy's Siena Division occupied the eastern part of the island, the zone comprising the Bay of Mirabello, Agios Nikolaos, Sitia, Ierapetra and the plateau of Lasithi. The Greek regions (nomarchies) occupied by the Regio Esercito were Epirus (Jannina, Thesprotia, Preveza and Arta constituting the 'reserved zone'); Thessaly (Trikala and Larissa, partially a reserved zone); Hellas (Etolia and Akarnania, Focide, Attica and Boeotia and Euboea); the Peloponnese (Achaia, Argolida and Corinth, Messenia, Arcadia, Laconia and Elis); the Ionian islands (Corfu, Cephalonia and Zakynthos); and the Aegean islands (Cyclades and southern Sporades, at the end of 1941).

The demarcation line with the Germans began at the eastern shore of Lake Presba and followed the ridge dividing Kastoria, Neapolis and Grevenà from Florina Kozani as far as Mount Olympus and the River Penaeus, which

[76] USSME, I 13, b. 105, *Con l'XI Armata nella guerra contro la Grecia*, typescript by General Geloso, p. 185.

[77] DDI, ser. IX, 1939–43, vol. 6, doc. 968, 'Belgrado 22 aprile 1941, Colloquio del ministro degli Esteri Ciano con il ministro tedesco': 'Ribbentrop was in full agreement with our territorial claims as I put them to him yesterday . . . The Führer concurs that no decision should be taken before the end of the general conflict. However, he feels obliged to inform the Duce that the king of Bulgaria, at a recent meeting with him, had claimed Salonika on the grounds that it is Macedonia's natural outlet to the sea. The Führer had reserved his reply, but Ribbentrop added that the request was viewed with sympathy by Hitler.'

formed the southern border of the German territory. The Germans installed a puppet government headed by General George Tsolakoglou in which the Greeks had absolutely no confidence, and which, according to General Geloso, was manipulated by the Germans and was certainly 'Italophobic'.[78] Not only did the executive in Athens enjoy no support or prestige in the country, it was devoid of any organizational and administrative ability.[79]

The reserved zone: the Pindus and Ciamuria

Among the various projects for the dismemberment of Greece, particular mention should be made of the 'reserved zone' comprising Epirus, the so-called Ciamuria (or Tsamurja, the name of a group of Greek districts) and the Pindus, the chain of mountains whose name the Italians used when referring to the zone comprising the towns and villages inhabited by the Aromanian minority (Kastoria, Grevenà, Jannina, Samarina, Preveza, Konitza and Trikala). Unfortunately, the scant documentation that still survives cannot be used to determine Rome's intentions for these areas. Palazzo Chigi communicated its plans for the partitioning to the commanders of the Eleventh Army, who, once in Greece, divided its various populations into Greek, Jewish, Bulgarian, Armenian, Aromanian and Ciamuriota and surveyed every village's number of inhabitants, its main political and economic activities, and its attitudes towards the occupiers.[80]

In early 1941, amid various proposals for the organization of the Hellenic territory, the idea was mooted of creating an Aromanian state, or a 'territorial union of Cephalonia, Corfu and Preveza by means of a "corridor" between Albania and old Greece'.[81] The MAE had already compiled an 'Aromanian dossier' before the war, and at the appropriate moment it would be brought out to demonstrate that a 'semi-nomadic Aromanian people' had settled in the Pindus mountains in western Greek Macedonia and Thessaly.

78 USSME, I 13, b. 105, *Con l'XI Armata nella guerra contro la Grecia*, pp. 184–5.

79 DDI, ser. IX, 1939–43, vol. 7, doc. 402, 'Ghigi, plenipotenziario d'Italia per la Grecia, al ministro degli Esteri Ciano, Atene 18 luglio 1941'; doc. 533, 3 September 1941.

80 USSME, N 1–11, 'Diari storici', b. 322, 'Comando Divisione di fanteria Pinerolo, Ufficio del CSM, sezione "I"'. See also I 15, b. 23, 'Comando Divisione Forlì, sezione "I", Colonie rumene in Grecia'. These, by way of example, were the figures for Kastoria: '(b) Israelite . . . circa 2,000 Israelites . . . they speak Spanish fluently . . .; (c) Aromanian: people of Aromanian stock are little represented in Kastoria, having been absorbed and assimilated by the Greek community. Important Aromanian communities are scattered across the entire zone of Kastoria and Grevenà . . . where the concentration of groups besides the uniqueness of their activity (sheep-herding) has kept their character pure and their political attitude distinct . . . they are anti-Bulgarian and anti-Greek, pro-Italian and pro-Romanian . . . They apparently amount to some several thousands in the zone of Kastoria.'

81 USSME, N 1–11, 'Diari storici', b. 664, 'Comando Divisione di fanteria Pinerolo – UAC al Comando del III CdA, 14 agosto 1941'.

According to a report by Randi, the Aromanians were descended from the ancient Romans: 'they lived among the mountains for centuries sheltering against the invasions of the barbarians, then to reappear with the name of *valacchi*, *vlasi* (in Croat *vlaj*, in Greek *vlakos*), *morlacchi* (a contraction of the Veneto *mauro-valacco*) or *aromuni* (*arumeni*)'.[82] This community of approximately 500,000 individuals was the 'most important minority on Greek soil'.[83]

Between 1939 and 1941, the 'Ciamurioti' – or the Muslim minority residing in north-west Greece in the areas of Gomenitsa (Igoumenitsa), Jannina, Belica, Sarandopores, Argirocastro and Konitza – were also subject to study by the Fascist regime. An article in *Geopolitica* claimed that the Epirus–Akarnania region belonged to Albania rather than Greece, and that it formed 'a single geographic system' with the Adriatic zone. The region was ethnically 'Dynaric' because 'Illyrians and Albanians once constituted the core of its population together with Italiots immigrated there in prehistoric times.' The millenary influence exerted by Rome and Venice over the region proved that Italy had 'rights' to it (possession of the Ionian islands implied extension of Italian influence to Epirus and Akarnania, as well as the extension of Albanian sovereignty to the Ciamuria).[84]

According to the findings of the Greek census conducted in 1936, the province of Thesprotia comprising the three districts of the Ciamuria was inhabited by 20,000 Orthodox Greeks, 26,000 Orthodox Albanians and 28,000 Muslim Albanians residing in the towns of Filiates, Paramithia and Margariti. But to whom, exactly, did the Italian authorities refer when they used the term Ciamurioti? According to Geloso, the Ciamurioti of Albanian tongue and Muslim religion, 'without pronounced Albanian ethnic features, were a Muslim people excluded from the exchange of populations between Turkey and Greece provided for by the Treaty of Lausanne (1923)'. Forced Hellenization and political persecution had fuelled fierce hatred of

[82] ASMAE, GABAP, b. 25, *Dalmazia*, typescript by O. Randi: 'In the fourteenth century, the Turkish invasion dispersed [the Aromanians] among Macedonia, Thessaly and the Pindus. The Aromanian communities (nomadic or settled) of the Pindus, of south-western Macedonia and Thessaly spoke *cutzo-vlach*, a variant of Romanian. They boasted their descent from Roman colonists in order to distinguish themselves from the Daco-Romanians, the Vlach minority of Romania, and from the Illyro-Romanians or Morlachs inhabiting Dalmatia and the Dinaric Alps.' See Colonna di Cesarò, *L'Italia nella Albania meridionale*; Graziani, 'Gli aromeni del Pindo', 1941; see also the monograph by Antonio Baldacci, professor at the University of Bologna, entitled *Il Pindo, uno stato da sé*, in ASMAE, GABAP, b. 25.

[83] USSME, I 15, b. 12, 'capo ufficio colonnello Arturo Scattini'. In July 1940, the Macedonian Aromanians, through the Italian plenipotentiary in Romania, Pellegrino Ghigi, asked for annexation to Albania so that a 'common ethnic living space' could be formed.

[84] Cappuccio, *Epiro, Acarnania ed isole Jonie*, 1941.

Athens, a hatred exacerbated by the agrarian reforms of 1919, which on the pretext of combating the Turkish latifundium system, had in fact led to the Christian-Orthodox colonization of the region.[85] During the Italo-Greek war, the general added, the Muslims had profited from the turmoil to avenge the abuses that they had suffered in the previous twenty years, and a spiral of feuds and vendettas had stained the region with blood. Immediately following the occupation, a number of Ciamurioti asked – through their local political leader Ahmed Dino – for Prevesa and the Ciamurioti districts to be annexed to Albania.[86] Rome appointed Gemil Dino Albanian civil commissioner for the Ciamuria. According to Jacomoni, the lieutenant of Albania, who more than anyone else had backed the separatist cause, Gemil Dino's administration should have coincided with the transfer of the forces stationed in Ciamuria (the 26th Army Corps) from the High Command of Armed Forces Greece to Superalba. This would have sent a clear signal to Athens and the Germans of Italian intentions in the region.[87] The commissioner (married to the daughter of the Albanian prime minister Shefqet Vërlaçi) was to receive all necessary support from Tirana in the campaign to 'Albanianize' the region, and his powers would extend from the Albanian frontier as far as Jannina. However, the population of that town (in which there resided 16,000 Muslims, 2,500 Jews and 14,500 Greeks), fearful of imminent annexation by the Albanians, raised a rebellion.[88] Consequently, owing to the tension caused by ethnic clashes in the region, and even before Dino's arrival, the military authorities ordered discontinuation of the separatist pro-Albanian policy. The commander of the 26th Army Corps, Guido Della Bona, explained to the army command that, if the Greek population were given the choice between Albanian or Italian annexation, they would certainly opt for the latter. According to Della Bona, 'spiritual and political assimilation into Italy' would be accomplished straightforwardly only if the operation were entrusted to select and prestigious personnel, and if Carabinieri were stationed in each village prior to annexation.

[85] USSME, I 15, b. 85, 'Informazioni fino alle ore 20 del giorno 8 maggio 1941': 'In Ciamuria from November until today around 600 persons have been murdered; the Greeks have been especially brutal in the Gomaniça and Grekohari zone . . . moreover, many Muslim families have been stripped of their possessions and cattle. It seems that there have been other killings in the Paramithia zone (12 May 1941).'

[86] ASMAE, AA.PP. – Jugoslavia, b. 105, 'telegramma di Ahmed Dino al MAE, 1 maggio 1941'.

[87] ASMAE, GABAP, b. 51, 'CS al GABAP – Ufficio Grecia, 18 luglio 1941'; USSME, I 15, b. 25, 'telegramma cifrato per il Com. sup. FF.AA. Grecia, 3 agosto 1941'; b. 27, 'Com. sup. FF.AA. Grecia al CS, 30 settembre 1941'.

[88] USSME, I 15, b. 22, 'Comando XXV CdA al Com. sup. FF.AA. Grecia, 20 luglio 1941, Relazione settimanale'; b. 25, 3 agosto 1941.

The 'Ciamuriota question' was then shelved for the duration of the war. The region was garrisoned by Italian military personnel who ensured that civil affairs were managed properly, and that the Albanian communities were protected, doing so in co-ordination with the plenipotentiary in Athens, Ghigi. The influence of the Lieutenancy of Tirana was drastically curbed.[89] When conducting an inspection of the region, the diplomat Carlo Umiltà reported as follows: 'there was not even a shadow' of an Albanian in Kastoria; Grevenà was Aromanian and Metzovo was a mix of Aromanian and Greek; Jannina, Arta and Prevesa were Greek; in all these localities the population was determined not to become part of the Albanian state: 'the idea of annexing these places to Albania was absurd and the entire population would have rebelled'. Umiltà added: 'the reasons that persuaded our government to make the proposal neither I, nor many other Italians and Albanians, in Rome and in Tirana, have ever been able to fathom'.[90] And at the end of 1941 he declared that 'of Ciamuria it is better never to speak further'. Rome fully agreed. Still today, given that the Fascist archives on Albania (deposited in the archives of the Italian Ministry of Foreign Affairs) are closed to researchers, we know little more about those reasons than Umiltà did at the time.

The actual occupation of the *spazio vitale* came about in circumstances that differed entirely from those envisaged by the Fascist regime's plans for expansion. The fact that Germany's assistance in the conquests was indispensable meant that Italy's ambitions for living space and an imperial community were thwarted. Armistices, frontiers and governments were established and controlled from Berlin while Rome played second string – although, once the Italians had gained a foothold in the Balkans and France, they sought to carve out a broader role for themselves than their ally was willing to grant.

[89] USSME, I 15, b. 27, 'rappresentanza d'Italia per la Grecia al Com. sup. FF.AA. Grecia, 3 novembre 1941, Situazione zone riservate'.
[90] Umiltà, *Jugoslavia e Albania*, 1947.

CHAPTER 4

Mussolini, the civil and military authorities and the co-ordination of occupation policies

This chapter describes the organs of the Fascist state and the structures responsible for decisions concerning the civil and military co-ordination of occupation policies. It discusses the role of Mussolini and examines the metropolitan and colonial apparatus, the intention being to clear the field of clichés and stereotypes which have long accompanied study of the Fascist state. I refer to claims of its intrinsic dysfunctionality or the irrationality of its decision-makers and of the Duce himself. The chapter deliberately eschews the use of notions like defeatism or carelessness or some presumed 'Italian' way of doing things as the *a priori* causes of the inefficiency of Italian bureaucracy and the Italian army. Unfortunately, owing to gaps in the archival materials it will not be possible to shed light on the tasks and roles of the various ministries, the PNF, the Milizia Volontaria Sicurezza Nazionale (MVSN, Voluntary Fascist Militia) and the judiciary in the territories conquered after 1940.

MUSSOLINI'S ROLE

Conceived in futurist and millenarian terms, the Mussolinian 'grand design' was to be achieved through Fascistization of Italy and totalitarization of the country. Historians such as Philippe Burrin, Emilio Gentile and Pierre Milza have highlighted a number of similarities between Fascist totalitarianism and the Nazi regime: the single party, mobilization of the masses into paramilitary organizations, the omnipotence of the charismatic leader, the obsessive use of propaganda and the institutionalization of a repressive system.[1] But they have also emphasized certain differences between Fascism and the Nazi or Stalinist versions of totalitarianism. The latter sought to eradicate the state, or considered it to be a contingent structure, whereas

[1] Burrin, *Fascisme, nazisme, autoritarisme*; Gentile, *Il culto del littorio*; Gentile, *La via italiana al totalitarismo*; Milza, *Mussolini*, pp. 658–826.

Italian Fascism closely identified with the state. Indeed, in the ideal view of the regime's evolution, the state would absorb the party and assume all its functions.

The Fascist dictatorship can be called neither 'Mussolinism' nor a classic authoritarian regime unable to impose the primacy of the party on the state and give concrete form to its totalitarian project. Its distinctive feature was the progressive centralization of powers to the person of Mussolini, the charismatic leader – in Max Weber's sense of the term[2] – of a regime intent on realizing its totalitarian designs. Before Italy entered the war, Mussolini had accumulated among his offices those of head of government, prime minister, secretary of state, general secretary of the Fascist Party and commander general of the MVSN. After 1933, he was chairman of the Supreme Defence Council and minister of war, the navy and the air force. In March 1938, following a 'spontaneous' vote by the Chamber of Deputies and the Senate, and a contemporaneous decision by the king, he was elevated to the rank of 'first marshal of the Empire': a manoeuvre functional to Mussolini's determination to do away with the monarchy as soon as a suitable opportunity arose. In early 1939, the Chamber of Deputies, an already powerless body, was replaced by the Camera dei Fasci e delle Corporazioni, an assembly of unelected Fascist dignitaries which consisted of the directors, heads, presidents and secretaries of the regime's collegial organs (the National Party Council, members of the National Party Directorate, the federal secretaries, the presidents of national associations like that for disabled ex-servicemen). Mussolini and the members of the Grand Council obviously sat in the Camera dei Fasci in a personal capacity. It was permanent in nature and when a member was removed from his post he was replaced by a designated successor. This system was directly controlled by Mussolini, who had the right to reject any nomination made by the party.

Gentile has pointed out that the PNF performed a decisive function in the Fascistization of society, and that it was an instrument of social mediation which operated through a system of political representation that

[2] Kershaw, *Hitler*, provided a definition of this concept and applied it to the case of the Third Reich. I believe that it can be extended in large part to Mussolini and Italian Fascism. Max Weber examines charisma from the point of view of the adepts' perception of it, not as a quality inherent in an individual. He examines the expectations that a given group of people (a society or a nation) place in an allegedly charismatic leader. The latter, believing it his destiny to fulfil his mission, requires the others to obey and serve him. If a given group of people recognizes the leader's virtues of heroism and grandeur, he will be proclaimed chief, and his partisans will become part of a charismatic community bound by a common faith to their leader and his mission. By rejecting routine, charismatic authority is unstable and doomed to self-destruction.

the end of parliamentarianism had not definitively eliminated. The PNF was not politically liquidated at the end of the 1920s (with the exit from the scene of the *ras* of Cremona, Roberto Farinacci). Mussolini used it to maintain order and in his attempts to organize the social body, to imbue the masses with Fascist ideology and to fuel the myth and the cult of his person. It was to the PNF that Mussolini gave the twofold mission of transforming the passive compliance of the masses into active participation and of forging the human material needed by the Duce to 'make History'. Yet, although the PNF performed crucial tasks for the regime, it had no decision-making autonomy in that it was entirely subordinate to Mussolini. Moreover, at the moment of Italy's entry into the war, the PNF had failed to carry out the tasks given it by the Duce: Italian society was far from being Fascisticized, and a Fascist ruling class able to take the place of the traditional élites had not been created. As we shall see in the next chapter, the PNF played a secondary role in the territories conquered after 1940. This is not to imply that Mussolini deliberately excluded it from his plans for conquest of the *spazio vitale*. More simply, given that the PNF had failed in its tasks, and given that its role was in any case subordinate to that of the state, the party transferred its main prerogatives of Fascistization to the territories of the *piccolo spazio* and worked alongside the other organs of the state in the territories of the *grande spazio*.

The concentration of powers in Mussolini's hands was partly impeded by the monarchy and the army, which were the only two institutions, apart from the PNF, to some extent able to oppose him. While it is true that Philippe Burrin's *compromis autoritaire* (Mussolini's compromise with the conservative forces in the country: the church, the monarchy, the army and the industrialists) set limits on his ambitions, it also restricted those of the king and his generals. Up until 25 July 1943, the 'dyarchy' worked in Mussolini's favour as he progressively stripped the king of his powers until he yielded and accepted Mussolini's decisions. As for the army, although it was not – to paraphrase the title of a book by Omer Bartov[3] – 'Mussolini's army', it wavered between loyalty to the king (and therefore bowing to the will of the Duce) and the desire of some of its cadres to exploit the opportunities for promotion offered by complicity with the regime. Until 1943, the army remained obedient to the regime and to its head, who did not hesitate to replace even the highest-ranking officers if necessary: to cite some celebrated examples, Emilio De Bono at the beginning of the Ethiopia campaign, Pietro Badoglio after the catastrophic campaign

[3] Bartov, *Hitler's Army*.

in Greece, or Rodolfo Graziani in the aftermath of the defeats in North Africa.

Until 1936 Mussolini personally ran the government and the PNF, as well as domestic and foreign policy. He monopolized numerous ministerial appointments and, unlike Hitler, he was ubiquitously present in all aspects of the life of the state. After the war in Ethiopia, he divested himself of some of these positions, for example by giving the job of foreign minister to Ciano, but at the same time he substantially curtailed the power of the collegial organs (as happened in Nazi Germany). Between 1940 and the fateful meeting of 25 July 1943, the Grand Council did not assemble even once (and the Council of Ministers was certainly not the place where important decisions were taken). This does not mean that Mussolini ceased to be the Fascist regime's centre of power. On the contrary, the stripping of the collegial organs of their powers, the delegation of public affairs, and his sole and absolute control and co-ordination of the state reinforced Mussolini's charismatic power and enabled him to work towards realization of his 'grand design'. Like Hitler, Mussolini was able to augment his power by the dynamism deriving from conflict among various other power centres, by the duel between state and party, the resolution of which was referred for arbitration to himself. This process radicalized – though less evidently than in Nazi Germany – the regime's policies, and it encouraged Mussolini's collaborators and his power centres to anticipate his wishes (the notion of 'working towards the Führer' introduced by Ian Kershaw with reference to the Third Reich can be extended to Fascist Italy), while at the same time increasing his charismatic authority and his power as the supreme arbiter.[4]

While waiting for the single party to wither away, and for the monarchy to be eliminated, the Duce built up his power. Had he not been obliged to reckon with the weight of certain hierarchs unwilling to cede their posts to technocrats, he would willingly have governed with a cabinet of general directors of the public administration, so profoundly pessimistic was he about human nature and so suspicious of the bureaucracy's opportunism. Milza has observed that Mussolini attempted to govern in this manner between January and May 1941 by sending Fascist ministers to the front. Only the vehement protests of those concerned induced him to abandon the experiment after the armistice with Greece. Milza's discussion is particularly insightful in its treatment of the conquered territories, where the *compromis autoritaire*, the recalcitrance of the hierarchs and the situation of

[4] Kershaw, 'Working Towards the Führer'; Kershaw, *Hitler 1889–1936*, chap. 13.

the war induced Mussolini to attempt the operation. After all, what were the governor of Dalmatia, Giuseppe Bastianini, the high commissioner for Ljubljana, Emilio Grazioli, the high commissioner for Montenegro, Serafino Mazzolini, or even the military governor of Montenegro himself, General Alessandro Pirzio Biroli, if not lieutenant-director generals belonging to the civil service? In the occupied territories, Mussolini (like Hitler) delegated some of his powers to trusted technocrats – lieutenants – many of whom did not belong to a ministry and periodically returned to Rome to confer with him. They received instructions and guidelines on the policies to implement in the conquered territories, whence they returned to work 'towards the Duce'.

Mussolini also exercised overriding decision-making power and control as military leader or, one might say, as a *condottiere*. Fortunato Minniti has pointed out that in Fascist Italy strategy coincided with the art of warfare typified by the figure of the *condottiere*, who 'drew up plans, made the decisions and carried through the operations'.[5] Conduct of the war was the Duce's political task, with the assistance of a military adviser, the chief of General Staff, while conduct of operations was assigned to the general commands of the army, navy and air force, these being co-ordinated, though not commanded, by the Stato Maggiore Generale (SMG, Joint General Staff). Mussolini emptied the SMG of its functions and took over as minister of war, delegating the ministerial function to the undersecretaries and to the chiefs of the Stato Maggiore (SM, General Staff) of the army, navy and air force. This decision gave the latter more power – in that their incumbency of government offices meant that they exercised full control over their forces – and removed it from the chief of the SMG. At the same time it gave the chiefs of the SM privileged access to Mussolini and further strengthened his power. The SMG's demotion, writes Minniti, was accompanied by a further cleavage at institutional level when Mussolini, following his appointment as First Marshal of the Empire, wrested from the king nominal command of the armed forces in the event of war and then took effective power by removing it from the chief of SMG, thereby adding strategic-operational military powers to his political-administrative ones. He thus wielded, albeit by proxy, effective powers of command and appropriated the king's prerogatives as commander of the nation's armed forces.

[5] Minniti, 'Profili dell'iniziativa strategica italiana'. The definition in the main text is taken from the entry 'Strategia' in the *Enciclopedia Italiana* (vol. XXXII, Rome 1936, pp. 823–4), written by General Carlo Geloso, later commander of the Italian troops in Greece. See also Rochat, 'Il ruolo delle forze armate nel regime fascista'.

The chief of SMG, Badoglio (who was replaced by General Ugo Cavallero and then in February 1943 by General Vittorio Ambrosio), was 'an office head charged with the compilation and issue of orders' squeezed between Mussolini and the SM of the armed forces. The curtailment of the SMG, which on 20 May 1941 took the name of Comando Supremo (CS, Supreme Command), and the centralization of powers to Mussolini, became manifest with the appointment of Ubaldo Soddu, under-secretary at the War Ministry, as deputy chief of the SMG. Mussolini thus sanctioned the pre-eminence of the army over the other branches of the armed forces. By virtue of his twofold appointment as deputy chief of SMG and under-secretary at the War Office, Soddu (and then Guzzoni) was able to act as intermediary between the SMG and the SM of the army in the same way as his navy and air force colleagues had been doing for some time. When Italy entered the war, the CS was responsible for military strategy and deployment of all the country's military resources in pursuit of objectives (disruption or destruction of the enemy's forces, capture of territorial positions) that, once achieved, would force the adversary to surrender. The SMs of the air force, navy and army would link conception to planning – that is to say, they would ensure that intentions matched what was technically feasible. The pivot of the system was Mussolini.

Aside from any considerations on the efficiency or otherwise of this arrangement, fully seven commanders-in-chief were directly dependent on Mussolini: Soddu, under-secretary of state at the Ministry of War and deputy chief of the SMG; General Mario Roatta, deputy chief of the SMRE and who, on the death of Italo Balbo and following the departure of Graziani, became its commander-in-chief; Admiral Domenico Cavagnari, under-secretary of state and chief of the Navy SM; General Francesco Pricolo, under-secretary of state and chief of the Air Force SM; General Graziani, commander of Italian forces in North Africa; the Duke of Aosta, Viceroy of Ethiopia; General Cesare Maria De Vecchi, commander of the Italian forces in the Aegean. To these may be added the commander of armed forces in Yugoslavia, General Vittorio Ambrosio (later replaced by Roatta), the commander of armed forces in Greece, General Carlo Geloso, and the commander-in-chief of the Fourth Army in France, General Mario Vercellino. Moreover, the men who occupied leading roles in the territories conquered after 1940 were given important posts when the regime was at its most critical juncture: Ambrosio was appointed chief of the SMG, Roatta took over from Ambrosio at the SMRE, and Giuseppe Bastianini became under-secretary at the Ministry of Foreign Affairs in February 1943. All these men had served in the occupied territories.

Mussolini co-ordinated and controlled occupation policies in the territories conquered after 1940. As in Rome until 1936, he was ubiquitously present, dealing with even the most minor of matters: we saw in the previous chapter that he would attend personally to even the smallest details of, for instance, individual tracts of frontier. He played a decisive part in defining the structures of government and administration and the tasks that they were to perform. He was the charismatic leader (in the Weberian sense), the supreme arbiter of a polycratic system, and he intervened to resolve the conflicts for power that broke out in the occupied territories (or in certain cases deliberately let them degenerate).

THE MINISTRY OF FOREIGN AFFAIRS

Mussolini's directives were co-ordinated – on his own order – by what can be described as a central sorting office: the Ministero degli Affari Esteri (although he could at any time and in any manner take direct action independently of it). While Ciano headed the ministry (1936 to February 1943), his cabinet almost entirely monopolized political activity, arrogating the powers of the Departments of European and Mediterranean Affairs (Direzione Generale degli Affari Europei e del Mediterraneo) and of Overseas Affairs (Affari Transoceanici). Specific work groups (or offices) were created within Ciano's cabinet to deal with issues of particular importance. One functionary, the plenipotentiary minister Luca Pietromarchi, headed three such groups (Spain, Economic War and Armistice–Peace (GABAP)) and supervised their respective director generals. The most relevant documentary material on these matters is contained in the GABAP archives, but unfortunately it is incomplete.

The GABAP was created at the end of June 1940, immediately following the armistice with France. After the armistice with Yugoslavia it was renamed the Ufficio Armistizio e Territori Occupati, although it was still referred to as the GABAP. The 'nerve centre' of occupation policies, it was used by Pietromarchi to channel all information arriving from the conquered territories among offices allocated to each of them: Croatia, Montenegro, Greece, France, Slovenia and Dalmatia (see appendix, table 17). Moreover, by order of Mussolini, all information, specific questions and dossiers addressed to each of the Foreign Ministry's departments from other state organs had first to pass through the GABAP. On 14 or 15 July 1940, the foreign minister Ciano ordered Pietromarchi to prepare reports on the peace then believed to be imminent and which affirmed Italy's demands on the assumption – indeed, the certainty – of absolute and complete Italian victory. The reports were to be submitted for scrutiny by a committee of ministers chaired by Ciano. Consequently, Pietromarchi had to gain prior approval of them from all the administrative authorities and ministries concerned. To do so, he used a system of inter-ministerial committees where representatives of those authorities could work together and compare ideas. In fact, little assistance was forthcoming from the other ministries. The work was done by functionaries at the Foreign Ministry and by selected technicians, mainly from the National Research Centre.[6]

The GABAP oversaw the activities of the functionaries and diplomats 'on the spot'. When the Foreign Ministry appointed the functionaries to be sent to the conquered territories, it gave priority to those with experience in the field; and diplomats who had served in the occupied territories were often transferred among them. Relationships with the allied government of Zagreb were maintained by the ambassador Raffaele Casertano. Given Italy's intention to penetrate Croatia politically and economically, consulates were opened in Mostar, Sarajevo, Dubrovnik (Ragusa) and Banja Luka, while the consulate in Belgrade was kept in operation. Appointed to Greece was Plenipotentiary Minister Pellegrino Ghigi, previously ambassador to Bucharest, although, on Mussolini's orders, his authority was subordinate to that of the commander of the Eleventh Army. General Cavallero initially designated Dino Grandi for the post of political commissioner. But Grandi declined the offer on the grounds that his presence would be entirely superfluous, and that the presence of a political commission – not foreseen in the plans drawn up by the SMG – would inevitably give rise to damaging conflict between the political and military authorities. He suggested instead the appointment of a secretary for civil affairs to flank the military authorities.[7] Among the senior officials at the Foreign Ministry, Michele Scammacca acted as an important point of contact with the Supreme Command, while in the occupied territories an almost equivalent role was performed by the liaison officers – an example being Vittorio Castellani of the Second Army. Moreover, at embassies and consulates, co-ordination between the MAE and the Regio Esercito was ensured by the military attachés.

[6] Pietromarchi, unpublished diary, 29 May 1943 (Fondazione Luigi Einaudi, Turin). On the same day, Under-Secretary Bastianini held a meeting to decide the strategy to adopt in preparing for peace. The meeting was attended by some thirty senior officials at the ministry. According to Pietromarchi, they examined the proposals of other countries, constantly updating information and relying on the discreet support of technocrats.

[7] ASMAE, GABAP, b. 23, 'Grandi a Cavallero, 23 aprile 1941'. Grandi, then president of the Commissione per il Diritto di Guerra, suggested that the prefect Piero Parini, then secretary-general of the Lieutenancy of Albania, should become secretary for civil affairs at the Military High Command.

THE ITALIAN COMMISSION FOR ARMISTICE WITH FRANCE

The principal task of the Commissione Italiana d'Armistizio con la Francia (CIAF) was to administer military, economic, diplomatic and financial relations with France in the period between the armistice of 24 February 1940 and 11 November 1942. The ordinance instituting the commission stated that its duties were implementation of the armistice agreement between Italy and France and its harmonization with that between Germany and France. Created at a time when peace appeared close at hand, and consequently when it seemed inevitable that the Italo-French armistice regime would be short-lived, the CIAF had to contrive a policy towards the French authorities and abandon the illusion of a victorious peace. From the outset – writes Rainero, the author of the most detailed study on the commission and on Italo-French relations between 1940 and 1943 – the CIAF seemed overwhelmed by the tasks that the complex military and civil relations between the two countries imposed on it as the only Italian authority responsible for them.

A mixed civil and military body taking orders from the Supreme Command, the CIAF had its central offices in Turin. Its organizational structure consisted of a presidency (*presidenza*) – its first president was General Pietro Pintor, from 27 June to 7 December 1940, followed by General Camillo Grossi, from 8 December 1940 to 16 June 1941, and then finally General Arturo Vacca Maggiolini – and four sub-commissions, collaborating with which were the corresponding French sub-delegations. On 20 August 1940 General Fernando Gelich joined the presidency as secretary-general. The presidency issued general directives, took broad decisions of principle, interpreted the provisions of the armistice convention, maintained relations with the French delegation, liaised with the equivalent German commission in Wiesbaden (the Commissione Tedesca d'Armistizio con la Francia, CTA) and attended to matters concerning the French colonial territories.

The sub-commissions were given specific tasks, execution of which required the establishment of offices and delegations in south-eastern France and the French colonies (see appendix, tables 18–19). Allocating responsibilities among the sub-commissions for the army (General Carlo Vecchiarelli), the navy (Admiral Ildebrando Goiran) and the air force (General Aldo Pellegrini) was straightforward. 'Less easy', writes Rainero, 'was precise definition of the jurisdiction of the Sub-Commission for General Affairs, whose remit comprised all questions of a non-military nature that required attention: some in relation to application of the clauses in the armistice which referred to them in particular; others not covered by the convention but which arose in relation to resumption of legal and economic relations between Italy and France.' For example, the issue soon arose of the status of the Italians resident in France. The Sub-Commission for General Affairs (abolished on 15 April 1943) was tasked with protecting Italian emigrants and freeing Italians detained in concentration camps. It supervised the distribution of ration books, ascertained the reasons for dismissals of Italian workers and on several occasions obtained revocation of forced residence orders and other measures restricting freedom of movement. Its most important sections were the civil Delegazioni Civili Rimpatrio e Assistenza (DRAs) instituted on 4 February 1941 (and converted into consular offices on 15 January 1943). Staffed by consular officials working in the capacity of reserve officers, between October 1940 and April 1943 the DRAs repatriated more than 70,000 Italians.[8] Also, according to Rainero,

> The CIAF had yet other responsibilities. Because the armistice regime regulated relations between Vichy and Italy, the CIAF was called upon to extend its competences and tasks even further. This had an obvious twofold consequence: on the one hand, the administrative apparatus rapidly expanded; on the other, bodies, commissions and committees proliferated . . . The CIAF was never static. It constantly changed, doing so to respond better to the needs of the Italian government and of the Supreme Command, and in order to cope with the new political and diplomatic situations imposed by the evolution of bilateral relations on the original structure.[9]

For example, on 5 November 1940 an independent Sottocommissione per l'Amministrazione dei Territori Occupati (discussed in the next section) was created, as were, in the same period, the Sub-Commission for Legal Affairs and the Sub-Commission for Armaments, whose task was to supervise the activities of the French weapons factories located between the Italian border and the Rhône, and to organize re-use of those same factories jointly with Fabbriguerra.

The resumption of economic relations led to the creation of a specific body which operated not in Turin but in Rome: the Italo-French Economic Commission. Convened once a month and consisting of two permanent delegations (the Italian one headed by Amedeo Giannini, the French one by Sanguinetti), effective from 19 February 1942, the commission concerned itself only with economic and trade relations with Vichy France,

[8] USSME, D 7, b. 8, 'Storia dell'armistizio, attività della Sottocommissione Affari generali, dall'inizio dei lavori della CIAF sino alla soppressione'.

[9] Rainero, *Mussolini e Pétain*, vol. I, p. 87, and more generally pp. 81–102 and 285–92, with explanation of the organization chart of the sub-commissions and the delegations, including those in the French colonies.

given that the French territory occupied by the Germans fell within the sphere of competence of the CTA. Working in parallel with the commission in Turin was the Sottocommissione Affari Economici e Finanziari (SCAEF, Sub-Commission for Economic and Financial Affairs, headed by Tommaso Lazzari), which initially attended to economic questions to be resolved with France. It dealt with matters concerning the spoils of war, the use of harbours in the French colonies, the acquisition of war matériel and the property of Italians in France. Its activities then extended to the control of maritime traffic, policing of the transalpine frontiers, the recovery of ships and goods, armistice accounting and surveys of indirect war damage. The main task of the Trade Sub-Commission was to develop trade relations between Italy and the part of France occupied by the Germans. Working in close connection with it, at the Italian embassy in Paris, was the *commissario commerciale* Teodoro Pigozzi (governing director of SIMCA, the car company owned by FIAT). This commissariat was created by the Ministry for Trade and Exchange in order to protect Italian commercial interests in occupied France. These various economic bodies did nothing to co-ordinate their activities, which created considerable confusion and numerous conflicts of competence.

The embassy in Paris re-opened on 4 February 1941 but resumed its functions only on 20 February 1942 – Gino Buti was appointed ambassador – and it had a subsidiary office in Vichy headed by the consul Ottavio Zoppi. As Rainero noted,

> In Paris, no longer the seat of the French government and therefore without a diplomatic corps and moreover under German military occupation, the activity of an ambassador was obviously pointless. An Italian diplomatic representative should have been appointed for Vichy, but this did not happen, largely because of pressure applied by the Germans, who thus preserved their sole and hegemonic presence in Vichy. However, the CIAF failed to understand the Germans' stratagem and insisted forcefully on the presence in Paris of Ambassador Otto Abetz, forgetting that he occupied a specific position in the German structure of military occupation, which was not the case with Ambassador Buti. Subordinate to the Ministry of Foreign Affairs and not to the CIAF, Buti was instructed to attend only to matters unconnected with the armistice.[10]

From the moment of Buti's arrival, a series of bureaucratic complications and conflicts among decisions and competences arose. In effect, because of ongoing developments in the war, the CIAF lost its function as sole intermediary between Italy and France and became just one interlocutor

[10] Ibid., p. 340.

with the French authorities, which took advantage of the situation to deal with the other Italian organs as well.

In the spring of 1942 the question arose of harmonizing the activities of the diverse bodies engaged in relations with the French authorities. The president of the CIAF wrote that it was in Italy's essential interest not to give France the impression that by acting in one sector it could obtain results that it could only vainly seek in another. Awareness grew within the CIAF that the other power centres – the PNF and the MAE most of all – were seeking in every way possible to wrest influence away from the commission, and especially from its president General Vacca Maggiolini, who enjoyed a close relationship with Mussolini.

After the occupation of 12 November 1942, the role of the Armistice Commission was gradually curtailed as its functions were transferred to the command of the Fourth Army (for example, the DRA was taken over by the MAE liaison office within the Fourth Army). The changeover did not come about smoothly, however, and the numerous conflicts that ensued between the CIAF and the Fourth Army Command were invariably exploited by the French authorities.

In early December, the head of the French delegation, Admiral Emile-André Duplat, asked Vacca Maggiolini whether the CIAF had been dissolved. The Italians and Germans decided to keep their respective commissions, and on 31 December 1942 the CIAF president notified Commander Vercellino of the reasons why his commission should not be abolished. He pointed out that the armistice had not been repealed; that the legal situation between the Axis powers was still the same as it had been in June 1940; that the armistice convention was the text which affirmed Italy's superiority over France; and that there were French territories – those between Marseilles, the mouth of the Rhône and Avignon – not garrisoned by Italian troops. The chief of SMG, General Cavallero, intervened in the dispute, reiterating to both parties that the CIAF was to remain subordinate to the purposes and requirements of the occupying troops. Nevertheless, the wrangle between Vacca Maggiolini and Vercellino continued until 10 March 1943, when the new chief of SMG, General Ambrosio, spelled out the residual competences of the Armistice Commission. On 20 March the military sub-commissions were disbanded and their functions were transferred to the Fourth Army. The CIAF, however, in a decision typical of the Fascist regime, was not abolished.[11]

[11] Ibid., pp. 411–34, and vol. II, docs. 60 and 61: *I rapporti tra la CIAF e la IV Armata*, 10 March 1943, pp. 357–8; *L'abolizione delle sottocommissioni militari della CIAF*, 30 March 1943, p. 359.

THE ADMINISTRATIVE STRUCTURES OF THE ANNEXED TERRITORIES: CIVIL COMMISSIONS, GOVERNORATES AND HIGH COMMISSIONS

Between the armistice of 17 April 1941 and the annexations in May of that year, the Italian military authorities exercised all decision-making powers in the Yugoslavian territories. Operating in the zones of likely annexation were two civil commissions (*commissariati civili*), these being transitional administrative structures under the command of army corps: one with its headquarters in Ljubljana and which took orders from the command of the 11th CdA, the other in Zara (then in Šibenik and finally Split, from 28 April) and dependent on the 6th CdA. An Ufficio Affari Civili (UAC, Civil Affairs Office) was set up at Army Command. Directed by Colonel Michele Rolla, this office co-ordinated the activities of the commissioners (after the annexations it continued to co-ordinate the actions of the civil and military authorities).

The civil commissioners Athos Bartolucci and Emilio Grazioli – both PNF functionaries – represented the highest governmental authority in the region and were appointed by the CS. They not only oversaw the civil services furnished by the state, *banat* and municipalities but also prepared the ground for the future annexation of those zones. To that end, they established PNF welfare centres; banned nationalist associations; introduced the compulsory use of Italian in the courts; forced public officials to adopt the Roman salute; froze Yugoslavian state funds; and blocked exports of capital and the activities of foreign businesses. Bartolucci – federal secretary and then prefect of Zara – requested the sending from Rome of 'as many Dalmatians as possible', 'at least one official from each ministry', and the appointment of district commissioners for all the areas occupied (Ildebrando Tacconi in Split, Giuseppe Franchi in Zara).[12] The posts of civil commissioners were abolished after the annexations.

In the province of Ljubljana a separate system was created which in theory took account of the ethnic features of the local population, the geographical location of the zone and specific local exigencies. Powers of government were exercised by High Commissioner Grazioli, appointed by royal decree on the Duce's nomination (previously civil commissioner of Ljubljana, a Fascist activist in Venezia Giulia and leader of the campaign to Italianize the Slovene minorities in that region, Grazioli had also served as *podestà* and provincial party secretary in Sesana and as PNF inspector

[12] ASMAE, GABAP, b. 46, 'Relazione aprile–maggio 1941'.

for the Carso zone). The high commissioner (*alto commissario*), a newly created post in the Italian administrative system, roughly corresponded to a prefect, but with more extensive powers in that he acted independently of the Ministry of the Interior. First private secretary to the high commissioner was Giuseppe Lombrassa, and the vice-prefect was Pietro David (Lombrassa replaced Grazioli from 15 June to 12 August 1943, and then from 12 August to 8 September his place was taken by General Riccardo Moizo).[13] The high commissioner appointed and replaced the local authorities and functionaries; he determined the legitimacy of the decisions and provisions of the authorities and local bodies; he was empowered to issue ordinances on matters concerning construction, policing, sanitation, contract procurement, spending and local finance. He was 'assisted' by a council consisting of fourteen representatives of local industry and commerce, and intended to symbolize the 'autonomy of the province' (in the Dalmatian provinces the members of the councils were Italian Dalmatians). However, this council was a charade, for it had no effective powers and met only five times in twenty-nine months.

On 19 February 1942, Grazioli defined the duties of the district chiefs – similar to sub-prefects – who were 'to represent the high commissioner in the district'. On 18 February 1943, the high commissioner decreed that the captains must henceforth be designated *commissari civili* (civil commissioners) and the districts *commissariati* (commissions). Each municipality was administered by a *podestà* assisted by a council consisting of notables with proven loyalty to Italy. The *podestà* of Ljubljana were the Slovenes Juro Adlešić (until 2 June 1942) and Leon Rupnik, while the district captains were Italians, many of them members of the militia (Lodovico Maffei in Ljubljana, Umberto Rosin in Logatec, Ottone Griselli in Novo Mesto, Emilio Cassanego in Črnomelj, Giovanni Sisgoreo in Kočevje), assisted by Italian party functionaries or Italianized Slovenes from Venezia Giulia, Carabinieri, revenue officers and municipal policemen.[14] The High Commission also supervised several police departments, 1,500 royal military police flanked by 500 former Yugoslav gendarmes, around 800 revenue officers (250 of them Slovenian) and the border militia – a force of around 400 men, the majority of them from the Italian region of Venezia Giulia.[15]

[13] ACS, MI, ACP, 1935–47, b. 5198, 'Lubiana'. According to Ferenc, *La provincia 'italiana' di Lubiana*, p. 44, the chief of cabinet was not Lombrassa but Eduardo Bisia.

[14] Ferenc, *La provincia 'italiana' di Lubiana*, pp. 56–7.

[15] The chief of the Italian police, Carmine Senise, sent an inspector – Ciro Verdiani – to organize the PS in Ljubljana, where Police Superintendant (Questore) Ettore Messina had been appointed chief of police. He was replaced by Domenico Ravelli in the spring of 1942. The OVRA also operated in the province, although in what capacity is not known.

The duties and powers of the governor of Dalmatia were even broader than Grazioli's. The office did not correspond to that of a colonial governor because it was not vested with command over armed forces. Rather, it resembled that of the propraetors of the Augustan period, who were selected personally by the emperor. Unlike the proconsuls of the senatorial provinces, appointed by the Senate, the propraetors were sent out to govern the imperial provinces – those, that is, under the emperor's direct authority. In the Roman period, as in the Fascist one, these were frontier provinces likely to revolt or under external threat.[16] The duties and powers of the governor were defined by the decree-law of 18 May 1941 and specified by decree no. 453 of 7 June. Although the governor had powers over what was part of Italian territory, he depended not on a ministry but on Mussolini himself. He was assisted by a general secretary, Carlo Bozzi (replaced by Carlo Villasanta in February 1943), and had a practically unlimited range of functions and exercised the powers of central government in regard to civil, governmental and local services.[17] He issued orders on all matters and personally co-ordinated the political activities of the prefects of Kotor, Split and Zara (a province divided territorially and where the laws of the Kingdom of Italy and Yugoslavia co-existed in the nineteen municipalities annexed in 1941). He submitted proposals for the gradual extension of the statute to Mussolini and he legislated, by means of ordinances, in areas where the laws of the kingdom had not yet entered into force. The Fascist state transferred its institutions *in toto*: from the Banca d'Italia to the PNF, which in principle would function as it did in all the other provinces of the kingdom.

The government of Dalmatia consisted of the governor's civil cabinet, secretariat and military cabinet. It was organized into a series of offices corresponding to the metropolitan ministries (see appendix, table 20).[18] On his arrival in Dalmatia, Governor Giuseppe Bastianini realized that there were no Italian administrative officials at work in either Split or Kotor, apart from the prefects, and consequently rapidly set about transposing the administrative and governmental structures of the kingdom. He took

[16] Martin, 'L'empire: un espace organisé', pp. 85–7.

[17] ACS, PCM, 1.1.13.16542, 'governatorato della Dalmazia', 1–6; ASMAE, GABAP, b. 46, 'Giornale ufficiale del governo della Dalmazia – Leggi e decreti, Regio decreto del 7 giugno 1941, n. 453'.

[18] Segreteria generale del governo (General Government Secretariat), Ufficio di Grazia e Giustizia (Office of Justice), Ufficio di Pubblica sicurezza (Office of Public Security), Ufficio Opere pubbliche (Public Works Office), Ispettorato di Sanità (Health Inspectorate), Ufficio economico-finanziario (Economic-Financial Office), Ufficio Dogane (Customs Office), Ufficio Corporazioni (Corporations Office), Ufficio Agricoltura (Agriculture Office), Ufficio Poste e Telegrafi (Post Office), Ufficio Alimentazione (Food Office), Ufficio Ragioneria (Accountancy Office), Cancelleria (Chancellery).

particular pains to eliminate every trace of the Yugoslavian administration and created an office (the Ufficio Stralcio) to pay the salaries and pensions of the dismissed Yugoslav personnel. The statute and fundamental laws of the Kingdom of Italy were extended to Dalmatia in October 1941. The report and outline decree were submitted for scrutiny to the Commissione Consultiva per il Diritto di Guerra, which approved them, and on 6 February 1942 the decree was published in the *Gazzetta Ufficiale del Regno*. On 26 November 1941, the governor set up the Ufficio del Lavoro per la Dalmazia: supervised by the PNF inspector for Dalmatia (Bartolucci), this performed the functions of a trade union and was divided into territorial sections run by the provincial Federazioni dei Fasci di Combattimento (Fascist Party Federations). Also instituted were the provincial *intendenze* (administrative offices), the district commissions which adjudicated tax cases, the provincial education boards and the provincial offices of the Genio Civile (civil and urban engineers). In December 1941, Bastianini introduced a compulsory work permit issued by the *podestà* or civil commissioners in the worker's place of residence; then, some weeks later, employment offices were opened and all the Yugoslavian trade unions and their federations were dissolved. This policy, which was intended to clear the way for corporative reform, came into effect in March 1942 with the creation of the Consigli Provinciali delle Corporazioni of Split and Kotor (that of Zara extended its remit to the province's new communes) and the abolition of the chambers of commerce, industry and crafts. Bastianini also brought the numerous local co-operatives within the administrative structure and created the Ente di Cooperazione della Dalmazia, a body representing all the co-operatives, consortia and mutual enterprises under its administrative control (Rosario Labadessa was appointed its 'extraordinary director').

In the Ionian islands, the purpose of the civil administration was to prepare the way for annexation to Italy, doing so by means of a special regime which was markedly autonomous from Athens and more evidently dependent on Rome. *Bando* (notice) no. 91 issued on 12 November 1941, article 2, defined the powers of the chief of civil affairs (*capo degli affari civili*) in the islands – the prefect Piero Parini – stating that he might issue ordinances on matters concerning the police, sanitation, construction, procurement and spending, and local finance, although he was not vested with military competences.[19] Thus empowered, Parini refused to issue Greek

[19] ASMAE, GABAP, b. 23, *Bollettino ufficiale degli Affari civili delle isole Jonie*, no. 22, 9 December 1941, art. 2.

officials with entry permits to the islands, and in order to separate the latter further from Hellenic territory, introduced the Ionian drachma and opened a clearing account different from the Greek one managed by the ACJ (Anonima Commercio Jonico). He also established a provisioning system separate from the Greek mainland.[20] Ordinance no. 122 of May 1942 radically altered the administrative structure and geographical extent of the communes of the Eptanisa. The presidents, councillors and secretaries were dismissed by Parini, and each commune was administered by a mayor selected from the notables of the local villages and appointed by the prefect. The mayors could be suspended or dismissed for non-fulfilment of their duties, or for reasons of public order. They were assisted by municipal councils with consultative functions, which consisted of representatives from each of the villages in the ward. Convened by the mayor at least once a month, these councils too consisted of notables, who were appointed after prior approval by the chief of civil affairs. Nominated in each commune by the prefect was a municipal secretary who, among other requirements for the post, had to be a native-born Ionian. All officials were obliged to swear an oath of loyalty to Italy. The commission continued in operation until the armistice of 8 September 1943.

In the Cyclades and Sporades, the local civil authorities remained in their posts unless there were political reasons for removing them, and so did the gendarmerie. Valerio Valeriani was appointed civil commissioner for the province of the Cyclades. Unlike in the Ionian islands, the commission's Ufficio Affari Civili was staffed solely by military personnel. Administratively, the islands depended upon the government of Rhodes. One may liken the administration to a regime of military occupation, and it differed substantially from the regime which obtained in the Ionian islands. The only tangible sign of Fascist plans for annexation was the reprehensible decision taken to have the two archipelagos depend administratively, economically and commercially on the government of Rhodes. This decision was harshly criticized by Valeriani, who stressed the difficulty and danger of transport among the islands and also pointed out that the lira circulated in the Aegean possessions, while the currency in the Cyclades was the drachma. The obligation of gaining prior approval from the Italian authorities for all executive decisions, orders of payment, increases in salaries and pensions, taxes and duties caused long delays and severely damaged the already precarious economies of the Hellenic archipelagos. Moreover, the Comando Superegeo (Aegean High Command) ordered that the islands

[20] USSME, N I–II, 'Diari storici', b. 319, 'Comando XXV CdA – UAC, 16 luglio 1941'.

must provision themselves from their own resources, and this increased food shortages even further. Valeriani decided to intervene directly by seeking to draw upon the islands' stocks as little as possible. He created welfare offices and, as long as he had the financial resources, ordered military works so that income and employment would be provided for the islanders. Owing to inflation and problems of navigation, trade among the islands rapidly dwindled. In a report written in May 1943, Valeriani declared that the island of Syros was 'dead', its industries were idle, maritime traffic had ceased and unemployment was rampant.[21]

The CIAF Sottocommissione per l'Amminstrazione dei Territori Occupati (see appendix, table 21) attended to all problems concerning administration of the zone between the Italo-French border and the military demarcation line drawn at the time of the 1940 armistice. Civil commissioners were appointed for the *communes* of Bessans, Bramans, Fontano, Isola, Lanslebourg, Mont-Genèvre, Ristolas and Séez, and also for Menton, where commissioners remained in office until 8 September (Aldo Loni, then Virgilio Magris, Giuseppe Frediani – former PNF secretary of Pisa, then party secretary for the provinces of Verona and Pavia and inspector of Fasci Italiani all'Estero (Fascists Abroad), finally Berri from 30 November 1942). The commissioner executed orders issued by the chief prefect (Marziali) of the CIAF Amministrazione dei Territori Francesi Occupati. The occupation regime remained unchanged even after France's complete occupation (see appendix, table 22). Besides the commands of the local garrisons, all the organs of the Italian state were introduced in the occupied zones: command quarters for the Carabinieri, the police force, customs officers, border militia, forest guards, revenue officers, while the Fasci di Combattimento were established at Menton and Fontano. Criminal and civil justice was administered by the military authorities. To be noted is that the majority of the officials stationed in the French *communes* were military personnel who proved unsuitable for administrative duties.[22]

THE PNF

The very few documents in the archives do not permit a description, nor even an outline, of the activities of the PNF and the MVSN. However, it appears that the party performed different roles in the annexed and militarily occupied territories. In the latter it had to place itself entirely at

[21] ASMAE, GABAP, b. 22, 'Valeriani al capo di gabinetto del MAE Babuscio Rizzo, 6 maggio 1943'.
[22] USSME, D 7, b. 8, 'Relazione sull'attività svolta dal 1° ottobre 1941 al 31 gennaio 1943'.

the service of the occupation troops (this topic is dealt with in detail in the next chapter), while in the annexed territories it was responsible for the Fascistization of the new provinces. It is likely that, in the event of a victorious conclusion to the war, the PNF would have been empowered in the territories of the imperial community, as it had been in the colonies, to issue advisory opinions on matters concerning the activities of public and private bodies and the economy; it would have been allocated funds to conduct study and research with a view to economic development; and it would have directed transport projects.

The regime reproduced its metropolitan structures in the Governorate of Dalmatia and in the Province of Ljubljana, where the federal secretaries of the PNF depended respectively on the governor and the high commissioner, while the party organizations took the place of the Yugoslavian recreational, political and cultural associations.[23] Introduced in the new provinces were the PNF's provincial federation of welfare centres (Federazione Provinciale dei Centri d'Assistenza), the provincial and municipal sections of the Massaie Rurali, the federal secretariats of the PNF youth organizations, PNF sections for female industrial workers and domestic workers (Sezioni delle Operaie e Lavoranti a Domicilio), university organizations, National Working-Men's Guild (Dopolavoro) and even the provincial committee of CONI (the Italian National Olympic Committee).[24]

In October 1941, Grazioli was appointed PNF federal secretary in Ljubljana. He directed forty-nine welfare centres established in the occupied zones of Slovenia to encourage the settlement therein of Fasci di Combattimento. He delegated management of these centres to federal vice-secretaries. These were party functionaries, many of them from Venezia Giulia, and who on their own admission could not speak Slovene. The centres were grouped into five zones directed by political commissioners, who, rather than assist the needy, collaborated in repression of the rebel movement. Given their close contact with the local population, they were able to recruit spies and informers, arranging for their transfer to Italy in the event of their discovery. At the end of 1941, nine provincial federations of Fasci di Combattimento were created in Ljubljana, Logatec, Novo Mesto, Črnomelj, Kočevje, Metlika, Trebnje, Ribnica, Sent Jernej and Vinica. The administrators of the welfare centres were also appointed political secretaries: Orlando Orlandini became federal secretary

[23] ACS, PCM, 1940–3, 1.1.13.16542.33, August 1941.
[24] Ferenc, *La provincia 'italiana' di Lubiana*, p. 68.

for the province in February 1942 (he was succeeded by Lombrassa in June 1943).

In Ljubljana, only Italian citizens were eligible to join the Fascio di Combattimento and the Fascio Femminile, and their numbers never amounted to more than 1,500. The Gioventù Italiana del Littorio di Lubiana (GILL, Ljubljana Fascist Youth Organization), which had a staff of fully eighty persons, organized sports activities and ran canteens, but the results in terms of membership were only modest. Only one-tenth of school-aged children in the city were enrolled with GILL. Equally unsuccessful were the activities of the Organizzazione Universitaria di Lubiana (OUL, Ljubljana University Organization), the OND and CONI. Finally to be mentioned is the attempt made to introduce corporations by creating the Unione Provinciale Lavoratori and the Consigli Corporativi Provinciali. In the province of Kotor, the PNF opened offices in Perast, Tivat, Herceg Novi and Risan; others were opened in the provinces of Zara and Split at Šibenik and Stankovići.[25]

The structure of the PNF and all its bodies clearly shows what the intentions of the occupiers were in the annexed provinces, but it does not seem from the few documents available that the party was given a preeminent role by occupation policies.

THE CIVIL AND MILITARY COURTS

As in the case of the PNF, the documentary sources on the Italian civil courts in the annexed territories are extremely fragmentary. As regards the annexed provinces, we know that the judicial system suffered from a chronic shortage of qualified personnel, and that huge delays caused the severe overcrowding of prisons and internment camps with detainees awaiting trial. One of the most difficult technical problems was translation of trial documents, and it was often necessary to recruit local personnel to run the prosecutors' offices, courts and prisons.

The overhasty decision to transpose the legislation of the kingdom, the creation of appeal courts and other Italianization measures produced chaos in the administration of justice in the annexed provinces. Equally fragmentary is the documentation on the special courts of the High Commission of Ljubljana and the Governorate of Dalmatia, which dealt with such matters as the border, internment and the enforcement of sentences (also the death penalty) for serious offences against the public order. In the occupied

[25] ACS, 'Carteggio federazioni provinciali PNF, Servizi vari', ser. II, 1922–43, bb. 979 and 1698.

territories, the military courts tried not only soldiers but also persons accused of political offences against the Italian army. The Hellenic, Croatian, Montenegrin and French courts were vested with residual competence for minor offences. The Second Army established its central court in Sušak and had various sections distributed among the army corps.[26]

THE BANCA D'ITALIA

In August 1939 the Banca d'Italia created an Ufficio Speciale Coordinamento (USC, Special Co-ordination Office), a section linking the bank's central administration to the Ispettorato del Credito (the savings and credit supervisory authority), directed by Giuseppe Pennachio, and tasked with preparing measures to be taken in emergencies. After 1941 the USC extended its activities to the annexed and occupied territories, where it attended to settlement of the former Yugoslavian state's assets, liquidation of the Yugoslavian national bank, the adjustment of compensation claims and the winding up of the state-owned and semi-public banks. It took over some of the duties of the Ispettorato del Credito, and its delegates attended the meetings of the joint committees. The USC supervised the extension of Italian banking law to the Dalmatian provinces and to Ljubljana, it regulated the establishment of affiliates and branches of the Banca d'Italia and other Italian banks and it oversaw liquidation of the branches of private credit institutions with headquarters abroad. Through the Ufficio per la Difesa del Risparmio e l'Esercizio del Credito it conducted inspections of banks in the Yugoslavian and Hellenic territories, including the Ionian islands.

In the annexed territories, the supervisory offices of the Banca d'Italia operated under the orders of the governor of Dalmatia, Bastianini, and the high commissioner Grazioli (the Dalmatian office was opened by governor's ordinance on 28 February 1942). They attended to liquidation of the Yugoslavian banks, prepared for the entry of Italian banks into the country and compiled registers of the banks operating in the annexed territories. The Ufficio Speciale per le Isole Jonie (a branch of the Ufficio Affari Civili for the Ionian islands staffed by officials from the Banca d'Italia) organized the issue of the Ionian drachma and assisted with the economic separation of the islands of the Eptanisa from the Hellenic mainland, supervising

[26] There is a large body of documentation on the military tribunals. Unfortunately it cannot be consulted because the military prosecutors' offices deposited their files in the Rome Central Archive only in 1998. Collating the archive will take years, and the method used is name-based rather than thematic, which will probably hamper future research.

currency circulation and impeding the inflow of other currencies. Provisional exchange offices were set up on the islands of Corfu, Lefkada, Cephalonia and Zante under the direction of Inspector Enea Fabrizi, who, assisted by an island-chief 'of fascist faith', supervised exchange operations and issued instructions on the permissible activities of private banks.

A further economic aspect was the activity of the Commissione Economica Permanente Italo-Croata (CEPIC, Permanent Italo-Croat Economic Commission), a section of the Ministry of Foreign Affairs. This was divided into various sub-commissions which dealt with matters concerning agriculture, industry, mining, forestry, communications and contract procurement, and which were authorized to undertake agreements on banking, insurance, public works and occupation spending. On the recommendation of Ciano, Count Giuseppe Volpi di Misurata – who represented the interests of large financial and industrial groups backing Italian expansion in the Balkans – was appointed president of the commission.[27]

THE REGIO ESERCITO

I would reiterate in regard to the Regio Esercito that this study does not examine the military and strategic capabilities of the Italian commanders, nor does it analyse the technological level of Italy's armaments. The literature on these matters has shown that, during the campaign of 1940–1, the Italian army suffered from a shortage of infantry units and divisions, the unwieldiness of the *celeri* (fast-moving) and motorized brigades, a surplus of non-divisioned units, the dispersion of forces and the scant mobility of services. The literature also emphasizes the fragmentation of the high command, and in particular a tendency for pointless use to be made of CdAs, and the lack of support chains.[28] These features of the Regio Esercito did not change after the occupations. Rather, they were exacerbated by the problems that arose from occupying such broad tracts of territory, amid growing rebellion and difficult relations with the governments of the occupied states and, above all, with the Germans.

The Italian armies were structured in such a way that in theory they could wage a high-speed war (*una guerra di rapido corso*) against a similarly

[27] The commission's work resulted in the Ciano–Pavelić exchange of letters of 30 May 1941; the Zagreb agreements of 27 October 1941; the Abbazia agreements of 16 November 1941; the agreement of 27–30 September 1941 on the exploitation of mineral and forestry resources; the protocol on creation of an Italo-Croat public works authority in Croatia of 28–31 January 1942; and the Venice agreement of 6 August 1942.

[28] Ferrari, 'Considerazioni sull'ordinamento delle truppe nelle campagne balcaniche', pp. 135–6; Rochat, *L'esercito italiano*.

equipped enemy with an equivalent level of training. After the armistices of 1940 and 1941, they could have defended the annexed territories and put down what were still unorganized and uncoordinated rebellion movements. But the decision to occupy such extensive areas of territory required the adjustment of logistics and armaments to the new circumstances when the insurgents had already become mobilized and deployed. After fighting a European-type war in a colonial setting in Africa, now the Italian army had to fight a colonial-type war in a European setting. On European territory, despite the experience of the large number of colonial veterans still in armed service, an extremely mobile and logistically agile enemy – which operated in small units and mingled with the civilian population after operations – caused great difficulties for the large Italian units with their heavy artillery. Further difficulties were caused by the excessive dispersal of forces in order to defend numerous logistical bases and communication routes, the slowness due to heavy and cumbersome equipment and the need to ensure that all supply lines were completely secure. Moreover, the enemy was often well informed about the deployment and movements of the Italian units and the operational intentions of their commanders, while the Servizi Informazioni (where Informazione means 'Intelligence') were incapable of furnishing timely information.

The troops in Greece and Yugoslavia were equipped with an average of one sub-machine gun for every 40 men, one machine gun for every 70–80, one mortar for every 100–150, one barrage gun for every 600–900, one small-calibre gun for every 500 and one medium-calibre gun for every 1,000. The presence of anti-aircraft guns and of 'our poor tanks was little more than symbolic', wrote Rochat. This was weaponry suitable for relatively straightforward occupation, but it was inappropriate for combat against the Balkan guerrillas. The evolution of the conflict worked in favour of the partisan troops, which grew increasingly more numerous, efficient and well commanded, while the average size of the Italian battalions diminished to around 4,000 men, with weaponry and equipment that was increasingly less suited to the manifold requirements of the war, and who were commanded by reservist officers (newly commissioned reserve subalterns and sub-lieutenants). As well as these chronic deficiencies, only some weapons were replaced, and then only after long months of exasperating bureaucracy. Nor were replacements sent for the numerous horses and mules killed during military operations or by disease: by 1943, there were no longer enough pack animals to transport arms, let alone munitions and provisions.

Map 12. Deployment of the Second Army 'Supersloda'

The soldiers deployed in the Mediterranean territories conquered after 1940 numbered approximately 850,000, which constituted two-thirds of all troops committed outside Italian borders. The Balkans constantly absorbed 650,000 men and the occupation of southern France and Corsica required a further 200,000 (see appendix, tables 23–35 for an overview).

The Regio Esercito sent the Second Army to the territories annexed and occupied in Yugoslavia; the Eleventh Army to Greece; and the Fourth Army to France, where it was deployed along Italy's western frontier until autumn 1942. The 14th CdA was sent to Montenegro after the revolt of July 1941 and was commanded by the CS of the governor Pirzio Biroli. It established its headquarters in Podgorica under the command of General Luigi Mentasti (replaced by General Ettore Roncaglia in July 1943). Kosovo, Debar and part of Metohija annexed to Albania were occupied by the troops of the Ninth Army, known as Superalba.

Each army consisted of a variable number of army corps (CdAs). On its arrival in an occupied territory, a CdA would be assigned jurisdiction over a zone, which was allocated among its divisions, regiments and brigades, battalions and mobile regiments, and cavalry and foot artillery units, as well as border guards, royal military police, revenue officers, police officers (placed at the service of the civil authorities in the annexed provinces), and Blackshirt legions. Each division was formed of at least two infantry regions comprising at least three battalions each, a three-unit artillery regiment, a Blackshirt legion with two battalions, a mortar battalion and some other minor units. In October 1942, there were fully thirty-four infantry divisions deployed in the annexed and occupied territories (including Albania), but only one in the whole of southern Italy. The figures on conscription ages show that the armies in the Balkans were not allocated younger conscripts (there were equal numbers of 34-old and 20-year-old soldiers). Divisions, or parts of them, could be dispatched for temporary service within the areas of jurisdiction of other CdAs: for example, the Divisione Cacciatori delle Alpi of the 11th CdA was sent to Herzegovina to serve under the command of the 5th CdA.

The Carabinieri of each division received orders from the commander of the Carabinieri Reali of each CdA, although they could be transferred for service with garrison commands when particularly important and urgent situations arose. They were normally engaged in policing duties but they were also used to put down riots and for mopping-up operations. They were responsible for the security of concentration camps and also undertook the functions of military police for the Italian troops. In the annexed territories, the Carabinieri battalions were not organized systematically into units and structures but, as in Italy, were deployed as ground forces structured into companies, lieutenancies and territorial stations. In the militarily occupied territories, the Blackshirts were ranked with regular soldiers and were not permitted to undertake any actions on their own initiative, least of all arrests or executions, unless they did so jointly with the Carabinieri and the military authorities, or with their prior permission.

The administrative tasks of the Regio Esercito

Given this preliminary information, understanding Italy's occupation policies requires more detailed knowledge of the administrative tasks and structures of the Regio Esercito in the occupied territories. The UACs of each army performed important functions within the various army commands. They assisted the commanding generals in the choice of the policies to adopt *vis-à-vis* the governments of the occupied countries, and they determined the decisions to be taken with regard to civil affairs.

The UAC of the Second Army was divided into three sections. The military section was responsible for the maintenance of public order and the use of the Croatian gendarmerie, and for diplomatic relations. It also handled relationships with the Croat administrative commissioner, the Ustaša youth organizations, the officials of the MVSN and the Milizie Volontarie Anticomuniste (MVACs, Anti-Communist Voluntary Militias). The economic and customs sections collaborated with the Croat general administrative commissioner on contract procurement, the requisitioning of property, transport, the use of harbours and the regulation of shipping, mines, woodlands, studies on the Croatian economy, and the activities of the port of Ploce. The legal-administrative section issued political and economic directives and dealt with judicial questions concerning religious and ethnic conflicts, the status of Jews in the second zone, the extraordinary and military courts, the granting of permits for expatriation from Italy to Croatia, passports and travel permits, and relations with the Italian Red Cross (the liaison office with the MAE was part of this section).[29]

Montenegro was the only case of direct rule among the non-annexed conquered territories. On 17 August 1941, Pirzio Biroli (who served as military governor until his replacement on 20 July 1943 by General Curio Barbasetti) created a Segretariato Affari Civili del Montenegro headed by Captain Ugo Villani (a functionary seconded from the Ministry of War) and staffed by civilian personnel responsible for the administration of civil affairs,[30] in particular the functioning of the former Yugoslav administrative bodies and offices. The secretariat was divided into eleven sections, each of which operated as a veritable 'mini-ministry'. Only the Ispettorato Bancario, an off-shoot of the Banca d'Italia which already existed during

[29] USSME, M 3, b. 63, 1 November 1942.

[30] ASMAE, GABAP, b. 51. Villani headed the Montenegro administration from 29 April 1941 to 1943: he was first appointed head of the High Commission's UAC, then head of the Civil Affairs Secretariat, then of the Liaison Office during the incumbency of Commissioner Guglielmo Rulli, and finally of the Civil Administration.

the period of the High Commission, continued to perform its functions independently. The districts were administered by the commanders of the military garrisons in each of the chief towns, assisted by officers entitled 'civil delegates' (*delegati civili*).[31] The Montenegrins 'participated' in the management of public affairs only as office workers or, at most, as district captains (as in the colonies). The governorate was intended to be a temporary arrangement until the Axis had achieved its victory. During his two years as governor, Pirzio Biroli – who depended directly on the Army Supreme Command as regards military affairs, and on the MAE as regards civil ones – believed that it was still too early to re-establish the commission, and the structures of the governorate were maintained until the armistice of 8 September 1943.

According to Giacomo Scotti and Luciano Viazzi, Montenegro was considered to be an Italian metropolitan territory like Dalmatia. Yet in actual fact the situation in Montenegro was different from that in the annexed provinces. The Yugoslavian *banovina* was run by a hybrid administration which in some respects resembled the administration of a colony and in others that of a province. The governor acted as prime minister (or prefect) enacting measures as regards health care and employment, and above all supervising economic and financial affairs: for example, when he decided on the conversion of the dinar into lire, a measure adopted only in the annexed territories.[32] He acted like a colonial governor by granting no measure of self-government; but contradictorily he also acted like a lieutenant-governor by cultivating relations with local collaborationist groups (Muslims, Četniks and *zelenasi*) in order to create a single nationalist front against the rebels. For example, in August 1941 Pirzio Biroli decided to form a committee comprising Montenegrin notables – called 'delegates of national renewal' (*delegati della rinascita nazionale*) – which in theory would act as a provisional consultancy body, with branches in outlying districts, and represent the needs of the population, flanking the garrison commanders. He appointed a Montenegrin assistant commissioner in each district and had the phrase 'On the advice of the Montenegrin Assistant Commissioner . . . I order . . .' inserted in local administrative ordinances. He even went so far as to announce that the assistant commissioners might

[31] Scotti and Viazzi, *Le aquile delle montagne nere*, p. 252; USSME, M 3, b. 4, 26 July 1941, 'Nota di Pirzio Biroli sull'Ufficio Affari civili per il Montenegro'; ASMAE, GABAP, b. 51: the Italian garrisons were established in Cetinje, Antivari (ancient place name for Bar), Podgorica, Danilovgrad, Nikšić, Šavnik, Čajniče, Pljevlja, Kolašin, Andrijevica, Berane and Bijelo Polje.

[32] In his report of 2 August the general proposed the creation of a National Bank of Montenegro with the Italian lira as the currency.

become district commissioners if and when the situation normalized.[33] The experiment failed: in October 1941 the committee for independence was dissolved and its members expelled from the country.

During his governorship, Pirzio Biroli concerned himself mainly with the maintenance of order: 'the indispensable premise in regard to *these primitive Balkan peoples* for conferring the character of dispassionate but resolute justice upon the violence of repression'.[34] In a report sent to Mussolini in June 1943, he admitted that military action had always predominated over every other activity in Montenegro. He concluded by stressing that his title might suggest that his governorate was an arrangement similar to the Lieutenancy of Albania. Yet, when comparing the two territories, it should be borne in mind that Montenegro – unlike Albania – was an enemy country subject to Italian military authority; it should therefore be considered a 'territory of occupation' and a 'zone of operations'. The lieutenant of Albania had functions very different from those of the governor of Montenegro: he did not rule an occupied territory, he was backed by a regularly constituted and recognized government and he was not a commander of armed forces. Even less valid is comparison with the governor of Dalmatia, who, besides being a civilian, exercised his authority over a territory annexed to Italy and therefore worked in completely different circumstances.[35]

In the case of Greece, Mussolini ordered that the royal plenipotentiary be vested with powers to decide political matters. He would assume control of the civil administration in the occupied territories, with the exception of the 'reserved zone' (Ciamuria, the Ionian islands, the Cyclades and the Sporades). He was to be served by a central secretariat and by peripheral offices liaising with the army corps. The Army Command would collaborate with the civil offices, and it co-ordinated defensive operations and the maintenance of order with the plenipotentiary.[36] The Army High Command

[33] USSME, M 3, b. 4., 'Com. sup., FF.AA. Albania, Ufficio Cettigne, 18 agosto 1941, Appunto sul Comitato dell'assemblea costituente montenegrina, firmato Pirzio Biroli'. The districts (*oblasti*) would have been: Cetinje, Podgorica, Nikšić, Antivari, Kolašin, Andrijevica, Berane, Bijelo Polje and Pljevlja. The general wrote: 'I believe that this participation by local elements in the life of the country, though only partial, may have favourable repercussions throughout Montenegro and then facilitate, in its time, the sharing of civil and military functions within the framework of the organization to be given to the country . . . The prediction that Montenegro should be able to live independently does not seem to have been borne out by what has been seen thus far. But for the sake of scruple the experiment should be made.'

[34] USSME, M 3, b. 4, fasc. 12, 'governatorato del Montenegro, Ufficio militare, 2 dicembre 1941, Relazione sulla situazione del Montenegro, firmato Pirzio Biroli', p. 9 (emphasis added).

[35] USSME, M 3, b. 12, fasc. 11, 'Relazione al duce sull'opera svolta dal generale Pirzio Biroli come governatore del Montenegro, luglio 1941–giugno 1943'.

[36] ACS, PCM, 1940–3, G 7/8 20506, 'Attribuzioni del plenipotenziario per la Grecia, GABAP – Grecia 5, luglio 1941'.

decided the jurisdictions of the various CdAs: the area bordering on Albania and the Ionian islands were assigned to the 16th CdA; Epirus and the Hellad to the 25th, the Peloponnese to the 7th; and Thessaly to the 3rd. Dispatched to secure the Athens–Corinth axis were two divisions, a grenadier regiment, a cavalry regiment (Aosta), a light-infantry regiment (*bersaglieri*), a battalion of CC.RR. and three artillery units. The rest of the peninsula was occupied by units, never smaller than battalions, which were quartered in the main towns. These policed the smaller towns and villages, while lorry-borne patrols and reservist units controlled zones further away from the garrisons. Stationed in the city of Athens were twenty-five Carabinieri patrols, three lorry-borne patrols with machine-guns, three motorcycle patrols, four platoons of grenadiers, anti-aircraft artillery, the coastal defence force and two battalions of the Regia Guardia di Finanza (RGF, Royal Finance Police).

The paralysis of the Greek government led to extension of the powers of the three CdAs in the zones under their jurisdiction. These zones, though, did not correspond to the territories of the Greek nomarchies, so that the same province might be occupied by several divisions belonging to different CdAs, a situation which increased the inefficiency of the regional, provincial and municipal administrations. Hellenic law was supplanted by the ordinances of the CdA, by the orders of the garrison commanders and especially by the directives of the Army High Command. On 9 August 1941, the UAC of the Eleventh Army issued reports on the occupied population, political activity, the press, censorship, communications and transport, the food situation, the state of agriculture, commerce and industry, the public services and the police.[37] This information was then used by the commands to decide on the policies to adopt and the contents of the announcements to publish. Finally to be mentioned is the Duce's directive of 1 November 1942, no. 157, which announced the appointment of Alberto D'Agostino as special *chargé* for economic and financial affairs in Greece (with an office headed by Ubaldo Rochira).[38]

[37] Among the first bodies to operate in occupied Greece were the 'I' (Intelligence) Centres (*Centri 'I'*), which kept the divisional and army corps commands informed on all developments in military, political, economic and religious matters. The USSME archives L 13, b. 85 and L 15, b. 11, contain a large number of 'I' Office reports, many of which also appear in the logbooks kept by the divisions to which the 'I' Offices pertained.

[38] ASMAE, GABAP, b. 21, 'incaricato speciale del Regio governo italiano per le questioni economiche e finanziarie in Grecia – Atene 27 luglio 1943, risposta al telespresso n. 61/15601/164; b. 21, Appunto per il duce, 17 marzo e 13 luglio 1943'. The arrival of the special *chargé d'affaires* and the extension of powers to the CdA raised problems of prestige and authority for the royal plenipotentiary Ghigi, whose function became purely nominal and consultative. The GABAP proposed that control of the situation be left to the military authorities with the *chargé* attending to technical-administrative

In metropolitan France, after the November occupation, almost all the competences of the CIAF were delegated to the Fourth Army: military matters, those concerning the stationing of troops, the occupation regime, and the maintenance of order pertained exclusively to the Fourth Army; only the territories of the *linea verde* remained under CIAF administration. After the occupation of Corsica, a Political and General Affairs Office (Ufficio Politico e Affari Vari) was set up under the 7th CdA. Directed by a general of the Carabinieri, this office divided into three sections: a political section, one for the war economy and one for currency control, finance, agriculture and industry. The UAC handled relations with the island's political and administrative authorities; it organized and controlled the French police force; and it supervised all aspects of social, political, economic, industrial and agricultural activity.[39] The CIAF maintained its mixed delegation for Corsica; but its competences overlapped with those of the Political Office, which made the bureaucratic apparatus of the occupation even more cumbersome.

POWER CONFLICTS

Each power centre in Rome and in the occupied territories worked 'towards the Duce'. It strove to prevail over the others and to arrogate as much power as possible in pursuit of its own interests. The Fascist system by which competences were allocated was not irrational, however; it may have been chaotic, but this does not necessarily imply that it was inefficient. To be sure, there were mix-ups and overlaps among power centres; yet Mussolini's pivotal position at the centre of the system induced the civil and military organs of the state to perform to the best of their abilities, lest they be overtaken by the others. The charismatic leader, the supreme arbiter, dealt with disputes among power centres as he saw fit: he either let them degenerate or intervened in favour of one side or the other.

While the system bred conflicts among various organs of the state (though they were not conflicts peculiar to the Fascist regimes nor to their territorial occupations), it also fostered the formation of alliances among power centres. The conflicts were indeed numerous, but there was

matters, but for four months nothing was done. Moreover, had Ghigi been replaced by the legation adviser Mascia, Günther Altenburg, who remained in his post, would have outranked him. In the end the authorities opted for Ghigi in view of his influence on the Germans and his good relations with the Greek prime minister Ioannis Rallis. On 21 May 1943, D'Agostino was replaced by Vincenzo Fagiuoli and on 22 July 1943 Bottari became head of office.

[39] USSME, N 1–11, 'Diari storici', b. 1279, 'Comando VII CdA, Ufficio Ordinamento e Personale, 21 dicembre 1942'.

no lack of accords and co-operative arrangements among power centres. Yet, although there is a large body of documentation on the conflicts, there is very little on the co-operations. I would emphasize, therefore, the numerous occasions on which diplomats and soldiers reached agreement on common policies: Ghigi and General Geloso in Greece; Carlo Umiltà and General Pirzio Biroli in Montenegro and Albania; the consul in Belgrade Francesco Mameli and General Renzo Dalmazzo – commander of the 6th CdA – in Bosnia-Herzegovina. Indeed, the documentary sources testify to numerous partnerships between soldiers and diplomats, a case in point being the alliance against the chief of the PNF delegation in Zagreb, Eugenio Coselschi. Ambassador Casertano, backed by the military attaché and by the Command of the Second Army, recommended that Coselschi be replaced, criticizing his work as 'half-baked, superficial and poor'.[40] However, despite this pressure, Coselschi remained in his post.

When reading Pietromarchi's diary, one is struck by his close relationship with Count Volpi and by his evident esteem for Bastianini, Ambassador Casertano and Colonel Giancarlo Re, the military attaché in Zagreb. Pietromarchi severely criticizes the generals and Italy's military organization: especially the Second Army, which he describes as a 'complement of 220,000 men who have done nothing but drain the resources of Croatia and create distrust with its policy of friendship towards the Četniks, who should instead be fought against'.[41] He accuses of cowardice an army which even as early as 1942 seemed about 'to melt like snow in the sun' and whose men no longer fought but fled.[42] He passed equally harsh judgement on Roatta, guilty of 'reducing the Second Army to the condition of the volunteer corps after [the defeat of] Guadalajara',[43] and passes even severer judgement on General Cavallero and Mario Robotti, who replaced Roatta as commander of the Second Army: he considered them among 'the most mediocre of our generals, who are certainly not conspicuous for their qualities. Thus, a front which from one moment to the next may become of vital importance is abandoned to an incompetent, while the army is in the worst of psychological and material states. This is the work of Cavallero. These are things that cause despair for those with the country's interests at heart.'[44]

[40] ASMAE, GABAP, b. 28, 'telegramma di Casertano al GABAP, Ufficio Croazia, 1 dicembre 1941'; b. 35, 'telegramma di Casertano al GABAP, Ufficio Croazia, 8 gennaio 1942'.

[41] Pietromarchi, diary, 23 April 1942. See also the entries for 25 April 1942, where he writes that 'the organization of the Second Army leaves much to be desired', and for 26 April 1942: 'Unfortunately, the Second Army, its 200,000 men notwithstanding, has not achieved success and our prestige is very low . . . our military organization could not be less efficient.'

[42] Ibid., 3 June 1942. [43] Ibid., 12 September 1942. [44] Ibid., 18 January 1942.

The best-documented conflict of interest between civil and military authorities arose between Bastianini and General Quirino Armellini.[45] The governor was one of the severest critics of the Second Army, which he described in conversation with Mussolini as 'the laughing stock of the Italian army . . . a disgrace'.[46] Bastianini's dispute with Armellini began when he decided to bring the army troops under his personal command and – as had happened in Ljubljana – ordered the military not to install defensive positions, garrisons and fortifications, occupy premises permanently or ban free movement. In the governor's view, the military should be used only for territorial defence. But according to the general, the governorate authorities were interfering in actions to put down the rebels and meddling in matters that were not their concern. Mussolini ruled that in 'normal' cases the maintenance of order should be the responsibility of the political authorities, while the military authorities were to have exclusive competence in 'special' ones. But who decided whether a case was normal or special?[47] Roatta realized that, 'if we carry on like this, things will go to rack and ruin' and suggested the removal of Armellini, even though 'provoking the replacement of his Excellency Bastianini [was] decidedly the better solution'. On 25 July 1942, the CS notified Supersloda that, by order of the Duce, General Umberto Spigo would replace Armellini as commander of the 18th CdA; Mussolini intervened in favour of the governor because he knew that acknowledgement that Armellini was right, and therefore the replacement of Bastianini, would amount to admitting that the regime in Dalmatia was a failure.

Other conflicts over competences broke out between the civil and military authorities in the province of Ljubljana. In this case the high commissioner Grazioli was obliged, unlike Bastianini, to accept the transfer to command by the military authorities of all the province's law enforcement agencies (CC.RR., RGF, metropolitan police, border militia, police precincts, PS).[48] In June 1942, a dispute was sparked between General Roatta and Renato Giardini, the consul in Mostar, by critical remarks made by the latter on the Italian occupation forces. Pietromarchi wrote to Casertano that, although he supported Giardini, he would propose the transfer of consul Amedeo Mammalella from Dubrovnik to Mostar, given that he was on excellent terms with General Dalmazzo. In September,

[45] ASMAE, GABAP, b. 31, 'Casertano a Pietromarchi, 12 settembre 1941'; USSME, M 3, b. 85, 'Promemoria circa le provincie annesse'.

[46] Pietromarchi, diary, 7 May 1942. [47] USSME, M 3, b. 51.

[48] Ferenc, *La provincia 'italiana' di Lubiana*, pp. 210, 218, 235, 251, 273, 318, 330–1, 335, 406; ACS, A 5 G, b. 415.

however, Giardini was still in his post, which prompted Roatta to fulminate, 'This functionary can no longer be tolerated.'[49] Apart from the toughness of the language, to be stressed in this case – less well known than the previous ones – is the conciliatory role played by Pietromarchi, who (as we shall see in the following chapters) often endeavoured to settle controversies with the military authorities, seeking where possible to pursue a common policy with them – his extremely poor opinion of the Second Army notwithstanding.

Another dispute between the civilian and military authorities concerned the consul in Corsica, Ugo Turcato. In December 1942, Turcato drew up a plan for the replacement of the French administrative authorities on the island with Italian technocrats. His project came to naught, however, because the command of the CdA instituted its own War Economy Office, prompting Turcato to write to the MAE, with a hint of scornful irony, that he had achieved 'almost nil' results. Despite his initial failure, the consul continued to work busily on his initial project.[50] The wrangle between General Giovanni Magli and Consul Turcato reached the topmost levels of the MAE and the SMRE in the persons of Bastianini and General Ambrosio, when the latter declared that Turcato 'was no longer a *persona grata*' and asked for him to be replaced with another functionary. However, on 2 August 1943, Turcato was still in his post.

Despite these altercations and conflicts, in the militarily occupied territories the civil and military authorities were fundamentally in agreement. In the annexed territories, by contrast, relations between them were much more strained, especially from early 1943 onwards, when Italy's situation in the war became so critical that the military authorities realized that the populations under their control were resentful of the social structures imposed by the Fascist regime. According to the commander of the 18th CdA, Spigo, Italy's political activities in Dalmatia had provoked 'an antagonistic state of mind in the entire population, regardless of race and religion, from the large towns to the villages and the countryside'. The general suggested that the political initiatives causing such offence to the Dalmatians should be halted.[51] For their part, the civil authorities, in the person of the governor Francesco Giunta, dismissed the Second Army as 'sick from two years of garrison duty, its morale sapped by the constant torment of permanent

[49] ASMAE, GABAP, b. 29.
[50] ASMAE, 'AA.PP. – Francia', b. 67, 'console Turcato al Mae 17 aprile, 5 e 7 giugno 1943'; USSME, M 3, b. 9.
[51] USSME, M 3, b. 85, 'generale Spigo a Robotti, 30 marzo 1943'.

rebellion, with little bite or passion among its officers . . . no longer able to continue its work'.[52]

Grazioli's political and administrative decisions were constantly criticized by General Robotti, commander of the 11th CdA, on the grounds that they conflicted with the army's criteria of security and public order. The spread of the rebellion reduced the competences of the High Commission and conversely increased those of the military authorities: for example, the Second Army opened a detached section of its military tribunal and abolished the extraordinary court of Ljubljana created in September 1941. From the end of 1942 onwards, Robotti was in effect Grazioli's direct superior.

Conflicts over the allocation of power were not peculiar to the Fascist regime, nor were they a feature unique to the Fascist occupations. Distinctive of them instead was the role of the charismatic leader. As long as Mussolini kept firm hold on the reins of power, the system 'worked towards the Duce'. At the regime's most critical juncture following the defeats at Stalingrad and in North Africa, Mussolini's lack of interest bordering on apathy towards the occupied territories led to the collapse of the entire system.

Essential for understanding Fascist Italy's occupation policies, therefore, is the role performed by Mussolini, and his direct ties with his civil and military 'lieutenants' in the annexed and occupied territories. The charismatic leader used his power to create an almost feudal system made up of faithful vassals ready to defend Italy's *spazio vitale* against German encroachment. The functionaries and the *commis d'Etat* were convinced that they personified the bureaucracy of a modern and efficient great power bringing development and prosperity to the occupied territories. The racist references to the 'crudeness' and the 'primitiveness' of the Balkans often made by the Italian civil and military authorities derived not only from the longstanding anti-Slav racism of many Italians; they also sprang from a conviction of the superiority of the 'Italian race', and of a Fascist state deemed more advanced than the Hellenic and Yugoslavian ones, and even more advanced than 'decadent' France's. As the next chapter shows in detail, the Fascist bureaucrats, functionaries and military officers were imbued with a 'civilizing mission'. Strikingly evident was the connection pointed out by Hannah Arendt between the two main instruments of imperial domination: race and bureaucracy.[53] Moreover, although it is not possible to quantify the

[52] ACS, PCM, 1.1.13.16542.136, 'governatore Giunta a Mussolini, 21 giugno 1943'.
[53] Arendt, *Le origini del totalitarismo*, pp. 258–309.

extent to which Fascist ideology was embraced and internalized, it was quite apparent in the actions of the 'men on the spot'.

The power centres which decided, co-ordinated and administered relations with the occupied countries mostly worked with scrupulous dedication, and they did so even after 25 July 1943. There is no evidence that the Fascist bureaucrats were sloppy in their work, nor that they sought covertly to sabotage the regime. As we shall see in the second part of this book, the senior civil servants cannot be accused of carelessness or of doing things 'the Italian way'. They did not represent the bourgeois and conservative élite, a-fascist or even anti-fascist, which worked to thwart Mussolini's ambitions; on the contrary, most of the time, with conscientiousness and even stubbornness, they persevered until matters were resolved, working all the while 'towards the Duce'. Likewise, the commanders of the Regio Esercito showed no reluctance to fight, nor any meekness towards their enemies, while they strove to adapt their men and means to guerrilla warfare and to political situations objectively difficult to deal with. I believe that the conflicts of competence described above testify to the vitality of the organs of the state, not to a regime resigned to defeat – which, however, does not mean that the Italian bureaucracy was a model of efficiency, nor that all the ministries were hotbeds of rabid Fascism.

The obstinate and aggressive reaction of civilian officials and military officers to German interference and the actions of the partisans belies any accusation of defeatism: in order to hold their own against a more powerful ally and to handle an increasingly critical military situation, they summoned up all their strength and acted as shrewdly and precisely as possible. Indeed, despite deficiencies and a chronic lack of resources, the civilian as well as military functionaries strove to cope with insurmountable difficulties, displaying enterprise and adaptability as they did so.

The Fascist regime invested massively, with perhaps its best energies and its best men, in all the territories that it conquered. Mussolini was not alone in believing that the imperial 'grand design' could be realized. Italy's failure to conquer the *spazio vitale* or to defeat the partisans can in no way be blamed on the vices of what is alleged to be an Italian national 'character'.

CHAPTER 5

The conquerors

Having discussed the roles of Mussolini, the political and military leaders, and the administrations of the occupied and annexed territories, I will now examine that of the 'conquerors'. The title of the chapter may seem provocative. Yet it is much less so than might first appear, because, in keeping with the structure of this study as a whole, it serves to highlight the discrepancy between the regime's projects and its actual achievements.

I shall first outline some themes of the propaganda which, after the war in Ethiopia, most stridently promoted the idea of conquest and the new civilization. I shall then examine the orders issued by generals and officers that attempted to forge the minds and bodies of the conquerors, how the regime kept up the morale of the troops, relations with the occupied populations, certain aspects of everyday routine and the escalation of violence.

Were the hundreds and thousands of soldiers sent to France and the Balkans indeed the race of conquerors that Mussolini wanted? To what extent did Fascist ideology mould the behaviour of the troops? Did it influence the thought and actions of the generals, officials and rank-and-file troops in the same ways? What factors conditioned the behaviour and perceptions of the occupied populations? What influence was exerted on the everyday lives of the Italian soldiers by the ideal of the new civilization, the *ordine nuovo* and the *spazio vitale*? All these questions can be summed up in one alone: to what extent were the soldiers who occupied the European territories after 1940 actually Fascists?

Before beginning my discussion, I must briefly state my sources: the 'historical diaries' (*diari storici*) or logbooks of divisions, corps and armies, the reports of the 'P' (*Propaganda*), 'A' (*Assistenza*) and 'I' (*Informazioni*) sections, and of the *Ufficio Servizi*. I would point out that the divisional 'P' units systematically reported to their respective army corps commands, these to the army commands and these in their turn to the General Staff of the Regio Esercito and thence to the Supreme Command. We may take these sources to be reliable because, inasmuch as they were secret reports, they had no need to dissemble on the actual state of morale among the troops. I have also drawn, *cum grano salis*, on memoirs, diaries, written testimonies and novels. These I examine not as factual accounts but as descriptions of emotions and experiences which seem plausible in light of the archival documents. Memoirs will help reconstruct the perceptions of the soldiers by describing the 'natural reality' that the soldiers sought to construct for themselves but which the official documents rarely convey.

THE ARISTOCRACY OF THE NEW CIVILIZATION AND THE CIVILIZING MISSION

The Fascist regime depicted the world war as an 'inevitable collision of two civilizations': the Fascist civilization against the illusion of materialism, individualistic and hedonistic liberalism, sterile positivism, and super-capitalism. In the war for 'conquest of the higher spheres of the spirit', the 'warriors and saints', 'the aristocracy of the new civilization' invested with moral responsibility and bearing a message of 'salvation', would fight against the plutocratic, democratic, communist and Jewish 'dragon'. In the decisive clash between 'spiritual races', the 'dynamic and virile Graeco-Roman peoples' would defeat the 'Judeo-Christian believers in peace and justice'.

To win the war, bring salvation and free the peoples subject to the tyranny of the West, the Italian race would have to prove that it was a united and strong national community, that it was able to meet the challenge of the modern world, achieve supremacy and carry forward a civilizing mission. The regime's task was to create the Fascist new man: dynamic, virile, heroic, submissive to the state and obedient to its leader; the black-shirted reincarnation of the peasant-soldier who had enabled ancient Rome to dominate the Mediterranean, a popular hero, the promoter of the new civilization. This endeavour was not only announced by the slogans and the mass rituals organized by the PNF; it was given concrete form by Fascist racial policy in its two variants, colonial (apartheid) and metropolitan (anti-Semitism and discrimination against minorities).

In order to fulfil its mission, the regime had to accomplish a radical shift to totalitarianism. In this it was assisted by a conjuncture of cultural, political and economic impulses which recast the national-racial and biological definition of the racial features 'destined to produce the future leaders of the revolution and the empire'.[1] The Fascist regime adopted a definition of

[1] Sertoli Salis, *Imperi e colonizzazioni*, 1941, p. 331; V. Mazzei, *Razza e nazione*, 1941, p. 10; Guglielmi, '*Impero e razza*'.

race similar to the German notion of *Volk*. It was founded on the idea that there existed an Italian 'blood community': the Italian race '[as] the unity of the nation's bio-anthropological substratum . . . akin and analogous to the bio-physical-psychic features handed down over the centuries under the law of heredity'.[2] 'Scientific' proof of the existence of different races would give Italians a unitary purpose, produce consensus and cohesion, and consolidate national and ethnic unity. It would serve above all to justify the Italians' supremacy over other peoples and to legitimate conquest and domination.

Just prior to Italy's entry into the war, the population and the majority of the Fascist party hierarchs had not yet 'assimilated the empire into their consciousness'. Still predominant in the country was the 'home footing policy' (*politica del piede di casa*) inherited from the liberal 'Italietta' (a mocking term for Italy between the end of the First World War and Mussolini) so vituperated by the regime, and against which its propaganda inveighed, albeit in vain: in actual fact, the bourgeois mentality largely prevailed over the Fascist 'spirit'. Mussolini believed that the war (as a mass character-building experience) would forge the Fascist new man. The conflict would deliver the final 'kick in the arse' needed to turn the Italians into a great and modern nation. It would therefore be the war that eliminated the divisions between the military and civilian spheres, while years of mass mobilization would meld the country into a single production unit. Sentimentalism and pietism would be supplanted by hatred defined as 'the desire to wreak maximum harm on the enemy until his annihilation'. Some intellectuals, writes Ruth Ben-Ghiat, justified this normalization of the homicidal instinct as a continuation of the 'cathartic violence' distinctive of *squadrismo* and other defining aspects of the Fascist revolution. Others argued that acquisition of 'warrior character' would ensue from internalization by the Italians of the concepts of purification and expansion which underpinned the notion of Fascist modernity.[3] The war would 'kill off' the Italians' bourgeois mentality and mark the advent of the Fascist new man in the conquered *spazio vitale*.

But in what way, between 1940 and 1943, did the 'aristocracy of the new civilization' pursue its 'civilizing mission' in the conquered territories? Were the leaders of the revolution and the empire aware of their mission and conscious of their supposed racial, moral and spiritual superiority?

THE LEADERS OF THE REVOLUTION AND THE EMPIRE

Immediately following Italy's entry into the war, Mussolini was forced to admit that the leaders of the revolution and the empire did not exist; that the

[2] V. Mazzei, *Razza e nazione*, 1942, p. 60. [3] Ben-Ghiat, *La cultura fascista*, pp. 281–2.

Italians were not yet the race of conquerors which he envisioned; that the party had failed in its enterprise of Fascistization; and that the new ruling class – the aristocracy of the new civilization – was not yet ready to assume power. The king and the Regio Esercito had not been replaced by the Fascist popular army commanded by Mussolini and his leaders of the revolution. Nevertheless, the Duce did not relinquish his imperial ambitions, and he used the king's army, which he controlled and commanded, to pursue them.

The purpose of this chapter is to demonstrate the affinity between two mentalities: that of career military personnel on the one hand, and that of the Fascists on the other. It was an affinity, writes the historian Fortunato Minniti,

> which we may consider, if not certain, at least probable given the numerous contacts between the two mentalities during the years of the regime's consolidation, in both myth and reality, and both for and against ideals, values, norms and laws. It was an affinity between mentalities, not between ideologies, because the soldiers lacked, by training as well as by discipline, the expressive means to give complete form to the values system of a profession generally regarded as a way of life.

The military and the regime fused myth and reality together, both when they remembered the First World War and also when they imagined Italy's future role in Europe. They aimed for a stronger position in Europe and the world founded on the certainty of the instability and mutability of the world stage and achieved even by war if necessary. Other beliefs were shared by the soldiers and the Fascists: the values of pragmatism and concreteness, a willingness to undertake a mission in the collective interest on the state's behalf, the hierarchical principle extended to society, warfare as a positive phenomenon because it was intrinsic to human nature and, especially, nationalism.[4] This convergence of mentalities linked with the question of Fascistization of the Regio Esercito, although it is unfortunately difficult to determine the extent to which the soldiers' code of values, their ideal of military discipline, and their political and moral role were compatible with the Fascist project for conquest of the *spazio vitale*.

The commanders of the Regio Esercito stationed in the conquered territories soon realized that not only were the soldiers under their command not a 'race of conquerors', they were entirely unprepared for the experience of military occupation. The battalions sent to the Balkans had not been formed with a view to undertaking a lengthy occupation. The soldiers were accustomed to fighting an enemy in uniform, whereas the guerrilla offensive against them was initially waged by units difficult to identify, and with the participation – direct or indirect – of civilians. Large numbers of Italian

[4] Minniti, 'Gli ufficiali di carriera dell'esercito'.

soldiers died in the first ambushes because they were caught unawares, and because they did not have the training necessary to deal with an extremely mobile enemy well acquainted with the terrain.

Circular no. 3c of 1 March 1942 was a sort of vade-mecum drawn up by the senior commander, General Mario Roatta, and distributed to ranks up to battalion command in all the territories annexed and militarily occupied by the Second Army.[5] It set out a series of anti-insurgency measures and marked an aggressive radicalization of the campaign against the partisans. Yet it was written well before the occupation system collapsed into permanent disarray under the partisan onslaught (see chapters 10 and 11).[6] Circular 3c was an attempt, made by a general and not by the secretary of the PNF, to inculcate the Italian troops with a 'conqueror's' mentality. But were Roatta's conquerors the same as Mussolini's? The answer is broadly 'yes'. Selected to command the army in Yugoslavia because he was one of the Duce's most trusted lieutenants, General Roatta intended to instil a 'Fascist conqueror' mentality in his soldiers. The circular is a clear example of the 'working towards the Duce' principle in action. It was Roatta's contribution to the Fascist endeavour to root itself in the dominated territory and extirpate all 'treacherous' elements loath to accept the new Fascist reality. The part of the document of interest here sets out the 'ten commandments' which the cadres of the Second Army had always to obey:

The army is fighting a war. This means: a war mentality, rejection of the negative qualities summed up by the expression 'bono italiano'; 'true grit'.
The information service must be particularly active and extensive.
Secrecy must be maintained at all costs, living together with a population . . . induces the 'bono' Italian to trust everyone he meets . . . This behaviour must cease.
Garrisons large and small must be organized for defence.
The efficiency of the rebels is often overestimated. You must react vigorously . . . against the tendency to exaggerate the capabilities of the adversary.
You must react promptly against enemy offensives, using as much massive force as possible. The treatment to be meted out to the rebels is not 'a tooth for a tooth' but 'a head for a tooth'!
Operations against the rebels are real and proper acts of war.
Being caught tactically off-guard is unacceptable . . . Errors of this kind will incur specific and severe punishment.
You must tenaciously fight to the bitter end . . . Do not believe the myth that the rebels treat certain types of prisoner humanely.

[5] Legnani, 'Il ginger del generale Roatta'.
[6] DDI, ser. IX, 1939–43, vol. 8, doc. 222, 'ministro a Zagabria Raffaele Casertano al ministro degli Esteri Ciano, Zagabria 31 gennaio 1942': 'The organization of the rebels is still good as regards the Četniks, these being the remnants of the Yugoslavian army; it is instead improvised and deficient among the partisan bands (communists).'

The situation and prestige of Italy in the new provinces, and in the occupied territories, require iron discipline from the entire army and a demeanour in every respect exemplary.

Roatta's concern was more than the obvious need to adapt tactics and strategies to guerrilla warfare. He wanted to transform the *boni italiani* into warriors, and, even if his intention was not to turn them into Fascist warriors, it coincided with the Mussolinian ideal of the dominator. Roatta used elementary methods: he threatened harsh punishment for disobedience; he rallied the troops ('have the guts to defend your arms'); he belittled the military valour of the enemy; he urged his men to treat the 'treacherous' local population with the greatest suspicion. He insisted that the troops conduct themselves in a manner befitting 'a victorious nation' and he deliberately created a relation between the racially superior occupier and the racially inferior occupied that legitimated the authority of the former and erected a barrier between them and the latter. He instilled in his soldiers the idea that their enemies were savages, so that the war was a struggle between civilization and barbarism.[7] The barbarian-partisans and the civilian populations which supported them constituted a racially inferior breed (bandits, Bolsheviks, the godless). They threatened the fatherland, civilization and order, and the troops were never under any circumstance to fraternize with them. The spirit and contents of Circular 3c did not reflect Roatta's ideas alone, however, as the following document of the 8th Army Corps (July 1941) illustrates:

The present tranquillity of Greece must not induce us to relax our vigilance . . . It should be impressed upon our soldiers that they must be constantly ready to respond *immediately and violently* to every act of hostility. The conduct of individual soldiers is a decisive factor in the suppression of any uprising within the population, which we must *control and dominate*.[8]

In 1941, General Carlo Geloso had declared: 'Wherever there are Italian troops, the justice of Rome shall reign with its implacable serenity but also with its 2000-year tradition of fairness.'[9] But then, in April 1943, he proclaimed:

Let all be informed that our anonymous fallen, our martyred soldiers, our combatants profaned in their eternal sleep by the crosses smashed down from their graves,

[7] Capogreco, *Renicci*, pp. 18–19.

[8] USSME, L 15, b. 27, 'Comando VIII CdA – Ufficio "I", generale Giuseppe Pafundi a tutte le divisioni dipendenti, 26 luglio 1941' (emphasis added).

[9] USSME, N 1–11, 'Diari storici', b. 554, 'generale Geloso al Comando del III e XXVI CdA, 29 novembre 1941'.

demand vengeance. Obeying this commandment is the sacred duty of Italians, of men and of soldiers atrociously offended in their noblest of sentiments and who must safeguard their honour as well as their very existence.[10]

The ideals of Roman justice and humanity evaporated. The enemy that had 'surpassed the wickedness of the savages and beasts of the forest which hunt down their prey and make sadistic orgy of their blood' did not belong to the human race. There could be no quarter against the barbarian-partisans, against the 'savages' and their accomplices. No longer applicable was 'the moral, juridical, military law'; rather, 'the most pitiless vengeance and the most cruel reprisals' were to be exacted.

One cannot determine with certainty whether the military commanders were motivated to implement occupation policies by their ideological conviction alone. Some of them executed their orders out of a sense of duty; others did so for fear of the consequences if they refused. Yet others found ways not to execute their orders. The same applied to the senior officers charged with the crucial task of transmitting the 'conqueror mentality', with giving a new identity and new values to their soldiers, with influencing their perceptions of themselves, the occupied populations and the partisans.

THE HONOUR CODE OF THE ITALIAN OFFICER

Minniti has convincingly argued that the consensus shown by career officers towards Mussolini and the regime was not solely 'interest-based' (prompted by individual benefits received or expected and by the career opportunities made available by the regime). Nor was it a 'trade-off consensus' (support in return for rewards by the regime for the armed forces): had this been the case, the disastrous operations of the winter of 1940 – with the consequent failure of political and strategic plans for the 'short war' – would have put an end to the army's support for the regime. This did not happen. The armed forces lent their support to the regime for reasons both 'interested' and 'spontaneous' (conviction that the ideological bases of Fascism were

[10] USSME, N I–II, 'Diari storici', b. 1237, 'Comando XI Armata, 7 aprile 1943; b. 1056, 18 aprile 1943'. The commander Mario Robotti advised the high commissioner of Ljubljana to circulate a notice among the Slovene population informing them that upon the first crime committed by the communists ('because', the General wrote, 'we have a large quantity of captured communists in our hands') one of them, who was 'certainly guilty', would be shot. For Robotti, this was not hostage-taking, in which case moral scruples might arise: for a communist 'even in prison, even at Gonars, is irreducibly an enemy of Italy and the regime'. 'I am convinced that the measure is necessary [for the administration of] sound justice', concluded the general.

correct), and also because of what can be described as 'due' support (loyalty to the king who had given supreme military command to the Duce).[11]

But what demeanour was expected of the Italian officer in the occupied territories? The military code of honour stipulated that an official of the Regio Esercito must always act 'the gentleman, even towards the enemy'. His behaviour was to consist of dignity, decorum, courtesy, seriousness, professional competence, deference and respect for both enemy and ally. He was expected to excel in every aspect of everyday life. The Italian officers' motto was 'firmness with compassion, unbiased and objective appraisal'. In his dealings with civilians, the officer was to make it plain that any hope of revolt was pointless, but also that a new life in collaboration with Italy was possible.[12] In his relations with the troops he was required to personify the ideal warrior. General Geloso constantly extolled the 'mentality of the war front', the need to 'arise and to awaken' and to develop a profound sense of self-confidence and of superiority over the occupied populations. The latter would respond to the advent of the conquerors by bowing beneath the weight of defeat and accepting that the victors were morally, militarily, socially and organizationally superior.[13]

The officer was expected to talk to his troops, to attend to their physical and moral well-being and to make daily 'training exercises sportively useful and professionally advantageous'.[14] Like a good father he would combine reward with chastisement and punish wrongdoers inflexibly but fairly.[15] The commander of the Fourth Army instructed his officers that they must at all costs avoid emotional attachment to their troops. Becoming closely acquainted with the ordinary soldier, wrote Mario Vercellino, did not require 'unwholesome familiarity, but instead understanding of his mind and attentive concern for his needs'.[16] The officer's neat appearance, and therefore that of his men, was essential in order to emphasize the victors' superiority: constant refurbishment of uniforms was therefore essential. Every military action was to be regulated by a set of procedures which constituted a fully fledged ritual. From the changing of the guard to the relief

[11] Minniti, 'Gli ufficiali di carriera dell'esercito'; Rochat, *L'esercito italiano*, pp. 183–9.
[12] USSME, N 1–11, 'Diari storici', b. 374, 'Pirzio Biroli alle divisioni dipendenti dal XIV CdA, 31 agosto 1941'.
[13] USSME, N 1–11, 'Diari storici', b. 1004, 'Comando Divisione Sassari, 7 settembre 1942, oggetto: Bono italiano'.
[14] USSME, N 1–11, 'Diari storici', b. 1237, 'Comando III CdA alle divisioni dipendenti, 28 aprile 1943'.
[15] USSME, N 1–11, 'Diari storici', b. 457, 'Comando III CdA a tutti i comandi dipendenti, 19 novembre 1941, firmato generale Angelo Rossi'.
[16] USSME, N 1–11, 'Diari storici', b. 1127, 'Comando IV Armata, 25 gennaio 1943'.

of a unit fighting at the front, everything was to be performed in a manner that affirmed the dignity of the Italian army.

The ideal self-image of the officers was therefore somewhat traditional: almost nineteenth-century, in fact. Courtliness, good manners and gentlemanly behaviour were traditional bourgeois virtues, certainly not Fascist ones. So did the bourgeois and paternalistic Italian officer who did not fraternize with the troops (unlike his counterpart in the Wehrmacht) truly embody the ideal type of the Fascist warrior, of the *uomo nuovo*? Not at all, but in contradictory and ambiguous manner he transmitted some of the ideal values of the Fascist conqueror: the victor's moral, military, social and organizational superiority.

THE MORALE OF THE SOLDIERS

The General Staffs of every division endeavoured to maintain the morale of their troops in four complementary ways: pastoral care, sports and social entertainments, reading and information, and brothels. Before examining each of these aspects, I would stress a distinctive feature of the Italian occupation: the long periods of time spent by the divisions and CdAs in the occupied territories. The Second, Eleventh and Fourth Armies occupied Greece, Yugoslavia and France until 8 September 1943, and only a few divisions moved or changed *dipendenza* (passed from one CdA to another). Long service in the same territorial area without leave was a factor with a crucial influence on relationships between the occupiers and the local population, the attitude of commanders towards their troops, and occupation policies. The long spells of duty served by soldiers in the same locality made discipline increasingly difficult to maintain, and it sapped the morale of the troops.

The army tables on leave permits granted show that, at the beginning of 1943, fully 50 per cent of soldiers had not been on home leave in the past twelve months: some soldiers had remained uninterruptedly with their divisions for more than two years.[17] The situation then deteriorated further,

[17] USSME, N 1–11, 'Diari storici', b. 1110, 'Divisione Emilia, nucleo Assistenza, 17 gennaio 1943'. As of January 1943, in the Emilia Division (stationed in the province of Kotor), fully 3,900 out of 6,826 soldiers, equal to 57 per cent of the total, had not been on leave for at least twelve months; more than 1,300 of them had not been on leave for at least fifteen months. The figures for the 26th CdA (which in November 1942 consisted of 1,088 officers and 23,887 soldiers) are equally eloquent: 12 officers and 3,996 soldiers had not been on leave for more than twenty-four months, 56 officers and 3,698 soldiers for more than twenty months, 22 officers and 4,130 soldiers for more than sixteen months. Hence, 12,000 soldiers, approximately 50 per cent of those on active duty, had spent fifteen months uninterruptedly in the occupied territories.

owing to the chronic shortage of transport and to the disorganization of the Regio Esercito. A fifteen-day leave permit kept a soldier away from his unit for a period of around one and a half months taken up by travel, quarantine camp and delays at various staging posts. In 1943, the suspension of leave for the Sicilian soldiers of the Fourth Army and the Sardinian ones of the Eleventh provoked numerous attempts to desert. Supersloda considered the possibility of constructing rest centres or of leasing hotels so that furlough could be taken *in loco*.

Any army occupying a foreign territory spends a more or less long period of time amid alien customs and a general climate of hostility: the defeated population harbours resentment and yearns for vengeance. The soldier is enclosed within his camp, subject to iron discipline, far from his family, friends and work. This was also the case of the Italian soldier. To what extent did welfare and propaganda respond to the exigencies of the war? What was Fascist about the propaganda for the troops and the army services?

Examination of the documents does not reveal clear evidence of deteriorating morale or of a decline in the fighting spirit of the Italian troops, either in the Balkans or in France, and at least until the spring of 1942. As reported by the army commands, the main preoccupation of the soldiers was the fate of their families in distant Italy, while their main complaints were the suspension of leave, the non-arrival of parcels and the lack of news from Italy. But the 'P' section of the Command of the 6th CdA reported that 'after long months of arduous existence among inhospitable lands and hostile people, the body and spirit have been tempered and are not dismayed by the prospect of a winter even harsher than the last one'.[18] Indeed, morale would have been excellent had it not been for the indifference with which soldiers were greeted when they returned home; and had it not been for the economic hardships suffered by their families, compared with those whose breadwinners had not been conscripted.

The factor most responsible for the deterioration of morale was immorality in Italy and licentious behaviour towards the wives of combatants. The soldiers then complained about the lack of tobacco and wine, and the dreadful quality of their rations and of their clothes. They suffered

[18] For example, until March 1943, reports compiled by the censorship commission at the Command of the 7th CdA in Corsica stated that 'the morale of the troops was good' (see USSME, N 1–11, 'Diari storici', bb. 991, 1105, 1201, 1225, 1272, 2001, 2005). It might be objected that that soldiers were aware that their letters were being censored and consequently took care not to criticize the regime or the military authorities. Nevertheless, the 'A' reports based on direct observation of the soldiers' behaviour and attitudes also confirmed the 'good morale of the troops'. (The military mail censorship commissions set up by the CS–CSM in all divisions outside Italy inspected correspondence sent by soldiers and addressed to soldiers on other fronts. See USSME, M 7, b. 279.)

economically because they were serving in a territory whose currency was constantly devalued, while their pay could not keep pace with inflation.[19] Statements by the 'A' and 'P' units to the effect that 'events of the past few days [the loss of northern Africa] have not shaken the morale and the spirit of the troops, which can be considered excellent',[20] may have been superficial but they were largely true. The writers of the reports understood that the soldiers were preoccupied more by their personal situations, and those of their families, than by the outcomes of battles on distant fronts (in regard to which they, in any case, received news carefully sanitized to keep up their morale). In light of the statistics on desertion rates in the armies deployed in the occupied territories, should one wish to establish a causal link between desertion and the efficiency of the propaganda and the welfare services provided for the troops, one may conclude that they were to some extent successful. In 1942, for example, of 1,589 soldiers brought before the military tribunal of the Eleventh Army, only 226 were charged with desertion.[21] Moreover, the Italian armies were relatively unworried about the effects of communist propaganda on the troops. It seems that little notice was taken of the leaflets distributed by the partisans, and very few Italian soldiers crossed over to the Resistance before 8 September 1943. Some CdA commanders in Greece reported that 'given the absence of subversive propaganda among the troops, no repressive measures have been taken', and again 'no forms of communist propaganda are present among the troops'.[22] The abrupt collapse of morale came only after 25 July 1943. Does this mean that Fascist propaganda was successful? Does it mean that the Italian soldiers truly believed that they were engaged in a mission, and that this kept their morale high despite military defeats and the rigours of service in the occupied countries?

Re-arming the spirit,[23] *pastoral care*

Mussolini had to rely on the military chaplains to sustain the morale of the troops, a fact that underscores the failure of the Fascist totalitarian project. The Fascist *uomo nuovo* would never have seen the light of day had his

[19] USSME, M 3, b. 56, 'Comando VI CdA, sottosezione Propaganda, al Com. sup. di Supersloda, 2 novembre 1942'.

[20] USSME, N 1–11, 'Diari storici', b. 1180, 'al Com. sup. FF.AA. Grecia, 3 aprile 1943'.

[21] USSME, L 13, b. 105, 'procura militare del re imperatore presso il tribunale militare di guerra del Comando sup. FF.AA. Grecia allo SMRE, 20 aprile 1943'.

[22] ASMAE, GABAP, b. 4, 'MAE – AA.GG. IV al CS, 31 dicembre 1942'; see also b. 23.

[23] The reference is to Mimmo Franzinelli's excellent *Il riarmo dello spirito*; also by Franzinelli, see *Stellette, croce e fascio littorio*.

spiritual guide been the Catholic priest instead of the party.[24] This the Duce had to acknowledge, and he implicitly admitted that, in a cultural setting where the soldiers tenaciously adhered to the Catholic and peasant tradition, the chaplain attended to their spiritual needs better than did the party functionaries. The chaplain personified the village priest at the front: it was he who knew best the complex and deeply rooted spirituality of the masses in what was a still profoundly rural Italy. This visceral attachment to religion was a psychological factor of essential importance for sustaining the morale of the troops. Mimmo Franzinelli has rightly pointed out that, 'thanks to faith, the cruel and bloody reality of the war was set within the reassuring domain of a Christianity which could rationalize sacrifices otherwise incomprehensible and unbearable'. In the terminology of the Curia Castrense (Army Chaplaincy), the chaplain was 'father and brother to his soldiers', 'the soldier of Christ and of the fatherland marching with his gallant lads to victory': part parish priest, part confessor, part officer, always ready to listen with compassion, to help in every way possible, to advise the soldiers and raise their spirits, safeguard their morality and bolster their courage.[25]

The celebration of mass on certain occasions like Easter, or the consecration of the soldiers to the Sacred Heart (a bombastic religious ceremony, intended to inspire them) acquired military connotations. For the chaplains most deeply indoctrinated with the regime's ideology, they were ideal occasions to emphasize the collective nature of the ritual and to exploit its choreography. The chaplains' principal task was to give ardour, courage and heroism to 'their' soldiers: '[w]ith the twofold strength of faith in God and love of the fatherland' they were to 'shape souls' and furnish 'a doubly unshakeable certainty based on two foundations of granite: God and the fatherland'. The chaplains – and in this they demonstrated indubitable flexibility and adaptability – contrived to adjust themes, symbols

[24] The Oberkommand of the Wehrmacht 'interdit aux officiers de prendre position sur les questions religieuses, autorisa les "sorties de l'Eglise" et écarta des aumôniers les pasteurs de l'Eglise de la Confession. Ses conférenciers parcouraient les garnisons pour proposer un nouvel idéal d'officier, le chef politique, qui devrait propager parmi ses hommes les valeurs ethniques (Volkstum) et leur expliquer que la . . . guerre serait de nature idéologique. Cette manœuvre de débordement par en bas s'appuyait sur la jeune génération des officiers de troupe, souvent formés par la Jeunesse hitlérienne' (Ayçoberry, *La société allemande sous le IIIe Reich*, p. 221).

[25] Franzinelli, *Il riarmo dello spirito*, p. 40. Father Angelo Bartolomasi spoke to the soldiers on the following topics: Religion and the Fatherland, Romanity and Christianity, Work and Prayer, Duty and Pleasure, Valour and Virtue, Morals and Morality, Form and Strength, Sacrifice and Benefit, Per Aspera ad Astra, Per Terrestria ad Celestia, Per Crucem ad Lucem, Combat and Victory, Winning Against Yourself to Win, God Fatherland Family, Faith Work Valour, Memory Hopes and Purposes, Duty Pain Passion, Believing Obeying Fighting, on the three symbolic colours (green, white, red), and on trust in God, the King and the Duce.

and images to the changing circumstances of the war. The image of the 'God of the Army', which accompanied the offensive phases of the military campaigns, was adroitly replaced with the image of the suffering Christ with whom the soldiers could identify amid the harsh realities of their lives. The soldier was depicted as a 'lay priest and a little redeemer, because the law for which Christ had died and for which the soldiers were now dying was one and the same: the law of redemption (Don Gnocchi)'.[26]

On 20 February 1943, there were more than 400 military chaplains (of a total of 2,375) serving in the territories occupied by Italy: 27 in the Aegean, 124 in Greece, 77 in Albania, 47 in Montenegro, 147 in Slovenia, Dalmatia and the territories of the former Yugoslavia, and 140 in the French territories (as well as 172 in Soviet territory).[27] Many of them served with the 'P' sections. According to Franzinelli, the military chaplains conceived their pastoral mission in four main ways. First, there were the torch-bearers of Nazism–Fascism – those who had joined the conflict with ideological intent – for whom patriotic-religious beliefs were of much less importance than loyalty to the Duce and to the Axis cause: these chaplains constituted a hyper-fascist minority (382 in total), and the majority of them served with the MVSN. Then there were the chaplains who supported the Duce *usque ad mortem et ultra*, who sacralized the Fascist imperial adventure by blending religious with Fascist language, and who mixed remembrance of the fatherland's history with evangelism. Thirdly, there were the chaplains for whom militarism was profoundly distasteful but performed their duties nevertheless. And fourthly there were those who conceived their pastoral work as personal sacrifice.

It is difficult to quantify the impact of pastoral care on the behaviour of the soldiers. We do not know how many soldiers listened to the prayers and homilies of the chaplains, or whether and to what extent they assimilated their content. Just as General Roatta sought with his ten commandments to forge the Italian soldier, so the military chaplain carried forward the civilizing mission: 'Italy once again claims for itself the sacred right to teach other peoples that only one spiritually strong nation, that only one ardent and pure faith, is able to create heroes, and with these heroes the new destinies of an entire epoch.'[28] The Soldier's Prayer is the clearest example of this clerical-fascist – or at least clerical-nationalist – conceptualization:

[26] Franzinelli, *Il riarmo dello spirito*, pp. 91–5.
[27] USSME, N 1–11, 'Diari storici', b. 1074; see also bb. 605 and 1166.
[28] USSME, N 1–11, 'Diari storici', b. 1166, 'SMRE, Curia castrense'.

O Lord our God, eternal and omnipotent – who chose Rome to be the centre of your faith and who made Italy the land of saints and heroes – it is to You that we raise this heartfelt prayer. Keep us pure in thought, word and deed. Cherish within our hearts a love of religion, family and the fatherland. Make us safe in the hour of danger, constant in the hour of sacrifice, strong in the hour of battle. Bless our august emperor king and all the royal family, the head of our government and all the institutions of the state. Extend, O Lord our God, the just power of the fatherland and let our flag – adorned with the sign of the cross – forever fly as the symbol of civilization and the promise of victory.

'Mens sana in corpore sano'

Throughout the occupations the Italian commands attended carefully to the physical well-being of their soldiers. They organized sports events, regimental or divisional football tournaments, and even games against local teams (for example, the 74th Infantry Regiment of the Lombardia Division played a match against the Ogulin town team). In the lexicon of the commanders, sport was 'important' because it invigorated the bodies of the soldiers. It kept them occupied and prevented unsupervised contact with civilians and jaunts into neighbouring villages and towns. Above all, it helped sustain morale. To the same end, the commands set up *case del soldato*, recreation centres where the soldiers could play draughts and chess, take part in bingo games or in some exceptional cases play bowls, basketball or volleyball.

The 'P' sections, with the assistance of the OND, created 'artistic ensembles' (*complessi artistici*). Consisting of soldiers from the ranks, these put on theatre performances and music concerts. However, military orchestras increasingly took the place of those that the OND created, which were costly and whose members could not be paid – further confirmation that the PNF was only minimally involved in the everyday lives of the occupying soldiers. Some CdAs organized schools for illiterate soldiers, which the military chaplains successfully ran even if they had to do without teaching materials and stationery.

Newspapers, cinema and radio

Some divisions organized travelling libraries, while the commands obtained newspapers and magazines from Rome. Among the books most frequently loaned were *La tradotta del fronte giulio*, *Il fante costiero*, *Il Giappone e le sue forze armate*, *Mussolini parla agli operai*, *Il consulente coloniale*, *Distruggiamo il bolscevismo* (we do not know to what extent these books were actually read, nor the literacy rate among the troops, especially if the semi-literate are included). The newspapers can be divided into various categories. There were the clandestine ones, often of ironic or satirical character which ridiculed the senior officers, though they were careful not to criticize the regime, Mussolini or the Regio Esercito. These were short-lived, however, owing to troop movements and the difficulty of finding printing presses and paper, and because of their very nature as mildly subversive. Sent from Rome were *Fronte*, *Notizie dal fronte*, *Tradotta*, *Marco Aurelio*, *Domenica del Corriere*, *Bertoldo*, *Gente nostra*, *Settimana enigmistica*, and *Notiziario settimanale PNF* (which arrived in very few copies: for example, in February 1943, the Command of the 14th CdA received 9,000 copies of *Fronte* but only 250 of the PNF's *Notiziario*).[29]

Notable among the locally printed newspapers and news-sheets were *Sentinella*,[30] 'a newspaper in grey-green[31] [for the soldiers in Dubrovnik] created to bring the latest news on the war and the world and to provide hours of wholesome entertainment for the soldiers fighting on this front' (first published on 8 September 1942); *Tascapane. Quotidiano informatore dei bianco-azzurri della Divisione Marche* (between 1,500 and 2,300 copies per day in mid-July 1942); *Pista*, the newspaper for the Fourth Alpini Division; *Vedetta*, issued three times a week by the Italian command in Crete for troops in the province of Lassithi; and *Picchiasodo*. Cyclostyled broadsheets were circulated in some hundreds of copies by the divisional 'A' sections: for instance, *Notiziario taurinense*, which published the Italian bulletins and summaries of the news, mainly sports, from the Stefani agency. The divisions also gave oral briefings on the military situation to the illiterate and semi-literate. They were organized through the ranks up to platoon commander, their purpose being to keep up the combative spirit and the vigilance of the soldiers.

The newspapers published information carefully selected to furnish 'wholesome entertainment' and to sustain morale. Well aware of this, the soldiers paid close attention to Radio Fante (Radio Infantry), the rumour mill fed by soldiers returning from leave who supplied news on important events in Italy or the war. On several occasions, news leaked out and rapidly circulated despite the efforts of the commands. In France, for instance, because of the huge number of sick and wounded soldiers from the Soviet front hospitalized in nearby Liguria, reports spread of the defeat, slaughter

[29] USSME, N I–II, 'Diari storici', b. 1083, 'Comando XIV CdA, 10 marzo 1943'.
[30] USSME, N I–II, 'Diari storici', b. 1267, 'Comando VI CdA'.
[31] Grey and green were the colours of the Regio Esercito uniform.

and suffering of the Italian troops and of Germany's failure to support them. The arrival of this news, reported the Fourth Army Command, had a much greater impact on morale than did the leaflets dropped by the Allies or the broadcasts by Radio London. In more or less the same way the troops discovered the dreadful reality of the war in the East or learned of the bombings of Italian cities, of which little mention was made by the military publications or those of the regime.

During lulls in military operations, films and newsreels were projected in the *case del soldato* or at the military cinemas. The most popular were the box-office successes of the time: *Cantate con me*, *Tamara*, *La voce nella tempesta*, *Cento di questi giorni*, *La cena delle beffe*, *La figlia del vento*, *Bengasi*, *Casa paterna*, *Ballerine*, *Ave Maria*, *Giuliano de' Medici*, *Casta diva* and *Signore senza alloggio*. According to a calculation by the 'A' unit of the Murge Division, monthly audiences consisted on average of 520 officers, 560 non-commissioned officers and 8,700 troops, while for the entire CdA the average monthly audience was 17,000 soldiers.

Also organized for the troops were EIAR radio broadcasts, which flanked others like *Notizie da casa* and *Notizie a casa*, music programmes, news bulletins, history discussions, political commentaries and religious programmes. After 1941 also broadcast was a weekly conversation entitled *Parole di ufficiali ai soldati*, the declared purpose of which was to keep the ranks informed on action by the army's various units.[32]

The army brothels

The army commanders considered that the 'sexual question' had a decisive impact on the troops' morale. In reports by the 'A' sections, under the heading 'The Most Urgent Needs of the Soldiers', one reads for instance as follows: 'To be emphasized, with regard to soldiers who have by now been stationed on the island for nine months, is the hardship caused by the difficulty of satisfying their physiological needs.' The commanders admitted that, 'although [they are] good by nature, [faced with] the allure of sex [the Italian soldiers] forget every most sacred affection, every most intimate restraint, every most manifest duty'.[33] Unfortunately, only rare references to brothels are to be found in the archives of the Italian army, probably because part of the documentation has been lost. According to the veteran Renzo Biasion, the 'girls' – some of them

[32] *Parole di ufficiali ai soldati*, transcriptions of radio talks broadcast in 1941, published by SMRE, Ufficio Propaganda, 1942.

[33] Franzinelli, *Il riarmo dello spirito*, p. 141.

underaged – were attached to the battalions like any other troop unit; they were given rations, and they serviced officers and other ranks in separate facilities.[34] The fact that the military brothels followed the armies in the field or were organized on the spot to 'satisfy sexual needs' was not peculiar to the Italians. The Germans had their brothels as well, although theirs were (at least in theory) stocked with women selected in accordance with Nazi racial principles, whereas the open brothels of the Regio Esercito did not use prostitutes of 'Italian race' but drew their supplies, so to speak, from 'the local market'. The Italian divisional commands attended to the organization of the brothels under their jurisdiction, applying few and simple criteria: only women free from disease were to be recruited, and they were to be periodically examined by doctors; and the brothels for officers had to be separate from those for non-commissioned officers and other ranks.[35]

Setting up brothels to dissuade the use of travelling prostitutes from whom the soldiers might easily catch diseases was regarded as a 'compelling necessity' by all the authorities, even the ecclesiastical ones (although they officially deplored the existence of the brothels).[36] The *case di tolleranza*, the army commanders maintained, averted 'sentimental relations which in the particular political-operational situation are harmful'; they restricted relationships between soldiers and uncontrolled – politically and hygienically – members of the civilian population; and they satisfied a basic need, with the consequent boosting of morale.[37] Although the archive documents do not permit quantification of the use made of the illegal brothels, nor of the legal ones, it seems that illegal and uncontrolled prostitution predominated over its 'institutionalized' counterpart.[38]

[34] Biasion, *Sagapò*, 1953.

[35] USSME, N 1–11, 'Diari storici', b. 325, 'Comando VIII CdA – Ufficio Servizi'. The brothels were to be decorated in a dignified manner and have the sanitary fittings specified by the head of the garrison's health service. They were to be run by women who were responsible for discipline, the observation of opening and closing hours and compliance with the health regulations. Tariffs were to be those customary in the area and differentiated by category of client. The brothels were to be discreetly sited, and they were to be kept under surveillance.

[36] USSME, M 3, b. 51, 'Comando XI CdA, 5 febbraio 1942'.

[37] USSME, N 1–11, 'Diari storici', b. 376, 'Comando XXVI CdA, 17 settembre 1941, Malattie veneree e case di tolleranza'. Recommendations by the army commands on prophylactics and hygiene went unheeded. Moreover, the authorized brothels were often unable to meet demand. As regards hygiene, not all of them had 'anti-infection rooms' (*camere anticeltica*) or the necessary 'hygiene facilities' (*comodità igienica*).

[38] USSME, M 3, b. 65, 'Comando VI CdA, sottosezione Assistenza, al Com. sup. di Supersloda – Ufficio "A", 10 febbraio 1943'. See also b. 70, 9 May 1943, 'Relazione mensile sul servizio A per il periodo 15 marzo–15 aprile 1943'. In February 1943, the 6th CdA (more than 35,000 men) was served by only a handful of authorized brothels: one in Dubrovnik, one in Castelnuovo; one was scheduled to open in Mostar, while those in Ploče, Metković and Risano were still being built.

Finding the madams to run the brothels was relatively easy, because the Italian commands, with the regime's tacit approval, ignored the racial laws. The Balkan populations, with the exception of the Albanians, were theoretically members of 'other races' with whom the 'civilizing race' was prohibited by law to mix. However, given the contingencies of war, Rome did not in fact oppose the recruitment of native-born prostitutes. Indeed, according to the author of *Sagapò*, prostitutes were well regarded in the occupied countries, both because the population considered them by ancient custom to be a respectable public institution, and because they enabled the soldiers to find sexual relief without pestering the local women. As we shall see later, the problems between occupiers and the occupied populations proliferated when the soldiers formed sentimental relationships with native women.

One thus finds that the propaganda directed at the troops and the forms of spiritual, material and sexual welfare provided for them did not stem from the PNF, although this was the organ responsible for inculcating the notions of the conquest of the *spazio vitale* and for forging the spirit of the Fascist *uomo nuovo*. The officers did not assist their soldiers 'in Fascist manner' but they were nevertheless able to maintain high levels of morale. They were less susceptible to the appeal of Fascist ideology than their commanders. Finally, the military chaplains transmitted symbols largely inspired by national-religious rhetoric; they exploited the imperial myths and the cult of the leader with the tricolour; they mixed gospel, fatherland and the civilizing mission together; but in the end they ordained the preeminence of the cross over the *fascio*.

PERCEPTIONS AND RELATIONSHIPS BETWEEN CONQUERORS AND THE CONQUERED

Perceptions of the occupied populations changed from zone to zone, sometimes from village to village. There were Italian soldiers who detested the local inhabitants, blaming them for their forced presence in an inhospitable territory. Others seemed driven by a Fascist or Catholic 'civilizing mission'. Then there were those who sympathized with the occupied population but did their duty as soldiers out of a sense of discipline, for fear of being punished or because they had no alternative. Finally, there were Italian soldiers who throughout the occupation came only occasionally into contact with the local population and were entirely uninterested in what happened to them. In general, however, incomprehension between occupiers and occupied was the rule, the reasons being disorientation and the impact of what for many soldiers were places profoundly different from their homeland. Diaries and memoirs from the occupations of Greece and Yugoslavia frequently describe the bewilderment provoked by the 'exoticism' of the countries and peoples with which the soldiers came into contact. For many infantrymen and young officials, arrival in the occupied territories was their first experience of being outside Italy, or even their villages or towns. For an officer from the Veneto, Greece was like 'a desert of white stones'; for a Neapolitan, Bosnia-Herzegovina was 'cold . . . with the finest of air, woods, woods, woods'.[39]

The memoirs of veterans often associate landscapes with fear. Sergeant-Major Antonio Useli, 11th Infantry Regiment – Casale Division, described the village of Kefalovrison as enclosed by a ring of low white mountains scoured by the sun and the wind. 'You never saw and never met a living person, and those few inhabitants of the place were all shut up in their houses. Of an evening you felt almost afraid. You didn't know where to go; there wasn't a single shop open, or rather there weren't any shops at all; you didn't even hear a dog bark.'[40] For the painter Biasion, the colours of Greece were of a brightness so intense that everything turned white, and the extraordinary blue of a sea devoid of sails and the enemy which sharp-cut the horizon beyond the island, an oriental landscape, almost African, which crushed any hope of escape. Heavily bombed in 1941, Heraklion (Crete) was an apocalyptic tangle of roofless houses and tottering walls, some of them with chimney-pots perched upon them like black birds.[41] Often described in memoirs are places of oblivion and escape, like Athens, 'city of easy pleasure and sinister trafficking'.[42]

Perceptions of the local populations sprang from the baggage of prejudices, some of them racist, which the soldiers brought with them. From observation and contact with the locals, the occupiers 'decoded' the uses and customs of the occupied and catalogued them according to archetypes and stereotypes. The Italian generals were the first to construct an image of the Balkan people as treacherous and savage; many officials regarded themselves as superior to people dismissed as crude and primitive.

In memoirs and testimonies one also finds attempts to understand different settings and societies and to explain their diversity on the basis of pseudo-scientific theorizing. Colonel Giuseppe Angelini was struck by the Bosnian villages, whose inhabitants all ate from the same plate using their hands, and by the women 'of every race and type, with the most varied

[39] Mafrici, *Guerriglia sulla ferrovia del petrolio*, 1981, p. 17.
[40] Testimony in Bedeschi, *Fronte jugoslavo-balcanico*, 1986, pp. 633–4.
[41] Biasion, *Sagapò*, 1953, p. 68. [42] Mondini, *Prologo del conflitto italo-greco*, 1945.

styles of dress'.[43] A lieutenant from the Pusteria Division conducted a simple socio-economic analysis of the town of Višegrad (in 1942): small trade and crafts were run by the Muslims and the Jews; the Orthodox Christians owned the hotels, the manufacturing firms and the pharmacy, and formed the town's affluent class; the farmers and the small landowners were almost all Orthodox Christians, while the farm labourers and factory workers were Muslims. At the bottom of the social hierarchy, according to the lieutenant, were the Muslims and the Jews, poor, dirty, ragged and hungry; at the top, the Orthodox Christians, with whom, he wrote 'it would be decorous to have relations'.[44]

A propaganda officer in Epirus noted that during a field mass attended by native children, 'the strident chorus of childish voices repeated "eja eja, alalà" with wide-eyed solemnity, for all their pallid and emaciated faces'. He then asserted that the 'snotty-nosed dirty and dark-skinned [children] of gypsies and mulattoes, little pariahs of society, testified in their numerous and diverse cross-breedings to the sum of the flaws and hereditary taints of their various original races'.[45] Luigi Mondini, an official at the embassy in Athens, stressed the love of the Hellenic people for the *res publica* handed down across the centuries with unaltered virulence, and he contrived to explain why the present-day Hellenic citizen bore very little resemblance to his distant forebears: the Greeks had been 'fused and confused' with too many invaders, transfusing many of their original features into the incomers but inevitably receiving in return an influx that greatly weakened the personality of the 'primitive stock', transforming the Greeks into a 'mongrel mixture of races and nationalities'.[46]

Unfortunately, because of the high illiteracy rate among the troops, it is impossible to determine how soldiers of lower social extraction perceived the occupied population – how, that is, the peasants in grey-green uniforms perceived the French, Yugoslavian or Greek peasants. One may presume that they felt sympathy for them and saw them as similar to themselves, and that they felt closer affinity to them than to their officers. The following striking passage appears in the memoirs of an Italian officer who served in Slovenia:

> Slovenian villages consisting of clumps of wooden houses leapt into the air under the dull explosion of shells. 'Poor devils', I heard some whisper behind me, certainly

[43] Angelini, *Fuochi di bivacco in Croazia*, 1946, p. 48.
[44] Testimony by Lieutenant Antonio Perissinotto, group command Val Tagliamento, I Gruppo Alpini Valle, in Bedeschi, *Fronte jugoslavo-balcanico*, 1986, p. 306.
[45] Campione, *Guerra in Epiro*, 1950, p. 166.
[46] Mondini, *Prologo del conflitto italo-greco*, 1945, p. 19.

alluding to the peasants of those small farming communities. It was the comment of the Italian peasant in grey-green commiserating with his Slovene fellow-worker, he too sucked into the maelstrom of the guerrilla war.[47]

As regards the civilians' perceptions of the Italian soldiers, one should eschew their *ex post facto* memories, where the Italians are invariably compared with the Germans and emerge as the 'good occupiers'. Between 1940 and 1943, the occupied populations viewed the Italians as the cause of their misery and as responsible for the deaths of relatives and friends. They harboured deep hostility towards the Italians, as well as contempt for them as the weak allies of the Germans, the servants of Germany. The Italians were responsible for privations, acts of violent repression, requisitions, the destruction of houses and crops and the closure of factories and businesses. There is no doubt, therefore, that the majority of the occupied civilians were hostile to the occupiers. Yet the archive documents show the concern of the commanders to 'moralize' the soldiers so that they did not grow excessively familiar with the locals.[48] Why were orders repeatedly issued which strictly forbade fraternization with civilians in both Yugoslavia and Greece? In what circumstances did familiarity prevail over hostility? And what influence was exerted by cultural and racial prejudices, and by Fascist ideology?

In general, the Italian troops did not enter into prolonged relationships with civilians. Contacts were 'purely occasional', owing to a certain reserve on each side due to ignorance of the other's language and differences of customs, mentality and religion.[49] But in some cases contacts were far from hostile: for example, the health-care services initially set up for propaganda purposes prompted expressions of gratitude from the civilians treated. In certain zones – for instance, Rijeka Crnojevića between Cetinje and Podgorica – the populations of entire villages, hamlets and farmsteads flocked to the small military hospitals.[50] It is also true, though, that medical care served to demonstrate the superiority of the Italians: some doctors probably treated civilians in the conviction that they were absolving their imperial mission, while others did so out of professional duty, because they were following orders or because they were prompted by 'Christian charity'.

[47] Mafrici, *Guerriglia sulla ferrovia del petrolio*, 1981, p. 259.

[48] USSME, N 1–11, 'Diari storici', b. 1191, 'Divisione Macerata, nucleo divisionale A, 15 aprile 1943'.

[49] USSME, N 1–11, 'Diari storici', b. 1121, '18 gennaio 1943, Relazione mensile Servizio Assistenza al Comando VI CdA'.

[50] Testimony by Lieutenant Mario Alpi, 3rd Battalion – 129th Infantry Regiment, Perugia Division, in Bedeschi, *Fronte jugoslavo-balcanico*, 1986, p. 234. The Croatian authorities reported that Italian medical officers were performing abortions on local women made pregnant by Italian soldiers. See USSME, M 3, b. 71, 'Com. sup. Supersloda – UAC, 28 gennaio 1943'.

Other contacts are difficult to interpret. In some zones of Greece, Italian soldiers were often to be seen sitting in shops or private homes conversing familiarly 'con borghesi e con donne'. The commanders found it extremely difficult to break a habit among the troops that was 'prejudicial' to Italian prestige.[51] One cannot rule out that the soldiers behaved thus not so much out of a desire to fraternize as, more simply, to enjoy comforts other than those available at the *case del soldato*. Moreover, during the harsh winters such places afforded shelter from the cold. It is therefore not proven that there was a desire among the Italian solders to fraternize with the civilian population. Emblematic in this regard is the attitude expressed by the mayor of Kata-Koriò near Jerapetra (Crete), who told Colonel Ilo Grella, commander of the 341st Infantry Regiment: 'You are Italians and invaders. As such we hate you and hope that you will soon go away, but as long as you live in my home, you may rest assured that nothing unpleasant will happen to you.'[52]

The area of relations between conquerors and conquered most difficult to construe is emotional attachment between soldiers and local women. It is not possible to quantify this phenomenon exactly because the documentation is lacking, but we know that the commanders distinguished the purely sexual 'needs' of the troops from 'sentimental relations'. Young soldiers, far from their loved ones, sought refuge, escapism, adventure and pleasure in more stable relationships, endeavouring to create a quotidian normality insulated from the war. They formed enduring relationships as soon as they realized that their stationing in a particular locality was going to be lengthy. The documents show that this was a widespread phenomenon in both the Balkans and France. Indeed, in Greece the epithet *s'agapò* ('I love you') was given to the Italian army, scandalizing Italian public opinion even after the end of the war. The War Ministry instructed the commands of the CdAs in the Alpes-Maritimes to impose stricter discipline on officers who 'flaunted relations with women, ignoring social distance, nationality and the damage that this [causes] to the morale of the troops'. The non-commissioned officers and other ranks were guilty of a 'deplorable laxity of conduct', not only in the towns but also in the villages and the countryside,

51 USSME, N 1–11, 'Diari storici', b. 859, 'Com. sup. FF.AA. Grecia al Comando del XXVI CdA, 13 giugno 1941'. Special foot patrols were organized and senior officers were ordered to supervise the behaviour of their men when they were off duty. General Geloso repeatedly prohibited soldiers from frequenting private houses, accepting cigarettes, drinks or food from civilians, leaving camp unaccompanied or using civilian transport, and he ordered that transgressors be severely punished. Nevertheless many soldiers spurned the *casa del soldato*, preferring to drink in the local cafés.

52 Testimony by Colonel I. Grella, Siena Division, in Bedeschi, *Fronte jugoslavo-balcanico*, 1986, pp. 662–3.

and even after curfew.[53] In May 1943, the CS received a memorandum on Slovenia which reported that numerous officers had formed relationships with local women of such intimacy that 'when they are with them they forget every duty of discretion and dignity'. There were, the report continued, officers who 'on the eve of their departure for round-ups or on reconnaissance missions' abandon themselves 'to pathetic scenes with their lovers, during which they disclose orders, times of departure, itineraries, and the presumed duration of operations', thus breaching military secrecy and facilitating 'ambushes by the partisans and unexpected attacks against columns on the march'.[54]

Some members of the 'superior race' flouted the regime's strictures against 'contamination by inferiors' by indulging in concubinage. Armando Mafrici recalls that circulars constantly dwelt on the theme of relations with Croatian civilians, with whom the Italians were to manifest the 'true grit' of the army's ten commandments, but which no 'easy-going lad from Emilia, Lombardy or Abruzzo [could] assume after months and months of hardship' even had he wanted to.[55] The local girls, explains Ugo Dragoni, were afraid of marrying local men 'apparently mild and attentive . . . but soon drunken and violent'. It was for this reason that the Italians were so successful with the women of the country, who were unaccustomed to kindness and affection. Their desire to be cosseted and cherished drove them irresistibly, Dragoni claimed, to fall in love with the occupiers.[56] The local women continued to frequent the Italian soldiers even when the Croat (and French) police threatened to shave their heads if they continued to fraternize with the Italians.[57] The officers distinguished only in abstract sociological terms between *milostive*, 'women from affluent families, who by their intelligence, culture and sophistication were regarded as far superior to the males of their class', and *gospe*, working women whom they found just as attractive. A description by an Italian officer of a girl he met in Karlovac is emblematic: 'With her dazzling gypsy smile she seemed to me just like a girl from southern Italy.'[58] Would an officer of the Wehrmacht have ever compared a Roma or a Polish girl to a German *Fräulein*?

[53] USSME, M 7, b. 476, 'Comando I CdA, 12 agosto 1943, firmato generale Romero'.

[54] USSME, M 3, b. 1410, 'CS – SIM, 15 maggio 1943'.

[55] Mafrici, *Guerriglia sulla ferrovia del petrolio*, 1981, p. 143.

[56] Dragoni, *Fiaschi in Jugoslavia*, 1983, p. 107.

[57] ASMAE, GABAP, b. 30, 'Supersloda – UAC alla legazione d'Italia, 21 ottobre 1941, firmato generale Vittorio Ambrosio'. In Corsica, the French authorities prosecuted a number of women for forming relationships with Italian soldiers. See 'ASMAE, AA.PP. – Francia, b. 67, 15 giugno 1943, Appunto per il barone Michele Scammacca'.

[58] Mafrici, *Guerriglia sulla ferrovia del petrolio*, 1981, p. 272.

Apropos this difference I cite 'the horror' expressed by an Oberleutnant in a report to his superiors where he describes a group of Italian officers relaxing in the company of Jewish women at the Café Grodska in Dubrovnik.[59]

Nevertheless, although there were instances of innocuous familiarity between Italian soldiers and the women of Greece, France and Yugoslavia, it should be emphasized that rapes and other acts of sexual violence were committed during the occupations. Of these we know little, because the files on Italian war crimes are still closed to researchers. We cannot ascertain to what extent these episodes of violence were an expression of Fascist ideology and to what extent the consequence of the physical circumstances of the occupation. Owing to the inaccessibility of the archives of the military tribunals, it is impossible to determine whether – as in the case of the Wehrmacht – troops were punished for unauthorized crimes committed against civilians and the enemy.[60]

THE EVERYDAY LIVES OF THE CONQUERORS AND THE IMPACT ON OCCUPATION POLICIES

Sanitary conditions

The poor sanitary conditions on all the fronts fought by the Italian armies indubitably exacerbated the decline in morale.[61] Broad coastal zones of Greece were infested with malaria, which affected large numbers of both officers and other ranks (see appendix, tables 36–7): indeed, the Italian army was unable to subdue an enemy that killed considerably more troops than did the partisans. Tents with mosquito netting were the privilege of the lucky few. After August 1941, the lack of anti-malaria prophylactics forced the transfer of numerous battalions, units and companies of the

59 Steinberg, *All or Nothing*, p. 46.

60 Bartov, *Hitler's Army*, pp. 59–106 and p. 95: 'The army's legalization of crimes toward the enemy, its toleration of disciplinary offenses by the troops toward the same enemy, and its enforcement of a brutal discipline as concerns the soldiers' combat performance, were all linked to each other, derived their legitimacy from the acceptance of the Nazi "world view", and must be seen together as forming the kernel of the war in the East, and by extension, as the most characteristic and essential features of the Wehrmacht.'

61 USSME, N 1–11, 'Diari storici', b. 1098, 'Intendenza XI Armata, Direzione di Sanità, 2 gennaio 1943'. In November 1942, the Eleventh Army had 5,528 officers and 119,397 soldiers and non-commissioned officers, while the Army Command had 1,020 officers and 14,044 soldiers. The morbidity rate in 1942 was 8.67 per cent (the figure does not include repatriated soldiers). The morbidity rate for the 3rd CdA (2,016 officers and 46,742 soldiers) was 5.19 per cent; that of the 8th CdA (1,404 officers and 34,724 soldiers) 6.94 per cent; and that of the 26th CdA (1,088 officers and 23,887 soldiers) 13.91 per cent.

Casale, Modena and Acqui Divisions, which were especially hard hit by marsh fever. Only in the spring of 1942 did anti-malarial treatment begin – with the involvement of civilian malariologists – with the preparation and stockpiling of drugs and the extension of areas covered by anti-malaria campaigns. So many soldiers were infected that the army command decided to create a detachment, or even a battalion, in each division consisting solely of malaria victims too sick to undertake combat duty. These soldiers were given light tasks such as escort duties, the guarding of works of art and storehouses 'so that an equal number of detachments can be released for operational duties'.[62] A table drawn up by the Intendance of the Eleventh Army for the period 15–30 September 1941 shows that 5.84 per cent of the occupation troops were infected with malaria – and this was when relapses had not yet reached the levels of 1942 and 1943 (see appendix, table 36).[63] In the case of the 26th CdA, for instance, from the beginning of the occupation until February 1942 (around eight months) fully 7,333 cases of malaria were diagnosed and thirty-five deaths were caused by the disease. From March 1942 onwards, the health section of the CdA recorded an average monthly rate of around 300 relapses and a slightly lower one (200 cases) of full-blown malarial infection.[64] Besides malaria victims, around 20 per cent of the troops were sick for other reasons (an average monthly total of around 5,000 men): more that 3,000 men were treated at the infirmaries, and around 1,500 were hospitalized, although fewer than 2,000 beds were available. Every month, around 1,500 men were discharged and returned to their units, and around 200 'non-recoverable sick' soldiers were repatriated.

The war memoirs of soldiers serving on all the fronts make frequent mention of the army's failure to replace poor-quality boots which in hot weather caused the eruption of unbearable sores on the feet. In Crete, 'owing to an absolute lack of new boots . . . together with the shortage of the materials needed to repair them . . . almost 40 per cent of the

[62] USSME, N 1–11, 'Diari storici', b. 1125, 'allegato 198, 16 dicembre 1942'.

[63] USSME, N 1–11, 'Diari storici', b. 631, 'Intendenza Comando Superiore FF.AA. Grecia', 3 October 1941.

[64] USSME, N 1–11, 'Diari storici', bb. 376, 554, 566, 972, 1122, 1125, 126a, 'relative al Comando del XXVI CdA – Direzione Sanità'. 'Diario storico' b. 859 contains a study on malaria in the province of Jannina prepared by Medical Captain Cebrelli in June 1941; USSME, N 1–11, 'Diari storici', b. 1098, 'Com. sup. FF.AA. Grecia – Ufficio Operazioni, 27 novembre 1942, Cura della malaria: recidiva invernale e terapia – cura dei gametofori'. The malaria victim was usually struck by a sudden fever: Biasion recalls that he collapsed onto a comrade, who carried him like a dead body. The victim's face turned deep yellow, and when the fever subsided, he was drained of all energy and severely depressed. The most common symptoms of relapse were periodic fevers, migraines and severe cramps in the joints: victims rested with their units for seven to eighteen days or were hospitalized.

soldiers in the division [went] literally unshod, to the extent [they could not] take part in training exercises'.[65] The military hospitals in Bosnia-Herzegovina were filled with soldiers suffering from severe chilblains which not infrequently required legs to be amputated because adequate treatment and medicines were lacking. In many cases, soldiers were incapacitated by pleurisy and pneumonia caused by their leaking footwear and threadbare clothing.

Venereal diseases – gonorrhoea and syphilis – were other pathologies that incapacitated the Italians. Soldiers reluctant to use condoms, and deaf to their commanders' exhortations to 'wear a helmet', contracted venereal diseases mainly from sex obtained outside the authorized brothels. Given that intercourse with prostitutes or local women was strictly prohibited, and subject to court martial and punishment (solitary confinement), the soldiers did not report their infections to the medical officers; instead, they resorted to local doctors (a practice equally prohibited) or more often treated themselves, causing the infection to degenerate.

Other diseases that afflicted the 'conquerors' resulted from dirt and poor personal hygiene. Many soldiers' clothes were infested with lice and fleas which provoked painful infections, as well as flea-borne typhus and scabies. These diseases proliferated during 'operational cycles' when soap and showers were rare luxuries, especially for the troops. Fleas were an integral part of everyday life: 'the seams of their clothing teemed with bloated white bugs which burst with a pop when squeezed between the fingernails'. For this reason, when the weather permitted, the soldiers stripped half-naked. Lieutenant Mafrici recalls that the uniforms of the officers were also infested with fleas.

Sarajevo had probably the worst sanitary conditions. Hundreds of cases of typhus were diagnosed among troops stationed in the town, and billeting in private houses or indeed any contact with civilians was prohibited. Other towns and villages were afflicted by epidemics of flea-borne typhus. The unit commands in these infested areas were told to instruct the troops on the importance of personal hygiene and to set up makeshift disinfestation facilities. The officers – who were responsible for the cleanliness of their soldiers – took coercive measures against the most reluctant to wash. They made their men boil their infested clothing and hang their blankets out to air; they prohibited them from any contact with civilians, and ordered them to take part in daily gymnastics sessions.[66] However, a medical officer with

[65] USSME, N I–II, 'Diari storici', b. 229, 'Divisione Siena al Com. sup. FF.AA. Egeo, 21 maggio 1942.'
[66] Mafrici, *Guerriglia sulla ferrovia del petrolio*, 1981, p. 178.

the Cacciatori delle Alpi Division reported that in spite of these preventive measures the hospitals treated hundreds of cases of scabies, a disease rampant in all the army's units.[67]

The conqueror: ragged and dissolute

'Our uniforms', writes Biasion, 'retained only faint traces of what they had been when they passed inspections by majors and colonels.'[68] The commanders could harangue, punish and insist on cleanliness and neatness, but the troops grew ever more unkempt because requests for clothes and boots went largely unfulfilled. Indeed, the troops came increasingly to resemble the occupied populations: in Crete, some soldiers took to wearing locally made clogs because their boots had worn out and there were no replacements available in the stores. The situation wore down morale and caused 'embarrassment in relations with the subject population' which 'disturbed the young officers in their exercise of command'.[69] Hyperinflation and the consequent shortage of goods dealt a further blow to the 'style' of soldiers who, the official doctrine insisted, had everything that they needed. When after a certain period it was no longer possible to put off the expense necessary to maintain decency and hygiene, it was often discovered that the goods required were impossible to find. The dwindling of supplies brought from Italy forced the soldiers to repair their uniforms and to make their own underwear and clothing. Contact with the civilian population, 'which observed and judged', required 'for the dignity of Italians and soldiers' standards that could be maintained only by using local resources, given the impossibility of relying on supplies from Italy.[70]

There was in some cases a huge difference between the image that the officers were supposed to give of themselves to the troops and their actual behaviour. Some officers slept comfortably in private houses where they were served hand and foot by their attendants.[71] The soldiers instead slept on straw covered with field blankets. They dug holes in the ground or built makeshift shelters from rocks or any other materials that came to hand. On ceremonial evenings, the officers feasted in their messes on Russian caviar,

[67] Testimony by Lieutenant Doctor Mario Laureati, 451st camp hospital, Cacciatori delle Alpi Divisione, in Bedeschi, *Fronte jugoslavo-balcanico*, 1986, p. 678.

[68] Biasion, *Sagapò*, 1953, p. 80.

[69] USSME, N 1–11, 'Diari storici', b. 229, 'Divisione Siena al Com. sup. FF.AA. Egeo, 21 maggio 1942'.

[70] USSME, N 1–11, 'Diari storici', b. 660, 'Comando Divisione Pinerolo – nucleo "P" al Comando del III CdA, 15 marzo 1942'.

[71] Biasion, *Sagapò*, 1953, p. 35.

tortellini, sole, mixed roast meats, fresh vegetables and even champagne and liqueurs. Photographs from the time show young officials debauched by alcohol with red venose noses and puffed eyelids. In contrast, isolated detachments with inadequate food supplies, driven by hunger and encouraged by their commanders, plundered the fields like locusts.[72]

With time, the behaviour of the occupiers deteriorated and discipline began to disintegrate. The first to give way were the senior officers. According to the CS, by the end of 1942 numerous senior officers had given themselves over to a licentiousness in which 'women and gambling figured large' and resorted massively to the black market in order to finance their habits.[73] In May 1943 an inquiry was launched that led to the cashiering of almost the entire SM of the Eleventh Army and the resignation of Geloso. Around thirty generals, colonels and senior officers were arrested, and even the chief of General Staff, Domenico Tripiccione, was investigated.[74] The inquiries by Admiral Domenico Cavagnari (set out in a report of fully forty-two pages with 182 probative annexes) uncovered numerous unlawful activities: 'private speculations', the importing from Italy of goods for sale on the black market, but especially relations with women coyly referred to as 'ladies of the night', relations 'which, according to the investigators, assumed unwholesome and sometimes comical aspects, given the age and high rank of certain officers'. The officers were accused of engaging in unseemly relations with 'Athenian scum' that had serviced first the British, then the Germans and finally the Italians, with the consequent draining of physical and moral energy, and the risk of contagious diseases which would undermine 'health and reduce performance'.

The foregoing digression on the health and living conditions of the Italian soldiers has shown that many of the 'conquerors' certainly did not correspond to the ideal of the *uomo nuovo* that the regime wished to convey. Even if the Italian troops, sick, stripped semi-naked to escape the fleas that infested their clothes, shod with clogs or worn-out boots, had initially been convinced of their 'civilizing mission' and of the superiority of the Italian race, it was unlikely that they were convinced any longer. Their physical condition, appearance and resignation to long service in the occupied territories influenced their perceptions of themselves and of the local inhabitants.

72 Mafrici, *Guerriglia sulla ferrovia del petrolio*, 1981, p. 111.

73 USSME, M 3, b. 20, 'CS, 13 gennaio 1943'.

74 On the investigation, see USSME, L 13, b. 105, and H 5, b. 34, in particular the report by Admiral Cavagnari dated 16 June 1943.

Life in the garrisons

When describing the daily lives of the Italian soldiers it is useful to draw a distinction between two main phases: *cicli operativi* (combat periods) and garrison duty, during which soldiers 'in war but at rest' were 'like the leaves of a tree warmed by the sun and cooled by the rain'.[75] Until the spring of 1942 (the autumn in Greece), garrison life passed by relatively peacefully. Indeed, it fostered in some soldiers what came to be called *comodismo di guarigione* (garrison softness) or a 'peacetime mentality', and the commanders took action to 'deterritorialize' the troops. As David Reynolds has written: 'impelling an army to fight, particularly an army of conscripts, is one problem; holding it together when not fighting is equally difficult'.[76] Geloso recommended plenty of physical activity, also for the commanders, together with realistic and intense training exercises. Officers and soldiers should be alert and ready to react immediately. Surveillance operations that resembled combat security operations as closely as possible should be mounted. The *comodismo* to which the commands referred was a state of mind, however; it certainly did not mean that life in the garrisons was easy or that the solders whiled away their days in idle pleasure. Everyday life was exhausting, although the 'exhaustion' was different from that provoked by combat. In certain respects it was similar to that experienced by Lieutenant Drogo, the protagonist of Dino Buzzati's novel, *The Tartar Steppe*.

The soldiers in the garrisons suffered from loneliness. They felt, they said, 'sad and lost' as they passed months and years gazing fixedly at the sea waiting for the enemy to land, days and weeks before they emerged from the garrison on round-ups and *cicli operativi*. Like Drogo, they were dulled by the torpor of habit, military routine, the monotony of service and guard duty. Their lives were confined to the company of their comrades, the mess hall, petty squabbles, games of cards or chess. Not even rest evenings relieved the tedium. While Drogo spent his time waiting for the enemy, looking forward to the decisive conflict, the Italian soldiers in the Mediterranean first deluded themselves that they had won the war, then had to fight a kind of war for which they were not prepared, and finally were defeated by their former allies.[77] Even when, like Drogo, they never fired a shot in anger, life in the garrison affected them profoundly, for it

[75] Biasion, *Sagapò*, 1953, p. 77. [76] Reynolds, *Rich Relations*, p. 61.

[77] Mafrici, *Guerriglia sulla ferrovia del petrolio*, 1981, p. 54; Angelini, *Fuochi di bivacco in Croazia*, 1946, p. 106.

brought with it a 'degradation' caused by the physical surroundings, the climate and a boredom relieved only by sporadic moments of utter panic. The occupied territories acquired an unreal and dreamlike insubstantiality which sometimes afforded fleeting escape from reality.[78] Much more often, however, they provoked moral deterioration and a loss of individual dignity. In the Greek islands, the unchanging climate, a sky never stirred by even the shadow of a cloud, a sea as bland as a sheet of marble frayed the nerves. The lack of women tormented the men as much as the lack of water. The sun beat upon the men's bodies and overheated their minds: 'erotic images, obscene fantasies soon began to alternate with bizarre visions which despite the intense light were dark and brooding'.[79]

At a stronghold on the island of Crete the soldiers spent most of their days sitting on the rocky foreshore. They threw sticks of dynamite into the sea, presenting the fish that they caught to their grateful officers. At all hours of the day they fried the fish or grilled the skewered meat of young goats purloined from the pens of the local peasants.[80] But not far away was another forgotten unit of soldiers. These were stationed in a marshy bay amid a handful of dwellings whose inhabitants were yellow with malaria. Already befuddled by quinine, they spent their days stealing raki, which they drank to ward off disease, and the nights singing and shooting their rifles to prove that they were alive.

From the late spring of 1942 onwards, however, life became less tranquil in almost all garrisons: no longer were they safe havens, as the enemy first infiltrated and then attacked them. As Dragoni recalls, the difficult psychological position of the troops was evident. They had been forced to shift from the mentality of the victor to that of men under siege, barricaded within their garrisons. Here too, as at the front line, they spent their nights fighting invisible attackers and cursing the impotence of their reaction against the emptiness. Dragoni and his comrades ironically adapted the words of *Lili Marlène* to this watershed phase of the war, emphasizing their

[78] Biasion, *Sagapò*, 1953, p. 114: 'As soon as the sun touched the surface of the water, the entire arc of the coastline, the cliffs, the sky, the mountains, the village perched on the hillside, the sparse carob trees scattered on the mountain spur turned a uniform sulphurous red, a colour which dyed all things, transforming them into immaterial and fantastic objects like those that haunt one's dreams'; Angelini, *Fuochi di bivacco in Croazia*, 1946, p. 53: 'The Una Valley (Herzegovina) lit by the last rays of the sun, the wail of a muezzin calling the faithful to prayer, and the numerous minarets soaring into the sky against the backdrop of a fiery sunset, gave Colonel Angelini the sensation that he had been suddenly transported into a new, almost unreal world, awakening his nostalgia for the unforgettable sunsets of Africa.'

[79] Biasion, *Sagapò*, 1953, p. 80. [80] Ibid., p. 40.

anger at the harshness of the present and nostalgia for the *pacchia perduta* (roughly, 'no more cakes and ale').[81]

The cicli operativi

During *cicli operativi* or combat periods the soldiers' living conditions deteriorated further. They received almost no welfare services, their hardships multiplied and opportunities for relaxation disappeared. Good cigarettes were 'sucked down in a sort of ecstasy' because those issued to the troops, already irregular in their quantity, were extremely poor in their quality (in Crete, which was one of the best postings, the ration was five cigarettes a day). The soldiers were usually issued with cigarettes manufactured locally in Croatia, Montenegro and Greece, or Tuscan cigars and pipe tobacco. But they also smoked whatever came to hand: the infantrymen compensated for the lack of cigarettes by making their own from roasted and shredded potato skins.[82] *Sapol*, a paste of soda, flour and oil, was used as shaving soap – an absolute luxury – while olive oil fuelled makeshift lamps when the stocks of candles ran out, as they soon did.

The quality of mess food worsened. Angelini recalls that for more than a month the only rations were the *rancio totalitario* (meaning, with heavy irony, 'totalitarian mess rations'), which consisted largely of barley. Lieutenant Sergio Pirnetti of the 3rd Battalion – 73rd Infantry Regiment – Lombardia Division, remembers that when a horse injured by enemy fire was put down within the defensive stockade, there was an immediate 'rush of soldiers who flayed the animal's haunches and back and cut themselves steaks. The meat was tough but it served to supplement the mess rations, which were always meagre.'[83] The soldiers could not hunt game – as they were able to do during rest periods away from the front – because out in the open they were easy targets for snipers.

Mopping-up operations in rugged mountain terrain – either cold and densely wooded or suffocatingly hot and arid – were exhausting. The sufferings of men who spent entire weeks on such duty are evinced by the logbooks on 'medical examinees' and hospitalizations. Conveying some idea of the

81 Dragoni, *Fiaschi in Jugoslavia*, 1983, p. 83: 'Dolce mia Balcania, Balcania del mio cuor / tu eri l'anno scorso la terra dell'amor / si stava bene qua da te / con molte donne in canapè / tipo Fifi Marléen tipo Fifi Marléen. / Passavan le giornate, non c'era cosa far, / si mangiava bene, non si beveva mal! / Ecco la guerra che piace a me: / dormire, amar, mangiar e ber . . . / E ora invece come si sta mal, / tutte le sere mi tocca sparacchiar! / Ribelli qui, ribelli là. Che seccatura doversi alzar / per nulla combinar, per nulla combinar.'

82 Angelini, *Fuochi di bivacco in Croazia*, 1946, p. 143.

83 Testimony in Bedeschi, *Fronte jugoslavo-balcanico*, 1986, p. 67.

hardship is the fact that Lieutenant Mafrici's battalion was forced to camp among the graves of a cemetery.[84] As men already physically overloaded by the weight of their backpacks and weapons marched across the frozen terrain of the mountains, they collapsed psychologically. They longed for the warmth of a stove, or even to lie down in the snow for a moment, yet the gruelling march continued relentlessly.[85] The exhausted soldiers asked themselves what they would do if the enemy attacked: 'Would we throw ourselves down into the snow? Would we shoot it out among the trees, trusting to our luck? What on earth would we do to counter a surprise attack?'[86]

Spells of duty grew ever more onerous. 'The constant pursuit of the partisans, who would be chased out of one place only to reappear in another, sapped the strength more than defence of the front line.'[87] Officers were rarely replaced, and the growing qualitative deterioration and quantitative reduction of the cadres greatly diminished the efficiency of units. Already depleted, the complement of officers was further reduced by the decision to replace captains aged over forty with young second lieutenants, either just commissioned or recalled from leave: 'with what effect on the deployment of units one can easily imagine'.[88] In the meantime, the enemy constantly improved its organization and grew ever stronger. The remaining army divisions had to extend their jurisdictions over vast territories, which further diluted the Italian fighting force. Early in the winter of 1942, the units deployed in Yugoslavia and Greece were dispersed among isolated positions, with no comforts and the burden of constant escort and surveillance duties.

How, therefore, did the Italian soldier react to the rigours and miseries of his life in the garrison or when he was on combat duty?

Internalization of violence and adaptation to brutality

Fighting an unrecognizable enemy in a hostile territory, on open ground amid woods and hills and mud, without the friendly shelter of a trench, and where nobody spoke his language: these were the hardships that the Italian

84 Mafrici, *Guerriglia sulla ferrovia del petrolio*, 1981, p. 77.
85 Angelini, *Fuochi di bivacco in Croazia*, 1946, p. 164.
86 Mafrici, *Guerriglia sulla ferrovia del petrolio*, 1981, p. 174.
87 Testimony by Corporal Major Domenico Epoque, Pinerolo Battalion, 3rd Alpini Regiment, Taurinense Division, in Bedeschi, *Fronte jugoslavo-balcanico*, 1986, p. 343.
88 Angelini, *Fuochi di bivacco in Croazia*, 1946, pp. 220–1.

soldier found most difficult to bear. An infantryman from the Brennero Division said that his was a war unique of its kind, fought against an invisible enemy and without a front, a war fraught with the terror of being shot in the back by guerrillas who lay constantly in wait like 'blood-thirsty beasts'. The infantryman continued: 'There is nothing more terrible than living in a community where you know that you're going to be killed but you don't know who your executioner will be. Where everyone and anybody could be your enemy. Where every look, every gesture, seems a threat.' The Italian soldiers did indeed shoot, but they were shooting at shadows, at 'bodiless enemies'.[89]

When the conquest campaigns concluded, the Italian soldiers were directly confronted with death. They witnessed the massacres of civilians in Croatia, the death from starvation of children, women and the elderly in Greece. They saw corpses heaped on the pavements of Athens, buildings in flames, bleeding tangles of bodies, horribly mutilated men and women: 'their poor flesh torn to shreds, the roads so drenched with blood that they turned brown'.[90] The Italian soldiers thus became intimately and brutally aware of death, of the 'sense of death'. Now began a process by which they internalized the violence that they had witnessed.

At first the Italian 'conquerors' had been the detached observers of outrages to which they felt extraneous. Their adaptation to brutality began when death touched their friends and comrades, and when they themselves had to visit death upon others. For many soldiers, 'vengeance for comrades captured and cruelly tortured by the rebels [was] a watchword which they all certainly obeyed'.[91] In reprisal for the frequent summary executions of suspected rebels, the partisans tormented the officers who fell into their hands, stripping and mutilating them (castration was frequent), torturing them and finally putting them before a firing squad. More humane treatment was reserved for simple soldiers: disarmed and stripped of their boots and uniforms, they were sent back to their units naked, though this was not for humanitarian reasons but because the partisans 'did not waste men and means on guarding and feeding captives ill suited to the war in the woods'.[92] In these circumstances, as Biasion recalls, it was 'probably

89 Testimony by Infantryman Bruno Remondini, gruppo Carri semoventi 75/19, in Bedeschi, *Fronte jugoslavo-balcanico*, 1986, pp. 628–9.

90 Testimony by the interim commander general of the Cacciatori delle Alpi Division, in Bedeschi, *Fronte jugoslavo-balcanico*, 1986, p. 164; ASMAE, GABAP, b. 35, 'console a Mostar Renato Giardini al GABAP – Ufficio Croazia, 30 aprile 1942'.

91 USSME, M 3, b. 8, 'governatorato del Montenegro – Ufficio militare, 27 marzo 1942, firmato generale Pirzio Biroli'.

92 Dragoni, *Fiaschi in Jugoslavia*, 1983, p. 75.

pleasant to be "the commander" and have people prostrate themselves before you when you spoke' and 'intoxicating to see the fierce, bearded men of the mountains bow their heads to you'.[93]

These experiences became a burdensome – sometimes unbearable – part of everyday reality. In some cases they fuelled the desire for vengeance and the urge to kill the enemy. In others, they bred the self-closure necessary to blot out hostile surroundings and repress the haunting thought that what had happened to one's comrade might happen to oneself. Rather than provoking notions of desertion or mutiny, they instigated the instinct for survival.[94] Hence, for reasons that did not directly concern Fascist ideology or the regime's propaganda or military orders, but rather the circumstances of the occupations and guerrilla warfare, the internalization of violence and adaptation to brutality were followed by concrete acts of violence and brutality – and with them normalization of the homicidal instinct.[95]

When the Italian army became caught up in 'the Balkan turmoil of fratricidal struggle conducted with bestial ferocity',[96] the previously ragged and dissolute Italian soldiers, friends of the local population and convivial drinkers in Greece's cafés, became the perpetrators of that same bestial ferocity. Indeed, Italian reprisals led to the destruction of entire villages, swelling the numbers of fugitives more terrified by the actions of the Italians than those of the partisans. After an initial period of passively witnessing violence, the death of friends and of innocent civilians, combined with fear of an invisible enemy that grew increasingly well organized and aggressive, triggered a violence and brutality which one may call 'redemptive' in that delivering death proved that one was alive and alleviated the constant sense of death. Biasion recounts the following episode:

[93] ASMAE, GABAP, b. 35, 'console a Mostar'.

[94] Mafrici, *Guerriglia sulla ferrovia del petrolio*, 1981, p. 89: 'I could not get to sleep that night. My mind kept returning to the murdered cavalryman, with his yellow face and unkempt hair, stiff with rigor mortis . . . At that moment I felt a profound and powerful need to live, to live and attach myself to something that would alleviate that oppression, that constant sense of death.'

[95] Testimony by Sergeant Francesco Negri, 1st Artillery Regiment, in Bedeschi, *Fronte jugoslavo-balcanico*, 1986, pp. 487–8. The sergeant remembers that, on 15 June 1943, the commander of the Exilles Battalion decided to burn down a village to warn the partisans and 'remind them of our strength and our combativeness'. Each unit was assigned a zone of the village, which it was to set on fire after seizing the cattle as spoils of war, thereby depriving the partisans of food. The homes of civilians were to be spared and the civilians sent back to the base as prisoners. At 9 in the evening, the flames began to spread, fanned by the night breeze. The soldiers ran excitedly from house to house with fistfuls of burning straw which they thrust under the roofs of the wooden houses. There was so much confusion that it was impossible to evacuate the cattle. The flames soon encircled the inhabited houses as well, and the terrified civilians (only women and children) fled.

[96] Angelini, *Fuochi di bivacco in Croazia*, 1946, p. 18.

> The sergeant appeared to have gone berserk. He ran from one position to the next screaming 'Cowards, they've killed Pagnotta!' He clenched his fists, he frothed at the mouth with rage, he wanted revenge at any cost and he wanted it immediately. He grabbed the machine gun and aimed it towards the enemy fire. It was absurd to waste munitions like that, but the sergeant's gesture galvanized the soldiers. 'Go on, Sergeant', they shouted. 'Shoot, kill' em all!' A frenzy of death had overtaken them. They wanted to wound and kill, they thirsted for blood.[97]

The experience of death bred a tendency to repress atrocities both suffered and committed. The longer the war dragged on, the more each man thought only of himself, 'forgetting' the devastated towns and his dead comrades. The analysis conducted by Pietro Cavallo of the emotions and images of Italians at war can also be applied to the soldiers in the occupied territories, especially as regards 1943. In the section 'La paralisi' in the chapter entitled *Il crollo*, Cavallo draws on the work of one of the founders of phenomenological psychiatry, Eugène Minkowski, who in 1943 distinguished two ways of relating to the immediate future: *activity* and *expectation*. Activity is a temporal phenomenon; it has meta-temporal features and is forward-looking. Contraposed to activity is expectation, an inverse movement whereby the future as specifically foreseen (not as a primitive structure) moves towards the individual. The distrust in the regime that spread among the Italians between the summer and autumn of 1942 was *expectation*, resigned indifference, the feeling that 'the future has changed its sign'. It marked the disappearance of a collective future and the advent of an individual future where the only hope was individual survival.

The disappearance of a collective future also drained the energies of the soldiers who experienced defeat at first hand; and 1943 saw the onset of a 'shrivelling of the soul'. Expectation of certain defeat, of imminent attack by the partisans, of death on the battlefield, bred an inability to imagine the future and restricted the capacity to live and act in the present. The draining of energy was neither sudden nor total. *Activity* did not disappear among the soldiers: it was manifest in combat and sometimes degenerated into acts of violence and brutality against civilians.[98] We shall see in chapter 10 that these were not isolated phenomena, nor were they confined to the Yugoslavian territories alone.

[97] Biasion, *Sagapò*, 1953, pp. 122 and 143; Brignoli, *Santa messa per i miei fucilati*, 1973, pp. 126–7.

[98] Cavallo, *Italiani in guerra*, pp. 257–96. The work by Minkowski referred to is *Le Temps vécu. Études phénoménologiques et psychopathologiques*, Paris, 1933.

RELATIONS WITH THE GERMAN SOLDIERS

The presence of Germans in the territories occupied by the Italians conditioned the behaviour of the Italian authorities towards the occupied populations. However, contacts between the troops of the two armies were less frequent than one might imagine, because the occupation was grounded on the principle of separate territorial jurisdictions. Italian and German soldiers had few opportunities to get to know each other, even during joint operations against the partisans. Even on an island such as Crete, the army commands sought to ensure that contacts were as few as possible. The few joint initiatives organized included a number of football games, the exchange of documentary films, and theatre performances put on by the 'P' section company. But very little else was done, mainly owing to the unbridgeable language gap between the two armies. The Italian authorities constantly observed the behaviour of the Germans towards the occupied populations. A CIAF document of 5 December 1940 commented on 'the accentuated cordiality of relations between German and French officers', that 'the handshake has been reinstated' and that 'when visiting installations, German and French officers sit together at the same table', concluding that, as Franco-German cordiality grew warmer, French dislike of the Italians increased proportionally.[99]

Relations between the two armies varied according to the occupation zone, the orders issued and the nature of the contacts established. For example, General Geloso insisted that his soldiers must always salute their German allies. Indeed, in order to foster 'ever more comradely' relations, he suggested that German-language courses be introduced for Italian officers, and more frequent sports events organized between the two armies.[100] He nevertheless acknowledged that, although the relations between the two armies were marked by 'a good climate of comradeship and mutual respect', 'any feature of familiarity' was absent.[101] Instead, according to the Command of the 214st mixed section of the CC.RR. stationed in Herzegovina, the soldiers were convinced that the Germans – who treated them with haughty indifference – were insincere.[102] Yet different judgement was passed on the Germans in the same period by the 'P' section of the Sassari Division: 'constant admiration for the valour and the sacrifices made [by the

[99] ASMAE, GABAP, b. 1, 'CIAF al GABAP, 18 dicembre 1940'.
[100] USSME, N I–II, 'Diari storici', b. 631, 'comandante a tutti i CdA, 30 settembre 1941'.
[101] USSME, N I–II, 'Diari storici', b. 1218, 'Comando IV Armata, SM – sezione Assistenza, 13 marzo 1943, Relazione del Servizio "A" del mese di febbraio 1943'.
[102] USSME, M 3, b. 56, '6 ottobre 1942'.

Germans] for the triumph of the common cause'.[103] Feelings were therefore mixed among the Italians: there was undoubted envy at the abundance of means and the comforts enjoyed by the Germans, a sense of inferiority (the Italian soldiers lived in poverty compared to their German counterparts of equal rank), respect and awe when they compared German weaponry, equipment and organization against their own:

> We came across a German battalion whose abundance of armoured vehicles was truly impressive. We noticed among other things a huge mobile kitchen with equipment that would have been the envy of an entire barracks in peacetime![104]

An officer recalled the arrival in Jerapetra (Crete) of the occupation corps, when the Germans took possession of the town and then had to wait for more than a day before the Italians arrived:

> On the outskirts of the town we encountered the first German soldiers, who gazed down at us from their gigantic Panzers with curiosity and amusement as we shuffled past. Our grand allies must have found the sight of our expeditionary corps, with its train of donkeys like a gypsy caravan, irresistibly comic.[105]

But at the same time the Italians felt themselves superior to 'barbarians' who failed to understand the mentality and nature of the occupied populations. General Giacomo Zanussi wrote that his superior Roatta admired the organizational abilities, the perfect discipline and the military *élan* of the Germans. But he would go no further than that: 'for, not only as an Italian but also as a man, he was distressed by the arrogance and haughtiness of the Germans, the boorishness apparent beneath their formal correctness, their inability to understand anything at variance with their mentality, the rigidity and paucity of their thought, which was either irreducibly simplistic or absolutely dogmatic'.[106] The Italian soldiers believed that they understood the behaviour, values, traditions and customs of the occupied populations and that they had 'adjusted' occupation policy accordingly. The Italian army, wrote a colonel in Attica, was considered less efficient than the German army, but the locals saw Italian civilization as closer to Greek civilization. Reports by commands which undertook joint operations with the Germans expressed veiled criticism of the harshness of their repressive methods and stressed that they had not fully understood how to treat civilians. Criticized especially was the Germans' practice of requisitioning private homes and their habit 'of going around wearing only their

[103] USSME, M 3, b. 56, 'Comando Divisione Sassari, 20 ottobre 1942'.
[104] Angelini, *Fuochi di bivacco in Croazia*, 1946, p. 251.
[105] Baldi, *Dolce Egeo guerra amara*, 1988, p. 227.
[106] Zanussi, *Guerra e catastrofe d'Italia*, 1946, p. 141.

underpants when off duty, in both the houses and streets of the villages and in the countryside', which offended Greek proprieties.

The Germans for their part made no attempt to conceal their sense of superiority over the 'junior partner', and indeed sometimes publicly mocked the Italians. In some territories, Croatia for instance, where a large part of the local population understood German, the soldiers of the Reich not infrequently sneered at the Italians in public, promising that on conclusion of the war Hitler would 'make a present' of Dalmatia to Croatia. The perceptions of the soldiers corresponded to those of the Italian politicians and generals as described in the first chapter. They sought to distinguish themselves from the German allies, to adopt their own code of behaviour and to have the local population notice the difference. Yet this did not correspond to a more 'humane' attitude towards civilians. In a fictitious dialogue, Dragoni has a female character, a *milostiva*, deliver a speech that reflects the ways in which the allies perceived themselves and were perceived. Although the description of the Italians is overindulgent, that of the Germans seems accurate:

> As an occupation force you have everything to learn from the Germans. Your allies with pistols in their fists take everything they want, behaving exactly as they wish as conquerors of the country. They execute without trial all those who resist them in some way . . . While you Italians are all heart, *the Germans have the arrogance of conquerors in their souls*. This is the difference between a warrior people and a people made to love like you.[107]

The Germans had 'the arrogance of conquerors in their souls', the Italians did not. But although they were not the 'race of conquerors' desired by Mussolini, this did not prevent them from being sometimes brutal and violent. The observation on the difference of behaviour between Italians and Germans is correct but, as Enzo Collotti points out, one must establish the extent and quality of that difference.[108] Italy's excessive politicization was often a result of its weakness, while Germany's ruthlessness corresponded not only to the greater strike force of its military and police apparatus but also to the greater extremism of its goals.

Nazism's careful concern to prepare the German population in general, and the armed forces in particular, ideologically and psychologically for the war was intended to achieve specific goals. Nazification of the Wehrmacht reached indubitably high levels, whereas Fascist indoctrination was partial and superficial. Moreover, the Italian soldier was not supported by the

[107] Dragoni, *Fiaschi in Jugoslavia*, 1983, p. 114 (emphasis added).
[108] Collotti, 'Sulla politica di repressione italiana nei Balcani', p. 195.

strong bureaucratic-military structure that Mark Mazower has described in the case of the German army.[109] Indoctrination engendered a distortion of reality (the title of the final chapter in Omer Bartov's book) in the German soldiers which was of crucial importance. Firstly, it taught them to believe utterly in the Führer's political and military promises and never to doubt the morality of their orders or the results of Hitler's prophecies. Secondly, it created an image of the enemy which profoundly altered perceptions of the occupied populations; and when the German soldiers encountered them in person they invariably believed that their expectations had been confirmed. Indoctrination achieved its purpose and profoundly motivated the German troops, legitimating their sacrifice and the atrocities committed against the enemy. Fascist indoctrination achieved neither of these objectives.

There were also differences in behaviour between the Germans and Italians which sprang from the power of the German war machine, and from conviction that final victory by the Wehrmacht was inevitable. These were two features entirely lacking from the Regio Esercito, which conquered its territories only thanks to German intervention and which was constantly aware of the inferiority of its military means. The German soldier had proof of his technological superiority. This awareness bred contempt for the life of the enemy and the conviction that any means could be legitimately used to assert that superiority. If there were any moral restraints on the German army, its conviction that no one would ever be in a position to pass judgement on its decisions and actions was enough to overcome them. Italy differed from Germany in this respect as well, as we shall see in chapter 11 when the regime's racial policy is discussed. There was also the ethical difference between the Italian and German military traditions. In the latter, according to Bartov, Collotti and Steinberg, the imperatives of loyalty and the military virtues were indubitably much stronger than any principle that warfare be conducted humanely.[110] We shall see in the final section of chapter 11 ('Italiani brava gente?') how the Regio Esercito embraced the values of humaneness and two thousand years of Roman civilization.

While the Fascistization of the Regio Esercito fell far short of the Nazification of the Wehrmacht, this does not signify that the regime had no effect on the Italian troops. Behind the Italian war propaganda essential to incite the troops to perpetrate repression in the Balkans lay the twenty-year campaign by Fascism and the virulent nationalism of the Venezia Giulia

109 Mazower, 'Military Violence and National Socialist Values', p. 134.
110 Bartov, *Hitler's Army*; 'Collotti, Sulla politica di repressione italiana nei Balcani'; Steinberg, *All or Nothing*.

region to strip every dignity from the Slav population living within Italian borders – *razzamaglia slava* (Slav riff-raff). During the Second World War, the question of the Balkans arose with renewed virulence as a metaphor for the unknowable infinite, of the unknown, of a nightmare tinged with the darkest colours. Collotti highlights a particularly significant passage from *Picchiasodo*:

> When a people dishonours itself by resorting to these methods to wage war, it deserves no pity. Even if someone may be better than the others, we must treat him no differently; because the race is still the same, and it is earning itself the title of the accursed race . . . Rather than purification, what is needed is purging by machine-gun.[111]

The passage clearly illustrates the type of behaviour that the regime wanted to foster in its soldiers, and chapter 10 will examine how these messages were received by the latter. It is difficult to say to what extent the orders of the Italian commanders were executed, and to what extent propaganda slogans and the rules were able to eliminate uncertainty or disorientation among the troops.

To conclude: this chapter has shown – confirming Collotti's thesis – the bewilderment of the Italian soldier, who, amid partisan insurgency and a hostile population, did not fully understand his role, was unsure of the reasons for the war, and did not endorse them when he did. He felt used merely as cannon fodder. When he hated the enemy he did not do so for ideological reasons but because he had been forced into the irksome situation of having to defend himself when he should instead have been acting the conqueror. The use of violence and brutality by the Italians was not characterized by the Germans' triumphalism and exultation over the enemy's defeat, nor by a sense of racial superiority. They were manifest in reprisals indicative of the weakness of soldiers who had no other means to assert their power. Only in certain cases did the Blackshirts commit reprisals against civilians, or atrocities of any kind, purely for the sake of ideology.[112]

[111] Collotti, 'Sulla politica di repressione italiana nei Balcani', p. 195.

[112] We do not yet have sufficient documentation on Carabinieri, special military police units and enlisted soldiers to conduct analyses of individual units or studies similar to that by Christopher Browning (*Ordinary Men*) on a specific unit of the German police in Poland.

PART II

This is the state of the Europeans: hatred, hatred, hatred and boundless suffering. And it is only the beginning of a crisis which, whatever the outcome of the war, will leave deep scars in the souls of the European peoples . . . The worst is still to come.

Luca Pietromarchi, *unpublished diary*, 30 April 1942

CHAPTER 6
Relations with the occupied countries

The chapter analyses Italian occupation policy in the militarily occupied territories that had governments of their own: Croatia, Greece and France. It examines in particular the relations between the occupying authorities and the central and peripheral organs of the occupied countries with which the occupation policies were negotiated (or on which they were imposed). Montenegro, which did not have an independent executive, will be treated in chapter 8, together with the annexed territories.

Examination of relations with the occupied countries will bear two considerations in mind: firstly, that the presence of the Germans exerted substantial influence on Italian decisions and policies; and, secondly, that, in both the Balkans and France, the Italian military authorities pursued the same objectives: guaranteeing security and maintaining order. The commanders and General Staffs were aware that the military administration was a provisional arrangement which would be discontinued with the (victorious) end of the war. They wanted to restrict the investment of men and resources as far as possible, preferring instead to collaborate with the local authorities. The action of the military chiefs was predicated on control, not on the direct management of public administrations, and the replacement of local administrators with officers of the Regio Esercito was a last resort. It should also be pointed out that the military authorities had no desire to arrogate civil powers to themselves. This is not to imply, however, that they did not subscribe to the goals of the regime, or that, when the opportunity arose to interfere directly in administration, they did not pursue strategies in harmony with the expansionist ambitions of Fascism.

CROATIA, AN OCCUPIED ALLY

A distinction should be drawn between Croatia – which, like Albania, was formally allied with Italy and had Italian troops stationed on its territory – and France and Greece, with which Italy concluded armistices following their defeats. In this section, I intend to highlight certain aspects of Italo-Croat relations: in particular, relationships between Rome and Zagreb, between the military authorities of the Second Army and the Croat local authorities, and between the military authorities and ethnic and religious minorities. I shall also examine the co-ordination of policies between Rome and the periphery.

May to September 1941: the summer of massacres

The treaty of 18 May 1941 between Italy and Croatia established the frontiers between the two countries 'for all time' and laid the bases for 'intimate reciprocal collaboration'. Italy would promote the political development of Croatia with every means at its disposal, and it would guarantee the 'political independence' and 'territorial integrity' of the country. Zagreb would organize its armed forces in close contact with Rome, which would attend to their training, combat preparation and fieldwork. At the end of May, the Ustaša government requested and obtained authorization to administer Croatia's affairs autonomously, and it also asked that the Regio Esercito should depart from the country 'as soon as possible'. Those Italian troops that remained in Croatia officially did so to give protection to a friendly country, and it was determined that the Italian troops would never be numerically inferior to the German ones.[1]

On 11 June 1941, the UAC of the Second Army reported to the SMRE on the 'terrorist activity of the Ustaše'. According to the supreme army commander, Vittorio Ambrosio, the Ustaša militia were hunting down the alleged enemies of the state and the regime, whom they identified as Jews, Orthodox Christian Serbs and Croats belonging to the Peasant Party headed by Vladimir Maček. Driven by an ultra-nationalism which deprived it of all sense of proportion – when not serving to disguise personal grudges or interests – the militia unleashed a reign of violence and terror. The murders committed by the Ustaše were of such ferocity that the UAC was prompted to report: 'their equivalent is only to be found in the darkest times of the Middle Ages'. The barbaric repression was first perpetrated by the militia

[1] ASMAE, GABAP, b. 28, 24 May 1941, 'Appunto di Roberto Ducci per l'eccellenza il ministro'.

and then organized by the central government, which issued specific orders 'on the annihilation of the Serbs'. The Germans gave their support to the operations, especially those directed against the Jews – and the Croats, bolstered by Berlin's support, left conduct of the operations to vicious criminals. Among the protagonists of the massacres in the summer of 1941 were Catholic priests, who led punitive raids against Orthodox Christians. Monks were to seen at the head of processions, haranguing the mob and inciting it to wreak dreadful vengeance. Far from applying the evangelical precept of turning the other cheek, the 'warrior priests' were always ready to 'double the dose'. They were extremely effective Ustaša propagandists and intransigent revolutionaries, convinced that the Catholic faith could be exalted and strengthened only by 'suppressing' (in the concrete sense) 'all the Serbs'.[2] Rome received reports of the destruction of entire Orthodox Christian villages.[3] Throughout Croatia, arrests, house searches, the devastation of homes, rape, torture and violence were routine.[4]

The Italian authorities were confronted by an issue with major political repercussions: how should the troops stationed on the ally's territory behave towards the persecuted civilian population? In order not to antagonize the Croats, the SMRE and the MAE decided that in areas where the troops of the Regio Esercito were stationed, under no circumstances should soldiers protect civilians. Thus, for example, when the island of Pag became a 'confinement locality' (*località di confino*) for Serbs and Jews, the commander of the Italian troops prohibited soldiers from concerning themselves with the conditions of the detainees – despite the knowledge that they were being used to build roads and military barracks, and that some forty of them were

[2] ASMAE, GABAP, b. 28, 4 June 1941, 'Rapporto del consigliere nazionale Eugenio Coselschi, capo della delegazione del PNF a Zagabria'. A well-known case is that of the Franciscan friar Simić, from the monastery of Verpolje, who led the Ustaše on nighttime expeditions against the homes of Orthodox Serbs.

[3] ASMAE, GABAP, b. 30, 14 July 1941, 'Promemoria per il duce, con allegata una relazione del 9 luglio redatta dal Comando dei CC.RR. della II Armata'. In the district of Glina more than 18,000 Serbs were murdered, 417 of them butchered inside the Orthodox church. Between Petrovac and Oštrelj, 90 per cent of private houses were burnt and razed to the ground, and more than 30 per cent of the inhabitants were murdered. Cattle were dispersed or slaughtered, and entire grain warehouses were destroyed. Among the villages devastated by Muslim bands utilized or incited by the Ustaše were Sumnjaci, Vaganj, Ičići, Odzat, Podgradina and Debelja; there were horrifying massacres at Podgreda, Rajixka, Dubrava, Jsakvci (this place-name is probably misspelled in Italian documents) and Podkraji.

[4] ASMAE, GABAP, b. 28, 'Comando II Armata – UAC allo SMRE, 11 giugno 1941, Milizia ustascia'. Massacres were particularly numerous in the districts of Ogulin, Gospić, Otočac and Tenin. According to Ambrosio's sources, more than 1,000 civilians were killed and an equal number of people arrested: USSME, N 1–11, 'Diari storici', b. 523, 'Divisione Sassari, comandante della divisione Furio Monticelli al Comando del VI CdA', 19 July 1941. When the Italians took over the garrison in Knin from the Croats, they found fourteen bodies in the cellars, some of them of women whose breasts had been cut off.

being murdered each day and their bodies thrown into the sea.[5] But the Italian army's neutral stance towards Croat domestic affairs was not enough for the government in Zagreb, which mounted a violent anti-Italian propaganda campaign aimed at the restitution of Dalmatia. 'Publicly and with complete lack of respect, the noun "Italians" was invariably preceded by the adjective "filthy" [*porci*].'[6]

In the month of July, Croatia's internal situation began to deteriorate dangerously. An informant working with the political police in Fiume reported on the worrying state of political and economic disorder in Croatia, writing that, in Zagreb, 'the town is lit up at night for fear of murders and rioting'. The first organized revolts against the Ustaše erupted following the German attack on the Soviet Union. To quash them, Ante Pavelić authorized reprisals in zones inhabited by Serbs and Jews which would 'purge them forever'. There ensued a spate of atrocities on which Mussolini, the MAE and the military commands in Rome were kept fully informed. The GABAP received a telegram from the deputy commander of the Marche Division which reported that famished women in the prison at Gacko were offered their spit-roasted children to eat. In the same town, the prettiest girls were herded into a single room – in a building (subsequently burnt down) on the road to Atovak – where they were tortured and then killed. Babies and children in Betković were murdered in their homes and their parents compelled to bury them. At Gospić, an Italian soldier discovered the corpses of five small children with their throats cut. When Orthodox Christians managed to escape, their children were killed, their 'livers and hearts cut out' and 'hung on the doorknobs of the abandoned houses'. At Metković, almost the entire Serbo-Orthodox population was massacred; at Ljubuški, sixty people were shot by firing squad.[7]

[5] ASMAE, GABAP, b. 28, 14 August 1941, 'lettera di Lionello Alatri, presidente dell'Unione delle comunità ebraiche al GABAP': there were 6,000 detainees at Pag, where they were confined in inhuman conditions; USSME, M 3, b. 55, 'Comando II Armata, Ufficio "I", notiziario a/c, no. 3', 13 October 1941. Initially there were at least 4,000 internees on the island, 900 of them Jews from Zagreb (confined in two 'open air' camps, one for men at Barbato, one for women at Metaini) and 'undesirables of Serb origin', who were detained in a third camp. In September 1941, when the Regio Esercito occupied the island, it discovered mass graves containing more than 1,500 bodies. According to an estimate by Italian officers, no fewer than 9,000 people lost their lives at the hands of the Ustaše. Around 8,000 were murdered in the camp at Slana. One reads as follows in the unpublished diary kept by Luca Pietromarchi (Fondazione Luigi Einaudi, Turin): 'This war is ghastly, smeared as it is with blood. Mastromattei, now on the island of Pago to reactivate the lignite mines, has reported to the Duce that the Ustaše have had 7,000 victims on the island. Their bones, he says, are bleached to an eerie white on the salt marshes.'

[6] ASMAE, GABAP, b. 28, 'Ministero dell'Interno – DGPS AA.GG.RR. al MAE, 22 agosto 1941'; b. 28, 'legazione di Zagabria al GABAP, 27 giugno 1941, Manifestazioni antitaliane degli ustasci – Sconfinamenti – Rapporti italo-croati – Delimitazione confini tra Dalmazia e Croazia'.

[7] ASMAE, GABAP, b. 34, 'Ministero dell'Interno – DGPS Divisione Polizia politica', 12 July 1941.

Following the slaughter, groups of Orthodox Christians, Muslims and dissident Catholics appealed to the Italians to be freed from the Ustaše and have their lives and work protected 'as befitting people of white race'.[8] Other groups of Orthodox Christians accused the Italians of having done nothing to halt the massacre, stigmatizing their 'abstentionism' as a sign of weakness and as tacit encouragement of the Ustaša regime. Italian authority and prestige was fiercely criticized by the civilian population; yet for more than three months Mussolini, the MAE and the SMRE did nothing. Although some divisional or regimental commanders did take sporadic and isolated action to protect civilians, in general the Italian soldiers watched the massacres in frozen immobility.

One of the most interesting items in the archives of the Army General Staff is the *diario storico* (historical diary or logbook) of the Sassari Division – 13,000 officers and troops – deployed on the border between Dalmatia and Croatia.[9] The *diario* describes massacres of the civilian population, and relationships with the local Croatian authorities and with the Serbo-Orthodox population, and it unequivocally settles a point of historiographical controversy: the Italian army commanders were induced to assume civil powers in Croatia not by the massacres, but by the danger that the violent disorders might spread to Dalmatia. It was a total lack of trust in the Croat government that induced the Italian authorities to intervene, in concert with the Germans. One may take as credible, however, the descriptions by Colonel Gazzino Gazzini, the division's chief of General Staff and compiler of the *diario*, of the profound distress felt by the Italian soldiers when they witnessed unlawful and barbaric acts, and especially outrages against women and children.

The division was stationed in the zone between Knin and Šibenik. The 'racial' characteristics of the region were 'complex', the *diario storico* reports, because the population consisted of 'an extremely large majority of Serbs of Orthodox religion, [with a] minority of Croats of Catholic religion'. After 18 May, the division command received various delegations of Serb notables who pressed for the annexation of the region to the Kingdom of Italy. The command knew that the reason for the appeal was 'terror of Croatian vengeance and reprisals' but nevertheless took it as 'an unequivocal sign of esteem for our race, the recognition of its . . . millenary political maturity'. The Croats were aloof and arrogant towards the Italians. They

8 ASMAE, GABAP, b. 28, 'console Alberto Calisse al GABAP – Ufficio Croazia', 18 June 1941; b. 33, 14 August 1941, letter with illegible signature addressed to 'His Majesty the Duce, King of Italy'.

9 USSME, N I–II, 'Diari storici', b. 523, 'Divisione Sassari, relativo all'estate 1941'. Quotations from the logbook in the next four paragraphs of the main text are in inverted commas.

adopted deliberately provocative behaviour so that the Italians would realize that they 'would do well to get out' (*avrebbero fatto bene ad andarsene*). The division command, for its part, branded Croatian policy as 'highly deficient and backward'.

The division command sought to determine whether the massacres were isolated phenomena or whether the Ustaše were executing specific orders issued by the government in Zagreb. When questioned on the matter, the Ustaša chief of Gračac informed the local garrison commander that he was acting on higher orders and showed him a letter from the government instructing the Ustaše to annihilate the 'Serbian race' (the compiler of the *diario* writes at this point that the report could be confirmed by almost all the officers). The Croats, Gazzini adds, did not have the 'political acumen or the respect to wait for the departure of the troops before giving free rein to their bestial lust for vengeance and blood'. In the early days of June, the searches, seizures and arrests of Orthodox Christians began. Armed Ustaše burst into private homes and shops, carrying away property, money and even beds. They divided up the booty before the eyes of civilians, and even of Italian soldiers, furnishing concrete proof of the absolute illegality of their actions. After brief interrogation, the Serbs arrested were brought before a firing squad. Nor were the elderly or children spared, while young women were first sexually abused and then barbarously murdered. Rumours spread that children were told to make the sign of the cross, and their throats were cut if they did so in the Orthodox Christian manner. The massacres were committed mainly at night, for this was when the Ustaše, transported on lorries frequently driven by Catholic priests – 'who in numerous localities proved themselves to be fanatical murderers' – travelled out to the Serb villages to commit carnage. At its mouth, the River Krka threw up dozens of corpses which the Italian officers dutifully photographed.

'On the one hand, being the guests of a sovereign state recognized by Italy entailed non-interference in the political affairs of that state. On the other . . . the soldiers could not long remain deaf to the Serb population's pleas for help.' The Italians felt 'a general sense of disdain' which then 'transmuted into a profound hatred for the Croats capable of such horrors' and which 'rooted itself in the hearts of officers and soldiers. This disdain was proudly and implicitly aggressive, although it did not manifest itself in acts of violence against the Croatian authorities. The garrison commands intervened repeatedly, urging the Croatian authorities to impose order. A number of Serbs were saved on the initiative of officers . . . hundreds of Serbs saved their lives by taking refuge within the precincts of the Italian barracks, or actually within the barracks themselves.' Small refugee camps sprang up to provide shelter for women, old people and children after weeks spent hiding in the woods or the fields, where they eked out an existence amid hunger, foul weather and the constant threat of Ustaša massacres.

On 16 July, the Italian troops stationed at Drniš and Gračac withdrew to Dalmatia. Only Tenin was still garrisoned by Italian troops. As soon as the division left, the Ustaše 'threw themselves headlong into massacre. Defenceless women, old people and children were the victims of the Croats' savage brutality. But utter cowards as they were, neither the Ustaše nor the regular Croatian army had the strength or the courage to take on the rebels in their strongholds.' The rumour spread through Tenin that as soon as the Italians left the town, women who had been seen in the company of Italian officers would be subject to a 'medical inspection' (a gynaecological inspection to determine whether they were pregnant or had had sexual relations with Italian soldiers). In Obrovac, the arrival of loads of barbed wire for use 'as fencing for a concentration camp to contain Serbs', provoked episodes of 'madness and suicide' and the flight of numerous inhabitants. The anti-Croat revolt began at the end of July. Its leaders were 'essentially communists', while 'the mass of Serbs who fled into the mountains knew nothing about communism, nor did they want to, their only struggle being [for] defence of their lives'.[10]

During the summer of 1941, pleas by the civilian population for Italian military assistance and protection multiplied. Numerous division and garrison commanders in the massacre zones advocated occupation in order to bolster the army's prestige. The Command of the Second Army declared itself in favour of occupation because the deteriorating situation threatened to spread to the annexed territories. An official at the Ministry of the Interior wrote that the 'pietism' shown by the army towards the Serbs suggested weakness on the part of the Italians or, worse, complicity in what was happening in Croatia. He recommended that Italy either adopt a more decisive and energetic stance or disregard Croatian affairs altogether: in which case it should retreat behind its borders, garrison them to ensure defence and prevent any infiltration. Half-measures would antagonize both the Ustaše, who saw the presence of the Regio Esercito as obstructing their campaign to

[10] USSME, N 1–11, 'Diari storici', b. 523, 'Divisione Sassari, comandante di divisione Monticelli al Comando del VI CdA, Sintesi del colloquio di Tenin del 31 luglio 1941'. Colonel Leonardi stressed that the rebel movement was not in the least communist, and that all the Serbs were ready to die rather than continue beneath the Croatian yoke. The colonel wrote: 'In their eyes [of the Serbs] I have read the pain of their souls, but also a cold determination to persevere with their struggle until the bitter end.'

eliminate the Serb Orthodox Christians, and the latter, who would accuse Italy of complicity in their cruel repression.[11]

Ambassador Raffaele Casertano explained to the head of the GABAP that 'pietism towards the Serbs and Jews' was a source of serious conflict with the Croats and was provoking hatred of the Italians. If there had been excesses, wrote the ambassador, they had been committed on the orders of the Zagreb government; moreover, if there existed a German plan to gain influence in Croatia, it could only benefit from the present state of tension. Casertano added that every form of Italian pietism must now cease and every form of unlawful aid given to Jews and Serbs must be eradicated. His recommendation was that the Regio Esercito should withdraw behind the kingdom's borders and give free rein to the Croats, thereby demonstrating Italy's respect for its ally's independence and sovereignty.[12] Casertano's solution was not taken up, however, the reason being that definitive withdrawal into the annexed territories would consign Croatia to the Germans.

At the end of August, Mussolini, responding to a German proposal that Croatia should be occupied in its entirety in the event of an uprising, ordered the country's occupation. This, he said, would ensure the security of the annexed zones, after which the Regio Esercito would be able to crush the insurrection and normalize the situation. Decisive and successful action would enhance Italy's authority and prestige among the Balkan peoples. Especially, however, it would push the Germans out of the occupied territories. The Duce ordered the Second Army to occupy all public buildings and to select pro-Italian Croatian civil servants. The local authorities would be accountable for 'hostile acts' against Italian troops. The Ustaša squads were disbanded and the units of the Croatian army demobilized. Prison camps were taken over by the Italian authorities, lists of their inmates compiled and evidence for the arraignment of the Croatian authorities collected. Perpetrators of crimes against Serbs were arrested, as were all those suspected of hostile acts against Italy. Pressure was applied on refugees to return to their homes, and adjudication boards were set up to settle minor disputes and personal squabbles. Plans were made to create reception centres for refugees returning to the Italian zone, and to find work for them. Serbs and Croats were urged to collaborate in the fight against the communists. Each village would have its chief, to whom the garrison commander

[11] ASMAE, GABAP, b. 30, 'Pennetta – Ministero dell'Interno – DGPS AA.GG.RR. al MAE', 15 agosto 1941.

[12] ASMAE, GABAP, b. 30,'GABAP – Ufficio Croazia al CS e per conoscenza al governo della Dalmazia, Zara, 6 agosto 1941'.

would consign a certain quantity of weapons. However, the village chief had to be accepted by the population; so that if the majority of it was Orthodox Christian, then the chief too had to be of that faith.[13] The aim, wrote Mussolini, was to transform the occupied zones into areas of exclusively Italian influence, to attract businesses away from Croatia to the Italian zone and to prevent the reverse from happening. Officially, the impression was not to be given that Italy had occupied the zone in order to take possession of it; rather that the occupation was temporary and intended to restore peace in the zone.

At no time did occupation policy have 'humanitarian' aims, and its purpose was never to 'save' Orthodox Christians or Jews from Ustaša persecution. In the space of a few months, the Italians changed from immobilism to an extremely decisive occupation policy. The Croats were considered on a par with a defeated enemy, or even worse. The occupation had features that closely resembled colonial methods and policies: Croatian sovereignty was annulled; the occupying power bypassed the local authorities to deal directly with the minorities, pursuing ends diametrically opposed to those of Zagreb.

September 1941–June 1942

The *bando* of 7 September 1941 formally defined the competences of the Regio Esercito.[14] Civil powers in the occupied zones were assumed by the commander of the Second Army, Ambrosio. An administrative commission was created under the orders of the Supersloda command. It was headed by Andrija Karčić – replaced in mid-March 1942 by Vjekoslav Vrančić – who liaised between the Italian command and the Croatian local authorities. The *bando* specified that the commission should refer administrative matters directly or indirectly concerning public order to the commander, and that the prefects would collaborate without 'any directive function'.[15] Offences committed by Croatian civilians and soldiers came under the jurisdiction of the Croatian military tribunals. Offences relative to military matters or to public order would be adjudicated by the military tribunal of the Second Army.[16] In the occupied zones, the *domobrans* and Ustaša militia would cease their manoeuvres and actions against the rebels, and their numbers

[13] USSME, N 1–11, 'Diari storici', b. 568, 'Divisione Sassari, allegato 21'.
[14] USSME, M 3, b. 45, 30 November 1941: the Supersloda UAC sent the dossier of instructions on interpreting the *bando* issued by the Second Army Command on 7 September 1941.
[15] ASMAE, GABAP, b. 33, 9 October 1941, 'Sintesi degli accordi stabiliti nella conferenza del 26 agosto 1941 a Zagabria tra i rappresentanti del governo italiano e quelli del governo croato'.
[16] ASMAE, GABAP, b. 32, 'MAE ad Ambrosio, 2 novembre 1941, telespresso 05871 firmato Mussolini'.

would not be increased. Only youth formations would be authorized in the Italian zone. The local gendarmerie would flank the Carabinieri in maintaining public order, and it would have independent jurisdiction only in dealing with common crimes.

Immediately after the occupation, the army command ordered the restitution of nationalized property to Orthodox citizens (the measure did not apply to Jews) and allocated local administrative posts (that of *podestà* or mayor, for example) to Orthodox Serbs in municipalities where the majority of the population were of Serb Orthodox faith. It ordered that medical care be provided with no discrimination on grounds of race or religion, and it granted refugees a period of time in which to change their dinars into kune (the newly introduced Croatian currency).[17] The decision was taken that Orthodox priests should return to their villages of origin. All these measures were criticized by the local Croat authorities, who claimed that the real intention behind them was conquest of Croatia. They viewed the 'pacification provisions' or those intended to 'normalize the situation' as amounting to annexation. When the garrison commands appointed members of the majority ethnic group to the post of *podestà*, the Croatian protests erupted, even though very few Croats would have accepted civil appointments in a village or town with a Serb majority. Protests were equally strident when the army command lifted the obligation on Jews to wear yellow badges. Although Ambrosio informed the Croatian government that no such concession had been made, he was not believed. He was consequently obliged to announce that that displaying the badge had again been made compulsory for 'Croatian citizens of Jewish race'.[18]

In order not to exacerbate tensions with Zagreb, the commander of the Second Army, Ambrosio, ordered his troops to adopt a policy of 'equidistance' between Serbs and Croats. He instructed his commanders not to undertake any pro-Serbian action, to 'protect the lives of all', not to talk of Croatian territory but rather of the 'first, second and third zone' and 'not to use the word *bando* so as not to offend Croatian sensitivities'. Moreover, given that the Croats proposed – with the Vatican's approval – to 'convert' Jews and Orthodox Christians to Catholicism, he ordered commanders not to interfere in religious affairs. Finally, he recommended extreme caution when selecting village chiefs in the second zone, while he authorized commanders in the third zone to let events take their course, reporting

[17] ASMAE, GABAP, b. 33, Ambrosio, 7 October 1941, 'Situazione nella zona demilitarizzata dalla pubblicazione del bando del 7 settembre a oggi'.

[18] USSME, M 3, b. 45, 'elementi di risposa alla nota 1378/41 del 23 settembre 1941, presentata dalla legazione di Croazia a Roma al Ministero degli Esteri italiano', signed Ambrosio.

on them but not intervening.[19] However, the equidistance policy failed to achieve its purpose and was ignored by the Ustaše and the civilian population.[20]

When the restitution of property to Orthodox Christians began, the Croatian local authorities paralysed the operation by invoking the clause in the *bando* which required that all decisions must be submitted to the army command for executive authorization.[21] Zagreb flouted agreements on food supplies as, day after day, trainloads of goods headed north to Germany.[22] Large numbers of the Ustaša irregulars dismissed by the September *bando* joined the gendarmerie. In the third zone, destruction, burning and violence against defenceless civilians continued and went unpunished. Suspicion between Italians and Croats was mutual, the lack of co-operation between them total: Ambrosio accused the Croats of deliberately seeking to diminish Italian prestige and authority in the eyes of the Serbs; conversely, Zagreb accused the Italian military authorities of deliberately exacerbating tensions and of disempowering the Pavelić government.

As the rebellion spread, the Second Army gave secondary importance to administrative matters and concerned itself primarily with combating the Resistance. General Mario Roatta, then head of the SMRE, drew on his past experience of service in the colonies to suggest that Supersloda should be grouped into large garrisons:[23] a tactic, he wrote, which would give greater incisiveness to the repression. And in some cases and in certain zones, the tactic did indeed halt the rebellion; more often, however, it led to the creation of zones 'infested' (as the military terminology put it) or even controlled by the Resistance. At the end of April 1942, during a briefing

[19] USSME, N I–II, 'Diari storici', b. 523, 'colonnello Leonardi al comando di divisione, 4 novembre 1941'; b. 543, 'Rapporto tenuto dal capo di SM della II Armata il mattino del 31 ottobre 1941 ai capi di SM del V e VI CdA e delle divisioni del Regio Esercito Lombardia, II Celere, Sassari e Bergamo'; b. 543, 'Comando V CdA a tutte le divisioni, 12 novembre 1941'.

[20] USSME, N I–II, 'Diari storici', b. 569, 1 October 1941, 'Notiziario giornaliero del VI CdA'.

[21] USSME, M 3, b. 45, 'Comando Divisione celere Eugenio di Savoia al Comando della II Armata – UAC', 28 September 1941, signed Brigadier General Lomaglio; ASMAE, GABAP, b. 33, 'telegramma di Casertano al GABAP – Ufficio Croazia', 13 November 1941; USSME, M 3, b. 6, 'Comando II Armata – UAC al GABAP – Ufficio Croazia', 10 January 1942, signed Ambrosio: 'The Croatian commissioner seeks to obstruct Italian pacification and consolidation operations in every way possible.' Attached to the document is a summary of information collected by the Command of the CC.RR. of the Second Army on the members of the Croatian general administrative commission: 'Andrea Karcic: notoriously anti-Italian; Antonio Ruzic, ministerial adviser to the commission, of notorious anti-Italian sentiments and an active irredentist propagandist'; similar comments are made about the following members of the commission: Kirać, Mavrović, Gallosich, Resch, Fucić, Gropuzzo and Franko.

[22] ASMAE, GABAP, b. 33, 'Questioni da sottoporsi ai delegati dello stato indipendente di Croazia nella riunione di Abbazia del 15 novembre 1941'.

[23] USSME, M 3, b. 6, 13 January 1942, 'Appunto per il duce sulla situazione in Croazia'.

with the Duce, Count Giuseppe Volpi reported that the Second Army was not as efficient as it should be, and that it was a drain on the Croatian economy. He suggested to Mussolini that the effectives should be made more agile and that the army in the second zone should be pulled back to the ridge of the Dinaric Alps. Mussolini replied, 'You are right, Volpi, it will be done in the second zone, which we shall not give back. I have already spoken to Cavallero about it.'[24] The Duce was also very explicit about the change to the Dalmatian border in a conversation with Giuseppe Bastianini, whom he told that the new provinces had to be enlarged, that the border should be moved to the ridge of the Dinarics and that Dalmatia was not to be divided but should instead belong in its entirety to Italy.[25]

Exactly one year after the occupations, once again mooted was the initial plan of annexing the entire eastern Adriatic coast and the inland zones as far as the Dinaric Alps. The compromise of the limited annexations of 1941 no longer made sense, Croatia had proved to be an unreliable ally and the Germans had the economic resources of the entire country in their grasp. The withdrawal of the Second Army in the second zone would cut the Germans off from the Adriatic. But if the plan was adopted, Italy would definitively lose Zagreb's friendship; and it was for this reason that Luca Pietromarchi and Raffaele Casertano did not approve of the project and continued to advocate a policy of close collaboration with Pavelić and the Croatian government.

In May 1942, after conducting a series of largely fruitless combat operations against the rebels in Bosnia-Herzegovina, Roatta – who had in the meantime been appointed commander of Supersloda – consolidated the Italian army garrisons and sought to mend relations with Zagreb, at least to the extent that he could count on co-operation from the Croatian troops. The Italian commands justified their reluctance to make significant concessions to the Croats on the ground that an excessive reduction in Italian military powers and presence would provoke 'a second round of the persecutions of the summer of 1941'. Roatta proposed that the Italian troops be withdrawn from the third zone, while, in the second zone, certain lesser powers should be left to the Croats. The Italian military authorities would continue to administer justice, issue *bandi* on matters to do with public order, impose sanctions and arrest Croatian citizens suspected of offences against the public order, the security of the armed forces,

[24] Pietromarchi, diary, 28 April 1942. [25] Ibid., 7 May 1942.

industrial installations and the railways.[26] On 1 June 1942, Roatta's proposal was accepted by the Croats. On the urging of Count Volpi – president of the Commissione Economica Permanente Italo-Croata (CEPIC) – and with Mussolini's crucial backing, it was established that the payment in kune of the occupation expenses would no longer be calculated according to the number of Italian solders present on Croatian territory but would instead be decided by the CEPIC. Volpi had already stressed at the end of April that a less expensive method for settling the debt would have to be found, for otherwise . . . 'Otherwise,' interrupted Mussolini, 'one day they will bring us on a plate the little body of the Croatia that we have brought into the world. We risk suffocating it in our embrace.'[27]

The Italians retained broad powers in the event of revolt and for military operations along the coast and on the islands. The army command reserved the right to re-establish garrisons and create new ones if militarily necessary, or if a breakdown of public order required it. The agreement stipulated that conflict between the Četniks and the Croats must cease. The two groups undertook 'scrupulously' to respect their previous commitments to the Italian commands and guaranteed that abuses and reprisals would halt. The new joint administration gave the Croatian authorities responsibility for routine matters, although they were obliged to inform the Italians on all measures introduced to maintain law and order. A military commission was set up within Supersloda to handle relations between the troops of the two states. All the garrisons in the third zone were dismantled except for the one in Karlovac.[28]

June 1942–July 1943

The spiral of violence, reprisal and revenge erupted once again on the very same day that the agreement came into effect. Alarm swept through the

[26] ASMAE, GABAP, b. 31, 10 May 1942, 'Roatta, Promemoria all'esercizio dei poteri civili nella seconda zona da parte del comandante delle FF.AA. della Slovenia–Dalmazia'. In the second zone, the Croatians were left with control over the possession of firearms, munitions and explosives; at their discretion they could ban popular celebrations and public assemblies, decide on freedom of movement, impose curfews, regulate the circulation of civilian vehicles and seize radio apparatus. Again in the second zone, the garrisons were dismantled at Jastrebarsko, Bihać, Bosanski Petrovac, Glamoč, Bugojno, Prozor and Konjic, and in July, at Drvar, Bosansko Grahovo, Livno, Tomislavgrad and Gacko; the railway protection units north of Mostar were withdrawn; then the garrisons at Imotski, Stolac, Ljubinje, Nevesinje and Bileća were closed down.

[27] Pietromarchi, diary, 28 April 1942.

[28] ASMAE, GABAP, b. 31, 19 June 1942, 'Roatta, Accordo tra il governo dello stato indipendente di Croazia e il Comando superiore delle FF.AA. in Slovenia–Dalmazia, firmato Roatta, Pavelić e Lorković'.

population, especially among those of its members who had pleaded for annexation to Italy.[29] 'As the immediate and predictable consequence of the agreement', wrote the consul in Dubrovnik (Ragusa) Amedeo Mammalella, 'there were massacres in all localities from which we had withdrawn our garrisons . . . In the town of Foča some thirty Serbs were murdered. A group of Četniks then reciprocated by killing forty members of the Ustaša militia.'[30] The Serb Orthodox and Muslim populations, added the consul, 'have seen the protection afforded by us during a year of military action suddenly evaporate'.[31]

During a fact-finding mission for the MAE, on 15 August 1942, the general of the CC.RR., Giuseppe Pièche, wrote a report that analysed the situation of the Ustaša regime and set out Croatian, Italian and German policy towards it. Pièche's report touched upon all the main aspects of Italy's occupation policy: relationships between a nominal protector unable to take effective action and a refractory satellite entirely devoid of authority; the behaviour of Italy's untrustworthy ally; and an internal situation which had by now collapsed into civil, ideological, ethnic and religious war.

The Croatian state, wrote the general, was a 'fluid and formal entity' whose internal situation was 'uncertain, obscure, precarious'.[32] The only true pro-Italian was Pavelić; the rest of the executive, and especially the powerful Marshal Slavko Kvaternik, were pro-German. The *poglavnik* did not have a 'totalitarian following', the population was 'Germanophile' and 'Dalmatian irredentist', and ministers prevented the head of government from undertaking any 'truly dictatorial action'. Elevated to power by circumstance, Pavelić was obscure, almost unknown: he had neither the reputation nor the prestige to construct a solid political base and form an efficient state apparatus. The country treated him with cold indifference or ill-concealed hostility: who, the people enquired, is this nonentity imposed by foreign bayonets?[33] Aboard a frail craft leaking at every seam, Pavelić

[29] ASMAE, GABAP, b. 32, 'Situazione sull'isola di Pago'. Bastianini wrote that 80 per cent of the population of Pag was in favour of annexation. According to some sources, the inhabitants of Brazza and Lesina wanted to obtain Italian citizenship.

[30] ASMAE, GABAP, b. 36,'console Mammalella alla legazione di Zagabria, 29 agosto 1942, Eccidi di Foca'. Mammalella reports numerous acts of violence against Muslims and the barbaric murders of women and children.

[31] ASMAE, GABAP, b. 36,'consolato di Ragusa al MAE, 1 agosto 1942, telespresso 4194/353'.

[32] USSME, M 3, b. 6, 5 August 1942, 'Relazione sulla Croazia al GABAP'.

[33] ASMAE, GABAP, b. 33, 'legazione a Zagabria al GABAP, 27 settembre 1941'. Another description of Pavelić is provided by the head of the military mission in Zagreb, General Giovan Battista Oxilia: 'At bottom, the *poglavnik* is not at all a bloody revolutionary, but rather a mystic, a religious and honest man, very attached to his family, perhaps also a sentimentalist and a dreamer, but owing to his prejudices he has not managed to carry forward a policy of pacification towards the Serbs of Croatia that, in my view, is indispensable in view of the country's present and future situation.'

clung to the tiller as he strove to steer a course among the whirlpools and reefs of domestic difficulties, inexorable German encroachment and Italian resentment.

According to General Pièche, the Ustaše were undermanned and consisted of 'morally tainted, unscrupulous and violent individuals who profited from the general chaos to commit abuse, outrage and murder, enriching themselves as they did so. The political cadres in government [were] no better in quality.' The rank-and-file, the general added, were loyal to Pavelić 'not out of political conviction or devotion – such virtues being unknown in the Balkans [sic!] – but because of their interest in gaining power, which they interpreted as synonymous with lawlessness and privilege'. The haphazard training of the politicians partly explained 'the horrifying excesses perpetrated in the massacre of nameless Jews and Serbian Orthodox Christians on the pretext of pursuing a racial policy' which concealed the real intention of seizing the victims' property. According to Pièche, the massacre of the Jews lined the pockets of the Croatian leaders with property amounting to fully ten billion lire, none of which figured in the national accounts. 'There did indeed exist a Jewish question which required solution, but addressing it with such inhuman and appalling ferocity was an error [with] extremely grave consequences. The massacres caused an enormous and disastrous reaction in Aryan circles, so that even those who had good reason to complain about the behaviour of the Jews were induced, if not to defend them, at least to commiserate with them.'

Even more grievous and unjustified, wrote Pièche, was the treatment of the Slavs, who were 'slaughtered in their hundreds of thousands'. Caught up in the violence were a huge number of Croats tied by kinship or interest to the Orthodox community: 'half of Croatia was attacked and reviled, half of Croatia became the Ustaše's sworn enemy'. The government's attempt to bring Orthodox Christians onto its side by conversion was unsuccessful because the archbishop of Zagreb, Alojzije Stepinac, 'an intelligent and astute man, with the temperament of an expert and able diplomat, the faithful interpreter of the Vatican's instructions, refused to endorse the manoeuvre'. This makeshift policy, 'illogical, incoherent and impracticable, irked the Roman Church, caused tensions with the Vatican' and 'significantly damaged the regime'.[34] Pièche was equally harsh in his criticism

[34] USSME, M 3, b. 45; ASMAE, GABAP, b. 34, 'Ministero dell'Interno – DGPS Divisione Polizia politica', 12 July 1941: 'The extent of the persecution of both the Serbs and the Jews (who are compelled to wear a yellow disc bearing the letter Z = Zidovi = Jew) has aroused the ire of Stepinaz, Archbishop of Zagreb, who in his capacity as supreme head of the Croatian Catholic Church has protested to Pavelić about the brutality of the methods used.'

of the Croatian policy towards the Muslim minority, which had first been cosseted, then suspected of connivance with the communists and consequently harassed, and finally again favoured. The general also analysed the behaviour of the Germans, who, he wrote, 'undermined the *poglavnik's* position with every means and in every way possible'. They manipulated Pavelić and drew on the resources furnished by the thousands of *Volksdeutschen* living in the country, who opened Nazi clubs, *Kulturbünde* and *Arbeitfronten*. They inundated Croatia with propaganda, publishing newspapers and magazines, opened schools in every part of the country, persuaded the Croatian Ministry of Education to institute a special section for German schools and organized lectures that extolled the greatness of Germany and proclaimed German–Croatian friendship. The Reichsbank funded purchases of land in Croatia by German subjects and minorities. The Todt Organization ('a nest of spies') invaded the country, and the Gestapo – 'a beacon that enlightens and guides every German who may be involved with it in any capacity' – was ubiquitous.[35] The Germans emptied Croatia of its resources, they removed its industrial base and deported workers. They did not organize the Croatian armed forces, so that conduct of operations against the rebels and the maintenance of public order were reserved to the Wehrmacht and the SS with the assistance of the *Volksdeutschen*.

Pièche's opinion on the Germans' behaviour was shared by numerous Italians on the spot, and by the GABAP, which had kept Mussolini abreast of the situation since January 1942. Giuseppe Solari Bozzi, general manager of the Stefani press agency in Zagreb, wrote that German propaganda had committed innumerable offences against Italy. With a lack of scruple inconceivable in an ally, for one and a half years the Germans had sabotaged Italy's every attempt to heal the rift with the Croats. They had Croatia in their grasp both militarily and economically. Above all they could count on the crucial support of the German minority in the country. The Croatian *Volksdeutschen*, armed and inducted into the SS and the *Hitlerjugend*, constituted 'a state within the state'. It furnished officials for the state administration and worked for the 'economic rebirth of the country and the education of its people'.[36]

[35] USSME, M 3, b. 5,'generale Pièche al GABAP e al CS, 5 agosto 1942, Relazione sulla Croazia'.

[36] Talpo, *Dalmazia*, vol. II, p. 902, annex 22 to chap. 5; ASMAE, GABAP, b. 31, 'GABAP – Ufficio Croazia, 15 gennaio 1942, Promemoria per il duce; sottofasc. Penetrazione tedesca in Croazia'; ibid., 'Attività tedesca in Croazia, governatorato del Montenegro – Ufficio "I" – allo SMRE – SIE e per conoscenza al GABAP, 28 giugno 1942, firmato tenente colonnello Andrea Maderni'; b. 28, 'Il germanesimo in Croazia, Berlino 23 maggio 1941'; ACS, MI, DGPS – AA.RR., 1942, 'Divisione Polizia politica alla DGPS, 7 dicembre 1942, Nota rimessa brevi manu dal generale Pièche'; ASMAE,

Given that large part of the native population spoke German, it was not difficult for Germany to penetrate Croatia culturally.[37] The country's Habsburg past favoured its subservience to the Reich: large numbers of Croats were intimately acquainted with the German language and culture; numerous powerful Ustaše were former Austrian officers and had friendships with Germans reaching back to their childhoods. The influential General Edmund Glaise von Horstenau – plenipotentiary at the German legation in Zagreb – was Austrian. Pièche also points out that Italy's real enemies in the former Yugoslavia were not so much the Serbs as the Croats, owing to the Austrian tradition which had permeated 'consciences and minds with anti-Italianism until it became a permanent and constant mental attitude'.[38] The Italians' situation was made even more difficult by the German legation, and by Ambassador Siegfried Kasche, who played the part of a *deus ex machina* that 'protected' the Croats by generously donating weapons and supplies. Kasche never missed an opportunity to encourage the Croats in their obstructionism against Italy's interests by supporting their 'double-dealing game'.[39] He took full advantage of a dislike for Italy seemingly ingrained in sections of the Croat population by expressing contempt for the Italian troops – and indeed everything Italian. He even went so far as to finance a Croatian irredentist organization, the Blue Legion.[40]

Pietromarchi very soon realized that the policy of Kasche and von Horstenau was not, as he put it,

> a peripheral policy pursued by pro-Austrian elements intent on destabilizing our positions in Croatia, but a directive from the centre. According to this directive, Croatia should be divided into two zones, with the Western karstic zone going to Italy, and the one rich in minerals, crops and timber to Germany . . . [This] in blatant contradiction to Germany's undertaking that it would recognize Croatia as Italian *spazio vitale*.[41]

GABAP, b. 37, 'legazione di Zagabria al GABAP, 15 gennaio 1943, firmato Casertano'. The Hrvatski (Croatian) Gestapo was created in December 1942. Divided into three sections – economic-industrial, military and political – it worked entirely under the supervision of the Gestapo. Indeed, in January 1943, the *poglavnik* appointed Branimir Altgayer, former chief representative of the German minority at the Croatian Prime Minister's Office, as under-secretary of state.

[37] ASMAE, GABAP, b. 31: a copy of this report was sent to Pietromarchi on 30 July 1942.

[38] USSME, M 3, b. 19, fasc. 8, 18 January 1943, 'La Croazia alle soglie del 1943'.

[39] ASMAE, GABAP, b. 37, 'legazione a Zagabria al gabinetto del Ministero degli Esteri', 8 March 1943.

[40] ASMAE, GABAP, b. 37, 'legazione a Zagabria al gabinetto del Ministero degli Esteri', 22 March 1943; b. 37, 'Casertano al GABAP', 19 March 1943', to be found in DDI, ser. IX, 1939–43, vol. 10, doc. 173. Equally explicit was a note from Bastianini to Mussolini written before the discussions held with Ribbentrop in February 1943, in DDI, ser. IX, 1939–43, vol. 10, doc. 52, 'allegato 7 (visto dal duce)'.

[41] Pietromarchi, diary, 23–24 June 1942.

And Italian policy? General Pièche's analysis seems still valid today. It was not the policy of a 'protector' but of a hesitant and weak 'tutor' without the strength to support and guide. It was a policy that requested, or worse pleaded, but that never demanded or ordered, that desired but was unable to fulfil its desires, that adapted or meekly submitted to circumstances and situations sometimes at odds with formal pacts. But Pièche acknowledged that it was pointless for Italy to remonstrate if it could not back up its protests with forceful action. It was ingenuous to reproach the Croats for their duplicity and tendency to swim with the German tide if the Italians were unable to raise effective resistance against Germany's hegemony. According to Pièche, Rome should give more support to Pavelić and apply pressure in Berlin to persuade the Germans to comply with the agreements entered upon: otherwise, he said, rather than a *spazio vitale*, the Balkans would become a *spazio mortale*. Pièche saw three threats to what he still believed would be Italy's victorious peace: the Germans, the Croats and the communists.

In August 1942, as Pièche was writing his report, General Roatta issued his 'directives for the winter period', which foresaw intensified action by the rebels but also had to take account of reductions in army manning levels. Roatta ordered more garrisons to be dismantled, although this was only done slowly because the Croatian army was not ready to replace the Supersloda troops. The Regio Esercito was pushed ever deeper into the shifting sands of Bosnia and Herzegovina by its failure to deal with the partisan movement or halt the ferocious internecine conflict in the former Yugoslavia. Evidence accumulated that men close to Foreign Minister Mladen Lorković were fomenting anti-Italian unrest in Dalmatia and encouraging collusion between Herzegovinian partisans and Croatian officers to eliminate the Četnik units created by the Italians.

On 7 November 1942, Casertano admitted that relationships between the PNF and the Ustaša party were superficial and that youth education had slipped out of Fascist control. Police collaboration consisted of no more than the exchange of information and technical assistance and was obstructed by the pervasive presence of the German police. The Croats greatly preferred the support of Germany to military co-operation with the Italians. Their economic collaboration with Rome had produced agreements of only secondary importance, and cultural collaboration was only the compulsory teaching of Italian in schools and a university course in Italian civilization – altogether a failure, therefore, compared to Germany's control over the nerve centres of the country.[42]

[42] USSME, M 3, b. 6, 7 September 1942, 'Relazione al GABAP sulla Croazia'.

In early 1943, the Resistance achieved important victories. At the same time food shortages became critical. The Ustaše were profoundly hated: isolated and devoid of any prestige, they were incapable of resolving the country's difficulties. Fully 80 per cent of the Croatian population were opposed to the regime; 10 per cent declared themselves 'apolitical', while only a tiny minority still supported the Ustaše.[43] The *poglavnik* dismissed Marshal Kvaternik, together with his son, the notorious chief of police, who was officially blamed for the massacres of 1941. Ministries were merged, a Council of State was appointed and police commissioners were sacked. Financial measures were taken to improve the food situation, but they were unsuccessful.

More tolerance was shown towards Orthodox Christians (but not Jews). An autocephalous Church was created, but the divide between the two populations was unbridgeable. The partisan revolt – backed by an efficient propaganda machine – won hearts and minds even in the middle class and, indeed, the high bourgeoisie. It received further impetus from the defeats suffered by the Axis and from the Anglo-American offensive in the Mediterranean. Soviet republics sprang up in many parts of the country.[44]

The situation described in General Pièche's last report from Croatia was disastrous. The country had collapsed into lawlessness, the black market was the country's only real stock exchange, industry was paralysed, commerce took the form of barter and the government was incapable of organizing food supplies. Trade with Germany and Italy was practically non-existent, and nobody thought it worth reviving. The business community was pervaded by an 'atmosphere of resignation', and the Croatian economy was moribund.[45] Croatia was no longer an independent state; rather, it was a 'sick infant . . . brought by its own fault to the brink of the grave, yet still stubborn and fractious when only from us can it obtain life-saving oxygen'.[46]

After February 1943, Rome relinquished political and economic control over the second zone and resigned itself to the fact that Croatia was entirely under German control. It still hoped, however, for 'the closest collaboration between diplomatic representations . . . and between the military authorities' so that 'no initiative [is taken] without prior consultation'.[47]

43 USSME, M 3, b. 19, 18 January 1943, 'Relazione al GABAP del generale Pièche'.
44 USSME, M 3, b. 19, 'colonnello Giancarlo Re, capo della missione militare italiana in Croazia, al CS, allo SMRE e al ministro d'Italia a Zagabria Casertano', 15 January 1943.
45 USSME, M 3, b. 19, 14 May 1943, 'Relazione del generale Pièche al GABAP'.
46 USSME, M 3, b. 19, 19 January 1943,'Relazione del generale Pièche al GABAP'.
47 ASMAE, GABAP, b. 37, 2 February 1943.

A note by the GABAP acknowledged that the Croats were now entirely anti-Italian ('100 per cent'). For the time being their dislike was concealed behind 'a smile on the lips', but soon, on the promptings of the Germans, it would be expressed openly: 'This is because both Croats and Germans are intent on gaining command of the Adriatic, for obvious reasons of national interest and in order to counterbalance our maritime power in that sea.' The Italian consul in Sarajevo, Paolo Alberto Rossi, conceded that Italy had lost the contest against Germany. Italy had, he wrote, been unable to counter the southward thrust by the German occupation forces with a northward counter-thrust consisting of military and political infiltration of the German zone. The time had come to withdraw from Croatia. At most, symbolic small garrisons should remain behind to assert Italy's military presence and defend its prestige as Croatia's ally and a Balkan power. The advantage would be that entire divisions would no longer have to endure the unremitting pressure of forces which they could not withstand.[48]

GREECE

Such was the vast extent of the zones occupied in Greece that the Italian army was unable to police the territory in its entirety. As in the second and third Croatian zones, the strategy was consequently adopted of installing large garrisons. The Italian troops were concentrated in the main towns, in zones most at risk of enemy landings and in those where rebellion was most likely. The most important centres were defended, while densely populated areas deemed easier to control were neglected. Given the presence of a national government, the occupiers did not consider it necessary to install an administrative apparatus. But this political decision by the Axis partners was contradictory for, although it did not impose a regime of direct rule, it left almost no decision-making power to the Greek executive. The ruling class and the majority of the Greek population had no faith in the government, judging it for what it actually was: an Axis puppet manipulated by the two Axis plenipotentiaries, Günther Althenburg and Pellegrino Ghigi, who were empowered to appoint and dismiss ministers and civil servants at will. Moreover, the Italian and German military and civil authorities acted independently of each other, and they often did so in disagreement. As a result of this confusion of powers, the Greek government rapidly lost control of the periphery and effectively ruled only the capital.

[48] USSME, M 3, b. 19, MAE, 29 May 1943, 'Promemoria per il generale Ambrosio, consolato di Sarajevo'.

In the Italian occupation zone, the commands of the CdAs and each individual division established direct relations with the local Greek authorities: an arrangement, they believed, that would to some extent remedy administrative inefficiency and the confusion of powers caused by the joint management of the *res publica*. In the nomarchies (similar to the Italian *regioni* and the French *départements*), the Greek state was represented by a civil governor (a sort of prefect) who issued orders to all civil servants and the gendarmerie. The Italian commands preferred to work with these civil governors rather than with the central Greek government. In 1941 and the first six months of 1942, the occupiers replaced eight governors and twenty-three mayors, suspended two of them and transferred four magistrates. The intention was to elevate the prefect to the 'dignity of representative in the provinces so that he is the sole regulator and superintendent of a province's political, social and economic life in accordance with the directives issued by the political and military occupation authorities'.[49]

The first months of the occupation saw great administrative confusion. As the Italian troops took over, civil servants and gendarmes were not reinstated in their posts. The result was paralysis of all public services and authorities, from the courts to the post office. On instruction by the Axis plenipotentiaries, the central government then decreed that all civil servants must return to work. And the civil servants slowly did so, not because they were in sympathy with the Tsolakoglou government, but because they had realized that their jobs were a source – albeit a meagre one – of income. The commander of the 8th CdA Giuseppe Pafundi wrote thus:

> The Greek administrative machine is starting up again: overall, it does not excel, neither for the qualities of the functionaries nor for their competence, nor for their dutifulness. I have received not a few reports of apathy, poor performance and an apparent lack of interest in the *res publica*.[50]

In an attempt to remedy the deficiencies of the public administration, the CdA commands ordered the Greek authorities to compile and present to the divisional commands declarations of loyalty, obedience and 'absolute, unquestioning and totalitarian' subservience.[51] At the same time, the

[49] USSME, L 15, b. 23, 'Com. sup. FF.AA. Grecia al CS', 27 July 1941; b. 85, 7 June 1941, 'Relazione sulla situazione di Prevesa'; USSME, N 1–11, 'Diari storici', b. 713, 'Comando III CdA al Com. sup. FF.AA. Grecia – UAC, 13 giugno 1942, Relazione sulla situazione politico-amministrativa per il periodo dal 16 al 31 maggio 1942'.

[50] USSME, L 15, b. 23,'Comando VIII CdA – UAC a Supergrecia – UAC, 10 agosto 1941, Affari civili – Relazione riassuntiva sulla situazione nel Peloponneso'.

[51] USSME, N 1–11, 'Diari storici', b. 325, 'Comando VIII CdA ai comandanti di divisione', 10 June 1941.

military occupation authorities arrogated numerous powers to themselves. For example, where public offices were understaffed, they appointed committees of local trusties (*fidati*) – supervised by the CC.RR. – in order to ensure the delivery of essential services. The commands were authorized to impound goods, foodstuffs, raw materials useful for the war effort and fuel; they supervised currency transactions (via the Finance Police); and they undertook public works, recruiting local labour for the purpose.

The occupiers had to deal with problems for which they were unprepared: rampant malaria, the cornering of resources by the Germans and the presence of more than 10,000 Cretan soldiers roaming the Greek countryside (they were subsequently interned in concentration camps and occasionally used as labour for the Eleventh Army's public works). Public order was disrupted not by ethnic and religious civil war, as in Croatia, but by severe food shortages. General Geloso feared a popular uprising provoked by the government's lack of authority and fuelled by British propaganda. He reminded Rome that these problems were not the army's responsibility; but the authorities in the capital took no significant and concrete steps to deal with them. In July 1941, the general set about improving the railway transportation of food, especially to Athens, and he introduced credit facilities for public utilities. However, Geloso's actions were not prompted by humanitarianism; rather, they were a way of working 'towards the Duce'. He pursued a policy that differed from that of the Germans – who ruthlessly exploited the Greek peninsula – in order to highlight the different nature of the Italian occupation and to 'earn the esteem of the people . . . on the expectation that Greek territory will in the future be part of the *spazio vitale*'.[52]

In a report on the activities of the Italian armed forces written during the first year of occupation, Geloso claimed that occupation policy had developed into a veritable system of government. But he admitted the difficulties of working with the peripheral civil authorities, which were inefficient and indolent, as well as indifferent to the public welfare. The Eleventh Army vetted, encouraged and coerced the Greek civil servants. It removed those deemed 'inept and untrustworthy' and settled disputes and squabbles between local authorities. Its opinion of prefects, sub-prefects, mayors and magistrates was that they were 'dishonest' and indifferent to the needs of less affluent members of society. 'Personal cliques' were rampant, while 'remnants of the numerous former parties that [had] always waged

[52] USSME, L 15, b. 23, 'Com. sup. FF.AA. Grecia al CS, 27 luglio 1941, Relazione sulla situazione politico-militare in Grecia allo scadere del primo mese della nostra occupazione'.

internecine war' regrouped. Though these professed friendship for Italy, they obstructed the work of collaborating civil servants. And then, Geloso admitted, men of ability, the intelligentsia, the clergy, and former senior officials were implacably opposed to the occupiers.[53]

The gendarmerie and the police force were 'hostile, deceitful and unreliable'. They unabashedly did as little as possible without incurring punishment while covertly working against the occupiers.[54] They were apathetic for moral reasons but also for material ones: their meagre pay fell far short of that required to maintain a decent standard of living – as the regime put it, they were 'decaying forces'. Yet their members could have been first-rate collaborators given that 'they were still ferocious persecutors of communists', but their ardent Anglophilia made them into the opposite of what the Italian occupiers wanted. Consequently, after vain appeals for co-operation, the occupiers decided – as in Croatia – to conduct mass purges and then to reorganize the police and the gendarmerie, obliging them to sign a 'declaration of loyal collaboration with the occupier' which was administered by the CC.RR. The Athens school for gendarmes was closed, and those gendarmes in service were issued with only a pistol and a limited number of cartridges. Their tasks were restricted to the prevention and investigation of common crimes and the transfer of prisoners.[55]

The Italians' main concern as regards the judicial system was to assert their authority by pre-empting the Greek magistrates. For example, on the twentieth anniversary of the March on Rome, the occupiers announced an amnesty for all offences punished by the military tribunals with either fines or less than three years' imprisonment. Some 6,588 Greeks benefited from the amnesty, though not those who had committed the same kinds of

53 USSME, N I–II, 'Diari storici', b. 613, 'Comando Divisione Cagliari, sezione "I", 21 marzo 1942, Relazione quindicinale del servizio "I"': 'In Laconia conflict persists among the prefect, the *podestà* of the chief town and bodies responsible for the province, as well as private individuals, who complain directly to Minister of the Interior Cerigotis'; b. 1089, 'II Battaglione mobilitato CC.RR. Genova, relazione riservatissima sulla Grecia, 30 maggio 1942': 'There is a rising tide of resentment in Patras against the prefect of Achaea, one Splglica, accused of lacking the necessary training for his post; of being unable to solve the province's problems; of being influenced by a clique of upstarts and speculators. The military authorities rightly hold him in scant consideration and regard him as untrustworthy, notwithstanding his attempts to prove the contrary.'

54 USSME, N I–II, 'Diari storici', b. 660, 'Comando Divisione di fanteria Pinerolo – Ufficio di SM, sezione "I", al Comando del III CdA, 5 marzo 1942, Gendarmeria greca'; b. 462, 'Comando Divisione Pinerolo, 4 luglio 1941'; b. 719, 'Comando truppe italiane in Creta, Divisione di fanteria Siena, sezione "I", al Com. sup. Egeo, 10 giugno 1942, Relazione sulla situazione politica ed economica della provincia di Lassithi'.

55 USSME, N I–II, 'Diari storici', b. 1047, 'Comando VIII Battaglione autonomo CC.RR.', December 1942. Mass desertions were reported at the end of 1942, while other gendarmes allowed themselves to be captured without offering resistance.

offences but had received sentences from the Greek courts. The importance of occupational policy on judicial matters did not escape Geloso, who pointed out that intervention in this branch of the public administration would assert 'Fascist ethical superiority . . . without creating martyrs or the terror of ferocity'.[56]

The provision of social welfare services was a useful propaganda device for the occupiers: giving aid to the civilian population would enhance the Italians' prestige. According to Geloso's figures, the local welfare committees, which operated under the auspices of the military authorities, assisted 38,145 needy people, and the school canteens provided meals for 20,670 children. However, the figures do not specify whether the needy were assisted only once or repeatedly, or for how long, or where the school canteens or soup kitchens were located. In any event, in a situation of general and grinding poverty like Greece's, the welfare that the Italians provided was almost irrelevant.

During the two years of the occupation, the Eleventh Army intervened in economic and financial matters on an increasingly broad scale. The Italian military authorities sought to ensure the distribution of bread and the sale of foodstuffs; they granted transport and travel permits; they created civilian stockpiling agencies; they allowed the managers to use vehicles to distribute bread; they requisitioned warehouses; and they seized hoarded goods. They mounted a campaign to persuade the civil authorities, the police force and manufacturers to contribute to the success of the pooling policy (obliging the Greek government to order compulsory quota contributions by farmers after the 1942 harvests). The Corpo della Sicurezza Agricola (5,500 agents) was issued with arms, and it acted in concert with the gendarmerie under the supervision of the CC.RR. After 12 January 1942, provincial food commissions consisting of prefects, heads of the agrarian service and provincial ration inspectors (*ispettori annonari*) were set up at the prefectures. These commissions ascertained the availability of produce; they attended to the organization and surveillance of stockpiles; they arranged the transportation of foodstuffs from province to province; and they fixed prices. Army officers were seconded to the commissions in order to supervise their deliberations and to 'suggest' the measures to be taken, thereafter reporting to the UACs of the CdAs, the divisional UACs and the embassy in Athens. Also created was an inspectorate of Thessaly prefectures, with headquarters in Volos. Supervised by the military authorities, this inspectorate co-ordinated the economies of the provinces under its

[56] USSME, L 15, b. 23, 'Com. sup. FF.AA. Grecia al CS, 27 luglio 1941'.

jurisdiction with a view to improving relations between the capital and the provinces. In Larissa, Trikala and Lamia, provisioning officers reported to an Italian officer attached to the inspectorate, and to the food procurement commission. Seconded to this latter body was Lieutenant Cipollini, whose task was to supervise the local agencies and liaise between them and the CdA command 'for the purpose of improving collaboration in the field of food procurement'.[57]

There were also joint Italo-German commissions, one for the procurement of food, another for the procurement of building materials. The former processed applications to purchase and transport foodstuffs. It issued authorizations for purchases, set prices and monitored them, organized stocks and increased the activities of civil agencies. The Italo-German commission on building materials was created by the Wehrmacht Baustoffamt (an offshoot of the Greek WiRüAmt) and Italian officers from the military and naval engineering corps were seconded to it as members.

The Regio Esercito gave technical assistance to the Greek provincial authorities for industry, communications and transport, the purpose being to exploit resources more intensely.[58] The policy was to improve existing infrastructure and plant, thereby affording 'the civil population with tangible evidence of Italy's commitment to the well-being of Greece'. As a result, trams were brought back into service, electricity delivery for industrial use was boosted and the gas supply was restored.

The Italian army worked closely with the Greek authorities to increase crop yields, mainly by distributing seeds for high-quality spring wheat. Collaboration in this area reached a level unthinkable in Croatia or France. To deal with the food crisis, so-called *orti del soldato* (military vegetable plots) were planted so as 'not to draw on local resources for procurement of the fresh vegetables necessary for the preparation of mess rations'. Each garrison was ordered to bring 100 hectares per battalion under the cultivation of cereals. Fields were also set aside for cropping experiments conducted by suitably qualified military personnel. The purpose of this initiative was 'to demonstrate in technically backward areas the advantages deriving to individuals and the community from advanced farming systems such as those used in Italy'.[59] Cultivation of the *orti del soldato* began in numerous areas of Greece (subsequently in Corsica), and the results would have been impressive had the units received the seeds and equipment that they

[57] USSME, N 1–11, 'Diari storici', b. 713, 'Comando III CdA al Com. sup. FF.AA. Grecia – UAC, 13 giugno 1942, Relazione sulla situazione politico-amministrativa per il periodo dal 16 al 31 maggio 1942'.

[58] USSME, L 15, b. 23, 'Com. sup. FF.AA. Grecia al CS, 27 luglio 1941, Relazione G'.

[59] Ibid.

required. In Greece, only the command of the Cagliari Division managed to cultivate, 'for the autarkic activity of feeding the troops', 150 hectares of wheat and 22 hectares of vegetables. Thus it could propagandize its self-sufficiency, claim that it took nothing from the civilian population's reserves of food and extol 'Italian genius', while at the same time improving the soldiers' mess rations. Nevertheless, the Cagliari Division was an exception.

Finally, health was also an area of close co-operation: in this case between the Greek medical authorities and the Second Army's health service, which worked together to reorganize the Athens street-cleaning service, and, to combat malaria, undertook small-scale operations in drainage and anti-mosquito spraying (similar measures were taken in Corsica).[60] Greece's severe medical problems were not resolved, however. Indeed, the occupying authorities did not even have the means necessary for the prophylaxis of their own troops. The commands more modestly made arrangements for medical officers to examine and (depending on the medicine stocks available) treat the civil population.

Although, as we have seen, Italy's occupation policy had a number of positive outcomes, these were far from Fascism's initial ambitions of conquest and dominion. For a brief period between early 1942 and the October of that year, a section of the Greek population, despite the food crisis and after outright hostility, credited the troops of the Regio Esercito with 'acting with fairness, prudence and generosity'. In some zones, the Peloponnese, for example, the Greek public administration collaborated with the Italian military authorities to such an extent that the commander praised various officials in public.[61] After the end of 1942, however, the situation changed. Increasingly, severe economic difficulties induced various sections of the Greek population to change from apathy to resistance: many Greeks now had nothing more to lose.

In April, a strike by public-sector workers gave the occupiers a concrete measure of discontent in Athens. The population of the town of Trikala hurled abuse at the prefect, in Karditsa the poor quality of the flour distributed by the troops provoked demonstrations at the gates of the Italian garrison; the prefect of Kastoria was assaulted by a group of women. In the

[60] USSME, N I–II, 'Diari storici', b. 1207, 'Comando VII CdA, 15 marzo 1943, Lotta antimalarica'. Nothing could be done in southern Corsica, despite the work of a 'malariologist' dispatched to analyse the situation, owing to the presence of large numbers of elderly soldiers afflicted by malaria and a high percentage of chronic malaria victims in the civilian population.

[61] USSME, N I–II, 'Diari storici', b. 1193, 'Comando VIII CdA al Com. sup. FF.AA. Grecia – UAC, ottobre 1942'.

autumn, the Andartes resistance fighters began to organize attacks against public officials, Axis sympathizers and army informers, the intention being to isolate the Italians. A report by the 3rd CdA stated that the rebels were bent on 'alienating every sympathy and eliminating co-operation by any pro-Italian element'.[62] The local authorities were paralysed from the end of 1942 onwards as civil servants deserted their posts *en masse*, either to join the Andartes or because they feared reprisals. The Italian occupiers now took no further interest in administration, instead devoting all their energies to putting down the Andartes.[63]

FRANCE

Before analysing policy during Italy's ten-month occupation of south-eastern France, I would emphasize that, from the armistice until November 1942, the Vichy–Rome relationship was in reality a Franco-German relationship sporadically punctuated by futile Italian intervention. The Italians' insistence on resolution of the territorial question precluded all dialogue between the two countries. And Germany's veto on any such resolution aroused Rome's suspicions concerning its ally's real intentions. The historian Romain Rainero explains that the dilemma for Italy was Germany's dominance in the relationship between the Axis victors and Vichy France. Much more frequently than its ally, indeed, the Fascist government invoked the Axis as the essential basis for Italo-German policy towards the defeated states – France especially. Rome therefore reacted cautiously to Vichy's stubborn resistance against German claims and to the Berlin government's generosity. Its reaction was marked by the same political hesitancy that had been apparent during the talks on the Villa Incisa armistice – when Mussolini's 'spontaneous' withdrawal of his demands for annexation and occupation almost exactly replicated Germany's behaviour during negotiations on the Réthondes armistice.[64]

The CIAF central office had by now been given responsibility by the Italian government to handle all relations with Vichy France. It believed that the unilateralism of most commitments in the armistice convention allowed Italy to exercise all rights of belligerence. France was prohibited

[62] USSME, N 1–11, 'Diari storici', b. 1070, 'Comando III CdA al Com. sup. FF.AA. Grecia – UAC, 12 novembre 1942, Relazione sulla situazione politico-amministrativa per il periodo dal 1 al 31 ottobre 1942'.

[63] USSME, M 3, b. 19, 19 February 1943, 'Promemoria del generale Pièche per il duce, notizie dalla Grecia relative al mese di gennaio 1943'.

[64] Rainero, *Mussolini e Pétain*, vol. I, p. 16.

from undertaking any acts of belligerence against the Axis, while Italy was obliged to abstain from exercising only those rights expressly excluded by the armistice convention. This thesis, writes Rainero, was the one officially adopted by the CIAF, although it frequently proved inapplicable 'for reasons of political expediency'.[65]

The Italo-German Wiesbaden agreement (29 June 1940) had a distinctive feature that became a constant of Italo-Franco-German relations until 8 September 1943. The Italians and Germans were unable to produce a joint final document because the power relation between the two allies was so asymmetrical. As Germany saw it, why should Italy have the same weight and influence as the Third Reich in regard to a country that had been defeated by the Wehrmacht alone?

Immediately upon conclusion of the Wiesbaden meeting, it became clear that there was no Axis policy towards Vichy France. The CIAF, given Italy's subordinate role in the alliance, had nothing else to do but administer the Villa Incisa agreement. But Germany, following the meeting between Hitler and Pétain at Montoire (24 October 1940), pursued its own 'French policy': this first attempt at collaboration had no concrete results, but it demonstrated very clearly the divergence between Italian and German policies towards France. There was then, however, an important attempt at collaboration between Italy and Vichy which concerned the episode of Mers el-Kebir (Oran), where, on 3 July 1940, a British naval squadron attacked and sank ships of the French fleet anchored in the harbour. The Vichy government responded by making French military installations in the province of Oran available for use by the Italian air force. It then proposed that the French navy should attack the British fleet deployed off Alexandria and liberate the French forces trapped in the harbour. On that occasion Mussolini opted for intransigence towards defeated France, on the ground that it was the only policy which – in view of Britain's imminent defeat – would secure for Italy the colonial and metropolitan territories that it claimed.

Intransigence towards France continued to characterize Italian policy in the subsequent months of 1940. The directors of the CIAF, General Pietro Pintor and then Camillo Grossi, faithfully executed Mussolini's orders even though they had realized since the summer that Britain would not capitulate. The policy of intransigency was kept in being by the continuing desire of not only Mussolini but the entire Italian ruling class to impose their territorial ambitions. At the end of 1940, as the logical consequence of that

65 Ibid., pp. 79–80.

political strategy, relations between the French delegation in Turin and the CIAF became cold and tense. Each side accused the other of bad faith and of thwarting its plans in any way possible. According to Rainero, Vichy France's non-observance of the spirit of the agreement was a stratagem to gain time, and also to foment retaliation against an Italy deemed to be not a victor but an exploiter of France's military failings.[66] Clashes were frequent during those months, and especially over control of the war industry and regulation of maritime traffic.

The general progress of the war, and the prospect that it would be much more protracted than expected, brought changes to the triangular relationship among Rome, Vichy and Berlin. A phase began of Franco-German dialogue that was matched by fruitless attempts to create the Franco-Italian equivalent. The period between 1941 and the total occupation of French metropolitan territory saw a shift of German policy that entailed great, almost ruinous, sacrifices for Italy. Germany calculated that if France (and for a certain period also Spain) contributed substantially to the defeat of Great Britain, it would inevitably resume its role as a Mediterranean power in the post-war order – with the result, also inevitable, that Italy's *spazio vitale* would shrink in both the southern Mediterranean and the French metropolitan territories under claim by the Fascist regime. The Vichy government decided to collaborate with Germany, while Rome (which for ideological reasons had no intention of renouncing its claims) persisted with its policy of intransigence: a policy that also served to demonstrate to both the French and German governments that Italy was fully able to take its own decisions, and therefore fully able to assert its authority.

The first six months of 1941 saw German attempts at rapprochement with Vichy energetically carried forward by the German ambassador in Paris, Otto Abetz. They also saw the rapid rise of Admiral François Darlan, who was appointed Vichy foreign minister, given the portfolios for the interior and the navy, nominated vice-president and finally designated Pétain's official successor. According to Rainero, 'the factor that sparked a certain German interest in resuming negotiations with Vichy was the outbreak in Iraq of the insurrection led by Rashid Ali al-Ghaliani. This seemingly offered the Axis interesting prospects of advance within the wider context of the anti-British struggle in the Middle East.'[67] The Franco-German negotiations began with a preliminary agreement on the aid to be sent via Syria to the Iraqi insurgents, and on the use of Syrian airports by the German

[66] Ibid., p. 161. [67] Ibid., p. 194.

air force. In exchange, Germany agreed to reduce occupation expenditure and to facilitate transit between the 'free' and occupied zones. Darlan met Hitler at Berchtesgaden on 11 May and their negotiations were concluded in Paris on 28 May 1941. The outcome was the stipulation of three protocols: the first concerning Syria and Iraq; the second the provisioning of German troops in North Africa; and the third western and equatorial Africa. Nevertheless, like the Montoire agreement, the Paris protocols were a failure. The episode confirmed once again to the Italians that the Vichy government considered Berlin its only interlocutor, and that it was intent on freeing itself from the constraints of the armistice with Italy.

On 18 June 1941, Arturo Vacca Maggiolini replaced General Grossi following the latter's sudden death. Vacca Maggiolini's term of office is of particular interest, for, unlike his predecessors, he enjoyed a privileged relationship with Mussolini. During his first interview with the Duce, the newly appointed head of the CIAF stressed the danger to Italy of France's co-operation with Germany. Mussolini replied that Italy's policy towards France must be tough and uncompromising, and that the agreement with Germany on the new world order must be viewed as the division of the world into two spheres of influence, one Italian, the other German.

During the summer of 1941, discussions between the German Armistice Commission with France and the CIAF centred on France's participation in the war effort, and particularly on the use of French bases in Tunisia (topics on the agenda at Merano on 13–15 May and Wiesbaden on 28–29 May). The failure of the Paris protocols – for which the German attack on the Soviet Union seems to have been partly responsible – engendered a further change in the Axis's policy (or, rather, policies) towards France. At the Munich conference (31 July–2 August), in exchange for the Axis's use of the bases in Tunisia, Vichy requested settlement of all territorial, military and political disputes with Italy and Germany. When questioned by the head of the German Armistice Commission Oskar Vogl, Vacca Maggiolini declared that he was opposed to any concession to the French that might be prejudicial to Italian claims.[68] Nevertheless, on 13 August he proposed to the Duce that the armistice regime with France be abolished and replaced with co-operation. He hoped that Germany would make adequate concessions to France (the return of prisoners and renunciation of indemnities and territorial occupation) while Italy would content itself with Nice ('an autonomous county which has personal union with the

[68] ASMAE, GABAP, b. 13, 'CIAF – Sottocommissione AA.GG. al MAE, 10 agosto 1941'.

House of Savoy'), leaving all other matters for negotiation at the end of the war.[69] Mussolini accepted the plan but stipulated that he wanted Nice to be annexed in the same way as Ljubljana.[70]

It would be wrong to conclude that the Duce had developed a new vision of the post-war world order, or that he was ready to relinquish Italy's claims. Rather, his position was an expedient based on conviction that the victory of the Axis would place the defeated country at the mercy of the victor. The Italians discussed the plan until the end of August; they had the temerity to advance requests to the head of the French delegation in Turin without consulting the 'senior partner'. But then the situation on the eastern front prompted Berlin to shelve the question and in September to reverse its position. Hitler 'decided that it [was] not possible to reach agreement with France at the present time'.[71] Rome was forced to adjust to Germany's new policy. Vacca Maggiolini suggested that Italy should adopt a wait-and-see attitude until the war had put France 'at the complete mercy of the Axis powers, which [would see] all their claims satisfied'. Mussolini declared that France would be 'narcotized' and that Italian policy towards France would consist in 'sitting on the fence'.[72]

Resumption of negotiations with Vichy was discussed at the Gardone conference (9–13 September 1941). Nevertheless, Germany did not shift its position except in regard to certain military matters. Although the meeting at Wiesbaden (December 1941), where Italy was a mere supernumerary, achieved no progress, it laid bare the determination of the Italian authorities to assert their prestige. It is in this light one should also construe the meeting between Ciano and Darlan of 10 December.[73] The impasse reached at Wiesbaden briefly resuscitated the Italian plan, and Rome was able to conclude two secret agreements with the French: one on food and clothing transport (Delta transport), the other on lorry transport and fuel delivery to the Libyan front (Gamma transport). The secrecy of the accords was vital if they were to be practicable; but it only lasted for around a month, with the consequence that the Gamma and Delta transport system was scrapped in the following February.

69 ASMAE, GABAP, b. 13, 'CIAF – Sottocommissione AA.GG. al MAE', 13 August 1941; DDI, ser. IX, 1939–43, vol. 7, doc. 476, 'Promemoria di Vacca Maggiolini a Mussolini'.
70 ASMAE, GABAP, b. 13, 'CIAF – Sottocommissione AA.GG. a Pietromarchi', 20 August 1941.
71 ASMAE, GABAP, b. 13, 'CIAF – Sottocommissione AA.GG. al MAE', 27 August 1941.
72 ASMAE, GABAP, b. 13, 'CIAF – Sottocommissione AA.GG. al Ministero degli Esteri', 6 August 1941.
73 ASMAE, GABAP, b. 13, 6 December 1941, 'Appunto di Pietromarchi per l'eccellenza il ministro (visto dal duce)'; ibid., 'CIAF al CS, 25 dicembre 1941, Trattative a tre a Wiesbaden'.

On 25 February, Vacca Maggiolini wrote a long memorandum to Ugo Cavallero explaining that France was in a position of singular difficulty and complexity. The country had suffered a disastrous defeat and was being paralysed by the armistice. The occupation, with the consequent difficulties of doing business, was disrupting the French economy. For twenty months, France had paid between 300 and 400 million francs every day to Germany, and its metropolitan territory was being exploited to the utmost. Moreover, France's uncertain position, in that it had still not suffered all the consequences of defeat, heightened the distress of the population and provoked a constant state of anxiety. 'What policy was expedient for the Axis?', Vacca Maggiolini enquired. If France, albeit with diminished power and prestige, were to have a place in the new world order to come, it was inadvisable to stoke the hatred already simmering between the French and the Axis. If France could be of service to the Axis in military terms, and if the resistance of its African possessions might create complications, then it was better to make concessions. The Axis should therefore adopt the 'collaborative idea', albeit implementing it prudently and gradually. But this, for that matter, the Duce had already decided. Germany, Vacca Maggiolini went on, had no intention of adjusting itself to Italy's policy towards France. Hence, in view of increasingly likely internal complications, it was wise to take appropriate military measures by deploying rapid intervention forces beyond the Alps, in Corsica and in Tunisia.[74]

In April 1942 the return to power of Pierre Laval – branded by the army high commands, the CIAF functionaries and Ciano a 'German stooge' – heightened Italian suspicions that France and Germany had contrived secret agreements.[75] Hitler, Ribbentrop and the chief of General Staff, Wilhelm von Keitel, reassured Mussolini, Ciano and the chief of the SMRE Cavallero as to the 'French question'; nonetheless, the Italians were still deeply suspicious of Berlin's actions and policy. And their doubts increased during the summer when the French, bolstered by their concession to the Germans of the *relève* agreement (see p. 219), issued a unilateral declaration asserting the principle of metropolitan and imperial territorial integrity – and met with no official disclaimer from the Germans. Between 12 and 17 June 1942, the

[74] DDI, ser. IX, 1939–43, vol. 8, doc. 333, 'presidente della CIAF al capo di SMG Cavallero', 25 February 1942.

[75] On 15 April 1942, Ciano wrote in his diary (DDI, ser. IX, 1939–43, vol. 5, doc. 65): 'Laval to take over as head of the French government: this is the result of scheming by the Germans while keeping us in the dark. The German representative in Paris informed our representative only after the event. And yet this is a matter of our direct concern. What promises were made to the French to achieve this outcome? We shall see.'

CIAF and the German Armistice Commission met in Friedrichshafen: but, as at all previous conferences, no joint political strategy was agreed. Even worse, relations between the two commissions deteriorated to the point that the Italian chief delegate sent his German counterpart three notes expressing profound disagreement on French loyalty and stressing the danger of concessions to France, the implicit message being disapproval of the French policy pursued by the German authorities.

During the summer of 1942, Italo-French relations moved rapidly towards open conflict. Talks between Duplat and Vacca Maggiolini (5–11 August 1942) were fruitless, and on 20 August the Vichy government denounced the Menton accords, these being modest documents on Italian military access to the zone occupied by Italy and on travel arrangements for French citizens in the occupied zones. 'The specific phases of this crisis', wrote Rainero, 'are many, and they in fact form part of a two-faced war policy which the French pursue extremely effectively, on the one hand by playing the card of their special "friendship" with the German authorities . . . and on the other by obstructing dialogue with the CIAF authorities while advancing their demand for cancellation of the armistice.'[76] The talks in Venice (22–28 September) only served to confirm once again the impossibility of escaping from the blind alley into which the lack of dialogue between the armistice commissions had led the entire Axis policy on France.

The total occupation of France sharpened conflict between the allies, and it further subordinated Rome to Berlin. The Germans insisted that the French ships captured at Biserta must be allocated for use by German troops, even though they had been assigned to Italy; and they were adamant on command of the troops in Tunisia. The scuttling of the French fleet at Toulon (27 November 1942) caused Italo-French relations to deteriorate even further: 'The scuttling of the French fleet was disastrous for Italian hopes of involving those naval units in the war, or at least, as Vacca Maggiolini had suggested, appropriating them by force.'[77] Italy was assigned seventy-eight French ships, most of them cargo steamers of various tonnages, two British ships and ten Greek ones. As Rainero points out, the consequences of this policy were soon apparent:

> At the general political level, these concrete developments in armistice relations had the disastrous result of convincing the French authorities and public opinion that organized plunder was being disguised as transfer or purchase. And that this was indeed the spirit in which these requisitions, or these 'purchases' and 'confiscations', were being undertaken, at least on the part of the Italians, [was confirmed] during

[76] Rainero, *Mussolini e Pétain*, vol. I, p. 404. [77] Ibid., p. 414.

the Duce's interview with General Vacca Maggiolini on 12 February 1943 . . . The closing sentence of the Duce's long speech put it bluntly: 'So remember my order: get as much as you can and send everything to Italy.' Indeed, since the previous November, this had been the rationale of the armistice policy carried forward by Vacca Maggiolini, and through him by the CIAF. Naturally, this state of affairs, perhaps confusedly perceived by the majority of the population but perceived nonetheless, had concrete repercussions manifest in growing opposition against the policy of collaboration with the Axis, its troops and its agencies – opposition which led to organized resistance, also armed, and thereafter to the guerrilla warfare waged by the Maquis.[78]

Although during the ten months of its occupation of south-eastern France the Fourth Army was not officially subordinate to the German general headquarters, it received tactical orders from Marshal Gerd von Rundstedt, commander-in-chief of the German army in the West (the OKW's authority over the Fourth Army was restricted to the co-ordination of operations). The Germans did not hesitate to enter the Italian zone (at Toulon on 27 November 1942) or to station troops permanently in some areas of the *départements* of Isère and Vaucluse, in Lyons and Marseilles – which were also ideal positions from which to control and monitor the zone occupied by the 'junior partner'.

Pétain managed to ensure that the occupation of the free zone complied with the provisions of the 1907 Hague Convention on wartime occupation. The French state was thus able to conserve its legislative, legal, administrative and economic prerogatives. The Supreme Command explained that this was voluntary self-restraint in the exercise of an occupying power's rights. It would apply to the extent that military interests and exigencies were not compromised (for example, in the event of enemy landings) and if the French executive organs were not obstructionist. The CS endeavoured to safeguard French sovereignty and the prestige of the legal government, refraining from acts of interference; it sought to solve problems through the French authorities, giving them a semblance of independence; it ordered the occupation forces to be immovable on questions of principle but flexible on those of lesser importance, seeking not to wound French sensitivities unless necessary. It ordered the Fourth Army to behave as similarly as possible to the Germans, even though its occupation activities were conducted independently from those of the ally. Italian troops should be correct but detached in their dealings with the French, show restraint towards the Italian colony and above all be irreproachable in their behaviour and discipline. In short, wrote the CS, 'seek as far as possible to guarantee our security and

[78] Ibid., p. 424.

provide for our needs, with the constant, albeit formal consent of the French and in agreement with [Germany]'.[79] The divisional commanders recommended officers and troops not to trust the French authorities, and to have no truck with locals claiming to be native-born Italians or sympathizers.[80]

It is important to stress that, from a military point of view, the annexation of the zones claimed by Italy was entirely feasible. For example, Corsica – with around 300,000 inhabitants – was occupied by more than 85,000 soldiers: four divisions (Friuli, Cremona and two coastal divisions), various units of light infantrymen (*bersaglieri*), grenadiers, alpine troops (*alpini*), CC.RR., sappers and service personnel, as well as the navy, the air force, a German armoured brigade and eight battalions of the MVSN. The decision not to annex was taken for political reasons spelled out by Mussolini, who ordered that the Italian occupation must not take the form of a definitive conquest lest hostility be provoked in the Corsican population.[81] General Giovanni Magli wrote (in 1950) that the task of the occupation force was to defend the island against external attacks. It was to concern itself with internal affairs only in so far as the island's security was affected. Social and economic affairs were to be administered by the civil authorities: that is, the prefect in Ajaccio and the four sub-prefects in Bastia, Corte, Ajaccio and Sartène.[82]

The attitude of the Italian army towards the French authorities differed substantially from that towards those of Greece and Croatia. For example, Admiral Oscar di Giamberardino, chief of the joint delegation for Corsica, decided with the prefect Paul-Louis-Emmanuel Balley that the police force would remain under French control: when a similar request had been made by the Croatian allies, the command of the Second Army had rejected the idea out of hand. The Greek gendarmerie were assigned only very minor tasks and had no freedom of movement – likewise the Slovene gendarmes and the few native-born gendarmes in Dalmatia. In Corsica, by contrast, 208 national police officials and 762 gendarmes serving with the autonomous Corsican company organized the enforced residence of foreign crime suspects and of *personae non gratae* to the Italian authorities; it monitored the movement of travellers and checked hotels and guest houses; it isolated suspected spies and disarmed the population.

[79] ASMAE, AA.PP. – Francia, b. 69, 'CIAF – Sottocommissione AA.GG.', 16 March 1943.

[80] USSME, N 1–11, 'Diari storici', b. 1097, 'Comando XV CdA, 13 novembre 1942, Contegno dei comandi delle truppe e cautele nel territorio occupato'.

[81] USSME, N 1–11, 'Diari storici', b. 991, 'Comando Divisione Friuli', 19 November 1942.

[82] Magli, *Le truppe italiane in Corsica*, 1950, p. 36; USSME, N 1–11, 'Diari storici', b. 1272, VII CdA, doc. 255, allegato 6.

Despite the permissive conduct of the occupiers, however, the French authorities did not co-operate; indeed, they were openly hostile. Liaison with the prefectures and sub-prefectures was of little use in ensuring 'with due tact that promises of collaboration [were] fulfilled efficiently and promptly'.[83] According to a CIAF report, the police commissioners, the prefect's private secretaries, the sub-prefects and the municipal administrations acted – often in concert – against the orders of the occupying authorities. One of the very few pro-Italian public officials cited in reports by the CIAF and the military authorities was Prefect Balley, 'who issued to the civil servants of the *département* of Corsica instructions of sincere collaboration'. However, these instructions were ineffectual because almost all the sub-prefects refused to implement them.

Between 12 November 1942 and 25 July 1943, the occupiers were unable to establish a *modus vivendi* with the French authorities. The Italians were crushed beneath the weight of the Germans, the military crisis of the Axis and the magnitude of territorial claims which precluded any dialogue with Vichy. The French civil authorities took every opportunity to hinder the operations of occupation forces by which they had not been defeated. The Italian reaction to German interference and French obstructionism is exemplified by two episodes in particular: Jewish internment (which is examined in chapter 11), and the *relève*, the agreement under which, in March 1943, the Reich sent around 650,000 French workers to Germany. The Italians regarded the *relève* arrangement as greatly damaging to their interests in the Italian occupation zones. For this reason, they deliberately omitted on several occasions to communicate information in their possession to the Germans, despite their knowledge of the devices used by the French authorities to avoid sending the workers conscripted.[84]

At Klassheim, on 29 April 1943, Ribbentrop advised Bastianini to accept the French request for the Italo-German demarcation line on the Rhône

[83] USSME, N 1–11, 'Diari storici', b. 1272, 'capo Ufficio politico Mazzarelli al Comando del VII CdA', 26 November 1942. Besides an intelligence office and counter-espionage unit, the Command of the 7th CdA had a political-military office headed by a general of the Carabinieri (Mazzarelli, later replaced by Colonel Quercia).

[84] USSME, N 1–11, 'Diari storici', b. 1201, 16 April 1943, 'Relazione sulla situazione politica del VII CdA relativa al periodo 5–15 aprile 1943': 'A large number of young men conscripted to work in Germany have been inducted into the police force, for which they serve in plain clothes. The purpose of this measure by the French is evidently to shelter as many young men as possible against conscription . . . The municipal authorities have issued certificates stating that men are farm labourers when they have never worked in agriculture. In some municipalities, substantial numbers have left for parts unknown: indeed, it is reported that they have joined the Maquis, helped by Gaullist elements who provide them with food.'

to be removed. But Mussolini rejected the advice, suspecting a Franco-German manoeuvre with a view to the future territorial arrangement of France. At the Munich conference of 8 May 1943, the Italian authorities reiterated that the demarcation line between the German troops and the Fourth Army did not alter the situation created by the armistice and had only tactical value. The Rhône demarcation line continued to separate the Italian and German zones. Consequently, any issue concerning the armistice that pertained partly or wholly to the territory under Italian control could not be settled by the Germans without Italy's prior agreement.

Distrust was even greater on the German side. Berlin took care not to inform Rome that Laval was willing to negotiate (with German permission) on Tunisia and to meet Mussolini personally to explore the possibility of normalizing Italo-French relations. Hence, even if Rome had relinquished its claims to the French territories, Berlin would still have impeded an agreement for fear that it might lead to a separate peace with the Italians.[85] Until 8 September 1943, Italy continued to be subservient to Germany in its relations with the French government, and it continued to be the victim of its own actions – still blinded by the now anachronistic ideology of the *spazio vitale* that prevented it from shifting to a realistic policy.

To be emphasized is that Mussolini and the Italian political and military leaders did not resign themselves to the role of bit players on the European stage. In all the conquered territories they co-ordinated occupation policies intended to affirm Fascist authority and prestige. In some cases – Greece and France, for example – they sought to pursue a policy which posited Fascist Italy as an autonomous pole in the Axis, the hope being to regain the ground lost because of the defeats of 1940 and German intervention in the conquest of the Balkans.

I stressed in chapter 4 the understandings reached among the authorities on the spot. One of the most quixotic aspects of Italy's occupation policy was its attempt to penetrate the occupied territories culturally. This was an area of especial importance to the Fascist regime, and the Italian authorities worked together to counter 'unjustified intrusion by the ally' – although they did so with derisory resources compared with those available to the Germans. In the Fascist view, the widespread knowledge of Italian was a key factor in creating a collective Fascist mind-set, especially so in the Balkans, whose inhabitants had an astonishing ability to

[85] Borgogni, *Italia e Francia durante la crisi militare dell'Asse*, pp. 253–4.

learn foreign languages. The work of schools and cultural organizations to promote Italian was therefore of decisive importance, given that the troops would be withdrawn when victory had been achieved: it was indispensable that they should leave behind schools, radio stations, bookshops, libraries – in short 'the authorized expressions of our very being . . . Fascist culture'.[86]

The military authorities worked closely with the PNF on development of the Fascist cultural project in all the occupied territories. In eastern Crete, for example, the military authorities, assisted by the Dante Alighieri committee of Rhodes, made the teaching of Italian compulsory. They organized courses for adults and lessons at the schools in the island's largest towns, and they awarded prizes of money and books. They had schoolchildren sing the *Inno dei Popoli Mediterranei* which the poet Elefteriou Alexiou composed on the tune of the Greek national anthem to extol 'the Mussolinian concept of the unity of the Mediterranean peoples'.[87]

But the measures taken by Rome were almost ridiculous compared to the German efforts. So ubiquitous was the Germans' penetration of Greece that, for example, when they turned their attention to archaeology, they first contacted the university in Athens, then held lectures at the school of archaeology and then reopened the excavations at Olympia.[88] The Italian authorities broadcast programmes and news bulletins in Italian and Greek, but their efforts were overwhelmed by those of the Germans. Telefunken took over Cable & Wireless and engineered an exclusive agreement on radio broadcasting with the Greek government. It ceded its rights (although it remained the majority shareholder) to the Greek company AERE and began broadcasting as early as October 1941.[89] In July 1942, the Germans granted the Italians an equal share in the broadcasting network.[90] But in July 1943, after six months of transmissions, the Italian broadcasting commission closed down for lack of funds. Besides 'culture by radio', the Germans organized exhibitions by visiting artists from Germany and also commissioned performances by Greek artistes (among them the subsequently acclaimed Maria Callas). A few days before the fall of the regime, the Italian broadcasting commission asked for its

86 Scodro, 'La propaganda nei paesi occupati', 1942, p. 168. On propaganda, see Mignemi, *L'Italia s'è desta*, Arnold, *The Illusion of Victory*.
87 USSME, N 1–11, 'Diari storici', b. 801, September 1942.
88 USSME, L 15, b. 11, 'Com. sup. FF.AA. Grecia – Ufficio Informazioni, Stralcio di relazione di nostro ufficiale'.
89 Etmektsoglou-Koehn, '*Axis Exploitation of Wartime Greece*', p. 323.
90 ASMAE, GABAP, b. 21, 'sottofasc. Le radiodiffusioni italiane in Grecia, MINCULPOP al GABAP, 1 dicembre 1942'.

funding to be raised to the German level, claiming that broadcasting cutbacks would leave even more space for the Germans. But such was the failure of Radio Atene that the authorities deemed it best to close the station down permanently.[91]

The Italians attempted cultural penetration in Croatia as well, in this case mainly through the Italian Institutes of Culture, which organized cycles of lectures, theatre and opera performances, and cultivated relations with local cultural élites (in March 1943, Giuseppe Ungaretti gave a lecture at the University of Zagreb on 'Leopardi, the Founder of Modern Lyrical Poetry'). There were institutes in Sarajevo, Banja Luka, Mostar and Dubrovnik (in which city an Italian lower-secondary school was opened), and also in Athens and Salonika, Patras, Volos and Trikala. Rome sent magazines and newspapers to cafés and restaurants (*Tempo* was published in Greek and Croat versions) and children's comics (for instance, *Za Vas Djeco* and *Giornalino per la gioventù*, which were distributed in Dalmatia and Croatia), books (*Cosa deve l'Italia a Mussolini* by Mario Missiroli and *Mussolini* by Giorgio Pini, translated into Croat), pamphlets, religious pictures and bilingual prayers, and films (newsreels were dubbed into Croat).[92] As in Greece, the Italian authorities also intervened in national legislation by having the teaching of Italian made compulsory.[93]

Even in France, although the occupation came about in highly particular circumstances, the Italians set out to promote the diffusion of Fascist culture. The Istituto di Studi Liguri of Bordighera launched a 'programme of cultural action for the Nizzardo and on the historical, archaeological and artistic heritage of the western Ligurian region'. The intention was to extend the programme to cover all the areas of Provence occupied by

[91] ASMAE, GABAP, b. 21, 'MINCULPOP – Ispettorato per la radiodiffusione e la televisione al Ministero degli Esteri, 28 gennaio 1943'.

[92] In Montenegro, a press service prepared releases to be sent to the Stefani agency for publication in the Italian press. It also supervised the Radio Cettigne broadcasting station and published the bilingual weekly *La voce del Montenegro* (with a print run of 7,000 copies sold in the main towns at less than cost price). Publication was permitted, under the supervision of the press service, of the historical journal *Sapissi* (published in Cetinje) and two Montenegrin periodicals: *Zeta* (published in Podgorica by the Montenegrin Nationalist Party) and *Il libero pensiero* (published in Nikšić).

[93] USSME, N I–II, 'Diari storici', b. 1317, 'Comando Divisione di fanteria Isonzo, Relazione quindicinale del 19 marzo 1942'. The ASMAE archive, Archivio Scuole, 1936–43, b. 181, 'legazione di Zagabria al MAE – SIE, 4 novembre 1941', shows that Croatian schoolchildren preferred to study German. Paolo Alberto Rossi, consul in Sarajevo, took measures to increase the teaching staff at the Istituto di Cultura Italiana and the Doposcuola (which had only one teacher) and promoted Italian 'cultural penetration' of the Muslim press in Bosnia-Herzegovina.

Italian troops after November 1942.[94] Interestingly, despite the desire to annex the Nizzardo rapidly, in the period 1940–3 the Italian authorities did not permit the Gruppi di Azione Nizzarda (GAN) to unhinge the already difficult relations between Rome and Vichy. The 'discretion' of the Italian authorities was probably due to the fact that relationships with the French government were handled by the CIAF, which preferred the more discreet action of the Bordighera Istituto to the aggressiveness of the GAN. Indeed, in January 1941 it ordered the arrest of two members of the latter organization. The consul in Nice, Quinto Mazzolini, even expressly prohibited Italians resident in the Nizzardo from joining irredentist movements (see chapter 9). This policy was at odds with the strategies of other organs of the Fascist regime, especially MINCULPOP, the ministry which supported the magazine *Il Nizzardo* and the actions of General Ezio Garibaldi. But it enjoyed the crucial backing of Mussolini, who endorsed the decision by the CIAF because he was convinced that, sooner or later, France would pay for its defeat.

The Bordighera Istituto di Studi Liguri was used as the model for the creation of an Istituto Nazionale di Studi Corsi (National Institute of Corsican Studies), directed by Gioacchino Volpe, who fostered initiatives such as the Comitato di Assistenza e Promozione di Studi sulla Corsica, whose president was Petru Giovacchini. The Istituto had branches in all the Italian large cities and its activities covered the entire country. It organized lectures on Corsica in the universities and held an exhibition on the *Italianità della Corsica* in Venice (sponsored by the MAE). Radio broadcasts in Corsican were increased, although, after the arrival in the island of the various CIAF delegations in July 1940, the pressing of claims for its annexation took entirely second place among the commission's activities. Throughout the period 1940–3 there was an evident discrepancy between actions in favour of annexation organized in Italy and the discretion of the CIAF authorities in both Turin and Corsica. On the one hand, more copies of the magazine *L'idea corsa* were printed in Rome; on the other, radio broadcasts in Corsican dialect were halted on orders by the CIAF, which maintained that the Corsican population was utterly opposed to annexation of the island.[95] After the occupation, the Duce approved the creation of an 'A' Centre under his direct supervision. This would flank the propaganda for the troops produced by the PNF with action 'able to attract the attention

[94] ACS, PCM, 1940–3, 1.1.13.7047.

[95] ASMAE, AA.PP. – Francia, b. 65, 'capo della delegazione mista per la Corsica, ammiraglio Giamberardino, alla presidenza della CIAF e per conoscenza al GABAP', 12 May 1942.

and sympathy of the island's population'. In February 1942, the Centro di Coordinamento e di Assistenza per la Corsica was instituted.[96]

Relations between the occupied countries and Italy were characterized by the intrusive presence of the Germans. In the case of Croatia, the Germans effectively controlled and ran the country, impeding any form of intervention in its affairs by Italy. The relationship with Zagreb was heavily compromised by the Dalmatian question and by an occupation policy which, in an attempt to undermine the German position, annulled Croatian sovereignty. The administration of civil powers had no effect on German hegemony in Croatia. Instead, it had the opposite effect of pushing the country definitively into the German orbit.

The situation in Greece was equally difficult, for Rome was conditioned by the presence of the Germans and unable to conduct an independent occupation policy of its own. As we shall see in the next chapter, Greece was economically plundered by the Nazis. All that was left for the Italians was defence and the maintenance of public order. Rome's reaction, favoured by the belated development of the Resistance, consisted in the *de facto* administration of the Greek provinces in collaboration with the local authorities. Events in the country give us a measure of the gap between the accomplishments of the occupation policy and the Fascist regime's ambitions for imperial dominion. In France, the relationship with the Vichy government was closely conditioned by Italy's territorial claims, which the French found unacceptable. Berlin granted no leeway to its junior partner. While in Athens the Nazis 'associated' Rome in the management of power, it did not do so at all in France.

Everywhere, the efforts of the Italian authorities came to naught. The intention to react was not enough to counterbalance German hegemony. In general, Italian occupation policy towards the governments of the occupied countries oscillated almost schizophrenically between the pleas of an impotent guardian and the intransigence of an occupier unable to impose its will and frustrated by contingent circumstances. It was Fascist ideology that impeded not only Mussolini but also his lieutenants in the occupied territories from constructing a collaboration policy that demonstrated concretely the difference between the Italians and the Germans. It was again

96 ACS, PCM, 1940–3, 3.2.6.1372 and 21790, 30 July 1943, 'Istituzioni culturali riguardanti la Corsica alle dipendenze della PCM'; USSME, D 7, b. 24, 'relazione quindicinale alla CIAF, 15–30 ottobre 1942, cap. 3, Corsica'; b. 25, 'relazioni quindicinali alla CIAF, 1–15 aprile 1943'. The programme provided assistance in various areas: food (shipments of flour), health, religion (agreements with the military ordinariate on the dispatch of priests), pamphlets and religious materials written in local languages, press and propaganda, illustrated magazines, and radio broadcasts.

Fascist ideology that obliged Rome to march at the side of the Reich 'until the bitter end', to occupy vast territories when the men, means and resources could have been put to much better use in defending the peninsula. And it was again because of Fascist ideology that the Italians perpetrated cruel oppression and attempted, in vain, to plunder the occupied territories in emulation of the Nazis.

CHAPTER 7

Economic valorization and the exploitation of the occupied territories

The chapter examines a particular aspect of occupation policies in the countries considered previously: economic exploitation. It shows the discrepancy between the regime's ambitions and its concrete accomplishments, and the role therein of Germany. After examining the obstacles to economic exploitation in each occupied country, the chapter analyses the costs of occupation, cornering of resources by the Germans, and the Italians' attempts at industrial, commercial and financial penetration. It discusses in particular the regime's long-term economic plans, of which, however, almost nothing could be accomplished owing to the circumstances of the war and interference by the Germans. They were plans entirely divorced from reality, which took victory for granted and were predicated on a post-war regime in which the influence of the Western powers would disappear and Germany would respect Rome's exclusive sphere of influence and withdraw into its economic space – pure Utopia, therefore.

LONG-TERM PLANS: 'VALORIZATION' OF THE IMPERIAL COMMUNITY

In 1940 and 1941, Fascist propaganda appropriated arguments from economic articles and monographs to propound the 'liberation' of the Mediterranean countries enslaved by the 'plutocratic powers'.[1] But Fascism's true intention was not to liberate those countries but to supplant the Western powers and Germany. Given Italy's extremely limited financial and industrial resources, the economic literature glossed over how such 'liberation' was to be achieved in practice. 'Liberation' was a euphemism for military conquest, since only thus could the Germans be supplanted and

[1] Anon., 'La produzione agricola e mineraria jugoslava', 1940; Cosentino, 'Il sudest europeo e l'Italia', 1942; Giordano, 'La nuova organizzazione dell'economia europea', 1940; Giordano, 'Il commercio estero della Jugoslavia e della Grecia', 1940; Maineri, 'I paesi mediterranei e la nuova Europa nel dopoguerra', 1940; Pracchi, 'L'Italia nell'economia degli stati balcanici', 1940.

weak Italian imperialism achieve economic penetration of the countries of south-eastern Europe and the Mediterranean (see appendix, tables 38–40).

But the senior partner in the Axis had an economy that was sufficiently strong to withstand any encroachment. And before the war it had already penetrated the Balkan markets without the use of force. Germany found it relatively easy to promote the principle of complementarity between its economy and those of the Balkan countries (industry, technology and capital in exchange for agricultural produce and raw materials).

The notion of economic complementarity between Italy and the countries of south-eastern Europe was not endorsed by all Fascist economists. There were those who argued that the country was not yet entirely industrialized. And then, some of them pointed out, the regime had long proclaimed the primacy of agriculture (see e.g. the journal *Autarchia*). Only after 1940–2 did Italian economists subscribe to the notion of complementarity and advocate the exchange of capital and technology for raw materials on the German pattern (which again highlights how closely Fascism had depended intellectually on Nazism since the end of the 1930s).

Because Italian politicians and the regime's propaganda machine were obliged to conceal that their real intention was conquest, and because they had to demonstrate how Fascist imperialism differed from capitalist imperialism, they insisted on the idea of 'valorization' (*valorizzazione*), by which was meant an 'economic mission' to civilize the economies of the countries that would eventually belong to the Fascist imperial community. The term had already been used for some time in the literature on colonial economics, with its doctrine that Fascism's mission in the colonies was to achieve the following five goals:

(1) colonization;
(2) autarky, which would guarantee food self-sufficiency and secure the military production indispensable for the armed forces *in loco*, so that the empire would not have to depend on supplies from Italy;
(3) the development of mining, agriculture, cattle-husbandry and the promotion of complementarity between the local economies and the metropolitan economy;
(4) improvement in the national trade balance and increased exports to foreign markets;
(5) enhanced output by production systems, with a consequent increase in local purchasing power which would be entirely to the advantage of the exporting metropolitan area.[2]

[2] Massi, *La valorizzazione economica dell'impero*, 1938; Taralletto, 'L'espansione coloniale nel nuovo ordine europeo', 1941.

With the exception of the first objective, the notion of valorization was extended to all the European territories of the imperial community, of which Albania was the epitome extolled by the Fascist literature.[3] The regime propagandized the following valorization measures: a fixed exchange rate between the Albanian franc and the Italian lira (1 Albanian franc for 6.25 lire), the creation of a 'lira-standard' with the opening of an Italian currency reserve at the National Bank of Albania, the lifting of restrictions on Albanian exports to Italy, and absolute freedom of export from Italy. An economic customs convention was signed (20 April 1939), which harmonized customs regulations and tariffs between the two countries; on the basis of this convention, Italy extended its commercial agreements with third countries, while Albania cancelled its own. Responsibility for the policing of frontiers was assumed by Rome, and customs revenues accrued to Italy, which then returned a proportion of them to Albania.

More than 'valorizing' the Albanian economy, however, Fascist economic policy proved to be good business for Italian exporters, who took advantage of the new customs regime to purchase Albanian products at below-market prices.[4] It was also of benefit to a number of Italian banks: for instance the Banco di Napoli, which took over the Albanian Banca Agricola, and thus monopolized agricultural credit and banking services to Italian soldiers and civilians in Albania; or the Banca Nazionale del Lavoro (BNL), which extended credit in the agricultural, hotel, industrial and commercial sectors and co-financed public works projects. The public funds allocated to Albania went mainly to Italian firms (800 million lire for roadworks, divided into eight accounting periods from 1939–40 onwards, and 1,200 million lire for land clearance and the upgrading of 1,167 kilometres of roads and railways and the construction of 290 kilometres of new roads). But was the purpose of these investments to 'valorize' Albania, as the propaganda claimed?

Certainly not. They served the same purpose as the investments made by the imperialist powers. Italian industrial initiatives were piecemeal, not part of an overall programme, and the state neither guided nor organized the private initiative envisaged by Fascist doctrine (see chapter 2). Italian economic penetration of the Albanian protectorate catered as far as possible to Italian industry's needs by exploiting already-existing potential, especially

[3] Pistolese, 'La valorizzazione industriale della nuova Albania', 1940; Giordano, 'Gli sviluppi economici nell'Europa sudorientale', 1941.

[4] Roselli, *Italia e Albania*, p. 12.

in minerals and raw materials processing.[5] Subsequently, after Italy's entry into the war, manufacturing and construction sites were closed (except for activities directly connected with the war effort).

The events of the spring of 1941 opened up unexpected opportunities in Mediterranean Europe for Italian commercial, industrial and financial enterprises. A series of studies identified the resources, products and industries of interest to the Italians.[6] Initially, scholars and ministerial experts hoped that Italy would export to the conquered territories the means and expertise for land reclamation, minerals extraction and the construction of roads, railways and harbours. Supplanting the 'plutocratic powers' would increase exports by the engineering industry (farm machinery, components for electricity-generating stations, machines for the building industry and road construction, shipyard equipment, pumps for ships, accessories for steam generators).

Croatia was important to Italy because of its timber reserves, cattle herds and rich deposits of carbon, lignite, iron, copper, chrome, manganese, pyrites, antimony and mercury.[7] Serbia, 'reduced to its effective proportions', came within Italy's sphere of interest because of its mineral wealth, especially the Bor copper deposits. Bulgaria, a 'country to be incorporated into the Mediterranean *spazio vitale*' once it had acquired its 'rightful' outlet on the Aegean, would become a trading partner of major importance given its rapeseed and soya production, wine production and the chrome deposits of Uskub.[8] Hungary was of interest for its river harbours, tourism, large-scale production of agricultural machinery, electrical goods, pharmaceuticals and timber (especially abundant in the Transylvanian regions) – and also because it could import skilled Italian labour to construct roads, railways, bridges and tunnels.[9] Greece – 'destined always to record a

[5] Ibid., p. 212: there were oil wells at Devoli and Patos. In 1936 Italy imported 237,000 42-gallon barrels, 1,497,000 in 1940, 1,334,000 in 1941, 1,601,000 in 1942, 1,100,000 in 1943. The Azienda Carboni Italiani had been operating the Priske mine (with a daily output of circa 50 tonnes) since 1939. SAMIA (Società Anonima Mineraria Italo-Albanese) mined copper in Delvenit and Bulshiza, and AMMI (Azienda Minerali Metallici Italiani) mined chrome.

[6] Giordano, 'L'Italia e la nuova economia balcanica', 1941; ASMAE, GABAP, b. 29, 'Relazione di un viaggio in Croazia avente per scopo lo studio delle condizioni economiche del nuovo Regno'; ibid., 'Notiziario di carattere economico della II Armata al GABAP – Ufficio Croazia', 24 November 1941.

[7] Gulinelli, 'La Croazia', 1941; Tocilj, 'L'agricoltura del libero stato di Croazia', 1941; Mori, *La Dalmazia*, 1942, chap. 5 ('La struttura economica', pp. 73–109).

[8] Giordano, 'L'economia bulgara', 1941; 'La Bulgaria nel nuovo assetto europeo', 1941 (article unsigned but presumably by the same author); I. Vlahov, *Geografia economica delle terre bulgare recentemente liberate* (which discusses southern Dobrogea, the Aegean regions, Macedonia and the annexed Serbian zones).

[9] De Cesare, 'Il riordinamento economico danubio–balcanico', 1941.

negative foreign trade balance' – had substantial mineral resources, but it had not developed a significant steel industry: the country's revenues derived mainly from cattle-husbandry and agriculture (olive oil, wine, tobacco).[10] In an article entitled 'L'inquadramento dell'economia ellenica nelle attività europee', Giordano suggested the *valorizzazione* of agricultural, natural and industrial resources to give self-sufficiency to the Greek economy, and subsequently enable the export and sale of Greek products via the ports of Bari, Venice, Trieste and Fiume.[11] By collaborating with Italy, Greece would obtain all the machinery, apparatus and aircraft that it needed to improve its production plants and develop public infrastructure.

Under the economic plan, orders would be allotted as follows: the Breda company would be commissioned to construct harbour installations, Cantieri Navali Italiani to build warships, Industria Triestina to supply electrical cranes for the port of Piraeus, and FIAT to furnish motor vehicles. Once British influence had been eliminated, Italian capital would expand in the banking sector (prior to 1941 Italian banking had been represented in Greece mainly by the Banca Commerciale Italiana e Greca, COMIT Hellas) and in the insurance sector. This, it was claimed, would enable Greece to achieve 'an affluence hitherto unknown'.[12] According to an official at the Italian Foreign Ministry in France, although Italy did not possess the immense capital of the Germans, there was no reason why it should not be involved in 'practical affairs' – and in view of the resumption of business after the war, those affairs were tourism, the hotel industry and agriculture. The expected changes concerning metropolitan France were to be consolidated by the ownership of capital goods, wherever they were situated. That would enable Italian capital, enterprise and labour to operate profitably in the future.[13]

In actual fact, the Fascist regime had no specific plans for economic penetration: consider the mines of Bor, which were exploited by the Germans although they were claimed by the Italians. Thus, although the Italians complained about German invasiveness, they had no alternative plan to put in place. Frequently, therefore, German activity did not encroach on the Italian sphere of influence because this did not exist or had been artificially

[10] Gulinelli, 'Il conflitto italo-ellenico', 1941.

[11] Giordano, 'L'inquadramento dell'economia ellenica nelle attività europee', 1941; Giordano, 'La valorizzazione della navigazione fluviale in Ungheria e Slovacchia', 1941; Pala, 'I porti dell'Adriatico orientale', 1941; Milone, 'La funzione mediterranea dell'Italia', 1941.

[12] Giordano, 'L'inquadramento dell'economia ellenica nelle attività europee', 1941; Franciosa, 'Aspetti geopolitici ed economici della Grecia', 1941.

[13] ASMAE, GABAP, b. 4, 'Girolamo De Bosdari al MINCULPOP, telespresso 8/04287', 7 September 1941.

inflated by the Fascist regime and its propaganda. The Nazis, by contrast, had the means with which to systematically plunder the resources of the occupied Balkan territories and to exploit natural resources and entire industrial sectors. The Italians – one reads in a memorandum circulated by the German Foreign Ministry – were forced to acknowledge that the victory in the Balkans has been achieved with German blood and should therefore be to the economic advantage of the Reich.[14]

SHORT-TERM EXPLOITATION OF THE OCCUPIED TERRITORIES

Before I broach the main topic of this chapter, a number of specifications are necessary. No quantitative information is available on commandeering and looting by the Regio Esercito in the occupied territories. It is likely, at least initially, that the phenomena were limited, for the Germans left little for the junior partner to plunder. There are large gaps in the documentation on the confiscations that followed round-up operations against partisans. We know that the Italian army requisitioned goods (especially foodstuffs) in quantities in excess of those to which an occupying power was entitled under international law. In a region of widespread poverty like Haute-Savoie, during the period November–December 1942 alone, the Italian troops obliged the prefectures to hand over ten tonnes of potatoes – in addition to which were the non-quantifiable amounts of food purloined from warehouses by Italian soldiers. Christian Villermet also reports the large-scale expropriation of firewood, coal, hay and straw, and animals – especially mules (the requisitioning of which caused significant damage to agriculture).[15]

Secondly, it should not be forgotten that Italy's economic exploitation of the occupied territories also failed for reasons not directly connected with German interference: most notably partisan insurgency (sabotage and the severing of communications), which hampered Axis operations and on certain occasions thwarted them entirely. Delays and inefficiency were also caused by poor co-ordination and conflicts of competence among the civil and military Italian authorities, shortages of fuel and vehicles, and the backwardness and continuing deterioration of roads and railways (except in certain French *départements*). It took an average of thirty-eight hours to travel from Salonika to Athens (circa 500 kilometres). Moreover, delays or the non-delivery of commodities pushed up prices and paralysed certain

[14] Etmektsoglou-Koehn, 'Axis Exploitation of Wartime Greece', p. 25.
[15] Villermet, *A noi Savoia*, pp. 93–110.

production processes, with the added problem of the cost of the soldiers and equipment required to protect convoys.

A further factor responsible for Italy's failure to exploit the occupied territories was a shortage of labour. It is difficult to estimate the percentage of the active population that stopped working because of imprisonment, internment, illness, death, participation in resistance movements, resettlement, exile or deportation (voluntary or otherwise) to the Reich or forced labour for the civil or military authorities, or who lost their jobs because of the economic collapse. There are no statistics on the percentage of the civilian population employed on an unpaid basis by the Regio Esercito (internees, for example), but it is certain that the Italian army recruited local manpower – work squads – to build fortifications and defensive installations.[16]

Even a cursory reading of the CdA monthly economic-political reports suffices to understand the reasons for Italy's failure to exploit the occupied territories. By way of example, the Peloponnese, 'a solid though not flourishing region', with a traditional agriculture-driven economy and an industrial system based on small family-run businesses and some medium-sized firms (producing olive oil, soap, lignite, tobacco, raisins, knitwear, pasta and ice) was in a state of economic collapse by the end of 1941. In the summer of 1942, all reports sent to the regional army command by the 6 CdA began with expressions such as 'situation critical', 'situation serious', 'paralysis of the sector'.[17] All that survived was the domestic market for agricultural produce, although this was almost entirely bartered on the black market.[18] A report of October 1941 predicted that, if local industry could not be guaranteed raw materials and fuels, all production would cease. Similar reports were filed from other Greek provinces, Albania, Croatia and the annexed territories.

A final consideration concerns the term 'occupation expenditure', which denotes the sum of money paid by the defeated country for the maintenance of the occupying troops and the construction of defensive installations. Complete figures are not available for Italy, but one may presume that the monthly costs of occupation considerably exceeded the sums levied from the occupied countries. The investments made in men, equipment structures,

[16] USSME, N 1–11, 'Diari storici', b. 566, 'Comando XXVI CdA al Com. sup. FF.AA. Grecia', 7 February 1942; b. 1272, Comando VII CdA, 9 December 1942, 'Acquisto legname e impiego di mano d'opera civile in Corsica'.

[17] USSME, L 15, b. 23.

[18] USSME, N 1–11, 'Diari storici', b. 1193, 'II Battaglione CC.RR. Genova al Comando dell'VIII CdA', 29 September 1942.

the state and semi-public bodies involved, and the special funds set aside for the conquered territories were not covered by the monthly payments received from the occupied governments – not even if requisitions and seizures are factored into the calculation. The occupations were a burden on the Italian state, while occupation expenses crushed and paralysed the economies of the occupied countries.

The governments of the occupied countries reacted by issuing paper money: this, however, provoked rampant inflation and had highly damaging repercussions for the occupiers themselves, because the misery, hunger and desperation of the civilian population made the maintenance of law and order infinitely more difficult (and costly).

GREECE

In May 1941, the Germany army in Greece introduced the *Reichskreditkassenscheine* (RKKS), a currency which the troops could use to purchase goods of every kind. Like the other countries occupied by the Nazis, Greece was forced to recognize the RKKS currency as legal tender, and the Greek central bank was obliged to exchange overvalued RKKS for drachmas.[19] The Italians emulated the Germans by introducing vouchers issued by the Cassa Mediterranea di Credito. In July, the RKKS circulating in Greece were equivalent to 105 million Reichsmarks (RM) and the Cassa vouchers to around 80 million RM. Despite price capping and punitive measures against speculation, inflation was fuelled even further, firstly because troops spent lavishly and considered Greek currency to be of negligible value, and secondly because of a shortage of small denomination banknotes (large numbers of 500-RKKS notes were printed).[20]

The Axis powers forced the Greek government to redeem occupation expenses in drachmas (see appendix, tables 41 and 42). In August the total monthly amount to be repaid was fixed at 1.5 billion drachmas, more than 700 million of which were charged for the quartering of troops. In September, the amount was raised to 4.2 billion drachmas. The occupying powers then decided to withdraw the occupation currencies: the vouchers issued by the Cassa Mediterranea disappeared rapidly, while around 35 million

[19] Etmektsoglou-Koehn, 'Axis Exploitation of Wartime Greece', pp. 325–31.

[20] USSME, L 15, b. 27, 'Comando Divisione Cuneo, sezione "I"', 10 June 1941; N 1–11, 'Diari storici', b. 859, 'Comando Divisione Julia, 25 maggio 1941, Calmiere'; L 15, b. 23, 'Comando XI Armata – UAC', 20 June 1941, circular issued by General Geloso ordering solders not to purchase foodstuffs locally except for fruit and vegetables. On the withdrawal of the Cassa Mediterranea vouchers, see ASMAE, 'AA.CC. – Grecia, 1941, pos. 28/1-30'.

RM in RKKS were still circulating in February 1942. Between August and December, the Greeks paid fully 25 billion drachmas to the occupiers, and for the year 1941–2 the costs of the occupation totalled more than 113 per cent of annual national product (in other countries occupied by Germany, they were as follows: 69 per cent in Norway, 24 per cent in Belgium and 18 per cent in the Netherlands).[21] The Greek finance minister, Sotirios Gotzamanis, struggled in vain to have the Germans understand that such an enormous sum would rapidly bankrupt the country.

In January 1942, given the catastrophic state of the Greek economy, the Italians suggested to the German minister Karl Clodius (deputy head of the Reich's Department of Economic Affairs) that Greece's occupation expenses should be reduced to 1.5 billion drachmas a month, divided equally between the two armies. The Italian proposal – made for political rather than humanitarian reasons – was prompted by the fact that Greece's resources were entirely in the grasp of the Germans, and Rome hoped that offering relief to the Athens government would improve Italo-Greek relations. However, the German military authorities in Greece rejected the proposal out of hand.[22] Their rejection, the plenipotentiary Pellegrino Ghigi explained to Ciano, definitively compromised Italy's campaign for economic penetration, because Greece's food supplies and finances were by now in catastrophic disarray, and 'a revision of the terms of payment of occupation expenses' was of vital importance. Carlo Geloso proposed that the Greek government's expenses be debited in the form of 'credits, coemptions and direct concessions', thus insulating the drachma against excessive pressure.[23] The question was once again discussed with the Germans. The Axis powers now set the payment at 1.5 billion drachmas per month and agreed that expenses in excess of 750 million could be reimbursed by the Bank of Greece at zero interest. Between March and June 1942, the German navy demanded credit for 26 billion drachmas, while in Athens prices had risen in May 1942 by a staggering 13,000 per cent since April 1941.[24] The Italian government now put forward a new plan to reduce the costs of

[21] ASMAE, GABAP, b. 21, 21 September 1941, 'Appunto per Pietromarchi sulla capacità di pagamento della Grecia, firmato dal capo ufficio Affari finanziari Bertone'.

[22] ASMAE, AA.CC. – Grecia, 1941–2, pos. 3/1-4/1-5, 'Rapporto della commissione degli esperti italiani per l'esame delle questioni finanziarie in Grecia, riunitasi sotto la presidenza di Volpi il 17 e 19 gennaio 1942'.

[23] ASMAE, AA.CC. – Grecia, 1941–2, pos. 3/1-4/1-5, 'Ghigi a Ciano, 29 settembre 1941'; ibid., 'Situazione finanziaria in Grecia, commento alla riunione tra esperti italiani e tedeschi tenutasi a Roma il 22 ottobre 1941'; ASBI, Direttorio Azzolini, cart. 51, fasc. 2, 26 August 1941, 'Rapporto dell'inviato della Banca d'Italia Vittorio Forte al governatore Vincenzo Azzolini'.

[24] Etmektsoglou-Koehn, 'Axis Exploitation of Wartime Greece', p. 495.

the occupation. Hitler's dismissive response was to forbid German occupation forces in Greece from using the word *Besatzungskosten* (occupation costs), which was to be to replaced with *Aufbaukosten* (construction costs), and to remind Mussolini that the costs of fortifications had been imposed by the Germans in the interest of both the Axis powers. Thereafter, the six-monthly sums that the Bank of Greece disbursed in addition to the occupation expenses continued to increase.[25]

In September, a Greek delegation journeyed to Berlin to discuss a reduction in occupation expenses and to propose imposing a ceiling on them whereby, taking account of inflation, they would not exceed 8 billion drachmas per month, to be divided equally between Italy and Germany. Although no agreement was reached, it was decided that two special commissioners with full authorization to decide economic and financial matters – Hermann Neubacher and Alberto D'Agostino – should be sent to Greece, where they would work in close collaboration with the Greek authorities.[26] In June 1943, Greece's occupation expenses amounted to 65 billion drachmas, which was equal to 10 per cent of the money circulating in the country at the time, while the weighted average price index was 40–45 times higher than it had been in November 1942.[27] On 6 August 1943, after the arrest of Mussolini, an inter-ministerial meeting was convened to discuss the financial situation in Greece. One reads in the report on the meeting that the Germans were using a proportion of the payment extracted from the Greeks to purchase goods for shipment to Germany, and it was agreed that the Italians would do the same, to which end they would demand fully 10 billion drachmas in addition to the amount due for the month of July: 'any attenuation on our part being futile, for it would be annulled by increases on the German side'. Given that Greece was no longer Italy's exclusive economic *spazio vitale* and that it would remain under occupation for strictly military necessities only, 'there seems to be no alternative but to raise the Italian levy to the level exacted by the Germans'. With Italy invaded,

[25] ASMAE, AA.CC. – Grecia, 1942, s.p.; according to Ministry of Finance figures for the March–August 1942 semester, the sums were around 17 billion drachmas for Italy and more than 67 billion for Germany.

[26] The Italians were opposed to the dispatch of German experts. See ASMAE, AA.CC. – Grecia, 1942, s.p., unsigned note, probably written by the head of commercial affairs Amedeo Giannini in the first ten days of October 1942. (This carton contains most of the documentation on occupation expenses in Greece for the year 1942.)

[27] ASBI, USC, prat. 106, b. 42, fasc. 1, 'Grecia generico, commissario italiano presso la Banca di Grecia Forte al governatore della Banca d'Italia Azzolini', 21 August 1943; fasc. 3, nc. 132, bob. 47, ftg. 1778, 'Dettaglio conti stato greco'. The amount paid to the German authorities for occupation expenses on 15 December 1942 was 138,431 million drachmas. The amount paid to the Italians was 51,873 million.

Mussolini in prison, the war and the *spazio vitale* lost, the Italian officials felt no compunction about aggravating the Greek population's difficulties further, and even at this late hour committed plunder entirely similar in its rapacity to that of the Nazis.[28]

There is a further point to consider concerning Italy's occupation expenses in Greece. Although they amounted to around half those borne by Germany, and although the Regio Esercito had almost double the number of troops (approximately 160,000) in Greece, a German soldier cost on average twice as much as his Italian counterpart. The Wehrmacht's high technological coefficient with respect to the Regio Esercito partly explains this difference in costs. It should also be borne in mind that strategic defence works 'in the common interest' represented, according to an estimate by Neubacher, 84 per cent of all construction work undertaken, which in its turn accounted for 50 per cent of total occupation expenditure.[29]

The Italians were thus not overridden by the Germans on the question of occupation expenses, and they managed to maintain a semblance of decision-making power. Nevertheless, the price they paid for Germany's decisive military support during the Greek campaign was high indeed: their almost complete exclusion from economic exploitation of Greece. But then, even if German interference in the Fascist *spazio vitale* had been more restrained, the Italians would not have had the wherewithal to penetrate Greece economically.

Businessmen and experts on the Balkans followed behind the Wehrmacht's economic-military staff (*Wehrwirtschaftsamt*). They requisitioned, looted and plundered goods and products of every description, while German diplomats had the frontiers redrawn so that Bulgaria, not Italy, was allocated southern Macedonia with the chrome mines of Ljuboten, which were later exploited by the Germans. During the first weeks following the armistice, around 95 per cent of Greek raw materials and industrial output was appropriated by the Reich and transported out of the country before the arrival of the Italian troops (see appendix, table 42).

In the first ten days of May, Germany cornered the entire output of the Greek mining industry: pyrites, iron, chrome, nickel, magnesium, manganese and bauxite. German agents stipulated exclusive supply contracts

[28] ASMAE, AA.CC., 1943, s.p., 'presenti Pietromarchi, Antonio Venturini, Giovanni Paolo De Ferrari del GABAP, Emanuele Grazzi del Dipartimento Affari commerciali, Vincenzo Fagiuoli, Marcolini per il Ministero delle Finanze e rappresentanti d'altri ministeri'.

[29] Etmektsoglou-Koehn, 'Axis Exploitation of Wartime Greece', p. 472, excludes transport costs, which were always charged to the Greek government, and the costs of quartering troops, animals and vehicles.

with electricity companies, the Vasileiades shipyards and the Bodosakis munitions company. Stocks of tobacco, leather and cotton were confiscated or bought at rock-bottom prices, and the Shell oil company was compulsorily purchased. Almost all exportable goods produced by the building, metallurgical, shipbuilding, agricultural and textiles industries were requisitioned, pre-empted or exploited by the Germans. Even olive oil production was much more successfully 'squeezed' by the Germans, although Fascist propaganda cited it as an example of Italian economic success in the occupied territories. Greek entrepreneurs were compelled to sign exclusive supply contracts with durations ranging from ten to twenty-five years and to sell their businesses for worthless occupation marks. Germany determined that trade relations with Greece were to be regulated according to the volume of Greek exports to the two Axis countries in 1939: 88.7 per cent of Greek exports was allocated to Germany and 4.9 per cent to Italy.[30] Germany's 'brilliant second' was left the residue of Greek manufacturing output and the onus of the military occupation, including responsibility for feeding the Greek population.

On 1 May 1941, the general manager of the Azienda Minerali Metallici Italiani (AMMI), which was part of the IRI industrial conglomerate, informed the Italian *chargé d'affaires* in Athens, Giovanni Fornari, that the German authorities had purchased almost all of Greece's minerals output on five-year renewable contracts.[31] Count Giuseppe Volpi di Misurata – the unscrupulous financier who represented the interests of COMIT, the Società Adriatica di Elettricità, the Regia Cointeressata dei Tabacchi del Montenegro and the Compagnia di Antivari[32] – was sent to Athens by the Foreign Ministry on 8 May 1941, together with a conspicuously large retinue of aides, to persuade Greek industrialists and state and semi-state bodies that they should do business with Rome rather than Berlin. Volpi's mission had no significant outcome, however. Then, in June, during bilateral economic negotiations in Berlin, the Italians demanded once again that their economic interests in Greece be respected.

[30] Rieder, 'I rapporti economici italo-tedeschi'; Fleischer, 'Deutsche Besatzungsherrschaft'; USSME, I 13, b. 105, 'Con l'XI Armata nella guerra contro la Grecia, dattiloscritto del generale Geloso', pp. 177–80. Documents on the chrome and magnesite mines are to be found in ASMAE, AA.CC. – Grecia, 1942–3, s.p., and in the same dossier, 1942, s.p., on the iron mines.

[31] ASMAE, GABAP, b. 53, 'telegramma della Direzione Affari generali – Ministero degli Esteri all'ambasciata di Berlino'; DDI, ser. IX, 1939–43, vol. 7, doc. 92, 'ministro degli Esteri Ciano all'ambasciatore Dino Alfieri', 12 May 1941.

[32] The former was the Italian state-owned tobacco company in Montenegro, the latter a trade and transport company owned by the Banca Commerciale Italiana.

However, not only did they return to Italy empty-handed, they were obliged to announce that the Reich had decided to reduce the amounts of coal and oil sent every month to Italy. The Italian authorities realized that the Germans had not the slightest intention of cancelling their contracts with Greek companies, and that it would be impossible to regain the goods requisitioned or looted by the Reich.[33] In March 1942, during negotiations on the ninth secret Italo-German protocol on economic co-operation, the Germans (who had obtained Italy's agreement to send 134,000 Italian workers to the Reich) assigned 50 per cent of Greek chrome production to the junior partner and transferred to Italy shares in Mines Laurium, the Serifos company, and the American-owned Socony Vacuum Oil. Only a few weeks later, however, the Italian authorities in Greece accused the Germans of being in breach of the provisions of the just-concluded agreement.

By October 1941, opportunities for share takeovers in Greece had grown so difficult and costly that Italian industrial groups were compelled to act with alacrity, but even so there was very little left for them to acquire.[34] Ital-Cable failed to gain control of Cable & Wireless, which was transferred to Telefunken. The Volpi Group failed to take over either the General Hellenic Company or its affiliates Société Anonime Électrique d'Athènes-Pirée and the Société Hellénique des Transports; and it bid unsuccessfully for Lake Kopais (cotton) and Anglo-Greek Magnesite. AMMI recovered 43,530 shares in the Società Miniere Lokris (nickel) appropriated by the Germans following the armistice, but it was unable to gain control of the company's production.[35] FIAT attempted to acquire the Société Hellénique

33 Etmektsoglou-Koehn, 'Axis Exploitation of Wartime Greece', pp. 331–2. The Italians demanded the following: (1) all chrome produced by the Domokos (Société Union Minières), Apostolides and Papassotiriou mines located in the Regio Esercito's occupation zone; (2) half of Greece's total annual production of iron pyrites; (3) acquisition of the Parnassus bauxite mines (Parnassus and Delphi), controlled by Hansa Leichtmetall AG; (4) management of the Anglo-Greek Magnesite Co. Ltd and 50 per cent of its output; (5) the entire output from the magnesite mines of Mytilene and Calcidia; (6) the transfer of Compagnie française des mines du Laurium shares to an Italian company; (7) lead and zinc production and the acquisition of iron and barite deposits; (8) the exclusive right to export coal in the Italian zone; (9) exclusive exploitation of all mineral resources discovered in the future. They obtained none of these concessions, apart from a promise of 50 per cent of Greek magnesite production.

34 ASMAE, AA.CC. – Grecia, 1941–2, pos. 3/1-4/1-5, 17 October 1941, 'Appunto per l'eccellenza il plenipotenziario Ghigi sulle attività nemiche in Grecia', unsigned.

35 USSME, L 15, b. 23, 14 July 1941, 'Relazione sulla situazione generale del territorio greco occupato'; b. 85, Centro "I", Athens 10 May 1941, 'Notiziario riservato n. 2'. The Germans wanted to acquire the electricity-generating stations on the River Acheloos controlled by FIAT and the Volpi Group because they supplied the Parnassus bauxite mine under German control. They proposed their exchange for shares in the reservoirs of Stymphalia and Ladonos in the Peloponnese. The Italian companies rejected the proposal.

de Produits et Engrais Chimiques but was forestalled by Krupp, and it also made unsuccessful bids in the steel and cement industries (where it was interested in four large factories in Attica-Boeotia, two of them belonging to the same company and located in Volos and the Piraeus, one in Eleusis – Titan – and one in Chalkis, with a total annual output of 340,000 metric tons). IRI made a vain attempt to acquire the Société Lanière de Grèce and hesitated until it was too late over a 80 per cent shareholding in the Société Huilière de Grèce. By the end of 1941, the few Italian industrial groups still interested in exploiting Greek industry had definitively abandoned financial ventures which they saw as unprofitable, or as doomed to fail in any case by the hegemony of the Germans.

Only CIOM (Commercio Italiano Oriente Mediterraneo) and AMMI continued to operate in Greece. The former purchased the lignite mine of Peristeri (Athens), an important source of fuel for the Athens electricity-generating station,[36] mines operating in Aliveri (close to Euboea: lignite, circa 150 tonnes a day), Neon Iraklion, Kalogreca, Kalovrita (in the Peloponnese: daily output between 3 and 25 tonnes of lignite), Laurium (mixed sulphurs), Larimna (in Euboea: nickel) and the pyrolusite mines of the Peloponnese (Zerbissia, Andritsena and Vasta Issari). The handful of Greek companies controlled or operated by the Azienda Carboni Italiani produced derisory quantities (or none at all in the case of chrome); and what they did produce was of no practical use for the Italian war effort – apart from the minimal amounts that the Army Intendenza (administrative section) could utilize *in loco* – given that it could not be transported to Italy. The mine at Peristeri produced less than 50 tonnes a day (compared to the projected minimum amount of 300), while the workforces at the mines in Attica and Euboea were depleted as labourers quit their jobs to bring in the olive harvest, for which work they were paid in kind. From late 1942 onwards, obstructionism by workers and technicians against the occupiers grew increasingly obdurate. But the Regio Esercito also controlled a number of mines directly (for which it fixed contract prices between buyers and sellers of lignite), supervised sea transport, requisitioned vessels (*motovelieri* or motorsailers), reorganized overland transport, secured fuel supplies, defined relationships between owners and workers, disciplined the workforce and furnished technical assistance. Given the circumstances, the results achieved in three months by the Regio Esercito were impressive (see appendix, table 43).

[36] ASMAE, AA.CC. – Grecia, 1941–2, pos. 3/1a-4/1-5, 'presidente dell'Azienda carboni italiani Giovanni Vaselli al MAE', 19 January 1942.

Attempts at penetration by Italian commercial companies were just as unsuccessful as those by industrial enterprises. The figures are eloquent: between July and December 1941, fully 85 per cent of Greek exports were shipped to Germany; the 1942 percentage fell to 76 per cent, with a total for Italy of 17 per cent. The Reich imported 47 per cent of all Greek products; Italy 6 per cent.[37] Vittorio Signorelli, head of the commercial office at the embassy in Athens, sent the Ministry of Trade and Exchange an approximate calculation of potential exports and imports.[38] Less than one month later Ghigi declared that Greece could not be considered Italian *spazio vitale* as long as Germany was allowed to export Greek goods in quantities that far exceeded those permitted to Italy.[39]

Also the German clearing system – described as a sort of 'disguised plundering'[40] – had harmful effects on Italy, in that the central banks of the occupied countries tended to cover the liabilities in the German trade balance by extending credit to the Berlin clearing office. The Germans established the DeutscheGriechische-Warenausgleichgesellschaft (DEGRIGES) in Athens. This was an agency which supervised the profits made on imports and promoted the export of German products to the Greek peninsula by setting the prices of Greek exports to Germany equal to those of German imports into Greece. The Italians created a similar organization: the Società Anonima Commercio Italo-Greco (SACIG, chairman Guido Viola di Campalto, managing director Boffa Tarlatta) with offices in Athens, Heraklion and Ioannina. The tasks of SACIG were to issue entry and exit permits for merchandise, supervise purchases by Fabbriguerra, supervise

37 Etmektsoglou-Koehn, 'Axis Exploitation of Wartime Greece', p. 375.

38 ASMAE, AA.CC. – Grecia, 1941–2, pos. 3/1-4/1-9, 'rappresentanza d'Italia per la Grecia al Ministero per gli Scambi e le Valute', 24 August 1941. Italy would import from Greece (in millions of lire): rosin (15), essence of turpentine, resin (35), tobacco (9), carob seeds (3), mineral ores (5), nickel (10), magnesite (1), animal skins (10), dried grapes (15), dried figs (1), silkworm cocoons (10), scrap iron and steel (5), precious metals (6), rags (2) and other goods (5), for a total of 105 million lire (sic); olive oil (25), carob beans (20), emery (2) and other goods (3), for a total of 50 million lire; and an overall total value of 155 million (sic). Italy would export to Greece foodstuffs (320 million lire), chemicals and pharmaceuticals (5 million), matches (22) and other goods (25), for a total amount of 372 million lire and a deficit to Italy of 215 million lire (sic); ASMAE, AA.CC. – Grecia, 1941–2, pos. 3/1-4/1-5, 'sottocommissione per gli Affari bancari'. The Italo-German meeting of January 1942 established the export quotas of agricultural produce. The Germans refused to concede to the Italians quotas larger than their own for any agricultural product except carob beans.

39 ASMAE, AA.CC. – Grecia, 1941–2, pos. 3/1-4/1-5, 'Ghigi a Ciano', 29 September 1941.

40 Etmektsoglou-Koehn, 'Axis Exploitation of Wartime Greece', p. 362. Research in the Italian archives shows that some of Etmektsoglou-Koehn's observations on the German case apply to the Italian one as well: (1) the trade figures for the period prior to the war are incomplete; (2) some accounts were settled individually and were not included in the general account, or were paid with occupation marks; (3) numerous debts were financed by the occupation funds; (4) requisitions by the Wehrmacht were obviously excluded from the clearing balance.

other purchases, draw up contracts and organize finance, payments and transportation. Owing to hyperinflation, it also functioned as a clearing house which offset the differences in drachma prices between imported and exported goods.[41] SACIG operated in parallel with the Ente Industrie Attività Agrarie (EIAA) and undertook similar activities in Ciamuria and Epirus with the ACJ (Anonima Commercio Jonico), and with the CIOM in the Cyclades. Administered by the Treasury, these companies complied with instructions issued by the Direzione Generale dell'Alimentazione – an inter-ministerial body consisting of officials from the Ministries of Agriculture, Foreign Affairs, Finance, and Trade and Exchange – and administered their own budgets. They assumed the risks of and appropriated the profits from transactions; they purchased Italian products for export, paying for them in lire and selling them for drachmas which they used to purchase local products then remitted to the stockpiling agencies in Italy, receiving lire in exchange.[42] SACIG was assigned special funds by the Ministry of Finance to purchase goods that could not pass through the clearing system. It was also provided with advance clearing funds, which it used to purchase all products for export via the clearing system, and a supplementary fund for the purchase of products which exceeded the clearing value.[43] In Greece, by the end of May 1942, SACIG had purchased products for 267 million lire and exported items to the value of 127 million.

However, very few of these goods were of service to the war effort, and the quantity of metals obtained was negligible (368,820 kilos of tin, brass, copper, bronze and nickel). On the German side, the DEGRIGES, Viola di Campalto complained, was 'yet another instrument of penetration used by Germany' and it only 'paid for its purchases after taking all products that might prove useful and only when the drachma had almost entirely collapsed in value'. SACIG was overwhelmed by its German counterpart because Berlin, which owed Athens considerable sums for purchases, had goods available for trade with Greece, while Rome had few or no products and commodities to offer in exchange.[44] A report by the Italian *chargé* for economic and financial affairs in Greece, D'Agostino, confirms that between 1 November 1942 and 31 May 1943 Italy exported

[41] ASMAE, AA.CC., 1941–2, pos. 4/1-6 to 4/1-9, 'Ministero per gli Scambi e le Valute', 31 October 1941: 'SACIG . . . has competence for continental Greece (excluding Ciamuria and southern Epirus, whose trade is supervised by the EIAAA), the Peloponnese and the island of Crete.'

[42] ASBI, USC, prat. 106, b. 42, fasc. 1, 'Grecia generico, Ministero delle Finanze – Direzione generale Tesoro, 8 luglio 1941, firmato dal direttore Paolo Grassi'.

[43] ASMAE, AA.CC., 1941–2, pos. 4/1-6 to 4/1-9, 'SACIG al MAE', 18 January 1942.

[44] ASMAE, AA.CC., 1941–2, pos. 4/1-6 to 4/1-9, 'presidente della SACIG al Ministero delle Finanze', 28 September 1942.

very little and imported even less, and at prices higher than in the previous period.

As for the financial penetration of Greece, immediately following the occupation various Italian credit institutions, most notably the Banco di Napoli and the Banco di Roma, lobbied for permission to open subsidiaries in Greece, their stated intention being to undertake a programme of 'economic reorganization and reconstruction' which would cost some billions of lire. On agreement with the Germans, the Inter-Ministerial Co-ordination Committee appointed Vittorio Forte, a senior official at the Bank of Italy, to the dual post of commissioner at the Bank of Greece and head of the Office for Banking Control in Greece. On taking up his appointment, however, Forte criticized the Fascist scheme for banking and financial penetration on the grounds that the Italian bankers were colonialist in mentality and had failed to realize that the Greeks were hardly likely to deposit their savings in the branches of Italian banks.[45] Moreover, he pointed out, the Greek banks were reluctant to sell the parcels of shares in their possession, because with devaluation of the drachma and spiralling inflation, any sale at all of shares would be highly imprudent; and even if a bank were willing to sell, it would demand a price that would make the transaction unprofitable.

Forte's criticisms highlight a profound divergence of views on financial penetration between the Bank of Italy and the private banking sector, which, although it did not have the resources to fulfil its extravagant ambitions, expected to receive full backing from the state institutions. Italy, Forte argued, could not 'suddenly become capitalist in the British manner and thus be obliged to look for investments abroad'. Bankers and industrialists meant to exploit the occupied territories by means of operations 'intended to achieve the greatest influence and the most profound penetration', riding roughshod over local interests. They had failed to grasp the difference between colonies and the European territories of the imperial community, where it would instead be more fruitful to adopt the German model, which was based on co-operation agreements between German and Greek banks that preserved their national 'façades'.[46] In reality, neither the German model envisaged by Forte nor the colonial scheme propounded by the

[45] ASBI, USC, prat. 106, b. 42, fasc. 1, 'Grecia generico, Giuseppe Pietro Veroi ad Azzolini, Espansione del Banco di Roma in Grecia, Roma 13 agosto 1941'.

[46] ASBI, Direttorio Azzolini, cart. 51, fasc. 2, 26 August 1941, 'Rapporto dell'inviato della Banca d'Italia Forte al governatore Azzolini'; USC, fasc. 3, nc. 132, bob. 47, ftg. 1686, 'Forte ad Azzolini, 16 July 1941'; Vigilanza, prat. 808, fasc. 1, 'Forte ad Azzolini', 28 September 1941, 'Accordi fra la Deutsche Bank e la Banca nazionale di Grecia, fra la Dresdner Bank e la Banque d'Athènes'.

Italian bankers was implemented, simply because Italian banks could not gain a foothold in Greece during the Second World War.

Hence, Italian penetration was a failure from the industrial, commercial and financial points of view. Nevertheless, the Italians did not resign themselves to German superiority. Convinced that they could go it alone, probably befuddled by Fascist ideology, they continued to propose strategies and policies with which to secure Italy economic possession of Greece, but which invariably proved futile or were obstructed or rejected by the Germans.

CROATIA

Croatia's occupation expenses cannot be even minimally compared to those of Greece: Croatia was an allied state, not a defeated and occupied enemy. The bureaucratic and military jargon termed the expenses 'purveyances of kune' (*somministrazioni di kune*): in April 1942 they amounted to 1,250 million kune (compared to the 8 billion kune then circulating in the country), and they provoked, owing to the amount of money in circulation, hyperinflation and a black market. According to calculations by the Intendenza of the Second Army, between 1 January 1942 and May 1943 the cost of living in Croatia increased by 335 per cent, which was an extraordinary amount, but not nearly as high as the 13,000 per cent recorded in Greece.

The Croatian minister of finance, Vladimir Košak, reacted in the same manner as his Greek counterpart Gotzamanis by asking the Italians to reduce the monthly payments. His request was granted, but only in June 1942 after the partial withdrawal of the Regio Esercito. Italy repaid loans in kune with war supplies, extra clearing-system settlements in commodities, and credit liquidations, also relative to banks of the former Yugoslavia.[47] On 6 August 1942, the Italians and Croats agreed that credit advances to Supersloda should be consolidated into 1 billion kune and settled after the end of the war with restitution to the Bank of Croatia. They were used to meet expenses relative to public works executed in Croatia by Italian companies and to the administration of Italian patents, the profits of

[47] USSME, M 3, b. 48, 'GABAP al CS', 25 March 1942; the document refers to aircraft parts for a total value of 48 million lire, and ten tanks. See also ASBI, USC, prat. 100, b. 4, fasc. 9, 'Forniture per la milizia ustascia', 9 April 1942: the document quotes correspondence between the Ministry of Finance, the MAE and the central office of the Bank of Italy USC on the question of the advance payment of kune by the Croatian government to cover the Second Army's expenses. In fact, Italy had taken out large amounts of credit with the Croatian Cassa di Risparmio at its Sušak, Ljubljana and Split branches, and with the Società Generale Bancaria Jugoslava at its Ljubljana branch, and smaller amounts of credit with Croatian Railways taken out by the Compagnia Danubio-Sava-Adriatico.

contractor companies and remittances by Italian workers. After 1 July 1942, payments for the Second Army's expenses were made through Croatia's general clearing account.[48]

The economic exploitation of Croatia did not greatly differ from the economic exploitation of Greece. On 12 June 1941, Amedeo Giannini sent a telegram (forwarded to the Duce) to Dino Alfieri informing him that in Croatia, as in all the territories of the former Yugoslavia, Germany intended to conserve and protect its every economic interest as a matter of principle. But this principle could not be reconciled with the inclusion of Croatia in Italy's *spazio vitale*. Giannini stressed that the German–Croatian economic agreement precluded Italian purchases because Germany had secured – for four months – 500 million dinars worth of imports and the same amount of exports. Consequently, he wrote, 'If the question of principle is not addressed and settled, we shall find ourselves quarrelling on individual cases every day.'[49] The question of principle was not settled, therefore; indeed, by the end of the first year of occupation the Italian authorities had come to realize that the Germans intended to appropriate all Croatia's industries, mines, commercial enterprises and even large amounts of landed property, and that they were advancing their interests with an imperiousness that the Croats were unable to resist.[50] Although the Germans had proclaimed the Italians 'guarantors of the independence of the NDH and of its consolidation', and although the Reich had recognized the pre-eminence of Italy's *spazio vitale* in the Adriatic hinterland, they had engrossed the Croatian economy with exclusive agencies and monopolies on river traffic, mineral resources (bauxite), tobacco, the supply of explosives and transfers of formerly Jewish-owned firms. Germany invariably refused to grant concessions to Italy and even breached previous agreements on the exploitation of forest resources and lignite deposits.[51]

With the exception of Giannini, no member of the Italian establishment wanted to remember that Ciano had been forced at the Vienna conference to concede Germany the right to economic penetration of even Italy's annexed zones. Small wonder, then, that in 1943 Croatia exported

[48] ASBI, USC, prat. 100, b. 4, fasc. 4, 'Commissione economica italo-croata, accordo del 6 agosto 1942, Venezia, firmato da Volpi, Košak, Riccardi, Lorkoviće Pietromarchi'.

[49] DDI, ser. IX, 1939–43, vol. 7, doc. 247, 'ambasciatore Alfieri al ministro Ciano', 12 June 1941; see also docs. 248–50, 263.

[50] USSME, M 3, b. 51, fasc. 2, 'legazione di Zagabria al MAE, 15 agosto 1942'; ASMAE, GABAP, b. 31, 7 November 1942, 'Appunto di Casertano al GABAP': 'Our endeavour to collaborate . . . in all sectors, with advisers and experts, encounters opposition in the Croatian government, which . . . in many cases has followed the practice of balancing our contribution and advice by consulting the Germans, when it has not preferred to do things itself even at the cost of making mistakes.'

[51] USSME, M 3, b. 51, fasc. 2, 'legazione di Zagabria al MAE', 15 August 1942.

80 per cent of its goods to Germany and that up to 70 per cent of its imports were from Germany; or that the Germans owned shares in 503 Croatian enterprises and the Italians in only 18; or that the productive sector of greatest interest to Italy – raw materials, especially minerals – was entirely in German hands and those of the Croatian *Volksdeutschen*.[52] Perhaps the general amnesia served the authorities because it made the Italians' reaction more determined, but in the event this proved futile: one after the other, all Italian attempts at penetration failed.

The only Italian companies in Croatia with significant levels of business were Montecatini, which opened offices in Zagreb and constructed a superphosphate factory, and the Azienda Ligniti Italiane (ALI), which ran the mines at Kolan; these produced a daily output of around 40 tonnes, all of which were utilized by Supersloda.[53] In the petroleum sector, the Croatian government transferred the plants of Hrvatska Standard, formerly the Vacuum Oil Company of Yugoslavia, to AGIP (in February 1942). AGIP applied to the Zagreb government for permission to form a river shipping company with Italian capital and to survey and exploit oil fields. However, its plans were thwarted by German petroleum companies, which invoked the clause in the Vienna agreement on Germany's prevalent economic interests in the former Yugoslavia.[54] Ital-cable attempted unsuccessfully to establish a radio telegraphy and telephony station in Zagreb.[55]

The CEPIC arranged a number of meetings between representatives of the BNL, Banco di Napoli and the Banco di Roma, and their counterparts at the Udruena Banka and the Trgovača i Industrijalna Banka (Industrial Commercial Bank) in order to discuss the creation of a jointly owned company for the development of Croatian industry. The project never came to fruition, however, because Volpi, who wanted to take control of the company, provoked the opposition of the Croats.[56] The episode is indicative that Italy's failure cannot be blamed solely on German rapaciousness and

[52] ASMAE, AA.CC. – Croazia, 1942, pos. 3/1, 'Ministero degli Scambi e delle Valute – Ufficio Scambi italo-croati al GABAP', 4 March 1942. In March 1942, the minister for trade and exchange, Raffaello Riccardi, sent a report to the DGAC (Direzione Generale Affari Commerciali) of the MAE in which he warned that the *Volksdeutschen*, backed by their own banks, were penetrating all industrial sectors in Croatia and endeavouring to gain control of the country's largest companies.

[53] USSME, M 3, 'V CdA al comando d'armata, 15 agosto 1943', stated that the mine in question had reduced its average daily output to around 70 quintals, and that the management refused to install the machinery needed to increase production because of the 'precarious' political situation.

[54] ASMAE, GABAP, b. 47, 'presidente dell'AGIP a Pietromarchi', 22 November 1941.

[55] ASMAE, AA.CC. – Croazia, 1942, pos. 3/1, 'III Riunione plenaria della Commissione permanente'.

[56] ASBI, USC, prat. 100, b. 4, fasc. 4, 'Commissione economica all'Ispettorato per la difesa del risparmio e l'esercizio del credito, 5 ottobre 1942'.

economic supremacy. The problems encountered by the Italians in Croatia stemmed largely from their attempt to pursue ambitions of hegemony and economic exploitation similar to those of the Nazis. The Croats, made intractable by the territorial question, used their negotiating power on economic matters to assert their decision-making autonomy. They decided to throw in their lot with the Germans, not because they had no other option, but because they hoped that co-operation with the Reich would increase their chances of regaining Dalmatia.

As to economic penetration, the CEPIC appointed a joint committee to handle relations among the departments concerned and to promote commercial co-ordination. It fixed the value of the kuna at 38 lire for 100 kune and stipulated a protocol with the Croats which established that Italy would export 750 tonnes of aluminium to the factories in Lozovak, on condition that the entire amount would be used to satisfy Croatia's domestic needs.[57] Italy would export rice, sulphur, cotton yarn, cotton and woollen textiles, garments, agricultural produce, chemicals and pharmaceuticals. It was also agreed that textiles to the value of 80 million lire would be exported to Croatia, as well as chemical products, medicines, clover seeds, sulphur, machines and other goods. Croatia would export horses, lignite, sheepskins, timber, alcohol, caustic soda, poultry, eggs and beans to a total value of 90 million lire, and it would reserve for Italy metals and minerals that had not been committed to third countries (i.e., Germany).[58] Excluded from the account were the import–export quotas for Fiume and Dalmatia, which were regulated by a separate agreement.

During 1943, commodity trades were organized in accordance with the minutes of the meetings held in Venice on 10–12 September 1942 and on the basis of a provisional trade agreement stipulated in Rome on 26 June 1941. Owing to their arms expenditure, the Croats repeatedly exceeded the clearing balance. Croatia purchased goods for which it was obliged to pay in advance to Italian exporters, while Italy for its part failed to pay the sum of 130 million lire (as of March 1943) to the Croatian state railways for the transport of troops and war matériel. The Croats estimated that extra-clearing exchanges amounted to approximately 400 million lire.

[57] ASMAE, AA.CC. – Croazia, 1941, pos. 1/1, 3/1, 4, 4/1-4/1-24, 4/2, 'Riunione della Commissione economica permanente italo-croata, Roma 23–25 giugno 1941'.

[58] It would reserve up to 8,000 tonnes of bauxite from Adria Bauxit of Drniš and up to 8,000 tonnes of coal dust from Monte Promina of Siverić; for the Dalmatienne factories in Šibenik: a maximum of 4,000 tonnes of 50 per cent iron ore from Vareš, 4,000 tonnes of pyrite ash and 5,000 tonnes of charcoal from Drvar, 2,500 tonnes of silica and 6,000 of manganese, as well as a further 60,000 tonnes of iron ore until 31 December 1941.

In regard to trade between Croatia and Dalmatia, the convention on the free-trade zone of 23–26 June 1941 (in force from 1 July to 31 December 1941) regulated customs relations between the two countries. The movement of goods was unrestricted within the free-trade zone, and complete commercial freedom as well as the free movement of persons was established. The contracting parties undertook not to adopt without prior agreement any measure to impede or restrict exports to the free-trade zone of products that might be necessary for the well-being of its population. The CEPIC signed a further two treaties (Zagreb, 27 October 1941, and Fiume, 1 November 1941) by which the customs frontier between Croatia and Dalmatia was abolished and the Croatian government assumed responsibility for supplying Dalmatia, Fiume and the Second Army.[59] The general secretary of Dalmatia, Carlo Bozzi, calculated the monthly food requirements of the two provinces at such exorbitant levels that it would have been impossible for the Croatian government to fulfil them without starving the population.[60] On 28–31 January 1942, the Permanent Commission signed an agreement on direct payments for the provisioning of Fiume and Dalmatia which stipulated that two accounts in kune accredited to ESCATA (Ente per gli Scambi Commerciali e gli Approvvigionamenti nei Territori Annessi) and SACA (Società Anonima Commercio Adriatico) should be opened to pay for Croatian goods, the shipment of which was authorized on settlement account and in the counter-value of special consignments.[61]

Italian financial penetration of Croatia was as insignificant as it was in Greece. Volpi's action as chairman of CEPIC overlapped with his capacity as president of the Banca Commerciale, which controlled the Hrvatska Banka. According to Volpi, strengthening the Croatian bank would enable Rome to steer the economic development of the Ustaša state. Initially, as in Greece, ambitious plans were made for the takeover of local banks by Italian ones (the former Italian minister in Belgrade, Carlo Galli, drew up one such plan for COMIT). But the Banco di Napoli in Dubrovnik 'performed extremely modestly'; the Dalmatian Discount Bank (Credito Italiano) did not open until April 1942 and did very little business; and

[59] ASMAE, GABAP, b. 33, Croatia Office, 17 November 1941, 'Appunto per l'eccellenza il ministro'.

[60] ASMAE, GABAP, b. 33, 'Verbale della riunione interministeriale tenuta il 10 novembre 1941 alle ore 11.30 per l'esame degli accordi italo-croati per l'approvvigionamento della Dalmazia e della zona occupata': 22,500 quintals of flour, 7,500 of pasta, the same quantity of rice, 6,000 of beef, 2,000 of pork, 1,000 of oil and the same quantity of other fats, 3,000 of sugar for a total expenditure of 100 million kune, while the monthly requirements of the Second Army were estimated, by Colonel Michele Rolla, at 6,400 quintals of meat, 36,000 of flour, 1,850 of lard, 3,300 of vegetables, 6,500 of potatoes, 1,100 of preserved pork, 30,000 of oats, 37,500 of hay and 33,500 of straw for 25,000 horses and mules, 15,000 quintals of corn-cobs and 116,000 of firewood.

[61] ASMAE, AA.CC. – Croazia, 1942, pos. 3/1, 'III Riunione plenaria della Commissione permanente'.

only the Hrvatska Banka traded to any significant extent.[62] In the spring of 1943, the Banca Nazionale del Lavoro and INA obtained permission to open a subsidiary, the Radna Banka, but this never began trading. In the insurance sector, the Croatian company Domovina, appointed to handle the insurance portfolios of the British, French and American companies, relied on the services of the German Münchener Rückversicherung.[63]

FRANCE

Figures are available on German occupation expenses in France: the 1942 financial statement itemizes occupation expenses to a total of 120.4 billion francs and a Franco-German clearing deficit of 30 billion. However, the amount that the French paid to the Italians is not known. Immediately after the occupation, Rome demanded credit to cover the expenses of the Italian troops to be stationed on French metropolitan territory and in Tunisia:[64] should Vichy refuse to grant it, Rome would issue occupation currency (equivalent to the vouchers issued by the Cassa Mediterranea in drachmas). By 20 December, the parties still had not reached agreement (even though the talks between Giannini and the French commercial delegation in Rome had been going on for more than a month). The foreign minister submitted a report to Mussolini that argued that, if the request for credit was not granted, the military authorities would have to demand it 'peremptorily' by imposing immediate economic sanctions. The Germans expressed no official interest in the question, as they had done in Croatia, and thus enabled Laval to stand his ground. The CS then announced that, without the funds in question, it would be impossible to fortify the zone assigned to Italy and, if Berlin refused to give its support, Rome would independently issue currency vouchers and confer upon its military commands the powers provided by the law of war.

An inter-ministerial committee was accordingly created with the task of devising an efficient method for confiscating currency, bonds and French

[62] USSME, N 1–11, 'Diari storici', b. 1267, 'Comando VI CdA – UAC, Notizie di carattere economico riguardanti il territorio di giurisdizione del corpo d'armata, 1942'.

[63] ASMAE, GABAP, b. 33, 'legazione di Zagabria al GABAP, 20 luglio 1943, Interesse italiano per l'economia della Croazia'. Enterprises beyond the Dinarics were dismantled in 1943. The CEPIC recalled its secretary and dismissed its personnel; SALPIC (Società Azionaria per i Lavori Pubblici in Croazia) cut back on all its running costs; the Compagnia Italiana Scambi Internazionali of the Breda Group recalled its representative; Rudnik, an affiliate of AMMI and the Astaldi construction company did likewise. Of the IRI Group companies, Ugar stopped all work at the Turbe sawmill and Dalmatienne closed down all its activities in Croatia, continuing in the occupied territories alone.

[64] ASMAE, AA.PP. – France, 1939–45, b. 70, 'Appunto del 13 novembre 1942'.

state securities.[65] Subsequently, the Italian minister of finance set out the reasons that counselled in favour of requisitioning the French state-owned banks rather than issuing vouchers. In February, the French delegation acceded to some of Italy's demands: Rome would no longer have to credit the French delegation in lire for purchases made in France by the troops of the Regio Esercito, and in exchange for those purchases the Italian government would be subject to the extremely mild obligation of examining the French delegation's requests with benevolence. The agreement fixed Italy's occupation expenses at 1 million francs a month, with effect from 1 January 1943.[66]

According to the economist Eraldo Fossati, during the 1930s, the proportion of imports from France in total Italian imports decreased from 7.1 per cent in 1931 to 2.3 per cent in 1938, while exports to France in total Italian exports fell from 10.7 per cent in 1931 to 3.1 per cent in 1937 – a marked downward trend. This situation was obviously also part of the more general context of worsening political relationships between Rome and France – also borne out by the fact that, during the same period, Italo-German trade increased from 13.2 per cent in 1931 to 26.7 per cent in 1938, and Italian exports from 10.7 per cent to 18.8 per cent.[67] In these quantitative terms, the resumption of trade between Italy and France, interrupted by the war, was one of the tasks undertaken by the CIAF.

Economic relations between Italy and France were administered mainly by an Italo-French economic commission responsible for matters not pertaining to administration of the armistice (which was the prerogative of the CIAF), and only regarding *France non-occupée*. 'This twofold administrative and geographical situation – Rome and Turin – to some extent prejudiced uniformity of treatment of various questions, disrupting the unity which previously existed in relations [between the two countries].'[68] On 23 August 1940, Rome and Paris signed economic agreements that should have boosted trade between the two countries; yet in early 1941 the Italian authorities noted that traffic had increased to only a minor extent. France had shipped goods to a total value of around 50 million lire, whereas it was obliged to supply Italy with industrial products and raw materials totalling just over 120 million lire in value. The Italians had done no better: they should have delivered agricultural products and 5 million tonnes of zinc to a total amount of 121 million lire, but had in fact shipped only

[65] ASBI, USC, prat. 108, b. 47, fasc. 1, 'Territori francesi occupati, CIAF – SCAEF', 9 January 1943.
[66] ASMAE, AA.PP. – France, 1939–45, b. 70, 'Gino Buti al MAE', 2 March 1943.
[67] Rainero, *Mussolini e Pétain*, vol. I, p. 113, cites Fossati, 'Commercio estero', 1940.
[68] Rainero, *Mussolini e Pétain*, vol. I, p. 114.

30 million lire worth. The signing of the petroleum agreement of 2 February 1941 led to the resumption of economic negotiations. Although total trade by each country was projected to reach 260 million lire in the period 1 March–31 August 1941, expectations on both sides were disappointed, owing to difficulties of transport – especially as regards products for shipment to Italy. Thus, in this period too, the quotas envisaged were not fulfilled. The subsequent period was characterized by much more modest undertakings, while a triangular exchange system was introduced whereby 18 tonnes of wheat were sent by Italy to France, and then to Libya from Tunisia.

Economic questions between Italy and France grew particularly intractable during the second half of 1941. In August, the French economic delegation in Rome applied for the attachment of French companies operating in Italy to be discontinued. The equivalent Italian delegation agreed to the release of small and medium-sized enterprises, while those belonging to large French industrial groups would be taken over by Italy in order to forestall German designs on their parent companies in France. As regards the other firms – of large size but not vital for the Italian economy – the hope was expressed that technological and financial collaboration would prevail.[69] This question and Italy's intention to disclaim article 10 of the armistice convention were discussed at the Rome meeting between Giannini and the head of the foreign trade section of the Vichy Ministry of Finance, Paul Leroy-Beaulieu. Article 10 was amended 'in the sense that Italy, in exchange for 2,000,600,000 francs (of which 32 per cent in gold at the price of 57,671 francs per kilo, 16 per cent reserved for the purchase of shares in French companies, and 52 per cent for normal financial activities between the two countries), relinquished its claim on a quantity of war materials'. Agreement was also reached on what was to be done with French firms in Italy.[70] Romain Rainero reports that by February 1942 some 32 per cent of the gold had been consigned to Italy, but only 20 per cent (equal to 416 million francs) of the 16 per cent of the sum consisting of shares had been paid. Just three operations were authorized by Vichy: the purchase of 219,804 shares in Dalmatienne (a company discussed in the next chapter) for 95.4 million francs; the purchase of 258 shares in Dacia Romana for 420,000 francs, and the purchase of 170 shares in the Union Italienne de Réassurance for 110,000 francs. FIAT acquired the Milan subsidiary of Tréfileries du Havre (half its stock); Montecatini bought 30,250 shares in the Italian subsidiary of Rhône Poulenc (Rhodiaceta Italiana); and Italgas

[69] Ibid., pp. 282–3, where Guillen's study, *Les entreprises industrielles françaises en Italie*, is cited.

[70] Rainero, *Mussolini e Pétain*, vol. I, p. 315. Twenty-one firms were liquidated, sixteen kept under attachment and twenty-nine released; see ibid., vol. II, doc. 33, for the names of the firms concerned.

acquired 10,600 shares (out of 16,000) in the Compagnie des compteurs (the Siry-Chamon plant).

As in the Balkans so in France the main obstacle to Italian economic penetration was Germany. As early as 1941, Quinto Mazzolini, the delegate for repatriation and assistance in Nice, wrote that Germany was carrying out a methodical plan to infiltrate the French territories: a plan irrelevant to the requirements of war but with the longer-term aim of incorporating France into a European economic system co-ordinated and directed by Germany, and that would exclude Italy from the manufacture of consumer goods, as well as from heavy industry. Germany intended first to re-organize French industrial sites and then use their output for the purposes of domestic production. According to Mazzolini, in order to carry out this programme of economic penetration, Germany had created what he called *centri direttivi* headed by highly trained German technocrats (for example, the Centre of German Economic Organizations in France) as well as Franco-German committees in every branch of industry and commerce. The *centri direttivi* were unconcerned with temporary collaboration in order to settle matters concerning the war; they were looking to the future and planning Franco-German economic co-operation on a much broader scale.[71]

When France was completely occupied, any Italian penetration of its industrial system was impossible, both because of manoeuvres by Berlin and because of the progress of the war and the disastrous state of relations between Rome and Vichy. Studies and projects on France's natural, industrial and financial resources were meaningless for all practical purposes in the territories designated for annexation as well as in the broader zone of influence that Italy hoped to acquire (a June 1940 study of French mineral resources hopefully included a map with a dotted line running from north of Geneva through Clermont-Ferrand as far as the mouth of the River Garonne on the Atlantic coast to indicate the boundary of the Fascist sphere of influence).

Nine-tenths of the French aeronautics, steel and metallurgy industries were exploited by the Germans alone. The car manufacturers Renault, Citroën, Peugeot and Mathis Ford signed exclusive contracts with the Germans on car and truck models, standardization of production, commercial organization and exportation. Italy's presence in the sector was instead entirely symbolic, in that apart from SIMCA (whose production had in

[71] ASMAE, GABAP, b. 1, 'DRA al MAE, 9 ottobre 1941'; AA.PP. – France, 1931–45, b. 47, 26 April 1941, 'Appunto per il capo di gabinetto, firmato Rumi'.

any case slumped from 25,000 cars a year to only 20 in 1941) no French company signed contracts with Italian manufacturers. And then shortages of raw materials severely obstructed the production of chemicals, textiles, scrap iron, paper, leather, glass, gas and building materials.

The Italians were unable to win contracts for public works (only in the film industry did they manage to conclude agreements on the creation of three Italo-French companies in Nice). In the *départements* to the east of the Rhône, the Germans obtained work orders at fifty-four factories (steel production, shipbuilding, ore smelting, munitions, outboard engines, telephone cables), and they continued to acquire and requisition manufacturing companies located in the territory occupied by the Regio Esercito. An army study of 1942 concluded that any trade in industrial products between France and Italy was impossible, for the industries in the two countries suffered from the same shortages: coal, steel, textile fibres, and so on. Whenever Italian industrialists wanted to place orders with French companies, the undertaking was thwarted by a lack of raw materials. Italy and France depended for their supplies on Germany, which deducted from quotas allocated to Italy any supplies granted to the French as part of Italian work orders (for example, if the Italians supplied coal or steel to the French, the Germans would deduct an equal quantity of coal or steel sent to Italy from Germany). All that was achieved under the commercial agreements in force was some rare and small-scale trading in chemicals and pharmaceuticals.[72]

Despite this situation and the worrying progress of the war, in early 1943 Major Filippo Milo travelled to France to examine the opportunities for industrial exploitation left for the Italians after the Germans had appropriated what they wanted. He reported that Germany had opted to take over mainly large companies like Renault and Devoitine, 'forgetting that small-scale industry existed in France as well'. It was difficult to find industrial plants that matched Italian needs because a large part of those surveyed and considered 'interesting' had been stripped of their machine tools; others had been severely damaged; and yet others were about to be requisitioned by the Germans. There only remained the small workshops of southern France, which were of dubious profitability and distant from railways. Milo made no mention of the possible relocation of Italian industries; instead, he advised that agreement should be reached with the French to achieve modest levels of production and exploit the marginal capacities of small workshops. This should be done by cultivating managers so

[72] USSME, D 7, b. 37.

poorly paid by the Germans that their only concern was to increase their earnings.[73]

This was consequently a strategy different from the one adopted in Greece and Croatia, and it stemmed from the particular 'regard' in which the Italians initially held the French. However, the difference between the Balkan territories and metropolitan France was short-lived. On 12 February 1943, Mussolini told Vacca Maggiolini that Italy's economic penetration of France should consist in the seizure and transfer to Italy of everything that might prove useful. It was consequently decided to occupy factories, to impound all stocks of raw materials, to issue occupation vouchers in francs for all purchases made by the military authorities and to abolish the customs frontier.[74] There ensued 'intense activity of acquisitions and orders which, combined with seizures of greater or lesser legality, gave Italian behaviour in that period the character of outright pillage serving to supply, in one way or another, an Italian war industry in utter disarray'.[75] Mussolini and the CIAF also wanted Nazi methods of economic exploitation to be emulated in order to counter-balance Germany's economic action, which was an obstacle even more difficult to overcome than the obstructionism of the French authorities and population.

In 1943, Italian plans to exploit the economy of south-eastern France were further frustrated by the Franco-German *relève* programme. Exemplifying the nature of these difficulties was a meeting held in March 1943 at which the Italian consul in Savoie and Haute-Savoie, Malfatti, and delegates from FIAT and the Acciaierie Vanzetti sought in vain to persuade the German authorities to exempt from the *relève* workers employed at the Société d'Ugine (which manufactured steel armour-plating, tank turrets, weapons, ammunition and cannon parts).[76] Two months later, at the

[73] ACS, Gabinetto Aeronautica, 1943, b. 135, 'Promemoria per l'eccellenza il sottosegretario per l'Aeronautica, non datato, firmato dal maggiore dell'Aeronautica, pilota Filippo Milo di Villagrazia': 'On the basis of strictly orthodox criteria the Germans requisitioned numerous machine tools, transporting them to Germany in the belief that they could be used to increase national output, leaving France mutilated. Some machines, removed from certain factories since the summer of 1940, were still waiting in station depots for transport to Germany in 1943. Very soon, the Germans replaced dismantlement with the more logical practice of exploiting French industry *in loco*, with local manpower. However, they committed the error of imposing minimum prices and excessively high work rates on the French industrialists. The situation is still unchanged.'

[74] Villermet, *A noi Savoia*, p. 165.

[75] ASMAE, AA.PP. – France, 1939–45, b. 70, 'Ministero degli Esteri, 24 marzo 1943, Appunto per il CS'.

[76] Italian workers were a problem within the problem. On 12 October 1942, the Delegation for Repatriation and Assistance (DRA) of Chambéry informed the CIAF that the German offices for enrolment of workers for Germany were feigning ignorance of the instructions issued by the Foreign Ministry. Instead of referring those Italian workers that applied to them to the DRA, they were sending them

Munich conference, Vacca Maggiolini asked for a three-month suspension of the Sauckel Action[77] east of the Rhône. He also demanded that the Italian authorities be asked for their prior approval of work orders which Germany intended to place with French companies located in the Italian occupation zone. He requested that Italy be accorded the right to confer work orders in French territory under German control until they were equal in value to those made in the Italian zone, and he concluded with the demand that German acquisitions should halt unless reciprocity agreements applied.[78] Some of the Italian demands discussed by CTA and CIAF delegates in Paris on 18–21 May 1943 were granted: Italy would specify the workshops that it wanted to be exempted from the Sauckel Action, and for three months no skilled worker aged over thirty-five would be sent to Germany. A list was therefore drawn up of factories willing to work on orders for Italy subject to suspension of the *relève*.[79]

At the end of May, the head of the CIAF informed the French delegation that Italy would use industrial plants located east of the Rhône to produce material of service to the Italian war effort. By 25 July, however, the Italians had managed to place work orders amounting to the risible sum of only 33 million francs. Among the few firms that had signed contracts with French firms were FIAT, ILVA (Genoa), Ansaldo, Microtecnica (Turin), Salmoiraghi and Boprini-Parodi-Delfino (Milan) and Magrini (Milan), as well as the Air Force and War Ministries.[80] Moreover, until July 1943, although around eighty factories suitable for Italian work orders had been identified, it was undecided which ministry would organize the purchase and transfer to Italy of the mass of materials acquired.[81] In short, it seems inappropriate to call Italy's activity

to Germany. Moreover, the Vichy government had extended the law of 1942 on forced recruitment to cover foreign workers, including Italians. See. ASMAE, AA.PP. – Francia, 1939–45, b. 55, 'Vacca Maggiolini al Ministero degli Esteri'.

77 Named after its head, who was charged with recruiting foreign workmen for Germany. There were four Sauckel Actions; the one referred to here is the second Sauckel Action intended to accelerate the enforced recruitment of French workers during the months of February and March 1943.

78 USSME, D 7, b. 59, 8 May 1943, 'Convegno di Monaco CIAF–CTA', p. 6.

79 Compagnie Produits Chimiques Alais Froges of Riopereux, Neyret Beylier and DSN of Grenoble, Fils de L. Bretton of Cluses, Carpano et Pons of Cluses, Société Viennoise de Constructions Mécaniques, Atelier de Constructions Mécaniques J. Pouchon of Vienne, Atelier Deiderichs of Bourgoin, Cartoucherie de Valence, Manufacture Française de Mèches Américaines of Tours, Hauts Fourneaux and Forges et Aciéries de Bompertius in Isère, Paul Declos and P. Gaillat of Marseilles, Keller et Deleux of Livet, Société des Hauts Fourneaux et Forges d'Allevars in Isère, Société Electrométallurgique de St-Beron in Savoy, Usine de Giffre di Marignier Compagnie Alais Forges et Camargues – Usine, Chedda / Haute-Savoie.

80 USSME, D 7, b. 37, 'Programma dei colloqui italo-tedeschi di Parigi, 18–20 maggio 1943 – Commesse italiane concordate con le industrie francesi alla data del 15 maggio 1943'.

81 USSME, D 7, b. 37, 'Notiziario CIAF, luglio 1943'.

'penetration', for the aim was not to install Italian industries, nor to control and manage French firms, but to seize some or all of their output illegally.

Turning to trade, once again France was far from able to supply the amount of raw materials and products that it had exported to Italy before June 1940. Moreover, following the armistice, direct agreements between private contractors were not permitted: commerce was restricted to the Italian government authorities, which opened clearing accounts for the purpose. On 5 March 1941, a six-month trade programme for a total of 280 million lire was drawn up to regulate the supply of North African phosphates and iron. The commercial commissioner at the Italian embassy in Paris, Teodoro Pigozzi, wrote as follows: 'In view of the situation of particular advantage in which the victory has placed Germany in regard to metropolitan France, I consider that our action should be directed mainly at North Africa, not least because our export capacity in textiles – though limited – could serve to satisfy the severe shortage of raw materials for clothing in those markets.'[82] Very similar conclusions were reached by a 1942 Regio Esercito report entitled *Studio sull'Agricoltura, l'Industria Estrattiva e le Industrie Francesi*, which maintained that it was impossible to establish trade in agricultural products between France and Italy. The report was of the same opinion as regards coal, because Germany had occupied the areas of France in which the mines were located and exercised exclusive control over their output. Moreover, Germany would not concede the same quantities of coke, gas and coal from Saint-Etienne that Italy had imported before the war. Iron and oil were no longer imported; only negligible quantities of aluminium; and the importing of scrap iron had almost ceased because of the slowdown in machine manufacture and the closure of scrap yards. Nor could imports of wool and cotton rags be maintained at pre-war levels. The report concluded that 'the German economy is bound to overwhelm that of metropolitan France. Italy should seek to lay the basis for the greatest possible development of its commercial relations with North Africa.'[83] The only branch of the financial sector that did significant amounts of business was vehicle insurance, which earned around 600 million francs in 1941 after taking over the portfolios of British and American companies.[84]

[82] ASMAE, AA.PP – France, 1939–45, b. 54, ''commissario commerciale dell'ambasciata d'Italia a Parigi, registrato al MAE il 23 gennaio 1943'.

[83] USSME, D 7, b. 53.

[84] USSME, D 7, b. 8, CIAF–SCAEF, 4 March 1943, 'Storia dell'armistizio, attività svolta dalla sottocommissione nel periodo 1° giugno 1942–31 gennaio 1943'.

The chapter has shown the extent to which the economic 'valorization' of the countries of the imperial community was a mirage, and the extent to which the short-term exploitation of those countries was superficial or negligible. Germany gained supremacy in all the productive sectors of the occupied countries. Those activities and spaces which Italy managed to carve out for itself were insignificant and frequently unprofitable. The importance given to the valorization project by Mussolini and the political authorities in Rome and the conquered territories was a reaction to German invasiveness, and it gave rise to a method of exploitation which, in the eyes of the occupied populations, was no different from that of the Nazis. Although the economic and financial situation of the Italian state was far from healthy on its entry into the war, economic experts and the high officials of the state persuaded themselves that the structural problems of the economy could be solved by territorial expansion, and thus still cleaved to a 'classical' conception of imperialism. The question asked by the Bank of Italy's commissioner in Greece is emblematic: 'Could Italy suddenly become capitalist?'

This chapter has been only a preliminary exploration of an area which has been neglected in comparison to analogous studies on Nazism. Gaps in the documentation are an important factor, of course, but I believe that further research should set economic exploitation in relation to the general situation of the Italian economy during the war. It might thus be explained why, in 1943, it was decided to exploit the resources of the occupied territories by adopting the Nazi strategy of plunder, but at a time when the disintegration of the Fascist regime had reached such a point that, as Giuseppe Bottai wrote in his journal on 12 March, 'no man could restore life and motion to this inert and cumbersome body'.

Finally, a topic not touched upon in the chapter, and which I believe warrants brief comment, concerns the consequences for the occupied countries of their economic exploitation. The work by Gabriella Etmektsoglou-Koehn has convincingly demonstrated the responsibility of the Axis, and therefore of Italy, for the famine in Greece.[85] The country was pillaged after six months of isolation caused by the war with Italy. Between May and September 1941, the German authorities transported to the Reich foodstuffs to a value of 4.2 million RM, paying for them with worthless occupation marks. Between July and November 1941, the Italians confiscated 87 tonnes of cheese, 308 tonnes of olive residues, 1,153 tonnes of wine and

85 Etmektsoglou-Koehn, 'Axis Exploitation of Wartime Greece', pp. 407ff.

40,000 tonnes of sultanas. The meagre harvest of 1943 provoked severe shortages in the conurbation of Athens, which comprised around 89 per cent of the total population and was entirely dependent on supplies from outside. As corpses piled up in the streets of Athens, the Axis partners wrangled on about who was responsible for feeding the country. Only in March 1942 did the Axis powers reduce the requisitioning of foodstuffs, but this was when the famine had already claimed in excess of 100,000 victims.

CHAPTER 8

The forced Italianization of the new provinces

This chapter examines the territories annexed *de jure* and *de facto*. It identifies and discusses four distinct but interconnected aspects of the forced Italianization of the new provinces: ethnic and racial mapping; the erasure of national identity, the internment, transfer and expulsion of native-born residents; the Fascistization of the latter (especially those of younger age) through education and the 'totalitarian' action of all organs of the state and the Fascist party; and the colonizing of further provinces. We shall see that the Italianization policy was implemented, to varying extents and with different instruments, in Dalmatia, in the province of Ljubljana and in the Ionian islands until mid-1942, when severe problems of public order (or ones arising from food shortages in the islands) largely thwarted the Fascists' plans: indeed, after June 1942 in all provinces, absolute priority was given to suppression of rebel movements (the subject of chapter 10). Also examined – albeit within the limits imposed by the fragmentary nature of the documentation – are the economic aspects of the Italianization policy in the new provinces, with brief discussion also of Montenegro and the forced Albanianization of the provinces of Kosovo and western Macedonia (Debar).

In the course of 1942, partisans in Slovenia and Dalmatia seized municipalities and their outlying areas, and made every activity by the inhabitants and the occupiers impossible.[1] In September of that year, with so many towns and villages no longer under the control of the Italian authorities, numerous schools could not be opened for the autumn term. Vicious reprisals were visited upon those who failed to obey the orders of the partisans. Native-born workers deserted their jobs *en masse*, while their Italian counterparts pleaded to be repatriated. Bridges, roads, water mains and factories were sabotaged or blown up. Telegraph and telephone installations were wrecked or they functioned only sporadically with makeshift

[1] USSME, M 3, b. 85, 'Bastianini alla PCM e al Ministero dell'Interno', 11 October 1942.

apparatus. Supplies, especially of foodstuffs, grew increasingly intermittent after the summer of 1942.

Work on the electricity power line in Dalmatia between Šibenik and Zadar proceeded very slowly. The town of Zadar received its energy supplies from an antiquated and extremely costly oil-fired generating station. Land clearance and agriculture in Aurana and its district were halted by a total breakdown of security and the constant plundering of crops. It was no longer possible to stock goods or to purchase them for the town markets in the country's interior, where the partisans seized cattle and foodstuffs by force of arms. The industrial undertakings that had sprung up in 1941–2, notably the shipyards of Curzola and a number of construction companies, were forced to cease operations, with severe losses, because the banks could no longer provide them with funding. Routine administrative, economic and political activity ground to a halt because the partisans occupied the countryside around the towns and mounted large-scale operations against them. In the coastal ports, the partisans landed and shipped men and equipment undisturbed.

The situation was equally disastrous in Ljubljana, and on the Ionian islands, the Cyclades and the Sporades, where the civil administrations functioned only fitfully. The forced Italianization of the new provinces was discontinued as a consequence in the summer of 1942. Powers were removed from the civil authorities and transferred to the Italian army. Emblematic is Mussolini's instruction to Mario Roatta: 'If [the high commissioner Grazioli] continues to bother you, send me a letter and I shall write and tell him bluntly that he is not to concern himself with anything apart from administration of the province.'[2] In January 1943 the military authorities took over from civil apparatuses no longer able to perform their functions, and on 10 July all civil powers were assumed by the Supreme Command, which delegated their exercise to the military authorities.[3]

ASCERTAINING ELIGIBILITY FOR CITIZENSHIP, DENATIONALIZATION, FASCISTIZATION AND COLONIZATION

Philippe Burrin has written that an example of how ideology served the Nazi regime's purposes through 'institutional undermining' is provided by the administration of the territories annexed to the Reich, where Hitler had room for manoeuvre on two fronts. On the one hand, installation of an

[2] See Talpo, *Dalmazia*, vol. II, p. 787.

[3] ACS, PCM, 1940–3, 1.1.13.16542.151, 'Ministero dell'Interno – Gabinetto 530–84, Esercizio dei poteri civili nella zona delle operazioni'.

administration largely extraneous to the directives issued by the ministries in Berlin allowed him to pursue a radical policy – for instance on expulsion of 'allogens' or citizens of foreign extraction – without any impediment being raised by what remained of the rule of law in the Reich. On the other hand, the annexed territories were a proving ground for the Nazification of society on a scale broader than that authorized by power relations in the Reich: for example, with the churches. Whereas Stalinism duplicated its structures in its annexed territories, the Nazi regime used its annexed territories for political experimentation, the results of which were to be subsequently applied in the Reich. Expansion was therefore the necessary condition for the transformation of society.[4]

Fascist Italy attempted to do the same in its own annexed territories, but achieved much more modest results. There is an indubitable connection between Italianization and experiments undertaken in the 1920s, when Fascism sought to solve the 'problem of problems', emigration. Those years saw a cross-fertilization among racial demography, eugenics, anthropology and population policy (*Volkstumpolitik*): an intermingling of science and racial policy which bred the racial laws of 1938 and continued during the period 1940–3, when the annexed territories were used for experiments to be transposed into the metropolitan provinces on conclusion of the war.

The Fascist demographic studies of the 1920s were a prelude to the subsequent racial doctrine that transformed the Italians into a 'master race'.[5] Population samples, observed 'scientifically' as if they were human breeding colonies, influenced studies in eugenics, both positive (the discipline which developed the principles of physical hygiene and gave rise to hygiene policy, pre- and post-natal care, child welfare clinics and dietetics) and negative (the German movement that advocated arranged births and marriages and the sterilization of the physically inferior – its most 'illustrious' followers practised constitutional medicine, and its leading representative, Nicola Pende, was one of the authors of the *Manifesto della Razza*). Most recent Italian historiography has convincingly argued that the Italian racial laws were not introduced in belated and hasty emulation of the Nazi policy. Rather, they

[4] Burrin, 'Charisme et radicalisation dans le régime nazi', p. 92.

[5] Ipsen, *Demografia totalitaria*, p. 253: 'Racism was viewed as part of broader demographic policy to which it was institutionally tied.' Initially, the regime's main concern was internal migration, and it created the Commissariato per le Migrazioni e la Colonizzazione and the Comitato Permanente per le Migrazioni Interne. In 1938 Demorazza (the Directorate for Demography and Race) was instituted as the section responsible for demography at the Ministry of the Interior, thereby demonstrating the close connection between demographic and racial policy. The governing council of Demorazza consisted of the presidents of the Istituto Centrale di Statistica, the Opera Nazionale per la Protezione della Maternità e dell'Infanzia and the Ufficio Fascista per le Famiglie Numerose.

were a carefully considered consequence of an independent scientific and ideological tradition.[6] Roberto Maiocchi, author of *Scienza italiana e razzismo fascista*, has analysed the racism of that period's 'scientists', showing that:

> racial doctrine cut across all the medical-biological disciplines and the historical and social sciences. It became – among anthropologists, for example – an explanatory model based on the nineteenth-century tradition. The paradigm was embraced in the 1920s and 1930s by a broad constellation of scientific disciplines and practitioners whose complexity – characterized by the presence of considerable internal nuances and differences – confirms its influence on Italian scientific culture, and contradicts the conventional wisdom that Italian racism was a 'foreign body' belatedly grafted onto that culture by mere political opportunism.[7]

As noted, the forced Italianization of the new provinces had four distinct yet interconnected dimensions:

- the ethnic and racial mapping of eligibility for citizenship (*pertinenza*);
- denationalization, or the erasure of national identity; the internment, transfer and expulsion of non-native-born citizens;[8]
- the Fascistization of the indigenous population, mainly its younger members, through education and 'totalitarian' action by all organs of the state and party;
- the colonization of further provinces.

[6] On Mussolini's racism and on the connection between 'defence of the race', demographic policy and eugenics in the 1920s and 1930s, see Sarfatti, *Gli ebrei nell'Italia fascista.*

[7] Extract from Francesca Cavarocchi's review of Maiocchi, *Scienza italiana e razzismo fascista*. Cavarocchi continues: 'The author dwells on the origins and development of Italian eugenics, showing both its difference from the German and Anglo-Saxon movements and its shaky and confused theoretical foundations. He thus restores complexity to a debate which, despite its obvious limitations, had considerable influence on Italian medicine in the early twentieth century. Although it eschewed the radical conclusions reached in Nazi Germany, Italian eugenics helped form Fascist racial policy by combining pro-natalism with the organicist campaign to improve the Italian race. Maiocchi also examines demography at the time . . . Once again he shows how nativism performed an evident political function by legitimating Fascist imperialism as the natural outlet for a "young" and expanding race. The long chapter on the ethno-anthropological sciences rightly emphasizes (though perhaps with some simplifications) that Italian population research prevalently rejected the biological paradigm and Aryanist racism but then resumed that same biological racism when its attention turned to African ethnic groups. Of great interest . . . is his discussion on the role of studies of classical antiquity in generating the rhetoric of Romanity and extolling proto-historic Italy as the crucible of a superior racial stock – a theme of central importance to Fascist ideology.' It is incorrect to claim that 'the biological-materialist version was largely uninfluential in Italy, for although the hierarchization of mental characteristics on physical-somatic bases was ill suited to describing the features and establishing the superiority of the "Italic race", it was nevertheless one of the main reasons for the large body of theoretical-propagandistic studies that accompanied and sustained the rise and fall of Fascist colonialism', also – I would add – in the territories annexed during the Second World War.

[8] Montandon, 'Trapianti etnici', 1940.

How many inhabitants did the annexed territories have? For the Italian authorities, answering the question was the prerequisite for controlling and organizing those territories. After the annexations, Mussolini ordered the president of ISTAT (the Central Statistical Institute), Franco Rodolfo Savorgnan, to have the next statistical bulletin include Ljubljana, the three Dalmatian provinces and the territories annexed to Fiume. Savorgnan replied that it was impossible to quantify the current populations of the new provinces, although the data collected by the Yugoslavian census of 1931 were available for the Italian authorities to use (see appendix, table 2). Population censuses were conducted in July 1941 and March 1942, by which time registry offices were already operating in all the annexed Yugoslavian territories. On 15 December, on the promptings of Giuseppe Bastianini, the Ministry of the Interior dispatched twenty-one municipal secretaries to conduct censuses of the population, verify birth certificates and compile municipal registers in the three provinces. Similar measures were introduced by the High Commission of Ljubljana, the prefecture of Fiume and the consular authorities in Croatia, Serbia, Albania and Montenegro.

Who was allowed to reside in the annexed territories? Native-born residents of Dalmatia, San Marino, Menton, Malta, Corsica, and Canton Ticino and Canton Grisons were *italiani non regnicoli* – that is, persons born in territories who were 'ethnically Italian but politically not part of the kingdom' – and they had privileges (compared to other foreigners) in regard to marriage, the acquisition of citizenship, public-sector employment and military service. However, these privileges did not give automatic entitlement to Italian citizenship.[9] The inhabitants of Dalmatia were no longer classified as *italiani non regnicoli* after the annexations, because the principle of *pertinenza* (eligibility for citizenship) was introduced when the new provinces became part of the Kingdom of Italy. Bastianini drafted a law which, by combining *jus soli* and *jus sanguinis*, became *lex lata* for Dalmatia and the province of Ljubljana. His intention was to select a limited number of autochthons in the *piccolo spazio* and grant them the right to live together with the *etnia imperiale*. According to Bastianini's draft law, the following categories were eligible for citizenship, provided there was no political or penal impediment against it: persons born in the annexed territories of a father also born in those territories; persons resident therein or in another part of the kingdom; those resident for at least fifteen years in

[9] In October 1941 the Foreign Ministry asked for Savoy to be included on the list. The document refers the PCM circular no. 4872 of 12 June 1936: see Bottiglioni, 'Italiani in dominio straniero', 1941.

the same territory or who had owned real estate there for at least ten years; those deemed eligible for reasons of outstanding merit; those born within the borders of the annexed provinces but resident abroad for justified and demonstrable reasons; and those who could prove Italian parentage to the third remove.

If *pertinenza* was established, the successful applicant was required to transfer his residence to within the kingdom's borders, and *pertinenza* was extended to his wife and minor-age children. The authorities could revoke such eligibility at any time before three years had elapsed from the end of the war.[10] However, even if an application were granted, a passport or a certificate of citizenship was not issued automatically: ascertaining *pertinenza* served to screen the population and to divide it into those individuals in favour of Fascism and those hostile to it.[11] Successful applicants were issued with a receipt of enrolment on the register. They obtained a sort of 'provisional citizenship' similar to that of the inhabitants of the Aegean possessions and mentioned in chapter 2.[12] The prefects and the high commissioner were authorized to exclude from the *pertinenti* register even individuals who fulfilled every requirement. The Ministry of the Interior had wanted collective citizenship to be granted to the Dalmatians, but Bastianini – urged by politicians from Venezia Giulia who feared invasion of the region by 'Slavs with Italian passports' – strenuously opposed the proposal. A dispute ensued which left the question in limbo until 15 February 1943, when, in the Camera dei Fasci e Corporazioni, Mussolini, that 'polycratic arbiter', sided with the ministry but also mollified Bastianini by declaring that the prefects were authorized to revoke the 'citizenship of persons unworthy of it'. Procedures to ascertain *pertinenza* got under way on 8 September 1943.

[10] ASMAE, AA.PP. – Italia, 1939–45, b. 77, 'Schema del provvedimento legislativo concernente l'acquisto della cittadinanza italiana da parte degli ex sudditi jugoslavi, residenti od originari dei nuovi territori (provincia di Lubiana, Dalmazia, zona fiumana) annessi al Regno (in allegato al caso Orlic Alessandra, 8 marzo 1943)'. B. 77, 'telespresso 34/r 3102/771, MAE – AA.GG. IV al Ministero dell'Interno – Ufficio Passaporti', also contains the complete text of the bill (attached to the 'Lah Dusan Case').

[11] ACS, PCM, 1.1.13.16542.14.40, 'governatore della Dalmazia alla PCM', 29 May 1942, 'Questione della cittadinanza'.

[12] ASMAE, GABAP, b. 44, DGAC – Ufficio IV, 5 February 1942, 'circolare 0003, Passaporti provvisori ai cittadini ex jugoslavi originari delle nuove province': 'Save in exceptional cases Italian passports are issued to persons in possession of Italian citizenship. Consequently, because the necessary legislative measures relative to the citizenship of persons originally from the territories in question have not yet been enacted, such persons cannot be issued with a standard national passport.' Point 3 of the circular specifies that 'originally' applies to those born in the territories in question, of a father also born in those territories, and in possession of Yugoslavian nationality at the time of annexation. On the census, see Ipsen, *Demografia totalitaria*, p. 298.

There are no reliable figures on the number of *pertinenti* (those eligible to apply for Italian nationality: henceforth 'eligibles') in each province (see appendix, tables 44–5). Considering the stringent criteria and the determination of the Italian authorities to restrict the number of eligibles to the greatest extent possible, it is likely that there were rather few of them. Moreover, the ethnic-racial mapping of the annexed territories also served the purpose of justifying expulsion of refugees who had crossed the borders of the new provinces. Only in one circumstance (for reasons explained in the final chapter), relative to certain Jewish refugees, did assessment of *pertinenza* serve to delay their consignment to the German authorities for deportation to eastern Europe.

Besides generating a centrifugal population movement (expulsions, resettlements, internments), establishment of *pertinenza* gave rise to a centripetal one whose consequences were not given due consideration by the Italian authorities. The Zagreb government referred to the criteria used by the Italians in their annexed territories to expel all Slovenes from Ljubljana, and it obliged those originally from the German zones who remained to take out Croatian nationality.[13]

A series of police measures made it difficult for eligibles to gain access to the kingdom. For example, citizens of the province of Ljubljana who were resident abroad and wished to enter that province had to apply to the consulate for a permit issued by the high commissioner, and then replace their old Yugoslavian passports with provisional Italian ones, or have the old ones stamped as 'Valid in every effect as a passport issued to an Italian citizen'. Residents in Dalmatia before its annexation were allowed to move freely among towns in the same province, but in order to travel to another province they had to obtain written authorization from the prefect. Residents intending to enter the governorate of Dalmatia had to apply to the governor for authorization: their applications, which were forwarded to the appropriate police station, had to state, besides personal details and occupation, the purpose and duration of the visit, give information about the applicant's moral and political conduct, and, for tradesmen and manufacturers, carry a statement by the competent trade-union office attesting to their commercial or industrial rectitude and solidity. Workers had to obtain permission from the commissioner for migration and colonization which was written on their passports or travel permits.

In parallel with the ethnic mapping of the annexed territories, the regime began to 'cleanse them' of all 'harmful or undesirable elements'. The

[13] ACS, MI – DGPS, AA.GG.RR., 1942, b. 8, 3 February 1942.

guidelines for Italianization of the new provinces had been established by Mussolini in a speech delivered to the Camera dei Fasci e delle Corporazioni on 10 June 1941, in which he declared that 'states must strive to realize the maximum of their ethnic and spiritual unity so that the three elements of race, nation and state come to coincide'. According to Mussolini, annexing too many 'alloglots' was an error, save in exceptional cases like Slovenia, where it was necessary for reasons of security and strategy. 'Special treatment' should be reserved for 'allogenic' ethnic groups subject to annexation, provided they demonstrated their 'absolute loyalty to the state': otherwise, 'when ethnicity conflicts with geography, it is the ethnic group that must be moved; population exchanges and forced exodus are providential'.[14]

Zealously following Mussolini's lead, and 'working towards the Duce', ambassador Raffaele Casertano announced that Serbs and Jews in Dalmatia must be 'sent to camps in Sicily' and that the irredentist authorities of Split must be expelled.[15] The PNF federal inspector in Albania, Pietro Almerigogna, proposed that non-native Slav residents in the new provinces and those present in the kingdom be allowed to opt for expatriation on surrender of their property. Suspect or undesirable persons would be transferred, and the conveyancing of property between Italians and Slavs would be prohibited. Only Italians were to be employed in the civil service, and Italian would be the only language used in public offices and on public transport. Priests were to deliver their sermons in Italian and wear the cassock and the Roman hat. Surnames and place names were to be Italianized and the resettlement of Italian households in border zones was to be encouraged.[16] Hence, not only party officials but also civil servants at the Foreign Ministry, despite their different experiences and cultural backgrounds, concurred that ethnic homogeneity must be imposed upon Italy's new provinces.

Governor Bastianini took action on 18 July 1941. He ordered the expulsion – within fifteen days – of all Yugoslavian public officials, an order which provoked panic among the hundreds of Croats whose offices had not yet been evacuated from Split.[17] Bastianini justified his order on the grounds that the offices of the former *espositura* (an ecclesiastical district) were obsolete and that the civil service was in urgent need of renewal. First expelled were officials ineligible for Italian citizenship or who, even if eligible, were

[14] Sala, 'Occupazione militare e amministrazione civile nella provincia di Lubiana', p. 78.

[15] ASMAE, GABAP, b. 28, 'Casertano a Pietromarchi', handwritten letter, 1 August 1941.

[16] ASMAE, GABAP, b. 45, 'PNF – Direttorio nazionale (segretario del partito Adelchi Serena) al MAE', 29 July 1941.

[17] ACS, PCM, 1940–3, G 9/1 12860, 'governatore della Dalmazia'.

deemed not of sufficient political reliability to be allowed to remain in their posts. A special committee determined the staffing requirements of the new administrative apparatuses and ordered the early retirement of redundant personnel. Expulsion orders were served on more than 50 per cent of Yugoslavian civil servants, the majority of them Croats (although how many actually left the annexed territories is not known). On the other hand, there were a number of *funzionari non pertinenti* who continued to work for the Italian administration, being paid from special funds, not as state employees. To ensure the co-operation of the civil servants who remained, Bastianini ordered that they were to swear oaths of loyalty to the Italian state. He also announced that in no circumstance could the governorate guarantee employment or eventual Italian citizenship (priests were also obliged to swear the oath of loyalty).

The governor then set about purging 'entire sectors of the populations of the three provinces under his authority: railway workers, nurses and doctors'. Ordinance no. 41 of 4 November 1941, which regulated enrolment on the professional register for legal practitioners in Dalmatia, forbade registration by those without Italian citizenship and 'equated' only *pertinenti* with Italian citizens. According to figures compiled by the secretaries of the Fascist organizations and by the police – reports Dragovan Sepić – a large number of Dalmatian lawyers were struck off the professional register because they were classified as Croats or Serbs. Similar ordinances were issued for notaries, doctors, veterinary surgeons, pharmacists, artists, tradesmen and street traders. The governor urged the rapid transfer to Croatia of all the male religious orders with lower houses on Croatian territory and monasteries in the three provinces of Dalmatia, and all Franciscan friars (except for those at the monastery of Saint Francis in Zadar). Bastianini accused the religious orders of being 'ferociously anti-Italian' and announced that he was minded to expel them *en masse*. He added that the Italian friars, especially the Franciscans, could have taken the place of all those zealots who offended Italy and Christ and disrupted the public order.[18]

Italianization of the new provinces by means of totalitarian methods proved impossible. The endeavour to create 'ethnically pure' administrations paralysed the principal administrative departments, and the problem soon arose of finding a sufficient number of civil servants not of 'Slav race'

[18] Sepić, 'La politique italienne d'occupation en Dalmatie', pp. 390–1; ASMAE, GABAP, b. 47, 3 July 1941, 'Religiosi in Dalmazia'. On 8 July the governor suggested the creation in Zadar of a single religious authority – an Italian metropolitan – who would ensure compliance with religious (and political) directives within Dalmatia. The metropolitan would have had authority over the bishoprics of Šibenik, Split and Kotor and the archbishopric of Zadar.

The regime endeavoured to give strikingly concrete form to the *Italianità* of the occupied territories in France by changing place names and planning large-scale public works which would parade Fascist Italy's imperialist ambitions.

Giuseppe Frediani, former PNF federal secretary in Verona and then Pavia, was sent to Menton as civil commissioner and tasked with drawing up plans to rebuild the town and give it a markedly Fascist appearance.

The plans were officially presented in the form of elaborate photomontages assembled by Frediani's friend, the photographer Giuseppe Chiolini. They were then collected into a large album, *Mentone dalla Ricostruzione alla Rinascita,* intended not only to illustrate the technical aspects of the 'reconstruction' but also to demonstrate the regime's political and administrative vision for the recently conquered territories.

Chiolini's 'photographic mosaics' comprise everyday images in strident contrast with the reality of the ongoing conflict. Juxtaposed with violent war propaganda are tourist publicity for the 'Costa Azzurra di Mentone', shop signs changed into Italian, and posters for theatre performances. There are announcements of bicycle races organized by the National Working-Men's Guild, activities by the Comitato di Tradizioni Mentonasche created to assert the town's *Italianità*, folk events and the presence of Menton's civil administration at the Milan Fair of March 1942.

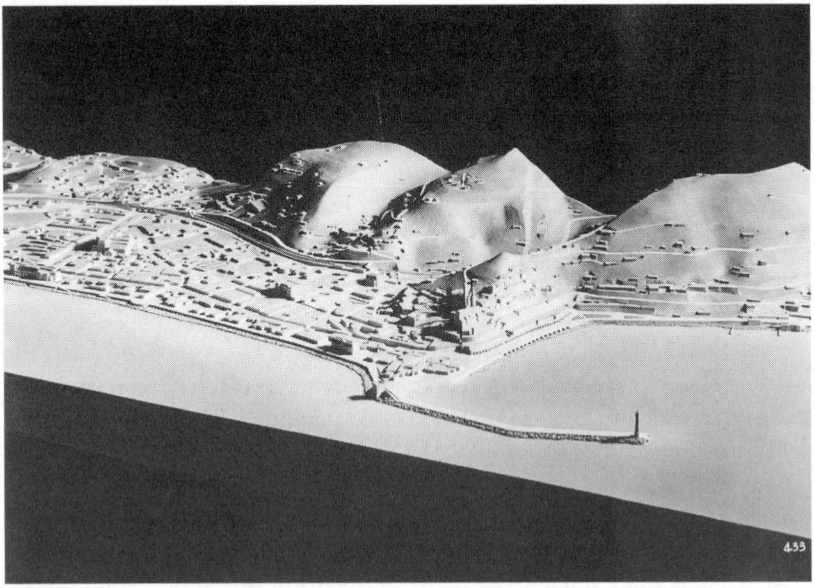

Figure 1. Relief map of the Fascist urban renewal plan for Menton produced by the Milan firm Primo Stabilimento Plastigrafico Italiano (Archivio Fotografico, ISR, Pavia, Fondo Frediani).

Figure 2–11. Pages from the photograph album illustrating the Fascist 'reconstruction' of Menton, *Mentone dalla Ricostruzione alla Rinascita* (Archivio Fotografico, ISR, Pavia, Fondo Frediani).

Figure 3.

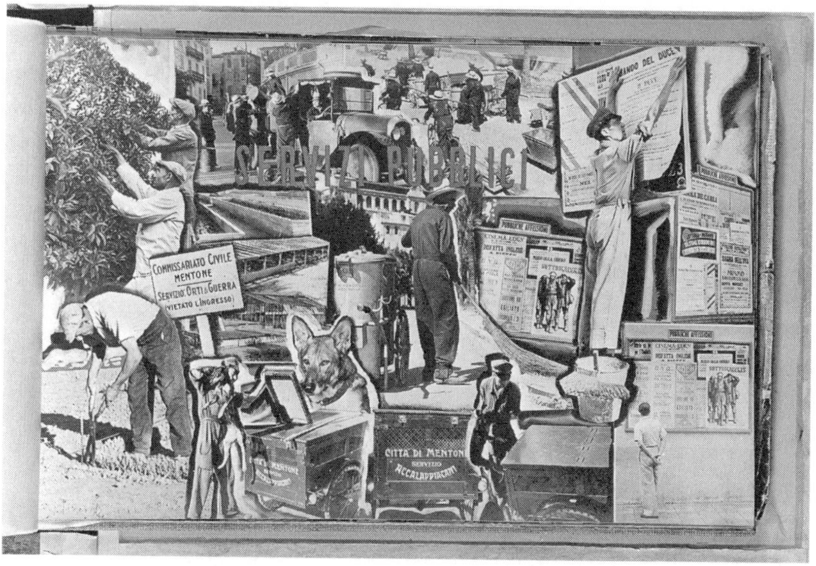

Figure 4.

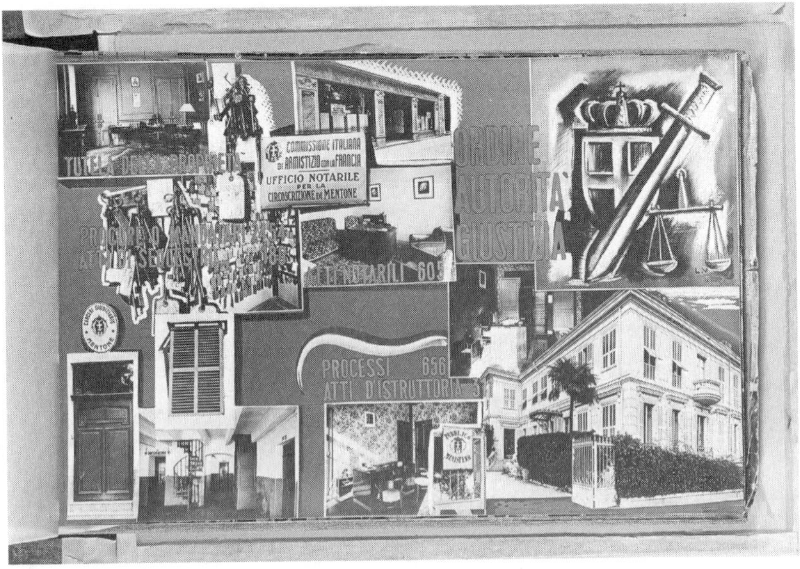

Figure 5.

Figures 6.

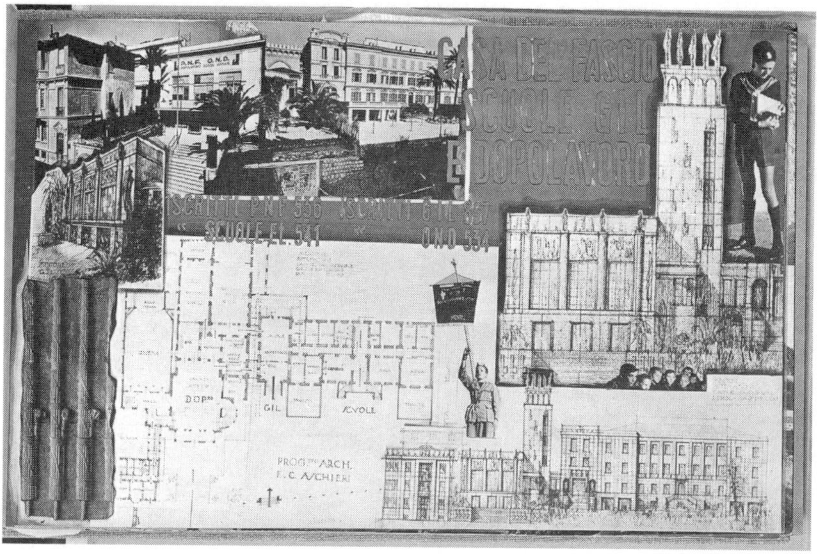

Figure 7.

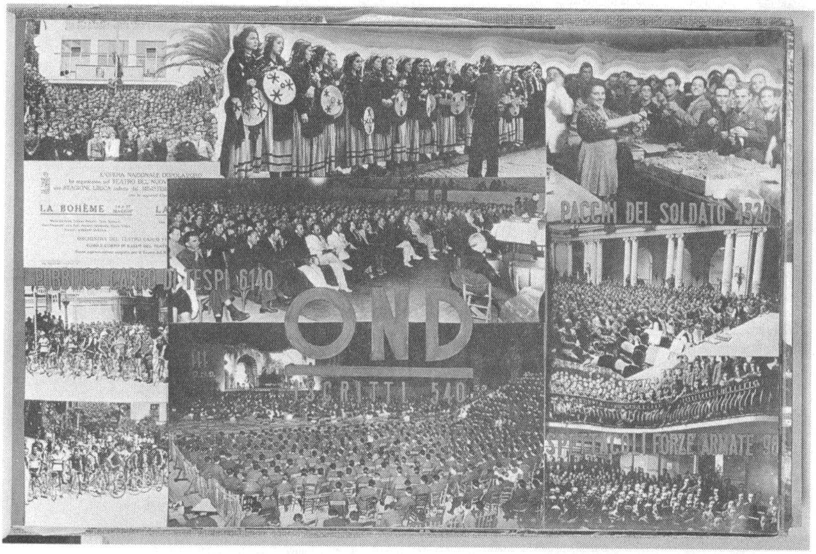

Figure 8.

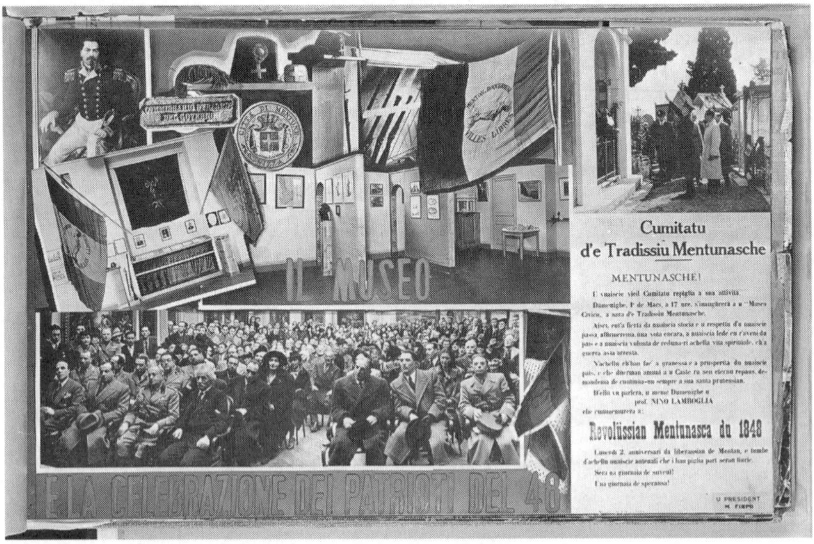

Figure 9.

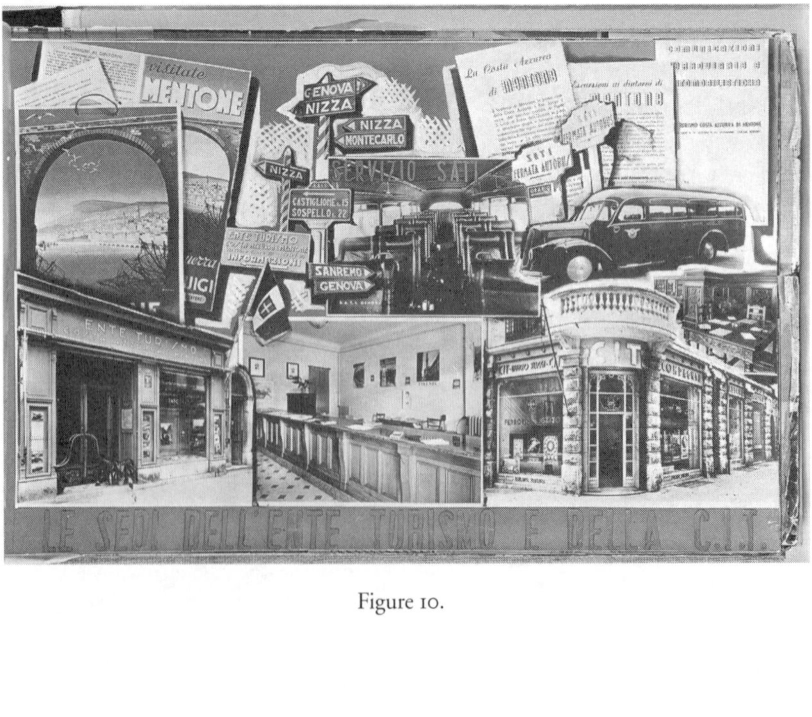

Figure 10.

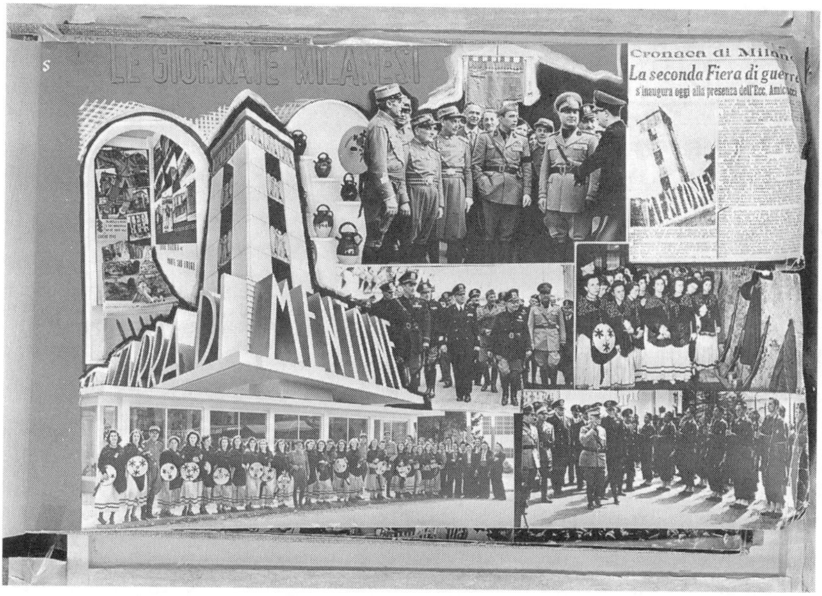
LE GIORNATE MILANESI
Cronaca di Milan
La seconda Fiera di guerr
s'inaugura oggi alla presenza dell'Ecc. Amic
MENTONE

Figure 11.

LJUBLJANA

The most systematic photographic record of the Italian and German occupation of Yugoslavia was compiled by reporters working for the Ljubljana newspapers, most notably Miran Pavlin and Jakob Prešeren, who took more than 2,500 snapshots (some of them in colour). But also valuable was the work of amateur photographers. A number of laboratories – for example, the studios of Josip Pelikan at Celje and Šelhaus at Škofja Loka – were commissioned by the occupiers to develop photographs, and they surreptitiously made copies of images documenting the most odious aspects of the occupation (reprisals and mass murders). These images were collected after the war by the photograph library of the Muzej Novejše Zgodovine (MNZ) of Ljubljana.

Figure 12. Ljubljana, 12 April 1941. Entry of the Italian troops into the city. The photograph was taken outside the Moderno Galerijo by Miran Pavlin, a correspondent for the *Jutro* newspaper (photograph collection, MNZ).

Figure 13. Ljubljana, 3 May 1941. Portraits of Mussolini and Victor Emmanuel III were affixed to walls and displayed in shop windows to celebrate annexation of the province of Ljubljana to Italy (photograph by Stane Zalokar, MNZ).

Figure 14. Immediately after occupation, Fascist slogans were painted on the walls of buildings throughout the province of Ljubljana (photograph by Miran Pavlin, MNZ).

Figure 15. Ljubljana, 1941. Residents queueing outside the National Bank to change their money into Italian currency. Photograph by Jakob Prešeren, who also took the only known set of colour photographs of the city during occupation (MNZ).

Figure 16. Ljubljana, 1941. Workers chisel the Slovene inscription from the façade of the commercial high school. The inscriptions on all the city's principal buildings were removed in the same way (photograph by Miran Pavlin, MNZ).

Figure 17. Ljubljana, 1941. The Italianization campaign involved the mass circulation of Italian newspapers and magazines (photograph by Jakob Prešeren, MNZ).

Figure 18. Ljubljana, November 1941. Call by the Resistance to boycott Italian theatre performances (photograph by Miran Pavlin, MNZ).

Figure 19. All trees within a distance of 100 metres from roads were cut down to prevent partisan ambushes (MNZ).

ATHENS

Between 1941 and 1944, the Greek journalist Kostas Paraschos, who worked for the Athens newspaper *Proia*, took around 850 photographs of everyday life under the Italian and German occupiers. On publishing a selection of his photographs in 1997, he wrote: 'I decided to take photographs to supplement my work with the underground press. I began with a little pocket camera, but I soon met almost unsurmountable obstacles. It was extremely difficult to find film and the equipment that I needed to develop it. And then the occupiers had banned not only travel and free movement by Greeks but even the taking of photographs . . . I kept my camera constantly at the ready in the rear pocket of my trousers or the inside pocket of my coat. I tried to snap anything that might be of interest, everything that testified to the occupation and the changes that it had made to our lives . . . I took photographs on the run, literally stealing them without being noticed. Not even my friends knew what I was doing . . . I shall never forget how an elderly passer-by in the Exarchia quarter swore at me obscenely when he saw me photographing a man half dead from hunger lying on the pavement . . . I did not use either a photometer or special lenses to take my photographs but relied solely on my experience. I developed my films myself, without the temperatures required by the chemical products . . . I developed almost all my films but I did not print them' (*E khatokhe*, pp. 7–9; the quotations captioning the photos that follow are from the same source).

Figure 20. 'Panespistiumi Street, outside the National Library. People scavenge through garbage in a desperate search for something to eat' (p. 40). 'Little by little famine took its toll . . . The occupying troops had to feed off the land, but the Greek land could not be cultivated as before. So numerous foodstuffs became unobtainable . . . People weakened by hunger fainted in the street and passers-by would hurry to help them. But then the sight became routine, and more and more people collapsed to the ground. Their helpers could no longer tell whether they were alive or dead. Passing Italian or German soldiers ascertained death by giving the poor bodies a kick. Another common sight was people picking through rubbish for something to eat, or anything that would fill their stomachs. And their hunger and misery soon made them victims to disease' (p. 39).

Figure 21. 'Here's a man happy at finding lots of dustbins to scavenge. He's sure to find something' (p. 43).

Figure 22. Kallidromou: a man lies exhausted on the pavement (p. 47).

Figure 23. '"Pedio tu Areos" (Field of Mars) on a fine winter's day: the little boy has found something' (p. 66).

Figure 24. Panepistimiou, outside the Tsitas pastry shop: people queueing to enter a soup kitchen.

Figure 25. 'Family portrait. But where is the father?' (p. 72).

Figure 26. 'Who will look after this small child in Athinas Street?' A poster offering rewards for wanted Greek patriots is affixed to the wall. 'The city woke up in the mornings to the sight of the rigid corpses of hunger victims in many of its streets (especially during the winter). The municipal lorries previously used to collect rubbish were now sent to clear the neighbourhoods of corpses. They took them to the mortuary in Massilias Street . . . where they made a horrific spectacle. All those corpses heaped in the open-backed vehicles were almost an image from hell. How can one describe such horror? Words like bestial, barbaric, wicked, cruel are too bland to convey the reality of the spectacle . . . The first to find a body would remove its shoes and any decent clothing, and the food ration book if it could be found' (p. 77).

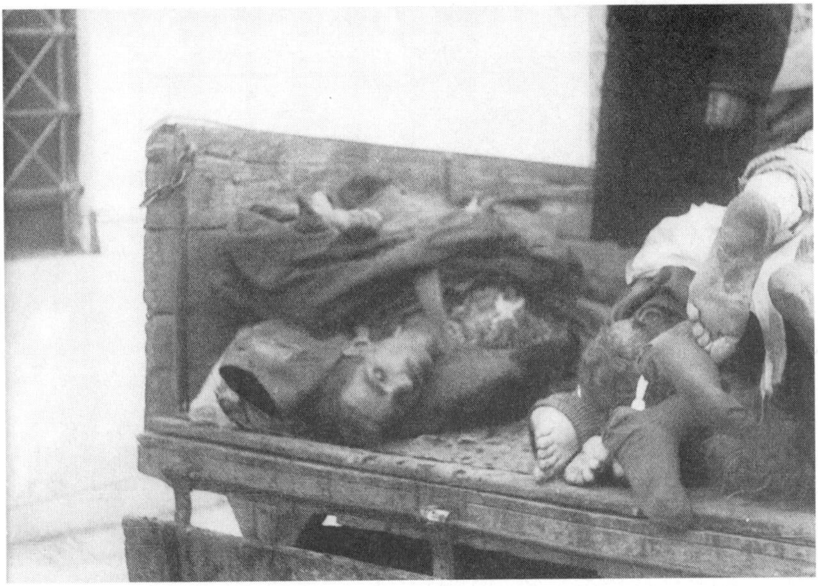

Figure 27. 'How could a sight like this be stomached? Many passers-by crossed the street' (p. 79).

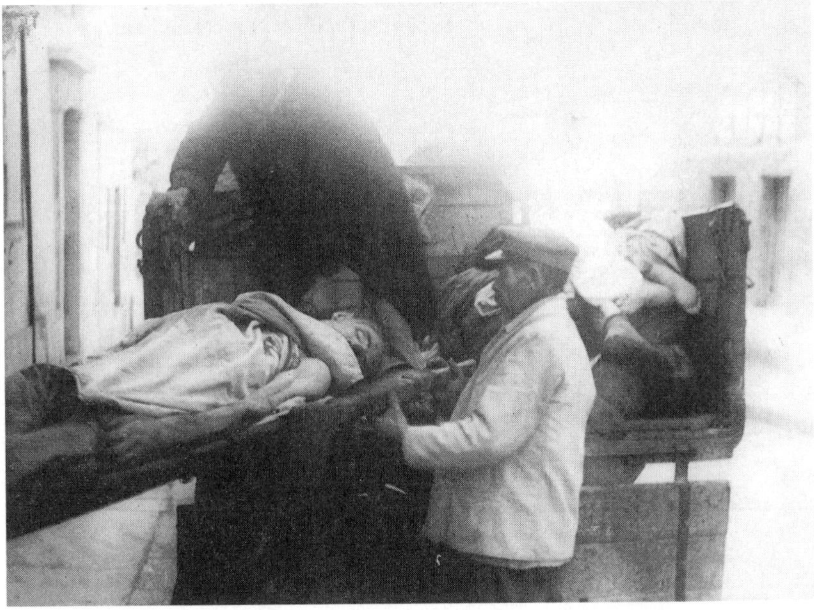

Figure 28. 'Municipal workers attend to their dreadful task' (p. 80).

ALBANIA, MONTENEGRO, SLOVENIA

From the personal photograph collection of Mario Camera (Novi Ligure, 8 September 1916–Novara, 1 December 1973), a sergeant in the Bassano Battalion, Pusteria Division, Alpine Regiment. Camera's unit was deployed first in Albania and then in Montenegro, where it mounted numerous operations against the partisans. Between 1940 and 1942, Camera used a Leica to take numerous photographs which graphically convey the everyday realities of the occupation. Unfortunately, however, no chronological information appears on the prints. Because Camera died many years ago, the photographs have been dated by drawing upon the memories of his family members. The negatives are conserved at Novara by Camera's son, Luciano.

Figure 29. Albania, 1941. A group of civilians set up a small market close to an Italian command post. They watch the soldier photographing them with a mixture of curiosity and fear, as shown by the woman standing at the door on the right of the picture. Provisional street signs, commercial advertisements and propaganda posters have been nailed to the wooden walls of the shop on the corner.

Figure 30. Montenegro, Crmnica area, July 1941. A group of men of various ages, in civilian clothing and carrying a white flag, surrender to the Bassano Battalion.

Figure 31. Montenegro, Crmnica area, July 1941. A group of men, of various ages, parley with officers of the Bassano Battalion (Neg. XI, fot. 10).

Figure 32. Montenegro, 1941. Command post of a Bassano Battalion company. A group of soldiers pose at the mess table with a local girl employed by the command. Communication dockets hang from the shelves among domestic utensils (Neg. X, fot. 35).

Figure 33. Montenegro, 1941. The mess (Neg. XI, fot. 32a).

Figures 34–5. Montenegro, 1941. Theatre show put on for the troops at the Bassano Battalion camp (Neg. III, fot. 12A and 10A).

Figure 35.

Figure 36. Outside Pljevlja, winter 1941–2. A halt in the woods during a round-up operation conducted jointly with a band of Četniks (Neg. VI, fot. 6a).

Figure 37. Outside Pljevlja, winter 1941–2. A band of Četniks line up outside a partly destroyed building for the funeral of a comrade killed during an anti-partisan operation conducted jointly with the Bassano Battalion. Note the formation's banner with the skull and crossbones in the foreground, and the typical fur busbies worn by the Četniks (Neg. VIII, fot. 6a).

Figure 38. Outside Pljevlja, 1941. Corpse of a member of the Bassano Battalion killed by partisans on his way to visit a woman at night (Neg. V, fot. 5a).

Figure 39. Outside Pljevlja, 1941. A village burned in reprisal by the Bassano Battalion (Neg. XI, fot. 3).

Figure 40. Eighteen photographs were found in the pockets of Italian soldiers captured by Yugoslav partisans. Giuseppe Piemontese appended them to his study *Ventinove mesi di occupazione italiana nella provincia di Lubiana* 1946. Among them was this tragic image of mass murder committed at an unknown location in Slovenia.

Figure 41. 500 Ionian drachmas, 1942 issue (from Crapanzano, *Soldi d'Italia*).

to run them. The prefect of Fiume, Temistocle Testa, admitted that without sufficient personnel it would be impossible to install an administrative system similar to that of the kingdom's municipalities. The under-secretary of the interior, Guido Buffarini Guidi, estimated that 1,052 posts were vacant in Dalmatia and Slovenia.[19] However, the ministries could supply only a very small number of officials, many of them without the necessary training. The Roman bureaucracy was utterly inefficient and the ministries were incompetent.[20] A census was conducted of all officials of Dalmatian origin working at the Rome ministries, and arrangements were made for them to be sent to the governorate. The results were disastrous. Bastianini reported that suitable employment could not even be found for those few Dalmatian officials who actually arrived in the governorate, and he suggested that the Ministry of the Interior should carefully appraise their abilities before dispatching them.[21] The civil authorities in all the annexed territories had to rely on native-born administrative personnel who, in theory, should have been expelled or transferred. The governorate and the High Commission reacted to the paralysis of the civil service by delaying Italianization, or by employing measures which increasingly differed from the original intentions. The figures are eloquent: by November 1942 MINCULPOP had despatched seven Dalmatian officials, the Ministry of Agriculture and Forestry ten and the Ministry of Trade and Exchange only one, while all the other ministries had sent around twenty. None of the ministerial officials of Dalmatian origin expressed any desire to return to their country of origin.

In Ljubljana, Emilio Grazioli divided the provincial executive into sections run 'on the principle of autonomy' by Slovene directors but supervised by Italian 'experts' at the offices for Slovene personnel (Fabrizio Boggiano-Pico), for German emigration (also Boggiano-Pico), for currency exchange (Arnaldo Rizzi, then Angelo Manfredini), for the economy (Carlo Scala), the technical office (Bruno Alivotti), and for transfer and settlement (Mario Zinna): 'There were more offices with Italian directors than sections with Slovene ones.' There was a shortage of middle-level officials – the backbone of the bureaucracy. In compliance with directives received from the Duce, Grazioli maintained former Yugoslavian civil servants in service – only later

[19] ACS, MI, ACP, 1935–47, b. 5176, 'Fiume e territori aggregati alla provincia di Fiume, prot. 1324/Tr, 28 febbraio 1942, Richiesta di personale per i territori annessi al Ministero dell'Interno, firmato il prefetto Testa'.

[20] ASMAE, GABAP, bb. 52–3, 'richiesta di Serafino Mazzolini al Ministero dell'Interno per l'invio di dieci funzionari di PS che parlassero serbo': Mazzolini, civil governor in Montenegro, was told that his request could not be granted in view of the Duce's order to create new mobile battalions.

[21] ACS, PCM, 1.1.13.16542.14.26, 'Ministero delle Corporazioni alla PCM, 5 febbraio 1943, Destinazione in Dalmazia del personale di origine dalmata'.

were they dismissed or pensioned off – and the high commissioner was also obliged to keep more than 2,300 Slovenian civil servants in their posts (see appendix, table 46).[22] The administrations of the new provinces also sought to recruit officials from the small Italian communities and from previous employees at the Italian consulates before the war.[23] A search was made in Fiume, Trieste and Gorizia for personnel with technical and language skills – a difficult task given the large number of Italians who had been drafted into military service and the small number of those with suitable qualifications. The only unconscripted Italian resident of Ljubljana was Niccolò Tramontana (born in Lissa), an official at the Ministry of Justice and latterly attaché at the Civil Affairs Department in Ljubljana. Well versed in Austrian law, and a speaker of Slovene, Croatian and German, Tramontana was a rare bird indeed!

The political and administrative purging of the annexed provinces was flanked by attempts to erase their Slav and Habsburg pasts: the names of towns and squares were changed, monuments were demolished, the institutions of the previous regime were abolished and the laws and organs of the Italian state were forcibly transposed. Bastianini banned all political and cultural associations and sports clubs not controlled by the PNF. He imposed Italian as the official language of the civil service, law courts and the ecclesiastical administration. He ordered the nationalization of public (i.e., Yugoslav) and private enterprises, and the immediate beginning of public works which served eminently political purposes. Bastianini wrote: 'The depressing spectacle of neglect contrasted with the Duce's determination to rejuvenate these lands.' He asked for 190 million lire to be allocated for a variety of purposes – reducing the unemployment rate, improving sanitation – and for the resumption of other public works (the harbour installations at Šibenik and the Firule Hospital in Split, as well as schools, roads, cemeteries and sewers), thus creating employment for some thousands of workers and improving the living conditions both material and, 'why not, moral of a large mass of people'.[24]

At the end of the first year following annexation, the governor drew up a balance sheet of his activities and explained that he had proceeded

[22] Ferenc, *La provincia 'italiana' di Lubiana*, p. 45: 25 officials worked in the Customs Service, 130 for the Financial Inspectorate, 150 at the Justice Inspectorate, 19 at the State Monopoly Agency, 43 at the National Theatre of Ljubljana, 61 at the Royal University, 10 at the Royal Academy of Music, 5 at the National Museum, 270 for the Post and Telephone Office, 1,059 at the School Board and 7 at Police Headquarters, besides railway workers and gendarmes; the total was 2,344.

[23] ACS, MI, ACP, 1935–47, b. 5196, 'Spalato'.

[24] ACS, PCM, 1.1.13.16542.14, 30 December 1941, 'Costruzione e manutenzione di opere pubbliche, Bastianini alla PCM e al Ministero delle Finanze'.

with 'the work of penetration, and of assimilating the administrative life of these lands to that of the motherland'. Every decision, he wrote, from the levying of taxes to the cancelling of mortgages on state property, had been taken to complete the process of transposing the laws of the kingdom. To that end, provincial councils had been created and auxiliary state agencies introduced: for instance, the province as an administrative unit, with all its peripheral apparatus.

In Slovenia, Grazioli transplanted the main welfare and social security provisions in force in the kingdom. On 26 December 1941, the fundamental laws of the Italian state were extended to cover the annexed territories: the Statute, the law on the powers vested in the head of government; the 1926 law on executive power to enact legislation; the law on the Fascist Grand Council; the statute of the PNF; and the statute of the Camera dei Fasci e delle Corporazioni. There was to be no further misunderstanding as to the real extent of Slovene autonomy: it was a mere propaganda device and it was to remain a dead letter.

The fact that the kingdom's fundamental laws were introduced into the new provinces did not signify that the process of substitution and integration was complete. Both in Dalmatia and Slovenia, the regime placed almost exclusive reliance on provincial legislation consisting of ordinances and decrees issued by the governor, the prefects or the high commissioner. On 1 April 1942, Bastianini proudly announced that the last remnants of the Yugoslavian administration had been 'eliminated', but he omitted to mention that chaos reigned in the local administrations.[25] For example, an ordinance of 15 October 1942 stated that Italian was to be the official language for all civil and criminal trials, with the consequence that judicial activity immediately came to a halt at courts where no one spoke Italian. The ordinance started from the erroneous assumption that it was only necessary to increase the already 'extremely widespread knowledge of our language' in the Dalmatian provinces. The Italian authorities were exceedingly ill informed, however, for there was no truth to their assertion that 'the few non-Italian speakers [could speak] the Venetian dialect of Dalmatia'.[26]

In regard to Italianization policies, mention should also be made of the transfer of the German minorities resident in the province of Ljubljana and in Dalmatia. While Bastianini had been ruthless in his treatment of

[25] An appendix in Missoni, *Luci ed ombre sulle Dinariche*, 1942, contains the full text of Bastianini's speech delivered on 12 April 1942 in Zadar.

[26] ASMAE, GABAP, b. 48, 'console generale d'Italia Amedeo Mammalella al Commissariato civile per il Montenegro', 21 May 1941.

the Croat civil servants of Dalmatia, taking the unilateral decision to have them expelled immediately and without compensation, in the case of the German minorities Berlin applied pressure on the junior partner to organize their speedy transfer.[27] The Germans also made arrangements for the few *Volksdeutschen* living in Dalmatia to leave the Italian zone without delay. Reichsführer Greifelt, appointed by the German government to deal with questions concerning the repatriation of German citizens, organized the emigration of around 900 of them resident in Dalmatia. Their transfer took place in the absence of a formal agreement, and their property was liquidated privately.

In August 1941, Italy and Germany concluded a treaty which stipulated that the *Volksdeutschen* of the province of Ljubljana – the majority of whom lived in the town of Kočevje (Gottschee) – would be offered the option of resettling in the part of Slovenia incorporated into the Reich: the zone of Brežice (from which an equal number of native residents would be deported to Croatia). The option was taken up by around 13,500 persons and their transfer was completed in 1942. Some 12,500 people left the town of Kočevje, while the total number of transferees from the province was 15,800.[28] Germany obtained compensation for the Germans who had left Italian Slovenia and, although not recognizing the *quid pro quo* principle, paid compensation to the approximately 17,000 refugee Slovenes in the Italian zone who had left all their property behind in German territory, and to the natives of Italian Slovenia who owned property in the German zone.[29] According to the High Commission, the town and land abandoned by the Kočevje Germans would be 'repopulated' with 'Slovene elements from the zones in the province of Ljubljana'.[30]

Turning the possessions into Italian provinces required more than *pertinenza* and denationalization, however. Essential for the purpose was the Fascistization of the eligibles, a task to be performed by the schools and by

27 USSME, M 3, b. 55, 'Comando II Armata – ufficio ≪I≫, 20 maggio 1941, Notizario 12': 'Intense German pressure continues to provoke the exodus from the zones occupied [by the Germans] of persons either hostile or indifferent to Nazism. The pressure is applied mainly to the clergy and professionals. Still active is nationalist propaganda among the Germans resident in the district of Kočevje and Novo Mesto.'

28 ACS, PCM, 1940–3, cart. 1.1.13.8204 1–13, 'Ministero dell'Interno, Gabinetto del ministro Buffarini Guidi al MAE e per conoscenza alla PCM, 9 febbraio 1942, Originari tedeschi in Dalmazia'. According to German documents published by Tone Ferenc, a total of 12,147 persons opted for transfer: 2,951 families with 11,747 members, of which 8,944 were 'pure' *Volksdeutschen* and 2,803 with 'mixed forebears', were transferred between October and December 1941. A further 2,687 *Volksdeutschen* were registered in Ljubljana.

29 ASMAE, GABAP, b. 28, 'Appunto del 19 novembre 1942'; see also b. 45, 'Accordo italo-germanico per la sistemazione economica degli sloveni nati nel territorio italiano di Lubiana e ivi pertinenti, Roma 10 dicembre 1941'.

30 ASMAE, GABAP, b. 45. The operation was organized by the Istituto Agricolo Immobiliare Emona.

the PNF. The perseverance shown by the Italian authorities in overcoming the obstacles that impeded the Fascist education of children amid conditions of semi-anarchy demonstrates the importance that Rome attached to it. Applying its doctrine of the hierarchy of races, the regime differentiated the role of education in the annexed territories from that of the colonial schools, these being founded on the principle of 'level of development and civilization'. The purpose of schooling in the African colonies was to make 'the black man not into a simulacrum of a European, but into a better black man . . . with affection for the regime'.[31] Racial segregation in the colonies thus bred two distinct types of school, one for subjects and one for colonizers. Male Africans were to 'work as clerical staff in the administration' and women, who 'belonged in the home', were to have no contact with outsiders. The educational system in Italian Africa (as of July 1936) comprised schools for Italians, for Libyans and for colonial subjects. The schools for 'nationals' (i.e., white Italian children) taught the same curricula as in Italy, with minor changes (the teaching of Arabic, for example) made to them in order to reflect local circumstances.[32] Used as the model in the new provinces was the system introduced in the Aegean possessions, where education served the purpose of 'Fascistizing' Greek children.

The Ministry of Education played a crucial role in the annexed provinces. As regards elementary education, the regime set about adjusting the former Yugoslavian system to Italy's, attending to the 'protection of childhood' with an ordinance (issued on 30 August 1941) which extended compulsory schooling to six-year-olds. Just before the 1941–2 school year, a 'School Charter' was promulgated, and hundreds of teachers were dispatched from Italy to the annexed provinces. Still open at the time were 563 elementary schools (123 in Zadar for 23,029 pupils, 412 in Split for 13,098, and 28 in Kotor for 4,329), and 35 lower-secondary schools (6 in Zadar, 19 in Split and 10 in Kotor). From 1941 onwards, all subjects in the first and second years of elementary school were taught in Italian (Slovene children were instructed in their own language, and Italian was optional).[33]

[31] Tritonj, *Politica indigena africana*, 1941, p. 80.

[32] Foresti, 'Il problema linguistico nella politica indigena del colonialismo fascista'.

[33] ASMAE, GABAP, b. 46, 'Giornale ufficiale del governo della Dalmazia, ordinanze del governatore, 1–15 settembre 1941'; ACS, PCM, 1940–43, 1.1.13.25615, 'Gabinetto del ministro dell'Interno alla PCM, 27 ottobre 1941, Norme di carattere generale concernenti l'ordinamento scolastico dei territori annessi'; ASMAE, GABAP, b. 46, 16 April 1941, 'Relazione di Luigi Arduini'. The Fascistization of Dalmatian youth was also carried out by the Case d'Italia and the Lega Culturale Italiana, an offshoot of the Lega Nazionale headed by the Dalmatian senator Antonio Tacconi. Prior to 1941, the Lega administered seven Italian elementary schools in Split, Dubrovnik, Šibenik, Krk (Veglia), Traù, Lesina and Curzola.

All first- and second-year elementary school teachers were dismissed unless they spoke fluent Italian and were judged to be pro-Italian by the authorities. Serb and Croat teachers were replaced by 531 Italians, while native-born teachers in the third and fourth years remained 'provisionally in service' – as did those in the lower-secondary schools, who had their dismissals postponed for three years. The education board (*provveditorato*) set up a special office which compiled dossiers on all non-Italian teachers and monitored their political and 'moral' behaviour. A single example suffices to show the consequences of these policies: all the non-native teachers on Arbe were ordered to leave the island, yet not until 30 October 1941 was there a single Italian or *pertinente* official available to take their place. The situation was the same in Veglia.[34]

Bastianini announced that enrolments with the GIL had constantly increased in the year since annexation (could it have been otherwise?), and that 263 scholarships had been awarded to university students. But he was lying when he declared that Dalmatia's educational problems had been solved. Attempts to Italianize the school system almost entirely failed: the Fascist school, 'the instrument for the political, cultural and moral preparation of the future generations', was only such on paper, and the universities did anything but 'forge the new ideas that with Mussolini's fascism have begun to regenerate the minds of men'. Schooling was imposed on the young and, for those who decided not to attend, 'we inculcate in them what millennia of civilization have given to our culture: should they wish to forgo the opportunity, we shall not forcefully keep them either at school or at home, we shall open wide the gates of our frontiers so that those who do not feel themselves deserving of the privilege may leave'.[35]

In Menton, too, the head prefect of the French occupied territories at CIAF (Marziali) was given the task of 'contributing as far as possible to imprinting typically Italian features' upon the local population. He accordingly expelled defeatists and anti-Italian agitators, established a culture and propaganda office (headed by the director of the Istituto degli Studi Liguri of Bordighera), and introduced the lira as legal tender. The Italianization

[34] ASMAE, GABAP, b. 28, 'Casertano al MAE', 20 June 1941; b. 40, 'Casertano al GABAP, 22 ottobre 1941, Problemi di mobilità per popolazioni occupate'; ACS, PCM, 1940–3, 1.1.13.16542.45. The Kotor and Split education boards (*provveditorati*) were established in May 1942; ACS, PCM, 1940–3, G 9/1 12860, 'Personale per la Slovenia'. Ettore Raymondi (chief inspector of schools), the general director of higher education, and 'educational experts' Attilio Depoli (headmaster of the *liceo scientifico* of Fiume) and Edoardo Ciubelli (dean of the Royal Technical Institute of Zadar and at the time provincial superintendant of education) had not yet been consulted in May 1941, although they had been appointed.

[35] Missoni, *Luci ed ombre sulle Dinariche*, 1942, 'discorso di Bastianini a Zara il 12 aprile 1942'.

campaign required the replacement of French officials, and when this was not possible – in the case of teachers, for example – personnel were kept under close surveillance. Thirty-six Italian elementary and lower-secondary teachers were sent to the three schools in Menton, and it was ordered that all lessons must be taught in Italian. There then followed institution of the *Fascio di Combattimento* (the Fascist Party organizations), the GIL and the OND. Persons of 'Italian race' were encouraged to return to Menton – though obstacles were raised against those of 'different racial origin', the reference being to Jews, given that the commissioner wrote in his report that 'these may prove awkward in the future' and 'it will be necessary to adopt the expulsion measures already used in other Italian countries'.[36]

Two things are demonstrated by the fact that the Italian authorities pursued a policy in Menton largely similar to that adopted in the annexed Adriatic provinces, even though the circumstances were very different: firstly, that the Italian civil and military authorities concurred on the essential purposes of the occupations; secondly, that they did not think that France and the Balkans should be treated differently (for political or strategic reasons or for ones to do with race). The territories of Mediterranean Europe conquered during the Second World War were all part of a single project to acquire *spazio vitale*.

Once the eligibles had been identified, members of other races transferred or interned, the past erased, the organs of the Italian state and its laws transposed and the few natives deemed worthy of Italian nationality Fascistized, the next stage was colonization. The long-term intention was that this would involve the internal migration of Italians, but the brief duration of the domination put paid to that project.

A note (published by Oddone Talpo) handed to Sir Francis d'Arcy Osborne, the British ambassador at the Holy See, referred to an undated notice sent by Bastianini to the prefects in which he outlined how Italy would colonize Dalmatia[37] and declared that 'without ethnic expansion' political and military expansion could only be provisional. Bastianini envisaged the resettlement of Italy's surplus population in the new provinces, where it would absorb 'whatever remained of the native population'. Italy's

[36] USSME, D 7, 'Relazione dell'attività del commissario civile di Mentone per il periodo ottobre 1941–maggio 1942'; ASMAE, GABAP, b. 7, 'commissario civile al MAE, 10 ottobre 1940, Stanziamento di un fondo per "italianizzare la biblioteca civile di Mentone".

[37] Talpo, *Dalmazia*, vol. II, pp. 996 and 998, which refers to a document classified 'PRO–FO 371/33505 – 28752 – Nota 8931/92 – Italian Colonisation of Dalmatia, 11 dicembre 1942', and to the annexed 'Instructions confidentielles du "gouverneur" de la Dalmatie Bastianini aux préfets de cette province'.

success, he wrote, would depend on whether it could purge the region of its ethnic features, an undertaking which would be facilitated by the rivalry (to be instigated by every means) between the Croats and the Serbs.

The civil commissioner Amedeo Mammalella (later consul in Dubrovnik) wrote that the Italianization of Kotor would rely more heavily on the 'petty bourgeoisie and the families of ancient Italian origin, which have always maintained a certain pride in their origins . . . than on the very few Italian citizens resident here'.[38] The commander of the Second Army proposed that civil servants of Dalmatian origin should be invited – or if necessary compelled – to resettle in Dalmatia, where their presence would make *italianità* flourish once again.[39] A total of around one hundred Dalmatian families emigrated: 'the problem of the Italian eligibles who could achieve tangible results for Italy is being solved only with scant sincere participation . . . The eligibles make the legitimate, human and understandable plea for themselves and their families to be ensured their daily bread . . . These aspiring Italians resentfully acknowledge the power of the Germans' when they compared the status of the *Volksdeutschen* minority with their own.[40]

Talpo argues that the plan for the forced Italianization of Dalmatia, according to which the arrival of the Italian Dalmatians would be preceded by the evacuation of an equal number of citizens of 'Croatian race' resident in the governorate, reflected neither Italian mentality nor methods. He maintains that the governor discarded the ideas of forcibly expelling unreliable Croats (as the Germans were doing in Styria and Carinthia, and as Ante Pavelić was doing with the Serbs), of using the Italian minorities, and of resettling Dalmatian-born Italians *en masse* in the provinces of Dalmatia. According to Talpo, Bastianini merely isolated Dalmatia in the belief that the Croatian population could be assimilated by virtue of the governorate's efficient structures alone. Talpo's interpretation is wrong on three counts: (1) the first solution was entirely consistent with Fascism's methods – as borne out by Mussolini's speech of June 1941 to the Camera dei Fasci; (2) the second solution was not discarded by Bastianini: instead, it was begun but then not completed because of a shortage of resources and developments in the war; (3) assimilation was not incompatible with

[38] ASMAE, GABAP, b. 48, 'console generale d'Italia Mammalella al Commissariato civile per il Montenegro', 21 May 1941.

[39] ACS, PCM, 1.1.13.16542.14.26, 'PCM al governatore della Dalmazia, 15 giugno 1941, Rimpatrio dalmati residenti in Italia, firmato dal sottosegretario Luigi Russo'; ACS, MI, A 5 G, b. 415, 'Comando II Armata – UAC alla legazione di Zagabria, 17 giugno 1941, Rimpatrio dalmati in Dalmazia'.

[40] ACS, MI, A 5 G, b. 415, 'Ministero dell'Interno, Ufficio dell'ispettore generale di PS', 2 March 1942.

expulsion and repopulation: indeed, those Dalmatians not expelled would, after appropriate Fascistization, become Italian citizens and be flanked by Italian colonists, not solely ones of Dalmatian origin.

The Fascist *Volkstumpolitik* in the annexed provinces was entirely consistent with Italy's tradition of colonial and metropolitan racial policy. Consider the persecution of the Slovene and Croatian minorities in the territories annexed at the end of the First World War, towards which, after 1936, Rome intensified segregationist measures that would have led to a 'civil death' similar to the one awaiting the Italian Jews. Julian Fascists like Angelo Scocchi and Italo Sauro urged the expulsion of the Slavs, the Italian colonization of the borderlands, expropriation, the prohibition of intermarriage and denationalization by schooling. The urban renewal of Trieste drove non-native-born residents out of their homes and into the province's outlying areas.[41] Consider also the forced Italianization of Alto Adige – which also involved internal colonization – culminating in the transfer of non-natives after the referendum of 1939. The solution of the 'Slav question' and the 'Alto Adige question' and the anti-Semitic laws were all aspects of the same racist policy pursued in the territories annexed between 1940 and 1943.

Talpo is correct to point out that Bastianini's orders obstructed the return of the Dalmatians; but his intention was that the arrival of the colonists would constitute the final stage of the Italianization process. It is also true that Bastianini isolated Dalmatia, but he did so only to forestall an invasion of refugees, and so that an accurate census could be conducted, and denationalization get under way.

In regard to the colonization of the annexed territories, to be noted is Roatta's proposal made to Mussolini on 23 May 1942 in Fiume. The general urged that, once the frontiers had been closed, the borderland population expelled, and 20,000 to 30,000 people interned, families of the Italian war dead should be given property confiscated from Slovene rebels whose families had been interned (see chapter 10). This demonstrates that the military authorities, too, endorsed the idea of colonization, probably mindful of the Roman Empire; and also of the Napoleonic empire, which installed colonies in the *départements* of Piedmont and the Rhineland by giving land to veterans who would thus be immediately available for military defence of the region.

As we shall see in the next section, the forced Italianization of the Ionian islands came about mainly in the economic sphere. The Italians sought to

[41] Sala, 'Programmi di snazionalizzazione'.

separate the islanders politically and physically from the Greek mainland, and they opened Italian schools staffed by priests. When some natives applied to marry Italian citizens, the Civil Affairs Office proposed that 'autochthons' should be considered *italiani non regnicoli*. Tomaso Perassi, a legal expert at the MAE, wrote to the ministry on the legal aspects of the question, arguing that a decision was still premature. If the islanders were considered *italiani non regnicoli*, they could marry employees of the state civil and military authorities. Perassi proposed that natives wishing to marry Italian citizens might apply for citizenship under the final paragraph of the law on citizenship (amended by royal decree no. 1997 of 1 December 1934), and in exceptional cases that the Ministry of the Interior should have discretionary power to grant citizenship to persons not resident in the kingdom.[42]

THE FASCIST ECONOMY IN THE ANNEXED PROVINCES

The forced Italianization of the annexed territories also had an economic dimension which was manifest in intervention by the state, especially by the Bank of Italy and the economic ministries. Unfortunately, the documentation allows only partial reconstruction of economic Italianization between 1941 and 1943. It should also be borne in mind that the annexed zones were poor and that their economies were based on agriculture, cattle-husbandry and fishery.

Dalmatia was decidedly underdeveloped, with almost all sectors of its economy dependent on the Croatian hinterland.[43] Agricultural production was not enough to satisfy local demand, and the country's main resource was wine: grapevines covered one-third of arable land excluding pasturage and woodland, and wine-making gave employment to two-thirds of the active population. The products of the fishing industry were sold on the domestic market, with only a small proportion exported. Kotor, whose main economic activities were the industrial installations of Perast and the shipyards of Teodo, was hit very hard by its separation from Montenegro, with which it had close economic ties, and it spent the years of Italian occupation in a state of economic paralysis. The largest enterprises in Split were cement works, one close to the harbour and four at Baia Castelli

[42] ASMAE, AA.PP. – Italia, 1939–45, b. 77, 10 October 1942.

[43] Mori, *La Dalmazia*, 1942, chap. 5; Calestani, 'Dalmazia e Italia', 1943; ASBI, 'Direttorio Azzolini', nc. 51, fasc. 1, bob. 24, 'relazioni su Spalato e zona limitrofa, Sebenico, Dubrovnik con Gravosa e Lopud, Cattaro, Metkovic'; USSME, N 1–11, 'Diari storici', b. 1267, allegato 4, 'La Dalmazia e zone limitrofe, monografia geografico-militare dei territori occupati dal VI CdA', 15 September 1942.

(Kaštel). This industrial complex had excellent potential for production (6 million quintals a year) and also for growth as long as it received the necessary raw materials: coal (400 tonnes a day) and electricity (supplied by the Almissa power station). The supplies of coal from the mines operated by the Società Monte Promina (part of the IRI group) and those at Drniš, Livno and Mostar were able to meet demand by the cement works. But when the mines were forced to reduce their supplies because of partisan attacks, the malfunctioning of vehicles or the interruption of road and railway links, cement production suffered greatly. The region's main mineral resource, bauxite (seventeen deposits of excellent quality), was almost entirely exploited by the Germans.

Governor Bastianini sought with every means possible to solve Dalmatia's industrial problems, believing that this would remedy political and social difficulties of crucial importance. He gave priority to the financing of those public works that would 'revitalize the local economy and resolve the question of industrial and financial penetration'. The Italian government allocated fully 500 million lire to extraordinary public works programmes in Ljubljana, Fiume, Split, Kotor and Zadar. In order to ensure his control over every industrial undertaking, Bastianini reserved the right to declare factories that he deemed vital for the nation's defence or its efficiency 'auxiliary to the war effort' (*ausiliari allo sforzo di guerra*). Some firms were supervised by the Ufficio Fabbriguerra set up under the aegis of the Dalmatian government to plan production schedules, organize the sale of products, regulate management and personnel, and vet hirings and dismissals. The managers and workers in these firms automatically acquired rank as 'civilian conscripts' with the related duties and sanctions.[44]

In the industrial sector, at the end of January 1942, the IRI group acquired 63 per cent of the capital of the French company Dalmatienne (a transaction mentioned in the previous chapter), which owned mills and two electricity-generating stations on the Dalmatian border with a maximum capacity of 2.5 billion kilowatts (of which only 550 million were used in the annexed provinces). Giuseppe Volpi propounded a project (never implemented) to develop the steel and synthetic rubber industries. His intention was that these should use up all the output from the electricity-generating stations so that no surplus energy was left for the mines being exploited by German companies.[45] Indispensable for the Italian project – which would 'set the lives of the people on the foundation of a new order' – was organization of Dalmatia's cement works into 'a single national industry'.

[44] ACS, PCM, 1942, 1.1.13.16542.71. [45] S. Romano, *Giuseppe Volpi e l'Italia moderna*.

Accordingly, in September 1941, deputy Luigi Scarfiotti was appointed extraordinary commissioner of the Adria-Portland, Dalmatia and Spalato cement companies. He transferred Adria-Portland and Dalmatia to the Istituto Finanziario Italiano (IFI). The latter then merged the companies into S. A. Cemeterie Riunite Adria-Dalmatia, which was exempt from taxes. According to a military document, FIAT acquired a 70 per cent share of the cement works.[46] The Consorzio per le Sovvenzioni su Valori Industriali (CONSUVI, which used the Bank of Italy's facilities although it had its own legal personality) extended credit to companies such as Pastifici Zaratini, Manifattura Zaratina Sigarette, Silurificio Whitehead of Fiume, Cantieri Navali of Quarnaro, Farmochimica Dalmata, and Raffineria d'Olii Minerali-AGIP.[47] Cantieri Navali, together with Dalmatienne and the Losovac factory, were declared 'auxiliaries'. In a speech made at the University of Milan, Bastianini claimed that private enterprise had been encouraged with every means possible in Dalmatia; sole agencies had been prohibited, thus preventing 'parasitism'; and self-styled industrialists who set up in business only 'to milk the state' had been eliminated. He was lying. The largest industries were controlled by Italian state-owned enterprises (IRI).

Partition of the province of Ljubljana by the Germans turned it into an economically non-viable entity, a 'region of loss-making agriculture without adequate cereal cultivation and underdeveloped cattle-husbandry'. It ceased to be the area's financial and business centre. Links with industry and commerce beyond the frontier were severed, and all companies located on German or Croatian territory were transferred elsewhere. Ljubljana declined into the equivalent of a frontier township.

According to Grazioli, the province should have been converted to agriculture – not for ideological reasons but because the land ('the boggy terrain of Ljubljana') was all that remained of value in the area except for artisan activity, which in any case produced in modest qualities and could not supply the country.[48] The new province would have to cope with the problem of conversion and the trauma of losing wealth which the Dalmatian provinces had never known. Of the few industries that remained, only timber and construction achieved 'satisfactory' yields, but they did so only

[46] ASMAE, GABAP, b. 47, 20 June 1941, 'Cementerie dalmate'; USSME, M 3, b. 63, 14 March 1943, 'Argomenti trattati nel colloquio tra il generale Mario Robotti e il prefetto Paolo Valerio Zerbino'.

[47] ASBI, 'Consumi', pratt. 11 fasc. 1, 22 fasc. 11, 75 fasc. 3, 86 fasc. 7, 95 fasc. 2 and 3, 111 fasc. 1, 121 fasc. 7, 172 fasc. 4, 179 fasc. 6, 198 fasc. 4, 271 fasc. 8, 410 fasc. 7, 413 fasc. 1, 416 fasc. 18, 418 fasc. 6, 513 fasc. 6, 515 fasc. 19, 774 fasc. 10 and 17.

[48] ASMAE, GABAP, b. 25, 1 July 1941, 'Relazione di Grazioli a Pietromarchi'; Facciotti, 'Le risorse minerarie delle nuove provincie italiane', 1941.

thanks to military purchase orders. The timber industry (three large firms and twenty smaller ones) was severely affected by the decline in exports and increased production costs due to the lack of raw materials. The same applied to the metallurgical, electrical, chemicals, paper, leather, textile and food industries (the largest company in the last sector being the Union Brewery).[49]

Price rises, accelerating inflation, low pay and increased unemployment, as well as the semi-paralysis of the industrial sector in its entirety, mainly afflicted clerical workers and factory hands and provoked social tension which the Ljubljana civil authorities found impossible to deal with. In the spring of 1942 the province was devastated by military actions and partisan reprisals. Stocks of fruit and vegetables and cattle herds were destroyed by looting; road and railway links were severed, with extremely damaging consequences for domestic trade; the frontiers with the German territories and Croatia remained closed; and mass arrests greatly depleted the labour supply.[50]

Mussolini decided to extend Italian banking law to all the annexed provinces. For the purpose of establishing a preliminary legal framework to regulate the credit sector, orders were issued to co-ordinate the action of provincial officials, those employed by the governorate and the Ispettorato per la Difesa del Risparmio e l'Esercizio del Credito, a section of the Bank of Italy responsible for banking discipline.

The Bank of Italy opened branches in Ljubljana, Šibenik, Split and Kotor (it also operated in Dubrovnik and Cetinje, and since the end of the First World War had done business in Pola, Fiume and Zadar; in 1942 it opened a branch in Menton). In a memorandum for the Duce written just after the annexations, an official at the Bank of Italy, Giuseppe Pennachio, discussed two 'closely connected' topics: organization of the banking system in the annexed territories, and the establishment of Italian banks. For these purposes he carried out a census of banks operating in all the new provinces and in Montenegro (a total of 250) with the assistance of the civil and military authorities and the Ispettorato per la Difesa del Risparmio e l'Esercizio del Credito. Pennachio distinguished among four categories of banks operating in the annexed territories and in Montenegro: (a) branches of banks headquartered outside the annexed territories; (b) banks headquartered in the annexed territories and with subsidiaries elsewhere; (c) local banks (except

[49] ASBI, 'Sconti anticipazioni e corrispondenti', prat., n.c. 1195, fasc. 1, 19 February 1942, 'Relazione sulla situazione economica della provincia di Lubiana'.

[50] Cuzzi, *L'occupazione italiana della Slovenia*, p. 252.

for co-operatives); (d) co-operative federations (inspections had been conducted on around 250 banks by the time of Pennachio's memorandum).

The main banks in category (a) were the branches in Ljubljana, Split, Sušak and Cetinje of the National Bank of the former Kingdom of Yugoslavia, other branches of state-owned or state-controlled banks, and other ordinary banks with headquarters outside the annexed territories. Among these were the First Croatian Savings Bank, the Bank of Croatia, the Bohemian Industrial Bank and the Yugoslav General Banking Company. Group (b) comprised two Ljubljana banks whose subsidiaries in territories occupied by the Germans were to be wound up, while in the case of group (c) it does not seem that foreign clearances appreciably influenced the decisions taken. The fourth group consisted of a large number of small banks doing business mainly in the agricultural, artisanal and service sectors and which resembled the Italian rural savings banks (Casse Rurali); Pennachio deemed many of these banks 'unsustainable'.[51]

The question of the establishment of Italian banks in the annexed zones was bound up with the liquidation of the National Bank of Yugoslavia, an operation that involved Germany, Italy, Croatia, Bulgaria, Serbia, Hungary and Albania as the successor states to the former Yugoslavia. The Bank of Italy played a leading role in the operation by pledging to take over the activities of the National Bank and its state-owned or state-controlled subsidiaries (the State Mortgage Bank, the First Agricultural Bank, the Small Business Bank and the Postal Savings Bank) in the annexed territories and Montenegro. An Italo-German Economic and Financial Commission was set up to deal with questions concerning state assets, the national debt, the percentages of the latter to be distributed among the successor states – termed the 'purchasing states' (*stati acquirenti*) – and liquidation of the state-controlled banks.[52] The successor states appropriated assets and undertook to honour debts, which they allocated among themselves according to

[51] ASBI, USC, prat. 100, b. 1, fasc. 1, 'Promemoria per il duce', probably written in the first half of September 1941. The ASBI–USC archives contain the general financial statements and those of all branches of the Yugoslav National Bank updated to May 1941 for the annexed provinces, i.e. Ljubljana, Sušak, Split and Cetinje. Of particular interest are the reports of 28 August and 10 September 1941: 'Banca nazionale del regno di Jugoslavia, in liquidazione, Rapporto del rappresentante italiano presso la Liquidazione, direttore di filiale della Banca d'Italia Walter Liguori', in ASBI, Segretariato, nc. 482, fasc. 9, bob. 103.

[52] ASBI, Segretariato, nc. 482, fasc. 9, bob. 103, 'Riunioni a Berlino della Commissione italo-tedesca per i problemi economici e finanziari relativi alla ex Jugoslavia – per la delegazione italiana il plenipotenziario Diana, per i tedeschi Fabricius – 4–14 ottobre 1941' (contains five reports). The committee was divided into eight sub-committees: (i) on state debts and monopolies; (ii) on liquidation of the National Bank; (iii) on liquidation of private banks and insurance companies; (iv) on postal savings banks; (v) on social questions; (vi) on trade; (vii) on state civil servants; (viii) on legal affairs.

territorial partitions and in proportion to the Yugoslavian population as measured by the 1931 census, its annual increase being calculated at 1.5 per cent.[53]

On 22 July 1942, an agreement signed in Berlin on disposal of the former Yugoslavia's state property laid the basis for the dividing up of assets and liabilities. In regard to the Yugoslav National Bank, a protocol stipulated that each successor state must open a liquidation account. The operation began with the winding up of the bank's ordinary business, including its clearing accounts. Liabilities to creditors located on the territory of each 'purchaser' were appraised by its central bank, and in the case of the state-controlled banks, the 'purchasers' compiled balance sheets and submitted accounting data. Discussion on the procedures relating to liquidation of the National Bank continued until 17 April 1943, when examination of the financial statement began.[54]

According to the CEPIC banking sub-committee, the creditors of the Yugoslav National Bank and its subsidiaries should be given full satisfaction, because fulfilment of the state's guarantees would ensure the swift and efficient resolution of the state-owned and private banks and contribute to the 'hoped-for rapid reconstruction of the economies of the annexed territories'. The State Mortgage Bank and the First Agricultural Bank were financially sound, while the deficit accumulated by the Postal Savings Bank would be substantially reduced if, following collection of loans taken out by the public authorities, the surpluses of the other two banks were used. All in all, even if the Italian state paid off all the outstanding debts of Yugoslavian banks, the financial burden would be only modest.

At the end of September 1941, Mussolini and the governor of the Bank of Italy, Vincenzo Azzolini, agreed that all banking operations with the kingdom should be transacted by Italian-owned banks alone; and they also

[53] ASBI, 'Affari coloniali – Filiali coloniali e dalmate', prat., nc. 2815, bob. 244. On 24 April 1942, Italy, Germany and Hungary decided that Serbia should assume 29 per cent of the debts of the kingdom of Yugoslavia, Croatia 42 per cent, Bulgaria 8 per cent, Hungary 8 per cent, Italy together with Montenegro and Albania 8 per cent and Germany 5 per cent.

[54] ASBI, USC, prat., nc. 303, bob. 63, 'Commissione italo-tedesca per i problemi relativi alla ex Jugoslavia, riunioni di Roma 17–20 aprile 1943, Resoconto delle riunioni tenutesi presso il Ministero degli Esteri, Esame del bilancio di apertura della liquidazione della Banca nazionale del regno di Jugoslavia (al 31 maggio 1941)'. The national banks of Hungary, Serbia, Croatia and Bulgaria assumed the assets and liabilities of the former Yugoslav National Bank until the end of 1942. The branches in Ljubljana, Split, Sušak and Cetinje remained under the commission's control, and the Bank of Italy did not proceed with their liquidation. The holdings of the Split branch were deposited at the bank headquarters in Belgrade and those of Sušak were moved to Zagreb, while those of Cetinje, Ljubljana and Mostar were confiscated in April 1941 and transported to Rome. A dispute broke out when Zagreb demanded the holdings at the Mostar branch instead of those at Sušak, which slowed the liquidation operations down even further.

decided that the number of credit institutes operating in the annexed territories should be reduced by liquidation, merger and nationalization. The Cassa di Risparmio di Fiume opened a subsidiary in Sušak and branches in Bakar, Kastav, Veglia, Arbe and Cabar; the BNL received authorization to open branches in the province's new communes.[55] In Dalmatia, the Banco di Roma was similarly authorized to open a branch in Šibenik, and the Banco di Napoli in Split and Zadar (where it mainly did business with the Italian military). The presence of the Banco di Napoli apparently served to establish links between Dalmatia, southern Italy and the Montenegrin and Albanian territories. Already operating in Zadar and Split were both the BNL (which converted its fishery credit branch into a subsidiary) and the Dalmatian Discount Bank, a subsidiary of Credito Italiano (which also had a branch in Šibenik besides the one in Dubrovnik).[56] Finally, the Banca Commerciale Italiana took over the First Dalmatian Mutual Loan Bank. All these operations were co-ordinated and supervised by the Bank of Italy's credit inspector, Mario Buttiglione, who sought to obtain repayment by the Croats of their credit with the central banks and to take over both debts and credits contracted outside the annexed territories.

As for the private Croatian banks operating in the annexed territories, Pennachio and the head of the MAE's Direzione Generale Affari Commerciali, Amedeo Giannini, agreed that it was not opportune to stipulate agreements with Croatia before negotiations with Germany had been concluded. At the same time, the representatives of the Ljubljana High Commission and of the Governorate of Dalmatia (Teobaldo Zennaro and Lello Gangemi), as well as of the Bank of Italy's Ispettorato del Credito, recommended that the Croatian banks be closed down as soon as possible because they were colluding with the Germans. Indeed, it was the obstructionism of the latter – who had an obvious interest in maintaining its ostensibly Croatian bridgeheads in Italy's new provinces – that protracted the negotiations for so long.[57] Given the Croats' reluctance to settle these matters, the Italians proceeded with liquidations unilaterally. They transferred loans to the Croats, demanding the balances in return.[58]

[55] ASBI, USC, prat. 102, b. 26, fasc. 1, 'Fiumano generico'.

[56] ASBI, USC, cpl., nc. 2, bob. 1, 28 September 1941, 'Colloqui Mussolini–Azzolini' (the meeting was held on 26 September 1941).

[57] ASBI, Segretariato, prat., nc. 482, bob. 103.

[58] In July, 100 per cent was paid to the creditors of the Serbian Bank, 70 per cent to those of the Bank of Bosnia-Herzegovina, 60 per cent to those of the Adriatic–Danubian Bank, 30 per cent to those of the First Croatian Savings Bank and 10 per cent to those of the Croatian Independent State Savings Bank.

The bank liquidation programme got under way in 1942. In March of that year, the branches of the Serbian Bank and the Bank of Bosnia-Herzegovina were wound up and transferred to the Banco di Napoli; they were then followed by the branches of the First Croatian Savings Bank and the Croatian Banovina Savings Bank (i.e. the savings bank of the independent Croatian state), which were assigned to the Banco di Roma; and finally the Economic Savings Bank, which was taken over by the Dalmatian Discount Bank. A liquidation commissioner was installed at the Adriatic–Danubian Bank of Kotor, which too was transferred to the Banco di Roma. In the insurance sector, companies with headquarters in Belgrade were no longer authorized to do business, while those belonging to enemy countries were attached and brought under the management of Italian functionaries. Portfolios were transferred to the Italian-owned insurance companies INA, Generali and RAS, and to the Società Mutua Assicurazioni Enti Cooperativi, and Pace of Milan, which together with Assicurazioni d'Italia, Assicurazioni Fiume, Assicurazioni Mutua and Assicurazioni Slavja of Ljubljana were authorized to do business on the territory of the governorate. If the programme for liquidation and takeover of the former Yugoslavian banks had been implemented in its entirety, it would have engendered the administrative 'purification' advocated by Bastianini, and it would have created a large number of unemployed former Yugoslavians without Italian citizenship who could thus have been easily expelled from the province.[59]

In Ljubljana the programme was a complete failure. Credit was not transferred to the former Yugoslavian state-owned or state-controlled banks (First Agricultural Bank: loans and bonds issued or guaranteed by the former Yugoslavian state and local public authorities to a value of 80 million lire). Nor was it possible to recover securities belonging to Ljubljana companies transferred elsewhere on the eve of the war. Negotiations with the purchasing states, especially Germany, on the subsidiaries of Ljubljana banks located outside the annexed territories – fifteen in total, of which seven were in Styria and Carinthia, three in Serbia, one in Hungary, one in Croatia and three in Dalmatia – had no concrete outcomes.[60] The only financial institutes to open branches in Ljubljana were the Banco di Roma and the Hrvatska Banka, an affiliate of the Banca Commerciale Italia. Italy protested to Germany that the interests of the Ljubljana banks in Styria and Carinthia had been overridden, and that banks and insurance companies

[59] ASBI, USC, prat. 103, b. 1, fasc. 1, 'Colloquio del governatore della Banca d'Italia con Bastianini', undated, first months of 1942, probably February. See also b. 28, fasc. 1.

[60] ASBI, 'Affari coloniali – Filiali coloniali e dalmate', prat. 2609, fasc. 1, 16 June 1942, 'Promemoria sulla situazione bancaria della provincia di Lubiana'.

(except for Generali and RAS) had been closed, and their property confiscated. The Reich then acquired majority shareholdings in two former Yugoslavian banks located in Ljubljana: the Yugoslav General Banking Company, which was converted into an ostensibly Croatian joint-stock company, and the Bank of Croatia (brought under the direct control of the Dresdner Bank). Considering that Germany did not permit foreign banks to operate in its annexed territories – the Italians objected – why should Italy allow them to do so? Italy 'was entitled to be equal to the Reich and be granted the right not to tolerate intrusions by foreign banks', wrote an official at the Bank of Italy. This applied especially to Ljubljana, where there was a plethora of banks – fully fifty-six of them.[61] A report of April 1943 stated as follows: 'It has not yet been possible to begin re-organization of the banking system in this province mainly because solution of problems of a general nature . . . , which is the precondition for such reorganization, is not yet forthcoming.'[62]

The Ionian islands require separate treatment.[63] In July 1941, the Italian Post Office sent Italian stamps overprinted with 'Isole Jonie' to the islands, with instructions that they were to take the place of drachma-currency stamps. The Anonima Commercio Jonico (ACJ) was created in the same month, and a clearing account distinct from that for the Greek mainland was opened. Measures were taken to engross the largest businesses on the islands, principally by introducing interest-bearing bonds to be paid against expropriation 'of Jews, expelled Greeks or voluntary expatriates'.[64]

Piero Parini wrote on 26 June 1941 concerning the currency question that, 'since everything possible must be done to separate the economy of the Ionian islands from the rest of Greece' in order to prepare for the introduction of a 'single currency', it was advisable to replace drachmas with vouchers issued by the Cassa Mediterranea. Once the provincial currency had been created, it would be easy 'at any moment' to introduce the Ionian

[61] ASBI, 'Affari coloniali – Filiali coloniali e dalmate', 36, nc. 2802, bob. 242, 'Promemoria di una riunione tenutasi presso il MAE, il 15 maggio 1942, in vista della riunione della sottocommissione bancaria'.

[62] ASBI, 'Affari coloniali – Filiali coloniali e dalmate', cpl. n. 4983, 10 April 1943, 'Relazione riassuntiva sulla situazione bancaria nella provincia di Lubiana nei riguardi delle aziende di credito private'; USC, prat. 101, b. 6, fasc. 1, 'Slovenia generico'. The following banks in the province were in severe difficulties: Ljubljana Credit Bank, Economic Co-operative Bank, Agricultural Loans Bank, the Mortgage Bank belonging to the Yugoslav Savings Banks, the Credit Company of the Savings Banks and the Federation of Co-operatives. According to the report, only the Agricultural Loans Bank and the Commerce and Industry Credit Institute could be kept afloat.

[63] ASBI, USC, prat. 105, b. 40, fasc. 1, 'Fabrizi', 16 June 1941, 'Relazione sulla situazione economico-bancaria delle isole Jonie'; USSME, L 15, b. 85, 'Comando XI Armata – Ufficio "I" all'Ufficio Operazioni, Informazioni fino alle ore 20 del giorno 24 giugno 1941'.

[64] ASBI, USC, prat. 105, b. 40, fasc. 1, 'Fabrizi all'USC', 13 August 1941.

lira at parity of exchange with the vouchers.[65] The representative of the Bank of Italy, Enea Fabrizi, suggested the institution of an Ionian drachma or an Ionian lira at a favourable exchange rate, the purpose being to safeguard savings in the islands and attenuate the hardships of workers on fixed incomes, while also reducing price disparities with Italy. The financial reorganization plan envisaged the elimination of foreign banks (the Commercial Bank of Greece, the Ionian Bank, the Bank of Agriculture, the Bank of Athens, the Jonian Bank and the National Bank) and intervention by the Bank of Italy – which would replace the Bank of Greece – the Banco di Napoli and the Banca Nazionale del Lavoro, which would take over all branches of the other banks.

At the end of 1941, after consulting the minister of finance Thaon di Ravel and Count Volpi, Mussolini decided to introduce the Ionian drachma. Fabrizi opposed the plan because formal annexation had not yet taken place and, although he took part in the operation, he left overall responsibility for it to the Foreign Ministry.[66] The operation to replace the Ionian currency was accomplished in May 1942. Bankitalia set up the special fund (Cassa Speciale) for issue of the Ionian drachmas, fixed the exchange rate with the lira at 1 to 8, organized the compulsory conversion of the old drachmas and controlled the introduction of other currencies, including German Reichsmarks. The inhabitants of the countryside could exchange a maximum of 10,000 old drachmas, the residents of towns 20,000 of them and businesses 200,000. In May 1942, the local banks transferred their surplus liabilities to the Cassa Speciale per le Isole Jonie, which deposited the equivalent sum in Ionian drachmas at the Bank of Greece on Corfu.

The branches of Greek banks were prevented from receiving funds from their headquarters in Athens, and when they had exhausted their cash supplies, revenues from credit collection and liquid assets, it was impossible for them to conduct business. This situation, claimed Parini, had been deliberately created in order to ensure the complete reimbursement of creditors. The risk to the Italians was that bank branches would procure funds by demanding credit collection. This would have wiped out profits, and liabilities would have gone unpaid, with the consequence that the Treasury would have to assume all financial obligations. Hence, before intervening in direct administration of Ionian branches of the Greek banks, the Italian authorities realized the credit (300 million Greek drachmas) held by the branches towards their parent institutes.

[65] ASBI, USC, prat. 105, b. 40, fasc. 1, 'Progetto di sistemazione valutaria delle isole Jonie'.
[66] ASBI, USC, prat. 105, b. 40, fasc. 1, 'Fabrizi all'USC', 12 January 1942.

After the sum had been paid, the Ministry of the Treasury authorized the Cassa Speciale delle Isole Joniche to make an equal amount in Ionian drachmas available to the Bank of Greece on Corfu. It imposed controls (implemented by Bank of Italy officials) in order to 'effect a policy of penetrating the Greek market and developing business for Italian banks', and it drew up a plan for the distribution of about 30 per cent of their holdings to depositors and creditors. According to the Italian authorities, checks carried out on spending by bank branches had revealed their real economic situation, which was presumably loss-making, and the time had come to 'close down the Greek banks, except for the Bank of Greece, whose presence in Corfu [would have been] certainly useful until the hoped-for annexation comes about'.[67]

At the beginning of July 1942, a report by the Bank of Italy recommended as follows: fix the exchange rate between the Ionian and Greek drachma, conclude a Greek–Ionian compensatory commercial agreement, create a commercial and financial clearing account among the Ionian islands, Italy and Albania, and appoint a representative for the Istituto Cambi (Exchange Rate Institute). Clearer definition was given to the functions of the Cassa Speciale (Special Fund) which held deposits by banks, public bodies and Italian and Greek private individuals, handled cash deliveries to the public banks and the armed forces, performed currency transactions on behalf of the Istituto Cambi, and took delivery of the Ionian drachmas dispatched by the Italian State Printing Office and Mint (Istituto Poligrafico).[68]

On 24 October 1942, Fabrizi wrote to Azzolini: 'The measures have had their desired effect, for the Greek banks now find themselves completely in our hands, to the point that they themselves plead for a definitive solution.' Fabrizi omitted to mention that the population was suffering immensely from the financial paralysis provoked by the Italians, and that one of the measures adopted by the occupiers was a freeze on the unemployment benefit paid by the Greek social security offices – a 'tragic situation which provoked the piteous lamentations of those affected'. 'Here', Fabrizi continued, 'we cannot let the people die of starvation',[69] as if it could ever be acceptable in continental Greece or anywhere else.

[67] ASBI, USC, prat. 105, b. 40, fasc. 1, 'Parini al MAE – GABAP – Ufficio Grecia', 29 August 1942; 'Fabrizi ai controllori, circolare segreta, Corfu 31 agosto 1942'. See also 'Fabrizi al governatore della Banca Azzolini', 28 August 1942, in ASBI, USC, prat. 105, b. 40, fasc. 1.

[68] ASBI, USC,. prat. 105, b. 40, fasc. 1, 'Riunione per le isole Jonie del 6 luglio 1942'; ibid., 'direttore generale del Tesoro Grassi all'amministrazione centrale della Banca d'Italia, 24 settembre 1942, Norme regolamentari sul servizio della Cassa speciale per le isole Jonie'; ASBI, 'Direttorio Azzolini', n.c. 20, 11 January 1943, 'Relazione conclusiva di Fabrizi ad Azzolini'.

[69] ASBI, USC, prat. 105, b. 40, fasc. 1, 'Fabrizi ad Azzolini', 28 August 1942.

At the beginning of 1943, by which time it was obvious that the outcome of the war would be disastrous and that the collapse of the Greek economy was inevitable, Aldo Torelli (who had replaced Fabrizi as the Bank of Italy's controller at the Cassa Speciale) wrote that the situation in the archipelago did not warrant such intransigent measures by the Italians. It would be better to 'leave things as they were and settle for economic restraint and protection measures more in keeping with the dignity of an occupying nation'.[70] The ratio between the Ionian drachma and the lira fell to 1:35. Numerous families scraped a living by selling their jewellery, furniture and clothing, while the queues of the poverty-stricken outside the public welfare offices grew ever longer. Parini sent a letter to the director general of the Treasury, Paolo Grassi, in which he blamed the devaluation of the Ionian drachma on the costs of the occupation. He recommended that a proportion of the drachmas should be paid in lire into the Italo-Ionian clearing account for purchasing goods from the island markets, and also in order to reduce the money supply. Torelli for his part recommended that a regulatory body for money circulation be instituted, or alternatively that the Cassa Speciale 'should close its tills and cease issuing new paper'. But this did not happen until the armistice.

In May, the streets were littered with torn-up new 1 and 5 Ionian drachma notes: 'useless clutter which no one wanted in their wallets'.[71] Forced Italianization by economic means was abandoned (the vice-director of the Bank of Italy was dismissed when he was caught dealing in black-market currency).[72] At the end of June 1943, as the Bank of Italy officials packed their bags and arranged for their offices to be dismantled, the economy of the Heptanesus collapsed. Torelli had the effrontery to write:

> Attachment to our country stimulates our desire to . . . come up with a solution which adheres as closely as possible to reality and to practicality, yet never neglects the general political situation, for this is the factor that must above all govern our actions intended to remind these people of Venice's ancient traditions still today manifest on the bastions of the Ionian fortresses in the form of the winged lion, that symbol of power and civilization.[73]

Torelli was obviously feigning ignorance, for the winged lion had long been impotent, and the Italians, far from demonstrating their civilization,

[70] ASBI, USC, prat. 105, b. 40, fasc. 1, 11 June 1943, 'copia della lettera al Servizio Operazioni fianziare e rapporti con l'estero'.
[71] ASBI, USC, prat. 105, b. 40, fasc. 1, 'Torelli ad Azzolini', 5 May 1943.
[72] ASBI, USC, prat. 105, b. 40, fasc. 1, 'Torelli ad Azzolini', 23 February and 11 March 1943.
[73] ASBI, USC, prat. 105, b. 40, fasc. 1, 'Torelli ad Azzolini', 5 May 1943.

had starved and impoverished the Ionians, who cursed Venetian lions and Fascist eagles.

Montenegro's situation was a hybrid of annexation and military occupation. The Italians' initial intentions were to create a Montenegrin National Bank, issue a national currency, supervise liquidation of the country's largest banks and take over its treasury services. Ciro De Martino, credit inspector at the Bank of Italy, was sent to Cetinje to set these operations in motion.[74] His frequent reports to Rome on the economic and financial situation argued that the economic bases for creation of an independent state were wholly lacking.

De Martino reported that agricultural output in Montenegro was entirely unable to meet domestic demand, and industrial activity was almost non-existent. The country did not even have a brick-making industry; indeed, it had no sources of revenue other than cattle-husbandry (with subsidiary activities in what he termed 'the primordial state'), tobacco cultivation and forestry. Montenegro consumed rather than produced: more than two-thirds of the goods sold in the country were imported; and exports could never make up the trade gap. The country's only exportable commodities were tobacco from the factory in Podgorica and bauxite from the mines of Berane and Andrijevica. In June 1941, it was easy for De Martino to predict that the winter would render the country's economic situation unsustainable. The importing of staple commodities could be financed by an Italo-Montenegrin clearing account, but where would the necessary funds be found? Should the Royal Treasury, De Martino enquired sceptically, really bother itself with Montenegro?

And yet Mussolini approved an ambitious public works programme for Montenegro similar to the one in Albania. Roads and bridges costing 46 million lire were to be constructed and sanitary installations for 18 million, building work was to include the construction of a royal palace and an Orthodox Christian cathedral for 13 million, and the port of Antivari was to be rebuilt for an estimated 10 million, all of which, including other projects, came to a total cost of almost 119 million lire. The Duce decided that the public works were to be executed using local technicians and labour, given that this would provide employment for more than 30,000 refugees.

[74] ASBI, Ispettorato generale, n. 314, 'De Martino ad Azzolini', 30 August 1941. De Martino proposed that the branches of the former Yugoslav National Bank be liquidated, while for the local banks, if they were financially sound, he envisaged revival of their activities under supervision. Operating in Montenegro, besides the National Bank, state-controlled and local banks, were: in Cetinje, the Bank of Montenegro, the Commerce Bank, the Civil Service Savings Bank, the Civil Service Credit Co-operative and the Serbian–Albanian Bank; in Nikšić, the Credit Bank; in Podgorica, the Bank of Podgorica.

He even announced the draining of Lake Scutari, an operation which would make at least 300,000 hectares of land available for the cultivation of produce to satisfy the 'needs of Montenegro, Dalmatia, Herzegovina and in large part those of Albania'.[75] However, none of these grandiose projects ever actually began.

In the autumn of 1941, with plans for independence now abandoned, the operation to convert dinars into lire began.[76] The occupation authorities feared that the population would protest against an operation so obviously geared to the country's annexation and subjugation. A propaganda campaign was therefore mounted to discredit the dinar, explain the measures facilitating the exchange of dinars in Kotor, Scutari and Kosovo, and drive home the advantages of price stabilization. The introduction of the lira was immediately followed by devaluation. But this meant that Alessandro Pirzio Biroli was obliged to set up price-control commissions at garrison commands and to enforce homeland Italian legislation on speculation and profiteering.

A total of 150 million dinars was withdrawn. They were converted into lire and assigned to the Ministry of Finance as an extraordinary fund out of which to pay for the administration of Montenegro. The sum was used to make back payments and those pertaining to the fourth quarter of 1941. The salaries were thus paid of all the Montenegrin civilian personnel kept in service, and of the officers and non-commissioned officers on active service in Montenegro; a debt contracted with the National Bank was repaid; and food supplies were increased. However, the sum in question was not enough, and spending by the administration was consequently reduced to the indispensable minimum.

In the late spring of 1942, De Martino wrote to Azzolini that the failure to meet local needs had generated spiralling demand for goods and services, hardship was increasing, and finding solutions to the many problems at hand was very difficult. The Italian market was no longer able to supply Montenegro, and quota restrictions left demand for purchases unfulfilled, added to which was the difficulty of transport by sea. De Martino sent Azzolini a copy of a report compiled by the UAC of Andrijevica, where the situation was described as 'typical of Montenegro as a whole': by May 1942, the population had increased by 60 per cent because of the influx of refugees. The housing stock was close to exhaustion, and public health was deteriorating day by day. Food production was meagre, and the

[75] ASMAE, GABAP, b. 53, 'MAE al Ministero delle Finanze', 1 July 1941.

[76] The operation, established by the royal decrees of 2 and 11 June 1941, nos. 492 and 493, was concluded by the end of June.

zone depended on grain imported from Kosovo. The economic situation was described thus: 'No business is done. Commerce is paralysed, while smuggling is rife.'[77]

The situations of the territories of Epirus, Ciamuria, the Cyclades, the Sporades and the Cretan province of Lasithi were similar to that of Montenegro and the Ionian islands. In an attempt to integrate them with Albania and the possessions in the Aegean, the Italians created administrative and economic apparatuses which effectively cut those territories off from the Greek peninsula.[78] Very little is known, and there is probably very little to say, about Italian financial and industrial penetration of the zones, whose economies had already been paralysed by the occupation at the end of 1941.

THE FORCED ALBANIANIZATION OF THE PROVINCES OF KOSOVO AND DEBAR

Account should be given of the tragic situation in the new Albanian provinces of Kosovo, western Macedonia (Debar) and Metohija, where Serbian, Montenegrin and Bulgarian minorities were subject to a ruthlessly enforced Albanianization against which the Italian authorities raised no objection. Where the Albanian and Italian flags flew side by side, denationalization and ethnic cleansing were the rule: Macedonian, Greek, Serbian and Montenegrin surnames and place names were 'Albanianized', and a long period of internment, summary executions and resettlement began. Bulgarian and Greek inhabitants were 'encouraged' to move from the zones of Albanian occupation to those occupied by the Bulgarians, and to Greece.[79]

Immediately following the partition of Yugoslavia, Sofia and Tirana clashed over Macedonia. The Germans sided with Sofia in order to avert conflicts with the Bulgarians over the German occupation of Salonika. They allowed the Bulgarian troops to advance as far as Ohrid, although the town had been entered first by Italo-Albanian troops. The Italian ambassador in Sofia, Massimo Magistrati, met with his German counterpart and insisted that Ohrid and Struga be allocated to Albania. Wolfram von Richthofen replied that Berlin preferred to resolve the question in favour of Sofia (Ohrid

[77] ASBI, USC, prat. 104, b. 38, fasc. 1, 16 May 1942.

[78] ASBI, Ispettorato generale, n. 314, 'Ministero delle Finanze, Direzione generale del Tesoro all'ispettore capo dell'USC, 8 luglio 1941. L'Ente industrie attività agrarie (EIAA) per la Ciamuria, la Società coloniale italiana nelle Cicladi e nelle Sporadi'.

[79] Malev, *Aspetti di una occupazione*.

was the birthplace of the revered Saint Clement).[80] The dispute was settled as follows: Tetovo, Gostivar, Kičevo and Struga, as well as the southern part of Lake Ohrid and the area surrounding Lake Prespa (a total of around 230,000 inhabitants) would form the Albanian province of Debar (Dibra in Italian); the town of Ohrid and the rest of Yugoslavian Macedonia would go to the Bulgarians.[81]

In Debar, the non-payment of salaries to civil servants, the suspension of stipends for the local clergy and the abuses committed by the public officials brought from Tirana exacerbated inter-ethnic tensions. The Albanian community, confident of Italian support, took vicious reprisals.[82] Withdrawal of the dinar triggered steep price rises, and staple goods grew increasingly scarce (a situation exacerbated by the presence of the occupation troops). The hardship of the poorer sections of society was made more acute by the ban imposed on movements by seasonal workers. The newly drawn borders severed economic links because the main towns in the area, which had traditionally received their supplies from Skopje, could not be provisioned by the distant markets of Scutari and Tirana.

The repression was especially violent in Kosovo, and the authorities sent from the Albanian capital were heedless of the suffering of the Serb and Montenegrin minorities, and even of the Slavophone Albanians, who pleaded for restoration of the *status quo*.[83] The Italians left the Albanians free to do as they wanted, for officially the troops of the Regio Esercito could not interfere in civil affairs. The lieutenancy could have intervened, but refrained from doing so because the orders from Rome for Albania were extremely clear: 'Show the maximum impartiality towards the two races, but should it prove impossible to reconcile their opposing claims, favour the Albanian side, since this will be of some utility to the kingdom, whereas showing benevolence to the Orthodox Kosovars would strengthen their separatist tendencies and cause serious embarrassments.'[84]

The Italian authorities undoubtedly had the power to stop the massacres. They did not do so for two reasons: firstly, because Rome wanted to demonstrate that it did not interfere in the domestic affairs of allies in the imperial community (it adopted the same strategy in Croatia during the

80 ASMAE, AA.PP. – Jugoslavia, b. 107, 'ambasciatore a Sofia Magistrati al ministro Ciano', 24 April 1941.

81 Verna, 'Yugoslavia under Italian Rule', p. 134; DDI, ser. IX, 1939–43, vol. 6, docs. 956 and 962.

82 USSME, H 5, b. 40 RR, 'Comando XIV CdA al Comando della IX Armata, 11 giugno 1941, Situazione nel settore di Dibra'.

83 ASMAE, GABAP, b. 51, 'Visita ufficiale ai centri del Montenegro effettuata dal commissario civile Serafino Mazzolini'.

84 Umiltà, *Jugoslavia e Albania*, 1947, pp. 136–42.

summer of 1941); secondly, because, apart from the violence of its execution, denationalization in Kosovo was no different from that in Dalmatia and Slovenia. The Albanians proceeded 'Italian-style' with the immediate removal from the administrative apparatuses of all officials not of Albanian ethnic origin, and they encouraged the return of Albanian emigrants from Yugoslavia.

A particular role in Albanian events, especially in the new provinces, was played by Carlo Umiltà, who was appointed civil commissioner for Kosovo and Debar on 25 May 1941. His main task was to 'set some sort of order upon so much confusion and begin to make life bearable for so many people of different mentalities, languages and aspirations'. He witnessed at first hand the real intentions of the new Albanian masters, 'who seemed [to have] no interest other than getting rid of Serb civil servants', some of whom they dismissed, while others had their salaries halved, making their lives impossible. Umiltà realized that the Albanians, whom the Yugoslavian agrarian reforms of 1921 and 1925 had 'transformed from landowners into farm labourers', wanted to 'exterminate the Slavs'. He wrote in his memoirs that he had sought in vain to dissuade the Albanians from their violence. He noted that, although the Albanians were more numerous than the Slavs, almost all of them were illiterate, 'and in general of an indescribable poverty and dirtiness'.[85] He was not opposed in principle to the Albanianization of the new provinces, but asked 'where would a capable and educated ruling class be found?' For this reason, he concluded, it would be better to restore public order and adopt a more suitable policy. He wrote in his memoirs:

> Before the war and after it, racial hatred destroyed everything. Slavs and Albanians burned each others' houses and slaughtered as many people as they could . . . The Slavs wandered the streets, trying to persuade army trucks to give them lifts to Montenegro or to Old Serbia, where they hoped to find asylum . . . The majority had to give up any idea of leaving Kosovo and they swelled the numbers of the hungry camped on the outskirts of the towns of Prizren, Jakova, Peja and Priština, where there was at least the safe protection of the [Italian] soldiers.[86]

With great difficulty and after months of negotiations, Umiltà managed to persuade the Serbs, Montenegrins, Orthodox Christians and Albanians of Kosovo and Debar to agree to a *besa* (truce), to form mixed 'municipal councils' and to restore essential services like the electricity supply. On his return to Tirana, he applied pressure on the general lieutenancy and

[85] Ibid., p. 107. On 29 May Umiltà left for Kosovo. The first town that he visited was Prizren: 'inhabited by Mohammedan Albanians, who made up its most miserable part, and by a certain number of Orthodox Slavs – the former masters – who formed the so-called bourgeoisie of civil servants and shopkeepers, together with an extremely large number of Orthodox clergy'.
[86] Ibid., p. 112.

the Albanian government to provide the personnel and resources with which to restart the administrative machinery.[87] He sent to the Foreign Ministry a plan for reorganization of the civil service which was to be undertaken jointly with the lieutenancy and the Albanian government. The plan provided for the transfer of officials who could speak Serbian, legislation to separate civil from military affairs, the opening of an office in Tirana and the appointment of prefects for Kosovo and Debar. Umiltà suggested that the municipal administrations could be run by Albanians, with the assistance of representatives of the Serb minority in Kosovo and the Macedonian minority in Debar. As for the justice system, he envisaged the application, at least initially, of Yugoslavian law and the flanking of Yugoslavian judges with Albanian ones. He decided to staff the schools with Albanian teachers. Finally, he intended to transfer responsibility for supplies, mines and communications to the Civil Commission or the Italian military authorities. However, almost none of his plans came to fruition because the Albanians, with the backing of the lieutenancy, refused to make any concessions to the other groups.

Although the high commissioner for the regions of Kosovo and Debar, Alizotti Bev (the former prefect of the Ottoman administration), admitted that without the assistance of the Yugoslavian functionaries the bureaucracy would be paralysed, he did not change his mind on the forced Albanianization of the eastern provinces. Albanian currency was introduced and dinars were withdrawn from circulation. The Yugoslavian schools were closed and their buildings requisitioned for use as Albanian schools (Lieutenancy decree no. 317, November 1941). But Bev failed utterly in his attempt to change the system of direct tax collection and thus reignited violence between Albanians and Slavs. The indiscriminate internment of Orthodox Christians resumed, and with it seizures of their property and the burning of the homes of 'criminals' who had allegedly absconded.

At the end of 1941 the *besa* broke down. As in Croatia, the Italians attempted to maintain their control over the Albanian administration, fearing that the situation would degenerate into chaos. The president of the council, Mustafa Kruja, disbanded the High Commission and created a special ministry for the redeemed lands of Debar, Kosovo and Metohija, which formed three provinces ruled by prefects (at Prizren, Priština and Peć) and sub-prefects (at Djakovika, Orahovac, Suhareka, Tetovo and Rostuse). Offices of the *questura* (police headquarters) were opened, and a provincial Fascist party secretary and an inspector were seconded to the Albanian

[87] Ibid., p. 121.

Ministry of Fascism, where they were supervised by Italian officials. Further battalions of Carabinieri and Blackshirts were dispatched to Kosovo, the Blackshirts being responsible – according to Yugoslavian historiography – for the destruction of entire villages and the arrest and murder of thousands of people. One learns from the scant Italian documentation available that mixed battalions of Italian and Albanian Blackshirts were created in Kosovo, as well as groups of native volunteers to be armed in the event of incursions by partisans from Montenegro. Officially, weapons were issued only when it was necessary to defend inhabitants against partisan attacks or against communist insurgency; the documentation in the archives does not enable one to determine whether they were used for repression or for reprisals against civilians.[88]

In 1943, the situation in Kosovo grew 'every day more turbulent owing to the presence of armed bands and the activities of the extremist parties' against the Italians.[89] The local communist bands established contacts with the Serb and Bulgarian communists. And rather than fight against the communists, the Albanians reached agreements with them against the Italians. In January, Francesco Jacomoni informed Pietromarchi that he had expelled a further 12,000 Montenegrins from Kosovo to Montenegro: those expelled lost their property and their jobs, and on arriving in Montenegro, burning with rage, became the leaders of further uprisings. The head of the GABAP wrote of the lieutenant governor:

> It is said that Jacomoni has all the vices of the regime. The description is correct. But what makes the greatest impression on me is the ingenuous egoism of the man, who is unconcerned about the severe repercussions in Italy of his policy of satisfying the Albanians' interests and self-conceit. Few men are as hated as he is. But he continues unperturbed. One day, when he wanted me to agree to the inclusion of a large part of the Sanjak of Novi Bazar in the territory administered by the Albanian authorities, I replied to him that his policy of wanting to rest on a bed of roses in Albania was costing the country tears and blood. His policy towards Montenegro had provoked a rebellion in which thousands of our soldiers had been massacred. Consequently, I told him, I could not accede to his requests.[90]

Finally, the large numbers of Montenegrins in the area of Berane persuaded Tirana (under Italian pressure) not to annex Metohija but instead bring it under military jurisdiction and have it administered by a civil commissioner 'for the mixed population regions' (the appointee was again Umiltà, who took up the post in 1942). On 6 July 1941, Ciano pledged

[88] USSME, N 1–11, 'Diari storici', b. 493, 'Com. sup. FF.AA. Albania', 6 January 1942.
[89] USSME, M 3, b. 19, 'generale Pièche al GABAP, 15 febbraio 1943, Notizie dal Kossovo albanese'.
[90] Pietromarchi, unpublished diary, 8 January 1943 (Fondazione Luigi Einaudi, Turin).

to the Montenegrins that their rights would be fully respected; nevertheless, Albanian harassment and looting led to the exodus of around 5,000 refugees.[91] According to Umiltà, the population of Metohija was more than two-thirds Albanian but of Serbian mother-tongue. Hence it was impossible in practice to take measures that met with everyone's satisfaction. The region was torn by the violence of the Albanian annexationists and by feuds among clans which 'concluded with truly frightful tolls of death and damage'.[92] At the end of April 1943, the Metohija commission was abolished and administration was transferred to the military authorities.

Bloody tribal feuds and vendettas swept Albania. The Resistance and the struggle against communism reached its height only in 1943 (the Albanian Communist Party had just 200 members in 1942 and 4,000 a year later). The year 1942 was marked by Albanian 'governmental' repression, while 1943 began with great ideological ferment and clashes between communists and the Balli Kombëtar (BK), the moderate and anti-communist national front officially founded in November 1942.[93] In early February 1943, General Giuseppe Pièche suggested the immediate transfer of powers to the military authorities, the purpose being to 'sweep away the Albanian political and administrative regime'. Jacomoni proposed instead that a government be set up with the collaboration of the loyal tribal chiefs in the country's northern regions. If the experiment failed, as a last resort powers would be transferred to the military authorities. Shortly before his replacement, the lieutenant general granted broad concessions to nationalists willing to collaborate: the appointment of an Italian government representative in Tirana to take care of Rome's interests, and the appointment of his Albanian counterpart in Italy; the conversion of the PFA into an Italian national party which assumed the name of Guard of Great Albania; the creation of an Albanian

[91] ASMAE, GABAP, b. 50, 'Relazione di Serafino Mazzolini a Ciano sull'opera svolta come commissario civile del Montenegro', late July 1941.

[92] Umiltà, *Jugoslavia e Albania*, 1947, p. 149.

[93] Fischer, *Albania at War*, pp. 125 and 133: 'The leaders of the BK claimed that the group was founded on the first day of the Italian invasion, and indeed, there probably was some informal organization among a few former politicians, but the organization and its platform were clearly a direct reaction to the founding of the [National Liberation Movement]. Albanian socialist historiography argues that it was put together by the reactionary middle classes . . . with the support of the fascist invaders . . . Milovan Djilas . . . described the BK as Albanian minority fascists.' See USSME, N 1–11, 'Diari storici', b. 972, Com. sup. FF.AA. Albania, 1 September 1942. According to the Italian military authorities, there were 'political' bands and gangs of common criminals operating in the country. The most dangerous of them were those led by Muharem Bajrktari, which was in contact with the British, by Abas Kupi with around 150 armed men, and by Mislym Peza, with around 100. Then there was Ram Muja Hoxha, a devoted communist known as the King of the Mountains, who led eighty-three armed men.

army; the independence of the Albanian gendarmerie, police force, financial police corps and militia.[94]

In March, when General Alberto Pariani took over from Jacomoni, the prime minister Eqrem Libohava had already been replaced by Maliq Bushati. Pariani immediately realized that Italians were faced by 'the last experiment', for if they did not 'successfully and rapidly . . . cure Albania's sickness', grievous consequences would ensue.[95] Pietromarchi acidly describes his opposition to Pariani's appointment in his diary:

> Jacomoni's policy has been a failure. In this moment of crisis we have not a single friend. We have bought the Albanians and now we watch as they offer themselves to the highest bidder. In a situation of such difficulty who do they propose to send in place of Jacomoni? Old Pariani, one of the authors of the present policy of appeasement towards the Albanians and principally responsible for the grave situation in which our army found itself when it entered the war. This shows that the illness from which Italy suffers is incurable. The old discredited men are rotated; the same errors are committed. Italy has returned to the worst of immobilism: from the Italy of Vittorio Veneto it has returned to the Italy of Franceschiello [the last king of Naples].[96]

In May 1943 the Germans occupied large parts of Kosovo and Albanian western Macedonia. In Peja, the Albanians, now liberated from the Italians, took revenge on Serbs who had collaborated with the Italians, and, 'on the pretext that Orthodox Christians were the sworn enemies of the Muslims and were conspiring against the current state of affairs', viciously persecuted them and their families. The most grievous abuses were committed by senior Albanian officials, for instance the chief of police in Priština, Nalbani, who blackmailed numerous Serbian shopkeepers, forcing them to pay huge sums to avoid imprisonment 'unless their women [were offered] as ransom'.[97] The spiralling ethnic violence induced those Montenegrins and Serbs who had not fled their homes to form bands with the declared intent of 'exacting vengeance for the murders and devastations perpetrated by the Albanians'.[98]

[94] On the Albanian flag, Fischer, *Albania at War*, p. 92, writes: 'The Italians took the old flag, a black double eagle on a red field, and added a fascio on either side, looking as if they were about to crush the old symbol. To make matters worse, the Italians topped the eagle off with the crown of Savoy, which itself is topped by a cross. In a country where 70 per cent of the people were Moslem, this was little more than woodenheadness.' The former Albanian flag was reinstated in May 1941.

[95] DDI, ser. IX, 1939–43, vol. 10, doc. 178, 'luogotenente generale in Albania, Pariani, al sottosegretario agli Esteri Bastianini', 1 April 1943.

[96] Pietromarchi, diary, 16 February 1943.

[97] USSME, M 3, b. 19, 'generale Pièche al GABAP, 28 maggio 1943, Relazione sul Kossovo albanese'. Someone at the CS commented on the general's report: 'It's incredible what you can dream up when you don't know the facts.'

[98] ASMAE, GABAP, b. 51, 'telegramma a mano del GABAP – Ufficio Montenegro al CS', 10 November 1941.

As we have seen in the course of this chapter, in one year of occupation the Italians began a project for the forced Italianization of the annexed territories. Although one cannot appropriately speak of ethnic cleansing and racial purification, the Fascist regime nevertheless sought to denationalize the native population by force. The intention was that, with time, not only would every trace of the recent past be erased but Fascistization would furnish the few natives of Italian stock with a new identity – a Fascist identity. Once the war was won, the experience acquired in Italy's new provinces would be imported into the peninsula. For this reason Mussolini obstinately defended his most loyal lieutenant, Giuseppe Bastianini. The extensive powers of the governor (or the high commissioner) and the fact that he depended directly on the Duce were indicative of the revolution that Mussolini intended to bring about in Italy.

The governor exercised totalitarian control over economic activities, the free professions and associations – in short, over every aspect of life in the new provinces. Ideally, he would have governed as a minor *duce* over a population 'racially improved' in that it had been purged of Jews (as we shall see in chapter 11)[99] and of all persons impossible to assimilate politically, or of a different race: the *Volksdeutschen*, the Croats and the Serbs. If the Italianization programme had been accomplished in its entirety, the new provinces would have been almost completely emptied of their populations. The only people left would have been the individuals of 'Italian blood' whom the regime had imbued with 'the Fascist spirit' and the colonists transferred from Italy.

The convinced commitment of politicians, but also of high-ranking officials (at the Bank of Italy, for example) and of bureaucrats and technocrats, to the Italianization project demonstrates that it was not the illusion of one visionary alone. The 'men on the spot', perhaps more than those who remained in Rome, devoted themselves with enthusiasm and professionalism to implementing the Fascist plans, and they relented only when the situation was definitively beyond their control. It was only the insurmountable difficulties encountered in the occupied territories that forced the Italian authorities to discontinue their campaign for forced Italianization.

The Italianization policies also reveal the extent to which the men sent to the conquered territories had internalized the regime's geo-political vision, and they also demonstrate that this was not mere propaganda. The distinction between the *piccolo spazio* and the *grande spazio* (the imperial community) was apparent in the differences between occupation policies:

[99] Sertoli Salis, 'La condizione degli ebrei nella comunità imperiale italiana', 1942.

while, as the journal *Critica Fascista* pointed out, in the occupied territories the intention was to leave an imprint of Fascist culture, in the annexed territories it was to achieve totalitarian Fascistization.

A final consideration concerns the provinces annexed to Albania. In Kosovo and Debar, despite the endeavours of Umiltà, Italy gave free rein to its allies. The Italians had no objection to the forced Albanianization of the new provinces; their only concern was that the excesses committed should not undermine public order and disrupt relations with neighbouring regions. It is very likely that the Italians would have supported the Ustaša campaign for forced Croatization if relationships with them had not been damaged by Dalmatian irredentism, and if the German influence in Croatia had not been so ubiquitous. They would have opposed mass murder, but they would certainly have had no qualms over deportations and resettlements to bring about the country's ethnic and racial homogeneity. Unlike Nazism, Fascism would have admitted European states and ethnic groups into the imperial community provided they submitted to Fascist domination.

CHAPTER 9

Collaboration

Philippe Burrin and Claudio Pavone have shown that dividing the occupied societies between 'white and black', classifying them into the rigid categories of 'collaborationists' and 'partisans' alone, is Manichean and obsolete.[1] The grey area of accommodation and compromise was broad and it comprised the majority of the population. The purpose of historical knowledge is served much better if reactions to the occupiers are differentiated according to the causes of a particular attitude towards them and the ways in which it was expressed. The upheavals provoked by defeat induced both individuals and entire sections of society to seek a *modus vivendi* with the occupiers, and they sought it for a wide variety of reasons. The degrees of compromise were numerous, and it is inappropriate to lump together the Greek gendarme, the French prefect, the Četniks and the anti-communist militiaman of Yugoslavia. A distinction must be drawn between those who fought alongside the occupiers for ideological reasons and those who collaborated in order to survive. Large numbers of workers, industrialists, shopkeepers, farmers and artisans had to reach some sort of accommodation with the occupiers if they were to continue to work and to earn a living. Some of the most vulnerable ethnic or religious minorities collaborated with the Italians because they considered them the lesser of two evils, or because they could ease their suffering by gaining material benefit from the occupation.

The first to acquire thorough acquaintance with collaboration and to realize that it had varying degrees, and that it was forthcoming for diverse reasons, were the civil and military authorities on the spot. An example is provided in a report written by the Italian consul in Sarajevo, Alberto Rossi, who found that on his arrival in that city he was warmly welcomed by the Muslim community. But, he explained, the Muslims were only accommodating to the Italians because their relations with Zagreb were so extremely difficult. For similar reasons, according to the

[1] Burrin, *La France à l'heure allemande*; Pavone, *Una guerra civile*.

CC.RR. (24th mixed unit) Murge Division (stationed in Herzegovina), the Jewish, Muslim and Serb communities treated the Italians cordially, while the Croats preferred the Germans. Reports by the 14th CdA 'on the spirit of the populations in the occupied territories' classified the attitudes of the Montenegrins to the Regio Esercito as follows: the Orthodox intellectuals (a 'tiny minority') were favourably disposed to 'the Anglo-Saxons' and they aspired to reconstruction of Yugoslavia, or to the creation of a Greater Serbia. They regarded the Italian occupation as being the 'least of all evils'. The majority of the Orthodox Christian population, described as 'simple and primitive', wanted the protection of the Regio Esercito but the clergy was aggressively anti-Italian. The Orthodox Christian inhabitants of the territories ceded to Croatia – Čajnice, Foča and Višegrad – hoped that their lands would be restored to Montenegro, while the Muslims harboured some 'sentiments of sympathy' for the occupation troops but collaborated only because they were hostile to the Serbs. The Jews of Montenegro formed a tiny community almost entirely concentrated in Višegrad: they dreaded German occupation of their town and pleaded for Italian protection. In Dalmatia, the Italian authorities distinguished among the attitudes of the civilian population according to ethnicity, religion and social class, remarking that the peasants were devoted to work, the professionals were hostile and most students were communist activists egged on by 'certain magistrates'. The clergy, they reported, were ambivalent and treacherous.[2]

One of the few accurate statements in General Mario Roatta's memoirs is his assertion that there was no such thing as a general and organized Balkan insurrection raised by all the region's peoples. There were indeed partisans and collaborationists; above all, however, there was 'a great quantity of people entirely indifferent to the state structure of the zone, and perhaps also to whoever might eventually assume power; they asked nothing more than to be left in peace to attend to their daily chores, take care of their property and practise their customs'.[3]

Of course, not all the local populations reached compromises with the occupiers: not only the partisans but also the educated classes and the intellectuals were generally hostile to the Italians. Greek and Yugoslav Orthodox Christian clerics were very reluctant to collaborate. Their Catholic counterparts – particularly the Franciscans of Croatia – owned large estates on the Dalmatian coast and consequently gave vent to the 'utmost violence and hatred' against the occupiers by mounting an unremitting and 'poisonous'

[2] USSME, N 1–11, 'Diari storici', b. 523, 'Divisione Sassari, comandante della divisione Furio Monticelli al Comando del VI CdA', 19 July 1941.

[3] Roatta, *Otto milioni di baionette*, 1946, pp. 172–3.

propaganda campaign against everything Italian.[4] But some populations were more hostile than others. In France, for example, even though the occupiers showed great restraint, the locals treated them with cool disdain. Emblematic is the reaction of the headmistress of a girls' school in Annemasse (in Savoy, on the border with Geneva), who instructed her pupils to show contempt for the Italians: they should refuse to speak to them and turn their heads away if addressed.[5]

Collaboration had indubitable advantages for the Italians, mindful as they were of the scant possibilities of penetration and their military weakness. If the Italian occupation forces could persuade the governments and administrations of the occupied countries to co-operate, they would be able to free resources with which to defend the territory, enforce security and maintain law and order, while at the same time exploiting the economies of those countries. And yet in none of the occupied territories, except for Greece and then only briefly, did the Italians enjoy the genuine collaboration of governments and public administrations. As soon as rebel movements were sufficiently strong to jeopardize security and order, the occupiers turned to native bands and militias for military assistance. But, before this, they had had little interest in *political* collaboration, either in the annexed territories or in those that they had occupied militarily. They baulked at reaching agreements with nationalist leaders, at promising autonomy or independence or at using the services of separatist movements.

At the end of 1941, the garrison and division commands held their first parleys with armed Bosnian and Herzegovinian bands; and in the summer of 1942 they resorted to the assistance of Dalmatian and Slovene bands. By contrast, in Greece, where the Italians still had the situation under control, when the commander of the Pinerolo Division, Cesare Benelli, asked for authorization to set up organized bands he was rebuffed by General Carlo Geloso, who ordered that no negotiations must ever take place with 'bandits'.[6] Only at the end of 1942, when the Resistance movement had begun to cause difficulties for the occupiers, did the Italians consider persuading the non-communist forces among the Andartes to come over to their side.[7] Whereas in Yugoslavia, aided by its mosaic of

4 ASMAE, GABAP, b. 46, 26 June 1941.

5 ASMAE, AA.PP. – 'Francia', b. 54, 'DRA – Annecy alla CIAF', 6 December 1942.

6 USSME, N 1–11, 'Diari storici', b. 839, 'Com. sup. FF.AA. Grecia ai comandanti del III, VIII e XXVI CdA', 13 May 1942.

7 USSME, N 1–11, 'Diari storici', b. 1237, 'Comando III CdA al Com. sup. FF.AA. Grecia, 26 marzo 1943, Promemoria del prefetto di Trikala'.

nationalities, ethnic groups, religions and political movements, they could rely on the assistance of armed bands and militias drafted into the Regio Esercito, in the Greek peninsula they were forced to abandon any such plans because the non-communist activists of the National Liberation Front (Ethniko Apelefterotiko Metopo, EAM) were convinced that the Allies would soon be landing in Crete or Epirus. Consequently, notwithstanding their fervent anti-communism, they refused to collaborate with the occupiers. The situation in France was similar to that in Greece.

How did the occupiers choose their collaborators? They did so by identifying a disaffected political faction, ethnic group or religious minority and fomenting its grievances so that it would sever its political, economic and social ties with the rest of the occupied society. Money and food rations (extremely valuable commodities in times of war) would be lavished on the breakaway group in exchange for the military assistance that the occupiers needed, but political promises were never made. In the Yugoslavian territories the Italians adjusted to the age-old law of the Balkans: 'The friends of my friends are my friends, the enemies of my friends are my enemies; but the enemies of my enemies are my friends.'[8]

The Italians' divide-and-rule strategy was a gamble: had it failed, the bonds that it was meant to sever would instead have been strengthened. The occupiers were aware of the precariousness of collaboration, a phenomenon inextricably bound up with the fortunes of war. They knew that they had to proceed with caution and that they could grant only minor concessions. Collaboration was based on the principle of *do ut des* ('I give so that you give'), on compromises and on delicate balances vulnerable to distant events: the Allied landings in North Africa, for example, or the defeat at Stalingrad.

It is now possible to draw up a typology of collaboration based on the extent of political and dependence on the occupiers:

(1) pro-Fascist collaborationists: numerically small groups, even more insignificant in term of military assistance to the occupiers; they included the members of the Azione Nizzarda and some Italophone residents of Dalmatia;
(2) groups of armed auxiliaries (the MVACs, Anti-Communist Voluntary Militias) drafted into the Regio Esercito;
(3) groups that furnished tactical and military support during military operations.

[8] Steinberg, *All or Nothing*, p. 38.

The second and third categories often merged together in Yugoslavia, according to military circumstances and type of operation. The militias assisted in campaigns against the resistance movements in Slovenia, Dalmatia and the occupied territories of Croatia – although in these last zones the commanders of the Regio Esercito would have preferred to rely on the Croatian army. The *domobrans* – and even more so the Ustaša militia – were a 'hotchpotch', unreliable and entirely unprepared for combat 'against an astute adversary, with perfect knowledge of the terrain, master of the ambush, who is never caught off guard, who is everywhere and nowhere'.[9] Given the complexity and difficulty of military collaboration with Zagreb, the Regio Esercito sought to enlist as many MVAC volunteers as possible, thereby bringing them under military orders and preventing them from joining the Resistance.

The most substantial tactical and military support was provided by the Yugoslavian Četniks: militant nationalists who had 'fled to the woods' as the Balkan expression put it. Consisting largely of Orthodox Serbs and monarchists, loyal to the Yugoslavian government in exile and led by Draža Mihajlović, the Četniks had organized themselves into armed bands of which many were enlisted under officers of the disbanded Yugoslavian army. In the zones of Croatia occupied by the Regio Esercito, the only features shared by these disparate Četnik bands were their hatred of the Ustaša government and their desire to fight the communists. Their political goal was the independence of Serbia, the birth of a Greater Serbia. But given the circumstances – the war and foreign military occupation of Serbia – they were willing to settle for autonomy and guarantees of their ethnic and religious rights and recovery of their property seized by the Ustaše. The Italians knew that the Četniks preferred the British and that if the opportunity arose they would turn their weapons against the Axis; nevertheless, given their willingness to fight against the partisans, the Italians wanted to ensure their military contribution. The Četniks collaborated with the Italians 'for reasons of short-term convenience'[10] in the awareness that if the partisans were definitively defeated their services would be superfluous and the Axis powers would turn hostile towards them. According to Jozo Tomasevich, in Yugoslavia as in all the Balkan territories there was a traditional inclination to use terror for political ends which set off 'a dreadful spiral of terror and counter-terror'.[11] So it was that the Četniks obtained

9 USSME, N I–II, 'Diari storici', b. 379, 'Comando II Armata, Ufficio Operazioni, 12 settembre 1941', signed Vittorio Ambrosio.

10 Tomasevich, *The Chetniks*, p. 196.

11 Ibid., pp. 256–61.

full licence to commit crimes and to wage personal vendettas without being punished. They had good reason to loathe the Ustaše and the Muslims who had massacred defenceless Orthodox Christians. They took revenge using the same methods as their enemies and under the pretext of waging a holy war. For example, against the Muslims in Bosnia-Herzegovina and the Sanjak they invoked the betrayal they had suffered during the First World War when the Muslims of Bosnia had joined forces with the Austro-Hungarian Schultzkorps. Bolstered by Italian support, the Četniks also committed acts of savagery against the communist partisans, who responded with equal violence.

The Italians had reasons other than suppression of the partisans for so actively seeking the Četniks' collaboration. According to Srdjan Trifković, the underlying reason for the Italians' accommodating policy towards the Četniks was the refusal by the Italian commands to fight a war in the Balkans on terms dictated by the Germans, under the command of the Germans, and in order to achieve the Germans' purposes. Besides keeping Nazi troops out of the Italian zones, the aim of Vittorio Ambrosio, Mario Roatta and Mario Robotti was to ensure that the Italian forces remained intact. Defeating Tito was of secondary importance.[12]

COLLABORATION IN THE ANNEXED TERRITORIES: SLOVENIA AND DALMATIA

During the campaign of April 1941, a number of Slovene political leaders in Ljubljana decided to establish a Slovene National Committee composed of the heads of the Catholic Popular Party, the Liberal Party and various socialists. The former *bān* Marko Natlačen was appointed president. The purpose of the committee was to obtain independence under Italian and German protection, on the pattern of Slovakia. On 4 May 1941 a group of Slovene notables sent Mussolini 'an act of submission' signed by former Yugoslavian ministers, academics, the mayor Juro Adlešić, representatives of the professional orders, and the leader of the Liberal Party Albert Kramer. The prince-bishop Gregorij Rožman then sent a similar message to the Duce.

The Italians rejected the request because they intended to annex the region. Initially, the policy of Italianizing the province excluded the local élites from any form of collaboration. Neither Emilio Grazioli nor Robotti thought that the direct involvement of the Slovenes would serve any useful

[12] Trifkovic, 'Rivalry Between Germany and Italy in Croatia', p. 898.

purpose, given that it appeared that the embryonic partisan movement could easily be crushed. Only at the end of 1941 did the Italian authorities realize the advantages that they could have gained by seeking to obtain the consensus of the Slovene population.

The distinctive feature of Slovene collaborators – generically called Belogardisti (from the Slovene *belogardizem* or White Guards; *Bela Garda* was the term used by the Yugoslavian communists after World War II for the armed Slovene anti-communists, a reference to the anti-communist fighters against the Russian Revolution and the early Soviet Union) – was the markedly clerical and conservative character of the movement (if it can be correctly called such). They pursued their action in a well-established political and cultural setting where the largest political organization was the Popular Party – or more exactly, what was left of it after most of its leaders had gone into exile in London with the royal government. Its main representatives in Ljubljana were Natlačen, Anton Dubrovnik, Škrbec, the mayor Adlešić and General Leon Rupnik. The Belogardista movement consisted of an anti-clerical faction (*plavogardiste*, from *Plava Garda*, the Blue Guard, the name given to the few followers of Mihajlović led by officers of the former Yugoslavian army), called 'liberals' by the occupiers; and 'black' (i.e. extreme right) monarchist and collaborationist formations like Lambert Ehrlich's Straža v Viharju (Keeping Guard in the Storm, and Slovene section of Dimitrije Ljotić's Zbor), whose action was insignificant. After the annexation, the leaders of the Popular Party founded the Slovene Legion (Slovenska Legija), while the 'liberals' set up the Falcon League (Sokolska Legija) (see. appendix, table 47). Then, in March 1942, the Slovene Alliance (Slovenska Zavesa) was created; it styled itself anti-communist and separatist and was renamed the Centro Nazionale Sloveno by the Italians. It was led by Natlačen, Bishop Rožman and General Rupnik, close collaborators with the Italian authorities who, in May 1942, created a military formation, the Styrian Battalion, made up of members of the Alliance, the Straža, the Zbor and Četniks. The declared intention of the Alliance and its armed wing was to collaborate with the Italians until the communists had been defeated, whereupon they would join forces with the Anglo-Americans.

The fervid anti-communism of the Popular Party and the National Liberal Party furnished the Italians with valid and influential political support in the province. Yet conceding greater political power to men like Natlačen and allowing General Rupnik to create the core of a future national army would have reignited desire for independence in the Ljubljana political class, confounded the reasons for the annexation and increased the number of the Italians' adversaries.[13] Nevertheless, the occupiers believed that they could harness the anti-communist movement and steer it away from its aspirations for independence. And all in all, at least until 1942, they managed to do so.

In the early months of 1942, Rupnik submitted to General Robotti a project for the campaign against the partisans based on the creation of Streifkorps (autonomous counter-insurgency bands) which would join the Regio Esercito troops in putting down the communist movement. The Italians rejected the proposal, preferring to form an anti-communist militia, the MVAC, enlisted in the 11th CdA. The first band, made up of 800 men, began operations in July 1942. The CdA command set up a MVAC Office headed by Colonel Annibale Gallo assisted by a Slovene colonel. Every CdA division and unit had a similar office, and every company consisted of 50- to 200-man formations commanded formally by a Slovene non-commissioned officer but in fact by an Italian liaison officer. The formations were politically very heterogeneous. Even priests enlisted, and they worked at the Curia of Ljubljana, not as chaplains but as non-commissioned officers or commanders responsible for organization of the militia.

By November 1942 the total number of enlisted men stood at around 4,000. Tomasevich and Ferenc put the figure at around 6,000 in August 1943, and Marco Cuzzi reports that the number of militiamen had reached 6,131 in July 1943. Only 1,800 of them originated from 'Italian' Slovenia; the majority were from 'German' Slovenia, while the rest came from Serbia, Bosnia and, especially, Croatia. The militiamen were initially used as interpreters and informers, but they were then dispatched to join the fighting against the partisans, where they proved themselves as effective as they were violent. During the anti-partisan campaign of September 1942, the Command of the Isonzo Division announced that it had killed 53 communists in combat, wounded 15 and shot 4, while 164 had surrendered. On the Italian side, 4 officers and 55 soldiers had been killed and 37 wounded, and 24 men were missing. The MVAC forces proved to be more 'efficient' than the Italian troops, having killed 66 communists and wounded 40.[14]

But from December 1942 onwards, the bands achieved less 'successful' results. There were numerous reports of infiltration by communists, thefts

[13] Cuzzi, *L'occupazione italiana della Slovenia*, p. 87.

[14] During operations by the Isonzo Division between 23 September and 4 October 1942, 194 communists were killed in combat, 3 were wounded, 2 were shot and 13 surrendered. The Regio Esercito lost 2 officers and 2 soldiers, and 15 soldiers were wounded. Four MVAC combatants were killed and 3 were wounded. In the month of October, more or less the same number of losses were inflicted and suffered, which confirms the effectiveness of the MVAC.

of weapons and bungled round-ups, while the partisans improved their combat organization.[15] Then, but only for a few months, the Italians managed to foment infighting among the Slovenes themselves. In early 1943, the partisan forces belonging to the OF (Osvobodilna Fronta) repeatedly created serious difficulties for the 11th CdA, and they adopted a strategy which proved highly efficacious: the Belagardisti put themselves forward as the 'dupes', the weak party obliged perforce to commit violence and therefore to be forgiven; and they considerably moderated their traditional hostility against the clergy. Although seizures of cattle, food and clothing belonging to the families of militiamen continued, the executions of collaborationists (except for those of particular importance) became rare.[16] The poor quality of weapons and the precarious circumstances of their families induced numerous members of the MVAC to cease collaborating with the Italians.

By the end of January 1943, wrote the commander of the Isonzo Division, public sympathy for the Belagardisti had almost entirely dwindled away.[17] Even at its apogee, the Bela Garda was never more than a minority movement, and the crimes that it committed against the civilian population alienated the majority of non-communist Slovenes. If the Italian occupiers had endorsed the idea of independence for Slovenia on the Croatian or Slovakian pattern, they would have received greater collaboration. But this possibility was discarded because Rome obstinately insisted that Ljubljana was 'an Italian province'.

The same applies to the three provinces of the Governorate of Dalmatia, where the forced Italianization of the local population and the anti-Croatian policy pursued by Giuseppe Bastianini precluded any significant collaboration with the Italians. The few armed native auxiliaries, the majority of them Italophone Dalmatians, were enlisted in the Regio Esercito. On 23 June 1942, with the assistance of the Četnik *vojvoda* Ilija Trifunović-Birčanin (the pre-war nationalist leader and Mihajlović's representative in Dalmatia), the first unit of the MVAC or BAC (Anti-Communist Band) was created.[18] It was commanded by Colonel Eugenio Morra, chief of the governor's military cabinet, and its 1,500 men (9 bands) were enlisted with

[15] USSME, N 1–11, 'Diari storici', b. 1319, 'Divisione Isonzo'.

[16] ACS, MI, *Servizi di guerra, 1941–5*; the document was written in March 1943. Barracks in protected zones had to be constructed for the Roma of the town of Črnomelj in Slovenia, who were threatened by the partisans because they were actively collaborating with the Regio Esercito.

[17] USSME, N 1–11, 'Diari storici', b. 1320, 'Comando Divisione Isonzo al Comando dell'XI CdA – Ufficio "I", 31 gennaio 1943, Relazione quindicinale sul servizio "I"'.

[18] USSME, M 3, b. 85, 'governatore della Dalmazia, 23 giugno 1943, Costituzione del corpo volontari anticomunisti della Dalmazia italiana'.

the Zara Division and divided between two battalions: the Twenty-Second or Greek Orthodox Battalion (bands 4 and 5) and the Twentieth or the Catholic Battalion (bands 1–3 and 6–8; another band composed mainly of Italian and Croatian Dalmatians was created on 21 May 1943).[19] Band 9 consisted of Italian and Orthodox Dalmatians and operated independently in Šibenik. Of interest is the oath sworn by inductees into the MVAC:

> Here before the Crucified Christ I swear to dedicate myself unto death to the annihilation of communism, fighting with weapons in hand under the orders of the Italian government to bring peace and prosperity to Italian Dalmatia in accordance with the Fascist law and the Fascist order. Should I not obey my orders, or should I break my oath, may God and the Italian government punish me and my family.[20]

The annexed territories differed from those occupied militarily in that the Italians did not permit members of the indigenous population to fight against the communists in bands operating independently of the Regio Esercito.

CROATIA

Until the end of 1941, the documents of the Italian diplomatic and military authorities designated both the communists (to whom they very rarely applied the epithet of 'partisans') and the Četniks as insurgents, rebels or brigands. Such was the turmoil in the former Yugoslavia that, on 28 December 1941, the military attaché at the Italian legation in Belgrade, Luigi Bonfatti, illustrated the chaos by describing the ease with which the warring factions changed their allegiances.[21] All the parties concerned, wrote Bonfatti, took up official postures which were profoundly at odds with reality. Furthermore, for the Croatian authorities the Četniks were 'enemies of the state' to be eliminated even if they were fighting against the partisans. Yet the 'I' (intelligence) service reported that the Croats had reached agreements with Četnik bands, the purpose of which was to undermine the Italians. The German command in Belgrade categorically refused to contemplate participation by Četnik bands in joint operations

[19] USSME, N 1–11, 'Diari storici', b. 1280, 'Comando Divisione Zara, Ufficio BAC, generale Vitale', 21 May 1943.

[20] USSME, M 3, b. 85, 'governatore della Dalmazia, 23 giugno 1943, Costituzione del corpo volontari anticomunisti della Dalmazia italiana'.

[21] USSME, N 1–11, 'Diari storici', b. 1371, 'legazione d'Italia a Belgrado, addetto militare Bonfatti allo SMRE, 28 dicembre 1941, visto e appuntato dal generale Roatta'.

by the Axis powers; yet it had no compunction about using their services in Serbia. The Germans suspected that the Italians were in contact with a number of Četnik leaders, in particular with the notorious Mihajlović. The Italians suspected that the Germans had engineered parleys between the Četnik leader and Milan Nedić. In short, mutual suspicion reigned. A further difficulty was that the Četniks were not an organization with a single leader who co-ordinated its political and military action. Each band had its own leader who decided independently with whom, when and for how long to collaborate.

Until the end of 1941, Rome hesitated over how to deal with the 'Četnik question'. In November 1941, the first talks were held between the Regio Esercito and Četnik leaders: Nikola Trifunović and Ragenović in Split; Ježdimir Dangić and Bosko Todorović on the upper reaches of the River Drin.[22] But Rome envisaged a different strategy. In a note to Ciano dated 28 January 1942, Luca Pietromarchi explained that the 'distinction between Četnik bands and communist bands' was 'more formal than real' because they were 'united in their hostility against the Axis'.[23] In February 1942, the official policy laid down by the head of SMRE was as follows:

(1) the Croats were to be treated firmly but fairly;
(2) there were to be no negotiations with the Četniks;
(3) an uncompromising campaign was to be waged against the communists.[24]

The commander of the Second Army, General Ambrosio, took a different position. He pointed out that 'bearing the fundamental problem in mind and the correlated expediency of reducing our adversaries to the minimum, in the event that the Četniks and communists can be kept separate', it would be advisable to 'attempt to reach an agreement with the Četniks . . . on prior agreement with Germany, accompanying it with parallel pressure on the Croatian government to comply with our ideas'.[25]

On 6 March, General Roatta, who as head of the SMRE had been suspicious of the Četniks, on assuming command of the Second Army suggested that no action should be taken against them, because this would create a united Četnik–communist front and endanger Italian garrisons.

[22] USSME, M 3, b. 61, 'Comando II Armata, Ufficio "I" allo SMRE', 2 February 1942, signed Roatta; ASMAE, GABAP, b. 35, 'Comando VI CdA al Comando della II Armata'.

[23] ASMAE, GABAP, b. 35, 28 January 1942, 'Appunto di Pietromarchi per l'eccellenza il ministro'. The note states the views of the Italian military attaché in Croatia, Giancarlo Re.

[24] USSME, M 3, b. 61, 'SMRE al Comando della II Armata', 13 February 1942.

[25] Talpo, *Dalmazia*, vol. II, p. 165, annex to ch. 1, doc. 11, 'SMRE al CS, 4 febbraio 1942, Rapporti con i croati e con i cetnici'.

He proposed that the Italian authorities should 'menar il can per l'aia' or pussyfoot, given that, although wide-ranging Četnik action against the communists was advantageous from a military point of view, it was not so from a political one. When such action had concluded, the Četniks would demand payment from the Italians and the Germans. And if they were not paid in the coin that they wanted, the Četniks, battle-hardened and bolstered by their successes, would most likely turn against the Axis forces. Sufficient support should be given to the Četniks to induce them to fight the communists, Roatta argued, but not enough support for them to be able do so across a broad front. The purpose was to have them fight not all the Croatian forces and authorities but only the communists, so that 'they slit each other's throats'.[26]

During the month of March, Roatta provided Rome with a map of the Četnik and communist forces which divided them up according to their zones of action and political aims. He reported that the head of the Četnik movement was Mihajlović, and that among the Četnik leaders in Bosnia were Major Petar Bacović (head of the Foča Četniks, known to the Italian authorities for avenging the shooting of Četniks with the execution of Catholic civilians) and Major Dangić, who according to the military attaché in Belgrade, Bonfatti, followed the orders of the Serbian prime minister Nedić. Then there were the Bosnian bands headed by Ljotić and Jefrem Jeftić, who fought ferociously against the Croats and aimed at annexation of Bosnia to Serbia (Jeftić's band operated mainly in the province of Višegrad). The Četniks of Herzegovina were represented by the former parliamentary deputy for Bosnia Dobroslav Jevdjević, and they paid allegiance to Dangić rather than to Mihajlović. They were intransigently anti-Croatian and inclined to alignment with the communists.

During the inter-allied military conference of Opatija – organized to prepare the 'Trio' anti-partisan operation planned to take place in Bosnia-Herzegovina between 20 April and 13 May 1942 – the Croats rejected an Italian proposal to involve the Četniks of Bosnia-Herzegovina in the campaign. And, with the support of the Germans, they prevailed. But then, at a conference held in Ljubljana (28 and 29 March), it was decided to conclude temporary and non-political accords with the Četniks of Herzegovina, but not

[26] ASMAE, GABAP, b. 35, 6 March 1942. Roatta wrote: 'at most allow their bands to operate in parallel with the Italian and German forces, as do the nationalist bands in Montenegro . . . Italian relations with the Četniks were summed up in the formula: because you say that you are favourable to us, please restrain yourselves with us and with the Croats. This happened. Subsequently, as the communist menace grew apace, the formula was made more specific: show your loyalty to us in practical terms by fighting the communists. And the Četniks accepted the formula and began to apply it.'

with those of eastern Bosnia (and especially not with Dangić's Četniks).[27] The military collaboration of the Četniks bore fruit – or at least it did so according to the tables compiled by Supersloda (see appendix, tables 48 and 49).

Thus, when the operations had been successfully concluded, the Italians would continue the collaboration with the Četniks and conduct further military action in Bosnia, shifting it eastwards as far as the River Drina, which was the demarcation line with the German zone.[28] The Germans, aware of the dangers of an extension of the Italian occupation and of an Italo-Četnik alliance, rejected the proposal. The wrangling between the Axis powers gave the communists the time they needed to regroup and to launch new offensives, especially in the territories occupied by the Second Army. The Italian commanders in Croatia held the Germans responsible for the situation, and their response was to continue collaboration with the Četniks in their occupation zone.[29] Mussolini openly supported the policy of his generals. And for once the CS made itself clear to Supersloda by issuing instructions that agreements could be reached with the Četniks only in the Italian occupation zones and that they were to be exclusively military in nature, despite the German veto on any form of negotiation.[30]

A turning point in relations between the Italians and the Četniks came in June 1942 with the Italo-Croatian agreement on the dismantling of garrisons in the third zone (the one most densely populated with Orthodox

[27] Italy's representatives at the Abbazia conference were: Vittorio Ambrosio, Mario Roatta and Giovan Battista Oxilia. The German representatives were: General Walter Kuntze, Commander South-East, representing the OKW, General Paul Bader, commander of the German troops in Serbia, Enno von Rintelen, German general at the CS and General Edmund Glaise von Horstenau. The Croats were represented by General Vladimir Laxa, the Croatian Army chief of General Staff (ASMAE, GABAP, b. 35). At the Ljubljana meeting, Roatta, Bader and Laxa drew up the orders and plan of deployment for Operation 'Trio' (USSME, M 3, b. 71). See also USSME, M 3, b. 58, 'Comando II Armata, Ufficio Operazioni, al generale Bader, 31 marzo 1942, Trattative con i cetnici'; ASMAE, GABAP, b. 32, 'Ufficio di collegamento con il Comando della II Armata alla legazione di Zagabria e al GABAP, 15 aprile 1942, Colloqui del generale Roatta con il poglavnik Ante Pavelic e il maresciallo Slavko Kvaternik'; b. 35, 'Comando II Armata, Ufficio Operazioni, a Pietromarchi, 25 aprile 1942, Interferenze politiche sulle operazioni in Bosnia'.

[28] ASMAE, GABAP, b. 35, comment by Pietromarchi attached to 'telespresso n. 128 dell'Ufficio di collegamento con il Comando della II Armata, 7 marzo 1942, in visione al capo di gabinetto del ministro, Blasco Lanza d'Ajeta'.

[29] USSME, N 1–11, 'Diari storici', b. 1371, 'SMRE – Ufficio Operazioni', 10 February 1942; ASMAE, GABAP, b. 35, 16 January 1942, 'Appunto per l'eccellenza il ministro Pietromarchi (appunto trattenuto un giorno dal duce)'. The SMRE considered the German forces 'insufficient' to put down the rebel movement. The Germans were only interested in the security of strategic communications concerning the production of coal, timber and bauxite, and their transport to the Reich.

[30] ASMAE, GABAP, b. 35, 'Michele Scammacca al MAE', 21 April 1942.

Serbs). The Ustaše massacred defenceless civilians in various towns and villages, and the Četniks responded with equal violence and barbarism.[31] The latter accused the Italians of having 'abandoned them to the partisan menace and having failed to prevent acts of violence by the Ustaša units'.[32] Given the small numbers of the Croatian troops and their inefficiency, the Regio Esercito resumed its garrisoning of certain zones and once again requested assistance from the Četniks, who seized the opportunity to ask for greater guarantees and more concessions. One of the most fervently anti-Croat Četnik leaders, Momčilo Djujić (decorated for military valour by Peter II and active in northern Dalmatia), managed to obtain the sums normally paid to the MVAC for his five thousand men and also greater autonomy of action (his bands 'officially' formed ten battalions designated 'MVAC-Dinara'). Owing to the situation that had arisen since June, to prevent any worsening of relations with Zagreb and to curb the excesses committed by the bands, the Regio Esercito sought to enlist as many Četniks as possible in the MVAC. Unfortunately, the statistics on the militiamen and the documents on the duties assigned to them are very incomplete. However, it is possible to give a number of examples to illustrate the criteria and the *modus operandi* of the Italian divisional commands.

In June 1942, the Messina Division had around one hundred militiamen, which it used for routine communications among its units. The members of the bands were issued with identity cards by the 'I' Section of the divisional command and each was armed with a rifle and eight cartridge clips.[33] During round-up operations they were used as guides or informers for identification of partisans who had merged back into the civilian population. They pointed out the homes of fugitive partisans to be burned, and they prepared lists of persons to be taken as hostage. However, the commanders did not trust the information furnished by the militiamen, knowing full well that they often acted on the basis of personal grudges or sympathies.[34] For this reason, until the end of 1942, they were rarely given garrisoning duties and all contact between them and the Ustaša militia was prevented.[35]

[31] USSME, M 3, b. 66, 'Missione militare di Zagabria a Supersloda, 27 giugno 1942, "Eccessi" dei cetnici contro la popolazione civile di Nevesinje'.

[32] USSME, M 3, b. 66, 'Comando VI CdA al Comando di Supersloda', 26 June 1942.

[33] USSME, N 1–11, 'Diari storici', b. 735, 'Comando Divisione Messina, 10 giugno 1942, Compiti e dipendenze delle bande di volontari anticomunisti'.

[34] USSME, N 1–11, 'Diari storici', b. 1007, '4° Reggimento bersaglieri ciclisti al Comando della Divisione Messina', 14 August 1942.

[35] USSME, N 1–11, 'Diari storici', b. 993, 'Supersloda – Ufficio Operazioni al comandante del VI CdA Renzo Dalmazzo, 24 settembre 1942, firmato Roatta'.

The Sassari Division created two types of militia unit: some performed the same duties as the Italian troops (A); others were given the task of defending the towns and villages in which the militiamen had their homes (B). The latter were tasked with creating a security zone and observing partisan movements so that penetration by the rebels could be halted, while the former were deployed in offensive actions. The anti-communist militiamen were not officially selected on the basis of religion, but in fact the majority were Orthodox Christians and Muslims offered enlistment provided they were resolute in the fight against the rebels, and with no commitment of a political nature being made.[36]

By 1 September 1942, the army had recruited (for payment in kune and/or kind) five formations of Orthodox Croats and three of Catholic Croats under the command of local chiefs, the majority of whom were former officers in the Yugoslavian army. Each formation was supervised by the Italian section commander in the zone and by two liaison officers responsible for training and discipline. The A-type units were assigned to Italian regiments or battalions, and their men wore a blue armband bearing the insignia of the division command and the name of their chief. The B-type units were under the command of the closest Italian garrison and wore headgear which varied according to the unit (the Dalmatian or the Bosnian cap). The troops were billeted as close as possible to the Italian commands, and a recruitment centre was opened in Knin with several branches. On 21 September 1942, the Sassari Division had fully nine battalions (each of which consisted of four companies of around 120 men, each company being divided into three platoons of approximately 40 men: hence a battalion numbered some 500 men, for a total of 4,500 militiamen).

The 6th CdA had twenty-one MVACs: four of them with headquarters in Treninje, Hum, Bileća and Grab in the Marche Division's sector; two in Ljubuški and Stolac in the Messina Division's sector; four in Nevesinje, one in Ulog, one in Gacko, three in Kalinovnik and four at Foča in the Murge Division's sector. The battalions of the 5th CdA differed from those of the 4th CdA in that they were supervised by Italian officers, but the commands did not interfere in their organization or in their arming. They were subordinate to the CdA only administratively, and specifically to the 'I' Office – which suggests that autonomous bands of Četniks were operating in the guise of MVACs.[37] At the end of 1942, according to Ustaša sources,

[36] USSME, N I–II, 'Diari storici', b. 1004, 'Divisione Sassari, Ufficio MVAC', 13 September 1942.

[37] According to the figures of the Supersloda Political Office, the Italian government allocated reserve funds amounting to a monthly sum of 350,000 lire for Supersloda political propaganda. The funds

there were thirty MVAC battalions, with a total of 10,000 men, operating in the territories militarily occupied by the Italians and in Dalmatia. According to the Supersloda liaison office with the Foreign Ministry, more than 10,000 of the volunteers were Orthodox, but only a few hundred of them were Croats.[38] As of 7 March 1943, the Četnik bands and the anti-communist militias had more than 30,000 men, 23,000 of them operating in the Croatian territories occupied by the Regio Esercito, and 7,000 in the annexed territories (figures from a week earlier corroborate this; see appendix, table 50).[39]

The Zagreb Foreign Ministry repeatedly sent documents to the Supersloda Command attesting to acts of looting and violence against Croatian citizens by militiamen. It urged disbanding of the militias and 'elimination' of leaders from Montenegro or Serbia (the Croatian documents reported the massacre of hundreds of Croats in the Neretva Valley, the burning of thousands of houses, with more than 40,000 refugees forced to flee the area; also the Vatican State Secretariat warned the MAE of the slaughter of Catholics in Herzegovina).[40] Despite the Croats' protests, the Četniks and the militias took part in two cycles of operations against the communists: the Velebit campaign (16–19 July 1942) and the Albia campaign (12 August–2 September 1942), during which 962 partisans were killed in the Biohovo area and along the upper Dalmatian coast.

By the end of 1942, the MAE officials (mainly Luca Pietromarchi, Roberto Ducci, head of the GABAP – Ufficio Croazia, and Raffaele Casertano) had grown wary of the militias and critical of the Italian generals' pro-Serbism. Vittorio Castellani wrote to the Foreign Ministry that the CdA and division commands had allowed themselves to be excessively influenced by the local situation and by sentiment and personal factors. He acknowledged that, except in towns directly garrisoned by Italian troops, the situation was militarily and operationally out of control, and he admitted that the anti-communist bands and the Četniks could not be trusted.[41]

were to be spent on gifts, wages for band members and their families, fees and gratuities to personages such as the bishop of Ljubljana, Gregorij Rožman, or the Croatian administrative commissioner, Vjekoslav Vrančić, bounties for captured communists, various indemnities, allowances for the needy and the construction of concentration camps (e.g. for Jews at Porto Re, March 1943). For the figures in detail, see ASMAE, GABAP, b. 41.

38 ASMAE, GABAP, b. 36, 'Ufficio di collegamento con Supersloda, 17 settembre 1942, Collaborazione militare croata nella zona d'occupazione'.

39 ASMAE, GABAP, b. 26, 'Formazioni della MVAC, Ufficio di collegamento con il Comando della II Armata, Pierantoni', 7 March 1943.

40 USSME, M 3, b. 54, 'ministro degli Esteri croato Stijepo Perić al generale Roatta', 19 October 1942.

41 ASMAE, GABAP, b. 36, 'Ufficio di collegamento con Supersloda, 17 settembre 1942, Collaborazione militare croata nella zona di occupazione'; b. 37, 12 January 1943. In his unpublished diary (Fondazione

Pietromarchi wrote in his diary that in view of events in North Africa, and in order to send troops to metropolitan France, some divisions should be withdrawn from the Second Army. The latter should evacuate certain zones and concentrate on the coast, protecting its units by creating a shield of Četnik bands, these being certainly more reliable than the Croats.[42]

Roatta and the Second Army generals insisted that, although the landings by the Allies in North Africa had increased their expectations of victory, the militias and the Četniks were continuing to perform valuable services in the campaign against the partisans. The military authorities had no other alternative, because the Croatian troops were increasingly inefficient and hostile, and the Germans did not have sufficient military resources to assist the Regio Esercito. Roatta's cynical ploy – 'so that they can slit each other's throats' – proved extremely useful at a time when the 'partisans preferred to attack the militias [rather] than the regular troops of the Regio Esercito, owing to their limited firepower, having only few automatic weapons'.[43] In the territory covered by the Sassari Division it was the MVAC that kept up pressure on the rebels, 'waging arduous and constant warfare by day and night, on mountain positions exposed to the rigours of the oncoming winter and under enemy attack'.[44] The reluctance of the CdA commands to disband the militia formations is therefore entirely understandable.

The position of the Supersloda CdAs became even more difficult at the end of 1942, when the Germans ordered the Italians to disarm the bands and the militias. During the discussions in Görlitz between Ciano and Hitler (18–20 December 1942; also present were Joachim von Ribbentrop, Wilhelm von Keitel and Ugo Cavallero), the Germans reminded the junior partner that, in the event of an Allied invasion of the Balkans, the Četniks would turn their weapons against the Axis. Only Cavallero among the Italian military authorities unreservedly took the Germans' side, and acting contrary to the wishes of the army commanders in Yugoslavia, he set about planning Operation Weiss (the first phase of which was to take place between 15 and 20 February 1943, and the second between 25 February and 25 March, the objective of which was indeed to disarm the Četniks).

Luigi Einaudi, Turin), Pietromarchi wrote on 14 October as follows: 'Protests have been raised over the treatment meted out to Croats and Muslims by the Četnik bands that we have armed. In effect, these bands are committing every kind of atrocity under the control, and therefore with the responsibility, of our officers. The repercussions are extremely serious throughout Croatia.'

42 Pietromarchi, diary, 31 December 1942.

43 USSME, M 3, b. 55, 'Comando II Armata, Ufficio "I", notiziario a/c', September 1942.

44 USSME, M 3, b. 54, 'Comando XVIII CdA al Comando di Supersloda', 24 October 1942.

At the end of January, not having received specific assurances from the CS, General Alexander Löhr, commander of the German forces in the Balkans, informed Roatta that he had decided to mount a series of operations in Herzegovina independently of the Italians. These operations should have been carried out by the 6th CdA assisted by 3,000 Montenegrin Četniks. Evidently, not only did the Germans not want the Montenegrins to be involved, but they intended to use their own forces to disarm the pro-Italian Četniks of Herzegovina. Moreover, Löhr told the Italians, when the territories had been cleared, Croatian garrisons would not be established. Instead, German troops would take over and together with special Croatian commissioners purge the population, sending all Orthodox Christians of arms-bearing age to the concentration camps. Thus – despite the presence of some thirty divisions – the result of the military and political ineptness of the Italian commanders was that the German command took control of the entire Balkan peninsula. By February, the Second Army was effectively subordinate to General Löhr, who already controlled the Italian forces in Montenegro, Albania and Greece.

Mussolini's 'changing of the guard' in February 1943 removed General Cavallero (he was replaced with General Ambrosio, who left his post at the SMG to Roatta, while General Robotti took command of the Second Army). Ambrosio, Roatta and Robotti altered the agreements reached with the Germans. In the same few days, Ambassador Casertano informed Rome that a number of Četnik bands were fighting alongside the Germans, and that Croats had even been assigned certain administrative functions. General Giuseppe Pièche sent the GABAP a report on Mihajlović in which he affirmed that it was still possible to collaborate with the Četniks against Bolshevism. The Četnik leader, he wrote, was not hostile to Italy but hated Germany.[45] On 25 February 1943, Ribbentrop once again discussed the question with Mussolini, and on conclusion of the meeting the CS wrote to the OKW that it would proceed with disarming the Četniks when it was possible.

The Supreme Army Command again explained to the SMRE and to the CS that disarming the collaborationists would mean losing an ally, gaining an enemy and irremediably damaging Italy's prestige among the occupied populations. Moreover, Supersloda had begun to concentrate its forces along the Dalmatian coast. Withdrawal from the interior was particularly difficult because the partisans were penetrating and taking possession of

[45] USSME, M 3, b. 19, 22 January 1943, 'Relazione del generale Pièche al GABAP'.

zones as soon as they were evacuated. In this phase of operations, the army commands insisted, they had to be able to rely on the Četnik bands and the militias, which acted as buffers against the partisans and had also assumed tasks of civil administration (2,000 Herzegovinian Serbs and the Muslim Četnik leader Popovak moved into Knin, Ogulin, Gračac and Otočac, provoking the fury of Pavelić).

In April 1943, the British discarded Mihajlović and began to exploit 'the communist vital force in order to disrupt the Italian defensive system in the Balkans'. In such circumstances, advised the Army Intelligence Service (SIE), the best strategy was to 'exacerbate the struggle between the two parties and to support the Četniks', for three reasons. The first was military for, although the bands were low in morale and disorganized, they could still be of considerable service. The second related to internal politics, given that conflict between the two factions prevented the partisans from taking part in joint actions. The third concerned foreign policy and the regime's attempt to set London against Moscow.[46]

In May, the Italian troops withdrew definitively from a large part of Croatia. There were no troops left behind to protect the civilian population, the MVACs or the Četniks against Croatian revenge and reprisals by the partisans, and especially by the Germans. The Prinz Eugen SS Division (which consisted mainly of *Volksdeutschen* resident in the *banat*) moved through Bosnia and the former Italian zones, arresting and attacking the Četniks. The commanders of the 6th CdA protested but were able to save only a handful of the Četnik leaders. In response to the German action, Supersloda refused to take part in Operation Schwarz. Robotti resigned himself to losing the Četnik formations but sought to save Italian face by leaving 'the odious part of the operation to the Germans'.[47]

Pietromarchi wrote in his diary that Italian prestige had touched rock bottom. The civilians who had compromised themselves for the Italians and then been abandoned to reprisals by the Ustaše, the Četniks or the partisans both despised the Italians and loathed them as directly or indirectly responsible for their suffering. The weak, added Pietromarchi, are always wrong, and unfortunately the worst was yet to come. The CS continued to strip the Balkans of defences in order to move divisions back to Italy. Such was the shortage of weaponry and equipment that draft quotas had to be reduced. The CS sought to remedy the situation by withdrawing divisions

[46] USSME, L 10, b. 38, 'SIE allo SMRE', 14 April 1943.

[47] ASMAE, GABAP, b. 38, 'al colonnello capo Ufficio "I" della II Armata, 18 maggio 1943, firmato colonnello Tommaso Grignolo'.

for other duties, with the consequence that only two divisions were left to garrison Dalmatia, while a further two were stationed on the Croatian coast.[48]

From March 1943 onwards, Germany no longer took any account of the exigencies of the junior partner, which for its part seemed resignedly to accept that two years of occupation and its war had failed. Mussolini made a final pointless protest: he wrote a letter to Hitler reminding him that during discussions with Ribbentrop and General Walther Warlimont it had been agreed that the Croatian Četniks would be disarmed when the partisan menace had been dealt with and Mihajlović's armed formations eliminated, according to jointly decided operational plans and joint contingents of forces. But the German action against the Četniks had begun 'without even the minimum prior notice being given to the Italian side'.[49] Despite the violence of the repression, however, the German soldiers failed in their purpose: some of the Četniks who had survived eventually joined the partisans.

On 8 June 1943, in a contradictory and not entirely truthful entry in his diary, Pietromarchi glossed over his own responsibility for the failure of Italian policy and castigated the military commands and Ciano. He wrote that the agreements on borders and the dividing up of the Adriatic had been predicated on a close understanding with the Croats. But the Second Army Command had taken an intransigent stance with Zagreb and rejected any offer of military assistance. It had formed an alliance with Croatia's worst enemies, the Serbs, whom it had armed and then unleashed to take vengeance against the Croats and the Muslims. The Italian military commanders had undermined the alliance policy and provoked the hatred of the Croats, the birth of intransigent Croatian irredentism and the decision of the Zagreb government to deliver itself bound hand and foot to the Germans. The latter, wrote Pietromarchi, had adroitly used the policy of which the Italian Foreign Ministry had always been the master: they had supported the Croats and the Muslims, and they had forced the Italians to demobilize the Četnik bands. In this way they had diminished Italy's

[48] Pietromarchi, diary, 3 May 1943.

[49] DDI, ser. IX, 1939–43, vol. 10, doc. 354, 'capo del governo Mussolini al cancelliere del Reich Hitler', Rome 22 May 1943; doc. 301 – 'allegato, colloquio del generale Löhr con il generale Robotti del 5 maggio 1943', which shows that Hitler made no mention of the imminent attack against Mihajlović's Četniks; doc. 380, 'addetto all'Ufficio di collegamento con il Comando della II Armata, Pierantoni, al capo del governo Mussolini, 1 giugno 1943': this document confirms that no interference by the Germans in the annexed territories was permitted and that the Italians continued to keep the Četniks in service.

prestige in the eyes of the Croats, Serbs and Muslims, and deprived the Regio Esercito of the only force still available to it.

'Minister Ciano is obviously to blame', wrote Pietromarchi, because he had been unwilling to countermand the policy of the military authorities in Croatia; and he had been indecisive in dealing with Cavallero, who in his turn had ordered Generals Roatta and Alessandro Pirzio Biroli not to contact the MAE. Palazzo Chigi had failed to provide the unity of direction which was essential for success. The military commands had not been made subordinate to the Foreign Ministry. The Germans, said Pietromarchi, were doing exactly what he had recommended: occupy Croatia in its entirety and instigate conflict among races and religious faiths so that they neutralized each other, give political supremacy to the Croats, and recruit the largest possible number of Bosnian Muslims, enticing them with good pay and numerous benefits. The Germans were maintaining their control over Croatia almost entirely by means of indigenous forces – which was what Pietromarchi had planned. Moreover, he went on, reprisals by the military commands in Slovenia, Croatia, Dalmatia and especially Greece had greatly damaged the Italian cause. Indeed, the archbishop of Zagreb, Alojzije Stepinac, had made a public protest in church against the Italians' inhumane methods. The Blackshirts had committed numerous excesses and some 'M' battalions had behaved like the notorious Lansquenet mercenaries, still a byword in Italy for death and destruction. '[The military] authorities wanted to act as mediators among nationalities divided by centuries of hatred and by recent atrocities. An impartial, moderate and humane policy was necessary. This, however, they were unable to accomplish. They let themselves be swayed by local passions. They espoused the cause of the Serbs and the Jews, who had offered them their women.'[50]

In his diatribe against Italian policy in Yugoslavia, Pietromarchi omitted to mention that the Italian military authorities had made numerous attempts to gain collaboration; and he also forgot that German hegemony was already a reality when the occupations began. He deliberately ignored the numerous doubts that 'his' GABAP had raised about the reliability of the Zagreb government and its subordinate organs during the two years of occupation. However, regarding the question of concessions to ethnic or religious groups, although Pietromarchi somewhat simplified a highly complex situation, he was right to point out that the civil authorities and

[50] Pietromarchi, diary, 8 June 1943. Lansquenets (from German *Landsknechts*) were mainly German mercenaries with a formidable reputation as effective and brutal combat troops during the Renaissance.

the Italian military commands in Croatia preferred not to adopt a policy of openness, its considerable benefits notwithstanding. Two examples illustrate this point.

Some Serb Orthodox minorities demanded – not because they were pro-Italian but because they were terrified of Ustaša persecution – union with Italy; others urged annexation; yet others pressed for regional autonomy, or for a military protectorate created under Italian control.[51] The Italian authorities were aware that the Serbs' appeals were self-interested and temporary – the fruit of resentment and the unbridgeable divide 'between the Serb ethnic group and the Croatian state'.[52] While on the one hand accepting would have meant definitively taking sides against the Croats, on the other playing the Serbs off against the Croats would increase Italian authority and prestige. Moreover, given that the Germans were adamantly opposed to any kind of political openness towards the Serbs, any concessions by the Italians would furnish the ally and the Balkan peoples with proof of Rome's decision-making autonomy. The Serbs, wrote the GABAP just before 25 July 1943, 'as Serbs and not as Yugoslavians, gravitate towards the Danube and not towards the Adriatic. It is therefore much more advantageous for us to cultivate the Serbs and foster conflict between them and the Croats, for as long as they are divided and enemies we shall always have at our disposal a Danubian mass to counterbalance and obstruct the ambitions and threats of an Adriatic Croatian mass.' The decision not to seek ethnic or religious collaboration sprang from the necessity not to make political promises. Despite the uncertainty of the conflict and difficult relations with Zagreb, Italy did not want to bind its hands by committing itself to groups that were numerically insignificant and with little political weight. As we know, this does not mean that the 'ethnic question' would not have been of key importance when the war was won, but at that stage of the war the Italians decided to pursue military collaboration only with groups able to provide support against the communists.

A number of Muslim groups in Croatia also requested administrative autonomy and Rome's protection. As in the case of the Serbs, this was a fortuitous and self-interested request born of the conviction that, as soon as the Croats felt that they were sufficiently strong, they would act with

[51] USSME, N I–II, *Diari storici*, b. 829, 'Comando Divisione Taurinense al comandante delle truppe in Montenegro, 22 agosto 1942, Trasmissione delle petizioni della popolazione ortodossa dei distretti Cajnice e Visegrad'.

[52] ASMAE, GABAP, b. 35, 'console a Mostar Renato Giardini al GABAP, 30 aprile 1942, Relazione politica sull'Erzegovina'.

ruthless violence against them.[53] The Muslims did not form a politically homogeneous entity: on some occasions they adopted a 'wait-and-see' policy; on others they aligned themselves with the communist partisans; on yet others they fought in the anti-communist militias, motivated by both anti-partisan and anti-Orthodox fervour (especially in eastern Bosnia and the Sanjak). In 1941, the grand mufti of Palestine, Amin al-Husanyi, proposed that Bosnia should be unified with Albania in order to prevent the dispersal of the Muslim community in the Balkan peninsula. Rome refused to consider the proposal on the grounds that the Muslim religious minority was 'an uncertain, vacillating element under the sway of all political factions, while the mass is susceptible only to the influence of the faction seemingly most powerful and on which success seems to smile'.[54] Thus, in the spring of 1943, as the Italian army retreated in disarray to the Adriatic coast, General Robotti refused to arm Muslim militias and instead only made what was obviously an empty promise to protect their villages[55] (unlike the Germans, who instead formed Muslim SS battalions to do so and thus secured the goodwill of a large part of the Muslim community).[56]

MONTENEGRO

In Montenegro, the occupiers were to some extent successful in their recruitment of collaborators; nevertheless, law and order in the territory still remained precarious. Legitimist, pan-Serb and monarchist formations enjoyed considerable popularity among broad sections of the population.[57] In contrast to Croatia, the ethnic homogeneity of the territory facilitated collaboration; but it also made the partisan bands more compact.[58] Governor Pirzio Biroli explained that it was imperative to restrict collaboration

[53] ASMAE, GABAP, b. 46, 'Comando ii Armata, Ufficio Affari politici, al MAE, 23 ottobre 1941, prot. 12 segreto, Situazione in Erzegovina, firmato Castellani'.

[54] ASMAE, AA.PP. – Italia, b. 86, 'console Alberto Calisse al GABAP', 13 December 1941. The mufti proposed to the Italian authorities that a Maghreb liberation army be created. His proposal was rejected in view of its perilous consequences in Italian North Africa: USSME, N I–II, 'Diari storici', b. 1404, 'CS – SIM, Promemoria del 27 novembre 1942'.

[55] ASMAE, GABAP, b. 38, 'generale Robotti allo SMRE, 8 maggio 1943'; USSME, M 3, b. 19, 'Collaborazione con elementi musulmani'; b. 67, 'Comando Supersloda, Ufficio "I", al Comando del VI CdA, 8 maggio 1943, Collaborazione con elementi musulmani'.

[56] ASMAE, AA.PP. – 'Italia', b. 92, 'Appunto del 9 aprile 1943'. The same envelope contains the note sent by the consul in Sarajevo, Paolo Alberto Rossi, to the MAE on 12 April 1943, with the heading: 'Visita del gran muftì – suo svolgimento e suoi effetti; consolato di Sarajevo al MAE, 1 maggio 1943'; and 'Ufficio di collegamento II Armata al MAE, 17 giugno 1943', which refers to the enlistment of Herzegovinian Muslims in the SS battalions.

[57] Cuzzi, 'I Balcani'.

[58] USSME, M 3, b. 5, 'telegramma del console a Belgrado Francesco Mameli al MAE', 26 December 1941.

with the natives to the military sphere alone, with the Montenegrins allowed to take action against the rebels using the same tactics and the same means as the latter in areas of rugged terrain which regular troops found difficult to traverse.[59]

Pirzio Biroli initially attempted to group all the anti-communist forces operating in the region into a single militia under the command of the Montenegrin general Krsto Popović. The plan was agreed to by the Zelenasi (the followers of the former secretary of the Montenegrin Federalist Party Sekula Drljević, who formed a militia division within the 14th CdA),[60] some senior army officers, separatist groups, legitimists and early collaborationists known as Krilaši (units encadred into the 14th CdA).[61] However, the Bjelaši unionists, who had a much larger popular following than the Zelenasi, joined forces with the insurgents. Besides these groups, various units of 'mad dogs' were operating in the country, principal among them the Officers Organization for Defence of the Montenegro People, which had direct links with Mihajlović via Mile Lasić and Pavle Djurišić in the Sanjak.[62] Ranged against these bands were groups of armed Muslims: Arnauti and the Skipetars of the Kaçak units. One gathers from Pietromarchi's diary that the Albanian bands operating in the border zones were encouraged by the lieutenancy to advance into Montenegrin territory, a manoeuvre that, according to Pietromarchi, fomented insurrection in Montenegro and caused great loss of life. Francesco Jacomoni wanted the Albanians occupying the Montenegrin territories to be given fully sanctioned possession of them through the institution of military and civil authorities dependent on the lieutenancy. Pietromarchi objected to the proposal, pointing out that Pirzio Biroli was engaged in a difficult attempt to pacify and establish collaboration with the Montenegrin nationalists.[63] It was for this reason that Ambassador Carlo Umiltà was sent to the contested zone and appointed, in July 1942, civil commissioner 'for the mixed population regions'.

During the winter of 1941–2, the lack of co-operation between the Italians and Germans on mopping-up operations against the communists led to mass border violations by rebels from Bosnia and Serbia. In 1942 these encroachments severely stretched the Italian divisions and the Montenegrin

[59] ASMAE, GABAP, b. 50, 'Pirzio Biroli al GABAP – Ufficio Montenegro', 1 December 1941.

[60] Drljević was the principal Montenegrin separatist leader and one of the political signatories to the declaration of independence by the Kingdom of Montenegro of 12 July 1941.

[61] Also called *krilavi*, name of the Montenegrin gendarmerie, in ASMAE, GABAP, b. 51.

[62] USSME, N 1–11, 'Diari storici', b. 731, 'Comando Divisione Pusteria, 11 luglio 1942, Accordi con il capitano Giurisic (Djurisić)'.

[63] Pietromarchi, diary, 22 June 1942.

collaborationists, whose duties were to 'guard communications and to protect minor localities in outlying zones'.[64] In Croatia, with its confused and ever-changing situation, a number of 'white' and Četnik groups joined forces on 9 March 1942, and General Blažo Djukanović was appointed, with Mihajlović's approval, as supreme commander of all the Montenegrin nationalist forces. These bands collaborated militarily – but without being inducted into the army – in putting down the communist movement. On 24 July 1942, Pirzio Biroli and Djukanović signed a pact of alliance and co-operation. The white–Četnik forces were to fight only the communist partisans. They were merged with Popović's militias to form three detachments of 1,500 men commanded by Djurišić (in the district of Kolašin), by Popović himself (along the southern coast and immediately inland from it) and by Bajo Stanišić (in the zone of the Ostrog fortress). Agreements were reached on weapons and pay, and on the aid to be given the families of dead and wounded combatants. A Montenegrin nationalist committee consisting of Zelenasi, 'whites' and Četniks of other political persuasion was set up under the chairmanship of Djukanović. Symbolic of the collaboration was a joint ceremony held by all nationalists – and over which the governor himself presided – to commemorate the Italians and Montenegrins who had lost their lives in the struggle against communism.[65]

During the winter of 1942–3, the communists launched an offensive in areas adjoining Montenegro. Pirzio Biroli proposed that a Montenegrin formation should be dispatched beyond the frontier to fight them; the Croats rejected the idea, however, and thus enabled the partisans to infiltrate the governorate. In the meantime, the German troops occupied increasingly larger portions of eastern Montenegro: by the end of May they had taken control of the stretch of territory from the Sanjak to the border with Albania and had immediately set about disarming the pro-Italian Četniks. Even Djurišić himself was taken prisoner. The united anti-communist front disintegrated and by May–June 1943 it consisted of only a handful of bands loyal to the Italians. The German campaign dealt the *coup de grâce* to collaboration in Montenegro. The commander of the 14th CdA, Ercole Roncaglia, wrote that the Herzegovina situation had been repeated in Montenegro on a much larger scale.[66]

[64] USSME, M 3, b. 12, 'Relazione del generale Pirzio Biroli, luglio 1941–giugno 1943'.

[65] USSME, N 1–11, 'Diari storici', b. 1220, 'Divisione Taurinense, 5 settembre 1942, Persone amiche e collaboratori montenegrini'.

[66] ASMAE, GABAP, b. 38, 'colonnello Grignolo al colonnello capo Ufficio "I" della II Armata, 18 maggio 1943'. See also a top secret note dated 17 May 1943 from Castellani to Under-Secretary Bastianini.

GREECE

Had the Italians wanted to make use of ethnic collaboration in Greece, they could have relied on the services of Ciamuriota hirelings and Aromanian criminals. But it was obvious to the Italian military authorities that collaboration with the minorities in Epirus and the Pindus would have provoked a breakdown of order in the rest of the Greek peninsula, and it would not in any case have involved forces of numerically sufficient weight: in short, the game was not worth the candle. Mussolini, the CS and the army high command came to the same conclusion, and decided that collaboration with the Greek authorities was the best option for Italian occupation policy.

General Carlo Geloso took a 'neutral stance' on Epirus and the north-western Greek territories inhabited by Albanian minorities. Although the Greeks may have been resigned to the loss of the Ionian islands, he wrote, they would never accept the ceding of Jannina to the Albanians, or of Kastoria to the Aromanians. The fomenting of separatist unrest and the organization of ethnic bands would merely have the effect of disrupting public order. In June 1941, Geloso declared that only when the war was won would a victorious Italy be able to impose its will.[67] Until that time, tensions should be avoided in every circumstance, for they threatened public order and provoked ethnic strife.[68] The head of the SMG, General Cavallero and the plenipotentiary Pellegrino Ghigi were also of the opinion that the Ciamuriota question should be put aside, lest further hotbeds of discontent and rebellion be created. Only the Lieutenancy of Tirana, for the opposite reasons, wanted the Albanian claims to be satisfied. Mussolini intervened on the question and gave his backing to Geloso.

The only measure taken in favour of the Albanian Ciamurioti was the preferential victualling of their region, which like the Ionian islands was declared a 'privileged province'. However, the shelving of the question raised a number of problems, for between 1939 and 1940 the Italians had fomented a revolt by the Albanian minorities against Athens. By way of example, the prefect of Igoumenitsa (a town with a large Albanian minority) was unpopular with all the Ciamurioti:

> The time has come to replace him. But with whom? This is a difficult problem. Replacing him with an Italian is not possible, because for the time being the Greek

[67] USSME, L 13, b. 105, *Con l'XI Armata nella guerra contro la Grecia*, typescript by General Geloso, p. 191.

[68] USSME, N 1–11, 'Diari storici', b. 554, 'CS al Com. sup. FF.AA. Grecia, il capo di SMRE Ugo Cavallero, 14 ottobre 1941'; the MAE's note was delivered to the CS on 8 September 1941.

administrative apparatus remains in effect even in the reserved zone. With a Greek? There is the danger that he would favour the Greeks over the Muslims. With a Muslim? He could not fairly protect the rights of all the population, two-thirds of which are Greek. To conclude, given that it is not expedient to leave things as they are, it is advisable to replace the present prefect, also because he belongs to the previous Metaxas administration, and appoint a suitable person from the place (a Greek), flanking him with an Italian civilian under the direct supervision of the CdA.[69]

It seems from the few documents found in the archives that the Italians changed their policy only when the EAM intensified its action. At the end of 1942, the Italians asked for and obtained military assistance from the Albanians.[70] The clashes between the Ciamuriota Albanians and the EAM were not ideological, however. They did not consist of conflict between Fascist collaborationists and communists; rather, they were a continuation of strife that had been ongoing in the region for years.[71]

Immediately after the occupation, the Aromanians declared their willingness to collaborate with the Italian armed forces. The Italian commands in Thessaly realized that the Aromanian minority could guarantee security in areas of rugged terrain difficult to garrison. Geloso was convinced, however, that, although the Aromanians may have differed from the Slavs by virtue of 'a higher degree of civilization', they were nevertheless opportunists. He therefore carefully avoided making any political pledges or promises to them, insisting that the solution to the question would be forthcoming 'at the peace table'. The Aromanians were not permitted to form bands, and they were used by the Italians only as guides and informers.[72]

The commander of the Pinerolo Division, Cesare Benelli, at first envisaged the creation of Aromanian militias in Grevenà, Kastoria, Kalabaka, Trikala and Karditsa to root out 'the Greek element for the most part hostile or indolent'.[73] He proposed the following: replacement of Greeks in the civil service, public services and gendarmerie with Aromanians and a number of 'Bulgarophones' from Macedonia; reform and supervision of the Greek

[69] USSME, N I–II, 'Diari storici', b. 554, 'Comando XXVI CdA – UAC al Com. sup. FF.AA. Grecia – UAC, 15 dicembre 1941'.

[70] USSME, N I–II, 'Diari storici', b. 1122, 'Comando XXVI CdA – UAC al Com. sup. FF.AA. Grecia, 30 novembre 1942, Relazione sulla situazione politico-amministrativa del territorio di giurisdizione'.

[71] USSME, N I–II, 'Diari storici', b. 1122, 'Comando XXVI CdA – UAC al Com. sup. FF.AA. Grecia, 30 novembre 1942, Relazione mensile sulla situazione politico-amministrativa del territorio occupato'.

[72] USSME, N I–II, 'Diari storici', b. 1070, 'Comando III CdA al Comando della Divisione Pinerolo, 28 dicembre 1942, Armamento di elementi fidati'.

[73] USSME, N I–II, 'Diari storici', b. 462, 'Comando Divisione Pinerolo al colonnello Arturo Scattini, capo Ufficio "I" del Com. sup. FF.AA. Grecia', 19 September 1941.

schools; the opening and protection of Aromanian schools, and also of Italian ones; the dissemination of Italian culture by all possible means; and a propaganda campaign mounted by means of newspapers, books, films and documentaries. He then realized that the Aromanian ethnic group was not at all wholly pro-Italian, and that the communities in Thessaly and in the zones of Grevenà and Kastoria had diverse political tendencies. He also discovered that the Aromanians had grown rapidly in numbers, because non-Aromanian shepherds, small shopkeepers and workmen had declared themselves members of the minority in the hope of financial gain.

The 3rd CdA, which comprised the Pinerolo Division, blocked any attempt at collaboration and declared itself sceptical over the use of Aromanian bands. It was especially suspicious of Diamandi (or Diamanti, the extremist leader backed by Bucharest), who had formed the Fifth 'Roman Legion' with the purpose of obtaining autonomy for the regions of Epirus, Pindus, Thessaly, Macedonia and southern Albania under Rome's protection.[74] His band of some hundreds of criminals rampaged through the Pindus inflicting dreadful violence on the Greeks. Some of its members were disarmed, and the army commands were ordered to cease using Aromanians as support for the Carabinieri (for whom they worked as extremely useful translators and guides). The military authorities refused to permit any form of self-administration by the Aromanians in the awareness that their irredentist aspirations, or appeals for annexation to Italy, were a masquerade by a minority movement seeking political and economic revenge.[75] The Bulgarophone minority in the Italian zone – a handful of villages situated close to the demarcation line with the Germans – also organized bands. Like their Aromanian counterparts, they waged a campaign of anti-Greek violence, not for ideological reasons but in order to avenge abuses suffered at the hands of the Greeks. As in the two previous cases, the Italians decided not to avail themselves of Aromanian collaboration.[76]

[74] USSME, N 1–11, 'Diari storici', b. 376, 'Comando XXVI CdA al Com. sup. FF.AA. Grecia, Ufficio CSM, 19 ottobre 1941'. See also L 15, bb. 25 and 12, 'Saluti rivolti dal sindaco di Grevenà alle autorità italiane'.

[75] USSME, N 1–11, 'Diari storici', b. 462, 'Comando Divisione di fanteria Pinerolo, Ufficio del CSM – sez. "I"; L 13, b. 105, *Con l'XI Armata nella guerra contro la Grecia*, p. 196.

[76] USSME, N 1–11, 'Diari storici', b. 642, 'Comando Divisione Pinerolo – UAC, 3 settembre 1941, Relazione sulla situazione politico-amministrativa'; b. 1232, 'allegato 295, fonocifra, da Comando Operazioni "D" al Comando del III CdA'; 'Comando Divisione Pinerolo – UAC, Relazione mensile sulla situazione politico-amministrativa nel territorio occupato per il periodo 1–31 marzo 1943', which confirms the existence of Bulgarophone and Aromanian armed bands. See also USSME, M 3, b. 19, 'generale Pièche, 29 giugno 1943'.

In March 1943, the plenipotentiary in Athens reported that the various Greek political associations tended to form three broad factions: 'realistic', nationalist and left-wing. These numerous organizations had only one feature in common: their hatred of Fascism and of National Socialism. Italy's most implacable enemy was obviously the Komunistikon Komma Ellados. The 'seditious movement' spread rapidly through the peninsula despite the harsh repression of the civilian population. At the end of June, the Greek partisans joined forces with the Albanians in Epirus, and by July the whole of Greece was in a state of 'open rebellion'.

There was no one left in the country on whom the Italians could rely for support: a void had opened up around the armed forces. Elements favourable to the Italians – informers, collaborators and civil servants – were subjected to reprisals by the Andartes, who also 'tortured women suspected of having granted their favours to Italian soldiers'.[77] The occupiers spent 1943 barricaded in their garrisons, having abandoned large tracts of Greek territory to the partisans. From the spring of 1943 onwards, neither the Greek authorities nor the Ciamuriota, Aromanian or Bulgarophone minorities collaborated with the occupiers, either for fear of reprisals or because the Italians were no longer to be seen.

FRANCE

In France, the Italians made no use of Corsican separatists or of the few Nice irredentists. The unfulfilled annexation frustrated the aspirations of the country's minuscule pro-Fascist organizations, especially Azione Nizzarda, whose existence (around 1,500 members) was, according to the MAE, 'pointless and damaging'. A note to the SMG chief Ambrosio from the Foreign Ministry reminded him that some of the occupied regions were subject to territorial claims. Consequently, separatist and irredentist movements were to be fostered, while ensuring that political penetration was not obstructed by the 'deaf and tenacious opposition of the French administration and police'.[78] The 6th CdA stationed in Corsica made itself clear on the matter: 'The Corsicans, although of Italian blood, have been for many years dominated by the French government and for the time being

[77] USSME, M 3, b. 19, 'generale Pièche, 19 febbraio 1943, Promemoria per il duce con notizie dalla Grecia relative al mese di gennaio 1943'.

[78] USSME, M 3, b. 9, 'sottosegretario agli Esteri Bastianini al generale Ambrosio, 28 maggio 1943'.

it would be vain to hope that they can be induced to sympathize with us.'[79]

The civil authorities, and especially the consul Ugo Turcato, demanded that the mayor of Bastia and his executive council be replaced *en bloc*, that the police and gendarmerie be purged because they were Italophobe and Gaullist, and that priests, schoolteachers and communications personnel be placed under strict surveillance. He suggested that Corsica should be annexed, exploiting rebellious impulses provoked by irredentists who had allowed the Italian military authorities to replace French civil servants.[80] The military authorities were firmly opposed to any such policy and refused to assume civil powers in the island. They dismissed Turcato's proposal as foolish and unrealistic: no French civil servant would ever agree to work for the Italians, and no irredentist would ever accept a post as a French functionary.

In the Alpes-Maritimes, some Italian ministers believed that they could utilize the Italian community, but they soon realized that the repatriation of emigrants for which Mussolini had been pressing since 1940 would make this impossible. The CIAF registered 70,262 Italians as returnees to the peninsula between July 1940 and April 1943. There remained behind political exiles and anti-Fascists, who were sought not for collaboration but for arrest. The documentation consulted reveals no attempt by Italian emigrants to organize themselves into bands, and the endeavour to exploit their 'sense of legal and moral inferiority' proved futile. The Italian workers in France wanted abolition of the administrative rules restricting their freedom of movement and economic activity, change to the arbitrary identity card system, abolition of the prohibition on the purchase of land and the right to travel between *départements*. They aspired to fair treatment before the law and elimination of internment or expulsion for even the most trivial offences. But these demands were not enough to induce them to take up arms against the French.

The consul general in the Alpes-Maritimes, Quinto Mazzolini, concentrated on developing the activities of the Casa d'Italia, the Casa del Fascio (which at the end of 1941 had 86 members in Cannes and 750 in Nice), the OND, the Società Dante Alighieri, the Associazione Combattenti (1,355 members), the Associazione Mutilati (365 members), the Associazione Nastro Azzurro and the Fascist youth associations (GILE, with 76

[79] USSME, N I–II, 'Diari storici', b. 1272, 'Comando VII CdA, 3 dicembre 1942, Organizzazione difensiva – contegno nel momento attuale'.

[80] ASMAE, AA.PP. – 'Francia', b. 67, 'console Turcato al MAE', 17 April 1943'; see also 5 and 7 June 1943.

clubs – Balilla, Piccole Italiane, Avanguardisti, Giovani Italiane, Giovani Fascisti – and a total of 248 members). The consul claimed that 'grandiose celebrations were held for every date of national solemnity' and that rallies, free film shows, gifts of tobacco, health care and free meals for the indigent were organized. In no case did he support the Gruppi d'Azione Nizzarda (GAN) or other insignificant irredentist groupings. There was limited consular activity, and whatever existed concerned only an extremely small group of residents, considering that there were around 150,000 Italians in the *département* of Alpes-Maritimes.

Even more circumscribed was consular activity on behalf of the approximately 4,000 Italian workers in the *département* of the Alpes-de-Haute-Provence. The consul admitted that in their case the main concern was to 'give a soul to that community, revive the spirit of cohesion and national solidarity that the harsh life of the mountains, the international difficulties of the time and the low intellectual level of its members had almost entirely extinguished'. Mazzolini opined concerning the Italian community as follows: 'It does not shine either for its previous behaviour or customs or discipline. It has very few intellectuals and high professionals, numerous illegal families, an even larger number of promiscuous Italo-French families; the phenomenon of mixed Italian and French children is almost general.'[81]

Although it cannot be ruled out that the French departmental archives might provide useful information, the documentation consulted in the Italian archives reveals no attempts at collaboration with the Milice Française and the Légion.[82] The latter was dismissed by a CIAF report as a paramilitary organization, which together with its flanking organization Amis de la Légion, claimed to be a single party modelled on the totalitarian state. However broad their administrative and political functions (ranging from intervention and control in economic affairs and the welfare system to participation in consultative assemblies) may have been, these organizations were strictly confined to simple 'collaboration' with the representatives of

[81] ASMAE, AA.PP., '1939–45 – Francia, b. 68, 18–19 marzo 1943, Relazioni del console Mazzolini al GABAP'.

[82] The Milizia Francese (Milice Française) was created on 31 January 1943 and replaced the Servizio d'Ordine Legionario (Service d'Ordre Légionnaire). According to Article 1 of its statute, it could be joined by all Frenchmen resolved to play an active part in the political, social, economic, intellectual and moral renewal of France. The head of government was head of the militia. It was directed by a general secretary appointed by the head of government (Joseph Darnand) and consisted of 'morally alert and physically fit' volunteers. Those wishing to join had to be French by birth, not Jewish, not members of secret societies, volunteers and approved by the departmental chief. The secretary was assisted by administrators, these too appointed by the head of government. The militia was divided into territorial federations, one for each French administrative region.

central power, who alone exercised constitutional authority. The 'representative' function of the Légion was treated with apathy and indifference by the French population: the entire movement had been artificially created and sustained from above.

In conclusion, the Italian occupiers pursued a relatively consistent policy in all the conquered territories. Ideally, collaboration with the occupied countries and peoples would have enabled Rome to exploit them economically and penetrate them politically and culturally. The occupiers had need of persons without political aspirations and who enjoyed authority in the country concerned. None of these conditions were fulfilled. Although the Italians had the means to do so, they decided not to exploit the centrifugal forces generated by political, ethnic and religious groups that could have served the 'divide-and-rule' strategy. They did not want to tie their hands and be forced to confront a rival nationalism. Largely responsible for this decision were the military authorities in the occupied territories, who believed that collaboration with ethnic or religious minorities was detrimental to the maintenance of order. The ethnic or religious groups – such as the Muslims of Bosnia-Herzegovina, the Ciamurioti and Aromanians in Greece or the Corsicans in France – were not sufficiently compact, and they had insufficient followings. Action by them would have compromised the already difficult relations with the governments of the occupied countries, with the risk that each of them would have moved even closer to the Germans.

In all the occupied territories, when the rebel movements threatened the occupation forces, the latter resorted to the use of bands and militias. The same principle was adopted everywhere: make no kind of political promise and restrict collaboration to military assistance. The solution preferred by the Italian commands and the political authorities was the use of native military forces – like the Ascaris in the colonies – enlisted in the ranks of the Regio Esercito.

The case of collaboration in the occupied territories is also of interest for comparison between Fascist Italy and the Third Reich, for which, as Joseph Goebbels put it, any talk of collaboration was only idle chatter. If Fascism had had the strength to dominate the occupied countries, the Fascists would have said the same about the Nazis. The 'race of conquerors' would not have wasted its time with the occupied populations. Instead, given Italy's situation as the underdog, as a power subordinate to the Reich, and also because of its resentment at the inferior rank conferred upon it by Germany, it would have pursued the alternative strategy of collaboration, thereby giving a tangible sign of its prestige, authority and decision-making autonomy, and marking its difference from Germany. It was circumstance and Italy's weakness in the Axis that made the Italian forces more tactically flexible and opportunistic than the Germans. Also influential was the Fascist conception of imperial expansion, which, unlike the German project, did not envisage the emptying of the conquered territories (except for the ones annexed). I therefore believe that Enzo Collotti is right to maintain that the search for collaboration in Yugoslavia and Greece was not a deliberate political alternative to the Nazi policy. Rather, it was a practical expedient prompted by the need to compensate for Italy's lack of military might.

CHAPTER 10

Repression

This chapter is divided into two parts. The first examines the principles and methods adopted in the 'struggle against the rebels'. The second presents facts and figures (as well as a series of tables in the appendix) on the concentration camps for civilian internees constructed by the Italians in the occupied territories after 1940. The chapter does not provide an account of military operations against the partisan formations (these operations have already been documented for Yugoslavia: see the bibliography), nor does it furnish a chronology of reprisals against the partisans and civilians. Rather, it reports the results of research conducted in the Italian military archives on the directives, ordinances and orders concerning repression of all forms of insurgency against the Italian occupying forces in the annexed and occupied territories.

The first objective of this chapter is to demonstrate the uniformity of repression in all the occupied territories. Circular 3c, known to historians as the manifesto for repression in the Yugoslav territories, was not an isolated episode. Nor was it the brainchild of a general who happened to be more Fascist than the others. Similar measures were adopted in all the occupied territories, even in Greece and Albania where repression in practice was no different – in degree or in kind – from that in the Yugoslav occupied territories. The second objective is to report the results of research in the Italian archives, and those of the International Committee of the Red Cross (ICRC), which has confirmed a number of previous findings and shed light on hitherto little-known features of the civilian concentration camps. The chapter deliberately omits discussion of the internment of Jews, since this is the topic of the next chapter. Nevertheless, statistics on Jewish internees have been included in the tables in the appendix in order to emphasize that Italian policy towards the Jews is an integral and inseparable part of the history of the Italian occupations during the Second World War.

Between 1941 and 1943, the administration of the occupied territories was marked by profound divisions between the Axis partners in regard to the form that repression should take, divisions that stemmed from the differing political-military weights of the two allies and also from their differing objectives of conquest. The violence with which partisan groups and civilians were repressed obeyed two different logics: the extremism of Italy's occupation policy often reflected its army's substantial weakness, while the ruthlessness of Germany's repressive methods reflected not only the greater striking force of its military and police apparatus but also the greater radicalism of its goals.

In the actual practice of repression, the Italian army's actions were no different in degree or kind from those of the Wehrmacht, the SS and the German police engaged in similar operations. The orders issued by the Italian authorities to crush the partisan bands and to root out support for them in the civilian population envisaged a wide range of measures: hostage-taking, the burning of (sometimes) entire villages, reprisals against the families of suspected insurgents, the evacuation of large inhabited areas, the deforestation of zones considered particularly hospitable to partisan formations, the deportation of large groups of civilians, the seizure and killing of livestock – and all these with impunity for any excesses that might be committed.[1]

Notwithstanding its similarity to the repressive methods used by the Germans, to be stressed is the ambiguity of Italian policy, which oscillated between conventional military occupation and imperial conquest. The Italians' repression in the Balkans (but not in France) was decisively shaped by the colonial experience. It was in the colonies that the Italians first resorted to mass repression, deportation and internment. In Ethiopia, Mussolini had given a 'salutary warning' to the indigenous population by sending a phonogram in which he ordered that 'every civilian or member of a religious order, man or woman, suspected of having aided attacks [against Italian troops] is to be immediately shot without trial'. On 5 June 1936 he instructed that 'all rebels taken prisoner must be summarily executed' and then one month later, on 8 June, authorized a systematic 'policy of terror and extermination against the rebels and their civilian accomplices', because 'without the law of tenfold retribution wounds cannot soon be healed'. As the military and colonial historian Giorgio Rochat writes: 'Any compromise in the imposition of Italian domination was discounted. Conquest and pacification of the empire were to be achieved by force of arms, and the resistance of the population could only be overcome with terror.'[2]

[1] Collotti, 'Sulla politica di repressione italiana nei Balcani', pp. 186–8, 198, 203.
[2] Rochat, 'L'attentato a Graziani', p. 184.

As Rochat has convincingly shown, this policy was not restricted to Ethiopia alone. It was implemented in other colonial possessions as well, like Libya, and especially in Cyrenaica, where its aim of driving the semi-nomadic tribes out of the most fertile lands of the Gebel and exercising close political-military control over them was part of a 'broader design to destroy the traditional society of the cattle-herders of the Gebel and convert them into a reserve of low-cost and constantly available labour'. Rodolfo Graziani – observes Rochat – had publicly demonstrated a 'pathological' lack of understanding of the Arabic culture of Cyrenaica: 'nomadism must be considered an immanent threat', he had written in 1932, 'and it is therefore necessary to eradicate it rigorously and permanently' for political and economic reasons, given that the nomads were by their nature the enemies of agriculture and progress, as well as potential rebels. In apparent contradiction of these assumptions, Graziani intended to confine the peoples expelled from the best areas of the Gebel to the pre-desert borderlands: an arid and steppe-like strip between the plateau and the desert where nomadic cattle-herding was the only possible activity. Rather than being encouraged to settle, therefore, the survivors of the proud tribes of the Gebel were condemned to barely subsistence-level nomadism. Confined in 'native reservations', they would thereafter languish in constant and absolute inferiority.

According to Rochat, around 100,000 tribespeople were deported. After taking account of emigrants to Egypt and those exempted from deportation, the total Cyrenaican population before Graziani's campaign can be estimated at around 200,000, and the number who died during the repression at around 50,000. In the years that followed, reconstituting Cyrenaica's cattle herds proceeded only very slowly because Fascist colonial policy gave priority to the agricultural development of the Gebel and to large-scale Italian immigration. Traditional cattle-herding became a secondary economic activity, the main purpose of which was to maintain an underemployed pool of manpower from which the developing economic sectors could draw subordinate and casual labour.[3]

After 1940, the Italians treated the Balkan peoples as violently as they had treated the African natives in the colonial past, and Fascist racism undoubtedly played a role in implementation of these policies, especially in regard to the Slavs. To be pointed out finally is that the same penalties were provided in law for the political crimes of instigation and conspiracy, and for offences and attacks against the occupation forces and the Italian

[3] Ibid., pp. 95–6 and 84–5; see also Ottolenghi, *Gli italiani e il colonialismo*.

state, in all the militarily occupied territories.[4] But this does not mean that application of the law was identical in all the territories. Considerations concerning the diverse purposes and the differing circumstances of each occupied territory determined the severity with which the law was applied.

Any discussion of repression in the Yugoslavian territories must necessarily refer to the notorious Circular 3c of 1 March 1942 issued by General Mario Roatta, commander of the Second Army. In what follows, this document will be examined as the paradigm for all repressive measures against civilian populations, and as marking the point when the anti-partisan campaign became radicalized.[5] General Roatta declared bluntly that the offensive was colonial in its intent and that military force must be massively used even against extremely minor objectives. Yet, as we shall see, his circular was more than a mere description of the methods necessary to maintain order and to put down the first – and by and large manageable – stirrings of organized rebellion. It also served specific political purposes. The anti-insurgency methods ordered by Roatta went beyond military exigencies to enter the political domain: mass internment and a scorched-earth campaign would lead to 'de-Balkanization' and 'ethnic clearance' – and then in the annexed territories to Italian colonization. The High Command of the Second Army had no objection to the 'evacuation of entire regions'. Though pointing out that the measure was a far-reaching and complex undertaking beyond the army's competence and capacity, it raised no objection to it

4 The occupation authorities listed the following as 'political crimes': devastation, massacre, armed insurrection, conspiracy to subvert the political, economic and social order; these crimes incurred the death penalty. Membership of a subversive organization was punished with imprisonment for three to five years; subversive propaganda with imprisonment for between two and eight years. Those convicted of attacks against the general public or against the public services and the sabotage of military facilities (roads, communications or means of transport) received the death penalty or between ten and twenty-four years of imprisonment. Village chiefs and heads of households were considered abettors of crimes committed by minors. The penalties for 'crimes of instigation and conspiracy' were equally harsh: the death penalty for the organization of an armed gang, life imprisonment for membership of an armed gang. 'Offences against the occupation forces and the Italian state' included: threats against and assaults on Italian soldiers and citizens, incitement to hatred, defamation of the nation and the constitutional organs, defamation by correspondence, the possession of hostile propaganda, corruption or inducement to corruption. 'Offences against the public order' included: unlawful movement, officiating over unauthorized religious ceremonies, breach of curfew, opening shops outside legal hours, crossing occupation demarcation lines, breach of orders and provisions issued by the military authorities. See USSME, N 1–11, 'Diari storici', b. 971, 'generale Carlo Geloso, comandante superiore delle forze armate in Grecia, 28 aprile 1942'; b. 328; M 3, b. 48; N 1–11, 'Diari storici', b. 2005, 31 July 1943, 'Bando del Comando dell'VIII CdA' ('proclamation contenant les dispositions relatives à la sûreté et à l'ordre public dans le territoire de l'île de Corse'), and 15 November 1941, 'Giornale ufficiale del governo della Dalmazia, pubblicazione dei bandi del duce del 3 e 24 ottobre 1941' ('disposizioni per i territori annessi al Regno d'Italia')'.

5 Legnani, 'Il ginger del generale Roatta'.

in principle.[6] The main difficulties foreseen by the High Command were technical-logistical in nature: in particular 'the evident impossibility of giving refuge on [metropolitan] territory to such large masses of people' and the shortage of concentration camps.[7]

The Italian military authorities classified occupied districts into those that it considered 'normal' (*in situazione normale*) and 'abnormal' (*in situazione anormale*: towns and rural areas where military action was in progress against armed rebels). In the latter, Roatta ordered the internment of all families from which able-bodied males aged between sixteen and sixty were absent without good reason, and then their deportation. The general justified mass internment as a measure warranted by the extremely dangerous nature of the rebels' actions. Suspect groups of the population in each zone *in situazione anormale* were to be identified, and hostages taken from them and kept in custody. In the event of treacherous attacks against Italian troops, if the perpetrators were not identified within forty-eight hours, the hostages were to be executed. The inhabitants of homesteads close to railway lines, roads, telephone lines and military depots were deemed accomplices to any acts of sabotage on these installations, and if they did not furnish information leading to the arrest of the saboteurs within forty-eight hours, they would be interned, their cattle confiscated and their homes destroyed.

Roatta also distinguished between *periodi di operazioni* and *periodi al di fuori di operazioni*. He announced that any able-bodied or wounded males, even if unarmed, captured during operations in the immediate vicinity of rebel groups would be treated as insurgents if they were wearing military uniforms (or parts thereof) or band membership badges, or carrying military equipment, munitions or explosives. Able-bodied males aged under eighteen and women captured during operations would be brought before the military courts; so too would males of any age and women found in combat zones, and all persons not resident in the zone. Individuals suspected of aiding the rebels would be interned. During military operations, moreover, civilians could be rounded up and interned singly, by family, in groups or even as entire villages should the circumstances require it.

Circular 3c is not the only document that demonstrates a connection between the type of repression and the political aims of the occupation. For example, reference can be made to the military operation mounted to disarm the population of Ljubljana (which began in February 1942). The

[6] ACS, MI, DGPS, A 5 G, b. 145, 'Com. sup. Supersloda, 8 settembre 1942, Internamenti'.
[7] ACS, MI, DGPS, A 5 G, b. 145, 'Comando XI CdA al Com. sup. Supersloda', 14 September 1942.

purpose of the operation obviously extended beyond maintaining order and putting down the rebel movement; it seems to have been intended to prepare the way for colonization of a province which had nothing Italian about it. The troops of the 11th CdA stationed in Slovenia blockaded the city with 'an impenetrable cordon of troops and barbed wire' and four floodlight towers, so that Ljubljana was turned into a sort of enormous concentration camp. The civilian population was rounded up and searched. Many dozens of arrests were made each day. In the university district, 921 individuals were detained in a single day, and in the quarter to the south-west of the castle, fifty-six 'subversives' were arrested on 27 February alone.[8]

It was during the Ljubljana operation that Circular 3c was issued. Thereafter the campaign degenerated to the point that Roatta himself drew the commanders' attention to the danger of excessive or needless destruction, reminding them that villages were to be destroyed only if they were situated in 'abnormal zones'. The Ljubljana operation continued. On 26 April 1942, the high commissioner of Ljubljana, Emilio Grazioli, and the commander of the 11th CdA, General Mario Robotti, decided that in the event of the murder or attempted murder of a member of the armed forces, the police force or the civil service, or of an Italian citizen collaborating with the authorities, the culprit would be shot. If after a 48-hour search the culprit had not been arrested, communists and 'abettors of activities against the state' would be brought before a firing squad 'possibly in the place where the crime [had been] committed'.[9]

On 23 May 1942, in Fiume, General Roatta held a meeting with Mussolini, who told him that 'the best situation is when the enemy is dead. So we must take numerous hostages and shoot them whenever necessary.'[10] The general described his own scheme for dealing with the situation in Slovenia. Firstly, he said, the frontiers with the province of Fiume and Croatia must be closed. The entire population living to the east of the former frontiers must be evacuated to a distance of three to four kilometres inland, and patrols organized to police the borders and open fire upon anyone attempting to cross them. Indispensable for success was mass internment – of some 'twenty to thirty thousand persons'. The property confiscated from Slovene rebels, whose families were to be 'cleared' (i.e. evacuated), would be given to the families of fallen Italian soldiers. The scheme could obviously be extended to Dalmatia. General Roatta elaborated further. With a view to future requirements, he said, concentration camps should be constructed

[8] USSME, M 3, b. 59. [9] USSME, M 3, b. 51.

[10] USSME, M 3, b. 71, 'Stralcio delle comunicazioni verbali fatte dall'eccellenza Roatta nella riunione di Fiume del giorno 23 maggio 1942'.

for 20,000 inmates. He foresaw at least 5,000 internments for reasons of public order, and the evacuation of 15,000 people, including women and children, as a precautionary measure.[11]

There is a striking and significant similarity between Roatta's scheme and the directives issued by Pietro Badoglio on the deportation of the Cyrenaicans: 'We must first create a broad and clearly defined exclusion zone between the rebel formations and the subject population. I am fully aware of the extent and gravity of this measure, which will mean the ruin of the subject population. But the way has been marked out for us and we must pursue it until the end, even though all the population of Cyrenaica should perish (20 June 1930).'[12] Equally significantly, General Graziani executed his orders so conscientiously that he surrounded the camps of the Cyrenaican tribes with double barbed-wire entanglements, rationed food supplies, restricted the grazing of livestock and made any movement outside the camps subject to possession of a special permit. Graziani ordered the confiscation of all livestock found outside the authorized areas and announced that 'the government [would have] no compunction over reducing the population to the most abject hunger if it [did not] obey orders'.[13]

Mussolini fully endorsed these methods and ordered the 11th CdA to prepare a report on the zones to be evacuated and the number of civilians to be interned. In June 1942, the project moved into the implementation stage. The authorities thus began 'clearance' of unemployed workers, refugees, beggars, the homeless, university students, teachers, office workers, professionals, parish priests, factory hands transferred to Slovenia from Venezia Giulia after 1922 and former Italian soldiers who had moved to Yugoslavia after completing their military service.[14] In the *Rapporto di Gorizia* of 31 July 1942, Mussolini 'blessed' the policy pursued in Slovenia and Dalmatia:

> I think it is better to go from soft methods to harsh ones, rather than the other way round. In the latter case you lose face. I am not afraid of words. I am convinced that we should respond to the terror of the partisans with steel and fire. We must get rid of the stereotype that depicts the Italians as incapable of being ruthless when necessary. This tradition of excessive pleasantness and kindness must cease. As you have said [addressed to General Roatta], a new phase has begun which will see the Italians ready to do anything for the good of their country and for the prestige

[11] USSME, M 3, b. 82, 'Supersloda al CS, 2 giugno 1942'. The document finishes thus: 'Remember that no concessions are to be made to anyone when evacuation orders are enforced . . . Roatta will inform the political authorities.'

[12] Rochat, *Guerre italiane in Libia e in Etiopia*, p. 60. [13] Ibid., p. 66.

[14] USSME, M 3, b. 76, 'Comando Divisione Granatieri di Sardegna', 25 July 1941.

of their armed forces . . . Do not concern yourself about the economic hardship of the population. They wanted it! Let them take the consequences . . . I would not be averse to a mass transfer of the population . . . Make no distinction among communists: be they Slovenes or Croats, if they are communists deal with them all in the same way.[15]

On 7 August 1942, Luca Pietromarchi held a meeting with the prefect of Fiume, Temistocle Testa, and urged him to abandon the policy of reprisals, which, he argued, heightened the climate of hatred without achieving any practical results. Pietromarchi instead suggested a 'population exchange' (*cambio delle popolazioni*), a policy that he considered 'much more humane and practical, and certain to consolidate Italian control over the region for centuries'.[16] Pietromarchi's proposal was rejected, and in Slovenia the Regio Esercito planned a cycle of seven military operations to be mounted between 5 July and the second week of September. On 18 June, General Robotti issued his orders for repression and the maintenance of order. Between 16 July and the end of August, partisan losses amounted to 1,053 men killed in action, 1,236 summarily executed by firing squad, and 1,381 captured, for a total of 3,670 partisans eliminated. Italian casualties for the month of August were 43 men killed in action and 139 wounded. The cycle of operations was prolonged until November. When it ended, writes Marco Cuzzi, the province had been brought to its knees, devastated by military action and reprisals. Food stocks and cattle herds had been drastically depleted by raids (both partisan and Italian), with the consequent threat of famine; and the blockade on transport had severely damaged business in the province.[17] The 11th CdA's bulletin for 5 November triumphantly announced that around 7,000 casualties had been inflicted on the enemy.[18] Unfortunately, the figures do not distinguish between civilians and combatants, nor do they permit specification of how many civilian hostages were executed and in what circumstances.

[15] USSME, H 5, b. 40, CS, 'I Ufficio Operazioni – scacchiere orientale', 12 August 1942.

[16] Pietromarchi, unpublished diary, 7 August 1942 (Luigi Einaudi Foundation, Turin).

[17] Cuzzi, *L'occupazione italiana della Slovenia*, p. 262.

[18] USSME, M 3, b. 84, 5 November 1941, signed by Robotti: 'Our silent work, although it does not give us the pride and satisfaction of mention in the dispatches, has produced its results: (1) demonstrating to the world that we are the masters in Slovenia, free to move upon its territory when, how and where we wish; (2) destroying all the logistical installations that these bandits have created to the detriment of the wretched Slovene population, extorted, mistreated and murdered; (3) in almost four months, increasing their losses to 1,807 killed in combat, 847 captured and shot, 1,625 arrested while bearing weapons. We may add at least half as many again (dead and wounded taken away by the brigands) to this total of 4,279 losses to reach the rounded-up figure of 7,000 losses.'

In Dalmatia, exactly as in Slovenia and for the same political purposes, reprisals were organized against the families of fugitive rebels, and they led to the internment of thousands of people.[19] To give just one example, an ordinance of 7 June 1942 announced that all men who had left their communities of residence to join the rebels would be registered on special lists compiled by the municipality. If any men on the list were captured, they would be shot. Their families would be considered hostages and they could not, for any reason, leave their commune of residence unless they possessed a safe-conduct pass issued by the PS or the CC.RR. Anyone caught outside the commune without a pass would be shot. The property of men registered on the list would be confiscated and sold to the highest bidder. The chief of each village must place himself at the disposal of the civil and military authorities and assist with the search for and identification of fugitives. In the event of any non-cooperation he too would be shot.[20]

The methods used in the struggle against the partisans in the *situazione anormale* zones of militarily occupied Croatia were similar to those adopted in the annexed zones. Regardless of the results obtained against the rebel formations, wrote the commander of the 18th CdA, Umberto Spigo, it was still necessary to render the zone uninhabitable for the rebels and make all its resources unusable. He asked the Army High Command for authorization to destroy all rebel homes and villages, including those on the coast, and to intern all their women, children, old people and male adults, who were to receive the same treatment as meted out in Slovenia.[21] The Sassari Division 'dealt forcefully with those who aided the rebel movement'.[22] The division command ordered that villages assisting the rebels must be razed to the ground or burnt, and residents guilty of aiding the enemy interned, or shot, according to the circumstances.[23] During negotiations prior to the Trio

19 USSME, N 1–11, 'Diari storici', b. 732, 'generale Ruggero Cassata, Comando truppe Zara – Ufficio Operazioni, al Comando del XVIII CdA; b. 1380, XXV Battaglione CC.RR., dislocato a Cattaro e provincia': 'Following higher orders in accordance with political orders, the Kotor station shall endeavour to induce the rebels in the zone of Scagliari to surrender by interning members of their families.'

20 USSME, M 3, b. 64. The ordinance first applied only to the province of Zadar; it was then extended to those of Split and Kotor on 1 February 1943.

21 USSME, M 3, b. 60, 'Comando XVIII CdA – Ufficio Operazioni al Com. sup. Supersloda', 12 August 1942.

22 USSME, M 3, b. 51, fasc. 2, 'Comando II Armata – Ufficio Operazioni, generale Roatta a tutti i comandi di CdA', 7 April 1942; N 1–11, 'Diari storici', b. 999, May–June 1942. The Command of the 5th CdA informed the Supersloda High Command that 132 houses, barracks and huts used as bases by the enemy had been destroyed during operations along the coast near Ogulin (M 3, b. 60, 7 June 1942).

23 USSME, M 3, b. 58, 'Comando II Armata – Ufficio Operazioni al generale Bader'.

joint anti-partisan operation, Roatta spelled out the principles of Circular 3c to his German counterpart, General Paul Bader, and to the Croatian SM, which fully endorsed the Italians' methods, and indeed proposed the wholesale evacuation of entire zones on simple suspicion or as a mere precaution.

Montenegro was a special case, for as early as July 1941 a revolt in the region had been followed by harsh reprisals against the civilian population organized and supervised by General Alessandro Pirzio Biroli. Among the measures taken to put down the revolt was the destruction of dwellings and the taking of civilian hostages – even of entire families – who were 'evacuated', that is, deported to concentration camps (the hostages were termed 'evacuees' because they could not be considered prisoners of war). Pirzio Biroli decided to show his 'clemency' towards women and internees aged over sixty for whom charges were inapplicable by ordering their immediate release. The hostages taken were by preference able-bodied men related to fugitive rebels, or if none were found, the most able-bodied members (even women) of their families, whose dwellings were destroyed.[24] The hostages and the 'evacuees' were sent to concentration camps in Albania. For those sentenced to death, the army corps making the arrest had to draw up a *denunzia* (denunciation) to which it attached the charge documents (declarations written and signed by witnesses, reports by the garrison command) and documentary evidence to be sent to the 14th CdA.[25]

In October 1941, with the revolt quelled, the governor sought once again to set relations between the occupation troops and inhabitants 'on the basis of absolute legality, this being the essential condition for the easing of tension and the resuming of normal relations'. He cancelled the authorization for army commands to intern suspects immediately, and he ordered the cessation of acts that, although justifiable for the purposes of repression, could not continue without becoming 'arbitrary and damaging to prestige and to the work of Italian penetration'.[26] Henceforth policing measures or restrictions on the freedom of civilians were to be approved by a Commissione Speciale per i Provvedimenti di Polizia (consisting of the head of the civil administration and a military prosecutor). In order to regularize the

[24] USSME, N I–II, 'Diari storici', b. 374, 'Comando Divisione Messina, 14 agosto 1941, Prigionieri e ostaggi'.

[25] USSME, N I–II, 'Diari storici', b. 374, 'comandante del XIV CdA Luigi Mentasti, Trattamento dei ribelli montenegrini'. Draft copies of the report on the meeting were not found in the archives.

[26] USSME, N I–II, 'Diari storici', b. 463, 'Com. sup. FF.AA. Albania, Ufficio SM, Cettigne 13 ottobre 1941, Commissione speciale per i provvedimenti di polizia'.

positions of all Montenegrin internees, Pirzio Biroli ordered the compilation of lists stating the names of all prisoners and hostages, the date of their arrest and the reason for their internment. The Special Commission examined each individual on these lists and decided whether his or her release should be granted. At the end of the year, the governor published a proclamation of pardon which permitted around 3,000 internees (according to Pirzio Biroli's estimate) to return to their villages, but not always to their homes, because many of them had been burned down. As a precautionary measure, Pirzio Biroli instructed the garrison commanders as follows: 'if necessary, adopt the system of taking a certain number of hostages from the civilian population and holding them as guarantors for the good behaviour of the population itself'. Every week – or every ten days at most – the hostages were to be replaced by others indicated by the village chiefs or by local notables. The hostage exchange ceremony was to be conducted with a certain solemnity; and it was also to be used as an occasion to issue further instructions to the village chiefs. Housed in specially equipped quarters (even in army barracks from which troops were ejected to make room for them), and treated with respect, the hostages were not to be ill-treated, nor used as forced labour; they were to be given decent rations and kept in hygienic conditions. The garrison commanders would be held directly responsible for the treatment of the hostages and severely disciplined if they did not follow the orders issued to them. The purpose of the operation, wrote Pirzio Biroli, was to turn the hostages into propagandists who would recount to their compatriots '*how the Italian soldiers had treated them kindly and thoughtfully* [emphasis in the original]'.[27]

Hence, General Pirzio Biroli, who had cut his teeth in the African campaigns and had the colonialist notion of administration and government based on the civilization/barbarism dichotomy, managed to implement a policy other than brutal repression and show a degree of moderation towards the Montenegrins. But his policy was attacked by Guglielmo Rulli, a functionary seconded by the Foreign Ministry to Montenegro who criticized the governor's 'soft' line for not 'depleting the local energies of resistance'. The presence of around 100,000 Italian soldiers was enough 'for the majority of able-bodied men . . . to be rounded up and kept in concentration

[27] USSME, N I–II, 'Diari storici', b. 463, 'governatorato militare del Montenegro – UAC, Cettigne 6 novembre 1941, Internamento e provvedimenti di polizia'. Selection was to be made from among close kin, preferably male, of the rebels, village chiefs and local notables. Only in exceptional cases were the hostages to be the wives and mothers, aged under fifty-five, of known fugitives. In no case were young unmarried females, aged under twenty-five or in advanced stages of pregnancy, to be taken.

camps as hostages, or at any rate in conditions where they could not cause damage'. Pirzio Biroli had placed his trust in the pride of the Montenegrins, 'still regarded in the superficial and romantic manner with which the old pre-Fascist Italy of the beginning of the century considered the Montenegro of King Nicholas'. But this was a population entirely hostile to Italy and which, 'because of its ethnic origin', considered itself 'the cream of Serbism and the vanguard of the Slav and Orthodox movement on the shores of the Adriatic'.[28] Instead of cowing the population into submission with reprisals and the shooting of hostages, and therefore keeping them under 'firm but fair control' – Rulli wrote – Pirzio Biroli had cossetted them with acts of clemency. But then, with the first signs of revival in the rebel movement, the governor resumed the methods of violent repression used in July 1941 and thus adopted the hard line urged by Rulli.

Whereas in all the Yugoslavian territories the Italian troops burned villages and interned civilian populations, in Greece they were bound to the Roman ideal of justice and ordered to refrain from abuses and to respect the property of native Greeks. What accounts for the difference?

Firstly, the Greek government lodged vehement protests with Rome on every occasion of civilian hostage-taking.[29] In Yugoslavia, by contrast, no one came to the defence of civilians because the territories in question were either Italian provinces or Croatian possessions, and the Zagreb government was even more zealous in taking hostages with a view to reprisals. Secondly, in Greece, the actions of individual units were kept more closely under control by the military commands. For example, General Giuseppe Pafundi, commander of the 8th CdA, wrote a memorandum stating that abuses by native informers, interpreters and collaborationists must cease, and so too must the harassment, violence and bullying by Italian troops against civilians – whose attitudes, he said, were now changing from initial suspicion to a closeness that, in his mind, should be fostered in the common interest.

But the difference of treatment between Yugoslavia and Greece cannot be attributed to a difference in the Italians' perceptions of the Balkan peoples. The Italian generals considered the Greeks to be an 'inferior race' just as they did the Yugoslavs. When the Resistance began, brutal repression took

[28] USSME, M 3, b. 4, fasc. 12, 'Rulli a Ciano', 10 December 1941.

[29] USSME, N 1–11, 'Diari storici', b. 972, 'PCM al MAE – Gabinetto', 23 July 1942. Dino Grandi, then chairman of the Consultative Committee on the Law of War at the CS, pointed out that under international law hostages were to be treated as prisoners of war. He consequently advised against hostage-taking.

the place of 'justice' and 'humanity'. Consider the methods with which the 3rd Battalion of the CC.RR. repressed 'banditry' in the zone situated between Megara and Amfissa. All bandits captured were to be shot immediately and their families arrested. Should any member of the household resist arrest, he or she was to be treated as a *favoreggiatore* (accomplice or accessory) and brought before a firing squad. No leniency was to be shown towards political or ecclesiastical authorities. In addition to these measures, the homes of *favoreggiatori* – or even entire villages – were to destroyed and burned ('make much use of 81-millimetre mortars', the document specifies) and the inhabitants deported.[30] Between August and December 1942, all the CdAs subordinate to the Eleventh Army adopted these methods.

In August, the Command of the Pinerolo Division instructed the garrison of Lamia 'to scour the zone of the Parnassus and destroy all shepherd huts'.[31] A week later, it ordered that all armed groups must be hunted down and eliminated – or failing that, their families identified and arrested *en masse*. On 27 September, the general of the 26th CdA, Guido Della Bona, ordered: 'Whenever unlawfully armed individuals are encountered, they are to be immediately fired upon without prior warning',[32] adding: 'In the event of armed aggression, evacuate villages to a radius of ten kilometres and then destroy them. Conduct censuses of the inhabitants of the villages. All able-bodied males whose presence cannot be accounted for must be taken away. Investigate those who are missing and determine the reason for their absence. If they are absent for no justifiable reason, arrest the family and seize all its food provisions.' The commander of the 3rd CdA, Jalla, ordered his troops to 'feel no pity whatsoever for the population'.[33] On October 1942, the Eleventh Army command issued 'Directives for the Struggle against Rebel Bands and the Execution of Round-Ups' which specified as follows: 'Do not hesitate to intern family members of male sex aged over eighteen as hostages.'[34] The 3rd CdA's 'Rules for the Conduct of Operations' and 'Orders for the Deployment and Security of Units', issued on 16 October 1942, instructed that, when Italian troops came upon rebels, they were in all circumstances to attack them. Should they themselves be attacked, they

[30] USSME, N I–II, 'Diari storici', b. 823, 'maggiore Bruto Bixio Bersanetti al Comando della Divisione Forlì', 18 May 1942: 'I need not be asked to authorize the application of these orders. Such authorization I have already given. It will therefore be necessary to inform me after the event.'

[31] USSME, N I–II, 'Diari storici', b. 984, 'Comando Divisione Pinerolo', 24 August 1942.

[32] USSME, N I–II, 'Diari storici', b. 972, 'Comando XXVI CdA', 27 September 1942.

[33] USSME, N I–II, 'Diari storici', b. 1070, annex 9, 'Comando III CdA al generale Jallà'.

[34] USSME, N I–II, 'Diari storici', b. 1054, 'generale Geloso a tutti i CdA dipendenti', 8 October 1942.

were to respond immediately with bayonets, hand grenades and mortars.[35] Thus, for example, a relatively minor round-up (23 September to 15 October 1942), in the Fthiotida–Phocis region situated in the zone of Parnassus and Giona, led to the internment of 430 persons in concentration camps and the forced evacuation of two villages.[36] In that same period, the military authorities in Grevenà warned the 'bandits' that 'at least ten hostages' would be shot for every Italian soldier killed or wounded.[37] Similar measures were taken by the Italian commands in the provinces of Debar and Kosovo annexed to Albania.[38]

By the end of 1942, the repression was being prosecuted with the same criteria and with a similar level of violence in all the annexed and occupied territories. In 1943, the Regio Esercito reacted to the more efficient organization of the partisans with immediate reprisals and round-ups in zones where the presence of bands was reported, with 'the destruction of all support centres and logistical bases in order to deprive the bands of supplies and aid', and with 'severe measures of repression against villages which, either through open support or passive indifference, have facilitated the activities of the rebels'.[39]

A summary table compiled by the Command of the 3rd CdA on operations conducted against 'bandits' in February 1943 in the sectors of Kastoria, Trikala, Lamia and Thebes–Aliartos reported that around 120 bandits and 32 *favoreggiatori* had been killed and 107 persons shot in reprisals, and that aerial bombardments had caused an unspecified number of deaths and injuries. The document does not state whether these were civilians, whether they had been interned in previous actions

35 USSME, N I–II, 'Diari storici', b. 984, fasc. 01/4555, annex 1, 16 October 1942; b. 1194, 'Comando Divisione Pinerolo, generale Cesare Benelli': 'In action against rebel groups, show no pity; if necessary, burn everything within a radius of ten kilometres from the place where acts of brigandage have been committed; all troops should be informed that they will not remain alive in the hands of the enemy: sell your lives dearly.'

36 USSME, N I–II, 'Diari storici', b. 1192, Notiziario 3d, 16 October 1942, 'Movimento ribelle'. Three days later, a further 340 suspects were arrested in the area between the Parnassus and Giona (Notiziario 4d).

37 USSME, N I–II, 'Diari storici', b. 1232, 'Comando Divisione Pinerolo al Comando di presidio di Grevenà'.

38 USSME, N I–II, 'Diari storici', b. 1089, 16 February 1943. General Renzo Dalmazzo, commander-in-chief of the armed forces in Albania, wrote to the 4th and 25th CdAs and to the commander of the Scutari–Kosovo sector as follows: 'Able-bodied men arrested in villages at the centre of revolts [must be] held in readiness for dispatch to concentration camps for possible subsequent reprisals.' All men found bearing arms were to be shot on the spot. Also to be shot was any person not resident in the area of the operation and who could not account for his/her presence there.

39 USSME, N I–II, 'Diari storici', b. 1266a, 'Com. sup. FF.AA. Grecia al Com. sup. tedesco per il Sudest, 26 febbraio 1943, Relazione mensile sulla situazione politico militare'.

or whether they had been captured during the operations.[40] The village of Domenikon had also been destroyed during the operations, again as a reprisal.[41] The CS demanded that Carlo Geloso give account for the shooting of hostages. He replied that the intensification of the rebel insurgency, the extreme mobility of the bands and the impending invasion of Greek territory justified such a vigorous reaction. Geloso wrote that the bands did not have territorial objectives to defend: it was consequently necessary to punish the local people for acts of collusion by interning them and destroying their dwellings. These methods were not excessive, Geloso argued, for 'we were fighting not against a recognized belligerent enemy but against irregular formations . . . who wore civilian clothing . . . who invariably killed any Italian soldier or officer that fell into their hands'.[42]

In Slovenia, wrote Colonel Brucchietti, commander of the 12th Battalion of the CC.RR., in April 1943, Italian action consisted in 'the burning and destruction of villages previously occupied by rebels'.[43] According to the commander-in-chief of the Second Army, internment was 'decided on rather broad criteria' but 'it removed from circulation individuals who would probably have joined the rebels'. At the end of February, as the Regio Esercito withdrew to the Adriatic littoral, the army commands 'emptied' several camps for civilian internees, transferring some internees from the evacuated zones to the annexed provinces; they freed other civilian internees in the Italian camps to ease overcrowding.[44] These operations involved women, children, old people and the sick, since – wrote General Robotti – their age and state of health prevented such individuals from making any 'active and personal' contribution to the insurgency. However, the emptying of the concentration camps did not signify the end of reprisals against the civilian population. In May, the governor of Dalmatia Francesco Giunta decided, without consulting the military authorities, to distribute leaflets that threatened vicious reprisals against the civilian population: for instance, the shooting of three hostages for every telegraph pole cut down.

40 USSME, N 1–11, 'Diari storici', b. 1237, 'Comando III CdA Zara', February 1943: 34 rebels killed in combat and 1 wounded; 148 captured, 70 interned; for 5 wounded on the Italian side. See. b. 1187, 'Comando Divisione Zara, Sintesi dell'attività operativa svolta al bimestre gennaio–febbraio 1943'.

41 ACICR, G 3/27, b. 149, 'Comando gendarmeria greca al CICR', Athens, 12 April 1943. The Italian figures match those compiled by the gendarmerie except for the number of houses burned down: around 100.

42 USSME, N 1–11, 'Diari storici', b. 1266, 'Com. sup. FF.AA. XI Armata al CS'.

43 USSME, N 1–11, 'Diari storici', b. 1114, 27 March 1943, 'Attività'.

44 USSME, M 7, b. 411, 'generale Robotti ai CdA dipendenti', 6 July 1943.

In Greece, General Cesare Benelli, commander of the Pinerolo Division, announced: 'In the event of acts of sabotage against the Larissa–Volos railway line, the following [fifty] Greek citizens detained in the concentration camp will be shot.'[45] In the same period, on the Greek peninsula, the Italians resorted to heavy aerial bombardments that struck military targets and civilians indiscriminately, while during rounding-up operations several villages were razed to the ground.[46] In Montenegro, where the situation was equally difficult, the army continued to stage public executions of communists in reprisal for the killing of Italian prisoners.[47]

As regards the French occupied territories, one of the very few documents found in the Italian archives states that the SM of the Fourth Army organized a sweep of the city of Nice between 6 and 10 May 1943. The operation was carried out by the army CC.RR. with the assistance of soldiers from the EFTF and the Army Intendenza (administrative section), which furnished fifty lorries for the transport of persons arrested and established a camp at Cais (Fréjus) to hold one thousand internees, and another one at Modane for a further thousand.[48] A document dated 24 December 1942 of the 7th CdA stationed in Corsica, on the taking of hostages, shows that on paper Balkan-style repression was the rule in the French territories as well.[49] But we do not know for certain whether these measures were implemented with the same harshness (only detailed research in the French archives could yield conclusive evidence).

The foregoing examination of the military regulations on repression in the occupied territories has demonstrated that Circular 3c was not the only such instrument in force. Comparison with similar regulations in other

45 ACICR, G 3/27, b. 149, 13 June 1943 (my translation).

46 ASMAE, GABAP, b. 23, series of reports sent by the royal representative in Athens to the GABAP between May and September 1930. The villages razed were located between Argos Orestikon and Neapolis, and between Lamia and Larissa. The aerial bombardment of civilian targets is a topic that historians have not yet examined.

47 USSME, N 1–11, 'Diari storici', b. 1321, 'Comando Divisione Emilia, 23 giugno 1943, Rappresaglia nella zona di Nikšić e Danilovgrad'.

48 USSME, N 1–11, 'Diari storici', b. 1326, 'Comando IV Armata – SM – Ufficio Informazioni, 1 maggio 1943, firmato generale Mario Vercellino'.

49 USSME, N 1–11, 'Diari storici', b. 1099, 'Comando IV Armata, 4 dicembre 1942'; b. 1201, 'Comando VII CdA, 22 giugno 1943, ordine di internamento in Italia di tutti i comunisti corsi'; b. 1272, 'il generale comandante del VII CdA Carboni ai comandi di divisione dipendenti', 24 December 1942: 'On the occurrence of any act damaging to military personnel and equipment, the following numbers of hostages shall be taken from the civilian population: three hostages in the event that the attack causes no damage to military equipment or personnel; five hostages in the event that damage is caused to military facilities; ten hostages for each Italian soldier wounded; twenty hostages for each Italian soldier killed; double that number in the case of an officer. This command has drawn up lists of persons to take as hostages and will proceed with their capture if and when necessary.'

territories has shown that Roatta's circular was not unique; nor was it produced it by an exceptionally Fascist general. Similar measures were introduced in all the other occupied territories, even in France, and there is no doubt that methods of repression in Greece and Albania were no different in kind or degree from those in the occupied territories of Yugoslavia.

THE CIVILIAN INTERNMENT CAMPS: THEIR LOCATIONS AND INMATES

It should be stressed that the internment of certain categories of civilians was not a practice unique to the fascist regimes. Moreover, internment was not a measure used solely for the purpose of what we would today call 'ethnic cleansing'. Although some of the camps established in the occupied territories did indeed serve the purpose of maintaining civil order, what justification could there have been for the internment – between November 1941 and May 1942 alone – of around 25,000 persons in the province of Ljubljana, of between 6,000 and 8,000 in the Fiume hinterland and of more than 2,000 Dalmatians?

Unfortunately, it is not possible to furnish complete figures on civilian internees in the territories under Italian domination between 1941 and 1943. There are numerous gaps in the documentation. Often only the names of camps are given, with no information about the number of prisoners that they held, sanitary conditions and food provisioning, mortality rates or the release and transfer of internees. Nor do the archives yield much information about the 'provisional camps' like those of Cighino (Èigjnj) and Trebussa Inferiore (Doljna Trebuša) in Slovenia, which were constructed at the beginning of cycles of operations and dismantled on their conclusion. Were these camps only for male detainees? Were they for rebels or for civilians taken hostage? How many of their inmates were executed in reprisal for attacks on Italian troops, and how many died from natural causes? Nor is there any detailed information on the inmates of the prisons in the occupied territories: no lists of names were found in the archives. We know, for example, that in Montenegro a *bando* of 8 August 1941 ordered the internment of rebels who had been sentenced by the military courts but not yet executed by firing squad, of 'prisoners', of 'hostages' or of the families of 'evacuees'.[50] But it is impossible to ascertain the names, places

[50] USSME, N I–II, 'Diari storici', b. 328, 'Comando Divisione Messina al Comando del XIV CdA': 'The local CC.RR. territorial command already has one hundred-odd prisoners to dispatch to

and dates of internment of these individuals. One can only agree with Spartaco Capogreco's assessment concerning the lack of reliable figures on internees in the Italian camps. The estimated number of Yugoslavs ranges from 100,000 to 150,000, and the figures are even vaguer for Albania, Macedonia, Greece, Corsica and metropolitan France (see appendix, tables 51–65).[51]

The Italian concentration camps were of two kinds: those for prisoners of war (POWs) and those for civilian internees. Whereas international law regulated the treatment of POWs, there were no precise rules covering civilian internees. Each state applied its own criteria. For example, the Italians allowed the ICRC to furnish assistance to POWs but refused permission for its representatives to enter the camps containing 'new Italians' – Slovenes, Dalmatian Croats and Serbs – because Rome considered the peoples of the annexed territories to be 'Italian citizens'.

As regards civilian internment camps, those that operated between 10 June 1940 and 8 September 1943 can be distinguished into two types: those run by the Ministry of the Interior – around fifty of them situated in central and southern Italy – and those established after early 1942 by the Regio Esercito in central and northern Italy, of which there were around ten (the Regio Esercito also administered some seventy POW camps, but these are not considered here).

The term *concentrati* denoted foreigners dispatched to concentration camps where they were subject to military discipline. *Residenza in comuni liberi* was confinement in specific towns or villages with relative freedom under police supervision. The criteria for such confinement varied considerably because wealth, nationality, family and race influenced both the decision and the place of internment. *Isolati* and *rastrellati* (persons detained during round-ups) constituted a transitional category, in that as soon as these individuals were identified they were either sent to concentration

concentration camps STOP because it is likely that this number will increase over the next few days and it being not possible to detain these persons here please indicate to which concentration camps they are to be sent STOP General Tucci' (4 August 1942); b. 374, 'generale Mentasti, Scutari 5 agosto 1941, Trattamento dei ribelli montenegrini'. According to the 14th CdA Command, all individuals who could not be held in the military prison – not only prisoners but also hostages and evacuees – were to be sent to the concentration camps in Albania.

[51] Capogreco, 'Una storia rimossa dell'Italia fascista', especially p. 212; Capogreco, 'L'internamento degli ebrei stranieri e apolidi'; Capogreco, 'I campi di internamento fascisti per gli ebrei'. The figures on the concentration camps in Yugoslavia are controversial. According to Djilas, *The Contested Country*, Serbian victims amounted to 125,000 in Croatia and 209,000 in Bosnia-Herzegovina, this being approximately one-sixth of the total number of Serbs living within the frontiers of the NDH.

camps or confined in *comuni liberi* (within which they could move freely but could not leave under any circumstances).[52]

Civilian internments were distinguished between 'protective' and 'precautionary' (*repressivi*). Precautionary internment applied to former career soldiers (military personnel in the former Yugoslav army resident in the annexed territories and already POWs: these were released and then re-arrested and treated as civilian internees, so that they were no longer covered by the Geneva Conventions), former civil servants, teachers, students, intellectuals, unemployed workers, individuals suspected of acts harmful to Italy, able-bodied males formerly belonging to rebel formations, the relatives of rebel accomplices and hostages in general. Protective internment was provided for individuals eluding recruitment by the partisans, those who asked of their own accord to be evacuated and those who had collaborated with the occupiers and begged for protection against partisan reprisals. The Army General Command instructed that protected internees were to be sent to Italy, where they would be reunited with their families and detained in adequate living conditions. Precautionary internees were also to be dispatched to Italy, but their treatment was to be differentiated according to category: former soldiers were kept distinct from teachers, intellectuals, students and the unemployed, who were organized into work squads. Finally, the families of rebels were to be subject to a harsher regime than families interned for their own protection.[53]

Another distinction concerns the camps established in the annexed territories and those in the militarily occupied territories. The camps were run by the Regio Esercito. However, in the annexed provinces, and only in zones *in situazione normale* (to use Circular 3c terminology), decisions on internment were taken by the prefects, who left the choice of internment camp to the competent CdA. If the zone was *in situazione anormale*, the prefect was informed of the internment by the military authorities. In the militarily occupied zones, the internment of civilians was decided by the CdA commanders on consultation with the division commands, which then informed the authorities of the occupied governments.[54]

52 ACICR, GL 7/74, b. 488, 6 January 1943, 'Promemoria per il conte Guido Vinci Gigliucci, delegato generale della CRI'.

53 ACS, MI, DGPS, A 5 G, b. 145, 'Com. sup. Supersloda, 8 settembre 1942, Internamenti'.

54 USSME, N 1–11, 'Diari storici', b. 1265, 'Comando VI CdA – UAC', 27 April 1942, signed General Dalmazzo. The general attached an 'Internment Proposal' which, besides name, surname and the usual details, required specification of the internee's zone of residence, occupation and religion, the reason for the proposed internment, the internee's present place of custody, and the camp suggested for his/her internment.

NOTES ON THE CAMPS FOR FORMER YUGOSLAVIAN CIVILIANS: THE CONCENTRATION CAMP ON THE ISLAND OF ARBE (RAB)

On 16 December 1942, General Roatta sent to the CS his reply to a note of complaint by the Vatican concerning the civilian internment camp of Arbe, where, the Holy See alleged, around 30,000 Slovene internees were being kept 'in dreadful conditions'.[55] Roatta replied that a total of 19,369 civilians had been interned by Supersloda, and 6,577 of them were confined on the island of Arbe:[56] among them were Slovenes and persons from all the annexed territories (Dalmatia and Fiume). He also affirmed that the number of internees on Arbe had never exceeded 10,522. The general's figures roughly correspond to those that I have found in dossier 110 of the Army General Staff archives and which I set out in the tables in the appendix. However, although Roatta's figures seem reliable, he omitted numerous details and he repeatedly lied in his reply to the Vatican.

First, the implication of his statement that 'mass internments have not been undertaken for some time' is that they must previously have taken place. When he wrote 'the decision to construct a camp for 5,000 internees in tents was taken on 1 July 1942', he was obfuscating: the island had in fact been selected as the site of a civilian internment camp for 20,000 people (5,000 of them 'protected' and 15,000 'precautionary'). It would be divided into four blocks, so that each of these would represent the figure of 5,000 internees.

We know from a document compiled by the under-secretary of state, Antonio Scuero, that once the camp was completed it would have held the internees at Padua (Chiesanuova) and Treviso (Monigo). There were 316 brick barracks to be built, each of them for one hundred internees. Roatta had been informed as early as August by the Army Intendenza that the barracks would not be completed by October, and that the internees would therefore have to spend the beginning of winter in tents – and this on an island notorious for its bitter north-easterly wind (the *bora*). The

[55] The Vatican's note was handed to the Italian ambassador at the Holy See in November 1942, and the MAE forwarded it to the Ministry of the Interior, to the CS and to the high commissioner of Ljubljana, Graziani, with 'a request for attention' (ACS, MI, DGPS, AA.GG.RR., b. 109, sottofasc. 1). The other civilian internees were held at Gonars (2,250), Monigo (1,136), Chiesanuova (3,522) and Renicci (3,884). Added to these were a further 2,000 persons detained at Ljubljana before 'evacuation' to camps in Italy. General Roatta stated that, in November, 3,041 protected internees had been transferred from Arbe to Gonars, where they were joined by a further 1,300 other internees, making a total of 4,341.

[56] USSME, N 1–11, 'Diari storici', b. 824, 'Comando XII Battaglione CC.RR.'. The command logbook for August 1942 states that around 5,000 people were interned during that month, among them 3,459 Slovenes.

Intendenza stressed that the site selected had numerous shortcomings – high construction costs, difficulties of transport and logistics – and recommended that other solutions be found. But no alternative was given serious consideration. At the end of November, 1,700 six-berth tents were erected, while the hospital and the infirmary were able to accommodate around 500 persons.[57] Roatta was well aware of all this when he replied to the CS. He admitted that 502 internees were in barracks and 6,075 were living in tents, but to the Vatican's accusation that numerous internees were almost naked he objected that 'in the summer there were some of them . . . but in the winter they were all given pullovers and sweaters'.[58] This was a lie. Only at the end of November, when temperatures were already close to zero, did the Intendenza set about purchasing winter clothing, 5,000 pairs of shoes (a large number of them for children), 5,000 blankets and some thousands of items of underwear.

As regards sanitary conditions in the camps, Roatta claimed that releases of sick internees and those with chronic diseases had been in progress for some time. Hospital 481 on Arbe (staffed by fourteen doctors) had a paediatrics department, a children's clinic and an obstetrics and gynaecology ward. Seventy-three children had been born in the camp, of whom fifty – according to Roatta – were in good health. But a ICRC report of April 1943 instead stated: 'Almost all the women who have given birth in the camps of Rab and Gonars have been delivered of stillborn babies.'[59] Roatta claimed that, notwithstanding all the efforts made to improve living conditions in the camp, from the date of its opening until November 1942 there had been 588 deaths. These, however, he blamed on the frail physical state of the internees when they had been admitted to the camp, or on their advanced age: hence the living conditions in the camp were anything but 'dreadful'. Roatta stressed that Arbe complied with the rules on rationing stipulated by the Ministry of War: full rations for working protected internees; medium

[57] The barracks therefore had either not been built or were unfinished. The Intendenza expected the consignment of a first batch of 1,000 internees by 6 December, a further 1,000 by 15 December, 1,500 by 31 December and 1,500 in January 1943; these dates, of course, were very approximate given the conditions at sea and the winter weather. Lodgings for the second batch would not be ready before the spring of 1943, and the authorizations for construction by the Pardi Company of Sušak of barracks for the two batches expired in December, while the army engineers would finish building the barracks for the first 5,000 internees only in February. A document sent by the Supersloda Intendenza to the Pardi Company on 4 August confirmed its order for the construction of a barrack block for internees at Arbe: 50 dormitory barracks, 7 for general services and stores, 6 for kitchens, 6 for washrooms, 5 for infirmaries, shops, chapels, 5 for lavatories, all of which had to be ready by 31 October 1942.

[58] USSME, N 1–11, 'Diari storici', b. 1130, 'generale Roatta al CS', 16 December 1942.

[59] ACICR, G 17/74, b. 488, 14 April 1943, 'Note à l'attention de M. Salis, délégué du CICR en Italie' (my translation).

rations for non-working protected internees; and minimum rations for non-working precautionary detainees. This was another lie: on 12 November the health department of the Intendenza issued a report on the situation of the Arbe internees which stressed that the increase in the mortality rate had coincided with the rapid fall in temperature and was due to enfeeblement of the internees by their inadequate diet.[60] Fully twenty-six deaths had been registered in a single day (24 November). A note dated 14 April 1943 sent by the ICRC to Salis, its representative in Italy, ran as follows:

> Island of Rab. The situation of the internees on this island is not satisfactory. Indeed, the Italian authorities themselves have just ordered the evacuation of 300 women and children to Treviso. But many of them were in such a poor physical state that they could not be transported to the steamer. Around 3,000 deaths have apparently been caused in the camp by entirely inadequate rations and wretched accommodation. Moreover, it is reported that the local authorities do not distribute food parcels for the internees, but keep them in the camp stores (at certain times up to 12,000 parcels have been withheld from internees in this way).[61]

As regards the inmates of the camp, the Diary (envelope 1114) of the 12th Battalion of the CC.RR. logs the movements of internees from January to June 1943. Between January and June 1,439 internees left Arbe: 829 were interned at Gonars, 300 at Monigo, 58 at Chiesanuova and 252 in Fiume while awaiting transfer elsewhere; in addition, 210 Slovenes were set free. In the two months that followed, a further 316 prisoners were released: 65 were transferred to other camps, while at the same time 281 new internees arrived at Arbe. In May, 171 persons were transferred to Gonars, and some hundreds of Jewish internees arrived from Italian camps in various parts of

60 USSME, N 1–11, 'Diari storici', b. 1074, 'Curia castrense', February 1943. In that month, the apostolic nuncio of Italy, Francesco Borgognini Duca, visited the civilian internment camps of Chiesanuova, Monigo and Renicci. The nuncio asked why some internees were showing evident signs of physical deterioration. Without enquiring too insistently, he found 'giustissima' (entirely satisfactory) the explanation given him by the military authorities that: 'On their arrival at the camp they were in a wretched state, given that most of them had been rounded up in woods where they lived without nourishment, without roofs over their heads and without clothing.' On the question of food rations, see USSME, M 7, b. 411, 'Intendenza del Com. sup. FF.AA. Supersloda, Ufficio Prigionieri di guerra, sezione Internati civili, 27 marzo 1943, Vettovagliamento per internati civili': 'Measures were taken to improve the rations for civilian internees in order to prevent any further increase in the mortality rate, which had already reached rather high levels.' The rations for non-working precautionary internees were 50 g of bread, 20 g of meat, 10 g of vegetables and 10 g of cheese, which were the same as those for non-working protected internees; the rations for working precautionary internees were increased to 250 g of bread, 20 g of meat, 54 g of pasta, 20 g of cheese, 8 g of grated cheese and 10 g of vegetables, which were the same rations as received by working protected internees.

61 ACICR, G 17/74, b. 488, 14 April 1943, 'Note à l'attention de M. Salis, délégué du CICR en Italie' (my translation). The Ex-Combatants Association of Slovenia gives the figure of 1,552 dead Slovenes (Capogreco, *Renicci*, p. 27).

Croatia. In May 1943, the Jews interned in the militarily occupied Yugoslav territories were transferred to Arbe: those interned in the 6th CdA's zone of jurisdiction in the first fifteen days of May; those under the jurisdiction of the 18th CdA in the second fifteen days; those under the 5th CdA thereafter. Vittorio Castellani insisted that the 6th CdA's 874 Jewish internees and the 615 of the 18th CdA must be relocated as rapidly possible because the 1,272 Jews confined at Porto Re (Kraljevica) were only a few kilometres away from Sušak and hence very close to the Italian border.[62] By 25 July 1943, some 2,661 Jews were confined in the Arbe camp.

For the refugees interned in hotels on the 6th CdA's territory, or those fortunate enough to enjoy complete freedom of movement on the islands of Lesina and Brazza, their arrival on Arbe must have seemed like a descent into hell; likewise for those from Porto Re, who had slept in real barracks, had been able to use latrines and had received dental treatment. Their status as protected internees meant that they enjoyed 'privileges' such as receiving a little water without soap, and living amid bedbugs and fleas, but in any case conditions 'better' than those of the other civilian internees. The UAC instructed the Intendenza to improve the quality of the camp facilities, allow certain social events, organize primary and lower-secondary school classes, create a library, organize entertainment, set up dental clinics, provide the services of barbers, tailors and carpenters, and even arrange sea-bathing excursions.[63]

On 16 August 1943, the order arrived from Rome that the Jews were to be released from the Arbe camp, although those who so wished could stay. At the end of August the MAE recommended that 'rapid and benevolent' examination be made of each individual case, so that the best arrangements could be made for all Jewish internees. The Ministry of the Interior was thus obliged to grant the transfer of Jews with relatives in Italy or in the annexed territories and to release all elderly and chronically ill internees

[62] On 28 May, 69 Jews arrived from Gravosa: 42 women, 14 men and 13 children. On 6 June, 110 Jewish internees arrived from Porto Re: 15 men, 92 women and 3 children; on 8 June, again from Porto Re, 232 Jews: 88 men, 120 women and 24 children; on 19 June, from Split (from a camp or in transit?) 591 Jews: 268 men, 256 women and 67 children. The next day 474 Jews arrived from Dubrovnik: 199 men, 215 women and 60 children. A further 402 Jews from the same city were interned at Arbe on 30 June: 181 men, 137 women and 84 children. Thus, on 1 July, the camp held a total of at least 1,878 Jewish internees.

[63] USSME, M 3, b. 67, 'II Armata – UAC, 10 luglio 1943, Sistemazione e trattamento ebrei nel campo di Arbe': 'The army's Jewish internees form a mass of 2,700 persons who have all the duties of protected civilian internees, with the same treatment; but for particular, exceptional reasons, contingent and political, it is deemed opportune to grant them – in disciplinary matters – a sincerely "Italian" treatment, so that if kindness is to be shown towards them by our military authority, this must be full, not half-hearted.'

able to fend for themselves. The MAE declared itself in favour of these measures for 'political and humanitarian' reasons.

The Military History Institute of Belgrade has published the following figures on Arbe, which perhaps should be adjusted upwards: a total of 9,537 persons, including 4,958 men, 1,296 women and 1,039 children; 7,293 were from the province of Ljubljana and from Fiume, and finally there were 2,244 Jews, including 1,027 men, 930 women and 287 children.[64] It is not known how many died as a result of the conditions at the Arbe camp, but there is no doubt that they numbered more than the 1,009 buried in the cemetery of Kampor. On 8 September 1943, 2,000 Jews were liberated by the partisans: some decided to join the partisans, others tried to flee. Three hundred remained in the camp and were subsequently deported by the Germans: none of them survived.[65]

NOTES ON OTHER CIVILIAN INTERNMENT CAMPS IN THE TERRITORIES MILITARILY OCCUPIED BY THE SECOND ARMY

Still today, the exact number of Italian concentration camps in the territories occupied by the Second Army is not known. According to a handwritten note found in the archives, there were twenty-four camps for Slovene, Dalmatian and Croatian civilian internees. Some thousands of Yugoslav civilians were interned in concentration camps situated in Italy. These camps depended on the Second Army only for the transport of internees. The *difese territoriali* (military authorities other than the Second Army) were responsible for their organization, internal discipline and services. According to the figures provided by Roatta in his reply to the above-mentioned note from the Vatican, as well as at Arbe, Yugoslavs were interned at Gonars (2,250), Monigo (1,136), Chiesanuova (3,522) and Renicci (3,884). A further 2,000 persons at Ljubljana were to be 'evacuated' to camps in Italy. To be noted is that, as a rule, after civilian internees had spent a period of time in the annexed or militarily occupied territories, they were transferred to the metropolitan camps, which, besides those already mentioned, were the camps of Fiume, Visco, Fraschette di Alatri, Cairo Montenotte, Pisticci, Ferramonti Tarsia, Ancona, Fiume, Lipari and Ustica, and the forced labour camps of Fossalon di Grado and Tavernelle.

The Second Army and its dependent corps were responsible only for the camps in the annexed and militarily occupied territories. Some camps, for instance the one situated on the island of Molat (with a capacity for 1,200

[64] Potocnik, *Il campo di sterminio fascista.*

[65] Löwenthal, *The Crimes of the Fascist Occupants*, p. 23.

internees), were run – at least for a certain period of time – by the civil authorities.[66] On 19 January, the Molat camp, termed 'a graveyard of the living', contained 1,627 people, of whom 522 were women and children. The Forte Mamula camp, situated at the entry to the inlets of Kotor (Bocche di Cattaro), was used for civilians of both sexes and for hostages, as was the Prevlaka camp located approximately two kilometres from Cape Ostro in the province of Kotor. Both camps were administered by the military authorities.[67] The decision to construct a camp for around 500 internees at Buccari (Bakar) in Dalmatia was taken between January and February 1942.[68] The camp operated between March 1942 and July 1943. One deduces from a report on food rations that it contained political (and therefore precautionary) detainees, some of whom were Croats. In August 1942, the Croatian authorities requested the Italians to make a 'selection of the Croatian internees',[69] but the criteria used for this selection are not known (was the reference to Jewish internees?). A document of 20 April 1943 issued by the Supersloda Intendenza on transfer of civilian internees ordered that non-Jewish inmates of the Buccari camp were to be given thorough medical examinations – there had been several cases of typhoid in the camp – and then transferred.[70] On 30 April 1943, some 893 persons were interned in the camp, and 842 non-Jewish internees had been transferred to it.[71]

We know that the camp at Scoglio Calogerà (around 150 internees) in the annexed Dalmatian zone required the commitment of a large number of personnel 'because of the layout of the living quarters', and that it was particularly 'inconvenient in regard to hygiene' (that is to say, there were no lavatories). For this reason, in March 1943, the Zara Division Command asked for permission to transfer the inmates to the camp of Ugliano.[72]

[66] ACS, MI, DGPS, A 5 G, b. 424. This camp began receiving internees in February 1942. By September of that year it was 'accommodating' at least 2,300 internees in transit to camps in Italy, probably the relatives of rebels. The prefect of Fiume, Testa, was instructed to organize departures in small batches, keeping families together; See b. 145, 'Com. sup. Supersloda, 8 settembre 1942, Internamenti'.

[67] USSME, N 1–11, 'Diari storici', b. 993, 4 September 1942; b. 1265, 'Comando VI CdA – UAC', 30 March 1942; ACS, MI, 'Servizi di Guerra, 1941–5', b. 58, 'documento alla prefettura di Cattaro e p.c.c. al governo della Dalmazia', 11 November 1942.

[68] USSME, N 1–11, 'Diari storici', b. 446.

[69] USSME, M 3, b. 67, 'capo di SM Ettore De Blasio al commissario generale amministrativo dello stato indipendente di Croazia, Vjekoslav Vrančić', 31 August 1942.

[70] USSME, M 3, b. 64: 107 under protective internment (19 men, 64 women and 24 children) to the Monigo concentration camp, 735 under precautionary internment (431 men, 269 women, and 35 children) to the Gonars concentration camp.

[71] USSME, M 3, b. 64, 'Comando II Armata al V CdA e all'Intendenza', 31 May 1943. One can estimate that, in April 1943, there were at least 52 Jewish prisoners at Buccari.

[72] USSME, M 3, b. 87, 'Comando Divisione Zara alla prefettura di Zara', 16 March 1943.

The Intendenza organized the transfer of 178 precautionary internees from Scoglio Calogerà to Visco. Besides these camps, the documents refer to those of Vodice and of Laurana, located close to Sušak.[73] A document dated 14 April describes the camps of San Martino di Brazza and Lesina as 'concentration camps for Jewish internees'. We do not know whether they were originally intended for Jews or whether they became such following the transfer of the internees by Supersloda after the spring of 1943. Nor do we know how many Jews they 'accommodated'.[74] The largest Jewish internment camp was that of Kraljevica (Porto Re), which was notorious for its unsanitary conditions:[75] it contained at least 1,157 Jews, all of whom were transferred to Arbe at the end of May 1943.[76]

THE ITALIAN CONCENTRATION CAMPS IN MONTENEGRO, ALBANIA, GREECE AND FRANCE

How many internees remained in the camps after the end of the revolt that began in July 1941? Where were they held? Where were the individuals arrested during the anti-insurgent operations and round-ups of 1942–3 sent for internment? How many internees were there in Greater Albania? How many Serbs and Montenegrins from Kosovo, Metohija and Debar were interned by the authorities of Tirana, and how many by the Italian army?

There is little information with which to answer these questions. As regards Montenegro, we know that a group of prisoners was sent to Durazzo together with other 'political arrestees' (150) from Kotor. The lieutenancy informed Rome that there was a shortage of facilities suitable for 'long-term internment'; yet at the end of July the number of prisoners was estimated at 1,000 'Serbian sympathizers, Jews and communists'.[77] The situation deteriorated to such an extent that the MAE and the Ministry of the Interior decided to transfer the communists to Italy, while 'families, women,

[73] USSME, N 1–11, 'Diari storici', b. 446. [74] USSME, M 3, b. 64.

[75] USSME, M 3, b. 64, 'Comando V CdA al Comando della II Armata – UAC', 6 June 1943.

[76] USSME, N 1–11, 'Diari storici', b. 1321. The Intendenza of the Second Army arranged for the transfer of 157 women and 5 children interned in the 2nd CdA's zone of jurisdiction (in which camp is not known) to Visco, of 620 precautionary internees to Chiesanuova, or to Visco in the case of families, and of 435 civilian internees from Prevlaka. See M 3, b. 64, 'Comando II Armata – UAC', 18 June 1943: 'The new situation must now be evaluated to see whether it is not necessary to ease conditions in Fiume as soon as possible, review the precedence given to the evacuation of Jews, and give the 5th CdA responsibility.' The Intendenza organized for the 18th CdA the transfer to Monigo of 180 protected internees from Boccagnazzo, 50 from Brazza and 50 from Almissa, as well as those rounded up in Punta Planka.

[77] ASMAE, GABAP, b. 52, 'luogotenenza di Tirana al MAE', 23 July 1941.

children and men of advanced age or in precarious health' would remain in Albania, or in the camps of Montenegro. A report by the Italian Red Cross informed the ICRC that, as of 18 February 1942, there were 142 Montenegrin internees in Albania: 904 of them at Klos and 517 at Preza (possibly Pecira?).[78] On 14 June 1942, around 580 'undesirable' Kosovan intellectuals were sent from Preza for internment in Italy: 360 to the island of Ustica, where Croats had already been interned, and 220 to the island of Ponza, on which other Montenegrins were confined.[79] According to ICRC documents, on 31 July 1942 there were 2,500 Montenegrin internees in Albania: 1,200 in the camp at Klos (300 women), 1,000 in the camp at Kavajë and 300 at Preza, plus more than 4,000 at Kukës. According to the metropolitan of Montenegro writing from exile in Cairo, as well as in the camps just mentioned there were internees at Scutari and Boureli.[80] Numerous internees from Albania and Montenegro were held in the transit camp of Antivari (Bar). In 1946, the Yugoslav War Crimes Commission concluded that a total of 26,387 Montenegrins had been interned by the Italians in Yugoslavia, Albania and Italy. However, this figure seems excessive unless Albanian, Kosovar and western Macedonian internees are included in the calculation.[81]

In Greece, a concentration camp for political internees and enemy subjects (British and Russian) was constructed on the island of Paxos, with two 'annexes' on the island of Othoni and at Lazarati: one in Fanos, others in the fortress of Acronauplia, close to Nauplia, a further two at Kalavryta and

[78] ACICR, G 17/501, b. 139, 'J. Pictet a R. Voegeli agent de liaison del CICR presso il consolato svizzero di Belgrado', 13 March 1942.

[79] ACS, MI, DGPS, Direzione AA.GG.RR., 1942, b. 14, 'copia di lettera del CS al Ministero dell'Interno – DGPS', 19 May 1942.

[80] ACICR, G 17/501, b. 139, 31 July 1942, 'Note pour M. Voegeli: internés monténégrins en Albanie'. The figure of 18,000 Yugoslav internees in Albania appears in two ICRC documents: ACICR, G 17 Grèce G 3/40 JL/GV, 1 November 1941, 'Téléphone de M. Dufour du Département politique fédérale à M. J. Lossier': 'M. Ramseyer, de la délégation du CICR à Ankara, a demandé au DPF de transmettre au CICR le message suivant: L'ambassade de Yougoslavie à Ankara désirerait être renseignée sur la situation des yougoslaves en Grèce. Cette mission diplomatique désirerait préparer également une action de secours en faveur des 18000 yougoslaves qui se trouvent actuellement en Albanie, principalement à Cavalla et à Tirana; et dont la situation est – selon certains renseignements – très difficile'; G 17/139, b. 501, 'Département politique fédéral, Division Affaires étrangères', b. 55.11.5.ZN, au CICR Genève, Berne le 3 novembre 1941': 'Notre légation à Ankara a transmis à votre intention un message à M. Ramseyer. Celui-ci vous informe que l'ambassade de Yougoslavie lui a fait part de son désir d'être renseignée sur l'effectif de ses compatriotes qui ont cherché asile en territoire hellénique et sur l'endroit où ceux-ci se trouvent actuellement. Cette mission diplomatique aimerait aussi préparer l'expédition de secours à destination d'habitants du Monténégro qui, au nombre de 18000, se trouveraient, bien que non militaires internés à Kavaia et à Tirana, dans le royaume albanais, et auraient à y faire face à des nombreuses difficultés.'

[81] Capogreco, 'Una storia rimossa dell'Italia fascista', p. 229. This author states that other sources put the number of interned Montenegrins at around 10,000.

Trikala. The Larissa camp in Thessaly was situated in a zone infested with malaria-carrying mosquitoes (more than 50 per cent of the camp population were afflicted by malaria, and many others by scabies or tuberculosis). It contained an average of around 1,000 British POWs awaiting transfer to camps in Italy, as well as Cretan soldiers and civilian internees.[82] Cretans were deemed to be combatants, and they were interned at Larissa in the Italian zone, and at Tatoï in the German zone, until the end of 1942, when it was decided that they could return to their island. They were taken to the Piraeus, but because no transportation was available, they remained confined for several weeks within the precincts of the port. The conditions of their confinement – wrote the ICRC representative D'Amman – were deplorable, and those who had been interned by the Italians suffered most of all: they were given no humanitarian aid, for which the Italians' constant excuse was that their embarkation was imminent.[83]

It seems that there were no concentration camps in the strict sense of the term on Crete or in the other Greek provinces. Instead, civilian internees were usually incarcerated in the Greek prisons; but there the conditions were even worse. A report by the ICRC described the prison of Volos as horrific: the prisoners had neither beds nor blankets; there was no glass in the windows; and the cells flooded whenever it rained. Large numbers of prisoners were confined to small rooms with just one tiny window: the stench was appalling. As in the case of Montenegro, however, the documents are too fragmentary for any meaningful figures to be provided.[84] The commissioner of civil affairs in the Ionian islands, Piero Parini, requested the Ministry of the Interior to transfer the political internees in the Paxos and Fanos camps to Italy. He argued that removal from the proximity of their families would undermine their morale and impede access to them by their supporters. One gathers from the commissioner's letter that only a small number of persons were concerned: 'some lawyers, two or three teachers, some would-be worker intellectuals, some university students and a doctor'.[85]

[82] ACICR, G 3/27, 'Délégation du CICR en Grèce au CICR Genève', 3 November 1942, signed by M. Junod; G 3/27 C.I., b. 148, *Extraits du rapport du voyage à Volo et Larissa du 15 au 18 octobre 1942 du délégué CICR Sauser*: 'Les prisonniers disent eux-mêmes que les autorités militaires font tout le possible pour améliorer leur sort. Par suite des incidents en Théssalie, quelques centaines d'otages ont été pris à Larissa, entre autre la presque totalité des médecins de Larissa. Ils ont été enfermés dans un camp séparé dont l'accès ne m'a pas été accordé.'

[83] ACICR, G 3/27, b. 148, 'D'Amman à la délégation du CICR en Grèce', 23 November 1942.

[84] ACICR, G 17/74, b. 488.

[85] ASMAE, GABAP, b. 23, 24 September 1942. Only on 10 June 1943 were fourteen political detainees from the Ionian islands sent to the Pisticci camp in Italy. There are two lists for the Ionians, one with ten names, the other with fifteen.

At the end of 1942, when the offensive against the Andartes began to intensify, the Italians set about interning civilians accused of aiding the rebels, and they also took hostages.[86] One learns from ICRC reports, and from those by René Burkhardt, that many of the camps for political detainees (communists) and Jews were situated in zones infested with malaria. There were penitentiaries and a concentration camp for Serbs sentenced to extreme forced labour and who were sent to hospital only when it was too late to save their lives.[87] In a note to the ICRC representative one reads as follows:

By 'Greek internees' I mean all detainees in the prisons and concentration camps (excluding the Cyclades, the Sporades, Macedonia and Crete) for a total – the figure has been communicated to me by the Greek Red Cross – of 11,456 persons. I therefore believe that the total figure of 20,000 is no exaggeration for Greece as a whole. This figure includes political and ordinary detainees . . . in both concentration camps and prisons. The only difference between these is that the concentration camps are in the hands of the occupation authorities, while the prisons hold detainees partly under the power of those authorities and partly under that of the Greek government . . . Of a total of forty-four establishments there are seven concentration camps and thirty-seven prisons. The number of inmates is roughly the same as in October 1942. At that time there were still 383 'communist' detainees who had been deported by the Metaxas government to the Cyclades and the Sporades . . . Added to this number are the prisoners from Macedonia and Crete, about whom neither the Greek Red Cross nor our delegation has been able to obtain any precise information.[88]

[86] USSME, N 1–11, 'Diari storici', b. 829, 29 September 1942. Operations in the area of Mount Parnassus made it necessary for 'the individuals evacuated [to be] gathered in a provisional concentration camp to be set up in the area of Levadeia'; b. 1070, 'Comando III CdA al Comando del Genio di CdA, 6 ottobre 1942, Campo di concentramento provvisorio': 'urgent delivery of barbed wire'. The camp was opened at Thebes, and at the end of 1942 it held 1,500–2,000 detainees; ACICR, G 3/27, b. 148, 'délégation du CICR au CICR Genève, 10 novembre 1942'; b. 149, 'délégation du CICR en Grèce, M. D'Amman à M. Gallopin, 10 juin 1943, Camp de concentration de Kalavryta'. The ICRC delegation in Greece wrote a report on this camp. Situated south-east of Patras, it was then moved to a school at Aghias on the coast not far from Patras. At the time of the transfer it contained 170 civilian detainees. The inmates of the camp suffered greatly from the cold, and they received adequate rations only after intervention by the ICRC. Two-thirds of them were poverty-stricken and did not receive aid in any form; among the internees were seventy- and eighty-year-old men.

[87] ACICR, G 3/27, b. 149, 'délégation du CICR en Grèce, section de Thessalonique, 1° activité CICR, rapport du délégué adjoint dr R. Burkhardt, hiver 1942–3'. The report also mentions that a concentration camp for Jews was set up at the railway station of Thessaloniki (15 March 1943). The camp's maximum capacity was 2,500 people but it contained as many as 12,000. In eight weeks, wrote the ICRC representative, 43,800 Jews had passed through the camp before being deported to Germany in sealed wagons. By 1 June 1943 all the Jewish Greeks in Thessaloniki had been deported, and by 1 July so had all those of other nationalities present in Greek Macedonia.

[88] ACICR, G 3/27, b. 149, 3 May 1943, 'Note pour M. Sandstroem, président de la Commission de gestion: détenus politiques grecs' (my translation).

Finally, as regards France, after the occupation began, a number of French camps continued in operation while others were closed and their inmates were transferred either to the German zone or to Italy. After the occupation, the Italian authorities asked Vichy to transfer the 485 Italians interned in the camp at Vernet to the Modane camp, which was located in the zone occupied by the Regio Esercito. They then organized the transfer of 6,000 French colonials interned at Fréjus in south-eastern France.[89] Following agreement with the Vichy government, and with the approval of the Germans, it was decided that 3,000 internees would be moved to Sorgues (north-east of Avignon) and a further 3,000 to the German zone. Only a small number of colonial soldiers in need of medical treatment or required by the Intendenza remained in the Italian zone.

There were at least three Italian concentration camps in France: the Sospel camp north of Nice, the Modane camp for 'communists', and the d'Embrun camp for 'subjects of enemy states [interned] for the security of the troops'. Moreover, non-dangerous citizens of enemy states, mainly Jews, were sent into 'forced residence' in localities selected by the CdA commands (see chapter 11). In Corsica, the Prunelli di Fiumorbo camp held individuals guilty of various offences against the occupiers until construction work had been completed on a concentration camp also intended to contain all persons under forced residence at Bagno di Guagno. On 18 November, the prefect of Ajaccio ordered the sub-prefects of Bastia, Corte and Sartène to intern all foreigners belonging to states hostile to the Axis (or suspected of being so), among them Italian citizens. These internees were held temporarily in the transit camp of Corte, whence they were transported to France. The general of the 7th CdA, Carboni, suggested that the more dangerous prisoners should be interned in Italy,[90] and some of them were indeed deported to Ferramonti Tarsia.[91] The Italian archives do not furnish more precise information on the number of internees.

[89] USSME, M 7, b. 476. The camps in question were those of Gallieni, Darbussières, Boulouris, Vallescure, Le Puget, Cais and La Legue, and they contained a total number of 28 officers, 316 non-commissioned officers, and 6,620 soldiers. Besides French citizens they also held Madagascan, Indo-Chinese and Senegalese inmates.

[90] USSME, N 1–11, 'Diari storici', b. 1201, 'VII CdA, Corsica; ASMAE, AA.PP. – Francia, b. 67, 31 gennaio 1943, telegramma in arrivo n. 3268 p.r.'.

[91] Folino, *Ferramonti*, pp. 250ff., reports the deportation of around fifteen persons from Corsica.

CHAPTER II

Policy towards refugees and Jews

The chapter deals with matters that are in part already known. But contrary to the approach used in the past, its analysis of events contextualizes Fascist policy within the broader frame of occupation policies after 1940. Some scholars have argued that until 8 September 1943 the Italians handed not a single Jew over to the Germans or to the authorities of the local governments. Others have maintained that the Italians protected the Jews in the occupied territories and even adopted a humanitarian policy towards them. Hannah Arendt has written of the humanity of an ancient and civilized people which rejected the Fascist anti-Semitic laws; Léon Poliakov has affirmed that 'the protective curtain which surrounded the Jews under threat arose from the humanist tradition of the Italian people'. Thus the history of the 'humanitarian rescue' of Jews by the Fascist political and military authorities has become 'the history of a paradox'.[1] For too long, statements such as the following have been taken for granted: 'The Italian troops did everything to show their sympathy for the Jews. They obeyed the orders issued by the High Command. They manifested every goodwill and made every effort to save the Jews from falling into the hands of the Germans.'[2]

This alleged 'rescue of the Jews' has been uncritically accepted for three main reasons: the authoritativeness of historians who use the Italian case to highlight the horror of the Final Solution; the policy of the young Italian Republic to promote the national myth of *italiani brava gente* (Italians, good people) by exploiting the purported 'humanity' of the Italian people and soldiers during the war; and the intent to contrast the Italians with their former allies so that Italian anti-Semitism and its tragic consequences are forgotten, with the racial policy being blamed on Mussolini and certain hierarchs, while the population is absolved from responsibility.

[1] Arendt, *The Banality of Evil*; Poliakov, *Le totalitarismes du XXe siècle*; Herzer, *Italian Refuge*; Poliakov and Sabille, *Jews Under the Italian Occupation*, p. 20.
[2] Poliakov and Sabille, *Jews Under the Italian Occupation*, pp. 157–8.

The facts should be examined anew in the light of the following questions: is it true that the Italian government did not hand over Jews in the occupied territories to the Germans? If they did not, was it to protect the Jews or was it for other reasons? Was protection afforded to all Jews, to those resident in the militarily occupied territories or to those resident in the annexed territories?

First to be pointed out is that the Italian occupiers distinguished among:

(1) Italian Jews resident in the annexed and occupied territories;
(2) native-born Jews resident in the annexed territories (*pertinenti* or 'eligibles' for Italian citizenship: see chapter 8), whose status was never clearly defined;
(3) Jewish refugees in the annexed territories;
(4) Jews of Croatian, Greek or French nationality resident in the militarily occupied territories; and
(5) Jewish refugees in the militarily occupied territories.

A definition of the term 'protection' is required. If the reference is to the diplomatic protection provided by a sovereign state for its citizens, then the Italian government extended such protection only to Jewish Italians resident in the territories annexed or occupied by the Third Reich in Europe. In no case did foreign Jews obtain diplomatic protection from Italy. The term 'protection' was used by the Germans when they accused the Italian authorities of 'protecting Italian Jews resident abroad', and the term also appears in Italian documents, mainly those to do with Yugoslavia, which speak of the 'protection of civilians (Jews included) who have collaborated with the Italian military authorities'.

The Italian political and military authorities did not conspire to disobey Mussolini's orders; on the contrary, they invariably 'worked towards the Duce'. Mussolini was kept constantly informed of policies and decisions concerning the Jews and he frequently intervened personally in their formulation. The assertion by Jonathan Steinberg that there existed a 'conspiracy to deceive and frustrate Nazi Germany's determination to destroy the Jews of Europe' is far from proven. Analysis of Italian policy towards the Jews in the occupied zones must necessarily take account of relations with the ally. Conflicts of interest with Germany reduced the Jews to pawns in a conflict between the Axis powers in the occupied territories. Italian policy, I submit, should be interpreted as an attempt to respond pointedly and assertively to Nazi interference in Fascism's imaginary *domaine reservé*.

The Jews of the conquered territories became 'pawns in the game' for three main reasons. Firstly, in the event of a German victory, the Italian government would be able to demonstrate its difference from Germany to the Mediterranean peoples and put itself forward as the 'positive' pole of the Axis. Given the Germans' insistence that all Jews be delivered to them, and given the importance that they attached to solution of the 'Jewish question', the Italians could haggle over the price that the Germans would have to pay. It is likely that Italy's resistance to the frequent German demands for the handover of Jews was a 'tit for tat' after Germany's refusal to cease hostilities with the Soviet Union (the 'vallo dell'Est' proposed by Mussolini to Hitler during their meetings at Klessheim and Feltre in April 1943). Nor can one assume that, if the Germans had sent troops to the Mediterranean and thus given the Italians decisive help against the Allies, the Jews of the occupied territories would not have been handed over to them. Moreover, the Jews interned in the Italian occupied territories would have been a useful bargaining counter in the event of negotiations with the Allies (it is also noteworthy that the Italian government did not cite its benevolence towards the Jews during the armistice negotiations).

Furthermore, the belief that the Italian government stopped deporting Jews as soon as it realized that deportation meant extermination is mistaken (we know with certainty that Italy had learned of Germany's Final Solution as early as mid-1942).[3] Also to be borne in mind is that certain Italian authorities considered deportations of Jews to be profoundly damaging to Axis policy in Europe. Luca Pietromarchi wrote:

> When the Balkans were about to be put to fire and the sword, Hitler asked us yet again to hand over the Jews in the second zone occupied by us in Croatia . . . We once again gave an evasive reply. In Greece the Jews were being used as forced labour. The Germans wanted us to adopt similar measures, except for Jews of Italian and Spanish nationality. In France, the Duce agreed to have Jews wear the Star of David. This is the civilization brought by the new order. Is it surprising that no one believes in an Axis victory? It is repugnant to anyone with a sense of human dignity. And thus the Axis alienates the best part of public opinion.[4]

According to General Mario Roatta, handing the Jews over to the Germans or the Croats would have damaged the prestige of the Italians and alarmed the Četniks, who would imagine that the same fate awaited them as well. We shall see that Roatta's opinion was shared by the Italian occupation authorities in Greece and in France.

[3] De Felice, *Storia degli ebrei italiani*, p. 412; Laqueur, *The Terrible Secret*; Pirelli, *Taccuini*, 1984, p. 364; Poznanski, 'Que savait-on dans le monde'; Shelah, *Un debito di gratitudine*, publishes the entries in Pietromarchi's unpublished diary (Fondazione Luigi Einaudi, Turin) for 10 and 27 December 1942, and for 2 February and 11 March 1943; Steinberg, *All or Nothing*, pp. 51–2.

[4] Pietromarchi, diary, 10 October 1942.

THE REFUGEE QUESTION

Analysis of policy towards the Jews in the occupied territories must first set it in relation to the 'refugee question'. Indeed, Jews were often refused entry, expelled, interned or consigned to the government authorities of the occupied territories because they were refugees, and not simply because of 'racial' discrimination.

Population movements took place on a particularly massive scale during the Second World War. Aside from compulsory or voluntary transfers, an incalculable number of people were forced to abandon their homes because of racial, ethic, religious and political persecution and by the ravages of war, hunger and disease.[5] Population movements varied according to the intensity of the fighting and epidemics, but also according to apparently less significant variables like climatic conditions or the difficulty of leaving villages due to the lack of trains or buses. In almost all the territories conquered by the Italians, public transport and telephone, telegraph and postal services functioned badly or had been closed down by the occupiers. Civilians were not allowed to board trains in transit (unless they possessed valid passports), and they were forbidden to move from one town to another in any kind of vehicle. Nevertheless, large numbers of refugees headed for the Italian zones because repression and persecution were less violent there than in Croatia, Serbia, Albania, Bulgaria or the part of France occupied by the Germans. And as the refugees abandoned their land and property, other groups moved in to appropriate them.

The decisions taken by other states or other occupying powers had significant consequences in the territories conquered by the Italians. For example, the Germans concluded an agreement with the Croats for the transfer to Croatia of between 220,000 and 260,000 'non-Germanizable ethnic Croats' resident in Slovenia.[6] The agreement led to the transportation to Croatia of some 54,000 Croats, but it also induced fully 17,000 persons to leave the zone incorporated into the Reich and seek refuge in the Italian zones. Montenegro was literally invaded by refugees from all the regions adjoining it: most of the 43,000 Serbs and Albanians resident in the zones of Yugoslav Macedonia occupied by the Bulgarians sought shelter in the country,[7] while

[5] Kosinski, 'International Migration of Yugoslavs'.

[6] ASMAE, GABAP, b. 28, 'rapporto dell'ispettore di PS Ciro Verdiani al Ministero dell'Interno', 17 June 1941, and 'telegramma della legazione a Zagabria al GABAP', 24 June 1941; b. 40, 'legazione di Belgrado', 6 June 1941, signed Francesco Mameli; ibid., 'legazione di Zagabria al GABAP', 19 November 1941, Croatian–German agreement on repatriation of Croats resident in inner Styria.

[7] DDI, ser. IX, 1939–43, vol. 8, doc. 653.

between April and June 1941, 6,000 Croatian refugees of Montenegrin origin moved into the district of Nikšić alone. Of the approximately 20,000 Serbs and Montenegrins who had colonized Kosovo between the 1920s and 1940s, only 5,000 remained behind, almost all of them in Peć; the others took refuge in the governorate. According to High Commissioner Serafino Mazzolini, no fewer than 30,000 people moved into Montenegro from the territories annexed to Albania.[8] The zones of the Sanjak received around 16,000 Muslim refugees from the zones occupied by the Germans and from those bordering on Croatia.[9] The largest population movement in Greece was from the provinces of Macedonia and Thrace occupied by the Bulgarians. Western Macedonia, writes René Burkhardt, the ICRC delegate, was flooded by some 110,000 refugees (35,000 in Salonika alone and 40,000 among Kozani, Ekaterini and the frontier zones).[10] Athens and the Greek provinces occupied by the Regio Esercito attracted fewer refugees because it was well known that many Hellenic zones and the capital were afflicted by famine. In France, the largest flow of refugees into the Italian zones consisted of Jews.

Providing for needy refugees and physically managing thousands of people posed economic and logistical problems for the Italian authorities, which were compounded by political ones concerning ethnicity and religion, and in particular by the problem of maintaining civil order. The parlous state of the refugees is exemplified by the city of Sarajevo, where hygiene deteriorated until an epidemic of typhus fever swept through three districts where refugees had been lodged. Almost all of these refugees were Muslims, and 'because of their religious beliefs they did not kill fleas but threw them out of the windows into the streets below'.[11] The spread of disease was encouraged by malnutrition, and numerous otherwise healthy individuals were

[8] USSME, H 5, b. 40 RR, 'Comando XIV CdA al Comando della IX Armata, 1 giugno 1941, Ordine pubblico nel Kossovo, rapporto del maggiore dei CC.RR. Tullo'.

[9] USSME, N 1–11, 'Diari storici', b. 1273, 'Divisione alpina Taurinense al Comando truppe Montenegro, 27 febbraio 1943, Relazione sulla situazione politico-militare-economica'. The zone in question was inhabited by around 110,000 Orthodox Christians and 80,000 Muslims.

[10] ACICR, G 3/27, b. 149, 'Délégation du CICR en Grèce, Section de Thessalonique, 1° activité CICR, rapport du délégué adjoint dr R. Burkhardt, hiver 1942–3'. On devastation and persecution by the Bulgarians, see b. 148, 'Comité des macédoniens et des thraciens de Athènes', Athens, 4 September 1942, addressed to the head of the ICRC delegation in Athens.

[11] ASMAE, GABAP, b. 39, 'ambasciata presso la Santa Sede al MAE, 7 ottobre 1942, Situazione dei cattolici nei territori dell'Erzegovina'. Seven hundred refugees reached Almissa, 900 Signo and 300 Drniš, all Croats and Catholics, in extremely poor physical condition and with little food. Mostar received 20,000 Catholic refugees fleeing reprisals by the Četniks and the communist partisans; see USSME, M 3, b. 63, 'V CdA al Comando della II Armata', 31 March 1943. Around 1,000 Orthodox Christians with household goods, cattle and personal effects, terrified by the arrival of the Croats, abandoned Otočac: N 1–11, 'Diari storici', b. 1280, '22 aprile 1943, Situazione politico-militare'; 4,000 refugees arrived in Knin, where they were 'dispersed among all the houses, in some fifty wagons, and

afflicted by hunger oedemas. Similar epidemics hit Višegrad, Rogatica and Tuzla.

What decisions were taken by the Italian authorities to deal with the refugee problem in the annexed and occupied territories? Caught unawares by the magnitude of the problem and entirely unable to stem the flow of refugees, the Italian authorities resorted to the cheapest and most drastic measures possible. In order to prevent an 'invasion' of the occupied territories by refugees, in both the Balkans and France they ordered the closure of borders and the expulsion of refugees who had entered Italian territory clandestinely.[12] These measures applied to all refugees regardless of race, religion or nationality, although in actual fact the occupiers did not have sufficient men or means to close and police the borders.

Particularly restrictive measures were applied to Jews attempting to enter the annexed provinces. In 1939 the consular visa necessary to enter Italy was no longer granted to aliens 'belonging to the Jewish race'. On 12 December 1940, Minister Leonardo Vitetti issued Circular 00017, which instructed the MAE offices abroad not to issue Italian entry permits to Jews and stateless persons. A further circular sent to the prefects of border towns – and also to the prefects of Kotor (Scassellatti), Split (Zerbino), Zadar (Orazi), Fiume (Testa) and the high commissioner of Ljubljana (Grazioli) – reiterated that refugees were prohibited from entering or transiting through Italy. These restrictions were never relaxed, and the Italian authorities – writes Klaus Voigt – invariably rejected requests to enter the country to join family members, doing so even when applications were supported by the Foreign Ministry or by high-ranking churchmen.[13] All foreign Jews from countries (occupied or not) with racist policies (Hungary, Romania, Slovakia, Bulgaria, France, the Netherlands, Belgium, Denmark and Croatia) were routinely turned back at the border, as were stateless persons and refugees in general ('runaway' and 'refugee' were synonymous in the Italian

in sheds'. The military authorities wanted to transfer them to prevent 'epidemics and difficulties of every kind' or at least divide them by ethnic group and religion. Tenin received 5,000 refugees, of whom 3,500 were Orthodox Christian and 1,500 Catholic.

[12] For example, across the Italian–Croatian demarcation line in Croatia, the Rhône demarcation line (between the Italian and German occupation zones) and the Swiss frontier, in USSME, M 3, b. 7, 21 November 1942, 'Disposizioni amministrative nei territori della Francia recentemente occupati'.

[13] Voigt, *Il rifugio precario*, p. 246. Decree law no. 1381 of 7 September 1938 ('Provvedimenti nei Confronti degli Ebrei Stranieri') and no. 1728 of 17 November ('Provvedimenti per la Difesa della Razza Italiana') stated that all foreign Jews who had entered Italy after 1 January 1919 had to leave the country within six months, on pain of expulsion, and that all Italian citizenships granted to Jews after that date were revoked. Following a ministerial directive – Circular 0007/4 September 1941 – the movement of foreigners and the issue of visas were limited to the 'strictly indispensable'; the dossiers were compiled 'with criteria of severity'.

authorities' vocabulary): 'that is, any non-Italian either entering to Italian territory or attempting to gain unlawful entry to it'.[14]

ITALIAN POLICIES TOWARDS JEWS

The annexed territories

Italian policy in the three Dalmatian provinces, the province of Ljubljana and the province of Fiume differentiated between resident Jews and refugee Jews. The distinction is a rather subtle one, for although native-born Jews ('eligibles' or *pertinenti*) were few in number they were regarded as 'suspect persons'.[15] Even eligible Jews domiciled abroad had to comply with the regulations on the entry and transit of aliens. After the annexations, the prefectures were empowered to order escortment to the border (*allontanamento*) as they saw fit (only the authorities in Rome could order expulsions, *espulsioni*). Grounds for *allontanamento* were illegal entry, non-possession of the requisite papers from an issuing authority abroad, or lack of means of support.

After the Vienna Conference, the territory of the Kupano and Sušak – in which around 400 Jews resided – was annexed to the province of Fiume; there were about ten Jewish families domiciled in Ljubljana (following the annexation, 59 married and 56 unmarried resident Jews and 19 minor Jews were interned at Ferramonti Tarsia).[16] Some hundreds of Jews resided in Split but only a handful in Zadar and Kotor. These thousand or so eligible Jews were subject to Italian anti-Semitic legislation.

Very little information is available about Ljubljana, but we know that several waves of refugees moved into the city and that, according to the High Commission, they numbered approximately 1,500 in total.[17] No figures have yet come to light in the archives on how many of them were escorted to the border (*allontanati*) or expelled. The information on Zadar and Kotor is equally fragmentary: in the latter town, the police interned seventy Jews, who were then followed by an influx of a further one hundred,

[14] USSME, M 3, b. 48. Foreign Jews who were citizens of countries in which there were no racial laws were almost all Jews of enemy nationality and subject in any case to strict surveillance.

[15] ASMAE, AA.PP. – 'Italia, 1939–45', b. 77, 24 July 1941, 'Rimpatrio e riespatrio di connazionali residenti all'estero', signed by Chief of Police Carmine Senise.

[16] On the transfer of Jews from Ljubljana to Ferramonti Tarsia, see Folino, *Ferramonti*, pp. 59, 65–97, 101 and 104–5. One learns from the lists of names published by Folino that the persons transferred to the camp had been deported from Ljubljana. They were not inhabitants of that province, however, but Poles, Czechs, Austrians, Hungarians, Bulgarians and Yugoslavs from Croatia, Serbia and even Macedonia.

[17] CBUCEI, Delasem, b. 44 m; ACS, MI-PS, 1930–56, A 16, b. 10.

most of them Serbs but nevertheless tolerated by the local population; the prefect recommended their escortment to the border.[18] On 22 July 1941, 192 persons (mostly families with small children) were arrested and interned in a concentration camp at Kavajë in Albania and then transferred to the camp of Ferramonti Tarsia.[19] How many refugees suffered this fate? And how many were expelled?

In June 1940, the prefect of Fiume, Temistocle Testa, ordered the detention of all Italian or stateless Jews between the ages of eighteen and sixty (around 300 persons).[20] Foreign Jews were no longer granted extensions to their residence permits, and their 'prompt relocation abroad' was recommended.[21] The few Jews still at liberty were interned at Caprino Veronese on the outbreak of hostilities against Yugoslavia. After the annexation, the prefecture of Fiume ordered that all refugees, Jewish or otherwise, were to be turned back at the border. According to figures compiled by the Ministry of the Interior, which are undoubtedly incomplete, the prefecture of Fiume escorted around 800 Jews to the border or expelled them between July 1941 and May 1942 (see appendix, table 66). In the absence of lists of names, it is not possible to estimate the number of refugees expelled more than once, and therefore the number of them who repeatedly attempted to enter Italian territory. One may suppose that if refugees refused entry were not interned by the Croats, they would again try to cross the border clandestinely, given that living conditions and possibilities of survival were better in the Italian zone than they were in Croatia.

During the summer of 1941, numerous Jews fleeing persecution attempted to cross the Croatian frontier. At least 400 managed to reach Sušak, where there resided a small community of Jews, and the Fiume authorities took measures to expel them. The security police mounted surveillance at the municipal registry office, and when the refugees went there to enrol on the register, promptly arrested and expelled them. After

[18] ACS, MI-PS, 1930–56, A 16, b. 10, 'prefetto Francesco Scassellati al Ministero dell'Interno'.

[19] CBUCEI, Delasem, b. 44 m, 'lettera al rabbino Riccardo Pacifici'. See also Folino, *Ferramonti*, p. 84, n. 287. Folino mentions a request by Michele Aladjem and Raffaele Conforti, who together with 187 Jews from the Kavajë concentration camp signed a petition for their transfer to other camps, claiming that the climate at Ferramonti Tarsia was severely damaging the health of many women and children.

[20] Capogreco, 'L'internamento degli ebrei'; ACS, MI-PS, 1930–56, A 16, b. 10, 'Regia prefettura del Carnaro al Ministero dell'Interno', 16 September 1940.

[21] ACS, MI-PS, 1930–56, A 16, b. 10, 'Ministero dell'Interno ai questori del Regno', 21 November 1939, signed by Chief of Police Arturo Bocchini. Two hundred Hungarian Jews were ordered to leave the kingdom on 25 June 1940; a month later, stateless Jews were expelled from Italian territory and registered at the frontier to be repelled if they attempted to re-enter in the future: ibid., 'Regia prefettura del Carnaro al Ministero dell'Interno', 24 July 1940.

the first expulsions, the refugees remained in the province illegally but were sooner or later discovered and deported. Expulsion and consignment to the Croatian authorities was ordered even for those many Jews who declared that they would rather be put to death than be handed over to the Ustaše.[22] The prefecture ordered that anyone furnishing moral or material aid to refugees was to be considered an accomplice of 'illegals' and taken into custody. Rabbi Otto Deutsch of the Jewish community of Sušak was arrested for this offence and interned at Ferramonti Tarsia.

In order to cope with the 'invasion of Jewish refugees', the chief of police in Fiume, Vincenzo Genovese, refused to issue officials of the Jewish community in Fiume with permits to travel to Sušak and demanded that he be given the names and addresses of those to whom they gave assistance in the town. Fearing that Genovese's intention was to expel the Sušak Jews to Croatia, and not wishing to be instrumental in their fate, the Fiume officials decided not provide them with any further assistance.[23]

In October 1941, the prefecture forwarded to the Ministry of the Interior a request for residence in the kingdom (provisionally at Sušak) made by a group of Croatian Jews who had entered the province on false documents.[24] A month later the ministry replied that the request had been rejected, and the applicants were to be expelled to Croatia. If there were Jews among them who could not return to Croatia for some reason, the ministry was to be informed so that it could arrange for their internment in Italy.

Between the end of 1941 and the spring of 1942 – wrote Pietromarchi to the Ministry of the Interior – very few attempts were made by Jews illegally to enter the zone of former Yugoslavia annexed to Fiume. Those few Jews who succeeded were expelled; only in exceptional cases were internments ordered. Moreover, instructions were given to the border police to increase their surveillance of the frontiers.[25] In March 1942, numerous Jewish refugees from the former Yugoslavia who had sought sanctuary in Sušak were driven out of the town to the Italian-occupied stretch of the Croatian coast, especially to the towns of Karljevica and Crikvenika. This order seems to have been in line with a more general policy to clear the

[22] USSME, N 1–11, 'Diari storici', b. 449, 11 August 1941.

[23] USSME, L 3, b. 185; CBUCEI, Delasem, b. 44 m: Cantori, secretary of the Jewish community of Fiume, informed the Genoa delegate that 'the superior authorities have ordered the expulsion to Croatia of refugees from that country who are presently at Sušak'.

[24] ACS, MI-PS, 1930–56, A 16, b. 10, 'Regia prefettura del Carnaro al Ministero dell'Interno', 2 November 1941.

[25] ACS, MI-PS, 1930–56, A 16, b. 10, 'Regia prefettura del Carnaro al Ministero dell'Interno', 31 January 1942.

zones annexed to Italy of all persons not in possession of residence permits (namely the non-eligibles of Sušak).

Some refugees were panic-stricken at the prospect of being forced to return to Croatia whence they had only recently escaped, and fled from Sušak to Trieste. They were assisted in their flight by profiteers who demanded extortionate payments for their services.[26] There sprang up a thriving business similar to the present-day migrant trafficking between the south-eastern shores of the Mediterranean and Italy. Croatian sailors rented out boats for the illegal crossing between the Balkan and Italian coasts at exorbitant prices. Then as today, the PS arrested some of the sailors and impounded the boats and cars used to transport the refugees, but were unable to halt the traffic. The prefecture reported cases of Italian officials issuing false documents to Croatian Jews (probably, as in the case of Edo Neufeld,[27] in return for illegal payments).

The documents of the prefecture of Fiume conserved in the state archives halt at May 1942, but one may deduce that the number of foreign Jews attempting to cross the border diminished because many had died in the Ustaša camps, had been shot as hostages or had committed suicide. Moreover, in the summer of 1942, the Germans and Croats concluded an agreement on the deportation of Croatian Jews,[28] with the consequence that the survivors of the massacres and the Ustaša camps were deported to eastern Europe by the Nazis. According to Voigt, at least 1,400 foreign Jews reached the province of Fiume during the occupation period,[29] and of these it is proven that more than 800 were turned back at the frontier. It is not known how many were expelled before or after this period or how many were refused entry.

The Italian authorities in Rome, Fiume and Dalmatia are to blame for more than just their decision to turn the refugees away (one could at least give the benefit of the doubt to their claim that scarce financial resources made the refugees impossible to look after, or that they were a threat to public order). They also knew perfectly well the fate that was awaiting the

[26] CBUCEI, Delasem, b. 44 m, 'Delasem Genova a Dante Almansi', 17 March 1942.

[27] ACS, MI-PS, 1930–56, A 16, b. 10, 'Regia prefettura del Carnaro al Ministero dell'Interno', 31 January 1942.

[28] ASMAE, GABAP, b. 42, 'Ufficio Collegamento con la II Armata, telegramma 19074 PR, Questione ebraica nelle zone occupate'; USSME, N 1–11, 'Diari storici', b. 859, 'Comando Divisione Murge al Comando del VI CdA', 13 August 1942: 'In regard to the agreements between the German and Croatian governments . . . all the Jews interned in the concentration camps of Stara Gradiska and Giacovo have already left. Those at the camps of Jasenovac and Labor-Gradu are about to depart . . . 3,000 Jews are concentrated at Osied. These will be deprived of all their belongings and with some clothing and without money sent to Russia in groups of 500–800.'

[29] Voigt, *Il rifugio precario*, p. 255.

Jews handed over to the Croats, and they were fully aware of the atrocities being committed only a few kilometres beyond the border. Indeed, the Italian authorities themselves described Jasenovac as a concentration camp where:

behind a barbed-wire fence, crammed into wooden barracks, are thousands of prisoners . . . clad in the barest minimum to hide their nudity, deprived of clothing and provisions; their conditions are horrendous, bestial even . . . hygiene is dreadful . . . the camp has no sanitation facilities, the sick are not cared for . . . The concentration camps of Dachau and Buchenwald are tragically famous. But individuals from these German camps say that compared with Jasenovac they are health spas.[30]

The Italian authorities therefore adopted measures against the Jews that refute the thesis that they mounted an operation of 'humanitarian rescue'. The anti-Semitic laws were applied with especial harshness in the province of Fiume to both Jewish natives and Jewish eligibles. For the Italian authorities, expulsion to Croatia amounted to the issue of a death sentence.

The three prefectures in Dalmatia expelled all refugees (not just Jews) and escorted all illegal immigrants to the frontier. Re-entry was also refused to a number of eligibles who, according to Giuseppe Bastianini, were 'undesirable Italian *pertinenti*' (most of them were Dalmatian residents of Croatia suspected of being irredentists).

Shortly after annexation, the chief of police wrote to the Ministry of the Interior that 'Jewish refugees from Croatia were constantly entering' the governorate, the majority of them via Split, where they managed to evade police surveillance. Very few came by train, however, for they knew that the checkpoints at stations were especially strict. The Croats used the situation as an excuse not to send food into Dalmatia, where, they claimed, it would be distributed to 'the most ferocious enemies of Italian–Croatian friendship'.[31] Regardless of Croatian pressures, the Italian authorities decided in any case to expel the refugees. Governor Bastianini justified this decision on the grounds of public order and the 'race' of the refugees, while also citing reasons to do with public health and economics (the cost of assisting the poverty-stricken and the expense of internment). On 22 August, the Ministry of the Interior instructed the prefectures to use every available means to repatriate refugees and, given the shortage of concentration camps in Italy, to intern only especially dangerous individuals. The ministry prohibited the use of forced residence orders for either Serbs or Jews, both groups it regarded as being 'extremely treacherous'. As in Fiume, foreign

[30] USSME, N I–II, 'Diari storici', b. 1371, 'X Battaglione mobilitato dei CC.RR.', July 1941.

[31] ASMAE, GABAP, b. 47, 'legazione di Zagabria al MAE', 12 August 1941, 'Approvvigionamento della Dalmazia'.

Jews detained by the police were either interned or placed on police record and expelled.[32]

By May 1942 the number of refugees had reached 2,748; many of them were individuals previously expelled from, or refused entry to, the province of Fiume. According to Voigt, a total of around 3,800 refugees entered Dalmatia.[33] In the eight months following annexation, an imprecise number of refugees were refused entry or expelled by Dalmatia, and more than 1,000 foreign Jews were dispatched to Italy for internment.

Governor Bastianini extended the anti-Jewish measures to cover 'Jews and their families domiciled in Dalmatia (Split especially) and possessing goods or landed property in the annexed territory'. Bastianini's aim was to rid Dalmatia forever of its small Jewish communities, and he announced on several occasions that the disappearance of foreign Jews from the Adriatic coast would be shortly followed by that of the Dalmatian Jews. He then set about applying the Italian anti-Semitic laws to the Dalmatian Jews (even ordering removal of their names from telephone directories and withdrawal of their ration books).[34] The application of these measures demonstrates once again that the annexed territories were used as testing grounds for the *nuovo ordine*, and that the policy implemented in them was a rehearsal of what would supposedly happen in Italy thereafter. The idea of 'riddance' from the Dalmatian Jews was part of the programme of forced Italianization which victimized not only Jews but also communists, the families of former Serb officers in the Yugoslav army, civil servants from the former Yugoslavia and Catholic priests.[35]

Internments were suspended at the beginning of 1942 owing to a shortage of places in the camps. The governor asked for 2,000 Jews to be temporarily interned in the concentration camp of Ugliano, although construction work on it had not yet been completed. Despite close surveillance of the frontiers, refugees continued to enter Dalmatia, provoking Bastianini's censure of the military authorities and his peremptory order that no further entries by Jews were to occur.[36] On 3 June he sent a telegram to Raffaele Casertano informing him that, by order of Mussolini, he should arrange for the expulsion from Split of 'the large number of Jews who [had taken refuge in that city] from adjoining regions in order to escape persecution

[32] ASMAE, GABAP, b. 40, 'Pietromarchi a Bastianini', 22 August 1941; b. 46, 'Ministero dell'Interno – DGPS, per conoscenza al MAE', 28 November 1941, 'Notizie pervenute dalla Dalmazia'.

[33] Voigt, *Il rifugio precario*, p. 260.

[34] ACS, MI, Demorazza, 1938–43, b. 3, 'prefettura di Spalato a Demorazza', 24 October 1941, signed by the prefect Paolo Valerio Zerbino.

[35] ASMAE, GABAP, b. 40, 'Bastianini al MAE e al Ministero dell'Interno – DGPS', 29 August 1941; ibid., 'governatore della Dalmazia al GABAP', 25 June 1941, telegram 20880 PR.

[36] ASMAE, GABAP, b. 42, 'alla legazione di Zagabria', 1 June 1942, telegram 19392.

and mistreatment by the Ustaša authorities'.[37] The order concerned some 1,500 Jews, whose expulsion, as we shall see, was attempted several times.[38]

Bastianini suggested that Zagreb should indicate a locality not far from Split where the Jews in question, 'currently resident on Croatian territory', could be sent with guarantees of their safety and with 'treatment of minimum human consideration'.[39] The Jews, he said, could be concentrated in the zones occupied by the Regio Esercito in Croatia (for example, in the town of Crikvenica, where around 300 Jews already lived). The MAE agreed that this was the best solution and consulted the commander of the Second Army, General Roatta, who initially rejected Bastianini's proposal, explaining that there were approximately 200 Jews resident in Crikvenica who were being afforded 'protection despite constant pressure by the Croats for their deportation to concentration camps'.[40] But Roatta then changed his mind, probably because he had learned that the Croats were rounding up Jews in preparation for their deportation by the Germans.[41] The decision to intern the Jewish refugees of Dalmatia in the militarily occupied territories of Croatia brings my discussion to the zones occupied by the Regio Esercito.

THE MILITARILY OCCUPIED TERRITORIES

Yugoslavia

Before examining the fate of the Jews who took refuge in Dalmatia, and were then deported to the second zone, I would stress that the Italian troops stationed in Croatia were confronted by the 'Jewish question' from the very first day of the occupation. At the end of the 1930s there were approximately 74,000 Jews living in Yugoslavia: one-third of them were Sephardic, with

[37] ASMAE, GABAP, b. 42, 'telegramma del GABAP al governo della Dalmazia', 3 June 1942; ACS, PCM, 1.1.13.16542, 'Ministero dell'Interno – Ufficio Cifra, da Zara alla PCM', 28 February 1942, signed Bastianini.

[38] CBUCEI, Delasem, b. 44 m, letter from Vittorio Morpurgo, secretary of the Jewish community of Trieste to UCEI in Rome, Split, 8 May 1942: 'Some dozens of refugees have already been sent back. Without warning, in the middle of the night, they are awakened and told to get ready to leave in the morning . . . Given that these poor souls know or fear the fate that awaits them, you can imagine the scenes of desperation that ensue . . . They are sent to places under Italian occupation . . . They can invoke the protection of the military authorities . . . but the protection may come too late, as happened at Caplijna and Priština, where it is not known what happened to those unfortunate internees transported to destinations unknown to us.'

[39] ASMAE, GABAP, b. 42, 'governatore Bastianini a Casertano', 3 June 1942.

[40] ASMAE, GABAP, b. 42, 'telegramma del governatore Bastianini al GABAP', 16 June 1942; USSME, M 3, b. 67, 'governatore Bastianini al generale Roatta', 7 July 1942.

[41] ASMAE, GABAP, b. 42, 'legazione di Zagabria al MAE', 6 August 1942.

a further 4,000–5,000 Jewish refugees from Germany, Austria, Czechoslovakia and Poland. And then around 38,000 Jews, including refugees, came under the sway of the Ustaše. The two largest Jewish communities – those of Zagreb (12,000) and Sarajevo (8,000) – lay within the German occupation zone. In the territories militarily occupied by Italy, about 150 Jews lived in Dubrovnik, 200 in Crikvenica and 120 in Mostar.

During the summer of 1941, some garrison commands intervened to assist the local populations under their control, including Jewish communities. In September, with a view to pacifying the occupied zones, the Italian commands pledged to safeguard the lives of civilians of all religious faiths and nationalities who collaborated with the occupiers. They promised the Jewish leaders of Mostar and Crikvenica that their communities would be left undisturbed as long as they refrained from acts hostile to the occupying authorities.

The military authorities regarded Croatian policy towards the Jews as counterproductive because it removed resources that could be much more usefully employed against the partisan movement. The UAC repeatedly sought to explain to the Croatian authorities that the 'Jewish question' was not a priority. The Italians' principal concerns were to maintain public order and to uphold their prestige by keeping promises made to the civilian population.[42] Moreover, the Army Command wanted to demonstrate to the Germans, the Croatian authorities and the civilian population that the reins of power were firmly in their grasp. For the same reasons, the Italians objected to the policy of nationalization without compensation pursued by the Ustaše against Serbs and Jews. The commander of the 6th CdA, Renzo Dalmazzo, explained that the policy was not only in breach of the *bando* of 7 September 1941 but also 'damaging to the purposes of pacification' because it provoked festering grievances. The general proposed the temporary suspension of the Croatian racial laws in order to foster the economic revival of the region, given that the nationalized businesses had been handed over to 'incompetents who will certainly drive them into bankruptcy'.[43] The Croats

[42] CBUCEI, Delasem, b. 44 m, Lelio Vittorio Valobra to Almansi, 29 January 1942: 'There are 490 former Yugoslav Jews in Mostar, some of them refugees, some members of the Mostar community. It appears that the Croatian authorities have asked for them to be handed over for internment in the concentration camps in the interior of Croatia. The president [of the community of Mostar, David Hajon] has already appealed to . . . General Ambrosio, asking for this group to be granted internment in Italy . . . This would be a procedure similar to the one adopted for the refugees of Crikvenica.'

[43] USSME, M 3, b. 67, 'generale Dalmazzo al Comando superiore di Supersloda – UAC', 22 July 1942. The consulate of Sarajevo intervened to protect Italian interests in companies which, owing to the presence of Jews on their boards of directors, had been brought under extraordinary administration (among them Ugar, a timber company in Turbe which supplied the Regio Esercito).

for their part repeatedly accused the military authorities of favouring Jews and Serbs. Exemplifying the Ustaše's resentment was the dispute over the yellow badge for Jews. A report by the UAC stated that the accusations of indulgence towards the Jews were false and tendentious, and that the Croatian authorities themselves did not enforce display of the badge. The military authorities, wrote the commander general of the 5th CdA, would have made wearing the badge compulsory if the Croats had requested it.[44]

In late 1941 and early 1942, as the number of refugees in the Italian zone constantly grew, the military authorities introduced a distinction between Jews resident in the occupation zones and Jewish refugees who had moved into those zones after the occupation. General Balocco decided that all Jews who had entered the zone under his jurisdiction after 7 September 1941 were to be expelled. The purpose of the measure, he wrote, was not persecution but security, and it concerned not only Jews but all 'undesirables' without permanent residence in the zone, foreigners especially.[45]

Between June and August 1942 a radical shift came about in Italian policy as a result of three sets of factors: local developments, relations with the Croats and relations with the Germans. In June, Bastianini ordered the expulsion of the numerous groups of Croatian Jews who had taken refuge in the governorate. On 19 June, the Italian–Croatian agreement, and the consequent dismantling of numerous Regio Esercito garrisons, considerably increased the flow of refugees from the interior of Croatia to the coastal areas. Again in the same month, the Germans decided to deport all Yugoslav Jews to the east European territories occupied by the Reich, in which enterprise the Croats were willing collaborators.

On 23 June 1942, the commander of the 6th CdA informed the Army Command that a German engineer had talked about a German–Croatian agreement on the deportation to German-occupied Soviet territory of all Croatian Jews, including those of Herzegovina.[46] The Second Army Command wrote to Rome that the agreement should not be implemented in the occupied zones. On 28 June the GABAP informed the Zagreb Legation and the liaison office that the MAE, 'for reasons of a general nature', entirely agreed with the Supersloda Command.[47] What were these 'reasons of a general nature'?

[44] USSME, N I–II, 'Diari storici', b. 543, 'allegato 41', 4 October 1941.

[45] USSME, N I–II, 'Diari storici', b. 543, 'allegato 489': before the beginning of the war, there were 14,000 Jews in Bosnia-Herzegovina, 8,000 of them in Sarajevo alone.

[46] ASMAE, GABAP, b. 42, 'Ufficio Collegamento con la II Armata, telegramma 19074 PR, Questione ebraica nelle zone occupate'; USSME, N I–II, 'Diari storici', b. 859, 'Comando Divisione Murge al Comando del vi CdA', 13 August 1942 (see above, p. //, n. 27).

[47] ASMAE, GABAP, b. 42, telegram 22694 PR, signed Blasco Lanza d'Ajeta.

Firstly, any sudden change in the Italian attitude towards the local population (not just the Jews) was unthinkable, particularly if it resulted from a decision taken by the Croats and Germans. Only a few days before the German–Croatian agreement, the consul Amedeo Mammalella had guaranteed Italian assistance and protection to the Orthodox Christians of Dubrovnik. A sudden reversal of this policy would have discredited the Italian authorities in the eyes of every section of the occupied population, whatever its religious faith.[48] Secondly, Zagreb's policy towards the Jews was regarded as foolish and as intended solely to create difficulties for Supersloda. Why should a request by the Ustaše be granted when it would entail Rome's subservience to the Germans? Thirdly, pursuit by the Italians of their own policy on a matter of such importance to the Germans as the Jewish question would demonstrate Rome's independence of action in its *spazio vitale*. Finally, it should be borne in mind that 1,500 Jewish refugees in Dalmatia were to be transferred to the second zone:[49] the knowledge that they would be handed over to the Croats upon their arrival in Croatia, and then to the Germans, would provoke turmoil which the Italian authorities wanted to avoid if at all possible.

The decision not to consign the Jews resident in the occupied territories to the Croats should not be mistaken for any desire by the Italian authorities to give asylum to Jewish refugees. The Italians made no attempt to impede deportations to eastern Europe: indeed, expulsions and refusals of entry continued throughout 1942 and 1943, swelling the numbers of the Jewish deportees. On 30 June 1942, the commander of the 5th CdA, Renato Coturri, wrote that the coastal area under his jurisdiction had been 'swamped by Jews and other political refugees who believe that they are now under the protection of our armed forces'. A further influx of refugees, said Coturri, would not only aggravate the already severe food shortages but create problems of security and public order. For these reasons he ordered that 'no further access to the zone' was to be granted to refugees and informed the army command that the presence on the coast of large numbers of Jews was creating political, economic and social difficulties. Any further

[48] ASMAE, GABAP, b. 36, 19 June 1942, 'Situazione politica nella seconda zona occupata'. Mammalella reassured the numerous Montenegrins registered at the consulate and the Orthodox Christian *pertinenti* that they had no reason for believing that Italy would cease providing them with protection and assistance.

[49] USSME, M 3, b. 69, teletyped message 1725 of 26 June 1942, signed by Army chief of staff General Ettore De Blasio; ASMAE, GABAP, b. 42, 24 July 1942, 'Appunto per il barone Michele Scammacca'. Supersloda planned to intern 300 refugees in the camps at Segna, Novi, Porto Re and Crikvenica, 300 on the island of Brazza, 500 on the island of Lesina, 250 at Caplijna and Dubrovnik and 150 on the island of Mezzo. On 6 August, General Roatta told the government of Dalmatia to form the groups and make arrangements with the CdAs.

waves of refugees were to be 'repulsed by forcing trespassers back across the demarcation line'. Given that the Jews were 'considerably depleting the area's already scarce food resources', Coturri prohibited the presence of all Jewish refugees in the area under his jurisdiction, reported all Jews who had illegally entered the area after 30 April 1942 to the military tribunals, and issued instructions that all attempts at 'infiltration' were to be ruthlessly suppressed.[50] He ordered that anyone caught in breach of the ban on entry into the second zone was to be escorted across the demarcation line[51] (where goods trains were waiting to deport them to the Nazi-occupied territories in eastern Europe).

Italy's position at the beginning of July 1942 was as follows:

- no further Jewish refugees were to be allowed into the occupied territories; expulsions and refusals of entry would therefore continue;
- 1,500 Jewish refugees were to be deported from Dalmatia to Croatia, but to the Italian-occupied zone, and under Italian custody;
- no Jews domiciled in the occupied territories were to be handed over to the Croats or Germans.

On 7 July, Casertano informed Rome that the Germans had objected to the fact that numerous Jewish refugees were living undisturbed in Mostar and Crikvenica. For the ambassador, Germany's expression of concern 'smacked of interference' and was probably the prelude to an official German protest. On 18 August 1942, the MAE sent a note to the Duce 'without comment or proposal by the ministry' (this being handwritten on the document) which informed him that Joachim von Ribbentrop, via the German embassy secretary in Rome, Otto Bismarck, had officially requested the Italian government to instruct the military authorities in Croatia to begin the mass transfer of Jews from the Italian-occupied zones to eastern Europe. Bismarck said that thousands of people would be involved and let it be understood that the purpose of the measure was 'in practice, to disperse the Jews and eliminate them entirely' (underlined in the text of the document). The fate of the Jews in the Croatian territories, therefore, was now an integral part of Italo-German policy.

The Foreign Ministry advised Mussolini to reply to the German ambassador that Italy would seek direct agreement with the Croatians; in the

[50] USSME, M 3, b. 67, 'Comando V CdA – UAC al Com. sup. FF.AA. Slovenia–Dalmazia', 30 June 1942.

[51] USSME, N 1–11, 'Diari storici', b. 1426, 24 July 1942; M 3, b. 66: in October 1942 General Coturri wrote to the Supersloda Command that the 1,500 Jewish refugees in Dalmatia assigned to his zone would cause severe problems of civil order.

meantime, the army would be ordered to place 'the five or six thousand Jews resident in the occupation zones' under strict surveillance.[52]

On 21 August, Mussolini received a summary of the document which stated that the 'Jewish question' in Croatia had reached its 'decisive phase'. The document concluded thus: 'we submit the above for your decision'.[53] Mussolini appended his *nulla osta* (no objection): a locution which, if unaccompanied by further instructions, meant in Italian bureaucratic parlance that the request had been noted but any decision in its regard was to be taken by the competent authority, which in this case was the Second Army Command. However, the German authorities interpreted *nulla osta* as signifying that the Italians had consented to the mass deportation of the Jews in the occupied territories.

In the same days as Ribbentrop made his request, the CdA was engaged in transferring the refugees from Dalmatia. However, the operation proceeded slowly: by the end of August only 450 of a total of 1,500 refugees had been transferred. The Jews, wrote General Dalmazzo, would not receive sufficient food and consequently would start dealing on the black market and take sides with the communists. Moreover, the majority of them were not interned in concentration camps but were 'on probation' (*libertà vigilità*) with the obligation not to leave their places of residence. They should, Dalmazzo said, be interned in concentration camps set up either on the Croatian coast or on an Italian island. Once the Jews had been interned, their nationalities could be established, and then, in co-operation with the consular authorities, arrangements could be made for 'returning them to their places of origin'.[54] Dalmazzo informed the Supersloda UAC that the 895 Jews resident in the area under his jurisdiction (75 in Caplijna, 450 in Mostar, 350 in Dubrovnik, 7 in Trebinje, 6 in Konjić, 3 in Prozor and 4 in Metković) had not caused difficulties of any kind. He consequently saw no reason for changing the policy towards them: they were Sephardic, and by tradition, culture, kinship and knowledge of the Romance languages, willing to take Italian nationality. Consul Mammalella, indeed, considered them to be an important bloc of favourable votes in the event of a referendum on unification with Italy.

A paradoxical situation had therefore arisen in the occupied territories: the refugees deported from Dalmatia would be interned but resident Jews

[52] ASMAE, GABAP, b. 42.

[53] Pietromarchi wrote in his diary on 20 August 1942 that Bismarck 'has asked our minister to order the consignment of the Jews in the zones occupied by us for "their extermination"'.

[54] USSME, M 3, b. 67, 'Comando vi CdA – UAC al Comando superiore di Supersloda', 9 September 1942.

would remain at liberty. But neither group, although they were Croatian nationals, or at any rate resident on Croatian territory, would be handed over to the Ustaša government. This was an interference in Croatian sovereignty that Rome would have to justify to both Zagreb and Berlin.

On 31 August, during an Italo-Croatian conference in Dubrovnik, Roatta informed the Croats that he would not hand over persons who were under virtual Italian protection until he received orders to the contrary.[55] The head of the GABAP, Pietromarchi, now intervened by pointing out that there were relatively few Jews left in the second zone and that some of them were probably eligibles. He urged Roatta to carry out a census using 'flexible' criteria. Deportation would be extremely damaging to Italy's prestige in the Balkans, for it would be taken to be a breach of the pledges made to the civilian population that no discrimination would be made on grounds of religion and race. Pietromarchi explained to Roatta that he believed that behind the German manoeuvre lay the Croats' determination to seize the property of the deported Jews. He also informed him that plans were afoot to construct internment camps for all Jewish refugees on one of the Dalmatian islands, probably implying by this that Supersloda's responsibility for internment was only temporary. The liaison officer Vittorio Castellani added a handwritten note to Pietromarchi's letter stating that for every Croat handed over to the Germans the Ustaše received thirty dinars, and that, 'aside from moral considerations', it would be degrading for Italy to sanction such a despicable trade.[56]

It was therefore decided that the internment of all Jews was to be the solution proposed by Rome to Berlin. It was now only necessary to coordinate the decision with Mussolini and the CS. However, before the head of the GABAP and Ciano could discuss the proposal with the Duce, the Croats and the Germans complicated the situation further. The Croatian

[55] USSME, N I–II, 'Diari storici', b. 993, 31 August 1942.

[56] ASMAE, GABAP, b. 42, 11 September 1942, 'Ufficio Collegamento con Supersloda'. Roatta's reply to the CS was judged apposite by Castellani, who explained that the general was in an extremely difficult position: 'He rightly tried not to give his Roman "friends" an opportunity to depict him as rebelling against orders or get him to slip on the proverbial banana skin.' On 13 September 1942, Pietromarchi noted in his diary: 'I met General Roatta on Via Veneto. He immediately asked me about the Jews to be handed over to the Germans. "It's not possible", he told me. "They've placed themselves under our authority. The Croats have already asked us to hand them over. I naturally refused. They then said that they would get the Germans to make the request. And now there's an order from the Duce." I explained to the general what had happened during my absence and the information given to Castellani. Roatta said he agreed. He would begin the correspondence with us and drag things out as long as possible.'

police headquarters in Mostar ordered all Jews to report to them, giving their names and addresses, countries of origin, a statement of their assets, and family composition.[57]

On 3 and 21 October, the German embassy counsellor in Rome, Johann von Plessen, complained to Blasco Lanza d'Ajeta that Rome had not yet instructed Supersloda on the measures that it should take. When informed of the Germans' complaint, the CS sent the MAE a report written by Roatta – his reply to Pietromarchi – in which he argued that 'for reasons of prestige' the Jews of the second zone should not yet be handed over because their eligibility had first to be established, and because 'we are still awaiting instructions on how already-ascertained Croatian eligibles should be handed over to the German authorities'. This document formed the basis for Rome's reply to Berlin. The Germans immediately asked what criteria would be used to determine eligibility.[58]

On 15 October, the commander of Supersloda reported the presence of some 3,800 Jews (including the 1,500 refugees from Dalmatia) in the Italian-occupied territories. The commander said that he was of the opinion that the Croats should assemble and deport the Croatian Jews, and that the internment of the Jews could only be justified to the occupied population as a measure necessary until eligibility for nationality had been determined.[59] He added that if non-eligibles were deported by the Croats, there would be no need for their internment. On the same day, General Giovanni Magli of the CS wrote to inform the Supersloda commander that the Germans had been told of the *nulla osta*, but he still believed that handing over the Jews was contrary to Italian interests in the region. The only possible solution was to intern all the Jews and then procrastinate by protracting the eligibility verification procedures as long as possible.

On 17 October, the Foreign Ministry sent the Second Army Command a note which specified the eligibility criteria: the Jews would have to produce documents and other evidence proving their *pertinenza* to the annexed territories. The MAE made no attempt to establish criteria with which to ensure that only a minimum number of Jews were consigned to the Croats. It merely sent Supersloda a document detailing how eligibility had been determined in Dalmatia – although this had had the unintended effect of

57 USSME, N 1–11, 'Diari storici', b. 859, 'Comando Divisione Murge al Comando del VI CdA', 13 September 1942.
58 ASMAE, GABAP, b. 42, 'CS al MAE', 10 October 1942, signed General Magli.
59 ASMAE, GABAP, b. 42, 'CS al MAE', 15 October 1942, signed General Magli.

helping foreign Jews because the procedures for establishing their eligibility were so laborious and time-consuming.[60]

Between October and December 1942, the MAE gathered information on the extermination of Jews by the Germans and sent it to Mussolini. The Duce was perfectly aware that handing the Jews over to the Croats was tantamount to complicity in their murder (although, like the generals and senior civil servants, he refused to accept that expulsion and refusal of entry meant exactly the same thing). One of the briefings sent to Mussolini was written by the Croatian minister of foreign affairs, Stijepo Perić, who said that he was entirely aware of the fate awaiting the Jews deported by the Germans. Mussolini also received a report from the Vatican secretary of state requesting intervention by the Italian ambassador to prevent the handover of Jews. General Giuseppe Pièche informed the GABAP and the Duce that the Croatian Jews of the German-occupied zone deported to eastern Europe had been 'eliminated' by poisonous gas pumped into the cattle wagons used to transport them.[61] Pièche urged the immediate internment of all Jews, both those entitled to Italian citizenship and the Croatian Jews awaiting consignment. Abandoning the Jews in the Italian-occupied areas – 'who alone in the Balkans have never caused us any trouble!' – would be a blatant disavowal of Italy's pledges and would harm its prestige; and this in a region where prestige was synonymous with strength. Such abandonment would have damaging repercussions among Orthodox Christians, and especially among the 20,000 anti-communist militiamen fighting alongside the Regio Esercito. Pièche concluded thus:

> If the handing over, and therefore the extermination, of 3,000 Jews in the second zone must go ahead at all costs, the Italian army should at least not dirty its hands in this affair (as unfortunately seems likely in view of the transfers of Jews to concentration camps that have taken place over the past few days). If the Croats insist on handing over the Jews to the Germans, they are welcome to do so, but they will have to round them up themselves, without involving us as intermediaries, or worse; and they alone will have to arrange their direct delivery to the Germans. For the army of a great power to do nothing to prevent such a sorry spectacle is already bad enough.[62]

Finally, at the beginning of December, General Roatta met Mussolini in Rome to discuss *inter alia* the 'question of the Jews' and stressed to the Duce

[60] USSME, M 3, b. 66, 17 October 1942. The MAE ordered the army command to send the lists of names by 15 November, and therefore very soon.

[61] ASMAE, GABAP, b. 42, 'Appunto per il GABAP del 20 ottobre 1942'.

[62] ASMAE, GABAP, b. 42, 'Appunto del 23 ottobre 1942, in allegato a Pièche, 4 novembre 1942, visto dal duce'.

the damaging repercussions which would ensue if Jews were consigned to the Croats. Mussolini was persuaded. As a result of these various representations on behalf of the Jews – made for political or military reasons or ones connected with the overall progress of the war – internment (which originally served to identify those Jews who were or were not to be handed over to the Croats) now saved some thousands of Jews from deportation to eastern Europe, if only briefly.

The Italians decided to intern all families whose heads of household were considered to be of 'Jewish race', those who claimed entitlement to 'positive discrimination' and Jewish citizens of third-party states even if they possessed a passport from their country of origin and a stay permit issued by the Croatian authorities. The MAE specified the criteria for internment thus: (1) Jewish nationals of other countries would still be subject to internment; (2) Jews possessing visas for neutral countries could leave for those countries only on obtaining a permit from the Military Intelligence Service (SIM) and the Legation in Zagreb; (3) Jewish Croatian civil servants would be released only if the Croatian authorities so desired; (4) those eligible for release could no longer remain in the Italian-occupied territories and could choose between continued internment or dispatch to Croatia; (5) a Jewish parent could not join a mixed Aryan–Jewish son and daughter and was to remain in internment; (6) those eligible for Italian citizenship could not be released from the camps, nor could they re-enter the annexed zones, and no application for citizenship by them would be granted. Jews were also to be prevented from moving to Italy: only Italian Jews could exercise the *diritto di chiamata*, or the right to summon relatives of first degree and spouses to Italy provided they could prove possession of sufficient financial means to maintain the family members thus summoned.[63]

After a first census carried out in December 1942 (see appendix, table 67), the information on the nationalities of the Jews interned in the occupied zones of Croatia was complete by the following February. The total number of internees amounted to 2,661; Jews from European countries, excluding Croatia, numbered 283; those from Croatia 2,378, of whom 893 fulfilled

[63] ASMAE, GABAP, b. 42, 'promemoria all'ufficiale di collegamento con Supersloda', 13 December 1942. The intentions of the Italians were not clear to the refugees: some of them greeted the news of their internment 'with great pleasure' (for example, the community of Mostar); others with a certain resignation; yet others sought in every way possible to obtain documents proving their *pertinenza* to the annexed zone. Several internees, convinced that they were to be handed over to the Croats, committed suicide (probably because they were unable to prove their *pertinenza*). Enacted in October was law no. CCXCZ–2502–2–1942, which stated that all Jewish-owned assets, credit instruments and securities were irrevocably and immediately the property of the Croatian state. This provoked further panic in the Jewish communities.

the requirements for Italian citizenship while 1,485 were not eligible and would have to be handed over to the Croatian authorities.[64]

On 26 October, the Germans were informed of the eligibility criteria and told that the procedures for internment and verification had begun. On 28 October, the Zagreb government and Bismarck were advised of the Duce's order to intern 'all Jews in the Italian-occupied zones of Croatia'. The leaders of the Jewish communities were briefed on the transfer of all Jews in zones directly and exclusively under Italian control. Internment countered the contention by the Croats and Germans that free Jews were 'harmful' and were likely to join the Resistance; and by sending the Jews to concentration camps the Italians demonstrated that they were taking independent action to deal with the problem. The measure would also reassure the Orthodox Christians, who were increasingly convinced that the Italians were about to abandon the second zone and leave them to the tender mercies of the Germans and Croats.[65]

On 9 December 1943, the Germans asked for the fourth time that the Jews in the second zone be handed over to them. Bismarck even suggested the route that the refugees should take to leave Croatia: they could be transported, he said, via sea to Trieste and thence to Germany. The MAE replied that, because of difficulties of maritime communications and a shortage of ships, arranging transport for the Jews would be less easy than Bismarck imagined.[66]

On 17 January 1943, the German ambassador in Rome informed the MAE that the government of the Reich intended to take action against the Italian Jews in the occupied territories, who hitherto had been protected. A note on the matter stated: 'Jews are enemies of the Axis, whatever the Fascist government may think, and despite its different policy. The Italian government is given one and a half months to arrange for the return to Italy of the Jews whom it intends to save.' 'For my part,' wrote Pietromarchi, 'I have advised that Italy's doors should be opened to all those who wish to take refuge in the country. Perhaps they could be sent to concentration camps or into forced residence. Prince Bismarck has added verbally that all European Jews must be exterminated by the end of 1943.'[67]

[64] USSME, M 3, b. 78, 'II Armata – UAC al CS', 20 February 1943.

[65] USSME, N 1–11, 'Diari storici', b. 1001, 'Comando Divisione Murge, Sezione "I"', 7 December 1942.

[66] ASMAE, GABAP, b. 42.

[67] Pietromarchi, diary, 18 January 1943. The chief of the GABAP commented thus on the German request: 'One cannot report those words without a sense of horror. We are in the midst of utter bloody madness. And one does not perceive in Germany the feeling of revulsion that such proposals arouse in all of us here, especially those who serve the state but do not allow themselves to be debased by such wickedness. I cannot help thinking that an act of this sort will be the fatal last straw.'

On 25 February, Ribbentrop himself raised the issue during a conversation with Mussolini. The Duce appeared to accept the idea of deportation, but he instructed General Mario Robotti – who had recently assumed command of the Second Army –'to invent whatever excuse he liked, but not hand a single Jew over to the Germans'.[68] It was accordingly decided that all internees in the Italian-occupied zone of Croatia were to be transferred to the annexed territories, and specifically to the Arbe camp in the province of Fiume (with the civilian Slovene and Croatian internees of that camp being deported to Gonars). Bastianini, who been appointed under-secretary for foreign affairs in the meantime, was irked by the idea that the Jews whom he had so energetically sought to expel from Dalmatia could now return to Italy in even larger numbers. He proposed that all of them should be interned at Porto Re (Karljevica) in the Croatian zone but was told by Colonel Michele Rolla, head of the UAC of the Second Army, that the Porto Re camp was too small to be suitable. Between May and the end of June, therefore, the Jews were sent to Arbe (see chapter 10).

Then, on 27 April 1943, the Army High Command ordered the CdAs to 'block all access routes to the Italian zones and turn back all Jews reaching the borders'.[69] The internment of 2,261 Jews from the occupied area of Croatia served propaganda purposes: it showed the Četniks and the Balkan peoples in general that the Italians were resisting German interference; and it demonstrated that Italy was taking an independent line in its relations with the Croats. Internment was not ordered for all Jews, and in no respect was it conceived and implemented as a 'rescue operation'.

The territories annexed to Albania

In the immediate aftermath of the partitioning of Yugoslavia, a number of Serbian Jews took refuge in Priština, where a small Jewish community lived. The authorities in Tirana discovered that many of the refugees were carrying false papers and ordered an inquiry, instructing the prefecture to refuse entry in the district to anyone without a proper permit. On 10 January 1942, the lieutenancy announced that anyone found in possession of false papers would be expelled.[70]

A major with the CC.RR., Giorgio Silvestro, then ordered a census to be conducted on all foreign nationals, including Jews. On 12 January 1942

[68] Poliakov and Sabille, *Jews Under Italian Occupation*, p. 148.

[69] USSME, M 3, b. 71, 'II Armata – UAC a tutti i CdA', 27 April 1943.

[70] USSME, N 1–11, 'Diari storici', b. 493, 'Presidenza del Consiglio di Tirana alla luogotenenza', 13 January 1942, signed Mustafa Kruja.

Silvestro applied to the German commander in Mitrovica for permission to eject Jews who had illegally entered Albanian Kosovo from German-occupied territory. He was told that the Germans had insufficient facilities to detain the illegal entrants and was asked to provide a list of their names. On the following day, Silvestro ordered the arrest of those caught in possession of invalid papers and of all Jews unlawfully present in Priština.[71] Able-bodied males from the zone were interned in Old Albania. The arrests of Serbs and Montegrins continued in the months that followed, and so did arrests of all 'Jews who had entered Kosovo after the declaration of war against Yugoslavia'. On 15 March, Lieutenant-Colonel De Leo instructed Silvestro 'to consign the first group of Jews held in the Priština concentration camp (51 individuals) to the German authorities'.[72]

Unfortunately, the other diaries of the 4th Battalion have not been preserved, and it is not possible to determine exactly how many Jews were expelled and how many were handed over to the Germans. Nevertheless, events in Albania disprove the contention that the Italians deliberately sought to protect the Jews, and they gainsay the claims of certain historians and memorialists: for example, Lieutenant-General Francesco Jacomoni, according to whom it was the German military command in Belgrade that furnished the names of the 300 Jewish refugees in Kosovo and their places of refuge (whereas we know that it was the Italians who gave their names to the Germans). Again according to Jacomoni, the lieutenancy and the Albanian government decided that Jewish refugees were to be transferred to the Gjirokastër district (but the Italian military sources instead show that they were arrested in Kosovo and deported in groups to the German zone).[73] Moreover, the case of the Jewish refugees in Priština once again demonstrates that the Italians had no particular qualms over delivering up the Jews, and that they did so under specific agreements between the Italian and German police.

Several groups of refugees reached the part of Macedonia annexed to Albania. It is not known, however, whether they were handed over to the Bulgarian or German authorities, or whether they were turned back at the

[71] CBUCEI, Delasem, b. 44 m, Haijim Azer, president of the Jewish community of Priština, to the Delasem Genoa, 19 January 1942: 'In this town of Priština there are around 80 Jewish refugees, men, women, children and babies from many different places, a large number of whom arrived many months ago. The leaders of the Jewish community of Priština have sought to establish the identity of all men, and it is possible to state that there is not a dangerous person among them and that they have not engaged in political activities but are only free professionals or shopkeepers. Consequently, the community . . . has assumed all responsibility regarding their morality and proper behaviour and guarantees that none of them will ever be involved in undesirable affairs.'

[72] USSME, N 1–11, 'Diari storici', b. 823.

[73] Jacomoni, *La politica dell'Italia in Albania*, 1965, pp. 288–9.

border – and if so, how many.[74] German sources report the existence of a Jewish organization which smuggled a thousand or so Jews into Albania. We know with certainty that the deportation of Macedonian Jews to eastern Europe under a Bulgarian–German agreement provoked alarm among the region's Albanian minorities, which were convinced that they were next on the list after the Jews.

Initially, only Jews living in the Bulgarian zone annexed after 1941 were handed over to the Germans, who then deported them to the extermination camps. The Macedonian and Thracian Jews amounted to approximately 20,000 individuals: of these, in Macedonia, 4,000 lived in Skopje, 3,000 in Botili, 800 in Štip and 300 in Pirot.[75] In Old Bulgaria, the destruction of the Jews – a community of some 5,000 persons – moved through the 'classic' phases of identification, expropriation and concentration, but not, for a certain period of time, that of deportation. When Bulgaria gave the go-ahead for the deportation of foreign Jews (the agreement of 22 February 1943 between Hauptsturmführer Theodor Dannecker and the commissioner for Jewish affairs Alexander Belev provided for the deportation of 8,000 Macedonian Jews, 6,000 Jews from Thrace and 6,000 Jews from Old Bulgaria), the ambassador in Sofia, Massimo Magistrati, invoked diplomatic protection for Italian and Albanian Jews domiciled in Bulgaria. The ambassador was acting on the orders of Ciano, who had instructed him that the Jews were of economic importance and were therefore to be protected: 'not because they are Jews but because they represent Italian interests abroad'. Despite the embassy's intervention, however, both Albanian and Italian Jews were rounded up and detained, although by virtue of diplomatic protection some of them were released from the concentration camp.[76] According to Pietromarchi, of the Macedonian Jews 'only around a thousand managed to escape across the Albanian border and, as we well know, only those able to reach Italian territory were saved. Many committed suicide to escape indescribable torment.'[77]

Pièche informed the MAE and the CS that Jewish families were being deported to Poland, where, as he put it, 'they have been suppressed'

[74] Grünbaum, *Escape Through the Balkans*, p. 38: 'Yesterday there were people here in Tetovo who had fled from the Germans in Skopje, but they were arrested and sent back there.' It is not known to what extent the Italian authorities collaborated (or if they collaborated) with the Albanian authorities.

[75] Petrović, 'La situation des juifs dans le sud-est de la Serbie et en Macédoine'. Some 7,122 Jews were deported from Yugoslavian Macedonia.

[76] Matkovski, 'The Destruction of Macedonian Jewry', p. 243: 'Those who were released from the camp as Italian or Albanian nationals – a total of 24 persons – had to leave Bulgarian territory. Some of them were deported by the police and others voluntarily left for Priština, which was then under Italian occupation.'

[77] Pietromarchi, diary, 27 March 1943.

(*sarebbero state soppresse*). He added that, while 'the Bulgarians have obeyed their orders faithfully and have impressed the Germans with a cruelty of which only an uncivilized people is capable, we [Italians] are fortunately extraneous to such horrors, which will leave their bloody imprint on history'.[78] Pièche was wrong.

Greece

In 1940–1 the number of Jews in Greece was estimated at 80,000.[79] The largest community (around 56,000 persons) lived in Salonika in the German-occupied zone. There were also communities on Chios, also in the German zone, in Kavala (2,200) and Drama (1,200) in the Bulgarian zone, and on Rhodes (2,200). In 1941, Jacques Sabille reports, around 900 Jewish families were living in the Italian-occupied zone but their numbers were constantly increasing. There were further Jewish communities on Corfu (around 2,000 persons), in Ioannina (1,950), Preveza (around 50, some 30 households),[80] Volos (882), Larissa (1,175) and Kastoria (900). In 1941, there were 3,500 Jews living in Athens; by 1943 their number had risen to 8,000.[81]

The Italian military authorities were suspicious of the Sephardic and Romaniote Jewish communities in the Italian zone, and they demonstrated that they had assimilated all the stereotypes of European anti-Semitism: 'the treacherous Jew', 'pro-British', 'leaders of the democratic-liberal international', 'the Jewish caste which pulls the strings of the economy'.[82] Until

[78] USSME, M 3, b. 19, 'generale Pièche al GABAP, 23 marzo 1943, Relazione sulla Macedonia bulgara'; DDI, ser. IX, 1939–43, vol. 10, doc. 367, 'ministro a Sofia Magistrati al capo del governo e ministro degli Esteri', 28 May 1943: no Jew was affected by the provision. See also doc. 412, 'sottosegretario agli Esteri Bastianini al ministro a Sofia Magistrati'.

[79] Carpi, 'Nuovi documenti'; Mohlo, *In memoriam*; Novitch, *Le passage des barbares*.

[80] USSME, N 1–11, 'Diari storici', b. 556, 'Comando XXVI CdA – Ufficio Informazioni al Com. sup. FF.AA. Grecia', 7 January 1942, signed General Guido Della Bona.

[81] Poliakov and Sabille, *Jews Under Italian Occupation*. Bowman, 'Jews in Wartime Greece', pp. 50–1, provides the following figures on the Jewish communities present in the Italian-occupied zone in 1940: 520 in Trikala, 1,175 in Larissa, 882 in Volos, 150 in Karditsa, 350 in Chalkis, 3,500 in Athens (10,000 in 1943 after the deportations of the Jews of Salonika), 337 in Patras and Agrinion, 1,950 in Ioannina, 250 in Prevesa, 384 in Arta, 2,000 in Corfù, 275 in Zante.

[82] USSME, N 1–11, 'Diari storici', b. 859, 'Comando Divisione alpina Julia al Comando del XXVI CdA', 26 May 1941, signed by Lieutenant Colonel Arturo Barbieri; L 15, b. 85, 'XI Armata – Ufficio "I", Informazioni sino alle ore 20 del giorno 26 maggio 1941': 'The Jewish community . . . is to be considered untrustworthy'; N 1–11, 'Diari storici', b. 660, 'Comando Divisione Pinerolo – UAC al Comando del III CdA', 27 February 1942: 'The Jewish caste . . . is a powerful means of incitement in the occupied territory because it monopolizes most of the commerce in a country whose soul is business and are therefore easily able to influence the masses by means of economic action'; b. 972, 'Comando XXVI CdA al Com. sup. FF.AA. Grecia', 6 October 1942; b. 542, 'Comando Divisione Puglie – UAC al Comando del III CdA', 20 January 1942: in Thessaly and Attica, the authorities

the end of 1942, these various small Jewish communities caused no problems of public order or security for the occupiers: they were well organized, with their own welfare services, elementary schools, clinics and food distribution organizations.

From 1943 onwards, after the deportation of Greek Jews by the Germans, a distinction can be drawn between Italian policy towards the Greek Jews in the zones occupied by the Regio Esercito, on the one hand, and towards Italian Jews resident in Greece on the other. Until 8 September 1943 there is no evidence that the resident Jews or those who took refuge in the Italian zone from other areas of Greece were subject to persecution, arrest or internment by the Italian military authorities.

On 3 February 1943, the German embassy announced that the German occupation authorities in Greece intended to deport all Jews, and it inquired whether similar measures were envisaged in the Italian zones. Ciano instructed Pellegrino Ghigi to arrange for 'Jewish elements' of Greek nationality on Italian-occupied territory to be sent to a concentration camp, suggesting one of the Ionian islands for the purpose. Ghigi replied, however, that the arrest and internment of many thousands of Greek Jews was politically counterproductive as well as being difficult to put into practice.[83]

After Ciano's dismissal from office, the under-secretary of foreign affairs, Bastianini, informed the Germans that the treatment of Greek and foreign Jews in the part of Greece occupied by the Wehrmacht was of 'no concern to the Italian government', adding that plans were being made for the transfer of Greek Jews resident in the Italian zone to concentration camps in Italy – plans which would be implemented as soon as transport could be arranged. Moreover, foreign Jews from allied and neutral countries domiciled in Greece would also be removed to Italy. There is no documentary evidence that these decisions were implemented, and it cannot be ruled out that Bastianini's reply was merely a sop to the Germans. Bastianini also pointed out that the presence of Jews in the occupied zones was primarily a problem of public order. Italian prestige was to be respected, and the Germans and the occupied governments were to comply with Italian decisions. The Italian authorities, Bastianini declared, had exclusive responsibility for the 'Jewish question' and would not tolerate any interference by the Germans. This policy was applied in all areas under Italian occupation, and by virtue of this principle requests for direct intervention by the German authorities had been refused in the occupied zone of France.[84]

requested the Army Command to ban street trading by Jews in order to prevent any possible contact with Greek peasants.

83 DDI, ser. IX, 1939–43, vol. 10, doc. 3.

84 Carpi, 'Nuovi documenti', p. 190, doc. 16.

Ghigi wrote to Pietromarchi that, 'for a thousand reasons ranging from our humanity to our prestige', the Jews in the Italian-occupied zone had not been interned. The Jewish communities were peaceable, isolated and easily controlled: in short, they were not a problem. Why, Ghigi asked, should the Regio Esercito waste time, men and materials on rounding up and interning civilians when the Andartes were growing more dangerous by the day?

The MAE closely watched the methods used by the Germans to deal with the Jews in the part of Greece occupied by the Wehrmacht. It was decided that they would be treated in the same way as the Italian Jews resident in Germany and in the German-occupied territories of western Europe. Bastianini announced that because Greece was part of Fascist *spazio vitale*, it was entirely legitimate for Italy to cultivate its economic and political interests in the country. A racist measure such as the annihilation of the Jewish community in Salonika would have caused excessive 'damage' to those interests.[85]

What happened in Salonika warrants more detailed description. In that city, according to the literature on the topic, even distant and often bogus family ties with an Italian were enough to persuade the consular authorities to issue a certificate of nationality permitting the recipient to reach the Italian zone. Sometimes it was sufficient to have an Italian-sounding surname or to declare oneself a fugitive from the Gestapo. Some officers of the Regio Esercito went repeatedly to the concentration camps, where they claimed that certain women were their wives and demanded their immediate release. On 16 March 1943, Pietromarchi noted in his diary that the Germans had given vent to their brutality against Salonika's 60,000 Jews. In batches of 10,000 a week, the 'poor wretches' were being loaded on cattle trains, with sixty people packed into each wagon, which were then sealed so that when they reached their destination awful carnage had been accomplished. This colony of Jews had been settled in Greece for centuries and was tolerated by the Turks: 'Then the Germans came to consign this people to their dreadful fate. There is no corner of Europe that has not witnessed the Germans' innate, ineradicable wickedness. And these are the bringers of *Kultur* and the artificers of the New Order!'[86]

On 24 April, Lucillo Merci, liaison officer with the Germans, wrote in his diary that he had given them long lists of the names, especially of women

[85] Ibid., p. 187, doc. 15. [86] Pietromarchi, diary, 26 March 1943.

and children, whom the authorities considered to be Italian nationals. 'Time is running out and the deportation trains to Poland keep rolling. For our part, we try to save as many Italian Jews holding Greek citizenship as possible.'[87] Berlin announced that all Jews without undisputed Italian citizenship would be deported: mere application for citizenship or simple entitlement was no longer enough. Bastianini consequently hastened to repatriate the Italian Jews, although he stressed that the situation was extremely delicate because some Italian Jews in Salonika, who were originally from the Grand Duchy of Tuscany, no longer possessed Italian nationality (others had renounced their Italian citizenship when Italy invaded Greece in October 1940). Above all, their deportation would lead to the irreparable loss of positions representing major Italian interests, which they intended to keep and protect.

Merci, with the help of officials at the consulate in Salonika, compiled a list of Jews who had economic ties with Italy or who held positions of influence in Greek commerce and finance, and he asked the Germans to suspend their deportation. On 23 April, Bastianini wrote to the representative in Athens and to the consul in Salonika, Guelfo Zamboni, that Italian nationality should be granted even in dubious cases and that deportation of Italian Jews should be prevented by transferring them to the Italian-occupied zone. On 21 June, the consulate organized the transfer of the last remaining Italian Jews in Salonika. The operation was complicated by the German authorities' insistence on scrupulously checking the documents of every Jew in order to verify his or her nationality. Rome continued to 'assist the Jews in every possible way, especially in relation to their property, which is in every effect Italian property'. But the action of the Italian consulate was successful in only a relatively small number of cases: Merci's diary and documents published by Daniel Carpi report that 'some hundreds of persons' were transferred to the Italian zone. On 30 April 1943, there were sixty-five Italian Jews still left in the German concentration camps; the others had been deported.[88]

On the assumption that Merci's statements are truthful, the transfer to the Italian zone of a relative handful of Italian Jews cannot be regarded as a

[87] Shelah and Rochlitz, 'Excerpts from the Salonika Diary of Lucillo Merci'. According to Merci (29 April 1943), besides Italian Jews, the categories of Jews entitled to protection were: '(1) Italian-born widows of Greek Jews; (2) women born in Italy and married to Greek Jews; (3) couples consisting of Jewish men and Aryan Italian women; (4) all cases where there is no reasonable doubt as to the claim for citizenship. The instructions aim at facilitating the transfer of those falling within one of the above categories to Italy or to the Italian occupation zone.'

[88] DDI, ser. IX, 1939–43, vol. 10, doc. 238.

humanitarian rescue operation. The Italians did not intervene on behalf of all Jews; they provided diplomatic protection for Italian (or virtually Italian) Jews because they represented 'economic and financial interests of the Italian state abroad'.[89] The Italian authorities took action because they feared that the Greeks or Germans would appropriate these 'Italian positions', confiscating or selling the assets of Jews. The General Affairs Directorate of the MAE put it thus: the Italian authorities had not 'intervened on behalf of the Jews but had acted in order to defend a position that is essential to preserve our rights in regard to our claims'.[90]

Confirmation that the interest of the Italian government was political and economic, rather than humanitarian, is provided by a MAE note stating that numerous Jews with Italian citizenship in the Mediterranean basin had considerable economic and financial influence. The government was seeking to protect them 'despite their membership of the Jewish race' because they represented 'conspicuous Italian interests in zones of particular political importance'. Such action would continue because application of the racial laws had served 'to undermine Italian economic positions'.[91] A total of 322 Jews were saved from deportation: 217 of them were Italian nationals, 92 had temporary certificates and 13 were foreigners related to members of these two categories.

After 25 July 1943, the MAE sought to relieve itself of any responsibility for the increasingly repressive measures that it was forced to take in Greece. During an inter-ministerial meeting held at the GABAP on 30 August 1943, Pietromarchi pointed out that, if civil powers in Greece were transferred to the Germans, then the Jews – even those of Italian nationality – would be deported. The head of the GABAP suggested that the Jews be transported to the Ionian islands, for if they were sent to Italy the problem would arise of supporting them. A week before the signing of the armistice, Pietromarchi recommended as follows:

We should disassociate ourselves from the Germans in order not to be blamed, even indirectly, for the acts committed by the Germans. The remaining Italian zones should be administered according to humanitarian principles, leaving the best possible memory of us behind. Also in regard to German conceptions, so

89 Shelah writes in his introduction to Rochlitz's article, 'Excerpts from the Salonika Diary of Lucillo Merci', that Salonika 'boasted a large and well-established Italian community with significant economic and social power. Italian religious, cultural and commercial institutions were prominent in the city and their preservation was of crucial importance. Quite a few Jews were Italian nationals, including some pillars of the community [such] as the Modiano and Moisis families' (p. 298).

90 ASMAE, GABAP, b. 42, 'Appunto del 10 ottobre 1942'.

91 ASMAE, AA.PP. – Italia, b. 77. The two documents quoted are undated; the second refers to the Italian Jews of Tunisia.

different from Italian ones, we should comply with the rules laid down by the law of war and with humanitarian principles.[92]

France

According to Léon Poliakov, when the Vichy government began deportations, between 15,000 and 20,000 French and foreign Jews were resident in France, and 12,000 to 13,000 of them (including around 8,000 foreigners) in the Alpes-Maritimes alone. Raul Hilberg has written that from June 1940 to 8 September 1943 the Italian zone was 'an inviolable sanctuary for Jews of all nationalities' and gave refuge to some 50,000 Jews (foreign and French).[93] For Klaus Voigt, by contrast, after November 1942 the flow of foreign Jewish refugees amounted to only around 5,000 persons, somewhat more if French Jews and refugees to Corsica are counted.[94]

As in all the other occupied territories, in France the Italian government extended diplomatic protection only to Italian Jews, its declared purpose being to prevent property confiscated from Jews with Italian nationality from falling into French or German hands. The approximately 1,500 Italian Jews resident in the German-occupied zones of France and in non-occupied France were not interned by the Germans or by the French. Instead, they were repatriated; they were not obliged to wear the yellow star until October 1942; and their property was managed by administrators of Italian nationality.[95] The Italian government's intention was to assert its authority *vis-à-vis* the French and not give way to the Germans even on matters concerning citizens of 'Jewish race'. Rome instructed the Fourth Army Command not to tolerate any French interference in the administration of property seized from Italian and foreign Jews and notified the Germans that no measures were to be taken against Italian Jews in the German-occupied zones without the express consent of the MAE.[96]

92 Pictromarchi, diary, 1–2 September 1943.

93 Hilberg, *La déstruction des juifs d'Europe*, pp. 561–70.

94 USSME, N 1–11, 'Diari storici', b. 1272, 'VII CdA Comando CC.RR. al Comando di CdA', 27 November 1942, signed Lanza d'Ajeta; ACS, MI-DGPS, Divisione AA.GG.RR., 1942, b. 4.

95 Carpi, *Between Mussolini and Hitler*, especially pp. 1–66. When the Germans had finished deporting foreign Jews without diplomatic protection, they began the deportation of Hungarian (1,500), Romanian (3,800), Bulgarian and then Greek (1,500) Jews. The Greek Jews living in France asked for diplomatic protection from the Italian delegation in Paris, which was unable (or unwilling) to grant it.

96 ASMAE, AA.PP. – Francia, b. 54, 'MAE al ministro Bonarelli presso la IV Armata, alle DRA di Nizza, Marsiglia, Tolosa, Tolone, Montpellier, Chambery, Annecy, Cannes, Nîmes e Avignone, alla CIAF e al console Ugo Turcato a Bastia', 22 December 1942; Carpi, *Between Mussolini and Hitler*, pp. 99–101.

After 12 November 1942, the question of the attitude to take towards French and foreign Jews (which in itself was of secondary importance to the occupying authorities) interwove with occupation policy and, as in Croatia, became an integral part of Italo-German policy.

The Vichy government organized a series of round-ups – undertaken by the French police – of foreign Jews in the Italian zone. Vichy authorized the operation because it had received orders from the Germans, and its purpose was also to prove to the Italians that Vichy still exercised full authority in domestic political affairs. The round-ups provoked an angry response from the Italian authorities, which regarded them as breaching the rights of the occupying power and which notified the French government that the internment of 'persons of Jewish race' was the exclusive prerogative of the occupier.[97] The CIAF bulletin stressed the duplicity of the French authorities: when reproached for not implementing the racial laws they blamed the Italian commands for not allowing them to do so, but then told the Jews that they had been forced to take action against them by the Italians and the Germans.

The Italian government's protest was purely political in nature. It should not be forgotten that the Fourth Army Command regarded refugees (Jews included) as a threat to security and to the public order. We know with certainty from Voigt's research that the CS promised the Wehrmacht Supreme Command that not only nationals of enemy states would be interned but also all Jews, regardless of their nationality.[98] Immediately after the occupation, the Army Command imposed the strictest surveillance of borders,[99] and on 12 December the understanding reached between the Italian and German Supreme Commands was confirmed by a communication sent both to the MAE and the Ministry of the Interior which attributed the decision to Mussolini in person: 'Following concerns raised by the Germans, it has been decided upon high that all subjects of enemy states deemed dangerous must be arrested immediately, and Jews resident in metropolitan French territory must be interned.'[100]

[97] ASMAE, GABAP, b. 3, 'Alberto Calisse al MAE', 24 December 1942; USSME, M 3, b. 78, 'Comando IV Armata'.

[98] Voigt, *Il rifugio precario*, p. 296.

[99] At the end of November, the Swiss authorities complained about the permeability of the borders between French Savoy and the cantons of Geneva and Valais, and the increase in border crossings from the Italian zone. The Bern legation wrote: 'There is no need to point out how politically infectious any contact, even limited [with the Swiss population] can be, especially by the old [Jews], who arouse compassion. It is obvious that if this mass of Jews continues to increase, there will form in the centre of Europe, between the two countries of the Axis, a powerful Jewish accumulator capable of irradiating energies contrary to our interests' (ASMAE, GABAP, b. 3, 'legazione a Berna al MAE', 27 November 1942, signed Attilio Tamaro).

[100] See Voigt, *Il rifugio precario*, p. 296, n. 6.

On 29 December 1942, the military authorities along the Italo-German demarcation line received instructions to expel foreign Jews and French undesirables to the French territories occupied by German troops.[101] At the beginning of 1943 they closed the Franco-Swiss frontier and created a special police force. Consisting of PS officials and agents, supervised by the SIM and the MAE, this agency reported information on Jewish persons, property and businesses, identified and arrested suspects, interned Jews, and organized the administration of concentration camps and forced residence. Appointed director of the special police office at the Fourth Army Command was Rosario Barranco (general inspector of public security), who also collaborated with the headquarters of the German security service in Lyons.

For reasons of cost, internment in the camps was restricted to politically suspect foreigners. The first camps were opened at the end of 1942, but information about them is fragmentary. We know, for example, that at Sospel to the north of Nice, a hotel and an army barracks were converted into a 'concentration camp' which at the beginning of February 1943 contained 238 internees (some Jewish), thirty-four of whom were women. The figures are not indicative, however, because many more than 238 people passed through the camp: some of them were released while others were sent into forced residence. The camp was closed in May of the same year, and the internees were transferred to Embrun and Modane (two camps on which significant information has not been found in the Italian archives).

Besides internment, the Italian authorities decided – again for reasons of security – to expel all foreigners not yet arrested, including Jews, from the military security zone along the coast. These persons were sent to what the French termed *résidence assignée* in the localities of Digne, Vence, Guagno in Corsica, Saint-Martin-Vésubie, Barcelonnette, Moustier-Sainte-Marie, Castellane, Enchastrayes and Château de Chavance. The measure came into force in the Alpes-Maritimes on 20 February 1943. Those affected were given five days to take up forced residence in the localities to which they had been assigned: if they did not comply, they would be arrested. The costs of maintaining indigent Jews were to be paid by the Refugee Aid Committee of Nice (Comité d'Aide aux Réfugiés or Comité Dubouchage, from the name of the street in which the Ashkenazi synagogue was located).

In early 1943, the occupiers in France found themselves in the same situation as in Croatia. Foreign Jews in the Italian zone had been interned in

[101] ASMAE, GABAP, b. 42.

concentration camps or sent into *résidences assignées*, and all those attempting to enter the zone had been repulsed. In France as in the Balkans, the Italians had no intention of protecting foreign or French Jews: rather, and more simply, they would not tolerate interference in matters which they considered their exclusive competence. In this sense – at least as regards decisions concerning Jewish refugees – Italian policy towards the authorities of the occupied countries and towards Germany was indubitably consistent. Confirmation of the Italian authorities' intolerance of any act damaging to their prestige and prerogatives is provided by an injunction issued to the prefect of the Alpes-Maritimes, Marcel Ribière, ordering him to suspend the provision that all foreign Jews must report to the police offices and take up forced residence in the German zone within three days. For exactly the same reasons, the Fourth Army Command instructed Ribière that the epithet *juif* was not to be annotated on the identity cards of foreign Jews.

The French authorities refused to submit to the directives of the Italian occupiers. In February, the French police in Savoie organized what they termed a 'manhunt' (but which in fact was a 'Jew-hunt': according to official Italian figures, there were 240 Jews in Savoie and 373 in Haute-Savoie). The regional commissioner for Jewish affairs, Léon Bérard, met the DRA in the presence of the prefect and explained his plans for the round-up. All foreign Jews were to be interned in the Italian zone or made to take up forced residence in the zones bordering on Switzerland. On 20 and 22 February the French police breached the agreement with the Italians by making several arrests and deporting the Jews detained to the German zone. The Italian authorities, incensed at what they regarded as a deliberate affront, ordered the French to release all the deportees immediately. Some days later, the head of the SMG Vittorio Ambrosio asked Admiral Charles Platon to revoke all the arrests and internments of foreign Jews, except for those accused of common crimes – who would go before the French courts. Ambrosio stressed that he was serving notification on the French government that the internment of foreign Jews was, and must remain, the exclusive competence of the Italian authorities.[102]

[102] USSME, M 3, b. 78, 1 March 1943, 'telescritto del generale Ambrosio inviato a tutti i CdA della IV Armata'. A similar notification was issued a month later to the Vichy government: in USSME, N 1–11, 'Diari storici', b. 1218, allegato 70, 'CS alla IV Armata, 22 aprile 1943, telescritto cifrato in arrivo. Generale Carlo Avarna di Gualtieri, portavoce del CS presso le autorità di Vichy': 'If, according to the law in force, competence to adjudicate pertains to a judicial authority external to the Italian-occupied zone, the transfer of the defendant cannot be effected without authorization issued by the Italian authorities and only in regard to the effects of the sentence and its execution in France.'

The effect (entirely unwanted) of these various decisions was to swell the flood of Jewish refugees from the *départements* beyond the Rhône demarcation line (3,000 to 5,000 arrived from the German zone after November 1942): for obvious reasons, they preferred forced residence or internment by the Italians to the fate awaiting them at the hands of the Germans. The Jewish aid organizations (like the above-mentioned Comité d'Aide aux Réfugiés) reacted to the situation by circulating information among the Jewish communities – with the result that the number of Jews fleeing to the Italian-occupied zone increased even further. The Jewish community of Nice, indeed, held a ceremony in its synagogue 'to thank the Italians'.[103]

Obviously, the German authorities could not tolerate these actions by the Italians. On 13 January 1943, Standartenführer SS Helmut Knochen informed the Reich Central Security Office that the Italian government was impeding all measures against Jews of every nationality in their occupation zone. On 26 January 1943, Heinrich Himmler, mindful of the significance of the dispute, contacted Ribbentrop, who on 25 February took advantage of a visit to Rome to ask Mussolini for clarification. The Duce told him that the misunderstandings resulted from a tactical stratagem by the French.[104] The senior partner then proceeded to apply pressure through the German ambassador in Rome, Hans von Mackensen, who proposed three solutions to Mussolini: leave it to the French police to deal with the 'Jewish question'; exclude the Italian military and give the task to the Italian police; or let Himmler and the SS resolve the matter. In March, having given Berlin further evidence that the Italian authorities were obstructing the deportation of foreign Jews in France, Mackensen arranged a meeting with Mussolini. In justification of the behaviour of his generals, the Duce adduced their 'sentimental humanitarianism', but then went on to say that the French police should deal with the matter.[105] Immediately after the meeting, Bastianini sent Mussolini a report by Italian army officers documenting German atrocities in eastern Europe. He attached to the report a letter in which he declared that Italy must not associate itself with such heinous acts. Mussolini then received a report from Dino Alfieri on the gas chambers, whereafter Pietromarchi and Ambrosio furnished him with further details on the extermination of the Jews.[106]

103 USSME, D 7, b. 24, 'Notiziario CIAF della prima quindicina di gennaio 1943'.

104 Klarsfeld, *Vichy–Auschwitz*, pp. 206 and 228.

105 Poliakov and Sabille, *Jews Under Italian Occupation*, pp. 33–4 and 68–72; Klarsfeld, *Vichy–Auschwitz*, pp. 243–4; Pietromarchi, diary, 31 March and 6 April 1943, on the audience with Victor Emmanuel III.

106 De Felice, *Storia degli ebrei italiani*, doc. 32; Klarsfeld, *Vichy–Auschwitz*, pp. 45–8 and 235–40; Ortona, *Diplomazia di guerra*, 1994, pp. 201 and 209.

On 20 March 1943, Mackensen received a note from Bastianini informing him that all measures regarding Jews were the exclusive competence of the Italians. The Italian Jews would be rapidly repatriated, and the German police need take no action against French and foreign Jews because the Italian military and police authorities would deal with them. On 19 March 1943, the inspector general of police, Guido Lospinoso – a direct subordinate of the Rome chief of police, Carmine Senise – was instructed to set up a racial police inspectorate in Nice and attend to the 'Jewish question' in collaboration with the Regio Esercito (Barranco's police section continued to operate).[107] Lospinoso's appointment was not the only important decision taken: on 26 March an Italo-German agreement was signed in regard to French or foreign Jews attempting to move from the German to the Italian occupation zones: they were to be temporarily interned while awaiting consignment to the German or French authorities, if this was requested.[108] It should be borne in mind, moreover, that in mid-March the Italian Ministry of Foreign Affairs had requested the commanders of the Fourth Army to turn back refugees who managed to reach the demarcation line.[109]

On arriving in the occupied territories, Lospinoso attempted to halt the flow of Jews entering the Italian zone, to conduct a census of them and to intern those from the Côte d'Azur in a camp on the Geneva border. However, because he was unable to obtain lists of the French Jews, their internment was postponed indefinitely. Lospinoso dispatched foreign Jews for internment or forced residence according to lists furnished by the Nice Comité d'Aide aux Réfugiés. Because of insurmountable difficulties of transport, the Jews in question could not be sent to Savoie (only a thousand

[107] On Lospinoso's activities, see Voigt, *Il rifugio precario*, pp. 311–22; Klarsfeld, *Vichy–Auschwitz*, pp. 49–54, 62–3, 78–81, 89–91 and the documents on pp. 258, 265, 277, 311, 330 and 335–41.

[108] USSME, M 3, b. 63, 'Comando iv Armata – Ufficio "I"', 26 March 1943; ibid., 'Comando I CdA – Ufficio "I" a tutti comandi di divisione dipendenti', 7 April 1943. The rejection order was transmitted by the CdAs to all their divisions: 'Jews . . . who have arrived after 26 March must be consigned, if requested, to the German or French authorities.' They would be 'sent into forced residence under Italian control *while awaiting consignment to the German or French authorities that request it*' (underlined in the document). In M 7, b. 496, the application of the directive is described in regard to certain specific cases, for instance, that of the parents of Eva Zussman: the document states that they were to be sent into forced residence 'while awaiting consignment, if requested, to the German and French authorities'.

[109] USSME, M 3, b. 78, 'MAE al CS, che comunica a Supergrecia, Superegeo, Superalba, al governatorato del Montenegro e a Supersloda, 24 marzo 1943, marconigramma cifrato 3526', signed General Angelo Rossi. The copy to the German ambassador is in ASMAE, GABAP, b. 42, dated 14 March 1943, 'Appunto per il GABAP (comm. Alberto Berio)'. See Poliakov and Sabille, *Jews Under Italian Occupation*, pp. 68–72.

or so reached Megève), and they were instead transported to the more internal zones of the Alpes-Maritimes.[110] Voigt writes:

> The information communicated by Barranco [see appendix, table 68] in a letter to the Rome chief of police, according to which 1,783 persons were registered for internment on 10 April, and specifically 763 men, 671 women and 349 children, seems to be accurate . . . As to national origin, approximately half were Polish. Only 97 had been registered as former German citizens, while 111 were termed 'former Austrians'. Again according to Barranco's report, of these 1,783 persons registered on 10 April, some 1,404 had already been interned, the majority at Saint-Martin-Vésubie and Megève.[111]

Lospinoso – Voigt notes – applied Mussolini's directives as laxly as he could, avoiding arrests, excluding the French police from all important decisions, and restricting contacts with the Gestapo to the collaboration already begun by Barranco with the detached commands in Lyons, Marseilles and Toulon. For Lospinoso, as a senior Fascist police official, internment was a practical problem to be addressed and solved in fulfilment of his duties and with the least possible trouble.[112] Not surprisingly, the German authorities objected to his methods. On 10 July 1943, they informed one of his assistants that, by virtue of reciprocity, the German Jews who had taken refuge in the Italian zone must be handed over.[113] On 15 July, the chief of police, Renzo Chierici, acceded to the German demand.[114] Published documents confirm that agreement was reached with Lospinoso on the consignment, and that he even furnished the Germans with lists of the Jews resident on the Côte d'Azur.[115] Were the Italians preparing to hand over all the Jews? Only German Jews? Only those who had entered the Italian zone after 26 March 1943 and had been interned in the meantime? The present state of research does not permit answers to these questions.

Before and after 25 July, a number of Italians sought to prevent the deportation of Jews. Particular mention should be made of Angelo Donati, who, although a Jew and therefore suffering discrimination, possessed a

110 At the end of April, the CS informed the Fourth Army Command that the 'Jewish question' was now the exclusive competence of the police. Thereafter, the military authorities merely provided information, seconded communications officers to the French authorities, requested the opening of hotels as forced residences for Jews and prevented entry by further Jews along the Rhône demarcation line.

111 Voigt, *Il rifugio precario*, pp. 317–18. 112 Ibid., p. 321.

113 Sarfatti, 'Fascist Italy and German Jews'.

114 Sarfatti, 'Consegnate gli ebrei', publishes a document dated 15 July 1943 written by the Italian chief of police, Chierici, which with reference to the French territories states baldly: 'You are to abide by the German police force's request for the consignment of German Jews.'

115 Caracciolo, *Gli ebrei e l'Italia*, pp. 86–8; Cavaglion, *Nella notte straniera*.

permanent safe-conduct pass between Italy and France. In mid-August (at a meeting at the MAE attended by the directors general Amedeo Giannini, Leonardo Vitetti, Luigi Vidau and Pietromarchi), Vidau pointed out that since the replacement of Italian troops by German ones in the French territories, several thousand Jews, almost all of foreign nationality, who had been protected against capture by the German police now found themselves in extremely difficult circumstances. Given that abandoning them to their fate was out of the question, Vidau proposed that agreement be reached with the Ministry of the Interior to 'close one eye' to their clandestine entry into the kingdom, consider them political refugees and deal with them in the most appropriate fashion. As regards the Italian Jews who became naturalized French citizens after losing their Italian nationality by leaving the kingdom after 1938, the Ministry of the Interior arranged for their return by restoring their Italian citizenship.[116] The MAE directive was welcomed by the Ministry of the Interior. Lospinoso issued instructions for the Jews in forced residence at the demarcation line to be transferred to *communes* situated close to the Italian border: from Vence they were to be transported to Vésubie, from Barcelonnette to Rocquebillière, from Castellane to Lantosque, from Saint-Gervais to Venanson, from Megève to Peria-Cava. After 8 September 1943, they were deported by the Germans.

ITALIANI BRAVA GENTE?

While it is true that the Italians interned thousands of Jews rather than hand them over to the Germans, they nevertheless expelled a large number or turned them back at borders in all the occupied territories. There were indeed 'good Italians' who rescued persecuted Jews and persons of other faiths and nationalities, but I do not believe the thesis that the Italians as a whole were *brava gente* who refused to give the Jews over to the Germans for humanitarian reasons. Citing individual acts in order to claim that humanitarianism is inherent to the Italian national character, asserting that it would be intrinsically impossible for Italians to harm Jews voluntarily, is to make claims that have no basis in fact.

I agree with Liliana Picciotto Fargion that Italian humaneness has for too long been deliberately extolled in order to emphasize the cruelty of the Germans by contrast. There has been much talk of anti-Semitism *all'italiana*,

[116] ASMAE, AA.PP. – Francia, b. 69, 11 August 1943, 'Appunto per sua eccellenza il ministro Raffaele Guariglia'.

of the Italians' natural good-heartedness, while their responsibilities have been forgotten. It is not the task of this study to judge the behaviour of the Italians in general, nor that of the thousands of soldiers sent to the occupied territories in particular. This chapter has analysed Italian occupation policy towards the Jews: more exactly, it has examined the decisions taken by generals and politicians, and also by Mussolini – who, as we have seen, performed a central and crucial role at this juncture as well.

In order to argue for the humanitarianism of Italian policy, one has to demonstrate that the Italian political and military establishment 'rescued' the Jews on the orders of Mussolini. This thesis is simply absurd, and it is disproved by the documents. Equally false is the idea that the political and military authorities conspired against Mussolini. The ten previous chapters have shown that they worked towards the Duce, not against him. The reasons that the Italians did not hand over some of the Jews in the occupied territories relate to the circumstances of the occupation, to the maintenance of prestige, to the exercise of authority over the occupied peoples and governments and to the nature of the Italo-German relationship.

Moreover, as Renzo De Felice has shown, the laws of 1938 did not put an end to consensus for the regime. Hence, the alleged humanitarianism of the Italian soldiers cannot be explained as their reaction against the regime's racism. And reactions against the racial laws were in any case decidedly muted. The initial shock provoked by their promulgation affected only the most sensitive of consciences; in the others it gave rise at most to a certain disenchantment with the regime, a sort of 'inner malaise'.[117]

Probably, the decision of certain individuals to aid the persecuted (Jews and non-Jews) was prompted by this malaise, which was exacerbated by the war and by the progressive disintegration of the regime and its institutions. As in Italy, so in the occupied territories a crisis of conscience alienated certain individuals from a regime no longer able to convince them with myths and symbols. At times of crisis, the Fascist rituals had compensated for privation and hardship with the fervour of enthusiasm; they had concealed the regime's difficulties behind a façade of order and efficiency; and they had distracted the masses from severe problems abroad, reassuring them with intoxicating displays of power.

In the occupied territories, the Fascist political liturgy was no longer able to legitimate power and to manipulate and control the masses; it was no longer able to express the beliefs, values and purposes of Fascist culture. The war was lived 'in a climate that today appears almost unreal, in which what

[117] De Felice, *Rosso e nero*, pp. 161–2.

mattered most was one's own career, not to undertake binding personal responsibilities, adhere strictly to canonized principles, and always blame others, the regime and Mussolini . . . when things went wrong'.[118] The agony of the regime affected those in power and simple soldiers alike.[119] Disorder, disobedience and amoralism increased as time passed and sometimes allowed the persecuted to break the law: hence, in certain cases, what appeared to be humanitarian action to help Jews reach the Italian zones resulted in fact from the corruption of soldiers and officials.

Finally, as we saw in chapter 5, prolonged contact with the 'inferior races' diluted Fascist racist and anti-Semitic ideology. Although Italian repression was certainly violent, the extreme brutality of the Nazis and the Ustaše irremediably tarnished the image of Italy's allies and, in some cases, led to 'compassion' for the persecuted.[120] During my research, I frequently came across documents that referred to the Italian 'humanitarian' tradition or spoke of 'humanitarian treatment'. In what, therefore, did the alleged humaneness or humanitarianism of certain Italians consist?

There is no doubt that the Italian political and military leaders regarded themselves as racially and culturally superior to the occupied peoples and to the Germans (although one cannot be equally sure that the rank-and-file troops did so). The diary kept by the head of the GABAP, Pietromarchi, makes frequent reference to the barbarities of the Germans. Some examples follow.

On 26 March 1942, Pietromarchi wrote:

> The Second Army Command has sent us a report from the Jewish community of Mostar which recounts the horrors committed against the Jews of the interior by the Ustaše: forced labour, girls raped before the eyes of their parents, all the abominations that only the most brutal delinquency can conceive. When one thinks that the progress of human sentiment and kindness has led to the prohibition, by law and protective agencies, of violence against animals, one cannot but shudder at such wickedness. We are indebted for this depravity, which dishonours all humanity, to the country of *Kultur*, to Germany. Such are the Germans' qualifications for supremacy among the races and for domination of the world.[121]

On 7 April 1942:

> We have been informed that in the past few days SS formations have conducted nocturnal raids into Slovakia and snatched from their families some 3,000 Jewish women, many of them of high social position, taking them to concentration camps

[118] De Felice, *Mussolini l'alleato*, p. 826.

[119] Gallerano, 'Gli italiani in guerra', p. 314; Rizzi, 'Il morale dei militari e dei civili', pp. 371–8.

[120] Petersen, 'Italia e Germania', pp. 52–8.

[121] Pietromarchi, diary, 26 March 1942.

in Germany where they are forced to service soldiers in the military brothels. Every day brings a new abomination.[122]

On 27 June 1942:

Germany's brutality and rapaciousness have alienated all the sympathies that it once enjoyed. Wherever the Germans may be, they arouse hatred. Politically, the German domination has been a disaster. No people has so defiantly challenged the sense of justice and humanity that was once Europe's thousand-year heritage. It has reawakened satanic forces of destruction which the Europeans believed had gone from their lives. The *Annals* of Tacitus, the darkest chronicles of tyranny ever written, pale in comparison to the horrors that the Germans have inflicted upon Europe during this war.[123]

The UAC of the Pinerolo Division described its treatment of civilians as 'fair' and as exhibiting the 'sense of high justice and humanity' distinctive of the 'Italian race'. The Balkan peoples were 'crude and primitive', and the violence of the Germans was the violence of 'barbarians'. A report by the General Command of the Second Army stated that mass executions by the Germans, internment in 'inhuman' conditions, murder, slaughter, the torture of Orthodox Christian and Jewish women and children had caused disquiet among the local commands. Italian officers and troops were distressed by the Germans' 'illegal and uncivilized' behaviour.[124] A document reporting on pacification in Croatia affirmed that 'for reasons of humanity', civilians should never be forced to return to their countries of origin.[125] Roatta's reference to the *bono italiano*, and Casertano's to a 'pietism' and 'sentimentalism' founded on the Italians' 'higher degree of civilization', testify to an endeavour to forge an Italian and Fascist identity by asserting the Italian race's difference from the Balkan peoples, the French and the Germans. The Fascist conqueror was neither good nor sentimental, neither primitive nor barbaric. Instead, he was 'fair' and 'humane' because he was Italian and Fascist.

The behaviour of certain Italian soldiers and officers also resulted from the partial failure to Fascisticize the Regio Esercito and the persistence of an ethic and a military code of honour which, unlike that of the Wehrmacht (as Omer Bartov has shown), prohibited and severely punished acts of violence against women and children. General Pièche wrote in a report to the MAE that removing Jews from a zone where they were particularly vulnerable

[122] Pietromarchi called the measures taken against the Jews 'monstrous'. 'They offend human nature in the most brutal of ways. Such wickedness will not be forgotten for centuries and it will brand the German people with infamy for all time' (diary, 26 July 1942).

[123] Pietromarchi, diary, 27 June 1942. [124] ASMAE, GABAP, b. 28.

[125] USSME, M 3, b. 63, 'Risposta al foglio 3065 del 23 febbraio 1942'.

was a 'wise measure'. Consignment to the Ustaše was equivalent to a death sentence, said Pièche: it would provoke unrest among troops 'accustomed to fighting the enemy fairly' who would baulk at having to consign those 'poor wretches' to certain death.

However, the humanitarianism displayed by some Italians, in certain circumstances, was often overridden by political considerations, while in other circumstances, and for similar reasons, it was paraded as the feature that distinguished Italians from Germans. Italian propaganda insisted that 'The Italians have a soul (*Seele*), the Germans do not.' It was convenient to blame the Germans for the war, for destruction and misery, for the inhumane treatment of civilians, for the slaughter of innocents (especially women and children) shot and hanged with neither pity nor justice, and especially so at a juncture when the civilian population was beginning to realize that the German troops were the destroyers rather than the artificers of a 'fair and humane peace'.[126] General Pièche, by now certain of Italy's defeat, connected the extermination of the Jews in Poland with Italy's political and moral necessity to distinguish itself from Germany, Bulgaria and Croatia:

> The population has been so afflicted by the brutality of the German persecutions that the campaign will leave deep scars in the history of warfare. There is an impressive body of evidence on the guilt of the German executioners. There have been numerous episodes of blackmail, violence and theft . . . The Gestapo have subjected numerous wealthy Jews to cruelty and torture in order to force them to give over considerable sums of gold and precious carpets . . . the victims have been warned that if they talk they will be killed. Numerous young girls have been forcibly removed from concentration camps and taken to places where they have been raped to satisfy the lust of drunken German agents. Increasingly frequently, Jews are fleeing in vehicles provided by the Gestapo or German units in exchange for large sums of money, while the severest punishment is inflicted upon those who seek to escape from the ghettoes . . . These sordid episodes cast a dark shadow on the events of this war. The German authorities reproach us for protecting the Jews and for not supporting them in their racial campaign, as Bulgaria has done. Yet I believe that our behaviour, inspired as it is by the principles of humanity, will one day be recognized as the most opportune at the present time.[127]

Even more significant and coloured by hindsight is the following account by Pietromarchi of an audience with the pope. It seems that the head of the GABAP – that shrewd observer of the conflict's tragedies – is preparing

[126] ASMAE, GABAP, b. 27, 'Rapporto del nucleo di collegamento con l'armata germanica a Belgrado', signed Colonel Fabbri, undated.

[127] USSME, M 3, b. 19, Generale Pièche to GABAP, 1 April 1943, 'Notizie sulla Macedonia greca e dalla Bulgaria'.

the Foreign Ministry's defence by evoking Italian humaneness for political ends:

This is one of the darkest ages of human history, perhaps the darkest – said the Holy Father – never has there been such slaughter. And yet, I replied, amid so much wickedness the Italians have been immune to the fever, to the sickness. We are perhaps the only people for whom the teaching of the Church has become our very conscience. The instinct by which our soldiers are repelled by atrocity has been bred by Christianity. And I mentioned how much Italy, and the Foreign Ministry in particular, had done to stop the massacres between Croats and Serbs, and to feed the Greeks when our own people were being rationed to 150 grammes of bread a day. The Holy Father was greatly interested in what I said, and when I concluded that one day account would be taken of our people's humanitarianism, he told me with great force of conviction that the Lord would reward Italy and protect her.[128]

And on 11 March 1943:

News has reached us from London that the massacres of the Jews in Poland are continuing. Eden has informed the Commons that not only Jews but also Poles and Yugoslavs are being slaughtered. Our embassy in Berlin has sent macabre details on mass executions in the death camps of Jews from all the occupied territories. Only those Jews who placed themselves under our protection are safe. Our military authorities, and for this they deserve all credit, have been unyielding in their opposition to the Germans' brutal methods . . . The Germans have taken great offence, which Ribbentrop showed no restraint in declaring in a note of 26 February which listed all our actions to help the Jews in the occupied countries. He added that our conduct was encouraging the other governments to behave in the same way. I have told my colleagues to preserve the document carefully, for it is irrefutable proof of our actions, precious testimony that will exonerate us from vile accusations in the future.[129]

Political considerations also prompted 'humanitarian' behaviour after 25 July 1943. On 19 August, the liaison office at the Second Army Command wrote that Italy's racial policy had not prevented observance of humane principles, our 'ineradicable spiritual heritage'. Such observance, he stressed, was all the more imperative because, from a political point of view, it would be 'opportunely valued and recognized'.[130]

It would be an error to believe that anti-Semitism did not exist among the ranks of the Regio Esercito. At least for the army's commanding officers, the Jews were an 'inferior race'. General Ambrosio wrote that the Croatian

[128] Pietromarchi, diary, 1 January 1943. [129] Pietromarchi, diary, 11 March 1943.
[130] ASMAE, GABAP, b. 42, 19 August 1943, 'telegramma in partenza 23675 PR', signed Augusto Rosso.

campaign against the Jews was conducted less zealously because of 'the lack of reaction shown by the race assailed'.[131] General Renzo Dalmazzo forbade fraternization between Italian soldiers and 'Jewish elements'.[132] General Renato Coturri wrote that the Jews were 'notoriously cunning' and 'had refined their ability to take advantage of every favourable opportunity'. The police, 'with little or no experience in recognizing Jews from their somatic characteristics', were unable to identify them. According to Coturri, Jews were 'elements who by nature and temperament were given to criticizing and grumbling' and 'the inertia in which they are forced to live, loafing in public meeting-places, accentuates their negative and parasitical qualities'.[133]

Nevertheless, I believe that Jonathan Steinberg is right to maintain that the Wehrmacht and the Regio Esercito inhabited two different moral universes. Positions such as that taken up by Pièche, however opportunistically, are not to be found in the Nazi documentation. And statements such as those by the Italian consul in Dubrovnik, who welcomed the settlement in that city of Sephardic Jews because their tradition, culture, relations and knowledge of languages would make them easily manipulable in the event of elections, would have been unthinkable for a German consul or ministerial functionary.

This demonstrates that Italian occupation policies differed from those of the Germans because the Jews and the 'Jewish question' were not central to them. The Italian refusal to deport Jews also stemmed from the nature of Fascist anti-Semitism, which had developed autonomously and was not a German imposition.[134] One should remember that promulgation of the racial laws indubitably helped resolve fierce controversy on the 'Jewish question'. It gave greater credibility to the Axis, but the grotesque *Manifesto della Razza* was an Italian product, an incoherent mish-mash of the biological and intellectual bases of the various currents of racial thought in the Italian scientific community, combined with the political and ideological principles of the regime.

Although Italian anti-Semitism cannot be equated with Nazi 'redemptive anti-Semitism',[135] neither can it be described as 'aimless'.[136] Its intention was not the extermination of the Jews, not even in the annexed and occupied

[131] ASMAE, GABAP, b. 34, 'generale Ambrosio allo SMRE', 28 September 1941.

[132] USSME, N 1–11, 'Diari storici', b. 583, 'Comando VI CdA – UAC alle divisioni dipendenti', 14 November 1941, signed General Dalmazzo.

[133] USSME, N 1–11, 'Diari storici', b. 1426, 24 July 1942; M 3, b. 66.

[134] On this, see Sarfatti, *Gli ebrei nell'Italia fascista.* [135] Friedländer, *L'Allemagne nazie et les juifs.*

[136] Carpi, *Between Mussolini and Hitler.*

territories. The aim of the Italian anti-Semitic laws was to exclude Jews from employment and to prevent them from exercising their rights, both political (including the right to vote) and public, and thus turn them into the pariahs of society. Government action was designed to separate Jews from non-Jews (the ban on mixed marriages, etc.) and to eliminate them from public life. The repressive measures enacted (the ban or restriction on working or receiving an education) caused the civil death of the Italian Jews and served 'objectively' to encourage their emigration.[137] From 1940 onwards, the Italian government interned foreign Jews with the declared purpose of transferring them at the end of the war to those countries willing to receive them; and the same fate awaited the Italian Jews. As Michele Sarfatti has written:

> Between the autumn of 1940 and the summer of 1941 a plan was devised – but not implemented – to solve the 'Jewish question'. It was based on a classification of 'members of the Jewish race' into two categories. Those who belonged to the first – which was by far the largest – would be expelled from the country during the following ten years; in the meantime, they would be subjected to even harsher persecution. The second category, which comprised persons 'of Jewish race' professing the Christian faith and who had Christian 'Aryan' spouses and Christian children, and including ascendant and lateral kin (if baptized) of the former, would, without change to their racial classification, maintain their right to residence in Italy and reacquire all rights lost in previous years.[138]

This provision would then have been applied throughout the Mediterranean imperial community. After conquest of the *spazio vitale*, there would have been no place in the *nuovo ordine* for either the Italian Jews or the Jewish communities of the Mediterranean.

[137] Sarfatti, 'La persecuzione degli ebrei in Italia', pp. 87–8.
[138] Sarfatti, *Gli ebrei nell'Italia fascista*, pp. 163–4.

Epilogue

'If men were not blind,' wrote Luca Pietromarchi in his diary on 23 January 1943, 'history would not be so replete with the tragedies and catastrophes of individuals and peoples. Italy committed errors just as much as all other countries before and after its entry into the war. But while the other, richer, countries were able to remedy their errors, the Italians were crushed by theirs.' Thus the chief of the GABAP commented on the fall of Libya and then went on to describe the history of Italy's war as the history of the incompetence, muddle-headedness, inertia and cowardice of those in command. These deficiencies, Pietromarchi wrote, condemned the regime and determined its fate. Only with different men and a different 'spirit' could Italy have reversed its fortunes and begun its history anew. But this did not happen, and at the end of March 1943, when the Allies attacked the Axis troops in Tunisia, despite staunch resistance the Italo-German armies were forced to retreat northwards. A month later they were defending themselves against massive Allied forces at Tunis and Bizerte, and on 12 May they surrendered.

In early 1942, Mussolini began to rid himself of his less trustworthy and more moderate lieutenants. After blaming the defeats on the generals and on the 'human material' – in which he had had insufficient time to instil the warrior virtues which make a country great – he dismissed Galeazzo Ciano, Giuseppe Bottai, Dino Grandi, Marshal Ugo Cavallero, Guido Buffarini Guidi, the minister of corporations Renato Ricci, the head of MINCULPOP Alessandro Pavolini, the minister of finance Paolo Thaon di Ravel and the ministers of public works Giuseppe Gorla and of communications Giovanni Host Venturi. The secretary of the PNF, Aldo Vidussoni, was replaced by Carlo Scorza. Mussolini made all these changes with a view to stiffening the regime's resolve for when the moment of truth came. The operation was unsuccessful because, as Pietromarchi wrote on 13 March 1943:

The truth is that in a regime like ours everything is tied down and controlled, everyone is involved in a particular situation. Either everything is destroyed or everything is left unchanged. It is a monolith. A change in the domestic situation can come about in only four ways: by decision of the Duce, by act of the king, by popular revolt or by invasion. As matters now stand, any change signifies defeat. In a month's time decisive events will come to a head, and any initiative on our part, whoever may take it, will be too late.[1]

On 24 June, the Allies occupied Pantelleria, and on 9 July they landed in Sicily. The talks between Mussolini and Hitler at Klessheim failed to produce the outcome that Italy desired: the dispatch from Germany of armaments and especially of aircraft. In an atmosphere of intrigue and amid the regime's death throes, preparations were made to oust the Duce. On 16 July, a group of hierarchs asked Mussolini to clarify the situation and to convene the Grand Council. The appointment was fixed for 24 July. On the 19th of the month Mussolini and Hitler met for discussions in Feltre. After listening to a long monologue by the Führer, the Duce scarcely uttered a word, even though he had asked the Foreign Ministry to prepare an *aide-mémoire* for him (written by Francesco Babuscio Rizzo and Leonardo Vitetti) on Germany's responsibility for Italy's predicament. Having learned of the bombings in Italy, and aware of the plotting behind his back, Mussolini then hastened back to Rome. At two o'clock in the morning of 25 July 1943, with nineteen votes in favour, seven against and one abstention, the Grand Council approved the motion tabled by Dino Grandi. On that same evening, after Mussolini had spoken to Victor Emmanuel III, he was arrested and Pietro Badoglio was appointed prime minister.

What was going on in the occupied territories? There are very few archival documents relating to 1943. Most of the army logbooks stop at January or February 1943, and those of the prefectures in the annexed territories are non-existent. We do not know exactly how the armies in the occupied territories lived through the events of 25 July and the subsequent forty-five days of Badoglio's government. The three Italian armies were 'under the custody' of the ally, and Germany had a plan of action ready in the event of a change of allegiance by Italy. This was Operation Alaric, plans for which were drawn up in the second half of May 1943. The password *Achse* was to be used for the simultaneous launch of all the operation's phases, one of which, called Schwarz, was to be an attack against the Italian armed

[1] Pietromarchi, unpublished diary, 13 March 1943 (Fondazione Luigi Einaudi, Turin).

forces and their disarmament. The part of the plan relative to the occupied territories in the Balkans was given the name *Konstantin*. In Greece, two German divisions in Attica were ready to swing into action. The Second Army was trapped on the Adriatic coast and the Fourth Army could be overwhelmed and disarmed at any time. During the month of June, a large number of civil servants left the annexed provinces and the Ionian islands, and the few Italian businesses there were closed down. The staff of all public offices were greatly reduced, and between July and August civil powers were transferred to the army.

The documentation that I have consulted in Italy shows no evidence of diplomatic negotiations by Italian authorities on the spot with representatives of the Allies or members of the Resistance.[2] As soon as the conclusion of the armistice was announced on 8 September 1943, the Italian troops in the occupied countries were overtaken by events. Badoglio gave the Supreme Command no instructions on how it should deal with Germany's predictable reaction to the news of the armistice. Between 2 and 14 September 1943, the head of SMRE Mario Roatta issued memorandum '44 op' which contained only ambiguous instructions – and nothing at all that resembled operational orders – on how to counter an attack by the Germans. The entry in Pietromarchi's diary for 8 September 1943 is tragic and pathetic. Pietromarchi reports a conversation with General Gastone Gambara, the last commander of the Second Army, during which he ventured that the Italians should 'throw themselves at the Germans' and thus provoke the latter into initiating hostilities (although how this 'gettarsi contro i tedeschi', as Pietromarchi put it, would not itself have constituted a hostile act is difficult to see). Pietromarchi suggested to Gambara that he could lead an insurrection, reach agreements with Tito and Dragoljub Mihajlović, ensure control of the Dalmatian harbours and then assault isolated German forces. The general replied that the Italian forces were 'greatly depleted' and indeed did not even have a single anti-tank gun. The meeting concluded with laconic wishes of good luck.

For the Fourth Army, abandonment and disintegration followed in rapid succession. The armistice caught the commanders by surprise as they prepared to withdraw their troops from France to Piedmont and Liguria. For the Second, Eleventh and Ninth (Superalba) Armies, the tragedy unfolded more slowly. It was not easy for the soldiers to turn their weapons against Germans overnight; moreover, since 25 July they had been preparing for

[2] Bruno Arcidiacono, a specialist on the Second World War, informs me that he has found evidence of contacts between the Italian military authorities and the Allies in the Balkans in the archives of the Public Record Office in London.

peace, not for a sequel to the war – especially a sequel fought against the Germans. The fact that the Italian soldiers were in foreign lands, barricaded in their garrisons and besieged by a hostile population, gave them greater compactness – their lack of orders notwithstanding. Capitulation to the Germans came about in various ways. It was sometimes preceded by negotiations. But in some cases entire divisions allowed themselves to be disarmed by the Germans and were deported to Germany. Some Italian soldiers fled, individually or in groups; others joined the partisans to fight against the Third Reich. From 8 September onwards, the territories militarily occupied or annexed by Italy were taken over by the German army. All the occupied peoples now suffered even more grievously than they had under the Italians, as the Nazis wreaked revenge, persecution, privation and devastation.

The research set out in this book has followed the path pioneered by Enzo Collotti in that it also starts from the premise that Italian Fascism can only be thoroughly understood if its ambitions are compared against its actual accomplishments. It has also sought to meet Renzo De Felice's criticism concerning the lack of studies on the 'post-war order', the place in it which Fascist Italy should have occupied, and the strategy devised by Mussolini and the regime to affirm this 'vision'. The most important result, I believe, has been proof of the existence of a project for the territorial conquest of Mediterranean Europe (although it was far from being a systematic programme for the Fascist conquest of a European and Mediterranean empire) and confirmation that Italian Fascism was a political and cultural revolution that aimed at the destruction of the liberal regime and sought to build a state taking the unprecedented form of totalitarian organization of civil society and the political system. The historical goal of Fascism was territorial expansion and the conquest of *spazio vitale* in which the New Man could live and prosper.

It is my firm conviction that these ideas – however vague, unoriginal or patterned on the Nazi model, and however grotesque and overambitious – warrant serious study. They represented, in fact (and not just for Mussolini, but also for top-ranking soldiers and civil servants), the endeavour to achieve the Utopia and the Uchronia of the New Order, the ultimate goal of Fascist conquest. It is only by constructing *a posteriori* the ideal type of the *spazio vitale*, *ordine nuovo*, conquest and Fascist expansion that the historian can measure the distance and divergence between the reality of the occupations and that ideal type (defined as an objectively possible but entirely ideal concept, a set of elements connected together without contradictions).

The Fascist imperial project of which the occupations formed an integral part was not an entirely original phenomenon. It belonged to the tradition of Western empires; but it differed from these in its determination to merge and unify the populations subjugated. Fascism intended to establish a racial hierarchy of peoples which would continue *ad libitum*. No other peoples would be allowed to mix with the 'civilizing race', and 'civilization' would not lead to assimilation of the conquered into the race of the conquerors. The *piccolo spazio* was to be the exclusive preserve of the civilizing ethnic group, which would dominate the peoples that inhabited the *grande spazio*. The conceivers of Fascism's imperial project proclaimed a 'civilizing mission' (though in actual fact the notion was mere propaganda) which presupposed the existence of the Other and the survival of the dominated. It consequently resembled not so much the Nazi conception of empire as the European imperialism of the late nineteenth century and the Japanese imperialism of the twentieth. Moreover, it preserved features of Napoleonic hegemony (for example, the idea that a system of values and beliefs can be violently forced upon a community or society). In contrast to the European colonial empires, Fascism intended to impose on the white, Christian and European peoples what the British and French had imposed upon those of Africa and Asia.

Fascism's attempts at conquest and domination were a failure. Italian occupation was unable to achieve its goals, for the reality of occupation was very different from the regime's projects and ambitions, and almost nothing of the post-war new order was accomplished. Research has shown that Italy's political, military and economic subordination to Germany came about before the military occupations and annexations began. The territories that were to be occupied by Italy were conquered by Berlin. Armistices, geographical spheres of influence, borders and governments were established and controlled by the Nazis. From the spring of 1941 onwards, the conditions that were supposed to lead to the triumph of the new order were not in place. Although Hitler could have reduced Italy to a satellite of the Reich, he gave it the status of the junior partner in the Axis. The Italian diplomats, hierarchs and military commanders reacted by seeking to create margins of manoeuvre for themselves in the occupied territories. As far as they were able, the Italian decision-makers endeavoured to achieve ideological, political and economic dominance of the Mediterranean following Mussolini's 'imperial intuition'. They wanted to extend the imperial space by extending its frontiers as far as possible. Driven by the idea of the superiority of Fascist civilization and of the 'Italian race', they attempted to organize the space conceded by Berlin in accordance with the orders issued by Mussolini, the central pivot of the empire.

My examination of the political co-ordination, military control and administrative management of the conquered territories has shown the key role performed in it by Mussolini. The charismatic leader exercised his power through a neo-feudal system of government, apportioning power among his loyal lieutenants. The Fascist regime massively invested its best resources in all the conquered territories. It was not only Mussolini who believed that the 'great imperial design' could be fulfilled. The high officers of the Fascist state were convinced that they personified the bureaucracy of a great, modern and efficient power which brought development and prosperity to the occupied peoples. The power centres that decided occupation policies worked towards the Duce, and by and large they did so with probity, dedication and punctiliousness. The conflicts of competence among them testify to the vitality of the state organs and of a regime that was not resigned to defeat.

Although the Italians were not the 'race of conquerors' that Mussolini wanted, they were nevertheless capable of brutality and violence. The extremism of Italy's policy and propaganda often revealed the regime's weaknesses. The extent to which the Regio Esercito was Fascisticized cannot be compared to the Nazification of the Wehrmacht. And even though it has been amply demonstrated that the two armies inhabited different moral universes, Fascist ideology nevertheless figured large in official directives and attitudes and in the racism of Italy's occupation policies.

My analysis of the relations among the occupiers, the governments and the local authorities in Croatia, Greece and France has shown the extremely narrow margins of manoeuvre conceded to Italy by Germany in territories that were nominally Italian *spazio vitale*. In the case of Croatia, indeed, the Germans effectively ran the entire country and obstructed any action by the Italians. Italo-Croatian relations were severely compromised by the Dalmatian question and by Rome's policy to annul Croatian sovereignty in order to undermine German power and influence. Italy's exercise of civil powers over almost half the country did nothing to counter German economic and political dominance, and in fact its effect was to push Zagreb definitively on to Berlin's side. Italian policy in Greece was conditioned by occupation in condominium; and Rome was entirely unable to implement its own occupation policy. Finally, the relationship with the Vichy government was characterized by Italian claims which the French found entirely unacceptable and, whereas in Athens the Nazis 'associated' Rome in the exercise of power, they did not do so in France.

This study has for the first time drawn a parallel between events in the Balkan territories and those in the French metropolitan territories after November 1942. This is a point on which I must dwell briefly. Italian historiography has tended to analyse events in the Balkans and in France entirely separately, on the grounds that the situations were so different, and arose at such different times, that they cannot be considered within a single interpretative framework. I believe instead that the French occupation should not be studied in isolation: it was part of the same plan of Fascist conquest and part of the same project for the post-war new order; it was driven by the same aspirations and it was marked by the same failure.

The efforts by the Italian authorities in both the Balkans and France – before and after the occupation of November 1942 – resulted in practically nothing. Italy's determination to assert its prestige and authority was not enough to counterbalance German hegemony. Relations with the governments of the occupied countries swung almost schizophrenically between the intransigence of the impotent and the demands of a weak and uncertain 'tutor' unable to impose its will. Fascist ideology prevented Mussolini and his lieutenants abroad from implementing a policy which displayed any concrete differences between the Italians and the Germans. It was ideology that induced the Fascist regime to reject its status as underdog, with the tragic consequence that it continued to emulate the Reich by occupying vast territories with men, means and resources that could have been much better employed in defending the peninsula.

My analysis of the economic exploitation of the occupied territories has furnished further evidence on the paucity of the regime's accomplishments. It has shown that the project for the economic development of the countries belonging to the imperial community was a mirage. This was not an original plan but instead a recasting of the classic model of European capitalist imperialism clothed with the standard themes of Fascist propaganda. While from a political point of view the Italians were unable to distinguish themselves as the positive pole of the Axis, economic competition with the Germans induced them to adopt a policy of exploitation which, in the eyes of the occupied populations, made Rome no different from Berlin. During the period 1941–3, the Italians were just as much responsible for the tragic consequences of the occupations as were the Germans, and in their attempt to exploit the economic resources of the occupied territories they made no distinction between the Balkans and France.

The policy of the forced Italianization of the annexed territories went ahead despite difficulties due to local circumstances and the general context of the war. In the annexed territories the Fascists pursued – more radically and mainly motivated by racist dogma – the policies of ethnic repopulation (*Volkstumpolitik*) and denationalization imposed in the 1920s and 1930s on the German-speaking minority of Alto Adige in Italy, on the Croatian and Slovene minorities of Friuli and Venezia Giulia, and on the Jews.

That the general division of the *spazio vitale* into *piccolo* and *grande* was not implemented in the occupied territories alone is evidenced by the forced Albanianization of Kosovo and Debar. In the hypothetical new order that would ensue from victory, the European territories of the imperial community, ethnically homogeneous and subject to Rome's dominion, would, unlike under Nazism, continue to exist.

The chapter on collaboration has shown that the Italians made use of small and ineffectual groups of collaborationists. They decided not to exploit the centrifugal forces of political, ethnic or religious groups, even though this would have served the divide-and-rule strategy, because they did not want to tie their hands or risk having to deal with rival nationalisms. In all the occupied territories, as in the colonies, the occupation forces sought to obtain military collaboration only when the rebel movements began to threaten security and civil order. Italian and Nazi policies were no different in this regard. If Fascism had been powerful enough to dominate the occupied countries, it would have had no interest in groups willing to collaborate. Instead, given the competition with the Reich, the Italians wanted to give tangible proof of their prestige, authority and decision-making autonomy by underscoring their differences with respect to the Germans. Circumstances and Italy's weakness in the Axis partnership engendered the greater tactical flexibility and opportunism of the Italian forces compared to the Germans. The search for collaboration in Yugoslavia and Greece was not a policy alternative to the German line; rather, it was a practical expedient suggested by the need to compensate for a lack of military resources.

Similar considerations apply to repression. My analysis of the methods used against the partisan movements and civilian populations in the various occupation zones has shown that their violence and brutality resulted from the occupiers' substantial weakness and that they derived from the methods employed in the African colonies. Moreover, repressive measures by the Regio Esercito were no different in degree and kind from those used by the Wehrmacht: hostage-taking, the destruction and burning of entire villages, reprisals against the families even of simple suspects, the evacuation of broad inhabited zones, the deforestation of areas considered hospitable to partisan formations, the deportation of large groups of civilians, the seizure and slaughter of livestock. The only differences between these measures and those of the Germans were their frequency and intensity.

I have examined Italian occupation policy towards Jews in terms of relations with the Germans and with the other occupied countries. My analysis has shown that, like many other refugees, those Jewish fugitives who were able to reach the Italian zones were expelled or escorted to the border and handed over to their persecutors – and also that in certain circumstances they were delivered up to the Germans. I have argued that no attempt was made by Mussolini, his government, senior Italian civil servants or military commanders to conduct what certain historians have called a 'humanitarian rescue' of the Jews. It may be true that some soldiers and some officials did, on occasion, take such action, but their purpose was to help the persecuted in general, not Jews in particular.

The Italians avoided handing over some of the Jews in the occupied territories to their persecutors for reasons to do with the circumstances of the occupation, the need to maintain prestige and exert authority over the occupied peoples and governments, and the nature of Italo-German relations. The alleged humanitarianism of the Italian people had nothing to do with it. The differences with respect to behaviour by the Germans stemmed from the different levels of Fascisticization of the two armies and from the fact that the 'Jewish question' was not of crucial concern to the Italians. A further reason was the nature of Fascist anti-Semitism, whose aim was the 'civil death' and emigration of Jews, whether Italian or resident in the territories of the imperial community. This was different from Nazi 'redemptive anti-Semitism'.

To conclude: Italy's occupation policies relative to the Fascist project for territorial conquest of Mediterranean Europe cannot be ignored. Rather, they should be fully incorporated into the history of the Fascist regime, of Italy and of the Second World War. This study is intended to be a point of departure for further analysis of these matters. It has proposed a summary of the Italy's military occupations, an overview that is certainly not exhaustive and each of whose themes should be deepened. Michael Marrus has written that research on the Holocaust has concentrated on the 'how' rather than the 'why' and that studies on specific aspects predominate over syntheses.[3] Yet investigation of both is necessary if we are thoroughly to understand the phenomenon. It is therefore my hope that future research will investigate the 'hows', confirming or disproving the 'whys' proposed in this book.

[3] Marrus, 'Reflections on the Historiography of the Holocaust'.

Appendix

Table 1. *Outlines of projects for the political organization of the Fascist imperial community*

Type of community/nationality	Political regime/situation	Territory/geographical zone
	First Circle	
Nationalities different by language but not by religion, and of 'Italian race'	Participation in the leader-nation's power: assimilation following denationalization and fascistization; possibility of a special administrative order	Corsica, French Alpes-Maritimes, Savoy, Dalmatia, Slovenia, Ionian islands, Canton Ticino, Grisons
Territories with little demographic importance, geographically close to Italy	Limited independence or direct domination, with possible annexation to the empire; *status civitatis* on the Dodecanese pattern	Balearic islands, Crete, Sporades, Cyclades, Cyprus, Malta
	First/Second Circle	
Western European nationalities different by language, but of Catholic religion and of 'Latin race'		Spain, France
	Second Circle	
Nationalities different by language and religion but of 'Europoid race'	Controlled independence; possibility of becoming a constitutionally integral part of the leader-nation	Croatia, Serbia, Epirus, Pindus, Bosnia-Herzegovina, Albania, Montenegro
Balkan nationalities different by language, but of Orthodox Christian religion and of 'Slav and Hellenic race'	Special economic relationship, but with links to Rome varying according to degree of civilization	Bulgaria, Romania, Hungary, Greece

(*cont.*)

Table 1. (*cont.*)

Type of community/nationality	Political regime/situation	Territory/geographical zone
	Second/Third Circle	
Communities 'inferior' by race, language and religion, but with one nationality	Controlled independence or a colonial regime	Turkey, Egypt, Middle East
	Third Circle	
Communities 'inferior' by race, language and religion and those 'without nationality'[a]	A colonial regime or similar; political status: subjugation or limited citizenship	All African territories, with possible exceptions in North Africa

[a] Jews were included in this category. Sertoli Salis wrote: 'The Jewish Problem (of nationality, race, religion and language) must be solved by excluding Jews from the Mediterranean. If we want peace truly to reign in the post-war era, and hatred among peoples to cease, we must devise fair and humane solutions for the various problems. Because the Jews have proved themselves impossible to assimilate into other populations, they must learn to live on their own account. It is of little importance where their new homeland will be. What matters is that they must be distant from our Mediterranean' ('La condizione degli ebrei nella comunità imperiale', 1942).

Table 2. *The population of Yugoslavia after partition by the Axis powers*

Territory	Population as of 31 July 1941
Annexed to Italy	
Ljubljana	336,279
Carnaro (Fiume)	81,711
Dalmatia	393,000
	810,990
Other annexed territories	
Annexed to Albania	754,000
Annexed to Germany (Slovenia)	727,000
Annexed to Hungary	1,208,500
Annexed to Bulgaria (Macedonia)	1,299,000
Other territories	
Montenegro	411,000
Croatia	6,193,000
Serbia	3,823,000
Banat	596,500
Total	15,822,990

Source: ASMAE, GABAP, b. 35. Figures are projected on the basis of the 1931 Yugoslav census.

Table 3. *Distribution of the population by religion in the western part of the Kingdom of Yugoslavia (1931 census data)*

Historical regions	Total pop.	Catholic pop.	%	Orthodox Christian pop.	%	Muslim pop.	%
Croatia proper	2,532,822	1,945,928	76.8	583,166	23.0	3,728	0.15
Srijem	218,989	63,228	28.9	155,392	71.0	369	0.17
Dalmatia	297,274	250,339	84.2	46,522	15.6	413	0.14
Bosnia	1,824,585	376,712	20.6	867,344	47.5	580,529	31.8
Herzegovina	400,704	160,695	40.1	124,471	31.1	115,538	28.8
Total	5,274,374	2,796,902	53.0	1,776,895	33.7	700,577	13.3

Note: Jews are not included in these population figures.

Table 4. *Municipalities transferred to the provinces of Zadar, Split and Kotor, official names*

Italian names	Native-language names
Zadar	
Bencovazzo	Benkovac
Bosava	Bozava
Chistagne	Kistanje
Eso Grande	Iz Veliki
Nona	Nin
Novegradi	Novigrad
Obbrovazzo	Obrovac
Oltre	Sale
Scardona	Skradin
Sebenico	Šibenik
Selve	Silba
Stancovazzo	Stankovici
Stretto	Tijesho
Timeto	Smilčić
Vodizze	Vodice
Zaravecchia	Biograd
Zemonico	Zemunik
Zlarino	Zlarin
Split	
Blatta di Curzola	Blato
Castella Inferiore	Donji Kaštel
Castel S. Giorgio	Kastel Sucurac

(*cont.*)

Table 4. (*cont.*)

Italian names	Native-language names
Castel Vitturi	Kastel Lukšić
Comisa	Komisa
Curzola	Korcula
Lissa	Vis
Melada	Melada
Solta	Solta
Spalato	Split
Traù	Trogir
Vallegrande	Velaluka
Kotor	
Cartolle	Krtole
Castelnuovo di C.	Hervegnovi
Cattaro	Kotor
Dobroto	Dobrota
Gruda	Gruda
Lastua Inferiore	Donje Lastovo
Lustizza	Lustiza
Mulla	Muć
Perasto	Perast
Perzagno	Prcanj
Risano	Risan
Stolivo Inferiore	Donji Stoliv
Sutorina	Sutorina
Teodo	Tivat
Zuppa	Grbali

Source: ASMAE, GABAP, b. 47.

Table 5. *Districts and municipalities annexed to the province of Carnaro*

Districts/ Municipalities	Population, July 1941 census
Cabar	*12,331*
Cabar	3,040
Draga (includes Trava)[a]	1,309
Gerovo	2,540
Osilnica	1,255
Plesce	960
Prezid	1,610
Crni Lug	1,617
Castua	*9,600*
Veglia	*19,442*
Ponte (Aleksandrovo)	2,844
Bescanuova	3,086
Dobrigno	3,618

(*cont.*)

Table 5. (*cont.*)

Districts/ Municipalities	Population, July 1941 census
Dubasnizza	2,861
Castelmuschio	1,923
Veglia	2,440
Vebrenico	2,670
Arbe	*6,998*
Sušak	*33,340*
Cerni Calve	2,143
Sušak	17,915
Buccari	2,069
Krassica	3,685
Grobnico	2,991
Jelenie	4,537
Total	81,711

Source: USSME, M 3, B. 54.
[a]The border with Fiume entirely ignored the Slovene ethnic group. Around 3,000 Slovenes consequently became citizens of the province of Carnaro.

Table 6. *Projection on data from the 1931 Yugoslav census*

	1931 Yugoslav census data	Projection for 1940
Zadar	180,000	211,900
Split	109,000	128,400
Kotor	33,800	39,800

Source: ASMAE, GABAP, b. 25.

Table 7. *Population of the province of Ljubljana on annexation*

District	Municipalities before the occupation	Municipalities annexed	Detached	Municipalities occupied	Inhabitants
Ljubljana (town)	1	–	–	1	91,612
Logatec	12	1	6	11	24,710
Ljubljana (district)	28	6	9	28	68,707
Novo Mesto	22	–	–	31	81,389
Kočevje	13	–	–	13	40,074
Črnomelj	11			11	29,787
Total	87	7	15	95	336,279

Source: Ferenc, *La provincia 'italiana' di Lubiana*, p. 35.

Table 8. *Military occupation of metropolitan France (Plan A)*

Governorate	Capital	Number of *communes*	Population
Alpes-Maritimes	Nice	151	514,000
Basses-Alpes	Digne	245	90,000
Bouches-du-Rhône	Marseilles	117	1,225,000
Drôme	Valence	378	268,000
Haute-Savoie	Annecy	315	260,000
Hautes-Alpes	Gap	184	89,000
Isère	Grenoble	566	573,000
Savoie	Chambéry	330	239,000
Var	Draguignan	151	399,000
Vaucluse	Avignon	151	246,000
Corse	Ajaccio	365	323,000
Monaco (high commissioner)	Monaco	1	23,000

Table 9. *Staffing requirements for the offices of each French governorate (Plan A)*

Governorate	Interior Ministry	Foreign Ministry	Ministry of Corporations	MINCULPOP	Total
Nice	17	3	2	2	24
Ajaccio	17	2	2	2	23
Digne	10	2	1	1	14
Marseilles	17	3	2	2	24
Valence	10	2	1	1	14
Annecy	10	2	1	1	14
Gap	10	2	1	1	14
Grenoble	10	2	1	1	14
Chambéry	10	2	1	1	14
Avignon	10	2	1	1	14
Draguignan	10	2	1	1	14
Total	131	24	14	14	183

Table 10. *Staffing requirements for the civil administration in the occupied French territories (Plan A)*

	Governor general's cabinet	Civil superintendency	Governor's civil offices	Civil commissions	Extraordinary Commission	High Commission Monaco	Total
Interior	4	67	136	88	30	3	328
Foreign		15	24			1	40
Justice		12					12
Finance		49					49
War		11					11
Exchange/Currency		8					8
Education		30					30
Public Works		15					15
Agriculture/Forestry		20					20
Communications		36					36
Corporations		13	14				27
MINCULPOP		4	14				18
Total	4	280	188	88	30	4	594

Table 11. *Geographical extent and population of Italian militarily occupied territories in Croatia*

Zone I (annexed: *zona annessa*)	7491 km^2	474,700
Zone II (militarily occupied)	24,300 km^2	970,000
Zone III (militarily occupied)	18,000 km^2	825,000
Total for zones II and III	42,300 km^2	1,795,000

Source: ASMAE, GABAP, b. 35, signed by Roberto Ducci, 17 January 1942.

Table 12. *Districts of Montenegro with significant percentages of Muslim inhabitants according to the census of 1931*

Districts	Population	Muslims
Andrievica	27,221	7,403
Antivari	32,926	13,796
Berane	6,940	6,403
Bijelo Polje	32,907	12,765
Pljevica	33,196	9,197
Podgorica	16,070	6,011
Prjepolje	42,904	4,324
Sjenica	23,606	10,927
Suvi Do	28,292	16,265
Other districts of Montenegro	6,790	6,319
Total Montenegro	383,998	95,686

Source: ASMAE, GABAP, b. 25. Tables 13–16 are based on a study by Colonel Bonfatti.
Note: The total includes population in districts where no Muslims lived.

Table 13. *Districts of Bosnia annexed by Croatia with significant percentages of Muslim inhabitants according to the census of 1931*

District	Population	Muslims
Bihać	39,139	13,962
Bosanska Krupa	46,936	15,087
Bugojno	42,894	11,769
Brčko	97,962	20,443
Čajniče	30,123	21,046
Cazin	47,280	35,313
Doboj	23,919	13,171
Foča	39,110	22,672

(*cont.*)

Table 13. (*cont.*)

District	Population	Muslims
Fojnica	25,125	8,587
Gračanica	55,727	32,265
Gradačać	50,663	14,521
Jajce	48,461	14,205
Kladanj	14,558	8,616
Ključ	37,259	10,901
Prijedor	54,869	16,113
Prozor	14,706	5,067
Rogatica	44,120	22,219
Sanski Most	46,664	11,652
Sarajevo	135,142	50,720
Srebrenica	35,142	17,332
Travnik	44,972	18,512
Tuzla	99,046	58,776
Visoko	54,670	26,253
Vlasenica	37,445	11,881
Zenica	35,413	20,207
Žepče	30,855	13,815
Zvornik	46,966	22,025
Other districts of Bosnia	614,582	38,567
Total	1,893,806	624,247

Source: See table 12.

Table 14. *Districts of Herzegovina annexed by Croatia with significant percentages of Muslim inhabitants according to the census of 1931*

Districts	Population	Muslims
Gacko	15,233	5,724
Konjic	32,167	16,693
Mostar	82,999	17,400
Nevesinje	25,283	5,917
Stolace	41,149	10,632
Trebinje	23,546	5,539
Other districts of Herzegovina	111,106	9,915
Total Herzegovina	331,483	71,820
Total Bosnia	1,893,806	624,247
Remaining districts of Croatia	3,049,085	4,510
Total Croatia	5,274,374	700,577

Table 15. *Districts of the former Yugoslavia (Vardarska Banovina – Yugoslav Macedonia and Zetska Banovina – Montenegro) assigned to Albania*

Banovina and districts	Population	Muslims
Zetska Banovina		
Ex Berano	24,023	5,911
Djakovica	45,378	32,810
Drenica (Serbica)	25,811	21,517
Peć	44,688	29,320
Podrima	36,191	31,597
Tutin	16,602	13,880
Vardarska Banovina		
Donji Polog (Tetovo)	70,983	46,543
Galičnik	12,051	5,532
Gnjilane	91,037	51,051
Gora (Dragas)	14,127	13,877
Gornij Polog (Gostivar)	32,666	26,635
Jablanica (Debar)	57,858	32,411
Kičevo	32,101	15,853
Nerodimije	38,383	24,894
Podgora	16,220	13,558
Gračanica (Priština)	57,858	32,411
Sar Planina (Prizren)	46,154	32,429
Struga	28,055	12,395
Total in new Albanian provinces	690,186	442,624
Total in new Albanian provinces as estimated in July 1941	750,000	440,000
Total in old Albanian provinces as estimated in July 1941	1,100,00	750,000
Overall total in Albania as estimated in July 1941	1,850,000	1,190,000

Table 16. *Muslim populations within 'Rome's Balkan Orbit'*

Bosnia	624,247
Herzegovina	71,820
Montenegro	95,686
Albania (old provinces)	750,000
Albania (new provinces)	440,000
Serbia	95,763
Bulgaria	148,514
Ciamuria	25,000
Total	2,251,030

Source: ASMAE, Affari Politici – Italia b. 92, *Relazioni*.

Table 17. *Executive officers at the Ministry of Foreign Affairs concerned with policies regarding the occupied territories*

June–October 1940

F. Anfuso, plenipotentiary minister first class, head of the Minister's Cabinet
B. Buti, director general, European and Mediterranean Affairs General Directorate
L. Vitetti, director general, General Affairs Directorate
L. Vidau, vice-director general, General Affairs Directorate, Head of Office IV – Confidential Affairs
A. Giannini, director general, Commercial Affairs General Directorate
Z. Benini, under-secretary of state for Albanian affairs
F. Mameli, plenipotentiary minister in Belgrade
L. Bonfatti, Colonel, military attaché in Belgrade
P. Ghigi, plenipotentiary minister in Bucharest
M. Scammacca, head of Office, Under-Secretariat of State for Albanian Affairs

Armistice–Peace Office

L. Pietromarchi, plenipotentiary minister first class, head of office
Secretaries: R. Giustiniani, L. Theodoli, G. Ciraolo, G. Ghenzi, M. Profili

August 1941 main changes

The Under-Secretariat for Albanian Affairs was replaced on 3 August 1941 by an Albania Office directly dependent on the Minister's Cabinet.

April 1942

B. Lanza d'Ajeta, head of the Minister's Cabinet
L. Pietromarchi, extraordinary envoy for the Minister's Cabinet, director general for affairs concerning Greece, Montenegro, Dalmatia, Slovenia, Croatia, the armistice and borders
Secretaries: C. Baldoni, G. Fornari, G. De Bosdari, M. Pletti, G. G. Cittadini Cesi, L. Theodoli, G. Ciraolo, G. Ghenzi, G. Profili, A. Russo, R. Ducci, M. Basso, G. P. De Ferrari, R. Bagli, C. Guazzaroni

February–25 July 1943

B. Mussolini, minister secretary of state
G. Bastianini, under-secretary of state
F. Babuscio Rizzo, head of the Minister's Cabinet
A. Berio, vice-director of the Armistice–Peace Cabinet

Table 18. *CIAF executive officers as of 25 July 1941*

President	Gen. Vacca Maggiolini
Army	Vecchiarelli
Administration of occupied territories	Vittorelli
Fabbriguerra	Vaglieco
Commercial Commission	Pigozzi
Sub-Commission for General Affairs	Liberati, Gelich
Mixed Delegation Corsica	Admiral Vannutelli

(*cont.*)

Table 18. (*cont.*)

Administration in the occupied territories:			
Menton	Magris, Frediani, Berri	Mont-Genèvre	Saporiti
Fontano	Castaldi	Isola	Giovenco
Lanslebourg	Zanetti	Ristolaz	Patrone
Bessans	Pertossi	Séez	Perna
Bramans	Giuà, Botto		

Source: ACS, fondo Ministero dell' Interno – A S G, b. 400.

Table 19. *CIAF sub-commissions as of 15 October 1941*

Army Sub-Commission
1 Alpine exchequer control delegation (Nice)
2 regional delegations (Marseilles, Valence)
5 control sections (Nice, Marseilles, Gap, Valence, Annecy)

Navy Sub-Commission
1 navy delegation (Toulon)
1 Italo-German delegation for the control of maritime traffic (Marseilles)
3 control sections (Marseilles, Toulon, Nice)
2 control units (Sète, Port Vendres)

Air Force Sub-Commission
1 air force control delegation Provence (Marseilles)
1 control section (Marignane)
1 flight assistance section (Lyons)
1 CTA liaison unit (Aix en Provence)

Armaments Sub-Commission
1 War Industry Control delegation (CIB) (Grenoble)
1 liquid fuels control delegation (Marseilles)
2 CIB sections (Lyons, Avignon)
3 units at German CIB (Toulouse, Clermont-Ferrand, Bourges)

General Affairs Sub-Commission
1 control body art. XXI (Lyons)
Repatriation and Assistance Delegations

Economic and Financial Affairs Sub-Commission (SCAEF)
1 ship and cargo recovery delegation (Marseilles)

Legal Affairs Sub-commission (Turin)

Trade Sub-commission
Commercial Commissariat for France (Paris)

Mixed control delegation Corsica (Ajaccio)
2 maritime traffic control sections (Ajaccio, Bastia)

Italian delegation at CTA (Wiesbaden)
General Delegation in Algiers and a *mixed delegation in Djibouti* consisting of various sub-delegations and control sections

Table 20. *Staff at the Civil Commission for Dalmatia*

PNF	Gianfelice
Interior	Benussi (Fiuman)
Agriculture and Forestry	Petronio (Istrian) and Lt. Col. Falconieri
Education	Ciubelli (Dalmatian)
MINCULPOP	Randi (Dalmatian)
Justice	Radnich (Dalmatian)
Finance	Raffone – administration; Pagano – customs; Bruscolini – taxes and duties; Caretti – accountancy; GdF Lt. Col. Simoni; Vitali – monopolies; Gualtieri – postal services
Communications	Giuliano
Public Works	Trifogli

Source: Nardi, 'I sessanta giorni del Commissariato civile della Dalmazia', 1941.

Table 21. *CIAF Sub-Commission for the Administration of the Occupied Territories, 31 January 1941*

Central Administration Office: 1 Prefect and 4 functionaries
Consul first class
Cabinet Office and Special Secretariat
Military Office
Justice Office
Notarial Office
Accounts Office
Finance Office
Health Services Inspectorate

Table 22. *Administrative structure of the commission in Menton*

Civil commissioner, supervised by a MAE consul
Vice-commissioner, supervised by a prefecture councillor
Municipal Affairs Office
Accounts Office
Welfare Office, headed by a functionary from the PNF Welfare Office
Agriculture Office
Culture and Propaganda Office, headed by the director of the Istituto di Studi Liguri di Bordighera
Secretariat and sundry offices

Table 23. *Army forces 1941–1943*

Non-commissioned officers	Italy	North Africa	Other theatres	CC.RR.	Recruits	Total troops	Officers
Oct 1941	1,474,932	117,957	539,867	117,079	301,341	2,551,176	113,500
Oct 1942	1,741,500	141,681	723,084	135,455	425,635	3,167,755	136,004
Oct 1943	1,924,055	121,684	797,178	143,194	546,161	3,532,272	146,251

Source: Taken from Rochat, 'Gli uomini alle armi', pp. 54ff.

Table 24. *CC.RR. abroad: non-commissioned officers and other ranks 1941–1943*

	NCOs	Other ranks	Total
1 October 1941	3,110	18,759	21,869
1 October 1942	4,167	26,009	30,176
1 October 1943	4,914	29,901	34,815

Battalion	Location	Officers	NCOs	Other ranks
XII	Sušak	13	110	630
XIV	Ljubljana	19	213	1,155
IX	Split	15	103	935
XV	Zadar	17	79	663
XVI	Šibenik	10	52	420
XXII	Zadar	6	61	437
Total		80	618	4,240

Source: USSME, M 7, b. 411, 'Comando della II Armata, Ufficio Ordinamento, 1° luglio 1943, btg. CC.RR.'

Table 25. *Example of the composition of an army corps: the 26th CdA*

Components	Units	SPE Officers	Officers	NCOs	Other ranks
Forces	CdA troops/services	44	209	274	4,004
	Modena Division	45	307	428	8,514
	Casale Division	41	356	435	7,277
Blackshirts	CdA troops/services				
	Modena Division				
	Casale Division	12	42	71	982
CC.RR.	CdA troops/services	1		14	101
	Modena Division	4	10	94	746
	Casale Division	2	9	49	387
RGF	Eighth Battalion	15	4	59	552
	Total	164	937	1,424	22,563

Source: USSME, N 1–11, 'Diari storici', b. 376, 'Comando XXVI CdA, Situazione complessiva delle unità dipendenti alla data del 1° ottobre 1942'; Rochat, 'Gli uomini alle armi', p. 64.

Table 26. *Composition of an Italian infantry division*

Components	Officers	NCOs	Other ranks	Horses and mules	Vehicles	Armoured vehicles
General Staff HQ	22	26	245	3	17	10
Infantry	11	11	105	381	4	6
Command	89	138	2,541	418	8	5
63rd	87	118	2,480	399	18	4
64th	110	124	2,959	52	14	5
363rd Regiment	14	13	300	56	18	1
Mortar Battalion	5	9	172	1,002	8	
59th Cannon Corps	71	122	2,064	72	14	5
Artillery	9	20	493	40	6	13
Sappers	29	18	429		4	
Health Service Commissary	6	6	144	87		
Transport	4	6	131	15	28	7
Reinforcements	55		1,129		75	7
Total Regio Esercito	512	611	13,192	2,525	214	63
CC.RR.	2	15	99		5	4
CC.NN. cyclists	9	23	236		7	13
GdF battalion	7	36	314		5	6

Source: USSME, N 1–11 'Diari storici', b. 1182, 'Commando Divisione Fanteria Cagliari, Sezione Personale e Segretaria, Situazione della forza presente il 20 marzo 1943'.

Table 27. *High Command, Second Army – Supersloda (11 October 1942)*

	Officers	NCOs
Command, troops and army services	1,724	24,851
6th CdA		
CdA command, troops and services	430	7,920
Messina Division	430	10,662
Marche Division	470	11,351
Murge Division	445	9,218
Emilia Division	410	9,517
Fourteenth Battalion Finance	16	691
Division	*2,201*	*49,359*
Total		
18th CdA		
CdA command, troops and services	821	13,298
Sassari Division	452	9,697
Bergamo Division	409	9,655
Zara Division	260	4,296
Fourth Battalion Finance	11	491
Total	*1,953*	*37,437*
5th CdA		
CdA command, troops and services	916	19,495
Granatieri Division	441	9,874
Re Division	464	11,624
Lombardia Division	441	10,505
1st Celere Division	232	5,132
5th GaF Unit	269	6,827
Total	*2,763*	*63,457*
11th CdA		
CdA command, troops and services	214	4,249
Isonzo Division	555	12,377
Macerata Division	343	7,619
Cacciatori Division	531	13,305
CC.NN. Unit	307	7,689
GaF Unit	203	4,194
Total	*2,153*	*49,433*
Total	10,794	224,537
On leave	1,203	21,757

Table 28. *Deployment of the Second Army's four CdAs*

11th	Province of Ljubljana Ensure the functioning of the Zolog–Postumia and Retlika–Novo Mesto–Ljubljana railway lines
5th	Province of Carnaro, Croatian zones under its jurisdiction, the town of Karlovac Ensure the functioning of the Karlovac–Ogulin-Sušak and Sušak–Gospić railway lines
18th	Zadar and Split, Šibenik, Croatian zones under its jurisdiction, Knin, Perković
6th	Kotor, Croatian zones under its jurisdiction, Tarčin, Mostar, Dubrovnik (Ragusa), Metković

Table 29. *Commanders of the Second Army 1941–1943*

April 1941–January 1942	General Vittorio Ambrosio
January 1942–January 1943	General Mario Roatta
January 1943–September 1943	General Mario Robotti

Table 30. *Numbers of officers and troops in Montenegro, 14th CdA (11 October 1942)*

	Officers	NCOs and other ranks
CdA command, troops and services	492	10,426
Ferrara Division	384	12,145
Venezia Division	592	15,847
Perugia Division	407	9,938
Taurinense Division	547	15,245
Alpi Graie Division	352	10,600
Total	2,774	74,201
On leave	497	7,526

Table 31. *Deployment of the 14th CdA divisions in Montenegro*

Taro (General Pedrazzoli), then Perugia (General Pentimalli), August 1942	Northern zone of the country, Čekanje and Antivari zone in the south
Venezia (General Bonini)	Eastern zone, HQ at Berane
Pusteria (General Esposito), then Taurinense (General Vivalda), August 1942	Southern zone, HQ at Pljevlja, garrisons at Nova Varos, Priboj border at Foča, Goražde and Višegrad[a]
Messina (General Tucci), then Emilia (General Romano), February 1942, Ferrara (General Zani), May 1943	Zone of Kotor, HQ at Castelnuovo, assigned to Supersloda but under the operational control of Gen. Pirzio Biroli
Cacciatori delle Alpi	Transferred to Croatia after summer 1941
Alpi Graie (General Girotti) March–November 1942	North-west, between Danilovgrad, Nikšić and Savnik

[a]ASMAE, GABAP, b. 26, 'Francesco Mameli al GABAP, telegramma in arrivo per corriere 7460 R, 21 novembre 1942'. The military attaché in Belgrade received a message from the CS accepting the OKW's proposal that German troops take over Italy's occupation of Višegrad and its district. If the governor considered it necessary, he could maintain a transitional command in the area. The troops were evacuated in mid-December 1942.

Table 32. *Ninth Army – Superalba High Command (11 October 1942)*

	Officials	NCOs and other ranks
Command, troops and army services	1,041	19,735
4th CdA		
CdA command, troops and services	339	7,192
Puglie Division	471	11,731
Firenze Division	444	11,014
Total	*1,254*	*29,937*
25th CdA		
CdA Command, troops and services	107	1,846
Acqui Division	632	13,992
Parma Division	425	12,253
Arezzo Division	473	12,404
Monferrato Cavalry Unit	33	790
Total	*1,670*	*41,285*
Territorial defence Albania	237	3,810
Carabinieri Albania	210	7,978
Border Guards	332	6,969
Finance Guards	73	2,566
Various	35	965
Total	4,852	113,245
On leave	554	8,307

Table 33. *Eleventh Army – Supergrecia High Command (11 October 1942)*

	Officers	NCOs and other ranks
Command, troops and army services	1,078	15,266
3rd CdA		
CdA command, troops and services	412	7,406
Brennero Division	412	8,198
Forlì Division	824	20,215
Pinerolo Division	559	15,565
Total	*2,207*	*51,384*
8th CdA		
CdA command, troops and services	469	10,431
Piemonte Division	478	11,731
Cagliari Division	541	13,565
Total	*1,488*	*35,727*
26th CdA		
CdA command, troops and services	304	6,342
Casale Division	430	9,471
Modena Division	394	10,015
Total	*1,128*	*25,828*
Piazza di Atene Command	106	1,690
Total	6,007	129,895
On leave	566	8,251

Table 34. *Fourth Army High Command (1 November 1942)*

Sections	Officers	NCOs and other ranks
Army HQ	87	641
Intendance	598	9,260
Artillery	72	1,267
Sappers	60	1,330
Tenth Batt., Army CC.RR.	12	457
Total command	*829*	*12,955*
	1st CdA	
CdA troops and services	483	9,380
Rovigo Artillery Division	264	4,933
Mantova Artillery Division	272	4,927
Pusteria Alpini Division	398	9,602
GaF	664	12,322
1st Alpini Valle Unit	149	3,926
Total	*2,230*	*45,090*
	15th CdA	
CdA troops and services	267	4,091
Legnano Infantry Division	320	6,825
Lupi di Toscana Infantry Division	312	7,639
Piave Motorized Division	440	6,464
GaF and reinforcements	476	10,051
Coastal defence units	450	11,153
Total	*2,265*	*46,223*
	22nd CdA	
CdA troops and services	411	6,606
Taro Infantry Division	347	9,413
Piacenza Artillery Division	260	4,728
Centauro Armoured Division	237	4,417
EFTF Armoured Division	305	5,419
GaF	393	8,118
Total	*1,953*	*38,701*
Total Army Command	7,277	142,969

Source: USSME, N 1–11, 'Diari storici', b. 1099. A German report of spring 1943 stated: 'The Fourth Army has no planes, no naval protection, no heavy artillery, no anti-aircraft guns. In addition, they are short of cement and iron in order to carry out coastal fortification' (Steinberg, *All or Nothing*, p. 109).

Table 35. *Deployment of the divisions in France*

CdA	Divisions	Deployment	Detachments (1 battalion)
1st CdA	Pusteria	Grenoble	Gap, Valence, Montélimar
	Valle	Chambéry	Albertville, Annecy
	20th Ski Unit	Briançon	
15th CdA	Legnano	Nice	One regiment in Grasse
	EFTF	Draguignan	
22nd CdA	Lupi di Toscana	Marseilles	
	Taro	Toulon	
Army Reserve	Piave	Brignoles	Aix

Table 36. *Cases of malaria in Greece*

Large units	Benign tertian, quartan malaria	Malignant tertian and pernicious malaria with fatal outcome	Relapse malaria	Total
Army units	111	12	11	134
3rd CdA				
Non-enlisted	41	3	6	50
Brennero	161	20	17	198
Forlì	119	2	6	127
Pinerolo	137	7	1	145
8th CdA				
Non-enlisted	45	13		58
Julia	15	1		16
Piemonte	243	137		380
Siena	28	8		36
Cagliari	35	18		53
26th CdA				
Non-enlisted	62	5	10	77
Casale	360	33	24	417
Acqui	360	17	7	384
Modena	270	7	6	283
Total	1,987	283	88	2,358

Source: USSME, N 1–11, 'Diari storici', b. 631, 'Intendenza Com. sup. FF.AA. Grecia, 3 ottobre 1941'.

Table 37. *6th CdA Military Health Service: pathologies recorded September–December 1942*

Disease	September	October	November	December
Scabies	71	94	142	125
Gonorrhoea	24	23	25	17
Syphilis	7	6	9	9
Chancroids	1	3	3	11
Parotitis	3	4	6	9
Abdominal typhoid	21	22	30	16
Paratyphoid	11	10	12	8
Trachoma	1	1	–	–
Malaria	181	301	88	13
Relapse malaria	80	47	10	–
Total	400	511	325	208

Source: USSME, N 1–11, 'Diari storici', b. 1269.
This table shows totals of daily figures.

Table 38. *Italy's share of Balkan trade prior to 1940*

	Exports				Imports			
	Value in millions of dinars		% share		Value in millions of dinars		% share	
	June 1939	January 1940	June 1939	January 1940	June 1939	January 1940	June 1939	January 1940
Germany	649,800	1,245,100	26.92	32.85	1,114,500	1,409,900	44.09	45.64
Italy	240,800	539,400	9.98	14.02	297,000	438,700	11.75	14.20

Table 39. *Yugoslav trade with Germany, Great Britain, Italy and the USA, 1939–1940*

	Imports		Exports	
	Value in millions of drachmas		Value in millions of drachmas	
	June 1939	January 1940	June 1939	January 1940
Germany	2,234	1,700	1,594	2,456
Great Britain	794	1,112	285	256
Italy	357	516	258	468
USA	473	724	565	1,186

Source: Giordano, 'Il commercio estero della Jugoslavia e della Grecia', 1940.

Table 40. *Italian imports/exports in south-east Europe*

	Imports from south-east Europe (%)			Exports from Italy to south-east Europe (%)		
	1936	Jan. 1938	July 1939	1936	Jan. 1938	July 1939
Bulgaria	0.5	1.0	0.3	0.1	0.7	0.9
Greece	0.1	0.8	0.7	0.2	1.0	1.1
Yugoslavia	1.1	1.3	2.0	0.8	2.1	2.6
Romania	3.7	2.1	3.9	0.4	1.2	2.7
Hungary	3.6	1.7	3.9	2.1	1.3	1.8
Turkey	0.9	2.2	1.7	0.5	0.6	1.7
Total	9.9	9.1	12.5	4.1	6.9	10.7

Source: Giordano, 'Le possibilità di sviluppare le esportazioni dell'industria meccanica italiana', 1941; Anon., 'Le relazioni economiche tra l'Italia e l'Ungheria', 1942.

Table 41. *Occupation costs paid in drachmas by the Bank of Greece (April 1941–October 1942)*

	Paid to Germany	Paid to Italy	Total in drachmas
July–December 1941	9,544,105,000	7,490,000,000	17,034,105,000
January–June 1942	48,346,000,000	10,780,000,000	59,126,000,000
September 1942	13,650,000,000	4,750,000,000	18,400,000,000
October 1942	20,246,209,403	9,000,000,000	29,246,209,403
Total	91,786,314,403	32,020,000,000	123,806,314,403

Source: Adapted from Ekmektsoglou-Koehn, 'Axis Exploitation in Wartime Greece', p. 479.

Table 42. *Goods and raw materials confiscated or purchased by the Germans in Greece (May–September 1941)*

Nickel	Tonnes 35,000
Chrome	20,000
Iron pyrites	70,000
Iron	175,000
Bauxite	100,000
Magnesite	40,000
Cotton	5,200
Jute	500
Leather	1,100 (1,750,000 pieces)
Silkworms	305
Chemical products	12,000
Drugs	7,135
Copper, zinc and lead	412
Olive oil	10,500
Grapes (including currants)	40,000
Tobacco	80,000
Total value in RM	45,700,000

Source: Etmektsoglou-Koehn, 'Axis Exploitation of Wartime Greece', p. 281.
Note: Quantities requisitioned by the Wehrmacht for troops in Greece are not included.

Table 43. *Increases in output by mines managed by the Regio Esercito (January–April 1942)*

Number of	January 1942	April 1942
Lignite mines	0	20
Average output in tonnes	250	1,000
Average consignment to railways (tonnes/day)	30	200
Average consignment to power stations (tonnes/day)	70	275
Average consignment to the army, gas works, hospitals, factories (tonnes/day)	10	90
Average output by the AthensPireo power station (kW/day)	200,000	350,000
Freighters operated by the DMIFG (number/tonnes)	0/0	3,700–3,900
Rail links constructed to mines (kilometres)	0	3
Rail links to mines under construction	0	8
Daily extra rations issued by the Army Intendance to miners (tonnes)	0	8,237

Table 44. 'Pertinenti' *registered at the Italian Consulate in Zagreb*

Province	Men	Women	Children	Aryans	Jews	Total	Of which, Italian speakers	Of which, illiterate
Albania	98	64	103	265		265	1	34
Dalmatia	71	43	14	128		128	8	
Montenegro	463	305	275	1,043	11	1,054	341	30
Carnaro	243	182	133	558	5	563	195	1
Ljubljana	349	433	214	996	8	1.004	154	
Total					24	3,014	699	

Source: ACS, MI, A 5 G, b. 415 'consolato d'Italia a Zagabria al MAE e p.c.c. al Ministero dell'Interno – DGPS, telespresso 2681/311', 3 March 1942.

Table 45. 'Pertinenti' *registered at the Italian Consulate in Sarajevo (April 1942)*

	Men	Women	Children	Aryans (excluding children)	Italian speakers (excluding children)	Total (excluding children)
Dalmatia	101	106	66	207	29	207
Carnaro	8	7	5	15	3	15
Ljubljana	14	10	7	24	1	24
Total						246

Source: ACS, MI, A 5 G, b. 415, 'GABAP – Ufficio Dalmazia, Registrazione dei pertinenti della città di Sarajevo', 30 April 1942.

Table 46. *'Current situation of former Yugoslavian personnel in the province of Ljubljana and in the provinces of the Governorate of Dalmatia'*

Province	Type of personnel	Number	Armed?	Uniform	Authority
Ljubljana	PS officials	–	–	–	Not included are persons awaiting retirement and those not *pertinenti* to the province[a]
	PS agents	233	no	old uniform	
	Gendarmes	190	no	old uniform	
	Financial police	187	no	old uniform	
Zadar	PS officials	–	–	–	
	PS agents	–	–	–	
	Gendarmes	38	musket	grey–green[b]	CC.RR. Zara. Mob. Batt
	Financial police	9	no	civilian clothing	Zara Finance Command
Split	PS officials	2	yes	civilian clothing	Proposed by the Prefect to remain in service
	PS agents	52	yes, not all	civilian clothing	
	Gendarmes	37	?	grey–green[b]	12 interpreters
	Financial police	6		civilian clothing	3 interpreters
Kotor	PS officials	–	–	–	
	PS agents	–	–	–	
	Gendarmes	4	yes	Italian CC.RR	Kotor Company
	Financial police	2	no		Kotor Company

Source: USSME, M 3 b. 54, 'Comando della II Armata – UAC, formazioni armate slovene'.
[a]ACS, MI, 'Affari Collettivi Prefetture 1935–1947, b. 5198 Lubiana'. The Special Police Division was increased to 400 officers on 1 June 1942.
[b]Grey and green were the colours of the Regio Esercito uniform.

Table 47. *Number of 'rebels' in Yugoslavia (20 February 1942)*

Zone	Communists	Četniks	Total
Slovenia, Dalmatia, 2nd and 3rd zones	50,100	3,100	53,200
Areas adjoining demarcation line	7,000	4,000	11,000
Total	57,100	7,100	64,200
Bosnia		23,000	23,000
Montenegro	8,000	5,000	13,000
Total	65,100	35,100	100,200

Source: USSME N 1 – 11, 'Diari storici', b. 1371, 'SMRE – ufficio operazioni, il 27 febbraio 1942'; ASMAE, GABAP, b, 35, signed by the minister.

Table 48. *Axis and rebel losses in Croatia, Montenegro and Bosnia from 20 April to 13 May 1942*

	Dead	Injured	Missing	Captured	Shot
Italians	220	556	173		
Germans	11	15	1		
Croats	82	149	121		
Četniks and collaborationists	74	102	3		
Rebels	1,646	719		2,626	259

Source: ASMAE, GABAP, b. 35.

Table 49. *Rebel losses on conclusion of Operation Trio*

Division	Dead	Injured	Prisoners
Marche	46	32	152
Murge	90	4	172
Emilia and Messina	3		612
Cacciatori	239	4	245
Taurinense	314	20	1,805
Total	692[a]	56[a]	2,986 of whom 544 captured and 2,442 surrendered

Source: USSME, M 3 b. 59.
[a]The figures refer to dead and wounded not taken away by the partisans. The Italian sources report that 'numerous' dead and wounded were 'recovered' by the rebels.

Table 50. *MVACs and Četniks, 28 February 1943*

	Orthodox Christians	Catholics	Muslims	Total
5th CdA	4,313			4,313
6th CdA	8,385	511	780	9,676
18th CdA	7,816	321		8,137
Total in occupied zones	20,514	832	780	22,126
Slovenia (11th CdA)				5,145
Dalmatia (18th CdA)				882
Kotor (6th CdA)				1,474
Total in annexed zones				7,501
Overall total				29,627

Table 51. *Concentration camps, capacity and number of inmates (30 December 1942)*

Location	Concentration camp no.	Capacity, officers	Capacity, other ranks	POWs/officers interned (30 Dec 1942)	POWs/officers interned on (26 Feb 1943)	Other ranks interned (30 Dec 1942)	Other ranks interned (26 Feb 1943)	In operation since
CAMPS FOR OFFICERS								
Chieti	21	1000		956	1002			July 1942
Busseto – Piacenza	55	100		92	168			June 1941
Vestone – Brescia	23	220		193	(?)161			"
Bagliano – Brescia	32	130		131	130			"
Razzanello – Piacenza	17	150		138	151			"
Montalbo – Piacenza	41	150		141	137			"
Cortemaggiore – Piacenza	26	170		174	189			May 1941
Veano – Piacenza	29	200		204	209			"
Forte dei Cavi – Alessandria	5	190		139	172			June 1941
Garessio	43	230		313	317			Oct 1942
Modena	47	1000		937	1015			"
Candeli – Firenze	12	38		36	37			Sept 1941
S. Romano – Pisa	27	49		35	45			Nov 1941
Villa Iscensione – Poppi	38	94		60	68			Jan 1942
Certosa di Padula – Napoli	35	490		441	(?)416			May 1942
Aversa	71	360		343	351			Apr 1941
CAMPS FOR NCOs/OTHER RANKS								
Aversano	91		4000			4014	1878	Feb 1942
Cresina – Bari	65		12000			3313	8970	Apr 1942
Servigliano – Ascoli	59		2000			2007	1008	Feb 1941
Villa Sereni – Bari	51		4000			147	126	Jul 42
Urbisaglia – Macerata	53		8000			5407	(?)6975	Oct 42
Monturano – Parma	70		8000			5763	7314	Aug 42
Sforzacosta	56		4000					
Cairo Montenotte – Genova	95		2060			932	(?)	Dec 41
Pian di Coreglia – Genova	52		3000			3461	3438	Oct 41

(cont.)

Table 51. (*cont.*)

Location	Concentration camp no.	Capacity, officers	Capacity, other ranks	POWs/officers interned (30 Dec 1942)	POWs/officers interned on (26 Feb 1943)	Other ranks interned (30 Dec 1942)	Other ranks interned (26 Feb 1943)	In operation since
Villa Marina – Roma	60							May 42
Passo Carese – Roma	54		6000			3796	3788	July 42
Pissignano – Foligno	77		4000			826	(?)809	Aug 42
Crunello del Piano-Bergamo	62		3000			3420	3104	Aug 41
Colle Compito – Lucca	60		4000					July 42
Laterina	82		6000			2753	2714	Aug 42
Carpi	73		6000			4113	5169	July 42
Cardoncelli – Benevento	87		4000					July 42
CAMPS FOR OFF./NCOs/OTHER RANKS								
Sulmona	78	370	2900	236	247	2745	2898	Aug 40
Gruppignano – Udine	57	22	4500	20	–	4505	4570	May 41
Carinaro – Aversa	63	500	500	353	357	53	58	Oct 42
QUARANTINE AND CLEARING CAMPS								
Torre Tresca – Bari	75	500	3626	216	144	2209	1785	May 41
Tuturano – Brindisi	85	50	6500	2	–	3585	3546	May 41
Genova Cavalleria	50	6	20	2	1	65	10	May 41
Fiume	83	500	500	46	–	17	920	Mar 41
Palazzolo della Stella – Naples	88	30	500					Mar 41
Capua	66	200	6000	111	155	5931	4785	Apr 41
S. Giuseppe Jato	98		1000	2	–	881	431	Dec 41
WORK CAMPS								
Locana Canavese – Aosta	127		200			93		Jan 42
Montelupone – Macerata	129		1150			150		Aug 42
L'Aquila	(?)108	500	500			250		Jul 42
Teramo (Montorio)	145		300					Jul 42
Carbonia – Cagliari	110		3000			2195		Jul 41

Margnano	115		300		460		May 42
Ruscio – Spoleto	117		200		95		Aug 42
Cinecittà	122		400		562		May 42
Avio – Trento	113		250		180		May 42
Pol di Pastrengo – Verona	148		250		250		?
Torviscova – Udine	107		2000		1000		Oct 42
CARE Bologna	156		100		101		Oct 42
HOSPITALS							
Bergamo	201	40	460		441	42	Jul 42
Lucca	202	50	565		554	–	Jul 42
Castel S. Pietro – Bologna	203	550			495	81	Sep 42
Alberoni – Piacenza					116	298	?
Morigi		33			222	186	Jun 41
Treviglio – Bergamo		13	232		196	119	Jul 41
Altamura – Bari	204	480	173		126	31	?
CIVILIAN INTERNMENT CAMPS							
Renicci – Arezzo			9000		3950	2374	?
Colfiorito – Viterbo			1500			931	
Gonars – Udine			5000		3687	9137	Jan 41
Chiesanuova – Padova			3000		3182	3346	Aug 42
Monigo – Treviso			3000		2850	2374	Aug 42
Pietrafitta (work camp)			600		600	589	Nov 42
CAMPS IN PREPARATION							
Castelraimondo – Macerata							
Acquapendente – Viterbo	93		8000				
Fontanellato – Parma	10	400					
Sus Malonne (barracks)	49	400					
Carpi – Modena	19	1000				144	
Nocera Inferiore (barracks)		180	1000	14		1337	
Visco (for civilian internees)	206	1000					

Source: USSME, N 1 – 11, 'Diari storici', b. 1130.

Table 52. *POWs and civilian internees in Italy, including the territories annexed to the province of Fiume, excluding the Governorate of Dalmatia and the province of Ljubljana*

Nationality	30 Nov 1942	31 Dec 1942	31 Mar 1943	30 Apr 1943
Gaullist French	627	681	2,330	1,914
British	70,155	71,227	70,521	68,898
American	24	446	742	556
Greek	1,653	1,531	1,686	1,690
Yugoslav	6,066	6,130	5,760	5,787
Civilian internees	22,195	22,062	20,724	21,141
Total	100,720	102,077	101,763	99,986

CAMP	Gonars	Monigo	Padova	Renicci	Pissignano	Arbe
Men	394	2,487	3,521	3,884	765	(?)
Women	2,523	699				(?)
Children		450				(?)
Total	2,917	3,636	3,521	3,884	765	7,472

Source: USSME, L 10, b. 32.
Note: The figures do not include civilian internees in the camps located in the militarily occupied zones and in Albania, although the overall number of internees comprises former Yugoslav citizens resident in occupied Slovenia, Dalmatia, Montenegro and Croatia. The total number of 22,195 civilian internees given for 30 November 1942 does not correspond to the one furnished by another table in the same document: 21,695. The difference of about five hundred internees is probably due to changes in data on the Arbe camp.

Table 53. *Nationalities of interned POWs*

		Numbers of POWs liberated on 31 December 1942
Greek	1,531	*
Serbian	3,079	*
Croatian	448	448
Slovenian	78	78
Albanian	1,597	1,597
Montenegrin	466	466
New Italian (inhabitants of the annexed territories)	297	297
Bulgarian, Hungarian, Romanian	105	105
New German and Russian	60	41
Total	7,661	3,032

Source: USSME, N 1 – 11, 'Diari storici', b. 1130.
Note: These POWs were interned in the following camps (the number refers to the camp): 5 – Forte dei Cavi (Alessandria); 12 – Candeli (Firenze); 23 – Vestone (Brescia); 26 – Cortemaggiore (Piacenza); 27 – S. Romano (Pisa); 32 – Bugliano (Brescia); 43 – Garessio; 50 – Genova; 55 – Busseto (Piacenza); 57 – Gruppignano (Udine); 62 – Crunello del Piano (Bergamo); 65 – Cresina (Bari); 71 – Aversa (Napoli); 75 – Torre Tresca (Bari); 78 – Sulmonia; 83 – Fiume; 95 – Cairo Montenotte (Genova); 110 – Carbonia; 113 – Avio (Trento); 115 – Cantiere Orlando e Margano; 117 – Ruscio (Spoleto); 127 – Locana Canavese (Aosta), and in the prisons of Turin. At the beginning of 1943, the release was ordered of all POWs holding passports from the Balkan states, including Slovenes, Croats, Montenegrins and Albanians, but excluding Serbs and Greeks. The documents do not state how many left the concentration camps.

Table 54. *Civilian internees on 30 November 1942*

CAMP	Gonars	Monigo	Padova	Renicci	Castel Sereno (work camp)	Pissignano	Arbe
Men	1504	1742	3183	3950	98	765	5349
Women	2614	661					176
Children	1569	447					4
Total	5687	2850	3183	3950	98	765	5529

Civilian internees on 31 March 1943[a]

CAMP	Gonars	Monigo	Padova	Pissignano	Renicci	Fiume	Visco	Colfiorito	Tavernelle	Cairo Montenotte	Arbe
Men	1665	872	3076		3500	184	1757	838	489	347	2505
Women	2021	869				199	352				123
Children	848	775				163	141				
Total	4534	2516	3076		3500	546	2250	838	489	347	2628

Civilian internees on 30 April 1943

CAMP	Gonars	Monigo	Padova	Pissignano	Renicci	Fiume	Visco	Colfiorito	Tavernelle	Cairo Montenotte	Arbe
Men	1335	1596	3346		3726	302 (?)	1242	931	549		2556
Women	2465	868				293 (?)	145				165
Children	1387					125 (?)					4
Total	5187	2374	3346		3726	720 (?)	1387	931	549		2721

[a] ACS, PCM 1940–3, G30.1.7368, Cabinet of the Ministry of the Interior, 13 February 1943: "the CS has informed this office . . . of the internment of *20,000 Slovene civilians at the camps of Arbe, Padova, Treviso, Gonars and Renicci*" (emphasis added to show that the figure refers to Slovenes alone). In ACICR, G 17/74, b. 488, according to a note of 14 April 1943, Gonars contained 5,000 civilian prisoners, the majority women and children, without clothes, underwear or shoes. Renicci had 4,000 internees in deplorable conditions, while Padova–Chiesanuova was 'relatively the best camp' and contained former Yugoslav soldiers. Around 1,000 oedemas were caused by poor diet (40 per cent fewer calories than the indispensable minimum for survival) at this last camp.

Table 55. *Internees at the camp on the island of Arbe from its opening on 27 November 1942 onwards*

	Period	Men	Women	Children	Average hospitalized	Total deaths:
July	27–31	1061	111	53	1406	422:
August	1–15	3992	1076	1029		men
	16–31	5333		1206		270
September	1–15	6787	1563	1296		children
	16–31	7327	1804	1392		48
October	1–15	7387	1854	1392		women
	16–31	7206	1991	1422		104
November	1–15	7207	2062	1463		
	16–27	6647	1560	926		
Total average	16 July–27 November	6146	1518	1087		
	Average daily number of internees: 8729; maximum 10,732					
	Average in hospital: 1,406					
	Total deaths: 422, of which 270 men, 48 women, 104 children					

Table 56. *Deaths in selected concentration camps between 1 January and 31 May 1943*

	January	February	March	April	May	Total
Visco			5	1	1	7
Arbe	190	20	11	11	6	238
Gonars	110	91	47	18	14	280
Monigo	20	12	34	25	13	104
Chiesanuova	19	5	4	3	0	31
Renicci	63	31	10	8	0	112
Fiume	21	6	4	0	2	33
Total deaths	423	165	115	66	36	805
Average number of internees	19,963	19,808	19,489	17,231	16,566	
% deaths	2.12	0.83	0.59	0.38	0.22	

Source: USSME, M 3, b. 64.

Table 57. *Civilian internees at the camps of Buccari and Porto Re on 29 June 1943*

	Buccari	Porto re
Capacity	1300	1800
Total number internees	225	1157
Protected internees	19	1157
Precautionary internees	206	
In barracks	225	
Catholics	218	
Orthodox Christians	7	
Jews		1157
Muslims		
Men	196	451
Women	23	606
Boys	3	53
Girls	3	47

Table 58. *Civilian internees on 29 December 1942*

		Type		'Race'			Religion			
	No. Internees	Precautionary	Protective	Slovene	Croatian	Other 'races'	Catholic	Orthodox Christian	Jewish	Muslim
				Army Intendance						
				5th CdA						
Buccari	573	393	180	– –	573	–	533	40	–	–
Porto Re	1,173	1,173	–		969	204[a]	–		1,173	
Total 5th CdA	*1,746*	*1,566*	*180*	–	*1,542*	*204*	*533*	*40*	*1,173*	–
				6th CdA						
Kupari	294	– –	294	– –	294			–	294	–
Mlini	97	– –	97	– –	97			–	97	
Gravosa	53		53	– –	53			–	53	
Isola di Mezzo	(?)377	(?)377			(?)377			(?)377		
Forte Mamula	379		379		379				379	
Prevlaka	(?)640	(?)640	–		(?)640			(?)640		
Total 6th CdA	*1,840*	*1,017*	*823*		*1,840*			*1,017*	*823*	–

					11th CdA n.a.					
					18th CdA					
Lesina	314	–	344	–	344	–	–	–	344	–
Brazza	217	–	217	–		–	–	–	217	
Scoglio Calogerà	129	129	–		129	–	82	38	–	
Total 18th CdA	*690*	*129*	*561*	–	*690*		*82*	*38*	*561*	–
Arbe	5,562	5,561	1	4,838	724		5,562			–
Gonars	5,687	3,850	1,837	1,759	3,928		5,687			
Monigo	3,172	2,191	981	2,621	551		3,172			
Chiesanuova	3,300	3,195	105	3,195	105		3,300			
Renicci	3,950	3,950	–	3,950	–		3,950			
Total Intendance	*21,671*	*18,747*	*2,924*	*16,363*	*5,308*		*21,671*			–
Overall total	*25,947*	*21,459*	*4,488*	*16,363*	*9,380*	*204*	*22,286*	*1,095*	*2,557*	–
Isola Meleda[b]	(?)2,400	(?)2,400	–	–	(?)2,400	–	(?)1,800	(?)600	–	–

Source: USSME, M 3, b. 64. No Muslims were interned at this time.

[a]Includes 122 Germans, 61 Hungarians, 6 Russians, 5 Romanians, 4 Czechs, 3 Ukrainians, 3 Poles, 1 Frenchman, 1 Italian.

[b]Dependent on political authorities.

Table 59. *Civilian internees on 1 February 1943*

Name	Number of internees	Type: Protected	Type: Precautionary	Religion: Catholic	Religion: Protestant	Religion: Orthodox Christian	Religion: Jewish	Religion: Muslim
			5thCdA					
Buccari	593	151	442	521		72		
Porto Re	1,172	1,172					1,172	
Total	*1,765*	*1,323*	*442*	*521*		*72*	*1,172*	
			6th CdA					
Mamula	560		560	190		295	10	65
Prevlaka	502		502	309		165	3	25
Gravosa	53	53		14		4	35	
Cupari	420	420		81	10	1	324	4
Isola di Mezzo	371	371		44		2	324	1
Total	*1,906*	*844*	*1,062*	*638*	*10*	*467*	*696*	*95*
			18th CdA					
S. Pietro Brazza	42							
Postire di Brazza	41							
Neresi	15							
Milna	45							
Bol	25							

S. Martino	72							
Lesina	215							
Gelsa	159							
Cittavecchia	(?)614							
Scoglio Calogerà	142		142	83		51		7
Total	*756*		*142*	*83*		*51*	*615*	*7*
			Intendance					
Arbe	2,857		2,857	2,850		4		3
Gonars	5,676	1,981	3,695	5,675		1		
Monigo	3,274	757	2,517	3,258		14		2
Chiesanuova	3,403	80	3,323	3,233		166	2	2
Renicci	3,865		3,865	3,844		17	1	3
Camp 83	876		876	876				
Total	*19,951*	*2,818*	*17,133*	*19,736*		*202*	*3*	*10*
Overall total	*24,378*	*4,985*	*18,779*	*20,978*	*10*	*792*	*1,872*	*112*
Governorate of Dalmatia	1,500							
Isola Melada								
Ugliano[b]	(1,116)							

[a]On the original document, this figure is handwritten, and is followed by a handwritten, underlined question mark. Because there is no more information on these 614 Jews, it is probable that the figure was included simply to ensure that the total figures were accounted for.
[b]Under construction.

Table 60. *Civilian internees on 1 February 1943: type of accommodation and gender and age breakdown*

Name of concentration camp	In tents	In barracks	In temporary billets	Men	Women	Boys	Girls
			5th CdA				
Buccari		593		226	270	56	41
Porto Re		1,172		462	612	51	47
Total		*1,765*		*688*	*882*	*107*	*88*
			6th CdA				
Mamula		188	560	560			
Prevlaka			314	243	238	15	6
Gravosa			53	16	26	4	7
Cupari			420	202	201	9	8
Isola di Mezzo			371	113	165	40	53
Total		*188*	*1,718*	*1,134*	*630*	*68*	*74*
			18th CdA				
S. Pietro Brazza				21	21		
Postire di Brazza				18	19	2	2
Neresi				8	7		3
Milna				19	23		
Bol				15	10		
S. Martino				34	38		8
Lesina				90	110	7	12
Gelsa				73	71	3	
Cittavecchia							1
Scoglio Calogerà	142			104	36	1	
Total	*756*[a]			*382*	*335*	*13*	*26*
			Intendance				
Arbe	1,057	898	902	2,694	163	807	835
Gonars	407	5,269	3,274	1,305	2,729	158	128
Monigo			3,403	2,493	495		
Chiesanuova				3,403			
Renicci	1,451	2,414		3,865			
Camp 83			876	876			
Total	*2,915*	*8,581*	*8,455*	*14,636*	*3,387*	*965*	*963*
Overall total	*3,057*[b]	*10,534*	*10,173*	*16,840*	*5,234*	*1,153*	*1151*

[a]Includes 614 internees arrested by the 18th CdA (this is probably the same group of 614 internees noted as handwritten in table 59).
[b]This total does not include the 614 internees in the previous footnote.

Table 61. *Civilian internees on 15 April 1943*

Name	Number of internees	Type		Religion				
		Protected	Precautionary	Catholic	Protestant	Orthodox Christian	Jewish	Muslim
				5thCdA				
Buccari	861	109	752	710	151			
Porto Re	1,160	1,160						
							1,160	
Total	*2,021*	*1,269*	*752*	*710*	*151*		*1,160*	
				6th CdA				
Mamula	383		383	94		289		
Prevlaka	399		399	283		116		
Gravosa	80	80		14		8	58	
Cupari	428	428		5		1	422	
Isola di Mezzo	377	377		44		2	330	1
Total	*1,667*	*885*	*782*	*440*		*416*	*810*	*1*
				18th CdA				
Postire di Brazza	115	115		12		1	102	
Milna	1	1					1	

(*cont.*)

Table 61. (*cont.*)

Name	Number of internees	Type		Religion				
		Protected	Precautionary	Catholic	Protestant	Orthodox Christian	Jewish	Muslim
S. Martino	122	122		9		4	109	
Lesina	365	365		22			342	1
Scoglio Calogerà	177		177	107		62	1	7
Total	*780*	*603*	*177*	*150*		*67*	*555*	*8*
Intendance								
Arbe	2,628		2,628	2,621		4		3
Gonars	4,503	4	4,499	4,460		46	1	1
Monigo	2,500	2,465	35	2,491		9		
Chiesanuova	3,015	2	3,013	2,862		150	2	1
Visco	2,390		2,390	2,388		2		
Renicci	3,183		3,183	3,159		18	3	3
Camp 83	619		619	607		12		
Total	*18,838*	*2,471*	*16,367*	*18,583*		*241*	*6*	*8*
Overall total	*23,306*	*5,228*	*18,078*	*19,883*	*151*	*724*	*2,531*	*17*

Note: No figures are available for February on the camps of Cittavecchia, Gelsa, Bol, Neresi and S. Pietro di Brazza, which were evidently closed down.

Table 62. *Civilian internees on 15 April 1943: type of accommodation and gender and age breakdown*

Name of concentration camp	In tents	In barracks	In temporary billets	Men	Women	Boys	Girls
			5th CdA				
Buccari		861		460	334	40	27
Porto Re		1,160		455	609	51	45
Total		*2,021*		*915*	*943*	*91*	*72*
			6th CdA				
Mamula				383			
Prevlaka		86	383	260	139		
Gravosa		80	313	28	39	5	8
Cupari		428		204	209	9	6
Isola di Mezzo		377		116	168	40	53
Total		*971*	*696*	*991*	*555*	*54*	*67*
			18th CdA				
Postire di			115	43	57	7	8
Brazza			1	1			
Milna			122	51	54	8	9
S. Martino			365	120	142	53	50
Lesina		177		132	45		
Scoglio Calogerà							
Total		*177*	*603*	*347*	*298*	*68*	*67*
			Intendance				
Arbe	895	1,377	356	2,505	123		
Gonars		4,503		1,654	2,004	431	414
Monigo		35	2,465	842	837	425	396
Chiesanuova			3,015	3,015			
Visco	520	1,398	472	1,775	454	79	82
Renicci	371	2,812		3,183			
Camp 83			619	380	147	48	44
Total	*1,786*	*10,125*	*6,927*	*13,354*	*3,565*	*983*	*936*
Overall total	*1,786*	*13,294*	*8,226*	*15,607*	*5,361*	*1,196*	*1,142*

Table 63. *Civilian internees on 27 June 1943*

Name	Number of internees	Type: Protected	Type: Precautionary	Religion: Catholic	Religion: Protestant	Religion: Orthodox Christian	Religion: Jewish	Religion: Muslim
				5thCdA				
Buccari	819	65	754	657		162		
Porto Re	1,163	1,163					1,163	
Total	*1,982*	*1,228*	*754*	*657*		*162*	*1,163*	
				6th CdA				
Mamula	509		509	194		244	10	61
Prevlaka	593	1	592	403		127	2	61
Gravosa								
Cupari	445	445		5		1	439	
Isola di Mezzo	385	385		52		3	329	1
Total	*1,932*	*831*	*1,101*	*654*		*375*	*780*	*123*
				18th CdA				
Postire di Brazza	114	114		10		1	103	
Milna								
S. Martino Lesina	118	118		7		4	107	
Scoglio Calogerà	364	364		22			341	1
	175		175	105		64	1	5
Total	*771*	*596*	*175*	*144*		*69*	*552*	*6*
				Intendance				
Arbe	2,232	69	2,163	2,174		9	46	3
Gonars	4,253		4,253	4,205		44	2	1
Monigo	2,213	2,203	10	2,210		3		
Chiesanuova	2,857		2,857	2,706	148		2	1
Visco	3,249		3,249	3,229		13	4	3
Renicci	1,619		1,619	1,616		3		
Camp 83	316		316	316				
Total	*16,739*	*2,272*	*14,467*	*16,457*		*220*	*54*	*8*
Overall total	*21,424*	*4,927*	*16,497*	*17,912*		*826*	*2,549*	*137*

Table 64. *Civilian internees on 27 June 1943: type of accommodation and gender and age breakdown*

Name of concentration camp	In tents	In barracks	In temporary billets	Men	Women	Boys	Girls
			5thCdA				
Buccari		819		451	318	28	22
Porto Re		1,163		453	611	52	47
Total		*1,982*		*904*	*929*	*80*	*69*
			6th CdA				
Mamula			509	509			
Prevlaka		269	324	334	249	6	4
Gravosa							
Cupari			445	193	204	28	20
Isola di Mezzo			385	136	185	28	36
Totale		*269*	*1,663*	*1,172*	*638*	*62*	*60*
			18th CdA				
Postire di Brazza			114	50	60		4
Milna							
S. Martino			118	57	61		
Lesina			364	161	179	8	16
Scoglio Calogerà		175		129	45		
Total		*175*	*596*	*397*	*346*	*8*	*20*
			Intendance				
Arbe	854	1,103	257	2,178	40	7	7
Gonars		4,253		2,353	1,244	328	328
Monigo			2,213	702	739	399	373
Chiesanuova			2,857	2,857			
Visco	231	3,249		3,249			
Renicci		855	533	1,159	295	66	63
Camp 83			316	97	135	44	40
Total	*1,085*	*9,460*	*6,194*	*12,631*	*2,453*	*844*	*811*
Overall total	*1,085*	*11,886*	*8,453*	*15,104*	*4,366*	*994*	*960*

Table 65. *Greek internees in Greece: Italian and German zones*

	Name of camp or prison	Number of detainees
Concentration camps	Larissa	933
	Trikala	125
	Tatoï (German zone)	325
	Nauplia	520
	Kalavryta	70
	Total	*1,973*
Places of deportation for communists in the Cyclades	Aghios Efstratios (Sporades)	90
	Anafi	97
	Folegandros	49
	Kimolos	8
	Naxos	4
	Euboea	35
	Total	*283*
Prisons in Athens and the Piraeus	Averoff – women	759
	Embirikion	200
	Syngros	1,300
	Vouliagmenis	280
	Aghios Sostis	160
	Dromocaition – girls	131
	Ambelokipi – adolescents	237
	Kifissia – adolescents	199
	Prison sanatorium	100
	Piraeus	247
	Piraeus military prison	24
	Piraeus Drapetsona	35
	Total	*3,672*
Prisons in the provinces	Oropos – Boeotia	70
	Corinth	53
	Nauplia	200
	Patrasso	500
	Pirgos – Elide	350
	Tirinto – Argolis	420
	Tripoli – Arcadia	430
	Sparta – Laconia	85
	Ghition – Laconia	80
	Kalamata – Messenia	250
	Atalanti – Locris	25
	Amphissa – Phokis	360
	Tebe	130
	Levadia – Beoetia	170
	Larissa	80

(*cont.*)

Table 65. *(cont.)*

	Name of camp or prison	Number of detainees
	Lamia	260
	Volo	350
	Karditsa – Thessaly	150
	Trikala – Thessaly	350
	Kalambaka – Thessaly	25
	Agrinion – Acarnania	250
	Missolungi – Acarnania	425
	Arta – Epirus	150
	Chalkis – Euboea	280
	Egina – island of Saronicos	458
	Syros – Cyclades	100
	Total	*6,001*
	Overall Total	11,929

Source: ACICR, G 3/27 CI, b. 148.

Table 66. *Refugees expelled, July 1941–May 1942*

Year	Month	Total ejected/refused entry
1941	July	31
	August	382
	September	166
	October	35
	November	4
	December	54
	January	no data
1942	February	17
	March	28 (including some Orthodox Christians)
	April	64
	May	41 (including some Orthodox Christians)

Source: Data from the Ministry of the Interior, Fiume.

Table 67. *Number of Jewish internees (by nationality) in the Italian-occupied Croatian territories (December 1942)*

Nationality	5th CdA	6th CdA	18th CdA
Croatian	1.106	947	300
German	50	141	
Hungarian	36	22	
Romanian	13		
Polish	3	2	
Russian	2		
Albanian	6		
Czechoslovakian	7	1	
Dutch	1		
Portuguese	2		
Annexed territories	22[a]		
	1,205	1,156	300

[a]According to military sources, the 22 in question had been interned in the territories of the 6th CdA. On 17 November 1942, 2,025 Jews were interned by Italian armed forces in occupied Croatia: 1,100 at Porto Re/Kraljevica (5th CdA); 908 at Lesina (6th CdA); 17 in Almissa and Knin (18th CdA). On 22 November 1942, Division Murge informed the Second Army chief of staff that 250 Jews from Mostar had been interned at Lopud. On 1 December 1942, the number of Jews interned by the 6th CdA had increased to 1,156. There were 294 Jews interned at Cupari, 97 at Mlijti, 53 at Gravosa, 379 at Isola di Mezzo, 333 at Lesina, some at Cittavecchia and some at Gelsa. The number of Jews interned by the 18th CdA increased too. On 1 December, 300 Jews were interned at Knin, Almissa, Brazza and Malarska.

Table 68. *Persons registered for internment in the occupied French territories*

Commune	*Département*	Number
Saint-Martin-Vésubie	Alpes-Maritimes	2,000
Berthémond	Alpes-Maritimes	50
Vence	Alpes-Maritimes	250
Venanson	Alpes-Maritimes	200
Castellane	Basses-Alpes	200
Moustier-Sainte-Marie	Basses-Alpes	60
Barcelonnette	Basses-Alpes	60
Saint-Gervais	Haute-Savoie	2,000
Megève	Haute-Savoie	500
Total		5,320

Source: Voigt, *Il refugio precario*, p. 317.
Note: List drawn up by Lospinoso for the Intergovernmental Committee on Refugees. The most reliable figure on internees for Saint-Martin is 1,250, for Saint-Gervais 1,200 and for Megève 1,000. The report omits Sallanches and Combloux (localities in Haute-Savoie). According to other sources, the total number did not exceed 4,150. The table does not include Jews in Corsica or all the Jews interned in concentration camps (e.g., Modane, Sospel, Embrun); USSME, L 3, b. 185, General Command of the CC.RR.: 'Many Jews who have fled from Marseilles have presented themselves spontaneously to the Force so that they may be included on the lists and reach their places of forced residence'; see also b. 59. In a paper given to a conference entitled '8 September 1943 e IV Armata', Alberto Cavaglion quoted Bronka Halpern's assertion that 'the Italians did not put the Jews in concentration camps but sent them to places of forced residence, one of which was S. Martin de Vesubie, a tourist resort in the mountains around sixty kilometres from Nice . . . the Jews lived in the houses and villas of the village, they had to report twice a day to the police station, and they were not allowed to leave the village' (*Nella notte straniera*, pp. 23, 25).

Archival sources

The sources cited in this book have been little used before. Indeed, during my research in the archives, I often found myself opening envelopes that had not been inspected by researchers since their contents had been catalogued. Unfortunately, as said in the introduction, not all the sources are accessible, either because of restrictions imposed by Italian law or because the work of cataloguing them has only just begun. Moreover, a great many documents have been lost, especially those for 1943.

While conducting my research, I was unable to consult the Yugoslavian, Croatian and Slovenian archives. In an exchange of e-mails (5 June 1998), Stevan Pavlowitch, an expert on Balkan history, told me that the bulk of the documentation relevant to my research could be found in the Italian archives in Rome. He informed me that Italian documents were conserved at the Institute of Military History and the Archiv Jugoslavije of Belgrade, and at the Institute for the History of the Workers' Movement of Zagreb. A large part of these documents can be consulted in the Zbornik collections (some of them published in the original Italian) and others have been made available to researchers through the numerous studies of Teodoro Sala and Enzo Collotti. As regards the Slovene archives, the works by Marco Cuzzi and Tone Ferenc – whose book contains a large documentary section – draw on the Ljubljana archives on the History of the Workers' Movement. Available in the case of Dalmatia is the abundant documentation published by Oddone Talpo in the appendix to his three volumes. I did not consult the documentation in the national and departmental French archives but instead relied on the outstanding studies by Romain Rainero, Christian Villermet and Jean-Louis Panicacci, which are based on precisely those archives. As far as Italian policy towards the Jews was concerned, I drew upon the book by Serge Klarsfeld, articles by Liliana Picciotto Fargion and Michele Sarfatti, and the works of Jonathan Steinberg, Menachem Shelah, Léon Poliakov and Jacques Sabille, which contain a substantial number of German documents concerning aspects of the Italian occupations.

The Diplomatic Archives of the Greek Ministry of Foreign Affairs and the Archives of the Greek Ministry of Defence do not contain Italian documents except for photocopies of the microfilms returned to Italy by the Allies.

The diplomatic archives of the Italian Ministry of Foreign Affairs contain the catalogued papers of the ministry's cabinet, on which Pietro Pastorelli has written an important article.[1] The set of documents of greatest importance for my research were the GABAP papers, the cataloguing of which, according to Pastorelli, has encountered two problems: the incompleteness of the papers, and the fact that they are scattered among the Political Affairs files. As regards France, a large part of the CIAF correspondence for 1940 is missing, and almost all that for 1943. It should be borne in mind that, after the accreditation in January 1942 of an Italian political representative in Paris, the papers on relations with France without direct relevance to the armistice were placed in the Political Affairs archives.

The CIAF's documents can be consulted at the USSME, fondo D 7, and at the ACS. The gaps in the GABAP archive mainly concern the years 1941–2 for Greece, and 1943 for Serbia. Only a handful of High Commission documents have been conserved in the case of Montenegro. The papers for Croatia are the most complete: only those removed by Luca Pietromarchi are missing. Other documents on the occupied countries are contained in the Political Affairs files. The diaries kept by Pietromarchi between 1940 and 1944 and conserved at the Fondazione Luigi Einaudi of Turin are indubitably a valuable source of information, and I believe they should be published in their entirety. As Paolo Soddu points out, diaries express the minds of those who write them, and whatever the author's purpose they say a great deal about him. Pietromarchi's diaries are no exception. It is pointless to look for revelations in them or evidence contrary to well-established historiographical findings. Their usefulness is more humble, so to speak, but this is not to imply that they are any less valuable to historians. They shed light on the spirit of the age and, in this case, on the attitudes of a crucial section of the Fascist ruling class towards dramatic events during the Second World War.[2]

The archives of the Italian Guardia di Finanza contain very few documents on the occupied territories, while it seems that those of the Carabinieri possess an interesting collection which it is unfortunately not possible to consult. The Banca d'Italia Archive is an extremely important source of materials, given that the archives of the economic ministries are closed to researchers. The archive has an excellent catalogue, which is available on CD-Rom for even easier consultation, and it is staffed by highly competent archivists. The Archives du Comité International de la Croix-Rouge of Geneva were opened only a few years ago and are still little used. They supplement the sources on internments and the concentration camps to be found at the USSME. As regards the military archives, I did not examine the documentation on regiments, battalions, platoons or special corps, nor did I conduct research in the archives of the Carabinieri, Italian navy or Italian air force.

Unless otherwise stated, the numbers used in the following index of sources refer to the actual envelope in the archive. The numerical references for the documents in the Commercial Affairs archive of the Foreign Ministry represent the reference numbers for individual dossiers.

[1] Pastorelli, 'Le carte di gabinetto del Ministero degli Affari esteri'.

[2] Soddu, *Pagine inedite del Diario di Luca Pietromarchi*, p. 476.

1. ARCHIVIO STORICO DELLO STATO MAGGIORE DELL'ESERCITO (USSME)

FONDO M 3, Documenti restituiti dagli alleati alla fine della seconda guerra mondiale (Documents returned by the Allies on conclusion of the Second World War):

CS: bb. 4–12, 14, 18–20, 30

CIAF: bb. 34–6

Second Army: bb. 44, 45, 48, 51–71, 75–9, 82, 84–6, 89, 90

FF.AA. Aegean: bb. 150–3

Other: bb. 309–11, 476 (Italian divisions in Yugoslavia and Greece); 483 (concentration camps); 96 (Fourth Army in France)

FONDO L 15, Carteggio sussidiario II Armata e Comando superiore FF.AA. Albania (in realtà Grecia) (Ancillary correspondence: Second Army and Army High Command Albania (in fact Greece)): bb. 11, 12, 16–18, 22, 23, 25, 27, 28, 31, 36–41

FONDO D 7, Commissione Italiana per l'Armistizio con la Francia (CIAF) (Armistice Commission with France): bb. 8, 10, 14, 24, 25, 37, 38, 44, 45, 48, 53, 58, 59

FONDO H 3, SIM – Notiziari Stati Esteri – Bollettini Seconda Guerra Mondiale (SIM – Country Reports – Bulletins):

Yugoslavia: bb. 32, 51, 60, 66, 67, 80

France: bb. 32, 33, 94

Greece: bb. 22, 46, 87

Albania: bb. 13, 80, 81, 87

FONDO H 5, SMRE classificato "RR" (General Staff of the Regio Esercito): bb. 1, 3, 34, 40

FONDO H 9, Carteggio col capo del governo (Correspondence with the head of government): bb. 9–12

FONDO I 3, Carteggio versato dallo Stato maggiore della Difesa (CS, SMG, seconda guerra mondiale) (Correspondence of the General Defence Staff (CS, SMG)): bb. 27, 29, 31, 107

FONDO L 3, Studi particolari (Special studies): bb. 58, 59, 85, 149, 185, 199, 200, 281

FONDO L 10, Vari uffici SMRE: bb. 21, 28, 32, 38, 81, 91, 96, 99

FONDO L 13, Documentazione acquisita dal 1968 (Documentation acquired since 1968)

Yugoslavia: bb. 160

General Geloso: bb. 85–94, 96, 97, 99, 100, 104–6

FONDO L 14, Carteggio sussidiario SMRE (Ancillary correspondence SMRE): bb. 22, 45, 50

FONDO M 7, Circolari vari uffici (Circulars of various offices): bb. 223, 260, 279, 284, 285, 288, 293, 297, 307, 313, 346, 411, 413

FONDO N I–II, Diari storici della seconda guerra mondiale (Historical diaries of the Second World War)[3]

CS, SIE: bb. 1393–1411

Yugoslavia

II Armata: bb. 235, 724, 993, 1222, 2084 v CdA: bb. 378, 449, 543, 1426; Divisione Bergamo: bb. 338, 379, 446, 514, 614, 732, 768, 1000, 1184, 1321; VI CdA: bb. 582–5, 1264–8; Divisione Pusteria: bb. 656, 657, 707, 821; Divisione Sassari: bb. 240, 523, 568, 569, 769, 999, 1004; XI CdA: b. 1056; Divisione Isonzo: bb. 336, 379, 465, 546, 1317–20; XVIII CdA: bb. 547, 646, 772, 782, 881, 996, 1068, 1188, 1290; Truppe Zara: bb. 568, 588, 697, 732, 1269; 58° Battaglione CC.NN.: bb. 770, 819, 1037, 1107, 1191, 1310

France

IV Armata: bb. 1099, 1127, 1218, 1326; 10° CC.RR. mobilitato: bb. 989, 1253, 1361, 1371, 1372; I CdA: bb. 987, 1100, 1186, 1312; XV CdA: bb. 1083, 1208, 1239; XXII CdA: bb. 1101, 1102, 1217, 1249; Divisione Taro: b. 1276; CC.NN. Mentone: bb. 1107, 1322; CC.NN. Nizza: bb. 1184, 1271

Corsica

VII CdA: bb. 990, 1120, 1201, 1287, 2005, 2006, 2010bis; Divisione Cremona: bb. 992, 1105, 1242; Divisione Friuli: bb. 991, 1105, 1225, 1272; Battaglione "M": bb. 1225, 1288, 2014

Greece

XI Armata: bb. 502, 503, 631–5, 736, 839, 840, 966, 1054, 1098, 1226, 1226a, 2245; CC.RR. Grecia: bb. 446, 448, 824, 946, 1114; Divisione Acqui: bb. 521, 550, 564, 1115, 1198, 1250; III CdA: bb. 268, 371, 457, 504, 567, 713, 789, 879, 1070, 1192, 1237; Divisione Julia: bb. 253, 319, 375, 459, 616, 661, 798, 1011; VIII CdA: bb. 246, 325, 457, 493, 659, 738, 1089, 1108, 1193; Divisione Pinerolo: bb. 215, 322, 462, 504, 542, 660, 984, 1194, 1232; CC.RR. Pinerolo: bb. 198, 215, 322, 462, 504, 542, 660, 705, 1047; XXV CdA: bb. 299, 641, 1199; Divisione Messina: bb. 272, 374, 463, 513, 589, 663, 735, 1007, 1066, 1162, 1191; XXVI CdA: bb. 196, 213, 328, 376, 554, 556, 971, 972, 1122; CC.NN. 95° Battaglione: bb. 611, 658, 771, 841; CC.NN. 130° Battaglione: bb. 504, 542, 660, 705; CC.NN. 28° Battaglione: bb. 522, 791, 880, 980, 1071, 1199, 1324; CC.NN. 82° Battaglione: bb. 558, 663, 734; Egeo e Cicladi: bb. 654, 719, 729, 730, 765; Divisione Regina: bb. 730, 840; Creta: bb. 447, 505, 565, 641, 719, 801, 982, 1090, 1180, 1261

Montenegro

XIV CdA: bb. 494, 647, 731, 820, 997, 1069, 1322, 2083; Divisione Lupi di Toscana: bb. 372, 464, 593, 710, 767, 1097, 2225; Divisione Marche: bb. 525, 546, 770, 857; Divisione Ferrara: bb. 663, 734; Divisione Murge:

[3] The cartons of the historical diaries contain documents relative to several divisions. I was able to examine those on the following divisions: Forlì, Cuneo, Cagliari, Brennero, Piemonte, Casale, Parma, Modena, deployed in Greece; Granatieri di Sardagna, in Yugoslavia; EFTF, in France; Venezia, in Montenegro.

bb. 709, 735, 859, 1001, 1121, 1233; Divisione Taurinense: bb. 711, 1002, 1003, 1220, 1221, 1273; Divisione Puglie: b. 542; CC.RR. Kossovo: bb. 168, 823

Curia Castrense (Army Chaplaincy): bb. 605, 959, 1074, 1166

Prisoners of War: b. 1130

2. ARCHIVIO CENTRALE DELLO STATO (ACS)

MINISTERO DELL'INTERNO

AFFARI COLLETTIVI PREFETTURE 1935–47: bb. 5176 (Fiume), 5196 (Split), 5197 (Kotor), 5198/1 (Ljubljana)

DEMORAZZA 1938–43: b. 3, fasc. 12 (Application of racial laws during the state of war); b. 4, fasc. 18 (Foreign Jews – not found); b. 5, fasc. 25 (Jews, voluntary enrolment); b. 6, fasc. 29 (Jewish petitions to the Duce's secretariat); b. 13, fasc. 46 (Birth premiums)

DIREZIONE GENERALE SERVIZI DI GUERRA 1941–5: bb. 18 (Internments and telegrams from Prefect Zerbino), 20, 50 (Fiume, evacuees and refugees), 58 (Ljubljana and Dalmatia, evacuees and refugees), 82/164, 86/216 and 221, 87/294, 90, 112/388 (Roma detainees, Ljubljana)

DGPS (DIREZIONE GENERALE PUBBLICA SICUREZZA) 1940–3, SEGRETERIA DEL CAPO DELLA POLIZIA SENISE: b. 10, fasc. 124/85 (Bimonthly reports of subversive episodes, Zara, May–June 1943); b. 11, fasc. 125

DGPS, DIVISIONE AFFARI GENERALI RISERVATI 1942 (3155.40 1942): b. 1, A 5 (Croatia reports); b. 13, C 2a (Ljubljana anti-fascism)

DGPS, DIVISIONE AFFARI GENERALI RISERVATI 1943 (3155.41–1943): bb. 1–5, 8, 17

DGPS, DIVISIONE AFFARI GENERALI RISERVATI, A 4bis STRANIERI INTERNATI DURANTE LA SECONDA GUERRA MONDIALE (UFFICIO INTERNATI STRANIERI): b. 1, fasc. 10 (Corsica), fasc. 4 (Arezzo); b. 5, fasc. 28 (Padova); b. 6, fasc. 39 (Treviso); b. 7, fasc. 56 (French internees), fasc. 57 (Greek internees), fasc. 59 (Yugoslav internees); b. 8, fasc. 64 A (exchange of Jewish internees); b. 10, fasc. 77 (Jewish valuables and property), fasc. 82 (Ionian islands); b. 11 (Concentration camps. Croatian internees: Greeks, ex-Yugoslavs, SS information requests)

DGPS, DIVISIONE AFFARI GENERALI RISERVATI, A 5 G SECONDA GUERRA MONDIALE: b. 19, fasc. 3 (Jewish Aid Committee); b. 60, fasc. 26 (Jews); b. 61, fasc. 26 (Zara); b. 63, fasc. 31 (Escortments to the eastern border); b. 66, fasc. 32 (Concentration camps, Lists: Kotor, Dalmazia Governorate, Split); b. 67, fasc. 32 (Concentration camps, Lists: Ljubljana, Split); b. 68, fasc. 32 (Fiume Italian Jews for internment); b. 400, fasc. 52 (CIAF); b. 401, fasc. 58 (CIAF); b. 405, fasc. 66 (Occupied territories); b. 408, fasc. 82 (German troops in Fiume); b. 415, fasc. 97 (Croatia reports); b. 415, fasc. 102 (General affairs, Ljubljana, new provinces); b. 424, fasc. 167 (Escortment rebel families to the eastern border); b. 425, fasc. 170 (Civilian internees in military concentration camps); b. 425, fasc. 180 (ICRC); b. 426, fasc. 181 (Internees at the Dalmatian government's disposal); b. 426, fasc. 191 (Internees deceased in concentration camps); b. 428, fasc. 203 (Police, Ljubljana, Fiume, Zagreb, Dalmatia)

DGPS, DIVISIONE AFFARI GENERALI RISERVATI 1930–56, A 16 STRANIERI ED EBREI: b. 1, fasc. a 3 (Jewish Aid Committee); b. 5, fasc. C 45 (Monaco); b. 8, fasc. D 16 (Refugees Croatia), fasc. d17 (Jews internees in Albania); b. 10, fasc. 22bis (Jews Kotor), fasc. 31,2 (Jews Fiume), fasc. 31,3 (Jews Fiume, police measures); b. 11, fasc. 41bis (Ljubljana); b. 14, fasc. 63 (Pola)

DGPS, DIVISIONE POLIZIA POLITICA, FASCICOLI PER MATERIA: packets 219 (Jews – not found), 221 (Foreign policy), 225 (Duce speeches)

DGPS, DIVISIONE POLIZIA POLITICA, CENSURA DI GUERRA: packet 32, fasc. 1 (Fiume, provincial censorship commission); packet 40, fasc. 1 (Ljubljana); packet 68, fasc. 1 (Split); packet 83, fasc. 6 (Zara)

MINISTERO DELLA CULTURA POPOLARE (MINCULPOP)

bb. 319–22 (France), 346–50 (Greece), 373–6 (Yugoslavia), 386 (Monaco Principality)

DIREZIONE GENERALE PROPAGANDA, NUCLEI PROPAGANDA ITALIA ESTERO: b. 4, 21 (Carnaro); b. 10, 64 (Pola); b. 15, 94 (Zara); b. 17, 23 (France); b. 17 bis, 27 (Greece); b. 24/125 (Mostra dell'Italianità della Dalmazia)

MINISTERO DELL'INDUSTRIA E DEL COMMERCIO

DIREZIONE GENERALE MINIERE, SERVIZI AMMINISTRATIVI 1878–1956: b. 114, fasc. 1155 (Consiglio Amministrazione Ufficio Metalli Nazionali); b. 115, fasc. 1164 (Lignite)

FASCIST ARCHIVES

SEGRETERIA PARTICOLARE DEL DUCE, CARTEGGIO RISERVATO: b. 61, fasc. 349/R, 71, fasc. 461/R, 174, 176, 177

BOLLETTINI E INFORMAZIONI 1940–3: b. 157, fasc. 12, 184, fasc. 60–2, 174

SEGRETERIA AMMINISTRATIVA DIRETTORIO FEDERAZIONI PROVINCIALI: bb. 678 (Fiume), 1242 (Ljubljana, Split, Kotor)

CARTEGGIO DELLE FEDERAZIONI PROVINCIALI, PNF, SERVIZI VARI, SERIE II: bb. 979 (Kotor), 1056 (Fiume), 1698 (Zara)

PRESIDENZA DEL CONSIGLIO DEI MINISTRI 1940–43 (the numbers refer to individual fascicles): 1.1.3.21195, 1.1.8.7.53456.3, 1.1.10.270.3.23.38, 1.1.10.270.3.23.41, 1.1.13.16452.1–180 (Governorate of Dalmatia), 1.1.13.301, 1.1.13.1654.148, 1.1.13.2382.d, 1.1.13.2944, 1.1.13.4705, 1.1.13.8204–13, 1.1.13.12940, 1.1.13.15964, 1.1.13.18388, 1.1.13.21002.a, 1.1.13.21002.13 (29780), 1.1.13.21195, 1.1.13.21843, 1.1.13.25615, 1.1.13.36146, 1.1.13.57412–1, 1.1.16.7.27000.127, 1.3.1.7966, 1.3.1.19388, 3.1.10 707.2, 3.2.2.27508, 3.2.6.1372, 3.2.6.1372/3, 3.2.6.21790, 3.2.9.22900, 4.1.1.18621, 4.12.55967, 5.2.2883–1, 5.4.23275, 7.1.2.48902, 7.1.228.4, 14.3.44888, 14.3.56245,

15.2.19328.8, g14.1.8843, g16.4.51963, g21.3.15102, g21.3.21589, g29.1.16798, g30.1.53825, g30.1.7368, g36/5 147.3, g7/8–12970–16002

OTHER ARCHIVES
CIAF (Civil Commission of Menton and Information Office): packets 3–4
IRI NERA: bb. 33, 73, 111, 112
IRI ROSSA: bb. 83, 124, 136, 137
ARCHIVIO PARINI: bb. 1, 39, 45, 46, 50–4, 56, 58–60, 62–6, 69
ARCHIVIO SCASSELLATI: b. 1
UFFICIO ITALIANO CAMBI (UIC – not consultable): cart. 80, 81 (Croatia); 103, 110 (France); 116 (Germany); 138–40, 145, 147 (Greece)
ARCHIVIO INGRAVALLE: bb. 2–4
GABINETTO AERONAUTICA 1943: bb. 4, 135
CIAF/SCAEF (catalogued 1997–99; I was able to examine some cartons thanks to the assistance of Dr. Paone)
JOINT ALLIED INTELLIGENCE AGENCY, PUBLIC RECORD OFFICE (microfilmed copies: the first number in each reference is that of the microfilm; those following the colon refer to the parts of the microfilm containing information on the occupied territories)

001: 99–231; 612–621	102: 27606–27671	306: 97810–97826
008: 4502–4726	115: 31720–31730	307: 98029–98034
009: 4730–4853	220: 56073–56115	309: 98961–98973*
025: 12135–12382	286: 87159–87243	310: 99277–99624
046: 24085–24140	306: 97489–97562	330: 11304–11305

3. ARCHIVIO STORICO-DIPLOMATICO DEL MINISTERO DEGLI AFFARI ESTERI (ASMAE)

GABINETTO ARMISTIZIO–PACE (GABAP)
France: bb. 1–20
Greece, Ionian islands: bb. 21–4
Serbia and annexed territories: bb. 25–7
Croatia: bb. 28–47
Montenegro: bb. 48–54
AFFARI POLITICI 1931–45
France: bb. 47, 51, 54, 55, 59, 65–70
Bulgaria: bb. 26–8
Principality of Monaco: b. 1
Yugoslavia: bb. 105–7
ARCHIVIO SCUOLE, DIREZIONE GENERALE ITALIANI ALL'ESTERO 1936–45: bb. 83, 92, 94bis, 95, 99, 142, 151, 162, 166, 181, 185, 186
ARCHIVIO SCUOLE 1922–45: bb. 58, 86, 91, 98
DIREZIONE GENERALE AFFARI COMMERCIALI (not catalogued; references are to year and position)

France: 1941, pos. from 17 to 43, 43/11 (2 envelopes), 5; 1940–2, pos. from 43/3 to 43/4–8, from 43/1 to 43/2–16; 1941–2, pos. from 43/5 to 43/10/9, from 43/10/11 to 60/2; 1942, no pos. (2 envelopes), pos. from 7/1 to 7/1–80, from 28/1–61 to 42/1, from 7 to 15; 1943, from 7/1 to 18, from 7/1 to 7/1–18 (2 envelopes), from 43/10 to 7/1, no pos. (3 envelopes)
Yugoslavia: 1937–40, pos. from 7/1 to 7/8; 1940, pos. from 1 to 8 (2 envelopes), from 8 to 32/1; 1940–1, pos. from 4/3 to 7/1; 1941, pos. from 1 to 4/1, from 4/1 to 43/1; 1941–2, pos. from 3/1 to 4/1–5; 1941–3, pos. from 9/1 to 43/3; 1942–3, no pos. (2 envelopes); 1943, no pos.
Greece: 1942, no pos.

4. ARCHIVIO STORICO DELLA BANCA D'ITALIA (ASBI) (REFERENCES ARE TO THE SERIES AND BUNDLE NUMBER)

UFFICIO SPECIALE COORDINAMENTO
Files 100, 1–5; 101 (Slovenia), 6, 7, 10; 102 (Yugoslavia), 26; 103 (Croatia), 28–30; 104 (Montenegro), 38, 39; 105 (Ionian islands), 40, 41, 365, 366; 106 (Greece), 42–4, 368; 107 (Banks), 45, 46, 372, 373; 108 (France), 47, 375; other envelopes: 2, 153, 187, 308–18, 345, 346, 361, 362, 369, 372, 375
Letter books 2, 4, 6, 19

DIRETTORIO AZZOLINI
Files 17, 20, 21, 34, 51

DIRETTORIO INTRONA
Files 18, 19
Letter books 4984

ESTERI
Files 132, 175, 179, 212, 279, 290, 301, 346, 450, 454, 485

VIGILANZA
Files 669, 749, 808, 809, 1151

CONSORZIO SOVVENZIONI VALORI INDUSTRIALI
Files 9, 11, 20, 22, 23, 43, 75, 80, 86, 95, 111, 121, 127, 172, 179, 189, 198, 232, 257, 271, 273, 289, 296, 301, 309, 357, 382, 384, 385, 396, 398, 405, 410, 413, 415, 416, 418, 420, 426, 513, 515, 774

ISPETTORATO GENERALE, CAMBIO DINARI
Files 308–14

SEGRETERIA PARTICOLARE
Files 146, 250, 444

UFFICIO AFFARI COLONIALI – FILIALI COLONIALI E DALMATE
Files Doc. Raitano, 815; Ionian islands, 9126, 9128; Fiume, 353, 354, 355 R; Zara, X 81, X 131, 2589, 2590, 2593; Šibenik, 2609, 17029, 17030; Split, 2594, 2595,

2604, 9122, 18450; Kotor, 402 R, 2602, 2603; Cetijne, 2606, 2608; Ljubljana, 2663, 2664, 2674, 2694, 2777, 2801, 2802, 2805, 2813, 440 R, 15083
Letter books 4983, 17074
Registers 9125, 1777

5. ARCHIVIO STORICO DELLA GUARDIA DI FINANZA (REFERENCES TO FILE, TOME AND FASCICLE)

Albania: 1/1, IV A, 1; 1/7, IV A, 41 A; 1/7, VI, 48
Battaglione Annemasse: 2/3, VI, 3–5
Battaglione Nizza: 2/6, II, 2, 3; 2/11, II, 1 and 3; 2/1, III, 7; 2/10, III, 2; 1/7, III A, 31, 31 C, 41 L

6. CENTRO BIBLIOGRAFICO UNIONE COMUNITÀ EBRAICHE ITALIANE (CBUCEI)

UCEI ARCHIVE
President's Office: 11 A -11 H
Newspapers and magazines: 27 AB
Various: 44 A (Deportee research committee), 44 H (Delasem), 44 M

7. ARCHIVES DU COMITÉ INTERNATIONAL DE LA CROIX-ROUGE (ACICR)

G 44/: 13/11–26, 53–37, 139–53
G 44/: 11–64, 146–72, 151–73, 73.01, 0.2
G 44/: 51/00–89
G 44/: 53–92
G 44/: 74–99, 99.01–11
G 44/: 139–130

RAPPORTS DE VISITE DE LA PUISSANCE PROTECTRICE
O CMS Commission mixte secours / Grèce 1940–46
O CMS 1940/45 Délégation CICR Rapports
G 68 Réfugiés divers dans différents pays, A–Z, 1939–46 (936)
G 83 III, IV 41–72

MICROFILMS
G 59/0/: 1.06, 2.02, 2.06; G 59/2/: 74–11, 151–15, 11–19, 51–25, 53–26, 147–31, 131–33, 139–35; G 59/3/: 140–57, 3–62, 74–72, 147–77; G 59/4: 104; G 59/7: 198, 222, 255, 289, 300, 308–310; G 59/8/74: 338, 339, 341; G 59/12/151: 359, 360, 360.01, 360.02

CARTONS DU GROUPE G 1939–50
81, 86, 87, 147–149, 192, 204, 358, 360, 362, 370, 380–383, 393, 464, 469, 470, 474, 482, 488, 493, 496, 501, 502, 972–973

Bibliography

GUIDES TO ARCHIVES AND BIBLIOGRAPHY

Cassels, A., *Italian Foreign Policy, 1918–1945. A Guide to Research and Research Materials*, Scholarly Resources, Wilmington, DE 1981.

De Felice, R., *Bibliografia orientativa del fascismo*, Bonacci, Rome 1991.

Missori, M., *Gerarchie e statuti del PNF*, Bonacci, Rome 1986.

PRINTED SOURCES

DIPLOMATIC DOCUMENTS, COLLECTIONS OF DOCUMENTS AND POLITICAL SPEECHES

Actes et documents du Saint Siège relatifs à la seconde guerre mondiale, 11 vols., Libreria editrice vaticana, Vatican City 1970–81.

Akten zur deutschen auswärtigen Politik, series E (1941–5), vols. 1–6, Vandenhoeck & Ruprecht, Göttingen 1969–79.

Documenti diplomatici italiani, series IX (1939–43), 9 vols., Istituto poligrafico e Zecca dello stato, Rome 1960–87.

Documents on German Foreign Policy, 1918–1945, series d (1937–45), 14 vols., US Government Printing Office, Washington 1949–64.

Mussolini, B., *Opera omnia*, edited by D. Susmel, 44 vols., La Fenice, Florence 1951–63, and Volpe, Rome 1978–81.

Noakes, J., and Pridham, G. (eds.), *Documents on Nazism, 1919–1945*, Cape, London 1974.

Piemontese, G., *Ventinove mesi di occupazione italiana nella provincia di Lubiana. Considerazioni e documenti*, S.C., Ljubljana 1946.

Relazione sull'opera svolta dal Ministero degli Affari esteri per la tutela delle comunità ebraiche (1938–1943), unpublished, Archivio Storico-Diplomatico del Ministero degli Affari Esteri, Rome.

Zbornik documentata i podataka o narodno-oslobodilackom ratu jugoslavenskih naroda, 11 vols., Institut d'Histoire Militaire de Belgrade, Belgrade 1975.

DOCUMENTARY WORKS: UFFICIO STORICO DELLO STATO MAGGIORE DELL'ESERCITO ITALIANO

Cronologia della seconda guerra mondiale, Rome 1948.
L'esercito italiano nella campagna di Grecia, Rome 1991.
Loi, S., *Le operazioni delle unità italiane in Jugoslavia (1941–1943). Narrazione – Documenti*, Rome 1978.
Montanari, M., *La campagna di Grecia*, Rome 1991.
Le operazioni delle unità italiane al fronte russo, 1941–1943, Rome 1977.
Rossi, F., *Mussolini e lo Stato maggiore. Avvenimenti del 1940*, Rome 1955.

DIARIES, MEMOIRS AND NOVELS

Alfieri, D., *Due dittatori di fronte*, Rizzoli, Milan 1948.
Anfuso, F., *Roma, Berlino, Salò (1936–1945)*, Garzanti, Milan 1950.
Angelini, G., *Fuochi di bivacco in Croazia*, Tipografia regionale, Rome 1946.
Armellini, Q., *Diario di guerra. Nove mesi al Comando supremo*, Garzanti, Cernusco sul Naviglio 1946.
Badoglio, P., *L'Italia nella seconda guerra mondiale*, Mondadori, Milan 1946.
Baghiou, J., *Come non vincemmo la campagna di Grecia. Fatti e retroscena*, De Vecchi, Milan 1971.
Baldi, G., *Dolce Egeo guerra amara*, Rizzoli, Milan 1988.
Bastianini, G., *Uomini, cose e fatti. Memorie di un ambasciatore*, Vitagliano, Milan 1967.
Bedeschi, G. (ed.), *Fronte greco-albanese. C'ero anch'io*, Mursia, Milan 1977.
Fronte jugoslavo-balcanico. C'ero anch'io, Mursia, Milan 1986.
Bettiza, E., *Esilio*, Mondadori, Milan 1996.
Biasion, R., *Sagapò*, Einaudi, Turin 1953, 2nd edn. 1991.
Bilenchi, R., *Cronache degli anni neri*, Editori Riuniti, Rome 1984.
Bottai, G., *Diario, 1935–1944*, Rizzoli, Milan 1982.
Bravo, A., *La vita offesa*, Angeli, Milan 1986.
Brignoli, P., *Santa messa per i miei fucilati. Le spietate rappresaglie italiane contro i partigiani in Croazia dal diario di un cappellano*, Longanesi, Milan 1973.
Campione, F., *Guerra in Epiro. Diario di un combattente della Divisione Siena*, Guida, Naples 1950.
Caracciolo di Feroleto, M., *E poi? La tragedia dell'esercito italiano*, Corso, Rome 1946.
Cavallero, U., *Comando supremo. Diario 1940–1943 del capo di Stato maggiore*, Cappelli, Rocca San Casciano 1948.
Ciano, G., *Diario, 1937–1943*, Rizzoli, Milan 1980.
De Bernières, L., *Captain Corelli's Mandolin*, Minerva, London 1994.
De Vecchi di Val Cismon, C. M., *Il quadriumviro scomodo. Il vero Mussolini nelle memorie del più monarchico dei fascisti*, edited by L. Romersa, Mursia, Milan 1983.

Dragoni, U., *Fiaschi in Jugoslavia. Ricordi polemici della campagna di guerra 1941–1943*, Il Quadrante, Alexandria 1983.

Fanizza, U., *De Vecchi – Bastico – Campioni. Ultimi governatori dell'Egeo*, Valbonesi, Forlì 1947.

Finestra, A., *Dal fronte jugoslavo alla Val d'Ossola*, Mursia, Milan 1995.

Grandi, D., *25 luglio. Quarant'anni dopo*, edited by R. De Felice, Il Mulino, Bologna 1983.

Graziani, R., *Ho difeso la patria*, Mondadori, Milan 1948.

Grazzi, E., *Il principio della fine*, Corso, Rome 1945.

Guariglia, R., *Ricordi 1922–1946*, ESI, Naples 1950.

Jacomoni di San Savino, F., *La politica dell'Italia in Albania*, Cappelli, Bologna 1965.

Kesselring, A., *Soldat bis zum letzten Tag*, Athenäum, Bonn 1953 [It. trans. *Memorie di guerra*, Garzanti, Milan 1954].

Lualdi, A., *Nudi alla meta*, Longanesi, Milan 1969.

Mafrici, A., *Guerriglia sulla ferrovia del petrolio. Croazia 1942–1943*, Corporazione Arti Grafiche, Rome 1981.

Magli, G., *Le truppe italiane in Corsica prima e dopo l'armistizio del 1943*, AUC, Lecce 1950.

Mazzantini, C., *A cercar la bella morte*, Mondadori, Milan 1986.

Mondini, L., *Prologo del conflitto italo-greco*, Treves, Rome 1945.

Ortona, E., *Diplomazia di guerra. Diari 1937–1943*, Il Mulino, Bologna 1994.

Pirelli, A., *Taccuini 1922/1943*, Il Mulino, Bologna 1984.

Puntoni, P., *Parla Vittorio Emanuele III*, Il Mulino, Bologna 1993.

Rahn, R., *Ruheloses Leben. Aufzeichnungen und Erinnerungen*, Diederichs, Düsseldorf 1949 [It. trans. *Ambasciatore di Hitler da Vichy a Salò*, Garzanti, Milan 1950].

Rintelen, E. von, *Mussolini als Bundesgenosse. Erinnerungen des deutschen Militärattachés in Rom, 1936–1943*, Wunderlich, Tübingen 1951 [It. trans. *Mussolini l'alleato. Ricordi dell'addetto militare tedesco a Roma, 1936–1943*, Corso, Rome 1952].

Roatta, M., *Otto milioni di baionette. L'esercito italiano in guerra 1940–1944*, Mondadori, Milan 1946.

Senise, C., *Quando ero a capo della polizia*, Ruffolo, Rome 1946.

Umiltà, C., *Jugoslavia e Albania. Memorie di un diplomatico*, Garzanti, Cernusco sul Naviglio 1947.

Visconti Prasca, S., *Io ho aggredito la Grecia*, Rizzoli, Milan 1946.

Zanussi, G., *Guerra e catastrofe d'Italia*, Corso, Rome 1946.

CONTEMPORARY LITERATURE

Ambrosini, G., *L'Albania nella comunità imperiale di Roma*, Istituto nazionale di cultura fascista, Rome 1940.

Anon., 'La produzione agricola e mineraria jugoslava', *Rivista di politica economica*, 30, 9–10, 1940, column 'Informazioni economiche e finanziarie'.

Anon., 'Le relazioni economiche tra l'Italia e l'Ungheria', *Rivista di politica economica*, 32, 7–8, 1942, 439–45.

Appiotti, G., 'Cenni geo-topografici sul Nizzardo e le sue funzioni militari', *Geopolitica*, 4, 31 July 1942, 299–311.

Baratelli, M., 'Unità romana nel Mediterraneo', *Gerarchia*, 20, 7, July 1941, 357–63.

Barendson, A., 'L'economia della Grecia', *Economia italiana*, 26, June 1941, 305–11.

Bernardy, A. A., 'La tradizione romana e veneziana della Dalmazia', *Civiltà fascista*, 7, July 1941, 532–42.

Bertelé, A., *Dal principio di nazionalità all'imperialismo. Origini, vita, superamento imperiale della nazionalità*, Poligrafica Editrice, Turin 1942.

Bobich, G., 'I discendenti degli illiri, i morlacchi', *Difesa della razza*, 3, 22, 20 September 1940, 30–6.

Bottai, G., 'Contributi dell'Italia al nuovo ordine', *Studi di civiltà fascista*, 6, 3, Rome 1941, 1–24.

Bottiglioni, G., 'Italiani in dominio straniero', *Geopolitica*, 3, 8–9, August–September 1941, 376–85.

Calestani, V., 'Dalmazia e Italia', *Rivista dalmatica*, 24, 1, 1943, 3–18.

Cansacchi, G., 'La luogotenenza generale d'Albania', *Jus. Rivista di scienze giuridiche, Università cattolica del Sacro Cuore*, 2, 2, June 1941, 1–53 (extract).

Cappuccio, L., 'Epiro, Acarnania ed isole Jonie territori geopoliticamente italiani', *Geopolitica*, 3, 5, 3 May 1941, 250–6.

Cocchiara, G., 'Le tradizioni della Dalmazia', *Difesa della razza*, 4, 22, 20, September 1941.

Colonna di Cesarò, G. A., *L'Italia nella Albania meridionale. Note e documenti, 1917–1918*, Campitelli, Foligno.

Cosentino, S., 'Il sudest europeo e l'Italia', *Economia fascista*, 3, 3, 1942, 21–6.

Curcio, C., 'La rivoluzione europea', *Economia italiana*, 25, August–September 1940, 515–18.

De Cesare, S., 'Il riordinamento economico danubio–balcanico', *Economia italiana*, 25, January 1941, 27–9.

Della Volpe, G., *Discorso sull'ineguaglianza*, Ciuni, Rome 1943.

Di Caporiacco, L., 'Cittadini e sudditi nel Dodecanneso', *Difesa della razza*, 6, 15, 5 June 1943, 12–13.

Ducci, R. (Verax), 'Gli ebrei e l'Italia durante la guerra', *Politica estera*, 1, 9, 1944, 21–44.

Evola, J., 'Elementi dell'idea europea', *Lo stato*, 9, 1940; reprinted in J. Evola, *Lo stato (1934–1943)*, edited by G. F. Lami, *Fondazione Julius Evola*, Rome 1995, 341–9.

Sintesi di dottrina della razza, Hoepli, Milan 1941.

Facciotti, F., 'Le risorse minerarie delle nuove provincie italiane', *Economia italiana*, 26, July 1941, 342–5.

Federzoni, L., *L'ora della Dalmazia*, Zanichelli, Bologna 1941.

Fossati, A., 'Carattere, oggetto e soggetti del commercio di importazione e di esportazione in regime di autarchia', *Rivista di politica economica*, 30, 6, 1940, 462–8.

'Commercio estero', in G. Demaria et al., *La situazione economica internazionale*, Cedam, Padua 1940.

Franchi, B., 'La Dalmazia nel pensiero degli artefici del Risorgimento', *Rivista dalmatica*, 23, 1, 1942, 3–14.

Franciosa, L., 'Aspetti geopolitici ed economici della Grecia', *Economia. Rivista di economia corporativa e di scienze sociali*, 19, 1, 1941, 25–35.

Gayda, V., *La politica italiana nei Balcani. I suoi sviluppi e le sue prospettive*, Istituto per gli studi di politica internazionale, Rome 1938.

Profili della nuova Europa. L'economia di domani, Edizioni del Giornale d'Italia, Rome 1941, 3rd edn.

Geloso, C., 'Con l'XI Armata nella guerra contro la Grecia', unpublished typescript, in USSME, l13, b. 105, undated.

Gianturco, M., *Lineamenti della nuova Europa*, Bocca, Milan 1941.

Gini, C., *Aspetti demografici del conflitto*, Federazione nazionale fascista dei dirigenti di aziende industriali, Milan 1942.

'Autarchia e complessi economici supernazionali', *Rivista di politica economica*, 32, 2, 1942, 77–97.

Giordano, A., 'Il commercio estero della Jugoslavia e della Grecia e gli sviluppi economici derivanti dal conflitto italo-ellenico', *Rivista di politica economica*, 30, 9–10, 1940, 791–4.

'La nuova organizzazione dell'economia europea e il bacino mediterraneo', *Rivista di politica economica*, 30, 9–10, 1940, 687–91.

'La Bulgaria nel nuovo assetto europeo', *Rivista di politica economica*, 31, 4, 1941, 840–2 (unsigned article but presumably by the same author) and 914–20.

'L'economia bulgara e il suo apporto nella sistemazione dell'economia dei paesi dell'Europa sudorientale', *Rivista di politica economica*, 31, 4, 1941, 338–41.

'L'inquadramento dell'economia ellenica nelle attività europee', *Rivista di politica economica*, 31, 7, 1941, 616–20.

'L'Italia e la nuova economia balcanica', *Economia. Rivista di economia corporativa e di scienze sociali*, 19, 2, 1941, 225–36.

'Le possibilità di sviluppare le esportazioni dell'industria meccanica italiana nell'Europa orientale', *Rivista di politica economica*, 31, 3, 1941, 237–40.

'Gli sviluppi della situazione nell'Europa sudorientale e le loro ripercussioni economiche', *Rivista di politica economica*, 31, 6, 1941, 519–23.

'Gli sviluppi economici nell'Europa sudorientale e gli interessi italiani', *Economia italiana*, 26, May 1941, 254–61.

'La valorizzazione della navigazione fluviale in Ungheria e Slovacchia e gli interessi dei nostri porti adriatici', *Rivista di politica economica*, 31, 8–9, 1941, 705–7.

Gray, E. M., *Le terre nostre ritornano*, Istituto geografico De Agostini, Novara 1941.

Dopo vent'anni. Il fascismo e l'Europa, PNF, Rome 1943.

Graziani, F., 'Gli aromeni del Pindo. Cultura e vicende storiche', *Difesa della razza*, 4, 5, 1941, 6–9.

Guglielmi, G., 'Impero e razza', unpublished typescript, in USSME, L 13, b. 59, undated.

Gulinelli, A., 'Il conflitto italo-ellenico', *Rivista di politica economica*, 31, 3, 1941, 231–7.

'La Croazia', *Rivista di politica economica*, 31, 8–9, 1941, 668–76.

Hassel, U. von, 'Die Neuordnung im Südostraum', *Berliner Monatshefte*, 19 September 1941.

Isnardi, G., *La Corsica*, Cremonese, Rome 1942.

Istituto di Studi Liguri, *Nizza nella storia, studi di N. Lamboglia e altri*, preface by M. Moresco, Garzanti, Milan 1943.

Istituto Nazionale per le Relazioni Culturali con l'Estero (IRCE), *Italia e Grecia. Saggi sulle due civiltà e i loro rapporti attraverso i secoli, scritti di E. Barie e altri*, Le Monnier, Florence 1939.

L'Italia e la difesa della razza, Istituto Nazionale per le Relazioni Culturali con l'Estero, Rome 1942.

Italie et Albanie, volume in the library of the Ministero degli Affari Esteri (without bibliographical references).

La Torre, M., 'Il compito direttivo dell'Italia imperiale', *Economia italiana*, 25, October 1940, 580–5.

'Ingrandimento dello stato italiano e del suo spazio vitale', *Economia italiana*, XXVI, June 1941, 283–90.

Landra, G., 'Presente e avvenire del razzismo italiano', *Difesa della razza*, 6, 12, 1943, 26–8.

Lodoli, R., 'Realtà e problemi di Lubiana', *Critica fascista*, July 1941, 315–16.

Lucatello, G., *La natura giuridica dell'unione italo-albanese*, Cedam, Padua 1943.

Magugliani, L., 'Impostazione geopolitica del bacino mediterraneo', *Geopolitica*, 4, 8–9, 1942, 374–82.

Mainardi, L., *Nazionalità e spazi vitali*, Cremonese, Rome 1941.

Maineri, B., 'I paesi mediterranei e la nuova Europa nel dopoguerra', *Rivista di politica economica*, 30, 9–10, 1940, 884–6.

Massi, E., *La valorizzazione economica dell'impero*, Edizioni della Federazione Nazionale Fascista dei Dirigenti di Aziende Industriali, Rome 1938.

Mazzei, J., 'La chiusura economica delle grandi unità statali e la subordinazione economica degli stati minori, premesse alla guerra attuale', *Economia fascista*, 3, 1942, 9, 6–15, and 10, 10–15.

Mazzei, V., *Razza e nazione*, Edizioni italiane, Rome 1941.

Messineo, A., 'Spazio vitale e grande spazio', *La civiltà cattolica*, Rome 1942.

Milone, F., 'La funzione mediterranea dell'Italia e l'avvenire del porto di Napoli', *Giornale degli economisti e Annali di economia*, 56, May–June 1941, 325–33.

Missoni, L., *Luci ed ombre sulle Dinariche. L'Italia nei Balcani*, Anonima Arti grafiche, Bologna 1942.

Montandon, G., 'Trapianti etnici', *Difesa della razza*, 3, 5 April 1940, 6–11.

Morandi, M., 'La comunità imperiale e l'Albania', *Civiltà fascista*, 6, April 1942, 370.

Mori, A., *La Dalmazia*, Cremonese, Rome 1942.

Nardi, O., 'I sessanta giorni di vita del commissariato civile della Dalmazia', *Rivista dalmatica*, 2–3, 1941, 57–65.

Nocera, G., '120 anni. Influenze straniere in Grecia e modifiche territoriali', *Geopolitica*, 4, 1, January 1942, 4–14.

Omarini, G. L., *Frontiere ideali*, L'artiglio, Lucca 1939.

Orano, P. (ed.), *Le direttive del duce sui problemi della vita nazionale. L'espansione coloniale*, Pinciana, Rome 1937.

Orestano, F., 'Nuovo ordine europeo', *Gerarchia*, 21, 1, 1942, 1–9.

Ottello, G., 'Spazi economici, scambi e collaborazione', *Economia italiana*, 27, July–August 1942, 321–30.

Pala, G., 'I porti dell'Adriatico orientale e la nuova sistemazione balcanica', *Economia italiana*, 26, October 1941, 474–9.

Pellizzi, C., 'Italia e Germania. Problemi del nuovo ordine', *Civiltà fascista*, 1–2, November–December 1941, 31–2, and 4 February 1942, 228–35.

Perticone, G., 'Il problema dello spazio vitale e del grande spazio', *Lo stato*, 11, 12, 1940, 522–31.

Pettinato, C., *La Francia vinta*, ISPI, Milan 1941.

Piccoli, F., 'La nazione e l'ordine nuovo', *Gerarchia*, 21, 7, July 1942, 281–4.

Pistolese, G. E., 'La valorizzazione industriale della nuova Albania', *Economia italiana*, 25, October 1940, 602–7.

Pozzi, R. A., 'Il valore razza nel problema coloniale', *Geopolitica*, 4, 1942, 11, 485–95, and 12, 538–47.

Pracchi, R., 'L'Italia nell'economia degli stati balcanici dal 1918 al 1938', *Geopolitica*, 2, 11, 1940, 491–5.

Quartara, G., *La futura pace*, Bocca, Milan 1942.

Reale Accademia d'Italia, *Italia e Croazia, scritti di A. Schiaffini e altri*, Rome 1942.

Regele, L. W., 'Südtirol in der Optionzeit und im zweiten Weltkrieg', *Österreich in Geschichte und Literatur*, 34, 5–6, 1990, 301–22.

Riccardi, R., 'Collaborazione economica europea', *Economia fascista*, 3, 1, 1942, 3–11.

'Rapporti economici italo-tedeschi', *Economia fascista*, 3, 3, 1942, 3–6.

Rivera, V., 'Prospettive di colonizzazione dell'Africa orientale italiana', *Rassegna economica dell'Africa italiana*, Rome 1939.

Roletto, G., *Rodi. La funzione imperiale nel Mediterraneo orientale*, Istituto Fascista dell'Africa Italiana, Milan section, Milan 1939.

Savelli, G., 'Corsica italiana. Sintesi razziale, Difesa della razza', 3, 5 June 1940, 23–7.

Schmidt, P. (ed.), *Rivoluzione nel Mediterraneo*, ISPI, Milan 1942.

Schmitt, C., 'Il concetto imperiale di spazio', *Lo stato*, 11, 7, 1940, 309–21; reprinted in Schmitt, *L'unità del mondo e altri saggi*, Pellicani, Rome 1994, 203–15.

Scocchi, A., 'L'Italia e i Balcani nel pensiero di Mazzini', *Geopolitica*, 2, 11, November 1940, 487.

Scodro, R., 'La propaganda nei paesi occupati', *Critica fascista*, 20, 20, 1942, 168.

Selvi, G., 'Le basi dell'ordine nuovo', *Gerarchia*, 21, 4, 1942, 162.

Nuova civiltà per la nuova Europa, Unione Editoriale d'Italia, Rome 1942.

Serra, E. (ed.), *L'occupazione bellica germanica negli anni 1939–1940*, ISPI, Milan 1941.
Sertoli Salis, R., *Le isole italiane dell'Egeo dall'occupazione alla sovranità*, Regio Istituto per la Storia del Risorgimento Italiano, Rome 1939.
Imperi e colonizzazioni, ISPI, Milan 1941.
'La condizione degli ebrei nella comunità imperiale italiana', *Rassegna italiana*, 56, 25, 1942, 241–51.
'L'elemento antropico e il nuovo ordine politico mediterraneo', *Gerarchia*, 21, 2, 1942, 68–73.
Soprano, D., *Spazio vitale*, Corbaccio, Milan 1941.
Spampanato, B., *Perché questa guerra*, Politica nuova, Rome 1942.
Starace, C., *Bibliografia della Corsica*, introduction by G. Volpe, ISPI, Milan 1943.
Stato Maggiore del Regio Esercito (SMRE) – Ufficio Propaganda, *Parole di ufficiali ai soldati, trascrizione dei discorsi radiofonici del 1941*, Rome 1942.
Tamagnini, G., 'Lo "spazio vitale" nell'organizzazione del nuovo ordine', *Rassegna italiana*, 56, 25, 1942, 157–62.
Taralletto, G., 'L'espansione coloniale nel nuovo ordine europeo', *Rivista delle colonie italiane*, 15, 11, 1941, 467–75.
Titta, A., 'Concetto di spazio vitale', *Gerarchia*, 20, 12, 1941, 646–8.
Tocilj, E., 'L'agricoltura del libero stato di Croazia', *Rivista di politica economica*, 11, 1941, 911–13.
Toniolo, A., Giusti, U. and Morandini, G., *La provincia di Lubiana*, Zanichelli, Bologna 1942.
Touring Club Italiano, *Guida d'Italia*, Rome, 1942.
Tritonj, R., *Politica indigena africana*, ISPI, Milan 1941.
Unione Editoriale d'Italia, *Nuova civiltà per la nuova Europa*, Rome 1942.
Vlora, A. K., 'L'italianità della Corsica', *Difesa della razza*, 6, January 1943, 14–17, and 20 May 1943, 4–7.
Volpi di Misurata, G., 'L'economia di domani', *Rivista di politica economica*, 30, 9–10, 1940, 625–6 (from *Popolo d'Italia*, 12 September 1940).

SECONDARY BIBLIOGRAPHY

Abramovici, P., *Un rocher bien occupé. Monaco pendant la guerre 1939–1945*, Seuil, Paris 2001.
Agazzi, E. (ed.), *La dittatura fascista*, Storia della società italiana, vol. XXII, Teti, Milan 1983.
Alcock, A. E., *The History of the South Tyrol Question*, Joseph, London 1970.
Amoretti, G. N., *La vicenda italo-croata nei documenti di Aimone di Savoia (1941–1943)*, Ipotesis, Rapallo 1979.
André, G., 'La guerra in Europa (1 settembre 1939–22 giugno 1941)', *Annuario di politica internazionale*, 6, 1, 1939–45.
'L'Italia nella seconda guerra mondiale fino all'intervento degli Stati Uniti nel conflitto', in *La politica estera italiana, 1918–1943*, ERI, Turin 1980.

and Pastorelli, P. (eds.), *La seconda guerra mondiale*, 2 vols., ISPI, Milan 1964–7.

Aquarone, A., 'Lo spirito pubblico in Italia alla vigilia della seconda guerra mondiale', *Nord e sud*, 11, 1964, 117–25.

Arcidiacono, B. and Burrin, P., 'Les occupations en Europes', *Relations internationales*, 79–80, 1994, 283–500.

Arendt, H., *The Origins of Totalitarianism*, Harcourt Brace, New York 1951 [It. trans. *Le origini del totalitarismo*, Comunità, Turin 1999].

Eichmann in Jerusalem. A Report on the Banality of Evil, Viking, New York 1963.

Arnold, W. V., *The Illusion of Victory. Fascist Propaganda and the Second World War*, Lang, New York 1998.

'Aspetti e momenti della crisi europea e della seconda guerra mondiale', *Storia contemporanea*, 7, 4, December 1976 (special issue).

'Axis Campaign Against Greece, 1940–1941', *Balkan Studies*, 23, 1, 1982, 3–236.

Ayçoberry, P., *La société allemande sous le III*e *Reich*, Seuil, Paris 1998.

Azzi, R., 'The Historiography of Fascist Foreign Policy', *Historical Journal*, 36, 1, 1993, 187–203.

Baird, J. W., *The Mythical World of the Nazi War Propaganda, 1939–1945*, University of Minnesota Press, Minneapolis 1974.

Barker, E., 'Fresh Sidelights on British Policy in Yugoslavia, 1942–1943', *Slavonic and East European Review*, 54, October 1976, 565–72.

Bartov, O., *The Eastern Front, 1941–1945. German Troops and the Barbarisation of Warfare*, Macmillan, London 1985.

Hitler's Army, Oxford University Press, Oxford 1992.

Bellomo, B., *Lettere censurate, 1940–1942. L'ottusità del potere si scatena sulla corrispondenza tra soldati e civili*, Longanesi, Milan 1975.

Ben-Ghiat, R., *La cultura fascista*, Il Mulino, Bologna 2000.

Bérenger, J., *Histoire de l'empire des Habsbourg, 1273–1918*, Fayard, Paris 1990.

Bernardini, G., 'The Origins and the Development of Racial Anti-Semitism in Fascist Italy', *Journal of Modern History*, 44, 3, 1977, 431–53.

Bessis, J., *La Méditerranée fasciste. L'Italie mussolinienne et la Tunisie*, Karthala, Paris 1981.

Bianchini, S., *6 aprile 1941*, Marzorati, Milan 1993.

Una biografia senza fine. Mussolini e l'Italia in guerra, studies by N. Tranfaglia et al., *Studi storici*, XXXII, 3, 1991, 597–637.

Bitzes, G., *Greece in World War II to April 1941*, Sunflower University Press, Manhattan, KS 1988.

Boban, L., 'Jasenovac and the Manipulation of History', *East European Politics and Societies*, 4, 3, 1994, 580–92.

Bono, S., 'Islam et politique coloniale en Libye', *Maghreb Review*, 13, 1–2, 1988, 70–6.

Borejza, J., 'Greece and the Balkan Policy of Fascist Italy', *Journal of Hellenic Diaspora*, 13, 1–2, 1988, 53–70.

Borgogni, M., *Mussolini e la Francia di Vichy (giugno 1940–aprile 1942)*, Nuova Immagine, Siena 1991.

Italia e Francia durante la crisi militare dell'Asse. L'ombra di Berlino sui rapporti diplomatici fra Italia fascista e Francia di Vichy, Nuova Immagine, Siena 1994.

Bosworth, J. B. and Romano, S. (eds.), *La politica estera italiana, 1860–1985*, Il Mulino, Bologna 1991.

Bowman, S., 'Jews in Wartime Greece', *Jewish Social Studies*, 48, 1, Winter 1986, 45–62.

'Could the Dodekanisi Jews Have Been Saved?', *Jewish Museum of Greece Newsletter*, 26, Winter 1989.

Breccia, A., 'Le potenze dell'Asse e la neutralità della Jugoslavia alla vigilia della seconda guerra mondiale', in Institute of Contemporary History (ed.), *The Third Reich and Yugoslavia, 1933–1945*, Belgrade 1977, 107–31.

Jugoslavia, 1939–1941. Diplomazia della neutralità, Giuffrè, Milan 1978.

Browning, C. R., *The Final Solution and the German Foreign Office. A Study of Referat D III of Abteilung Deutschland, 1940–1943*, Holmes & Meier, New York 1978.

'Wehrmacht Reprisal Policy and the Mass Murder of the Jews of Serbia', *Militärgeschichtliche Mitteilung*, 33, 1, 1983, 31–47.

Ordinary Men. Reserve Police Battalion 101 and the Final Solution in Poland, HarperCollins, New York 1992.

Burgio, A. (ed.), *Nel nome della razza. Il razzismo italiano nella storia d'Italia, 1870–1945*, Il Mulino, Bologna 2000.

Burrin, P., *Hitler et les juifs. Genèse d'un génocide*, Seuil, Paris 1989.

La France à l'heure allemande, Seuil, Paris 1995.

'Charisme et radicalisation dans le régime nazi', in H. Rousso (ed.), *Stalinisme et nazisme. Histoire et mémoire comparées*, Complèxe, Brussels 1999, 79–95.

Fascisme, nazisme et autoritarisme, Seuil, Paris 2000.

Caffaz, U., *L'antisemitismo italiano sotto il fascismo*, La Nuova Italia, Florence 1975.

Caforio, G. and Del Negro, P. (eds.), *Ufficiali e società. Interpretazione e modelli*, Angeli, Milan 1988.

Capogreco, C. S., *Ferramonti. La vita e gli uomini del più grande campo d'internamento fascista*, Giuntina, Florence 1987.

'I campi di internamento fascisti per gli ebrei, 1940–1943', *Storia contemporanea*, 22, 4, 1990, 663–82.

'L'internamento degli ebrei stranieri e apolidi dal 1940 al 1943. Il caso di Ferramonti Tarsia, in Italia judaica. Gli ebrei nell'Italia unita, 1870–1945', proceedings of the IV Convegno Internazionale, Siena, 12–16 June 1989, Ministero per i Beni Culturali e Ambientali, Ufficio Centrale per i Beni Archivistici, Rome 1993.

Renicci, un campo di concentramento in riva al Tevere (1942–1943), Fondazione Ferramonti Tarsia, Cosenza 1998.

'Una storia rimossa dell'Italia fascista. L'internamento dei civili jugoslavi (1941–1943)', *Studi storici*, 42, January–March 2001, 204–30.

Caracciolo, N., *Gli ebrei e l'Italia durante la guerra 1940–1945*, Bonacci, Rome 1986.

Carageani, G., 'Gli aromeni e la questione aromena nei documenti dell'Archivio storico diplomatico (1891–1916)', *Storia contemporanea*, 22, 4, 1990, 633–62.

Carpi, D., 'Rescue of Jews in the Italian Zone of Occupied Croatia', in *Rescue Attempts During the Holocaust*, proceedings of the Second Yad Vashem International Historical Conference (Jerusalem, April 8–11, 1974), edited by Y. Gutman and E. Zuroff, Ktav, New York 1978, 465–525.

'Notes of the History of the Jews in Greece During the Holocaust Period. The Attitude of the Italians, 1941–1943', in *Festschrift in Honor of G. S. Wise*, Ben-Shahar, Tel Aviv 1981, 25–62.

'Nuovi documenti per la storia dell'Olocausto in Grecia. L'atteggiamento degli italiani 1941–1943', *Michael*, 7, 1981, 118–200.

'The Italian Diplomat Luca Pietromarchi. On His Activities for the Jews of Croatia and Greece', *Yalkut Moreshet*, 33, 1982, 145–52.

'L'atteggiamento degli italiani nei confronti degli ebrei della Tunisia (giugno 1940–marzo 1943)', *Storia contemporanea*, 20, 6, 1989, 1183–246.

Between Mussolini and Hitler. The Jews and the Italian Authorities in France and Tunisia, University Press of New England, Hanover 1994.

Castronovo, V., 'L'industria di guerra, 1940–1943', *Italia contemporanea*, 160, 1985, 43–55.

Catalano, F., *L'economia italiana di guerra. La politica economico-finanziaria del fascismo dalla guerra d'Etiopia alla caduta del regime, 1935–1943*, Istituto Nazionale per la Storia del Movimento di Liberazione, Milan 1969.

Cavaglion, A., *Nella notte straniera. Gli ebrei di Saint-Martin-Vésubie e il campo di Borgo San Dalmazzo (8 settembre–21 novembre 1943)*, L'arciere, Cuneo 1981.

Cavallo, P., *Italiani in guerra. Sentimenti e immagini dal 1940 al 1943*, Il Mulino, Bologna 1997.

Cavarocchi, F., review of Maiocchi, R., *Scienza italiana e razzismo fascista*, La Nuova Italia, Florence 1999, in *Passato e presente*, 18, 50, 2000.

Centre Nationale de la Recherche Sciéntifique (CNRS), *La guerre en Méditerranée*, Paris 1971.

Centro di Documentazione Ebraica Contemporanea (CDEC), *Ebrei in Italia. Deportazione, Resistenza*, Florence 1974.

'Le leggi contro gli ebrei', *La rassegna mensile di Israel*, 1–2, 1988.

Cervi, M., *Storia della guerra in Grecia*, Sugar, Milan 1965.

Ceva, B., *Cinque anni di storia italiana, 1940–1945*, Comunità, Milan 1964.

Ceva, L., 'Testimonianze sulla guerra di Grecia', *Risorgimento*, 31, 1, 1979, 103–6.

Le forze armate, Utet, Turin 1981.

'Vertici politici e militari nel 1940–1943. Interrogativi e temi d'indagine', *Il politico*, 46, 4, 1981, 691–700.

'Il diario del maresciallo Ugo Cavallero', *Rivista storica italiana*, 97, 1, 1985, 296–324.

Coen, F., *Italiani ed ebrei. Come eravamo. Le leggi razziali del 1938*, Marietti, Genoa 1988.

Cohen, A., 'La politique antijuive en Europe (Allemagne exclue) de 1938 à 1941', *Guerres mondiales et conflits contemporains*, 150, 1988, 45–59.

Collotti, E., *L'amministrazione tedesca dell'Italia occupata, 1943–1945*, Lerici, Milan 1963.

(ed.), *L'occupazione nazista in Europa*, Editori Riuniti, Rome 1964.

'L'alleanza italo-tedesca, 1941–1943', in Storia della società italiana, vol. 22, *La dittatura fascista*, Teti, Milan 1983, 452ff.

'L'Italia dall'intervento alla guerra parallela', in *L'Italia nella seconda guerra mondiale e nella Resistenza*, Angeli, Milan 1988, 21ff.

Fascismo, fascismi, Sansoni, Florence 1989.

'Sulla politica di repressione italiana nei Balcani', in L. Paggi (ed.), *La memoria del nazismo nell'Europa di oggi*, La Nuova Italia, Florence 1997, 182–208.

Collotti, E., and Klinkhammer, L., *Il fascismo e l'Italia in guerra. Una conversazione fra storia e storiografia*, Ediesse, Rome 1996.

Collotti, E., and Sala, T. (ed.), *Le potenze dell'Asse e la Jugoslavia. Saggi e documenti, 1941/1943*, Feltrinelli, Milan 1974.

Conway, M., *Collaboration in Belgium*, Yale University Press, New Haven 1993.

Courtois, S. and Rayski, A. (eds.), *Qui savait quoi?*, La Découverte, Paris 1987.

Crapanzano, G., *Soldi d'Italia. Un secolo di cartamoneta*, Fondazione Cassa di Risparmio di Parma, Parma 1996.

Crespi, R., *Squadristi in Albania*, Nazionale Ed. Propaganda, Milan 1981.

Cuzzi, M., 'I Balcani, problemi di un'occupazione difficile', in R. Rainero and A. Biagini (eds.), *L'Italia in guerra il terzo anno – 1942*, Stabilimento grafico militare, Gaeta 1987.

L'occupazione italiana della Slovenia, 1940–1943, SME, Rome 1998.

Dallin, A., *La Russie sous la Botte nazie*, Fayard, Paris 1981.

De Felice, R., *Storia degli ebrei italiani sotto il fascismo*, Einaudi, Turin 1961, 1993.

(ed.), *L'Italia fra tedeschi e alleati*, Il Mulino, Bologna 1973.

Il problema dell'Alto Adige nei rapporti italo-tedeschi dall'Anschluss alla fine della seconda guerra mondiale, Il Mulino, Bologna 1973.

Mussolini il duce. Lo stato totalitario, 1936–1940, Einaudi, Turin 1981.

'Un nuovo documento sulla condizione degli ebrei nella zona d'occupazione italiana in Francia durante la seconda guerra mondiale', in *Israel. Saggi sull'ebraismo italiano*, edited by F. Del Canuto, Carucci, Rome 1984, 179–84.

'Ebrei, antisemitismo e razzismo in Italia dall'unità alla persecuzione fascista', *Storia contemporanea*, 19, 6, 1988, 1013–321.

Mussolini l'alleato, Einaudi, Turin 1990.

Rosso e nero, Baldini & Castoldi, Milan 1995.

Deakin, F. W., *The Brutal Friendship. Mussolini, Hitler and the Fall of Fascism*, Penguin, London 1966.

Del Boca, A., *Gli italiani in Africa orientale italiana*, 3 vols., Laterza, Bari 1979–83.

Del Boca, A., Legnani, M. and Rossi, M. G. (eds.), *Il regime fascista*, Laterza, Bari 1995.

Del Canuto, F., 'I falascià fra politica antisemita e politica razziale', *Storia contemporanea*, 19, 6, 1988, 1189–221.

Della Seta, S., 'Gli ebrei del Mediterraneo nella strategia politica fascista sino al 1938. Il caso di Rodi', *Storia contemporanea*, 17, December 1986, 997–1023.

Destopopoulos, A. I., 'La guerre gréco-italienne et gréco-allemande', *Revue d'histoire de la deuxième guerre mondiale*, 34, 136, 1984, 22ff.

Djilas, A., *The Contested Country. Yugoslav Unity and Communist Revolution, 1919–1953*, Harvard University Press, Cambridge, MA 1991.

Dufraisse, R., 'Le Troisième Reich', in J. Tulard (ed.), *Les empires occidentaux de Rome à Berlin*, PUF, Paris 1997, 449–82.

Dufraisse, R., and Kerautret, M., *La France napoléonienne. Aspects extérieurs, 1799–1815*, Seuil, Paris 1999.

Duroselle, J. B., and Serra, E. (eds.), *Italia e Francia*, 1939–1945, 2 vols., Angeli, Milan 1984.

Duus, P., 'Imperialism Without Colonies. The Vision of a Greater East Asia Co-Prosperity Sphere', *Diplomacy and Statecraft*, 7, 1, March 1996, 54–72.

Duus, P., Myers, R. H., and Peattie, M. R. (ed.), *The Japanese Wartime Empire, 1931–1945*, Princeton University Press, Princeton 1996.

Etmektsoglou-Koehn, G., 'Axis Exploitation of Wartime Greece, 1941–1943', PhD thesis, Emory University, Atlanta, GA 1995, unpublished.

Faldella, E., *L'Italia e la seconda guerra mondiale. Revisione di giudizi*, Cappelli, Bologna 1960.

Fenet, A., *La question du Tyrol du Sud. Un problème de droit international*, Librairie générale de droit et de jurisprudence, Paris 1968.

Ferenc, T., *La provincia 'italiana' di Lubiana. Documenti, 1941–1942*, Istituto friulano per la storia del movimento di liberazione, Udine 1994.

Ferrari, D., 'Considerazioni sull'ordinamento delle truppe nelle campagne balcaniche, 1939–1943', in *L'Italia in guerra, 1940–1943*, *Annali della Fondazione Luigi Micheletti*, 5, Brescia 1990–1, 125–40.

Ferratini Tosi, F., Grassi, G. and Legnani, M. (eds.), *L'Italia nella seconda guerra mondiale e nella Resistenza*, Angeli, Milan 1988.

Ferro, M., *Histoire des colonisations*, Seuil, Paris 1994.

Fino, E., *La tragedia di Rodi e dell'Egeo*, Rome 1957.

Fischer, B. J., 'Italian Policy in Albania, 1894–1943', *Balkan Studies*, 26, 1, 1985, 101–12.

Fischer, B. J., *Albania at War, 1939–1945*, Purdue University Press, West Lafayette, IN 1999.

Fleischer, H., 'Deutsche Besatzungsherrschaft zwischen Hegemonialpolitik, Ausbeutung und Germanisierung. Das Beispiel Griechenland', in N. Frei and H. Kling (eds.), *Der nationalsozialistische Krieg*, Campus, Frankfurt and New York 1990, 205–19.

Folino, F., *Ferramonti un lager di Mussolini. Gli internati durante la guerra*, Brenner, Cosenza 1985.

Foresti, F., 'Il problema linguistico nella politica indigena del colonialismo fascista', *Movimento operaio e socialista*, n.s., 7, 1, January–April 1984, 133–55.

Franco, H. M., *Les martyrs juifs de Rhodes et de Cos*, Congrégation israélite du Katanga, Elisabethville (Lubumbashi), Congo 1952.

Franzina, E., 'Una storia mentale degli italiani in guerra', *Quaderni storici*, 25, 2, 1990, 621–36.

Franzinelli, M., *Il riarmo dello spirito. I cappellani militari nella seconda guerra mondiale*, Pagus, Treviso 1991.

Stellette, croce e fascio littorio. L'assistenza religiosa a militari, balilla e camicie nere, 1919–1939, Angeli, Milan 1995.

Frei, N., *Der Führerstaat. Nationalsozialistische Herrschaft 1933 bis 1945*, Deutscher Taschenbuch Verlag, Munich 1987 [It. trans *Lo stato nazista*, Laterza, Rome 1992].

Freppaz, C., *La Haute Tarentaise dans la tourmente. La guerre 1939–1945*, Didier-Richard, Grenoble 1978.

Friedländer, S., *L'Allemagne nazie et les juifs*, Seuil, Paris 1997.

Gabrielli, G., 'Un aspetto della politica razzista nell'impero. Il "problema dei meticci"', *Passato e presente*, 15, 41, 1997, 77–105.

Gallerano, N., 'Gli italiani in guerra 1940–1943. Appunti per una ricerca', in Ferratini Tosi, Grassi and Legnani, *L'Italia nella seconda guerra mondiale e nella Resistenza*.

Gentile, E., 'Fascism as Political Religion', *Journal of Contemporary History*, 25, 2–3, 1986, 229–51.

Il culto del littorio, Laterza, Bari 1993.

La via italiana al totalitarismo, NIS, Rome 1995.

Le origini dell'ideologia fascista, Il Mulino, Bologna 1996.

Germinario, F., *Razza del sangue, razza dello spirito. Julius Evola, l'antisemitismo e il nazionalsocialismo (1930–1943)*, Bollati Boringhieri, Turin 2002.

Giardina, A. and Vauchez, A., *Rome. L'idée et le mythe du Moyen Âge à nos jours*, Fayard, Paris 2000.

Goglia, L., and Grassi, F., *Il colonialismo italiano da Adua all'impero*, Laterza, Bari 1993.

Goodman, G. K. (ed.), *Japanese Cultural Policies in Southeast Asia During World War II*, Macmillan, London 1981.

Gross, J. T., *Polish Society Under German Occupation. The General Government, 1939–1944*, Princeton University Press, Princeton 1979.

Revolution from Abroad. The Soviet Conquest of Poland's Western Ukraine and Western Belorussia, Princeton University Press, Princeton 1979.

Grottanelli, V., 'La ricerca etnologica nel periodo coloniale. Una testimonianza e una riflessione', *Storia contemporanea*, 16, 5–6, 1985, 1133–52.

Grünbaum, I., *Escape Through the Balkans*, University of Nebraska Press, Lincoln 1996.

Guillen, P., 'Les entreprises industrielles françaises en Italie pendant la période fasciste', *Studi in memoria di Mario Abate*, Università degli Studi di Torino, Turin 1986, 553–60.

Gunzberg, L., *Strangers at Home. Jews in the Italian Literary Imagination*, University of California Press, Berkeley 1992.

Herzer, I. (ed.), *The Italian Refuge. Rescue of the Jews During the Holocaust*, Catholic University of America Press, Washington 1989.

Hilberg, R., *La déstruction des juifs d'Europe*, Fayard, Paris 1988.
Hirschfeld, G. (ed.), *The Policies of Genocide*, German Historical Institute, London 1986.
Hondros, J. L., *Occupation and Resistance. The Greek Agony, 1941–1944*, Pella, New York 1983.
Hoppe, H. J., 'Germany, Bulgaria, Greece. Their Relations and Bulgarian Policy in Occupied Greece', *Journal of the Hellenic Diaspora*, 11, 3, 1984, 41–54.
'Bulgarian Nationality Policy in Occupied Thrace and Aegean Macedonia', *Nationality Papers*, 14, 1–2, 1986, 89–100.
Iatrides, J. (ed.), *Greece in the 1940s. A Nation in Crisis*, University Press of New England, London 1981.
Institut pour l'Étude du Mouvement Ouvrier, *Les systèmes d'occupation en Yougoslavie*, Congrès International sur l'Histoire de la Résistance Européenne, Belgrade 1963.
Institute of Contemporary History, Belgrade, *The Third Reich and Yugoslavia, 1933–1945*, 1977.
Ipsen, C., *Demografia totalitaria. Il problema della popolazione nell'Italia fascista*, Il Mulino, Bologna 1997.
Israel, G. and Nastasi, P., *Scienza e razza nell'Italia fascista*, Il Mulino, Bologna 1998.
Istituto nazionale per la Storia del Movimento di Liberazione, *L'Italia nell'Europa danubiana durante la seconda guerra mondiale*, essays by E. Collotti et al., Milan 1968.
Istituto Storico della Resistenza in Piemonte, *Una storia di tutti. Prigionieri, internati, deportati italiani nella seconda guerra mondiale*, Angeli, Milan 1989.
Jamini, A. L., 'Il salvataggio degli ebrei a Fiume durante la persecuzione nazi-fascista', *Movimento di liberazione in Italia*, 37, July 1955, 42–7.
Jerkov, A., 'Le direttive per l'occupazione in Jugoslavia', *Balcanica*, II, 2, 1983, 92–6.
Jourdan, A., *L'empire de Napoléon*, Flammarion, Paris 2000.
Jovanovich, L. M., 'The War in the Balkans in 1941', *East European Quarterly*, 23, 1, 1994, 105–29.
Kaser, M., 'Albania and Foreign Protection', *Slavic Review*, 47, 3, 1988, 526–9.
Kershaw, I., *Hitler*, Longman, London 1991 [It. trans. *Hitler e l'enigma del consenso*, Laterza, Rome-Bari 1997; French trans. *Hitler. Essai sur le charisme en politique*, Gallimard, Paris 1995].
Hitler, 1889–1936. Hubris, Penguin, London 1998 [It. trans. *Hitler, 1889–1936*, Bompiani, Milan 1999].
'"Working Towards the Führer". Reflections on the Nature of the Hitler Dictatorship', in I. Kershaw and M. Lewin (eds.), *Stalinism and Nazism. Dictatorship in Comparison*, Cambridge University Press, Cambridge 1998, 80–106.
Hitler, 1936–1945. Nemesis, Penguin, London 2000 [It. trans. *Hitler, 1936–1945*, Bompiani, Milan 2001].
Kershaw, I., and Lewin, M. (ed.), *Stalinism and Nazism. Dictatorship in Comparison*, Cambridge University Press, Cambridge 1997.

Klarsfeld, S., *Vichy–Auschwitz*, Fayard, Paris 1985.

'Le jeu de Vichy entre les italiens et les allemands', *Monde juif*, 49, 149, 1993, 74–83.

Klinkhammer, L., 'La politica tedesca nei confronti dell'Italia prima e dopo l'8 settembre e il disarmo delle truppe italiane', in B. Dradi Maraldi and R. Pieri (eds.), *Lotta armata e resistenza delle forze armate italiane all'estero*, Angeli, Milan 1990, 84–114.

Zwischen Bündnis und Besatzung. Das nationalsozialistische Deutschland und die Republik von Salò, 1943–1945, Niemeyer, Tübingen 1993 [It. trans. *L'occupazione tedesca in Italia, 1943–1945*, Bollati Boringhieri, Turin 1993].

Knox, M., *Mussolini Unleashed, 1939–1941. Politics and Strategy in Fascist Italy's Last War*, Cambridge University Press, Cambridge 1982.

'Conquest, Foreign and Domestic, in Fascist Italy and Nazi Germany', *Journal of Modern History*, 56, 1984, 1–57.

'The Fascist Regime, Its Foreign Policy and Its Wars. An "Anti-Anti Fascist" Orthodoxy?', *Contemporary European History*, 4, 3, 1995, 347–65.

Common Destiny. Dictatorship, Foreign Policy, and War in Fascist Italy and Nazi Germany, Cambridge University Press, Cambridge 2000.

Hitler's Italian Allies, Royal Armed Forces, Fascist Regime, and the War of 1940–1943, Cambridge University Press, Cambridge 2000.

Kosinski, L. A., 'International Migration of Yugoslavs During and Immediately After World War II', *East European Quarterly*, 16, 2, 1982, 183–98.

Krnic, Z., 'The German Volksgruppe in the Independent State of Croatia as an Instrument of German Occupation Policy of Yugoslavia', in Institute of Contemporary History, *The Third Reich and Yugoslavia 1933–1945*.

Kuby, E., *Verrat auf deutsch. Wie das Dritte Reich Italien ruinierte*, Hoffmann & Campe, Hamburg 1982 [It. trans. *Il tradimento tedesco*, Rizzoli, Milan 1983].

Kuzmanova, A., 'L'agression de l'Italie fasciste contre l'Ethiopie et les pays balkaniques', *Etudes balkaniques*, 22, 1, 1986, 31–41.

Laqueur, W., *The Terrible Secret*, Weidenfeld & Nicolson, London 1980.

Legnani, M., 'Sul finanziamento della guerra fascista', *Italia contemporanea*, 160, 1985, 25–42.

'Il ginger del generale Roatta, le direttive della II Armata sulla repressione antipartigiana in Slovenia e Croazia', *Italia contemporanea*, 209–10, December 1997–March 1998, 156–74.

Loker, Z., 'The Testimony of Dr Edo Neufeld. The Italians and the Jews of Croatia', *Holocaust and Genocide Studies*, 8, 1, 1993, 67–76.

Löwenthal, Z. (ed.), *The Crimes of the Fascist Occupants and Their Collaborators Against Jews in Yugoslavia*, Belgrade 1963.

Maiocchi, R., *Scienza italiana e razzismo fascista*, La Nuova Italia, Florence 1999.

Malev, C. T., 'Aspetti di una occupazione. Gli italiani in Macedonia occidentale', in *L'Italia in guerra, 1940–1943*, Annali della Fondazione Luigi Micheletti, 5, Brescia 1990–1, 171–84.

Mallett, R., 'The Anglo-Italian War Trade Negotiations, Contraband Control and the Failure to Appease Mussolini', *Diplomacy and Statecraft*, 8, 1, 1997, 137–67.

Marrus, M., 'The Nazi and the Jews in Occupied Western Europe, 1940–1944', *Journal of Modern History*, 54, 4, 1982, 687–714.

'History of the Holocaust. A Survey of Recent Literature', *Journal of Modern History*, 59, March 1987, 114–60.

The Holocaust in History, Brandeis University Press, Hanover NH 1987.

'Reflections on the Historiography of the Holocaust', *Journal of Modern History*, 66, March 1994, 92–116.

Marrus, M., and Paxton, R. O., *Vichy et les juifs*, Calman-Lévy, Paris 1981.

Martin, J.-P., 'L'empire: un espace conquis et Le modèle romain', in Tulard, *Les empires occidentaux de Rome à Berlin*, 45–78.

'L'empire: un espace organisé', in Tulard, *Les empires occidentaux de Rome à Berlin*, 79–108.

Matkovski, A., 'The Destruction of Macedonian Jewry in 1943', *Yad Vashem Studies*, 3, 1959, 203–58.

Matsas, J., and Altsech, M., 'The Participation of the Greek Jews in the National Resistance, 1940–1944', *Journal of the Hellenic Diaspora*, 17, 1, 1991, 55–68.

Mayda, G., *Ebrei sotto Salò. La persecuzione antisemita, 1943–1945*, Feltrinelli, Milan 1978.

Mazower, M., 'Military Violence and National Socialist Values. The Wehrmacht in Greece, 1941–1944', *Past and Present*, February 1992, 129–58.

Inside Hitler's Greece, Yale University Press, New Haven 1993.

'Hitler's New Order, 1939–1945', *Diplomacy and Statecraft*, 7, 1, March 1996, 29–53.

Dark Continent. Europe's Twentieth Century, Penguin, London 1998.

Messina, R., 'L'immagine della guerra nelle riviste illustrate, 1940–1943', *Italia contemporanea*, 164, 1986, 40–66.

Michaelis, M., 'The Attitude of the Fascist Regime to Jews in Italy', *Yad Vashem Studies*, 4, 1960, 7–41.

Mussolini and the Jews. German–Italian Relations and the Jewish Question in Italy, 1922–1945, Clarendon, London 1978.

'La politica razziale fascista vista da Berlino. L'antisemitismo italiano alla luce di documenti inediti (1938–1943)', *Storia contemporanea*, 11, 6, 1980, 1003–49.

Michalopoulis, D., 'The Moslems of Chamuria and the Exchange of Populations Between Greece and Turkey', *Balkan Studies*, 26, 2, 1985, 303–13.

Micheletti, B., and Poggio, P. P. (eds.), 'L'Italia in guerra, 1940–1943', *Annali della Fondazione Luigi Micheletti*, 5, Brescia 1990–1.

Mignemi, A. (ed.), *L'Italia s'è desta. Propaganda politica e mezzi di comunicazione di massa tra fascismo e democrazia*, Istituto Storico della Resistenza di Novara 'P. Fornara', Edizioni gruppo Abele, Turin 1996.

Miletić, A., *The Volksdeutschen of Bosnia, Slavonia and Srem Regions in the Struggle Against the People's Liberation Movement (1941–1944)*, in Institute of Contemporary History, *The Third Reich and Yugoslavia, 1933–1945*, 615ff.

Militärgeschichtliches Forschungsamt (Research Institute for Military History), Freiburg in Breisgau, Germany, *Germany and the Second World War*, vol. III, *The Mediterranean, South-East Europe and North Africa, 1939–1941. From Italy's Declaration of Non-Belligerence to the Entry of the United States into the War*, edited by Gerhard Schreiber, Bernd Stegemann and Detlef Vogel, trans. by Dean S. McMurry, Ewald Osers and Louise Willmot, translation editor P. S. Falla, Clarendon Press, Oxford 1995.

Milward, A., *The German Economy at War*, Athlone, London 1965.

The New Order and the French Economy, Clarendon, London 1970.

Milza, P., *Mussolini*, Fayard, Paris 2000 [It. trans. *Mussolini*, Carocci, Rome 2000].

Minerbi, S., 'Il progetto d'insediamento ebraico in Etiopia, 1936–1943', *Storia contemporanea*, 17, 6, December 1986, 1083–1137.

Minniti, F., 'Profili dell'iniziativa strategica italiana dalla non belligeranza alla guerra parallela', *Storia contemporanea*, 23, 6, 1987, 1113–97.

'Gli ufficiali di carriera dell'esercito nella crisi del regime', in A. Ventura (ed.), *Sulla crisi del regime fascista, 1938–1943. La società italiana dal 'consenso' alla Resistenza*, Marsilio, Venice 1996, 75–123.

Mitrović, A., *Ergänzungswirtschaft. The Theory of an Integrated Economic Area of the Third Reich and Southeast Europe (1933–1941)*, in Institute of Contemporary History, *The Third Reich and Yugoslavia, 1933–1945*, 7–45.

Mohlo, M. (ed.), *In memoriam. Hommage aux victimes juives des nazis en Grèce*, 2nd edn edited by J. Nehama, Nicolaidès, Thessalonica 1973.

Mollard, A., *La Résistance en Savoie, 1940–1944*, Mollard, Chambéry 1972.

Los muestros, hors série n. 1, February 1993.

Mulligan, T. P., *The Politics of Illusion and Empire. German Occupation Policy in the Soviet Union, 1942–1943*, Praeger, New York 1988.

Myers, R. H., and Peattie, M. R. (eds.), *The Japanese Colonial Empire, 1895–1945*, Princeton University Press, Princeton 1984.

Naimark, N. M., *The Russians in Germany. A History of the Soviet Zone of Occupation, 1945–1949*, Belknap Press of Harvard University Press, Cambridge, MA 1996.

Nehsovich, S., 'Mussolini's Decree on Greater Albania', *Macedonian Review*, 19, 2–3, 1989, 126–43.

Novitch, B., *Le passage des barbares*, Ghetto Fighters House, Israel 1982.

Les nouveaux cahiers, '*Etre juifs dans la douce Italie*', 118, 1994.

Nuti, L., 'I problemi storiografici connessi con l'intervento italiano nella seconda guerra mondiale', *Storia delle relazioni internazionali*, 1, 2, 1984, 369–93.

Orlandi, R., *Le isole italiane dell'Egeo (1912–1947)*, Bari, undated (after 1990).

Orlow, D., *Nazism in the Balkans*, University of Pittsburgh Press, Pittsburgh 1968.

Ostenc, M., 'Historiographie du fascisme italien. Examen critique', *Revue d'histoire de la deuxième guerre mondiale*, 35, 139, 1985, 3–23.

Ottolenghi, G., *Gli italiani e il colonialismo. I campi di detenzione italiani in Africa*, Sugar, Milan 1997.

Paggi, L. (ed.), *La memoria del nazismo nell'Europa di oggi*, La Nuova Italia, Florence 1997.

Panicacci, J.-L., 'Les juifs et la question juive dans les Alpes Maritimes de 1939 à 1945', *Recherches régionales. Côte d'Azur et contrées limitrophes*, 4, 1983, 239–331.

L'occupazione italiana di Mentone (giugno 1940–settembre 1943), Istituto Storico della Resistenza in Cuneo e Provincia, 24, December 1983, 3–18.

Les Alpes Maritimes de 1939 à 1945. Un département dans la tourmente, Serre, Nice 1989.

Paraschos, K., *E khatokhe. Fotografika tekhmeria 1941–1944*, Ermis, Athens 1997.

Parlato, G., 'Polemica antiborghese, antigermanesimo e questione razziale nel sindacalismo fascista', *Storia contemporanea*, 19, 6, 1988, 1189–221.

Paris, E., *Genocide in Satellite Croatia*, American Institute for Balkan Affairs, Chicago 1969.

Pastorelli, P., 'La politica estera fascista dalla fine del conflitto etiopico alla seconda guerra mondiale', in De Felice, *L'Italia fra tedeschi e alleati*, 113ff.

'Le carte di gabinetto del Ministero degli Affari esteri, 1923–1943', *Storia delle relazioni internazionali*, 5, 2, 1989, 313–48.

Pavlowitch, S. K., 'The King That Never Was. An Instance of Italian Involvement in Croatia, 1941–1943', *European Studies Review*, 8, 1978, 465–87.

'Momcilo Nincic and the European Policy of the Yugoslav Government in Exile, 1941–1943', *Slavonic and East European Review*, 62, 3–4, 1984, 401–18, 531–51.

The Improbable Survivor, Hurst, London 1988.

Pavone, C., *Una guerra civile. Saggio storico sulla moralità nella Resistenza*, Bollati Boringhieri, Turin 1991.

Pelagalli, S., 'Le relazioni militari italo-germaniche nelle carte del generale Marras, addetto militare a Berlino (giugno 1940–settembre 1943)', *Storia contemporanea*, 21, 1, 1990, 5–94.

Petersen, J., 'Italia e Germania: due immagini incrociate', in Ferratini Tosi, Grassi, and Legnani, *L'Italia nella seconda guerra mondiale e nella resistenza*, 49ff.

Petracarro, D., 'The Italian Army in Africa, 1940–1943. An Attempt in Historical Perspective', *War & Society*, 9, 2, 1991, 103–27.

Petrović, D., 'La situation des juifs dans le sud-est de la Serbie et en Macédoine annexés par la Bulgarie durant la seconde guerre mondiale', *Etudes balkaniques*, 1–2, 1997, 28–37.

Picciotto Fargion, L., 'Anti-Jewish Policy of the Italian Social Republic, 1943–1945', *Yad Vashem Studies*, 17, 1986, 17–49.

'Italian Citizens in Nazi-Occupied Europe. Documents from the Files of the German Foreign Office, 1941–1943', in *Simon Wiesenthal Center Annual*, 7, 1990, 93–141.

Il libro della memoria. Gli ebrei deportati dall'Italia, 1943–1945, Mursia, Milan 1991.

Pieri, P., and Ceva, L., *Badoglio*, Utet, Turin 1974.

Pitamitz, A., and Praga, G., *Storia della Dalmazia, 1870–1947*, Dall'Oglio, Milan 1981.

Poliakov, L., *Bréviaire de la haine*, Calman-Lévy, Paris 1951.

Les totalitarismes du XXe siècle, Fayard, Paris 1987.

Poliakov, L., and Sabille, J., *Jews Under the Italian Occupation*, Editions du Centre, Paris 1955.

Pommerin, R., 'La controversia di politica razziale nei rapporti dell'Asse Roma–Berlino, 1938–1943', *Storia contemporanea*, 10, 5, 1979, 925–40.

Potocnik, F., *Il campo di sterminio fascista. L'isola di Rab*, ANPI, Turin 1979.

Poznanski, R., 'Que savait-on dans le monde', in Courtois and Rayski, *Qui savait quoi?*, 24–37.

Raffaelli, S., 'Prodromi del purismo xenofobo fascista', *Movimento operaio e socialista*, 7, 1, 1984, 79–86.

Rainero, R. H., 'Le coup d'état de Metaxas et ses échos dans l'Italie fasciste', *Revue d'histoire moderne et contemporaine*, 36, 3, 1989, 439–49.

Mussolini e Pétain. Storia dei rapporti tra l'Italia e la Francia di Vichy, 2 vols., Stato Maggiore dell'Esercito, Rome 1990–2.

Raspanti, M., 'I razzismi del fascismo', in Centro Furio Jesi, *La menzogna della razza. Documenti e immagini del razzismo e dell'antisemitismo fascista*, Grafis, Bologna 1994, 73–89.

Revelli, N., *La strada del davai*, Einaudi, Turin 1966.

L'ultimo fronte. Lettere di soldati caduti o dispersi nella seconda guerra mondiale, Einaudi, Turin 1971.

Il mondo dei vinti. Testimonianze di vita contadina, 2 vols., Einaudi, Turin 1977.

Revue d'histoire de la seconde guerre mondiale, special issue, 'L'Italie dans la deuxième guerre mondiale', 92, 1973.

'L'Italie dans la deuxième guerre mondiale', 34, 136, 1984, 1–110.

Reynolds, D. (ed.), *Japanese Cultural Policies in Southeast Asia During World War II*, McFarland, London 1985.

Rich Relations. The American Occupation of Britain, 1942–1945, HarperCollins, London 1995.

Rickard, C., *La Savoie sous l'occupation*, Ouest-France, Rennes 1985.

Rieder, M., 'I rapporti economici italo-tedeschi tra alleanza, occupazione e ricostruzione', in Zamagni, *Come perdere la pace e vincere la guerra*, 309–56.

Riedmann, J., 'Auswirkungen der Politik Italiens auf das österreichische Bundesland Tirol von ca. 1928 bis 1938', *Annali dell'Istituto storico italo-germanico di Trento*, 15, 1989, 321–46.

Rigoni Stern, M., *Quota Albania*, Einaudi, Turin 1981.

Rizzi, L., *Lo sguardo del potere*, Rizzoli, Milan 1984.

'Il morale dei militari e dei civili nelle lettere censurate', in Ferratini Tosi, Grassi and Legnani, *L'Italia nella seconda guerra mondiale e nella Resistenza*, 371–8.

Roberts, R. W., *Tito, Mihalovic and the Allies, 1941–1945*, Rutgers University Press, New Brunswick, NJ 1983.

Robertson, E. M., 'Race as a Factor in Mussolini's Policy in Africa and Europe', *Journal of Contemporary History*, 23, 1988, 37–58.

Rochat, G., 'L'attentato a Graziani e la repressione italiana in Etiopia, 1936–1937', *Italia contemporanea*, 118, 1975, 3–38; reprinted in Rochat, *Guerre italiane in Libia e in Etiopia*.

'Mussolini chef de guerre, 1940–1943', *Revue d'histoire de la deuxième guerre mondiale*, 100, 1975, 43–66.

'Appunti sulla direzione politico-militare della guerra fascista, 1940–1943', *Belfagor*, 32, 1977, 7–30.

'Lo sforzo bellico, 1940–1943. Analisi di una sconfitta', *Italia contemporanea*, 160, 1985, 7–24.

'Gli uomini alle armi, 1940–1943. Dati generali sullo sforzo bellico italiano', in *L'Italia in guerra, 1940–1943*, in *Annali della Fondazione Luigi Micheletti*, 5, Brescia 1990–1, 33–72.

L'esercito italiano in pace e in guerra, Rara, Milan 1991.

'La giustizia militare nella guerra italiana, 1940–1943. Primi dati e spunti d'analisi', *Storia contemporanea*, 20, 4, 1991, 505–97.

Guerre italiane in Libia e in Etiopia, Pagus, Treviso 1991.

'Il ruolo delle forze armate nel regime fascista. Mussolini e le forze armate', in Rochat, *L'esercito italiano in pace e in guerra*, 209–19.

Rochat, G., and Venturi, M. (ed.), *La Divisione Acqui a Cefalonia, settembre 1943*, Mursia, Milan 1993.

Rochlitz, J., *Righteous Enemy. The Italians and the Jews in Occupied Europe, 1941–1943 (Extracts from the Private Diary of Count Luca Pietromarchi)*, collection of documentary materials for the film by Joseph Rochlitz, *Righteous Enemy*, 1988, National Center for Jewish Film, Waltham, MA 1991.

Romano, J., *The Jews of Yugoslavia, 1941–1945. Victims of Genocide and Freedom Fighters*, Federazione delle Comunità Ebraiche di Jugoslavia, Belgrade 1982 (translated from the Serbo-Croat).

Romano, S., *Giuseppe Volpi e l'Italia moderna*, Bompiani, Rome 1979.

Roselli, A., *Italia e Albania. Relazioni finanziarie nel ventennio fascista*, Il Mulino, Bologna 1986.

Sadkovich, J. J., 'Fascist Italy at War', *International History Review*, 14, 3, 1992, 526–33.

'The Italo-Greek War in Context. Italian Priorities and Axis Diplomacy', *Journal of Contemporary History*, 28, 1994, 439–64.

Sala, T., 'Occupazione militare e amministrazione civile nella provincia di Lubiana (1941–1943)', in *L'Italia nell'Europa danubiana durante la seconda guerra mondiale*, Istituto Nazionale per la Storia del Movimento di Liberazione, Milan 1967.

'Guerriglia e controguerriglia in Jugoslavia nella propaganda per le truppe occupanti italiane, 1941–1943', *Movimento di liberazione in Italia*, July–September 1972.

'Programmi di snazionalizzazione del "fascismo di frontiera" (1938–1942)', *Bollettino dell'Istituto regionale per la storia del movimento di liberazione nel Friuli Venezia-Giulia*, 2, 2, May 1974, 24–9.

'1939–1943. *Jugoslavia neutrale e Jugoslavia occupata*', *Italia contemporanea*, 138, 1980, 85–105.

Sarfatti, M., *Mussolini contro gli ebrei. Cronaca dell'elaborazione delle leggi del 1938*, Zamorani, Turin 1994.

'Consegnate gli ebrei', *L'Unità*, 27 April 1996.

'Fascist Italy and German Jews in South-Eastern France in July 1943', *Journal of Modern Italian Studies*, 3, 3, 1998, 318–28.

'La persecuzione degli ebrei in Italia dalle leggi razziali alla deportazione', in *La persecuzione degli ebrei durante il fascismo. Le leggi del 1938*, Camera dei Deputati, Rome 1998, 81–110.

Gli ebrei nell'Italia fascista. Vicende, identità, persecuzione, Einaudi, Turin 2000.

'Il razzismo fascista nella sua concretezza. La definizione di "ebreo" e la collocazione di questi nella costruenda gerarchia razziale', in Burgio, *Nel nome della razza*, 321–32.

Schreiber, G., 'Les structures stratégiques de la conduite de la guerre de coalition italo-allemande au cours de la deuxième guerre mondiale', *Revue d'histoire de la deuxième guerre mondiale*, 120, 1980, 1–32.

'Political and Military Developments in the Mediterranean Area, 1939–1940', in Militärgeschichtliches Forschungsamt, *Germany and the Second World War*, vol. III, *The Mediterranean, South-East Europe, and North Africa.*

Schulte, T., *The German Army and the Nazi Politics in Occupied Russia*, Berg, Oxford 1989.

Schwarz, R., 'Sources on the Holocaust in Italy (1950–1980). A Bibliographical Essay', *Il politico*, 55, 3, 1990, 527–37.

Scotti, G., *Il battaglione degli straccioni. I militari italiani nelle brigate jugoslave 1943–1945*, Mursia, Milan 1974.

I 'disertori'. Le scelte dei militari italiani sul fronte jugoslavo prima dell'8 settembre 1943, Mursia, Milan 1974.

Bono italiano. Gli italiani in Jugoslavia, La Pietra, Milan 1977.

L'inutile vittoria, Mursia, Milan 1989.

Scotti, G., and Viazzi, L., *Le aquile delle montagne nere. Storia dell'occupazione e della guerra italiana in Montenegro (1941–1943)*, Mursia, Milan 1987.

Sekelj, L., 'Antisemitism in Yugoslavia, 1918–1945', *East European Quarterly*, 22, 2 June 1988, 159–72.

Sepić, D., 'La politique italienne d'occupation en Dalmatie, 1941–1943', in *Les systèmes d'occupation en Yougoslavie*, Congrès International sur l'Histoire de la Résistance Européenne, Institut pour l'Étude du Mouvement Ouvrier, Belgrade 1963, 390–1.

Serra, E., 'I rapporti italo-tedeschi durante la non-belligeranza dell'Italia', *Rassegna di politica e di storia*, 1, 1955, 8–15.

Setta, S., 'Cesare Maria De Vecchi di Val Cismon. Diario 1943', *Storia contemporanea*, 24, 6, 1993, 1057–113.

Shelah, M., *Heshbon Damim. Hatzlat Yehudi Croatiah al yiday ha-italkim, 1941–1943 [Blood Account. The Rescue of Croatian Jews by the Italians]*, Tel Aviv 1986.

Un debito di gratitudine, Stato Maggiore dell'Esercito, Rome 1991.
'The Occupation of Dubrovnik by Waffen SS Division "Prinz Eugen" on 12 September 1943', *Mediterranean Historical Review*, 6, 1, 1992, 105–11.
'Kroatische Juden zwischen Deutschland und Italien. Die Rolle der italienischen Armee am Beispiel des Generals Giuseppe Amico, 1941–1943', *Vierteljahrshefte für Zeitgeschichte*, 41, 2, 1993, 175–95.
Shelah, M., and Rochlitz, J., 'Excerpts from the Salonika Diary of Lucillo Merci (February–August 1943)', *Yad Vashem Studies*, 18, 1987, 293–323.
Singleton, F., *Twentieth-Century Yugoslavia*, Macmillan, London 1976.
Soddu, P., *Pagine inedite dal Diario di Luca Pietromarchi*, edited and with an introductory note by P. Soddu, in *Annali della Fondazione Luigi Einaudi*, XXXI, 1997, 475–95.
Soulet, J.-F., *L'empire stalinien. L'URSS et les pays de l'Est depuis 1945*, Librairie générale française, Paris 2000.
Spinosa, A., *Mussolini razzista riluttante*, Bonacci, Rome 1994.
Steinberg, J., *All or Nothing. The Axis and the Holocaust, 1941–1943*, Routledge, London 1990 [It. trans. *Tutto o niente. L'Asse e gli ebrei nei territori occupati, 1941–1943*, Mursia, Milan 1997].
Talpo, O., *Dalmazia. Una cronaca per la storia 1941–1944*, 3 vols., Stato Maggiore dell'Esercito, Rome 1990–5.
Tomasevich, J., *The Chetniks*, Stanford University Press, Stanford 1975.
Toscano, M., *Le origini diplomatiche del patto d'acciaio*, Sansoni, Florence 1956.
Storia diplomatica della questione dell'Alto Adige, Laterza, Bari 1967.
'Gli ebrei in Italia, dall'emancipazione alle persecuzioni', *Storia contemporanea*, 17, 5, 1986, 905–54.
Toscano, M., and Sofia, F. (eds.), *Stato nazionale ed emancipazione ebraica*, Bonacci, Rome 1990.
Trifković, S., 'Rivalry Between Germany and Italy in Croatia 1942–1943', *Historical Journal*, 36, 4, 1993, 879–904.
Tulard, J. (ed.), *Les empires occidentaux de Rome à Berlin*, PUF, Paris 1997.
Napoléon. Le pouvoir, la nation, la légende, Librairie générale de France, Paris 1997.
Vaccarino, G., *La Grecia tra resistenza e guerra civile, 1940–1949*, Angeli, Milan 1988.
Van Staaveren, J., *An American in Japan, 1945–1948. A Civilian View of the Occupation*, University of Washington Press, Seattle 1994.
Varsano, S., 'Ebrei di Salonicco immigrati a Napoli, 1917–1940. Una testimonianza', *Storia contemporanea*, 23, 1, 1992, 119–26.
Verna, F., 'Yugoslavia Under Italian Rule, 1941–1943. Civil and Military Aspects of the Italian Occupation', PhD thesis, University of California, Santa Barbara 1985, unpublished.
Viault, B. S., 'Mussolini et la recherche d'une paix négociée (1939–1940)', *Revue d'histoire de la deuxième guerre mondiale*, 107, 1977, 1–18.
Vigezzi, B., 'La neutralità dell'Italia nel 1870, 1914, 1930 (e nel 1948)', *Storia contemporanea*, 23, 6, 1992, 633–62.

Villermet, C., *A noi Savoia. Histoire de l'occupation italienne en Savoie, novembre 1942–septembre 1943*, La Fontaine de Siloé, Les Marches 1991.
Voigt, K., *Zuflucht auf Widerruf. Exil in Italien, 1933–1945*, 2 vols., Klett-Cotta, Stuttgart 1989–93 [It. trans. *Il rifugio precario. Gli esuli in Italia dal 1933 al 1945*, La Nuova Italia, Florence 1996].
Vujosevic, J., 'L'occupation italienne de la Yougoslavie', *Revue d'histoire de la deuxième guerre mondiale*, 87, 1972, 35–52.
Warmbrunn, W., *The Dutch Under the German Occupation, 1941–1945*, Stanford University Press, Stanford 1963.
The German Occupation of Belgium, 1940–1944, Lang, New York 1993.
Woolf, S. J., *Napoleon's Integration of Europe*, Routledge, London 1991.
Zamagni, V. (ed.), *Come perdere la pace e vincere la guerra*, Il Mulino, Bologna 1997.
Zuccotti, S., *The Italians and the Holocaust. Persecution, Rescue, Survival*, Basic Books, New York 1987.
The Holocaust, the French, the Jews, Basic Books, New York 1993.

Index

NEW STUDIES IN EUROPEAN HISTORY

Books in the series

Royalty and Diplomacy in Europe, 1890–1914
RODERICK R. McLEAN

Catholic Revival in the Age of the Baroque
Religious Identity in Southwest Germany, 1550–1750
MARC R. FORSTER

Helmuth von Moltke and the Origins of the First World War
ANNIKA MOMBAUER

Peter the Great
The Struggle for Power, 1671–1725
PAUL BUSHKOVITCH

Fatherlands
State-Building and Nationhood in Nineteenth-Century Germany
ABIGAIL GREEN

The French Second Empire
An Anatomy of Political Power
ROGER PRICE

Origins of the French Welfare State
The Struggle for Social Reform in France, 1914–1947
PAUL V. DUTTON

Ordinary Prussians
Brandenburg Junkers and Villagers, 1500–1840
WILLIAM W. HAGEN

Liberty and Locality in Revolutionary France
Rural Life and Politics, 1760–1820
PETER JONES

Vienna and Versailles
The Courts of Europe's Dynastic Rivals, 1550–1780
JEROEN DUINDAM

From Reich to State
The Rhineland in the Revolutionary Age, 1780–1830
MICHAEL ROWE

Re-Writing the French Revolutionary Tradition
Liberal Opposition and the Fall of the Bourbon Monarchy
ROBERT ALEXANDER

Provincial Power and Absolute Monarchy
The Estates General of Burgundy, 1661–1790
JULIAN SWANN

People and Politics in France, 1848–1870
ROGER PRICE

Nobles and Nation in Central Europe
Free Imperial Knights in the Age of Revolution, 1750–1850
WILLIAM D. GODSEY, JR

Technology and the Culture of Modernity in Britain and Germany, 1890–1945
BERNHARD RIEGER

The Russian Roots of Nazism
White Émigrés and the Making of National Socialism, 1917–1945
MICHAEL KELLOGG

The World Hitler Never Made
Alternate History and the Memory of Nazism
GAVRIEL D. ROSENFELD

Madness, Religion and the State in Early Modern Europe
A Bavarian Beacon
DAVID LEDERER

Fascism's European Empire
Italian Occupation During the Second World War
DAVIDE RODOGNO, translated by ADRIAN BELTON

Family and Community in Early Modern Spain
The Citizens of Granada, 1570–1739
JAMES CASEY